1 MONTH OF
FREE
READING

at

www.ForgottenBooks.com

By purchasing this book you are eligible for one month membership to ForgottenBooks.com, giving you unlimited access to our entire collection of over 1,000,000 titles via our web site and mobile apps.

To claim your free month visit:
www.forgottenbooks.com/free925322

ISBN 978-0-260-06195-9
PIBN 10925322

STATE OF NEW YORK

MINUTES AND TESTIMONY

OF THE

Joint Legislative Committee

Appointed to Investigate the

ublic Service Commissions

uthorized by Joint Resolution of January 21, 1915, and continued
by Joint Resolution of April 24, 1915; further continued by
Joint Resolution January 20, 1916 and March 6, 1916)

VOLUME III

TRANSMITTED TO THE LEGISLATURE MARCH 30, 1916

ALBANY
J. B. LYON COMPANY, PRINTERS
1916

JOINT COMMITTEE OF THE LEGISLATURE

FROM THE SENATE

Hon. GEORGE F. THOMPSON,
        Chairman
Hon. ROBERT R. LAWSON,
Hon. JAMES E. TOWNER,
Hon. CHARLES J. HEWITT,
Hon. JAMES A. FOLEY.

FROM THE ASSEMBLY

Hon. J. LESLIE KINCAID,
        Vice-Chairman
Hon. R. HUNTER McQUISTION,
        Secretary
Hon. WILLIAM C. BAXTER,
Hon. AARON A. FEINBERG,
Hon. FREDERICK S. BURR,
Hon. CHARLES D. DONOHUE.

COUNSEL TO THE COMMITTEE

Hon. MERTON E. LEWIS,
        Deputy Attorney-General

Committee organized at the Hotel Biltmore, New York, on une 24, 1915.

CONTENTS

HEARINGS — VOL. III

WITNESSES — VOL. III

PRELIMINARY REPORT

STATE OF NEW YORK

No. 42

IN SENATE

MARCH 30, 1916

Preliminary Report of the Joint Legislative Committee appointed to investigate the Public Service Commissions, and to ascertain what, if any, change in the Public Service Commissions Law are desirable.

To the Legislature:

Your Committee, appointed pursuant to joint resolution of the Legislature, passed January 21, 1915, heretofore made final report thereunder April 20, 1915. In accordance with the recommendation in said report your Committee was, by a further joint resolution, passed April 24, 1915, continued with the same powers as in the original resolution, which said joint resolutions read as follows:

"By Mr. Brown.— Resolved (if the Assembly concur), That a joint committee of the Senate and Assembly is hereby created to consist of four members of the Senate to be appointed by the President of the Senate and five members of the Assembly to be appointed by the Speaker of the Assembly, to investigate and examine into the organization of the Public Service Commissions of the first and second districts, and the administration of the functions of such commissions, with a view to ascertaining what changes, if any, in such organization and administration, or either, is advisable in the interest of the public welfare and the efficiency of such commissions. Such Committee shall make its report to the Legislature thereon as speedily as possible and may recommend the enactment of such laws, if any, as the Committee may deem proper; and it is further

"Resolved, That such Committee is hereby authorized to choose from its members a chairman and to sit within and outside the city of Albany, to subpoena and compel the attendance of witnesses, including public officers and employees, and to require the production of books and papers, including any public record or document pertaining to the subject of investigation, to take and hear proofs and testimony, and have all the powers that a legislative committee is provided by legislative law, including the adoption of rules for the conduct of its proceedings. Such Committee may employ a secretary, counsel and such other assistants as may be necessary for the purpose of the investigation.

"It is further Resolved, That the sum of $5,000, or so much thereof as may be necessary, shall be paid from the funds appropriated for the contingent expenses of the Legislature, by the Treasurer on the warrant of the Comptroller upon the certificate of the chairman of such Committee for the expenses of such committee and its investigation.

"Referred to Finance Committee. Jan. 20. Reported and Adopted."

Jan. 21. The above resolution was handed down in the Assembly, amended to read as follows, and adopted:

"Resolved (if the Assembly concur), That a joint committee of the Senate and Assembly is hereby created to consist of five members of the Senate, to be appointed by the President of the Senate, and six members of the Assembly, to be appointed by the Speaker of the Assembly, to make an investigation of the Public Service Commissions of the first and second districts with reference to their organization and their powers and duties together with their administration of the same and further to examine into the question of duplication of functions by the Federal Interstate Commerce Commission and the Public Service Commissions of this State to determine whether useless effort and expense on the part of the State and the corporations affected is being caused thereby, with a view to ascertaining what changes, if any, in such organization, powers, duties and administration, or either, is advisable in the interest of the public welfare and the efficiency of such commissions. Such Committee shall make its report to the Legislature thereon as speedily as possible and may recommend the enactment of such laws, if any, as the Committee may deem proper; and it is further

" Resolved, That such Committee is hereby authorized to choose from its members a chairman and to sit within and outside of the city of Albany, to subpoena and compel the attendance of witnesses, including public officers and employees, and to require the production of books and papers, including any public record or document pertaining to the subject of the investigation, to take and hear proofs and testimony, and have all the powers of a legislative committee as provided by the legislative law, including the adoption of rules for the conduct of its proceedings. Such Committee may employ a secretary, counsel, and such other assistants as may be necessary for the purpose of the investigation.

" It is further Resolved, That the sum of five thousand dollars or so much thereof as may be necessary, shall be paid from the funds appropriated for contingent expenses of the Legislature, by the Treasurer on the warrant of the Comptroller upon the certificate of the chairman of such Committee for the expenses of such Committee and its investigation.

" The Senate concurred in the Assembly amendments."

The following committee was appointed: Senators G. F. Thompson of Niagara, Chairman, Cromwell of Richmond, Mills of New York, Lawson of Kings, Republicans; and Foley of New York, Democrat. Assemblymen Maier of Seneca, Knight of Wyoming, McQuistion of Kings, Kincaid of Onondaga, Republicans; and Burr of Kings, and Donohue of New York, Democrats.

April 21, 1915:

"By Mr. G. F. Thompson.— Resolved (if the Assembly
concur), That the Committee appointed under joint resolution heretofore adopted by the Senate and Assembly January 21, 1915, creating a joint Committee for the investigation of the Public Service Commissions Law and of the administration of the Public Service Commissions of the first
and second districts, be, and it hereby is continued and further
authorized and directed to examine and revise the Public
Service Commissions Law and such other laws or parts of
laws as may be necessary to harmonize all existing provisions
of statute law applicable to the regulation of public utilities,
and to report to the Legislature on or before the first Monday in February, 1916, and to submit to such Legislature
as a part of its report such legislative bills as in the judgment of the Committee may be deemed to be necessary and
proper for the purposes aforesaid; and be it further

"Resolved, That such Committee have and retain during
its continuance as a Committee all the powers conferred upon
it by the Legislature and the resolution under which such
Committee was created; and it is further

"Resolved, That the printing necessary for the work of
said Committee be done by the public printer at the expense
of the State and that the sum of $15,000, or so much thereof
as may be necessary, shall be paid from the funds appropriated for contingent expenses of the Legislature, by the
Treasurer on the warrant of the Comptroller, upon the certificate of the chairman of such Committee for the expense of
such Committee and for the expenses of such investigations
as the Committee shall conduct.

"To Finance Com.   Committee discharged.   Adopted.
April 22.   In Assembly.   Adopted."

PROCEEDINGS OF COMMITTEE

Pursuant to such resolution, the Committee reconvened at the
city of New York on June 24, 1915, Hon. George F. Thompson
of Niagara, presiding; Hon. J. Leslie Kincaid of Onondaga,
chosen vice-chairman; Hon. R. Hunter McQuistion, continuing as

secretary; Hon. Merton E. Lewis, first deputy attorney-general and Clarence E. Shuster, Esq., of Rochester, N. Y., continuing as counsel and associate counsel, respectively, of said Committee.

Thereafter and during the further proceedings of the Committee the following members thereof resigned:

Hon. Ogden L. Mills of New York; Hon. William J. Maier of Seneca; Hon. Charles D. Donohue of New York, and Hon. John Knight of Wyoming, and were succeeded by the appointment to said Committee of Hon. James E. Towner of Putnam; Hon. Charles J. Hewitt of Cayuga; Hon. Joseph M. Callahan of Bronx, and Hon. Wm. C. Baxter of Albany.

During the further proceedings of the Committee, Hon. Merton E. Lewis retired, as counsel to the Committee, and was succeeded therein by Bainbridge Colby, Esq., of New York, who was later succeeded as counsel by Frank Moss, Esq., of New York. J. Frank Smith, Esq., of Lockport, was appointed as an associate counsel to the Committee.

The Committee began its hearings on July 15, 1915, at the Bar Association Building, Forty-fourth street, in the city of New York, and later continued such hearings at the rooms of the New York County Lawyers' Association, No. 165 Broadway, in the city of New York, and the coroner's court room, in the Municipal Building in the city of New York, at which latter place its hearings are now being held.

The life of the Committee has been further extended from time to time by joint resolutions passed January 26, 1916, and March 6, 1916, reading as follows:

"By Mr. George F. Thompson.—Whereas, By joint resolution of the Senate and Assembly passed January 21st, 1915, that a joint Committee of the Senate and Assembly was created to make an investigation of the Public Service Commissions of the first and second districts with reference to their organization and their powers and duties, together with their administration of the same and further to examine into the question of the duplication of functions by the Federal Interstate Commerce Commission and the Public Service Commissions of the State, to determine whether useless effort and expense on the part of the State and the corporations affected is being caused thereby, with a view to ascertaining what changes, if any, are necessary in such organization, powers, duties and administration or either is advisable in the interest of the public welfare and the efficiency of said commissions;

"And Whereas, By joint resolution of the Senate and Assembly adopted April 22, 1915, said Committee was thereby continued and further authorized and directed to examine and revise the Public Service Commissions Law and such other laws or parts of laws as may be necessary to harmonize the existing provisions of statute law applicable to the regulation of public utilities and to report to the Legislature on or before the first Monday in February, 1916, and to submit to said Legislature as a part of its report such legislative bills as in the judgment of the Committee may be deemed to be necessary and proper for the purposes aforesaid; and

" Whereas, Said Committee has not yet concluded its duties and desires additional time in which to perform the same,

" Resolved (if the Assembly concur), That the time within which such a report to the Legislature is required to be made, as in said resolution provided, be and the same hereby is extended to and until the first Monday in March, 1916.

"Adopted, Jan. 20, in Assembly. To Ways and Means Committee. Jan. 26. Reported and adopted."

" By Mr. G. F. Thompson.—Whereas, By joint resolution of the Senate and Assembly, passed January 21, 1915, a joint Committee of the Senate and Assembly was created to make an investigation of the Public Service Commissions of the First and Second Districts with reference to their organization and their powers and duties, together with their administration of the same and further to examine into the question of the duplication of functions by the Federal Inter-State Commerce Commission, and the Public Service Commissions of the State, to determine whether useless effort and expense on the part of the State and corporations affected is being caused thereby, with a view to ascertaining what changes, if any, are necessary in such organization, powers, duties and administration or either is advisable in the interests of the public welfare and the efficiency of said commission;

"And Whereas, By joint resolution of the Senate and Assembly adopted April 22, 1915, said Committee was thereby continued and further authorized and directed to examine and revise the Public Service Commissions Law and such other laws or parts of laws as may be necessary to harmonize the existing provisions of Statute Law applicable to the regulation of public utilities and to report to the Legislature on or before the first Monday in February, 1916, and to submit to the said Legislature as a part of its report such legislative bills as in the judgment of the Committee may be deemed to be necessary and proper for the purposes aforesaid;

"And Whereas, By a joint resolution of the Senate and Assembly passed January 26, 1916, said Committee was granted to and until the first Monday in March, 1916, within which report to the Legislature is required to be made, as in said resolution provided;

"And Whereas, Said Committee has not yet concluded its duties and requests additional time in which to perform the same;

" Resolved (if the Assembly concur), That the time of such Committee to conduct its examination and investigation be and hereby is extended until the first day of July, 1916, and that the powers and duties of such Committee as set forth in said resolution herein mentioned be and the same hereby are continued until that time. The said Committee may make such preliminary reports to the Legislature at any time, and is continued after July 1 and until January 10, 1917, for the purpose of preparing and presenting its final report.

"Adopted. March 6, in Assembly. Adopted."

Such last quoted resolution extending the time for purposes of hearings and investigation until the 1st day of July, 1916, and for the purpose of making a final report until the 10th day of January, 1917.

The report of this Committee, submitted to the Legislature on

April 20, 1915, contained the following recommendation (page 42):

> "As a result of this investigation your Committee believes that an extensive and careful examination of the Public Service Commissions Law, the Transportation Corporations Law, the General Corporations Law, and the Stock Corporations Law should be had. In view of the brief period remaining in which this Committee is permitted, under the resolution creating it, to act, it would seem to your Committee desirable that a resolution be adopted under which such a general revision may be had, providing for a comprehensive and thoroughly digested system of law, relating to the regulation of public utilities."

During the progress of the investigation made by this Committee, prior to its final report of April 20, 1915, a very considerable body of evidence had been submitted to the Committee, pertaining to the foregoing recommendation, but which, for lack of time, had not been thoroughly digested and studied. Since the resumption of hearings of the Committee, pursuant to your joint resolution, beginning at New York on July 15, 1915, much additional testimony and data has been collected by the Committee in respect thereto, all of which data has been and still is being carefully examined and a thorough study thereof made, on the part of the Committee, and its counsel, but, owing to the unexpected but very important developments resulting from the investigation into the administration of the Public Service Commissions Law by the Commission for the First District, and the time necessarily devoted thereto, it has not been practicable for the Committee to prepare and submit its recommendations in full, with the proposed legislative changes and revisions in support thereof at this time, and largely for that reason your Committee was compelled recently to procure an extension of its existence until the 10th day of January, 1917.

At the resumption of its hearings on July 15, 1915, your Committee began an extended examination by public hearings, as to the state of the laws referred to in its recommendation. Considerable testimony and constructive criticisms in respect thereto were submitted by various officials of the city and others. It was the expectation and contemplation of your Committee at its resumption of hearings to devote its whole time to this branch of its inquiry, however, during the first month of its investigation, your Committee had presented to it, voluntarily, by substantial citizen and civic interests, particularly in the borough of Brooklyn, evidences of public dissatisfaction with the manner of the construction of the elevated third tracking in that borough, then in process, pursuant to the provisions of a certificate granted by the Public Service Commission for the First District to the New York Municipal Railway Corporation, and which said third track construction is to be a part of the so-called Dual Subway System of Rapid Transit for the City of New York. The matters thus brought to the attention of the Committee were deemed by it of such vital public importance, that it thereupon began an investigation of the entire rapid transit situation of the city of New York, and particularly in respect to the additional facilities for rapid transit contemplated in what is known as the new subway system. This investigation is still in progress. The interests both of the city and the corporations affected as well as the controversial matters involved in the investigation are of such importance that your Committee has concluded that its report in detail in respect thereto should be withheld until its final report as required by your joint resolution, to be submitted January 10, 1917.

In the course of this investigation it became necessary for your Committee to examine carefully into the transactions leading up to the making of the contracts by the Public Service Commission for the First District on behalf of the city and the Interborough Rapid Transit Company, and the New York Municipal Railway Corporation, respectively, which contracts were entered into on March 19, 1913. Under the provisions of these contracts, the city of New York is constructing additional subways for rapid transit, the same to be leased and operated when completed by the Interborough Rapid Transit Company and the New York Municipal Railway Corporation, respectively, each of which said railroad corporations in pursuance of the provisions of the contracts, contribute money toward the cost of the construction thereof, as a part consideration for the lease and right to operate such subway railroads. In addition each of said railroad corporations is subject to supervision and regulation by the Public Service Commission for the First District. Thus, it became necessary in the investigation of the subway contracts to reopen the investigation earlier made by your Committee into the administration of the Public Service Law by the Commission for the First District, and particularly as to the part taken by the individual commissioners in the making and carrying out of such contracts.

Growing out of that phase of its investigation, the Committee presented charges against the Hon. Edward E. McCall, chairman of such Commission, on the grounds set forth in the statute, in relation to the removal of commissioners. These charges were in due course heard before the Governor, and thereafter the said commissioner was removed from his office as such by the Governor on the 2d day of December, 1915.

During the progress of the investigation, Commissioner George V. S. Williams resigned on December 27, 1915, and Commissioner Robert Colgate Wood resigned on January 4, 1916.

By reason of the vacancies, occurring as aforesaid, together with the expiration of the terms of office of Commissioners Milo R. Maltbie and J. Sargent Cram, the entire membership of the Commission of the First District has been changed, since the appointment of your Committee on January 21, 1915.

Your Committee submits herewith, as a part of this report, all of the testimony and exhibits taken before your Committee from the 15th day of July, 1915, up to March 1, 1916.

PROPOSED LEGISLATION

Your Committee has, in process of preparation, a comprehensive revision of the Public Service Commissions Law, together with amendments to the Railroad Law and the Transportation Corporations Law of the State. Considerable additional study will be necessary to complete the labors of your Committee, in relation thereto, and as the matters are of such vital public importance, and in view of the extension of the time of your Committee until the 10th day of January, 1917, it is deemed advisable to withhold the presentation of such proposed changes in the law until the final report is made.

RAPID TRANSIT ACT

There is, however, one subject of very great public interest which your Committee deems of such importance as to require immediate legislation and to that end recommends the adoption of the amendments proposed in relation to the Laws of 1891, chapter 4, as amended, and known as the " Rapid Transit Act " for the creation of a municipal commission to exercise the powers thereunder.

The Rapid Transit Act, so-called, was an act to provide for rapid transit service in cities of more than one million inhabitants, and as such has been applicable from its enactment to the present time, only to the City of Greater New York, and will continue to be applicable only to said city for many years to come.

Immediately prior to the enactment of the Public Service Commissions Law, the powers and duties provided for in the said Rapid Transit Act were vested in a body known as the "Board of Rapid Transit Railroad Commissioners." Upon the enactment of the Public Service Commissions Law, all of the powers and duties of the Board of Rapid Transit Railroad Commissioners was transferred and vested in the Public Service Commission for the First District, which said powers have since continued to be vested in and to be exercised by such Commission.

The contracts hereinbefore referred to, known as the " Dual Subway Contracts " were entered into on behalf of the city by the Commissioners of the First District, in their capacity as Rapid Transit Commissioners, and the construction of such subways and the contracts therefor, together with the supervision of such construction has been carried on by the Commissioners of the First District, in their capacity as Rapid Transit Commissioners, and not as Public Service Commissioners.

Under the Public Service Commissions Law, all of the expenses for the maintenance of the Commission in the First District except the salaries of the Commissioners, the counsel to the Commission, and the Secretary to the Commission, are paid by the city of New York. The expense of maintaining the Commission in the First District is now aggregating more than three million dollars per annum; of this amount, all but the officers' salaries, amounting to $91,000, is paid from the treasury of the city of New York, and is appropriated for purposes of the city government, and as such is deemed a city government expense. Of the total expense of maintaining the Commission in the First District, approximately five-sixths thereof is required in the exercise of their Rapid Transit powers, while one-sixth, or approximately a half million dollars, is required in the exercise of their powers of supervision and regulation of the Public Service Corporations, doing business within that district.

The Public Service Commissions Law was designed primarily to furnish an efficient and expeditious method of regulating the service, facilities and rates of corporations and persons furnishing transportation and other public utilities within the State of New York, and in the main provides the organization and machinery through the Commissions, for that purpose.

The Commission of the Second District is vested with powers that are exclusively regulatory, whereas, the Commission of the First District, by the inclusion of the powers of the Rapid Transit Commission, is called upon to perform two separate, and in many essential particulars inconsistent and antagonistic functions, namely, constructing and maintaining railroads for transportation of persons and property while regulating and supervising the operating transactions of such railroad enterprises. Thus to the extent that the Public Service Commission for the First District constructs and maintains the subway transportation facilities, it is also called upon to regulate and supervise its own transactions in relation thereto.

This conflict of powers residing in the same Commission is in considerable part responsible, in the opinion of your Committee for the delinquencies in the administration in the First District disclosed by this investigation, and by reason of which there seems just ground to believe that both the city of New York, its inhabitants, and the public utilities corporations have suffered loss or been unwarrantably burdened with unnecessary and improvident obligations.

Such conflict of powers necessarily involves neglect of one or other set of duties and as might naturally be expected those powers and functions which seemed the more important received the greater attention, which in this instance was the Rapid Transit construction; whereas, the more truly beneficial service must result to the public at large and to the citizen individually, from a consistent and effective regulation of service and rates. The actual result, as disclosed by this investigation, is discouraging from either view point. The administration of the regulatory functions has been inefficient and extremely unsatisfactory both to the public and the consumer, and there is a wide spread feeling of distrust of the Commission as partial to the corporations and interest to be regulated and supervised. As to the Rapid Transit work: the conclusion is unavoidable that unwise and improvident contracts have been approved and entered into by the Commission thereby imposing upon the property of the taxpayers of the city and upon the users of its transit facilities, for many years to come, burdensome and unjust demands if not to imperil the solvency of the city itself.

Further inconsistency in their functions and relations is that, as Public Service Commissioners they are constituted as a state body, comprised of state officials, appointed by the executive of the state and exercising purely state powers and functions; and city officials, appointed by the state, exercising purely municipal powers and functions.

The Public Service Commission of the First District, in exercising its powers both as Public Service Commissioners, and as Rapid Transit Commissioners has been compelled by the very nature of the powers and duties, to keep separate and distinct as far as practicable their activities and transactions in each field.

As Rapid Transit Commissioners, they have deemed it essential to maintain a large and expensive engineering force, supervising contracts and construction. Likewise, elaborate and costly systems of record, statistics and accounts, no part of which is essential or required for the exercise of its powers as a regulating body.

Thus in transferring the powers and duties to the proposed Rapid Transit Commission as is recommended herein this experienced working and field organization of engineers, inspectors and other experts now used by the Commissioners of the First District in its subway work can and should be turned over intact to such proposed Transit Commission, thereby avoiding delay in the progress of the work and expense incident to the creation of a new organization. The possible objection that a body of new commissioners will render delay in the construction of the subways inevitable is fully met by the fact that the present membership of the Public Service Commission for the First District is practically new to the powers and duties of that body.

The construction by the Public Service Commission, as Rapid Transit Commissioners of the new subway system in New York City, involves contracts and expenditures, aggregating approximately three hundred million dollars. This vast enterprise of money and property is by the Public Service Commissions Law imposed upon the Public Service Commission for the First District, and is an enterprise of such magnitude that your Committee believes that it can only be efficiently and economically carried out for the best interests of the City of New York, by a separate and distinct body, devoting its entire time and abilities to the problems involved therein, exercising exclusively the powers and duties provided for in the Rapid Transit Act, and directly responsible to the taxpayers and electors of the City of New York.

The proposed amendments to the Rapid Transit Act, makes it necessary that amendments to the Public Service Commissions Law, be had in order that in transferring powers from the Public Service Commission of the Second District to a new and separate board of Rapid Transit Commissioners, the said Commission in the First District be divested of the powers and duties which it is now exercising in relation thereto, reserving, however, to the Public Service Commission for the First District, the same jurisdiction, powers and duties of supervision and regulation over the proposed Rapid Transit Commission, and the facilities constructed and created by it, as are now exercised by the Public Service Commission over railroads.

MUNICIPAL REPRESENTATION ON BOARDS OF DIRECTORS

It is further recommended by your Committee that an amendment to the Stock Corporations Law, providing for representation by the city, upon the board of directors of every corporation leasing or operating any railroad or other transit facilities belonging to the city.

The need for legislation giving municipalities representation on the boards of directors of corporations leasing or operating transit facilities owned by any such municipality is peculiarly demanded at this time as a protection to the rights of the City of New York growing out of the subway contracts existing between the city and the Interborough Rapid Transit Company and the city and the New York Municipal Railway Corporation, respectively.

Under those contracts the parties have assumed relations and will enjoy rights in their nature similar to that of copartners, which relations and duties will subsist in all probability for the entire period of the lease, namely, for the period of forty-nine years from the date of the commencement of operation under the leases. The city and corporations under the contracts each contribute millions of dollars toward the construction of the railroads, and will share in whatever net profits or earnings accrue from the operation thereof. The credit of the city of New York is, in effect at least, behind the operation of the railroads as well as the construction thereof. The manner and character of the operation of the railroads as well as the business and financial management of the enterprise by the lessee corporations are of as vital concern to the taxpayers of New York city as to the stockholders of the said corporations.

And finally your Committee's investigation has demonstrated that regardless of its broad powers the Public Service Commission inherently is, and perhaps properly must, be limited in its control over the transactions incident to the business and financial management of the corporations it supervises. The city, either as copartner or as owner and landlord of this subway enterprise, must be protected in its large investment of money and credit by more direct and accurate information with respect to the business thereof than can be afforded by Commission supervision.

Rate Decisions

The regulation of rates under the present law, and particularly in relation to gas service, has been very inadequate and provocative of widespread popular dissatisfaction in practically every part of the State where such questions have arisen.

The matter of rate adjustment must always remain a subject of first importance in any system of public regulation which might be adopted. The interests affected are in large part antagonistic, the parties involved hostile and the rights of each substantial and entitled to the full protection of the law. Under such circumstances orderly procedure, while proper and right, necessarily involves the parties in large expense and irksome delays, either or both of which not infrequently results in injustice and if carried too far or endured too long must imperil not only the rights of the immediate parties in interest, but in a matter of such public concern as the cost to the public of a necessary commodity like gas or electricity, may undermine the integrity of the State itself.

The Committee recognizes the fact that in contested proceedings on rate adjustments time and opportunity for each side to submit its case must be allowed and that thereafter the commissioners must employ further time for a proper study and consideration of the evidence in order to render just and proper relief. Furthermore the amount of such time properly required in any such inquiry must depend largely upon the facts and circumstances developed in each case. Arbitrary limitations by statute applicable alike to all cases has not proved satisfactory and obviously never will.

In all rate cases the corporation exacting the rate complained against is necessarily on the defensive and, right or wrong, will in most such cases strive for delay against a final decision which may reduce its revenue. Such practices may not be without some excuse, and possibly in some cases justifiable. However, your Committee feels that aside from such methods there has grown up within the organization of the Commission a disposition to deal with rate cases in a more or less indirect manner through over-elaboration of details and complex and involves computation resulting ofttimes in the decision being more the judgment of the Commission's subordinates than the independent judgment of the Commissioners expressly charged with that duty, and further resulting in creating in the minds of the complainants the suspicion that their interests have been prejudiced by a too generous consideration for the rights of the corporation complained of.

In order to correct this condition your Committee recommends as an addition to the powers of the Commission in respect to rate adjustments the power to compel reparation to the consumer, by

the corporation complained of, of excess payments made pending
the final determination of every such case. Your Committee accordingly recommends amendments to the Public Service Commissions Law carrying out its foregoing recommendation.

WATER COMPANIES

Governmental control over public franchises and privileges and
the regulation and supervision of the corporations and persons
exercising the same by Commissions has now become a fixed
policy of most of the states, some of which have extended their
powers of control and supervision to every class of corporations
rendering a service deemed to be of a public nature, whether
through the exercise of public franchises or by reason of the
relation of the service rendered in conjunction with a service dis-
tinctively recognized as a public utility; such for instance as in
this State: car corporations, sleeping-car companies, freight and
freight line corporations, baggage and transfer corporations, and
stock yards which while not required by law to be franchise holding corporations are nevertheless made subject to the Public
Service Commissions Law.

In its report dated April 20, 1915, your Committee at page 40
under the subject of franchises suggests that

> " The powers of the Commissions over the exercise of fran-
> chises might however with propriety be enlarged so as to
> apply to all public franchises sought to be exercised in
> respect to all class of public utilities of the State."

In line with its foregoing suggestion your Committee, as a
result of its study of this matter, is now prepared to and does
recommend that all water corporations and waterworks corporations furnishing potable water for public and private use and
consumption within the State be made subject to the Public
Service Commissions Law and placed under the supervision of
the Commission for the Second District.

Water companies, like gas and electric corporations, both of
which have been subject to the Public Service Commissions Law
since its enactment, are required by law to operate under public
franchises. The service rendered by water corporations is neces-

sarily of a public nature and the character of facilities essential to the supplying of water compels the use by such corporations of the public streets and highways; thus, in every essential feature the same fundamental reasons exist for placing water corporations and their service and facilities under the regulatory powers of the State as other franchise holding corporations. Furthermore, the State owes no greater duty and the Legislature can enact no constructive legislation of more vital public and private importance than that which will afford effective protection to the public health against disease and pestilence while supplying water adequately for the daily need and convenience of the individual citizen and the protection of both public and private property against conflagration and disaster.

The Committee has taken a large amount of evidence which is submitted herewith which clearly discloses the fact that water companies in many parts of the State have acquired all of the available supply of water for needs of the people for such localities, and are now engaged in delivering such water to the consumers at exorbitant prices. The evidence further discloses the fact that in many localities the service is inadequate and unsatisfactory.

CONCLUSION

Your Committee believes that the legislative changes recommended herein are all required in the public interest and to that end urges the enactment at this session of legislation carrying into effect each of such recommendations.

Dated, *March* 24, 1916.

GEORGE F. THOMPSON,
Chairman.

ROBT. R. LAWSON,
JAMES E. TOWNER,
C. J. HEWITT,
JAMES A. FOLEY,
AARON A. FEINBERG,
JOSEPH M. CALLAHAN,
FREDERICK S. BURR.

I am opposed to divestment of constructive functions of the Public Service Commission of the First District; otherwise I concur.

R. HUNTER McQUISTION,
Secretary.

I concur except as stated in attached memoranda.

J. LESLIE KINCAID,
WM. C. BAXTER.

Minority Report of the Joint Legislative Committee for the Investigation of the Public Service Commissions of the State of New York.

To the Senate and Assembly:

Believing that the majority report of the Joint Legislative Committee appointed to investigate the Public Service Commissions of the State, in so far as it deals with the question of the transfer of the control over construction of rapid transit lines from the Public Service Commission of the First District to a new commission does not fairly or adequately state the conditions and that the recommendation of such a transfer is unwise, we respectfully submit the following minority report:

To meet the peculiar transit conditions existing in New York City in 1907 with respect to existing lines and the imperative need for additional facilities both the control over the operation of railway lines and the construction of new lines was placed in the Public Service Commission of the First District. Governor Hughes in his first message to the Legislature in 1907 urged the desirability of such action. He said:

> " The board that is to have the power to supervise generally these operations should have the power of initiating plans and of making contracts for the construction and operation of new lines. Instead of two boards dealing with different phases of the same problem, there should be one board empowered to deal with it in its entirety." * * * " The urgent need of an increase in transportation facilities, and the unique conditions existing in Greater New York, justify the creation of a separate board to deal with the entire matter of transportation in that part of the State." * * * " Provision should be made for the retention by the board of estimate and apportionment of the city, of all the powers, including powers of approval, which it now enjoys."

The City of New York has entered into contracts known as the dual subway contracts for the construction and operation of new rapid transit lines and extensions and additions to existing lines which involve a total expense of approximately $350,000,000. These contracts were made with the approval of both the board of estimate and apportionment and the Public Service Commission. The responsibility for the work under these contracts is vested in the Public Service Commission of the First District. Its acts are subject to the check and control of the city authorities in the following important respects:

1. Contracts for all construction work must be approved by the board of estimate and apportionment, which board must also prescribe a limit to the amount of bonds available for work under contracts involving the expenditure of city money.

2. Contracts must be approved as to form by the corporation counsel.

3. Condemnation proceedings may only be conducted by the corporation counsel.

4. Routes and general plans adopted by the Commission must be approved by the board of estimate and apportionment and by the mayor.

It is now proposed by the majority report of this Committee that the responsibility for the construction of rapid transit lines be transferred from the Public Service Commission, a body free from control by the city administration, to a new commission consisting of the mayor, the comptroller and five other members to be appointed by the mayor. Whether or not this centralized power under the mayor at the time of the creation of the Public Service Commission could have been provided for with adequate safeguards, it would be entirely improper to attempt it now. At the time the city obligated itself under the dual contracts, it was contemplated that the work would be done subject to all the checks and safeguards then provided and no legislation should now be enacted that in any way weakens the protection furnished the city.

Assuming that any such transfer would not impair the effective prosecution of the work, it would occasion without doubt serious financial loss to the city. It involves not only a change in personnel but also a change in system. It would mean the division of the present staff of the Commission in the midst of the work which is under way. The Commission does not have two distinct and separate staffs, one in charge of construction and one in charge of regulation. A division of its staff would inevitably slow up the work and delay construction. Aside from the fact that additional transit facilities are demanded at the earliest possible moment, some idea of the financial cost to the city which a year's delay would mean is apparent from the fact that the annual interest and sinking fund charges for the investment under these contracts will amount to about $20,000,000 a year.

The fact that only about fifteen per centum of the annual expense of the First District Commission is now chargeable to regulatory work does not mean that this is the total cost of that work, for the construction staff is used very largely in an advisory capacity on problems of regulation. It is safe to say that if separate staffs were maintained under two heads instead of one the total cost would be twenty-five to thirty per centum higher than at present. The fact that not only new lines are being built but practically all of the elevated roads in this city are being reconstructed and that service must be maintained during this period, it is essential that the regulation and control of existing lines be co-ordinated with the construction work. Such difficult construction work as joining the Seventh Avenue subway to the old subway line at 42d street and at the same time carrying the new Broadway line underneath must be done without interruption to the present service. If the engineering staff of the Commission did not have such situations well in hand there would be a conflict of control between the regulation of traffic and the supervision of construction, and delays and serious accidents with loss of life might result.

Mayor Mitchell and Comptroller Pendergast, whom it is suggested should be made members of the proposed new commission, have already expressed disapproval of the entire plan. It is a well known fact that these officials with their present duties have all the work they can do.

We respectfully submit that this proposed legislation would cause serious delay in the completion of this important transit development, so urgently needed by the city of New York; that, at least temporarily, it would materially decrease the efficiency in handling the work; and that the cost to the city would be greatly increased.

ALBANY, N. Y., *March* 28, 1916.

Respectfully submitted,

J. LESLIE KINCAID,

WM. C. BAXTER.

IN THE MATTER OF THE INVESTIGATION BY JOINT COM-
MITTEE OF THE LEGISLATURE, PURSUANT TO THE
RESOLUTION OF JANUARY 15, 1915, TO INQUIRE INTO
THE PUBLIC SERVICE COMMISSIONS OF THE STATE
OF NEW YORK

TESTIMONY

JANUARY 27, 1916

NEW YORK COUNTY LAWYERS' ASSOCIATION BOARD ROOM,
165 Broadway, New York City

The Committee was called to order, pursuant to adjournment, Chairman Thompson presiding.

Quorum present.

Chairman Thompson.— This Committee will do no work to-day, and, without objection, we will suspend until to-morrow at eleven o'clock.

Whereupon at 12:10 o'clock P. M., an adjournment was taken to eleven o'clock A. M., January 28, 1916, at the same place.

JANUARY 28, 1916

NEW YORK COUNTY LAWYERS' ASSOCIATION BOARD ROOM,
165 Broadway, New York City

The Committee was called to order, pursuant to adjournment, Chairman Thompson presiding.

Quorum present.

Chairman Thompson.— There will be nothing to-day, either, except that I will guarantee the Committee will be busy all day in an attempt to earn its money. We will suspend now until to-morrow at eleven o'clock, and I expect to be able to go on then, or possibly tomorrow we might not go on, but we will be ready to do so the first of next week, and I expect to take practically every day of the week, and get excused from the sessions of the Legislature at Albany, and work every day when I get ready to go on with the work.

Whereupon an adjournment was taken at 12:55 o'clock P. M., to 11 o'clock A. M., January 29, 1916, at the same place.

[27]

JANUARY 29, 1916

NEW YORK COUNTY LAWYERS' ASSOCIATION BOARD ROOM,
165 Broadway, New York City

The Committee was called to order, pursuant to adjournment,
Chairman Thompson presiding.

Chairman Thompson.— We will now suspend until 2:30 o'clock,
at which time we will make any announcements that are necessary.

AFTERNOON SESSION

Chairman Thompson presiding.

Chairman Thompson.— The Committee will come to order.
The Chair announces the appointment of Mr. Bainbridge Colby
as counsel for the Committee, concerning matters of continued
investigation in New York. This conclusion was arrived at to-day,
and we will begin Monday morning to continue the investigation,
in the same course which the Committee suspended week before
last, and, of course, being an investigating Committee, as to the
subjects of investigation we have not any announcements to make
as to what the investigation will find, because if we knew exactly
what the investigation was to find it is our idea there would be
no need of an investigating Committee. This Committee has been
a Committee of investigation to ascertain facts that were not fully
known before the Committee's work commenced, and the investigation will continue on that line, and Mr. Colby will be present
at the Committee meeting on Monday morning and the work will
proceed, and we are going to devote all of our time and attention
to it and let the results count for themselves, whatever they are.

If there is no objection we will suspend until Monday morning
at 11 o'clock at this place.

Whereupon at 2:45 o'clock P. M., an adjournment was taken to
Monday, January 31, 1916, at 11 o'clock A. M. at the same place.

JANUARY 31, 1916

New York County Lawyers' Association Board Room,
165 Broadway, New York City

Meeting called to order by Chairman Thompson, at 11 A. M., a quorum being present.

Mr. Colby.— I am ready. Is Mr. Hedley present?

Hedley, Frank, being duly sworn testified as follows:

Mr. Quackenbush (counsel to Mr. Hedley).— I was asking about a stenographer. I was wondering whether or not we could take the minutes.

Chairman Thompson.— We made it a rule some time ago that we would not allow our record to be taken except by the official stenographer for many reasons.

Mr. Quackenbush.— I want to say, Mr. Chairman, that it is a mere matter of convenience. It might expedite things if we knew just what you wish to know.

Examination by Mr. Colby:

Q. Where do you reside, Mr. Hedley? A. I reside in Yonkers, sir.

Q. What is your position with the New York Railways Company? A. Vice-president and general manager.

Q. Do you fill that position with other companies engaged in the transportation field in New York? A. Some of the other companies, yes, sir.

Q. Name them? A. Interborough Railway Company, I am also vice-president and general manager.

Q. Any other companies? A. That's the only railway company, sir.

Q. You mean the only company engaged in the transportation of passengers within the greater city of New York? A. That is correct, sir.

Q. The Interborough Rapid Transit Company is the company operating the existing subway line? A. Yes, sir, and the elevated line.

Q. The New York Railways Company of which you are also vice-president and general manager, controls and operates the surface lines throughout the boroughs of Manhattan and the Bronx, is that right? A. The majority of them, yes, sir. Not all of them. We have nothing whatever to do with the Third Avenue street car system and nothing whatever to do with the Second Avenue system.

Q. With these exceptions, however, it may be said with sufficient accuracy that the New York Railways Company controls and operates the surface lines in Manhattan and Bronx boroughs? A. No. Manhattan but not the Bronx.

Q. How long have you occupied the position as vice-president and general manager with these companies? A. With the subway and elevated for several years before the subway was opened and with the street railways since January, 1912.

Q. Do I understand from that that you were vice-president and general manager of the elevated line prior to the opening of the present subway? A. No, sir. I was not vice-president and general manager at that time. I was first general superintendent and then I was made general manager and then vice-president and general manager.

Q. And you had risen to that important office before the subway was completed and placed in operation? A. If I recall it right I was general manager of the elevated before the subway was in operation. I am not sure of that, sir.

Q. What position have you filled since the subway began operation with the Interborough Rapid Transit Company? A. I had been general manager and vice-president or general manager ever since it commenced operation.

Q. How long have you been vice-president of the Interborough? A. I should say about nine years.

Q. And general manager for the same period? A. General manager from the time the subway was opened.

Q. Are you an engineer by profession? A. I am a mechanical engineer.

Q. Holding degrees as such? A. No, sir.

Q. A graduate of a scientific school? A. In a practical way. I learned the trade in a practical way and I followed engineering ever since.

Q. Were you connected with any of the financing or construction companies at the time the construction of the Interborough was undertaken, I mean the construction of the subway was undertaken? A. No, sir. That is to say, not before it was opened. I have been connected and am still connected with what is known as the Subway Construction Company.

Q. Tell me what that company is? A. That is the company that does construction work, subway construction work.

Q. Was it organized for the purpose of doing construction work for the New York subway? A. I assume that it was. It was organized prior to 1903. This fall I came with the company.

Q. You are still connected with that company? A. I am vice-president of that company in charge of construction.

Q. Who is the president of that company? A. Mr. Theodore P. Shonts.

Q. What is its capital? A. I don't know, sir.

Q. Do you know the names of its directors? A. No, sir. I don't know its directors. I cannot name all of them.

Q. Will you name those whom you can recall? A. I think Mr. Berwind is one. I think Mr. Belmont is another.

Q. You mean Mr. August Belmont? A. Yes. Mr. Andrew Friedman is another.

Q. He is dead. A. Yes. I think Mr. Cornelius Vanderbilt is another. I don't know the others.

Q. Are there any other companies related to or affiliated with the Interborough Company of which you are an officer? A. Yes, sir. I am an officer if you consider a director an officer. I am a director of the Queens County Line. I am a member of the board of Directors of the 145th Street Crosstown Line and of the 23d Street Line. I think that's all. I will fill out a complete list and send it to the counsel but I think that is all there is to it.

Q. Do all these companies with which you are identified pay you a salary? A. No, sir.

Q. From what companies do you receive compensation? A. I receive compensation from the Interborough Rapid Transit Company, from the New York Railways Company and from the Subway Construction Company.

Q. Will you specify in each case the compensation the company pays you? A. Why I think it is $6,000 from the Subway

Construction Company. I don't remember what the others are. Let me see if I can figure it from what it should be. I think that is on the statement that you requested of us, Mr. Colby. I have no statement containing that data. It was sent to Mr. Morse. I am not sure how it is divided. I think it is $6,000 for the New York Railways. I mean $6,000 for the Subway Construction Company, $12,000 from the New York Railways and $32,000 from the subway and elevated. However, the statement that I sent you is correct because the statement is from the distribution of the auditor's figures. That is in detail.

Q. Can you tell me approximately how the $32,000 that you receive as an annual salary from the subway and Manhattan Railway is proportioned between the companies? A. I think it is about half and half.

Q. So that it would appear that your annual salary from these various companies aggregates $50,000? A. That is correct, sir.

Chairman Thompson.— Would you have time to take another salary from another railway if that was operating in the city of New York?

Mr. Hedley.— There would be no question but what I would have time to take it, Mr. Chairman, but I don't know of any other railway just now that is looking for a man of my size that wants to add to my personal pay roll. If they do I am open for something more.

Chairman Thompson.— Do you receive any other compensation from any of the corporations mentioned? Do you receive any other compensation from any of the companies for a salary?

Mr. Hedley.— No, sir.

Chairman Thompson.— Will you specify how your salary is received, on what theory it is paid?

Mr. Hedley.— Well, I have invented a good many very valuable devices and when I originate a new device I patent, take out patents on it. I pay for these patents and I pay the attorney's fees and government fees out of my own pocket. If the railway companies that I am employed by desire to use these patents they do so and I give them their right to do so without payment of

any royalty to anyone.   They have a free right to purchase these
devices anywhere they can secure them in the open market.
There have been cases where the devices have proved meritorious,
have added to the safety of passengers, to the incomes of the operating company and in some cases the board of directors have
by resolution paid to me sums of money.

Q. The board of directors of the companies that you represent?
A. No, sir.   The board of directors of the companies that I am
employed by may pay me but none of the companies of which I
am a member of the board of directors.   In other words, I have no
voice.   It is entirely voluntary with the company through its
board of directors whether they pay me anything or not for the
patents.   I give them the free right to use them.

Q. Mr. Hedley, you said something about the companies being
able to purchase these devices in the open market if they regarded
them as meritorious.   What campanies had you in mind?   A. I
mean the companies I am employed by, the Interborough Rapid
Transit Company and the New York Railways Company.

Q. And is that the only way in which they could acquire the
right or license to use your patent devices?   A. No.   I give them
the license to use and then if they want to buy they can get it
wherever they can get it the cheapest and best.   I give them a
free license to use it.   They can have it manufactured by any
party they may like to have it manufactured by.   I have nothing
whatever to do with it.

Q. You refer to some resolutions of various boards of directors
authorizing and directing the payment to you of sums of money
for your patents.   What companies had you in mind as having
taken that action?   A. The Interborough Rapid Transit Company.   That is the company that I am employed by, that is one of
them.   There are many other companies that I am not employed
by that are paying me royalties.

Q. When did the board of directors of the Interborough Rapid
Transit Company by a resolution authorize the payment to you
of a substantial sum of money for your patent?   A. Well, I
wouldn't say that it was a substantial sum of money when you
consider the value of the devices, but it seems to me that this
occurred about 1909.   That is the best of my recollection.

2

Q. Was this formal resolution, I mean this formal recognition more than once? A. Yes, sir. It occurred twice.

Q. And no oftener to your knowledge? A. Yes. I was forgetting another case, it was so far back. In 1903 when I came with the company I had a patent that they thought was very valuable. I told them they could put it on and they did put it on. They gave me a sum of money.

Q. You are speaking of the Interborough Rapid Transit Company? A. Yes, sir.

Q. And then in 1909 they did it again? A. Yes, sir. With another device.

Q. Then about four years ago they did it again with another device, did they not? A. Yes, sir.

Chairman Thompson.— If I may interrupt a minute. The Committee notes the presence of Senator Simpson of New York, one of the Senators.

By Mr. Colby (continuing):

Q. Did the Subway Construction Company ever formally award you a sum of money for your patent devices — in other words, with the exception of the three instances you have mentioned, was any such action ever taken by any company with which you are connected officially? A. No, sir.

Q. No such action was taken by the board of directors of the New York Railways Company? A. No, sir.

Q. Any constituent company? A. No, sir.

Q. Nor by the Manhattan Elevated Company? A. No, sir.

Q. Or its predecessors? A. No.

Q. What was the device that in 1912 was the basis of this award that you have testified to? A. That was a device that I had been working on for about fifteen years. I was working on that long before I came into the employ of the company.

Q. I asked you what it was? A. I am telling you exactly so that you will understand it. It is a machine that prints the records in the machine itself and shows the motorman what time he has coasted in making a trip from one end of the road to the other. That coasting time is valuable because from that you can determine whether the man is operating economically or not.

Q. In other words it registers the application or attachments of the electrical power to the motor, is that right? A. No, it registers the time that the train is passing over the road when it is not using any power either for driving the train or for stopping the train. The device is on all the subway and elevated cars or a sufficient number on each train so that it amounts to a saving of about six hundred thousand dollars to the company.

Q. You call that the coasting clock? A. Yes, sir.

Q. You give prizes to the motormen for the best record? A. Yes.

Q. In other words if they can maintain their schedule and cover their route with a minimum of applied electric power it is considered a good thing from the operating standpoint? A. Yes, sir. We recognize that by payment.

Q. And this invention called the coasting clock measures the time of application or cut off of power? A. Yes.

By Chairman Thompson:

Q. You buy your power on peak load basis, do you not? A. We don't buy any power.

Q. You use your own power? A. Yes, sir.

Q. And you produce it by a steam plant? A. Yes.

Q. Do you have the same annoyance with peak load that other producers of power have? A. We do not have that trouble.

Q. It don't bother you as to how much of a peak you might have? A. It would but we have sufficient surplus power all the time to take care of that.

Q. The question of peak load don't interfere with your power? A. It does not because we furnish enough generating units in the power plant to take care of that. The question of peak is taken care of on our cars in the subway in one way and the elevated in another way.

Q. Well the best use of power is to keep an average load just as near an average load per day as you can? A. Yes, sir, certainly.

Mr. Colby (continuing):

Q. You patented the coasting clock device? A. I did, sir. I have worked on it for a number of years. I took in our Mr. Doyle, our superintendent of car equipments.

Q. The patent is taken in your name? A. Yes, sir. In the name of myself and Doyle.

Q. I direct your mind to the action taken by the board of directors in 1912 in relation to this subject. What amount of of money did they pay you? A. They paid me $7.50 per clock per year; half of it to Mr. Doyle and half of it to me.

Q. That was the only payment authorized by the board with reference to this invention? A. That's all.

Q. How many of these clocks are now installed or in use by the Interborough Rapid Transit Company or the New York Railways Company? A. Well on the subway there is about four hundred, I think, somewhere around there, and I have eight or nine hundred on the elevated. I can't give you the correct aggregate figures.

Q. I wish you would put yourself in position to do that. Who manufactures the coasting clock? A. The clock part, which is a mechanical part, is made by the Time Register Company, Endicott, N. Y. I think that was the name of the concern. They make the clock part and the General Electric Company or the Westinghouse Company have both made portions of the electrical parts. You see this device is partly electrical and partly mechanical.

Q. From whom does the Interborough Rapid Transit Company buy the clocks completed? A. The Interborough has always bought these clocks direct from the manufacturers.

Q. From the Time Register Company or its successor? A. Yes.

Q. To your best recollection there are about thirteen or fourteen hundred now in use? A. Yes.

Q. And you and Mr. J. S. Doyle, the superintendent of car equipments, also an official or employee of the company, are receiving $7.50 per annum for each clock? A. Yes, $7.50 between us.

Q. Dividing it equally? A. Yes.

Q. That is one of the three devices that you refer to in your former testimony? A. That is so.

Q. What was the particular device which in 1909 was the basis of some special compensation from the company? A. That was known as the anti-climbing device. It is a device that goes on the end of the cars, either fixed or bolted on the end or made

a part of the car construction to prevent cars from telescoping
in a collision. It is a device that is made with rolled steel. When
I first got it out I patented it myself. That's owned by me
solely. I paid my counsel fees, paid the Washington fees and
sent some $2,700, I think it was, to the steel company for making
up a special set of rolls, all of which I personally paid for. The
company studied it with its engineer and immediately after it
was put on the market it was taken up by a great many railroads.
There are a great many railroads using it today. The Interborough Rapid Transit Company adopted it on both its subway
and elevated cars. It has in a great many cases saved human
life and property for the Interborough Rapid Transit Company
and elsewhere. The Interborough Rapid Transit Company
directors apparently recognized that and they passed a resolution, as I said I believe it was in 1912, to pay me a sum of money
for every car on which this device was attached and they have
been doing so ever since. That action was taken in 1912.

Q. You say they have been paying you that ever since this
action was taken in 1912? A. I think so. The record will show.
I can furnish you with a complete record showing all these facts.

Q. I shall ask you to exhibit to me the resolution or resolutions authorizing that action. When did you patent the anti-
climbing device? A. I think it was about a year or so before the
board of directors passed this resolution that I am telling you
about.

Q. Approximately in 1911? A. Yes.

Q. As I understand this anti-climbing device it consists of a
sort of protection to the end of the car platform? A. Yes.

Q. It is a sort of preventative in the event of collision or accident arising from any source? A. Yes.

Q. To prevent telescoping? A. Yes.

Q. Was this idea suggested to you by the experience of the
Manhattan Elevated or the subway, which you had observed?
A. It grew out of thirty years' experience.

Q. When did you begin the work of this anti-climbing device?
A. Oh I have seen the necessity for it for a great many years,
twenty-eight or thirty years. I saw the necessity of it for all that
time and I should say that it was perhaps two or three years before I patented it that —

Q. I think I understand the situation perfectly, Mr. Hedley. Now I want to ask you what do the companies by whom you are employed pay you by way of additional compensation for these devices? A. Well I wouldn't say by way of additional compensation. They pay me $10 for each car it is put on.

Q. The Interborough Rapid Transit Company? A. Yes.

Q. The Manhattan Elevated Company? A. Yes, sir. That's the same. The Interborough Rapid Transit Company operates the Manhattan Elevated.

Q. These inventions you own exclusively? A. Yes.

Q. The patents are in your name? A. Yes.

Q. How many cars are equipped with this anti-climbing device on the subway? A. All of them, sir.

Q. How many? A. About twelve hundred.

Q. That is the total number of cars now operated down in the subway? A. Yes. We are operating about twelve hundred. I can give you the correct figures on this.

Q. Well this will do. How many on the elevated lines? A. About sixteen hundred on the elevated lines.

Q. That makes in all twenty-eight hundred? A. That's about right, sir.

Q. And you receive $10 a car from these cars per annum? A. No, $10 a car for a total. They put these on all the cars and pay me $10 a car and they have access to it for all times.

Q. When did that arrangement begin? A. About 1912.

Q. And since then you have received approximately $30,000 for that? A. Yes, that is from these companies that I am employed by. There are thousands of cars using it on other companies.

Q. Did you receive the same price from other companies? A. Some of them I got more. If I can get more I make them pay more.

Q. How many companies use this anti-climbing device? A. I should say thirty or forty.

Q. Steam railroads? A. Steam railroads with the electrical equipment, yes, sir.

Q. They are scattered throughout the country? A. Yes, sir. throughout the world.

Q. How many companies pay you more than $10 per car for the use of this device? A. Not very many.

Q. That's just a little incomplete as an answer. Can you approximately tell me? A. There was one company that I have in mind that paid me more.

Q. Did this company pay more than $10 per car? A. Yes.

Q. How many companies pay less than $10. A. Quite a lot, quite a lot, of course, pay me less than $10 per car now.

Q. What is the lowest price that any company has paid you for this device? A. The lowest price that I remember is $5.

Q. How many of the companies have paid you that? A. Some of them have paid more than that. When the demands have been made direct to me they have paid no less than $10. When the demands are made to the Railway Improvement Company, that I used to be a stockholder in and in which I no longer have connection therewith, the Railway Improvement Company have the right to sell these anti-climbers to anyone other than the companies that I am employed by. Then they make their own deal with the outside railway companies as to what royalty they get but under no circumstances can they make a deal with any railway that will be made less than $5 a car.

Q. And if they deal directly with you and you are an officer of the company they have got to pay you $10 per car? A. That was made in 1912 and I recall it and a resolution was passed at that time, this award of $10 per car. In fact I think it's worth more.

Q. How many companies buy the right to use this device directly from you? A. None of them. I don't give them,— (Interruption by Mr. Colby).

Q. The companies that do not use this device are whom? A. The Interborough and the New York Railways Company. The New York Railways Company have not used any of the devices. They are not necessary on a street car.

Q. In other words the subway and elevated companies are the only ones that use this device, deal with the Improvement Company? A. That's correct.

Q. And the Railway Improvement Company sell this device at varying figures, the only restrictions therein being that they must pay you $5 per car for this device? A. I think that's the way the agreement reads.

Q. That is a written agreement, is it not? A. I think it is.

Q. I don't want to ask you any question that is stray of the boundaries of direct relevancy to this inquiry, Mr. Hedley, but it appears that there is only one company that pays more for the privilege of using this device than does the Interborough Rapid Transit Company in which you are an officer, that all with the exception of that one company and the Interborough Rapid Transit Company deal with the Railways Improvement Company on apparently easier terms than either the Interborough or the elevated deal with you for this device. It seems to me that I should therefore ask to have you name the companies,— (interruption by witness). A. Well the statement that you have made is not entirely true. I would like you to understand that I am perfectly willing to tell you everything. I have nothing to conceal. I have got a clear conscience and I will tell you everything you want to know. Why the Hudson and Manhattan, the McAdoo tunnel, the Pennsylvania railroad are people paying $10 per car. They pay $10 per car to me.

Chairman Thompson.— You said one company paid you more than $10. A. I think it was the Southern Pacific, and Electric Apparatus. I am not sure but I think they paid $15.

Q. How many cars have they? A. I haven't the slightest idea, several hundred I believe.

Mr. Colby (resuming):

Q. How does the Interborough pay you on this device, from month to month as new cars are equipped with it? A. As new cars are equipped they send me a check and voucher at the rate of $10 per car.

Q. What did you receive last month on this account? A. Oh, we have got some new cars coming in. I think I got eight or nine hundred dollars.

Q. What did you receive last year on this account? A. Oh, I don't know.

Q. Can you give us that amount approximately? A. No, I don't think I can.

Q. Have you any workshop? A. What do you mean?

Q. Well, where do you do your work upon these measurements of your devices or where is your workshop for the purpose of perfecting these various devices that you have spoken of? A. No, I have no workshop outside the workshop I have in my own house.

Q. How extensive is that workshop? A. I have got about everything there that I know of. I haven't used it very much of late. I have any amount of tools, as far as bench tools are concerned.

Q. Have you a private dwelling in the city, Mr. Hedley? A. No, sir.

Q. Where do you live? A. In Yonkers.

Q. You live in a house there? A. Yes.

Q. And it is in that house where this workshop is? A. No. It used to be in that house but I have moved it out in the country house.

Q. What was the other device that you sold to the Interborough Rapid Transit Company, which you licensed the Interborough Rapid Transit Company to use? A. That is the third rail cleaning device.

Q. Will you explain that to us briefly? A. That is a device for sweeping the snow or sleet off the third rail when there is a snow or sleet storm. That's known as the Hedley Third Rail Scraper. I patented that before I came in the employ the last time of these companies. I was then employed in Chicago. The first year I came down here they had a lot of trouble with a sleet and snow storm. Perhaps you remember they didn't run these cars for a while.

By Chairman Thompson:

Q. On the subway? A. On the elevated.

By Mr. Colby:

Q. The devices were installed on all the elevated cars? A. They were purchased in the open market, in fact most of them were manufactured in shops in —

Chairman Thompson.— You mean in the Manhattan Elevated shops?

Mr. Hedley.— Yes.

Chairman Thompson.— And in the Interborough shops?

Mr. Hedley.— In the Manhattan shops at that time. They were applied to the Manhattan cars and the company had the free right to use it and do use it now without payment of royalty. They had however recognized the value of it and they paid me a sum of money for the patent.

Chairman Thompson.— How much?

Mr. Hedley.— Five thousand dollars if I recall it.

Chairman Thompson.— For all your rights?

Mr. Hedley.— Yes.

Chairman Thompson.— And that was for permanent use?

Mr. Hedley.— Yes.

Chairman Thompson.— That is sort of a whisk broom?

Mr. Hedley.— No, it has no bristles on it whatever. It's really a steel scraper.

By Mr. Colby:

Q. What other devices, if any, have you patented and disposed of to the companies by whom you are employed? A. I have patented a great many other things that the company is using and in all these things I always paid my personal patent attorney's fees and my Washington fees and all money connected with the matter I paid personally. I have done that in a great many cases, for the Interborough Rapid Transit Company are using these devices for which I have not received and may not receive any compensation therefor. I haven't even got my money yet for that that I paid in.

Chairman Thompson.— How much does it cost to get out a patent?

Mr. Hedley.— It costs anywhere from $75 to $5,000.

Chairman Thompson.— Have you got any patents that cost you $5,000?

Mr. Hedley.— I can't recall any just now.

Chairman Thompson.— Have you got any that cost over $200?

Mr. Hedley.— Oh, yes.

Chairman Thompson.— Got any that cost over $500?

Mr. Hedley.— Yes.

Chairman Thompson.— How many? Well, generally they cost between $100 and $200 as a rule, don't they?

Mr. Hedley.— I think that is the proper price.

By Mr. Colby:

Q. Will you enumerate briefly the devices that you obtained and which are used by the Interborough Rapid Transit Company on the subway or the elevated line? A. I obtained the railroad truck which is used very largely on the Interborough Rapid Transit Company and on many other companies, for which the Interborough Company has paid no royalty. I patented a number of things in connection with low level and double deck cars. I patented a device for interlocking the car doors with the controller.

Q. Was that called the Hedley door? A. No.

Q. You don't mean the door at the side of the car that is opened or which is opened by the guard of the platform? A. I mean the center side door. It is a device for locking the center side door so that it cannot be opened by the guard when the steps are down.

Q. Not for opening or shutting it, but for locking it? A. No, not for opening or shutting it. I patented a device for regulating the ventilation of the car that was graduated according to the number of people that there were in the car. If there were more people, more air, less people and of course less air.

Chairman Thompson.— It is a safeguard against too much ventilation?

Mr. Hedley.— No, I would not say so. It is a safeguard against getting too much ventilation, and retaining as much ventilation as is necessary without regard as to whether the car is crowded or not. That was the idea of the device. I patented another device that regulates braking efficiency on the car with a view to maintaining the maximum braking efficiency that you can have on any car whether it is loaded or empty.

By Mr. Colby:

Q. In simple terms that is a device for maintaining the efficiency of the brakes on the car, isn't it? A. Yes, sir.

Q. In other words a more simple braking system? A. No. I wouldn't call it a simple braking system.

Q. Well, what does it do? What is it? A. I think I would describe it to you in simple language in this way. If you get a hundred thousand pound car, the foundation brake on that car has got to be arranged so that you will use about ninety to ninety-five per cent of the correct load of the car for breaking purposes and now if the load of one hundred thousand pounds is stopped in that car then your braking efficiency is immediately gone down to about half or about forty-five per cent. This device is supposed to be applied to a car with a hundred thousand pounds capacity if you please and then if it is loaded with a hundred thousand pounds more that you will have the same ninety-five per cent braking efficiency on the two hundred thousand pounds.

Q. Now, what is the device? Have you investigated to accomplish these desirable results? A. That's described very fully in the patent of which I can give you a copy.

Q. Would you give me a simple statement of the nature of the mechanism? A. Well, this is to increase the pressure. You see, under this device the brakes may project so that it is pressed down to one inch and you get more air; if it comes down to two inches of course you get more still.

Q. What is that done for, to save air? A. That's to increase the pressure.

Q. That's applicable to any railroad company in the country? A. That's done so that if you have a train of empty cars and you are running along at forty miles an hour, you can stop in a thousand feet while that same train if it were loaded, instead of stopping in a thousand feet you would run about fifteen hundred feet.

Q. Will you please continue your enumeration of these different devices that you have patented? A. When I say a great many of these things were patented I mean they were patented between Mr. Doyle, our superintendent of car equipments, and myself.

Q. You might distinguish just which ones you patented yourself and the ones that were patented jointly between you and Mr. Doyle? A. The trucks that I mentioned is entirely mine and the anti-climber is entirely mine. The others have all been joint patents. We had a patent on a low level car, several patents on that. There is a patent on double deck cars. There is a patent on an electric contact shoe. That is on all of the subway cars and the chances are it is going on all the elevated cars too. It looks as though we would have to put that on. If he didn't have we would have to move the trolley rail. To move the trolley rail would cost about six hundred thousand dollars.

Q. How much did you get for the patent? A. The patent up to date cost me about $200 of my own money and I have never had anything back yet. I paid for the securing of the patent, counsel fees, and so forth. The company uses it and have never paid a dollar for it. Then there is the straphanger that I have seen referred to in the papers.

Q. I have sometimes heard that term myself.

Chairman Thompson.— That is the thing that is most in use by the citizens of New York, isn't it?

Mr. Hedley.— I hope it will continue to be used because if it isn't, the city of New York and the Interborough Rapid Transit Company both may go into the hands of a receiver.

Q. I really like to hang on to a strap because I feel that for the time at least I am bringing about a dividend for the company? A. That listens very satisfactorily. But getting back to this matter of the strap that you refer to, the company has been permitted to use it and never paid a penny for it.

Chairman Thompson.— And you paid out about $200. ·

Mr. Hedley.— Yes. I don't know, it may have been less.

Chairman Thompson.— Well, a patent runs anywheres from $100 up?

Mr. Hedley.— Well, I suppose it does

Q. Will you continue your enumerations? A. That's about all I think of. There may be a lot of others. I cannot think of them now but I will be glad to give you a list of them.

Q. I wish you would give me a complete statement of the patents. That is, I would like a statement of the devices patented by yourself. individually or jointly with Mr. Doyle.

Chairman Thompson.— Or jointly with anybody else.

Mr. Hedley.— I will give you a complete list.

Q. Can you let me have this at 2 o'clock? A. I don't know. I think I can. I will try.

Q. Were these devices that you have enumerated all developed and completed within the last few years? A. No, sir. They have been developed for the last twenty years.

Q. Is that true of all these devices? A. Oh, no, some of them are very new. Some of the patents are pending yet.

Q. Will you mention any patent, the period of whose development and perfection antedates your connection with the Interborough Rapid Transit Company? A. Oh, yes. The car truck did. There's another thing there also. I patented a cylinder cock.

Q. Now with the exception of the car trucks were there any patents that antedate your connection with the Interborough Railway Company? A. No, except the third rail cleaner, that's the sleet scraper. I think that's all.

Q. The rest you have worked upon and developed and perfected while you have been in the employment of the Interborough Rapid Transit Company? A. That's correct.

Q. Some of these experiments involved a number of failures, did they not? A. No. Any that we are using proved successful.

Q. I mean that in perfecting these devices to a usable degree of perfection you have been obliged to discard some completed devices as imperfect. In other words there has been considerable use of material and waste of material in perfecting them to the point where they could be used. A. No, sir, I wouldn't say that. There has been some work of course that would be partially completed and when we got there perhaps there was something lacking and we would change it.

Q. Whom do you mean by we? A. Why myself and Mr. Doyle or anyone in the engineering department associated with the Railway Company.

Q. It would be very extraordinary for inventors to carry into certain and practical form any idea that has occurred to them, would it not? A. It cannot be done. They have an instance of that at 14th street. We are spending a lot of money on that and we find it necessary to make a great many changes. We have made a great many changes. It isn't completed in a satisfactory form yet. Of course the company is doing that, doing it, because we want to save the lives of the people. We want to make it safe at that point. I have paid for all these patents. I own them myself and Mr. Doyle together and the company will use it without payment of any money to us.

Q. That the company is paying for the mechanical and practical work of developing and perfecting your patents? A. Yes.

Q. Well, isn't that the real cost of the patent? A. No. Sometimes it is and sometimes it is not. In a number of these instances I don't suppose the company spent anything. I don't believe they spent a cent.

Q. How many double deck cars have you built? A. Only one.

Q. How many have you completed, or partially completed? A. Nothing but the one, sir. We built a model car in the car house.

Q. You mean the Interborough Rapid Transit Company? A. No, sir, the New York Railways.

Q. The patent is in the name of yourself and Mr. Doyle? A. Yes.

Q. How many shops has the Interborough Rapid Transit Company? A. We have shops at 99th street and Third avenue. We have got shops at 148th street and Lenox avenue, 129th street and Third avenue, that is between Second and Third avenues. They are the principal shops. We have many other smaller places.

Q. That is where the experiments are made on these patents? A. When we have anything new to make we would make it at 148th street or at 99th street, one of these two shops.

Q. How long have you been in receipt of $50,000 per annum from the traction companies? A. Oh, it's less than a year. I think it's about eight months.

Q. What was your salary prior to that? A. My salary was $40,000. It isn't enough either.

Q. You are entitled to receive more salary? A. I feel that I am, yes, sir.

Q. Have you taken it up with the board? A. No, sir. I wouldn't ask for it.

Q. What is the total revenue you derive from the Interborough Rapid Transit Company, the Manhattan Railway Company, the Subway Construction Company and all these companies with which you are connected? A. I have told you all of it outside of the securities.

Q. I don't refer to the securities. You have mentioned a salary of $50,000 and you mentioned the income from the patent devices amounting to a certain amount? A. Well, I have given you the amount of my salary.

Q. Well, now how much do you receive from the coasting clock? A. Well, at $7.50 a machine.

Chairman Thompson.— That's approximately $9,750, that's about $5,000 apiece for Mr. Hedley and Mr. Doyle.

Q. Well, there are other devices which produce you an income? A. Yes, I have already stated them.

Chairman Thompson.— How much do you get out of the straphanger device?

Mr. Hedley.— Not a cent. Not from the Interborough.

By Chairman Thompson:

Q. Do you get any income from any corporation? A. I don't think I have ever had anything out of that.

Q. You have arrangements by which you do get an income? A. By which I will. I haven't any now.

By Mr. Colby:

Q. You were president of the Railway Improvement Company for a number of years? A. Yes, sir. I caused the Railway Improvement Company to be organized. I organized it for the purpose of having a company that would sell the device that I was interested in and only to the railway companies, outside of the railway companies that I was employed by. I retained the presidency of that company all the while I was connected with it, and the reason I did that was that I insisted that the companies that I was employed by could not purchase a penny's worth of material from the Railway Improvement Company. I was president of that company up to February of last year, and the Railway

Company that I was employed by never did buy a penny's worth from the Railway Improvement Company.

Q. Did not the Railway Improvement Company deal in materials and economical devices? A. They did, sir, but I wanted to have my record absolutely clear.

Q. Even if the company, of which you are or were an officer, was thereby deprived of obtaining material contracts? A. They never did that while I was connected with that company. I had given instructions that they were not even to quote the Interborough Rapid Transit Company on anything, and they didn't. As far as these devices are concerned, they could buy these from the manufacturer out in the open market, and do it today.

Q. How does it come that Mr. Doyle, also an employee of the Interborough Rapid Transit Company, was the treasurer of this Railway Improvement Company? A. Because he owned the same amount of stock as I did in that company. He had the same amount of stock as I did, and I wanted him to know of the position that I was taking, that I did not believe it proper for him to be interested in any officer in a supply company.

Q. Is not Mr. Doyle the purchasing agent of the Interborough Rapid Transit Company? A. No.

Q. Is he interested in the matter of the purchasing? A. No, sir. He is the superintendent of car equipment of the Interborough Rapid Transit Company.

Q. In other words, the position very closely related to the character of merchandise that the Railway Improvement Company was engaged in promoting? Is that not correct? A. Mr. Doyle makes out requisitions for materials.

Q. What I mean is this: You were dealing in railway equipment? A. No, not in the broad sense.

Q. I mean in the true sense you were dealing with devices that was a part of the equipment of the railway? A. Substantially, yes, sir.

Q. Mr. Doyle is the superintendent of car equipment of the Interborough Rapid Transit Company? A. Yes.

Q. How much stock does he own in the Railway Improvement Company? A. He owned the same as I did, and I think it was 130 shares.

Q. Par value of what amount? A. Par.

Q. Did you receive a salary as president? A. No, sir.

Q. Did you receive a dividend as a shareholder? A. No, sir.

Q. Did you ever make any money out of the Railway Improvement Company? A. No, sir, not by dividends.

Q. Is the company solvent? A. Oh, yes, I believe so. I don't know of its financial standing since February, a year ago. I sold every interest that I had in it.

Q. To whom did you sell your stock? A. I sold it to Mr. Andrew Pazermann.

Q. What is his address? A. He lives at the Ansonia.

Q. His business address? A. I think he is at 61 Broadway.

Q. Is Mr. Kenyon your Patent Attorney? A. Perhaps Mr. Kenyon has passed on some patent papers for me.

Q. Was he associated with you in the Railway Improvement Company. A. He was. That is, he had some legal work advising us on papers.

Q. Mr. Kenyon was a member of the board of directors? A. He was. I don't think he is now.

Q. Who were the other members of the board of directors? A. The other member of the board of directors I think was, the only one I can remember, is Senator Fairchild, Congressman Fairchild.

Q. When did you sell your stock to Mr. Pazermann. A. I sold it in February, 1915.

Q. You had owned it for five years or more? A. About that time, I don't remember just how long.

Q. Had it ever paid a dividend? A. No, sir. There was so much extra work, engineering work, on the outside, private engineers, in experimenting, that we were not in position to pay a dividend. I understand the company is making money now.

Q. Was Mr. Pazermann anxious to secure your stock? A. Yes.

Q. Did he ever make any offer to buy your stock prior to 1913? A. Yes, he had been after it for several years, at least two or three years for me to sell before I did.

Q. Did he want to get you out of the company? A. Well, I don't know. I don't know of any reason why he should.

Q. And ordinarily a man would like to have a man in your important position own stock in the company? A. I don't know that that would be so. As long as I own stock in his company I recognize the fact the company of which I was an employee would certainly never buy anything from him, that is the Railway Improvement Company. I mean that the company that I was employed by would never buy anything from this Railway Improvement Company.

Q. As I understand it, Mr. Pazermann bought not only your stock, but Mr. Doyle's? A. Yes.

Q. Was he trying to get control of this company that paid no dividends? A. Yes. The statement showed it could pay a dividend if they wanted it.

Q. Did you and Mr. Doyle have some talk about disposing of your holdings in the Railway Improvement Company? A. Yes, two or three days before we did.

Q. Did Mr. Pazermann pay you cash for your stock? A. Yes, sir. He paid some cash and gave me his note for the balance, and has since paid that. I have got the cash for this stock.

Q. How much did you get? A. For a hundred and thirty shares, I got twelve thousand five hundred dollars. Just a little bit below par, and the note has been paid.

Q. That's pretty good stock, despite the fact that it has not paid any dividends? A. Of course it is. I would advise you to buy some, if you can get it.

Q. After holding it for four or five years, why did you sell it, when it was just getting in condition to pay dividends? A. Well, I had no particular reason for selling it.

Q. Didn't you consider that you had buttressed yourself against criticism as between the Railway Improvement Company and the Interborough Rapid Transit Company, if any sales should be made between the two corporations? A. I think I had a very c'ean record on that. I know I did. I know I had a clean conscience.

Q. Your conscience might probably have been just a little elastic? A. Not a bit.

Q. Then why did you sell your stock? A. It was only a matter of the price of the stock, namely twelve thousand five hundred dollars, and rather than have any trouble for minds that have not been properly trained, I would rather sell the stock and leave no room open for criticism.

Q. To what minds as improperly trained have you reference?
A. There are always people whose minds are not properly trained.

Q. Is it or is it not a fact that you sold your stock in this improvement company to Mr. Pazermann after this Committee had opened its sessions? A. I sold it in February.

Q. This Committee began its hearings in January, 1915. A. I never heard of this Committee until four months ago. That is news to me.

Q. When did you resign as President of the Railway Improvement Company? A. In February I got out bag and baggage.

Q. And did your fellow corporate employee, Mr. Doyle, also resign at that time? A. Yes.

Q. You resigned simultaneously? A. Yes.

Q. He sold his, then you sold yours? A. Yes.

Q. And you had held it since the organization of the company?
A. Yes.

Q. And you remained with the company during its time of adversity until it showed promise of producing a dividend? A. Yes, sir.

Q. You had brought the stock to a point where it began to show a possibility of profit? A. Yes, sir.

Q. Do you mean to tell me that you did this with no idea in your mind that this joint Legislative Committee was on your trail? A. I did not.

Mr. Colby.—We will now take a recess until 2 P. M.

Whereupon, a recess was taken to 2 o'clock P. M., same day and same place.

AFTERNOON SESSION

The Committee was called to order at 2:20 P. M., Chairman Thompson in the Chair.

The Chairman.—All witnesses under subpoena for 2 o'clock — that don't mean those under subpoena for 11 o'clock this morning, does it?

Mr. Colby.— No.

The Chairman.— Those for 11 o'clock are not excused yet, but all those for 2 o'clock today are now excused until tomorrow morning at 11 o'clock, the subpoena to stand. You are directed to appear to-morrow morning at 11 o'clock.

FRANK HEDLEY, recalled.

Mr. Colby.— Shall we resume, Mr. Chairman?

The Chairman.— Proceed.

Examination by Mr. Colby:

Q. Had you a contract of employment with the Interborough? A. I had one, but I don't remember whether it has run out or not. I have had a contract with them for employment.

Q. You consider yourself under a contractual engagement to the Interboro? A. Why, I do for each year, yes.

Q. Has it been customary to renew or re-execute your contract of employment from year to year? A. It has been renewed, but as I say, I don't recall whether it has run out or not, but a resolution of the board of directors is passed every year appointing me to the position that I now hold, for a year.

Q. Have you a copy of your last contract with the Interborough? A. Yes, I must have a copy, if it has not run out; and if it has run out, I will have a copy.

Q. Will you let me have that contract? A. Yes.

Q. Have you a contract of hiring or employment with the Manhattan Elevated? A. No, sir. The Interborough Rapid Transit Company operate the Manhattan, so that from the Interborough Rapid Transit Company contract, if it still is running, it will include the running of the Interborough — the elevated.

Q. Have you a contract of employment with any company other than the Interborough? A. No, sir.

Q. At the present time? A. No, sir.

Q. And have you had contracts of employment with other companies at any time during your relations with the Interborough as an officer? A. No, sir.

Q. Have you been able to complete a list of the various patented articles or devices that you own individually or in conjunction with Mr. Doyle? A. No, sir, I asked that a list be prepared immediately I went upstairs, and my young men are preparing it. They will bring it down here as soon as it is ready.

Q. Have you received any stated share of the purchase price of your devices when bought by the Interborough from the manufacturing or selling companies? A. No, sir.

Q. You never have participated in the sale of the proceeds of your patented devices to the Interborough? A. Not when the Interborough has used them; no, sir. I have not received a penny compensation from any outside concern for devices that the Interborough used that I own or have an interest therein.

Q. Your interest in the devices in so far as they are used by the Interborough is only in royalties for the privilege — A. Well, my interest is to get these devices for the use of the Interborough and let the Interborough use them freely, which they do, unless in special cases where the board of directors have elected to pay me something. They do not have to do it, but they do in the cases that I have told you of, and that is all.

Q. You organized the Railway Improvement Company, did you not? A. Yes, sir; I was one of the organizers of that company.

Q. What was its capital stock upon its organization? A. I don't remember.

Q. Was it paid for in cash. A. All stock that was issued was paid for in cash except the stock that Mr. Doyle and myself got as the owners of the patents.

Q. What patents? A. The patents that the Railway Improvement Company were going to sell to railroad companies outside of railroad companies that I was employed by.

Q. What were those patents? A. Why, the coasting time recorders, anti-climbers, sanitary hand straps. That is all I recall just now.

Q. What interest in those devices did you turn over to the Railway Improvement Company as consideration for this stock issued to you and Doyle? A. Why, they have a right to sell the anti-climbers to any other railroads excepting the railroad companies that I am employed by. They have the same right on the sanitary hand-straps. And the patents I think Mr. Doyle and I assigned to the Railway Improvement Company. I think we did. I am not sure.

Q. I would like to know whether the stock was issued for the selling right or for the ownership of the devices themselves? A. Well, it was issued for the— what was considered to be the privilege of having the exclusive sale of those patented devices to railroads other than the Interborough.

Q. In other words, the stock was issued for a restricted right of sale and that alone? A. Well, the only restriction was that they could not sell anything to the Interborough that employed me.

Q. Yes. I assume of course that you retained the ownership in the patents, because you were collecting royalties thereon from the Interborough at that time? A. I don't recall that I did retain the ownership.

Q. How could you collect royalties other than as the owner of the right? A. Because they have, under a contract, agreed to pay me royalties.

Q. Whether you are the owner of the patents or not? A. Well, I did own the patents, but I am not sure but — though I can find out for you — just what we did with that — whether I did really assign the patent or whether I gave them the exclusive right to sell to other railroad companies. I don't remember, sir.

Q. Could you have assigned your patents to the Railway Improvement Company and continued to collect royalties — A. Oh yes.

Q. — thereon? A. Oh, yes sir. There are frequent cases of that kind, the patentee sells his patent to a manufacturer and assigns the patent outright, and in the sale he makes a provision that for all time during the life of the patent they are to pay him so much for every machine or device that is sold.

Q. I will leave the subject of the patents for the moment, Mr. Hedley, until I have the complete list, so that I can close this branch of my inquiry without repetition. A. All right, sir.

Q. You received a letter from the Chairman of the Joint Legislative Committee, dated January 27, 1916, requesting certain information, did you not? A. I received a letter requesting certain information. I don't recall the date, sir.

Q. Would you recall the communication if I showed you a copy of it? A. I think I would, sir.

(Counsel hands witness a copy of letter.)

The Witness.— Yes, I think I received a copy of this. This looks the same as I received.

Mr. Colby.— May I ask you, Senator Thompson, if that has been made a part of the record?

Chairman Thompson.— Yes, I think so. I am not sure.

Mr. Perley Morse.— It has not been.

Mr. Colby.— I would like to have this letter entered as a part of the record and set forth as read.

Q. You replied to this request? A. Yes.

Chairman Thompson.— Take it as an exhibit.

(The letter was marked Exhibit No. 1 of January 31, 1916, and is as follows:)

THE SENATE OF
THE STATE OF NEW YORK
ALBANY

GEORGE F. THOMPSON,
  47th District, Chairman,
    Committee on Public Service.

DEAR SIR:
  — re *Joint Legislative Committee to Investigate Public
  Service Commissions.*

Please be kind enough to send to our accountants, Messrs. Perley Morse & Company, Certified Public Accountants, 61 Broadway, New York, N. Y., immediately, answers to the following questions:

Question No. 1.— What are the names and addresses of all corporations, firms or individuals, subject to the provisions of the New York State Public Service Law, in which you have had a financial interest during the years 1914 and 1915?

(a) What is the par value of stock owned or controlled by you in such corporation; is it preferred or common?

(b) What is the par value of bonds owned or controlled by you in such corporation; what is the description thereof?

(c) What interest have you in such firms or individuals and what have you received on the investment?

This relates to investments standing in your own name or that of another, provided you control same, either personally or as agent or trustee.

Question No. 2.— Have you any interest in any firm or corporation from whom purchases have been made during 1914 or 1915 by any corporation of which you are an officer, director or employe? If so, state the amount of such interest, nature and value thereof; when acquired and price paid by you therefor.

Question No. 3.— If you have any such interest mentioned in Question No. 2, have you loaned money to or borrowed money from any corporation, firm or individual, or any employee thereof, subject to the provisions of the New York State Public Service Law during the years 1914 and 1915?

Has any corporation, firm or individual, or any employee thereof, subject to the New York State Public Service Law loaned money to or borrowed money from you during the years 1914 and 1915?

In answering this question, please give names, dates and amounts. This relates to loans standing in your own name or that of another, provided you control same, either personally or as an agent or trustee.

Yours very truly,

Chairman, Joint Legislative Com-
mittee to Investigate Public
Service Commissions.

Q. Mr. Morse, the accountant of the Committee, called my attention to the fact that this copy bears the date of January 27, 1916. It was a form letter, and inasmuch as your reply was dated January 19, 1916, I assume that a copy of this letter under an earlier date than it bears was sent to you, Mr. Hedley? A. Yes, sir, that looks exactly the same as a letter I had, without reading it in detail.

Mr. Perley Morse.— You received that on the 13th of January?

The Witness.— I don't remember when I received it or when it was dated.

Q. I hand you a letter apparently written by you dated January 19, 1916, and ask you if it is your reply to the request for the information above referred to, received from the Committee. I think it is unquestionably correct — A. (Witness looks at letter.) Yes, sir, that is my reply to the Chairman of this Committee and to the accountant of the Committee.

(Assemblyman Burr takes the Chair.)

Mr. Colby.— I will read this reply from Mr. Hedley, and ask that it be set forth in the record and entered as a letter received by the Committee from Mr. Hedley, Mr. Chairman.

> Hon. GEORGE F. THOMPSON, *Chairman, Joint Legislative Committee to Investigate Public Service Commissions:*
>
> SIR.— Pursuant to your former request of January 13, 1916, the undersigned has transmitted to your accountants, Messrs. Perley Morse & Company, 61 Broadway, in answer to your questions Nos. 1 and 2, the names and addresses of all corporations, firms or individuals subject to the provisions of the New York State Public Service Commissions Law, in which he has had a financial interest or with whom he has had personal business relations during the years 1914 and 1915. Also the names and addresses of corporations, firms or individuals who have had, according to his knowledge or information, financial relations or business transactions with corporations, firms or individuals subject to the provisions of the New York State Public Service Commissions Law, in which the undersigned had a financial interest or with whom he has had personal business relations during the years 1914 and 1915.
>
> In answer to your question No. 3, the undersigned states that he has not loaned money to or borrowed money from any corporation, firm or individual, or any employee thereof, subject to the provisions of the New York State Public Service Commissions Law during the years 1914 and 1915.
>
> In addition to the above information, you have requested the exact extent of such financial interest through stock or bond ownership or otherwise, from whom acquired, and the price paid and the return which such investment has yielded.

It is respectfully submitted that such matters are not material proper, legal or pertinent to the subject your Committee was appointed to investigate, which is the Public Service Commissions with reference to their organization, powers and duties, and their administration of the same, with a view to ascertaining what changes, if any, in such organization, powers, duties and administration are advisable in the interest of the public welfare and efficiency of such commission, and to examine and revise the Public Service Commissions Law and such other laws or parts of laws as may be necessary to harmonize all existing provisions of such law applicable to the regulation of public utilities.

The line of inquiry to which objection is taken if pursued would become, as was said by the Supreme Court of the United States, simply a fruitless investigation into the personal affairs of individuals, and would constitute, as the undersigned is advised by counsel, an invasion of the liberty of the individual, the protection of which is guaranteed by our State and Federal Constitutions.

The answers given to your questions have been thus limited, not because of any desire to withhold pertinent information from your Committee, but in the hope that when attention is called to the scope of your inquiries, your Committee will be glad to limit the questions to the sphere which has been clearly defined both by the Federal Courts and the courts of this State. If, however, your counsel does not agree with the decision taken, the undersigned will co-operate to expedite a judicial decision as to the propriety of such questions.

(Signed)   FRANK HEDLEY, Vice-President and General Manager.

Q. You refer to a decision of the Supreme Court of the United States, and you quote the words " Simply a fruitless investigation into the personal affairs of individuals." What case are you referring to there, Mr. Hedley? A. I don't personally know of the case. That part of the letter was prepared by counsel for me.

Q. Wasn't the letter in its entirety prepared by counsel? A. Very largely, yes, sir, although I did look it over during its course of preparation.

Q. We have received letters from a number of officers of the Interborough and they all refer the Committee to this case in the Supreme Court of the United States. They all quote the same sentence from this case. You don't know what the case is? A. I don't, no, sir.

Q. You don't know the Supreme Court ever used that language? A. I don't know the Supreme Court ever used that language.

Q. You don't know in what connection that language was used? A. Personally I don't know; no, sir.

Q. To what extent is it your opinion, as stated here, that this inquiry should be limited? A. Why, my opinion was and is now, although I may be wrong — I frequently am — that if I bought stock fifteen or twenty years ago, or bonds in a company that has sold or done business with a corporation that comes under the Public Service Commissions of this State, that it does not seem to me to be any business of this investigation commission as to when I bought that stock, how much I paid for it, who I bought it from, and how much return I have been receiving from it.

Q. Would you say that applied to the Railway Improvement Company? A. Why, I would say in a general way it applies to anything, to any business that I was ever engaged in.

Q. Would you say that where you have utilized the materials, the labor, the shops, of the Interborough Company, of which you are a highly salaried officer, for the development and protection of certain devices, and then had taken a patent in your own name, and had transferred the selling rights of the patent generally to the Railway Improvement Company for stock, that this Committee has no interest in ascertaining the circumstances of the issuance of that stock to you? A. Yes. That is a little different matter to what I first cited. But the question as I understood it from that letter was too broad. It did not only go back for four or five or six years, but it went back for all time. If I bought stock twenty years ago — in some cases I did buy stock twenty years ago — under that question I would have to find out who I bought it from, how much I paid for it, and how much return it was paying me. Now, with the Railway Improvement Company, it is a different proposition entirely, as I view it. The Railway Improvement Company was a corporation which, I have stated, I caused to be incorporated. I wanted to keep and did keep that corporation absolutely clear from the companies that employed me. We would not and did not buy anything from them, and I would not permit it. Now the sums of money that you spoke of that the company spent in developing these things were insignificant sums of money, and they have had tremendous benefits out of the development of these things. If I, for instance —

Q. Just a minute. Let me just interrupt you there. You say insignificant. You don't mean to imply unsubstantial? A. Yes, I do.

Q. Of course the Interborough deals in figures of such magnitude. A. When I say that, I mean a few hundred dollars. I confine myself to a few hundred dollars, sir. Now, the railroad company, if I should not patent those things, why, to a very large degree some one else would. And then the Interborough would have to pay very large sums for royalties.

Q. But you have already testified in the case of one of these devices that they paid ten dollars for each device where everybody else paid about five. A. No, I didn't say everybody else. I beg your pardon. I said some others paid ten and some paid more and some paid less than ten. Those are the facts.

Q. Let us get the facts exactly. · A. If a thing is worth ten dollars —

Q. Just a minute. Let us get exactly the facts. I think we are discussing the coasting clock — or is it the anti-climbers? A. The anti-climbers.

Q. You testified that some thirty or forty corporations were using it? A. I should think that was about right. May be more.

Q. You testified that two were paying at least as much as the Interborough were paying you as royalties. A. Oh, there is more than that paying —

Q. I endeavored to find out who were paying more and you said the Southern Pacific you thought paid more. A. I think that is right. I think the Southern Pacific did pay more.

Q. You also testified this corporation with which you were identified for five years until February last year has the right to sell it for five dollars per installation? A. That is, five dollars comes to me. They put a royalty on of whatever they please.

Q. The ten dollars you receive from the Interborough comes to you, so the comparison is fair. It sold through the Railway Im-

provement Company in which you were a stockholder and of which
you were president five years. You were satisfied with five dollars per installation, but dealing with the company of which you
are vice-president and manager, you want ten dollars? A. No, I
beg your pardon, sir. The price for the anti-climbers is scaled on
the kind of car it goes on. If it goes on an elevated car — which
it has gone on, the elevated cars in Boston, and in Philadelphia,
and on the Hudson & Manhattan cars, they all pay me ten dollars.
The same as the Interborough. But if it goes on a street car,
they don't pay the ten dollars; they pay less. Anyone who uses it
on a like car, the same as the Interborough uses it, pay me exactly the same as the Interborough.

Q. You get ten dollars a car for any anti-climbers sold to the
Railway Improvement Company? A. Yes, sir, all sold to the
Boston elevated and the Chicago elevated and the Philadelphia
elevated, the Boston and Philadelphia subways, all have paid me
ten dollars a car; the Pennsylvania railroad; the Long Island railroad. They have all paid ten dollars a car.

Q. Whom did you consult about this letter that you wrote to the
Committee? A. I consulted with a counsel for this company,
Mr. Quackenbush.

Q. He wrote the letter? A. Yes, he practically wrote the letter.
I went over it with him.

Q. Why did you consult counsel on a matter so simple as this?
A. Consult Thompson's?

Q. Counsel. A. Oh, counsel.

Q. On a matter so simple as this, asking merely what your interests were? A. I did not think it was a simple matter. I
thought it was asking questions which were beyond the scope of
this Committee, and I wanted to find out whether it was or not.
Not that I would care, because I have nothing to conceal.

Q. You did not go to counsel because you considered you were
on delicate ground? A. No, I am not on delicate ground. My
conscience is clear, sir.

Q. What is the Agasote Millboard Company? A. The Agasote Millboard Company, if I understand it, is one of the companies that I put on my list in answer to Mr. Thompson's letter.
That is the company that makes a composite board. It is some

kind of a compressed board made out of paper or fibre of some
kind.

Q. Do you know where its office is? A. Yes, its office is down in
the lower part of Broadway here.

Q. You held stock in it at one time? A. I did at one time
have, I think, 33 — 33, or 38 shares of stock.

Q. Can you tell me its capital stock? A. No, sir; I don't know
anything about that.

Q. Is it in active business? A. Oh, yes. Yes, it is in active
business.

Q. What is its product used for in connection with the Interborough? A. Why, some of it is used in car ceilings, the top
head-lining business. And that is all I recall that the Interborough ever used it for, though we may have used it for other
purposes.

Q. This Agasote millboard can be used for the roofing of a car?
A. That is what I am referring to. The roofing, the head-lining.

Q. I am distinguishing between the interior and the exterior of
the roof. A. Yes, well we have used it for both. We have some
cars where the interior is the exterior. No false lining at all.

Q. When was this company organized? A. I don't know, sir.

Q. Did the Interborough buy its product from the Agasote Millboard Company? A. The purchasing department of the Interborough have bought some material from the Agasote Millboard
Company.

Q. In substantial amounts? A. That I don't know, how much
it would amount to, sir.

Q. I gather from the tone of your answer that they have possibly through curiosity or experiment purchased some of this millboard. What I asked you is did they make substantial or periodic
or continual purchase from the Agasote Millboard Company.
A. Well, now, that "substantial" as you referred to a while ago,
means a big thing sometimes to the Interborough. When we are
getting new cars I suppose that there may be forty or fifty dollars
worth of that Agasote stuff used on some of the new cars. That is
about as near as I can guess. I can find out for you, sir, just —

Q. I don't want to tax your memory. A. Just how many dollars we have paid them for years past, if you wish.

Q. Did Mr. Doyle own some stock in the Agasote Millboard Company? A. Not that I know of.

Q. Were you an officer? A. No.

Q. Whom did you sell your stock to? A. Mr. Outerbridge.

Q. Which Mr. Outerbridge? A. The president of the company. He is the president —

Q. I mean, what is his first name, Eugene H.? A. Yes, sir.

Q. When did you sell it? A. I sold it only a few weeks ago. I sold it for what I paid for it.

Q. Did you sell it as long ago as February, 1915? A. Oh, no, within a few weeks I sold that, because I wanted to get rid of it.

Q. Did you pay cash for your stock? A. Yes, sir.

Q. Did you pay par for the stock? A. I paid 50 cents for the common stock and I paid par, or within a point or two of par, I don't remember, for the preferred stock. And I asked Mr. Outerbridge how much I paid for it. He said "I will look it up. You paid the same as I did. You paid about par." That is the best of my recollection.

Q. When you say fifty cents, you mean fifty per cent of the par value? Par value, I assume, was $100. A. On the common it is a hundred; on the preferred it was a hundred, and I paid a hundred dollars.

Q. How much of the preferred did you own? A. I think I had twenty-eight shares of the preferred, I think it was.

Q. And how much of the common? A. Five or six of the common.

Q. What is the Prepayment Car Sales Company? A. That is a company that had the selling right for the pay-as-you-enter cars, on the original pay-as-you-enter car patents. I believe that is where they started in business.

(Chairman Thompson resumes the Chair.)

Q. Did the New York Railways Company buy cars from this company? A. No, sir.

Q. Did either the Interborough or the New York Railways Company have any dealings with this company? A. No, sir, except in one thing, that I can recall — no, they didn't buy that. No, I don't recall anything, although there may have been, because

I am not the purchasing agent. I have nothing to do with the purchases.

Q. Whom should I ask that question of, Mr. Hedley? A. We have a vice-president in charge of purchases, Mr. Ross, D. W. Ross. I don't buy anything for the railway company. I have troubles enough of my own.

Q. You state in your communication of January 19th with reference to the Prepayment Car Sales Company, you made a contract with the Prepayment Car Sales Company giving them authority to sell certain patented devices relating to cars. A. Yes, sir.

Q. Have you got that contract? A. Yes, sir, I have got a contract. That means that I made a contract with them to sell my patented devices to other railroads, not including the New York railways.

Q. What devices of yours were included in this contract? A. The low-level car, and several of the other patents which I cited to you this morning, are incident to the low-level car requirements.

Q. Is it not a fact, Mr. Hedley, that a corporation cannot take out a patent? A. I don't know, sir; I don't know.

Q. Do you know of any corporation claiming to be the originator and inventor of a patentable device? A. No, I have not known a corporation to take a patent out, but I did not know it would not be possible for me to do it.

Q. It is true that the statute gives this qualified monopoly, this patent protection, only to the originator or inventor of some new and useful device? A. That is my understanding.

Q. Do you claim that you are the inventor in fact of these various devices? A. Why, I don't claim it. I know that I am.

Q. Of all of them? A. Yes, sir, in connection with Mr. Doyle.

Q. They are the children of your brain and the result of your mechanical training and skill, are they? A. They certainly are.

Q. Not to any extent are they the results of the ingenuity of the mechanics and workmen generally of the Interborough? A. If they were I would give them the credit for it. I have got a lot of good men —

Q. Did any employee of the Interborough make any patentable

3

invention while you were vice-president and general manager?
A. Yes, sir, but not these patents I am referring to.

Q. Any that the Interborough Company have seen fit to take up
and utilize? A. Yes, sir. We encourage that spirit among our
men, to develop things, to get up new and useful devices that will
save life and limb and reduce our operating expenses.

Q. Will you mention some of the devices which the Interborough is using which have been patented by others than you and
Mr. Doyle? A. Yes. There is some devices which were patented
by Mr. H. D. Stott, superintendent of motor power.

Chairman Thompson.— He was asking you for a patent by a
mechanic in the employ of the company.

The Witness.— He is a mechanic.

Chairman Thompson.— He is a foreman, one of the officers.
He means a regular mechanic, a fellow that works in the shop.
Got any of them where they get ten dollars a car?

The Witness.— That is where I work, and took out some of
these patents.

Chairman Thompson.— He is asking for some regular patent.

The Witness.— Well, we have got a mechanic, yes. Let me see,
now. I don't know that we have got a man that is below the rank
of foreman who ever did anything, if that is what the question is
intended to mean.

By Mr. Colby:

Q. Do you recall the name of any foreman who ever invented
a valuable or useful development or application or traffic device,
operating devices? A. No, I don't,— I don't recall a man in the
class of foreman. But an engineer I do. Those things are usually
invented by an engineering mind.

Q. Can you name the engineer? A. Yes, sir, Mr. Waldron, our
signal engineer, has invented some very useful devices.

Chairman Thompson.— Chief signal engineer?

The Witness.— Yes, sir. That have increased by their installation the capacity and tremendously increased the factor of safety
in subway operation.

By Mr. Colby:

Q. His name, please, Mr. Hedley? A. Waldron.

Q. What is his salary from the Interborough? A. Oh, I think it is about $3,600 or $4,000 a year, somewhere around there.

Chairman Thompson.— Waldron?

The Witness.— Yes.

Q. Well, what did he invent, what do you call it? A. Why, he invented one thing that I recall, and that is the time feed control system of signals.

Senator Lawson.— We have heard about speed control before. We have heard about that before.

The Witness.— That is a very creditable device, that one he got up.

Q. Did he patent it? A. Oh, yes.

Q. Did the board of directors vote him a special reward for it? A. I don't know that the board of directors did — I think they did. I know we paid him the money for it.

Q. How much did you pay? A. If I recall it, we paid him $1,500.

Q. For the right to use it or for the ownership of it? A. Right to use it in the subway and elevated.

Senator Lawson.—Exclusively the Interborough?

The Witness.— No; the Interborough takes the right to use it, and then he himself has the right to dispose of it to others, for other railroads, outside of the Interborough, so that the Interborough does not pay anything for royalties to anyone.

Senator Lawson.— Did he ever assign the right to use it to the Federal Signal Company of Rochester?

The Witness.— I don't know. I don't know what disposition he made of it.

Senator Lawson.— Is it workable?

The Witness.— It is working in the subway now. It is the signals you see when approaching an express station. They permit a man to run by those signals at a pre-determined speed.

Senator Lawson.— I know about them. That is all.

By Mr. Colby:

Q. But it was not apparently near so valuable as the anti-climber? A. It is not such a broad patent. It is only applicable some places. Now, for instance, the only place we are using it, care to use it, is where you are approaching an express station or approaching a dangerous interlocking point.

Q. Can you recall any other employee who ever hit upon something valuable and useful to the company? A. Why, Mr. H. T. Stott, I think, some five or six years ago, did patent some power-house apparatus.

Chairman Thompson.—Who is he?

Mr. Hedley.— He is our man in charge of power-houses, superintendent of motor power, his title is.

Chairman Thompson.— Head of that department?

Mr. Hedley.— Head of that department; yes, sir.

Q. What salary does he receive? A. Oh, I think Stott gets, twelve, eighteen, twenty thousand dollars a year, somewhere around there. He is worth all that and more too, the best power-house man there is in the world.

Q. I suppose he knows what he receives. A. He knows what he is getting; yes, sir.

Q. You and Mr. Doyle seem to have been very fortunate in hitting upon the really and truly valuable devices, don't you? A. Well, judging from the amount of money I received from them from outside companies, I think that statement is true?

Q. Well, confine the question, judging from the amount of money you received from the Interborough Company? A. Well, we have got the devices, the most of the devices that have been recognized by the Interborough and others as being of great value, yes.

Q. I think you have testified that — I have not the notes of the testimony before me — that you and Mr. Doyle made a royalty of $7.50 per anti-climber — per coasting clock.

The Chairman.— Per year?

The Witness.— Yes, sir.

Q. That is more than you are paying Mr. Waldron for this time speed control system of signals, isn't it? A. Yes, a very different device, entirely.

Q. Well, as I see it, this time speed control system is the very secret of your safe and successful operation of your system, and makes it possible for you to carry this traffic which, according to experts, is greater than your capacity? A. Well, it helps. It is one of the things. There is no one thing that does it down there. That thing helps.

Q. Can you specify anything more vital or essential to the operation of a system operating upon such headway as the subway does than a dependable, accurate and scientific system of signals and time speed control? A. That is one of the essentials, but —

Chairman Thompson.— Just answer the question. His question was if you conceive of anything more important —

Mr. Hedley.—Yes, the developments in the air-brake, all of which have been made down in the subway.

Q. You will agree, however, that it is a matter of prime importance to your operation, to have a system of speed control, timing and signalling that is scientific to the last degree? A. Oh yes, it is necessary.

Chairman Thompson.— The air-brake is the only thing that you mention that is greater in importance, as I take it.

Mr. Hedley.— The motors have a great deal to do with it. The signalling has permitted us to run a certain number more trains. Now, the improvement in efficiency of the brakes, of the character of brakes, has permitted us to run a great many more trains, so that if you are going to put that on a value, why, the speed time control signal, from a money point of view, is insignificant, a small amount. You take, as compared with the coasting clocks, the coasting clocks are actually saving on the subway and elevated railroads annually over $600,000 a year to the company.

Chairman Thompson.—And the other thing don't do anything only save lives?

Mr. Hedley.— It saves lives, and it increases the capacity of the property. We are able to run more cars.

Chairman Thompson.— The thing that saves dollars is worth more than the thing that saves lives?

Mr. Hedley.— I didn't say so. The first consideration is the thing that makes transportation in New York as safe as it is possible to make it under the known state of the art.

Chairman Thompson.— That is, the Waldron patent goes to the safety operation?

Mr. Hedley.— That patent does.

Chairman Thompson.—And the other patents, the coasting clocks, go to the question of saving money for power. That is the difference in the application of the two patents?

Mr. Hedley.— Yes. Now you refer to the anti-climber — they are both safety measures. The anti-climber does not earn anything, but it does safeguard the lives of the people and stops the destruction of property.

By Mr. Colby:

Q. Would you say that the ——— A. Been recognized the world over.

Q. Would you say that the — one of the important differences between the valuation of the time speed control system of signals and the coasting clock, which enables you to distinguish between the skill of your motormen in economizing power — would you say one element of distinction was that one belongs to you and the other to Waldron? A. None whatever, sir. None whatever. I do not set what I receive from the Interborough Rapid Transit Company. As I have told you, the Interborough Rapid Transit Company has a full right to use all or any of my patents without payment of a dollar. As I have also said, the Board of Directors on several occasions, by special resolution, have recognized that something of value has been produced, and they have paid me for it. They set the sum; not me.

Q. How many men in the employment of the Interborough are occupied in the development and perfection of these various devices? A. Why, that varies — and I would not say they are occupied in the development. Sometimes we may have more or less men on. And I show you how impossible it is for me to guess about that with this device we are trying to put at 14th street now, on that gap device. We are closing up the gap on the curved platform. Sometimes we have half a dozen men working at that. Sometimes we run into trouble and have only one or two working at it. Then again we have a dozen.

Q. You and Mr. Doyle are the patentees of that? A. Yes, sir. I have taken out all the patents in Mr. Doyle's and my name, and as I say, I have paid for them, paid the counsel fees. The company will have the right to use them without payment of a dollar to me.

Q. That has been a very baffling problem, to close up the gap on a curved platform? A. Yes, sir.

Q. It has been so recognized? A. Never been done.

Q. Have you been long at work to find some solution of that problem? A. Eight or nine years.

Q. How many working on it? A. Anywhere from two to a dozen or one to a dozen.

Q. Of the employees of the Interborough? A. Off and on.

Q. Have you made many models? A. No, I think we made — we made four or five models, yes, but, not — we only made one model in full size. We will make a small model and so build it up of wood, one-quarter size, so as to make it as cheaply as we can.

Q. You have tried a good many devices that have been satisfactory? A. Yes, we have tried many things on that, to get something that is right.

Q. Have you and Mr. Doyle taken out various patents on these devices? A. Yes, we have made several applications on that.

Q. What I mean is that from time to time you would hit upon some suggestion or device, and promptly patent it? A. Yes, sir.

Q. You have used up a good deal of material and labor in these eight years that you have been working on it? A. Oh, yes. We would like to have somebody produce something for us that would do that. We have many accidents there, and want to avoid them.

Q. Have more than one of your shops been at work on that? A. Yes, sir.

Q. How many of your shops have been at work on that problem? A. Why, there is two departments have taken a try

at it. One was the car department and the other was in the chief
engineer's department.

Q. How extensive is the car department? A. Why, the car
department have done practically all of it. The investigation of
the chief engineer's department and the device they set up, which
I went and looked at, was not satisfactory at all.

Q. I asked you how extensive is the car department? A. The
car department?

Q. Yes. How many men does the car department include?
A. Oh, there is about a couple thousand men there; about fifteen
hundred men, I think, in the car department, altogether.

Q. How many men of that 1,500 have been busied on this
problem? A. Well, for the last eight years, I would say from
one to perhaps a dozen, and many periods where we had nobody
at all. We have been trying to solve it for the last eight or nine
years.

Q. What other department has given its energies? A. The
civil engineer's department, the chief engineer.

Q. How many men there have worked on it? A. One or two
men probably set up a little wood sample I saw, and I told them
not to work any more on it. I could see they were not on the
right track. And I took it out of the hands of that department
and put it in the hands of the car department entirely to develop it.

Q. How do you come to be the inventor of all these models?
A. Why, because in these cases, Mr. Doyle and I, we get together
and we sit down and we talk them over, and he has one thought
and I have another thought, and in each one of these things we
have patented it has some of his ideas in it, fundamental with
him, and some of them have been fundamental with me, and we
put our brains together, so to speak, and make up the unit, and
we patent it jointly.

Q. But you make the employees of the Interborough carry out
your ideas and reduce them to working models? A. They do the
physical work with their hands, of course, in making the things
for use on the railroad company.

Q. Neither you nor Mr. Doyle pay the expenses of the workmen who are occupied for various periods for eight years, as you
testify? A. Oh, no.

Q. As many as twelve in one department and a number in another department, such as the civil engineers department. You pay nothing for the labor involved in the perfection — A. I personally do not pay the payrolls of the Interborough Rapid Transit Company.

Q. I don't ask you that. Of course I know you don't pay the payrolls of the Interborough Rapid Transit Company. I say you have paid nothing for materials or labor, the working out, development and perfection of these devices which you and Doyle have patented? A. No, I have paid nothing and I received nothing

Q. Why should you receive anything for Interborough labor? A. I don't expect to, and I don't. Why should I pay it.

Q. Of course, an inventor, you will admit, has a very soft snap, if somebody is paying for the maintenance of an efficient high grade shop of mechanics and workmen to carry out his impulse and his thought and his suppositions, looking to a working device. You will admit that, will you not? A. I will admit that if an inventor knows his business he won't spend too much of his own money on his own patents.

Q. I don't think you are in danger of falling into that improvidence, sir. A. I hope not.

Q. You have testified with great particularity and some emphasis that you always paid the lawyer for filing your application and paid all the expenses of these various devices for which you are collecting royalties, some from the Interborough. Now I ask you is it not a fact that the real cost and the chief expenditure involved in the working up of these ideas, the perfection of these devices, you did not pay for at all, but the Interborough paid for it exclusively? A. No, no.

Q. How can you say no in the light of the testimony you have just given, that you depended wholly upon the labor and material of the Interborough for working up these Doyle-Hedley devices? A. I told you this morning that as far as the coasting clock was concerned, I worked on that before I came to New York at all.

Q. No work ever done on that in the shops of the Interborough? A. Very little.

Q. What do you mean by very little? A. I mean perhaps a hundred dollars or may be two hundred dollars was not spent.

Q. Well, may be that is an exception. A. No, that is not an exception.

Q. Well, will you mention anything you have invented that you or Doyle have taken patents for that has not been worked up in whole or in part in the Interborough shops? A. Why, we, in the first place, only invent things that are applicable to the railroad company.

Q. Just answer the question. A. Of course they are worked up in the railroad company's shops.

Q. In other words, everything applicable to the railroad company has been worked up in the Interborough shops? A. Yes, sir. It is no use Mr. Doyle and I furnishing the brains if we don't have the workmen work out those things and use the thoughts —

Q. When was the coasting clock patented? A. Oh, seven or eight years ago.

Q. You were then connected with the Interborough, were you not? A. Yes, sir. I have the list of those patents here now.

Q. Have you? A. My boy sent them down. I have not had an opportunity of looking them over.

Q. I won't refer to them until you have had a chance to look them over.

Chairman Thompson.— You look them over and see if they are all right.

Mr. Hedley.— The only thing I have in mind is whether he has really got them all here.   (Witness examines list.)

Q. Mr. Hedley, when you or Mr. Doyle undertake to begin a series of experiments looking to advancing some idea that is in your mind, bringing it to practical form, with a view to patenting it, is there any intimation to the foreman of your shops that that is your purpose? Is there any initiation of that specific kind of work in your shops? A. No, sir. No, sir; in no case that I have known of.

Q. Are the expenditures made by the Interborough in connection with the Hedley-Doyle patents kept in any special account? A. No, sir. They are not made in connection with the Hedley-Doyle patents. Whether we should patent a thing or not we would make those expenditures. You see, whether Doyle or I were going to patent it or not, if we had conceived certain new ideas that would add to the safety or efficiency or economy of anything, we get the shop men and put them to work on certain drawings to make and produce certain things. Now, the company would pay for that whether Mr. Doyle and I in the end patented it or not. So that in the work such as you have referred to as experimental work, that is paid by the railroad company in developing patents that Hedley and Doyle have, that same expense would be made whether Hedley and Doyle patent it or not. There is a great many things that we try and experiment with, if you so please, that we don't patent.

Q. But the Interborough pays the expenses? A. The Interborough pays for everything developed in the Interborough shops.

Q. But you and Doyle get the patent? A. We get the patent, the United States letters patent. The Interborough has the free use of it, if she wants it.

Q. You never have assigned any of these patents to the Interborough simply because you and Doyle were employees of the Interborough and the Interborough paid you and also paid the expenses of your work? A. No, the patents have not been assigned to the Interborough.

Q. Do you allow your employees generally to patent any device or invention they come upon in the course of their work? A. Yes, sir; we want them to get up new devices.

Q. And yet you have been able to specify only one thing patented by anyone except the head of a department or major officer of the Interborough? A. I think that is right.

Q. How many mechanics has the Interborough in its employ? A. Oh, I suppose three or four thousand altogether.

Q. How many civil engineers? A. Oh, probably twenty.

Q. How many mining engineers? How many electrical engineers? A. Well, we have got not many men who are classed as electrical engineers. Many men who are more or less electricians call themselves electrical engineers.

Q. But you have a considerable number of electrical engineers? A. No.

Q. Have you any? A. Two or three.

Chairman Thompson.— How many have you that call themselves that?

Mr. Hedley.— I don't know. All these young students over to
the institute, they call themselves electrical engineers. I may say
we have three or four hundred of those.

Chairman Thompson.— That is how you became an engineer,
because you called yourself that?

Mr. Hedley.— No, sir. I don't call myself that unless I am
driven to it.

By Mr. Colby:

Q. What I mean is this; that you have a large number of employees who are graduates of technical schools who have had the
best technical training, who are men of promise and capacity, and
of unusual ability in their respective professions. That is true, is
it not? A. No doubt about that.

Q. And yet all this great number of technically trained, scientific, expert men, although working in the shops and doing nothing else, concentrating upon these problems, have only been able
to turn out one invention, while you and Doyle have turned up a
score or more? A. Well, that ought to be creditable, I think, I
don't think I should be condemned for that.

Q. I am merely asking you if that is not the fact. A. That is
the best of my recollection, yes.

Q. You have many duties aside from your mechanical duties,
have you not? A. Oh, yes.

Q. What are your duties as general manager and vice-president of all these companies? A. That would take about a week to
tell you, I guess.

Q. See how far you can get in five minutes. A. Why, I am in
charge of the operation and maintenance and construction of the
property. That means that the head of every department reports
to me and we discuss all matters of importance and arrive at conclusions. That refers to all of the departments that I have mentioned, including the operation. The operation I give a good deal
of personal attention to. I watch it very carefully. I know what
is going on all the time, and see to it that in so far as my ability

and experience goes, that the people of New York get the best
transportation facilities that we know how to provide, and my
job is to see that they get it. I made an effort, and have been
fairly successful, I think.

Q. You are the head of the department, are you not? A. Why,
you might put it that way, or I am the head of the departments,
every department.

Q. You are the general executive manager of that company,
are you not? A. Yes, sir, except in some of the departments I
have nothing to do with. The auditing department and the treasurer's department and the purchasing department don't come
under my jurisdiction. All the other departments in the organization do.

Q. Have you anything to do — A. And the legal department
does not.

Q. Have you anything to do with the financing of the company
and its financial problems? A. No, sir. They are discussed with
me sometimes, but I have no official duties in connection with
them.

Q. You are a member of the Board of Directors? A. No, sir,
I am not, and would not be. I am an operating man.

Q. Have they tried to make you a member of the Board of
Directors? A. Have spoken of it several times.

Q. But thus far you have evaded it? A. When I try to discourage a thing with my own company, I am usually successful.

Q. Do you think being a member of the board or executive committee would impair your usefulness to the company? A. Yes, in
many cases I know it would. I can do better work for the company if I am not — if I attend to my regular job than if I am
sitting discussing things with the Board of Directors.

Q. In other words, you haven't time for both? A. No, I don't
believe I have, and do both justice.

Q. Your duties as vice-president and general manager take up
practically all your time, do they not? A. Yes, except the time
that I steal off to have some fun. I do that once in a while, but I
am always on the telephone day and night. They always know
where I am. I don't go off the job anywhere for an hour that
they don't know where I am. They know I am right down here
now this moment. They know 24 hours of the day where I am.

Q. How much of your time do you spend in inventing? A.
That is my fun. That is part of my pleasure. And I have got
several things in mind now that I think over when I am sitting
by myself, some of which look pretty good to me, too. I think I
will work them out.

Chairman Thompson.— I wish you would tell us something
of that. I have not had any fun like that since —

Mr. Hedley.— We have got an open game of competition down
here, if any of you can bring in something to our factor of safety
and save us some money, why, we will pay you for it and pay
you well — better than I had paid me.

By Mr. Colby:

Q. Isn't it a fact, Mr. Hedley, that anything that is good that
comes along in your shops — A. No.

Q. — is taken by Hedley and Doyle and promptly patented,
no matter who did it? A. No. No. It is not a fact at all.

Q. Well, isn't it a fact — A. I resent the question, because —

Q. I think the question would be something that you might resent if it were not for the evidence you have already given here.
I think it is a quite extraordinary fact that over a period of some
six or eight years, all the useful, valuable devices evolved in your
shop with all these employees, happen to have been devices of
yourself, Mr. Doyle and possibly Mr. Stott or Stitt, who is also one
of the major officers of your company. That is a fact, isn't it?
A. Yes, sir. I have not said anything else here but facts.

Q. That is a surprising coincidence? A. Yes, sir, a very creditable one, too.

Q. Isn't it a fact that it is a practice of corporations dealing
with employees or inventors to have the patents taken out in the
name of the inventor and licensee and have the patent then assigned to the corporation? A. I don't know what the practice is,
but I do know that no application for U. S. patents would ever be
made by me with my name on it unless I was the inventor or partial inventor.

Chairman Thompson.— I am afraid if you worked for less
than two dollars a day that they would take it away from you.
That is what they would do.

The Witness.— I have worked for two dollars a day. We don't do that with the organization of the Interborough. A man earning two dollars or forty dollars, if he will invent something that will economize our operation or add to the safety of the public we will pay him good money for it.

Q. Isn't it a fact that has only occurred in one instance, and you have paid only $1,500? A. I have testified to the full facts here about it.

Q. That is what you have testified to? A. Yes, sir.

Q. So that the fact is hardly as sweeping or broad as your statement of the company's policy? A. Well, I have not stated anything that is not the full facts, both sweeping and broad.

Q. Is it not a fact that the employer owns the invention of his employee? A. No, they do not own mine that I ever knew of.

Q. I mean in the absence of some express agreement or some express stipulation? A. No, not that I ever heard of.

Q. Never heard of such a rule of law? A. No. I always thought I was the owner of my own brains. I think so still.

Chairman Thompson.— You did not reserve that in your contract of employment with the Interborough, I take it? There is nothing in your contract of employment with the Interborough that reserves your right with the patents?

Mr. Hedley.— I would not make a contract with anyone like that.

Chairman Thompson.— Nothing in there with reference to it?

Mr. Hedley.— I am sure there is not.

By Mr. Colby:

Q. Do you personally adopt or approve the use or purchase of various devices for use on the surface or subway cars? A. Why, no, I would not say that my approval is necessary.

Q. Is it influential? A. Oh, it is influential, yes. No doubt about that.

Q. In other words, you have a good deal to say as to what devices shall be adopted on the cars of the Interborough Company? A. They give a great deal of consideration to my opinion in those matters, yes. If I think a thing should be used, it has a better chance than if I should say I do not think it ought to be.

Q. How long have you exercised this function of passing on such devices? A. Oh, ever since I came to New York the last time; 1903.

Q. Nothing could be incorporated in the specifications, we will say, for a car on the subway, without your knowing it or without your approval? A. Well, it might get by and me not notice it. I read over those specifications. If it is a car, that is prepared in the car equipment department; if it is a generator, it is prepared in the superintendent of motor powers department; if it is a civil engineering problem, those specifications are prepared in the civil engineer's department.

Q. Are they all submitted to you? A. Yes, I read them all over. Not line for line. But in a general way I am familiar with what they are doing.

Q. Have you ever specified the use of devices patented by you or Mr. Doyle? A. No.

Q. You have seen that the specifications specified yours and Doyle's devices, have you not? A. Yes, I have seen that those devices will be furnished by the railroad company. Wherever we have mentioned in the specifications patents that Mr. Doyle or I own, as my recollection goes, we have always furnished the device ourselves — that is the railroad company has, and the railroad company goes and buys it in the open market. wherever it can, the cheapest, without payment of royalty.

Q. What duties has the general manager and vice-president of the New York Railways Company? A. The same as the subway and elevated.

Q. What are your duties for the Rapid Transit Construction Company? A. Rapid Transit Subway Construction Company?

Q. Yes. A. I am vice-president in charge of construction there. My duties there are to look over the organization, the work, and approve of or disapprove of the staff that is employed on the various contracts from the engineering down, and to have reports direct from those engineers as to the progress of the work, the manner in which the work is being done, and so on and so forth. General supervision as a general manager would have of a subway construction job.

Q. Is the Rapid Transit Subway Construction Company the company that is building the new Dual System? A. We are building a part of it. We bid on several sections and we were the successful bidders, and the contract was awarded us, and we are doing the work.

Q. How many miles of the new subway is the Rapid Transit Construction Company building? A. Oh, I don't know as to the mileage. We —

Q. Approximately? A. We have got about ten and a half million dollars' worth of the work.

Q. Is this company entirely independent from the Interborough Rapid Transit Company or the New York Railways Company? A. So far as I know it is. I don't mix it at all. I manage the business for the Subway Construction Company and I manage it just as though it was entirely separate, entirely. It is, as far as I am concerned.

Q. It is a contracting company, is it? A. Yes.

Q. It sustains the same relation to this new work as, for instance, such a contract or as Thomas A. Gillespie would sustain to the work if he got the contract? A. Just the same.

Q. Instead of an individual it is a corporation? A. That is correct.

Q. So that you are working for another corporation and not an affiliated company or not a company affiliated with the Interborough Rapid Transit Company? A. I don't recognize it is affiliated in a financial way. I suppose it is. The same men are on the directors of the Subway Construction Company as on the directors of the Interborough, I believe. I told you that this morning. I think they are the same men. As far as I am concerned, I run the Subway Construction Company's business just as though I was not with the subway and elevated. We are going to make some money out of our subway construction for the company.

Mr. Quackenbush.— The stock of the Construction Company is owned by the Interborough Rapid Transit Company. I think Mr. Hedley did not quite get your question, or perhaps may not be familiar with that.

By Mr. Colby:

Q. But the corporation as I understand it, Mr. Hedley, and possibly I should examine someone else on this interesting point— the corporation as I understand it is dealing with the subject matter of the dual system, and the work is undertaken quite as a person or corporation independent of the Interborough? A. Yes, that is the way the work is being conducted. It is being conducted as a construction job on precisely the same basis as a man like Degnon.

Q. Or O'Rourke? A. Or O'Rourke, or any of those people.

Q. Now, the Interborough owns the stock, Mr. Quackenbush tells me, of the Rapid Transit Construction Company, and yet is it not a fact that all this construction that is going on is being done for the city and the Interborough jointly, and the Brooklyn Rapid Transit?

Mr. Quackenbush.— I can answer that question, perhaps. Contract No. 3 expressly contemplates the existence of this construction company and provides that —

Chairman Thompson.— You mean Certificate No. 3?

Mr. Quackenbush.— We call it Contract No. 3. Certificates relate to the elevated. The subway is called Contract No. 3, as distinguished from Contracts No. 1 and 2 and 3. That is, the new Contract, No. 3, of March 19, had in mind this construction company, and provided that neither the Interborough nor any company affiliated with it should make a profit out of construction, except when the construction company came into the work through open and competitive bidding, and that is what Mr. Hedley has explained to you was the case in these contracts amounting to something over ten million dollars. We bid against these other people and we were the lowest bidders. Otherwise we could not make a profit out of it.

By Mr. Colby:

Q. From whom does the Interborough buy its cars? A. We have had cars from many places. Wherever we can get the best car for the least money. The last lot of cars we had were from the Pullman Company in Chicago. We have bought them from half a dozen other car builders.

Q. Mention them. A. We have bought them from the St. Louis Car Company, from J. J. Brill, from the Wason Company; we have bought them from Stevenson.

Q. Did you deal directly with the companies you mention, or with their selling agents? A. Well, we deal with the company or their representative. In most cases we deal directly with the car company, and they usually send their representative from the works to finally negotiate the contract.

Q. Is the Railway Improvement Company connected with any of these car companies? A. No.

Q. Are they agents of any of these car companies? A. No, not that I know of, while I had anything to do with the Railway Improvement Company.

Q. How many cars have you bought within the last year from the Pullman Company, approximately? I assume you cannot answer exactly. A. Well, I can give it to you pretty close. Seven hundred and eighty-six cars, in about a year.

(Assemblyman Burr takes the Chair.)

Q. Mr. Hedley, will you excuse me? My attention was distracted there for a moment. How many did you say from the Pullman? A. I said 786 during the past year.

Q. From the Pullman Car Company of Illinois? A. Yes.

Q. These other companies, how many from the St. Louis Car Company? A. We have bought all our cars during the last year from the Pullman Company. We have not bought any from these other companies in the past year.

Q. Have you — you have not bought anything from Brill or Wason? A. Not during the past year.

Q. You have in former years bought extensively from these companies? A. Bought several hundred of the subway cars from Brill and several hundred — I say we bought — the company bought several hundred from the St. Louis Car Company. About a hundred or two from the Wason Manufacturing Company. We bought a hundred or so from the Stephenson plant, and may be one or two others that I have forgotten.

Q. You don't know with whom the company dealt in any of those transactions? A. The individual?

Q. Yes. A. I do in a general way.

Q. Let us take them in order. Whom did you deal with in the Pullman Company? A. Why, a Mr. Slagle closed that contract.

Q. You don't know his initials? A. No, I don't, sir.

Q. Is he a New York man? A. Lives in Chicago, I believe. I think he is the general manager of the contract department or something of that kind.

Q. How about the St. Louis Car Company? A. The St. Louis Car Company, we have not bought any cars from the St. Louis Car Company for — see — I guess about three years ago, I think a man named Meisner closed that. I don't know whether that was not closed with Wendell & McDuffy.

Q. Wendell & McDuffy? A. Yes, Wendell & McDuffy, I think it was. I think they negotiated that contract. Either they or a man named Meisner who is the secretary of the St. Louis Car Company, I think.

Q. Where is the office of Wendell & McDuffy? A. I think it is 71 Broadway.

Q. That is the address of the Railway Improvement Company? A. In the same building, as I understand it. I have never been down there.

Q. Any connection between the firm of Wendell & McDuffy and the Railway Improvement Company? A. Not that I know of. There was not when I was handling the Railway Improvement Company — not handling it, but when I was controlling it.

Q. Who composed the firm of Wendell & McDuffy? A. McDuffy — that is right — McDuffy held some of the Railway Improvement Company's stock, I believe, at one time. I guess he did.

Q. Who composed the firm? A. Wendell & McDuffy?

Q. Yes. A. I don't know, sir.

Q. Do you know any of the members of the firm except Wendell & McDuffy? A. No. Wendell is dead. No; I don't know of my own knowledge any other members of the firm.

Q. Whom did you deal with in dealing with Brill? A. Why,

that was Mr. Kerwind, the president, and Hulings, I think. Hulings is the general manager of sales, or something of that kind.

Q. These cars were not bought by you or through you? A. No, I don't close these contracts. Mr. Ross, their vice-president in charge of purchase —

Q. David W. Ross? A. Yes. I don't mean by that that I don't have a great deal to say about just where the contract ought to go for cars, as to the ability of the shop to turn them out and make deliveries and so on and so forth. Final negotiations as to how much money we paid for them. Mr. Ross does that; not me.

Q. What about Wason Manufacturing Company? You would refer me for accurate information to Ross on that point, would you? A. Well, I know those fellows pretty well, all of them. A man named Pierson used to come down for the Wason — nice fellow, too.

Q. When you buy cars, do you send specifications of all of the devices that the cars shall carry? A. Well, when we buy the cars, we buy the car body with the fixtures that go with the car body, but that is all. Now, that sometimes mean that we will buy a car body even without the seats. The seat frames will be in there. Then the purchasing department buys the seats of the seat manufacturer, and — like, for instance, these cars, new cars that you see coming down in the subway now have a white enameled railing in the center of the car. We buy a car and our purchasing department buys those white enameled railings and puts them in.

Q. When are the sanitary straps bought and put in? A. Those sanitary straps, if I recall it right, the last lot were bought by the railroad company and sent to Pullman and Pullman put them in. That is as I remember it.

Q. Bought from whom? A. I don't know where the purchasing department bought them. I could find out for you.

Q. Well, I will ask Mr. Moss. A. Ross — R-o-s-s.

Q. Ross. And where do they get the door controlling device for the cars? A. That is the air device, I suppose you mean. We buy —

Q. Yes, that air device. A. The air machine, the air engine, as we call it. Why, that — those air engines come from two places.

The most of them come from one place, and I wish they all came from one place. The Burdett Rountree. That is a Chicago concern. I think that is their name. They have furnished the most of them. And the Consolidated Car Heating Company have furnished some of them. They furnish very few.

Q. Is Rountree, R-o-w-n, or R-o-u-n? A. R-o-u-n.

Q. Where is the Consolidated Car Heating Company's office? A. In Albany, I think. I think they have a representative in New York.

Q. And Burnett Rountree Company, is that the name? A. No, I think it is Burdette & Rountree.

Q. Of Chicago? A. Yes.

Mr. Colby.— Mr. Chairman, it is now four o'clock, and I said that I would — we would adjourn at four. I would like to ask just one question of Mr. Hedley before we take a recess until to-morrow morning.

Chairman Burr.— Would you like half an hour more?

Mr. Colby.— I just want to ask him one question.

By Mr. Colby:

Q. You have stated that you do not think you receive a sufficient salary. A. Oh, well, that is —

Q. What do you think you are entitled to receive for your labor? A. That was more or less conversational. But I never set any figure on what my value is. I think it is worth a good deal, though. I have got a good opinion of myself.

Chairman Burr.— Never have had to ask them for a raise?

Mr. Hedley.— Oh, yes, I have asked for a raise.

Chairman Burr.— We will adjourn until 11 o'clock to-morrow morning at this place.

Whereupon, at 4 o'clock P. M., the Committee adjourned to meet at 11 o'clock A. M., February 1, 1916, at the same place.

FEBRUARY 1, 1916

NEW YORK COUNTY LAWYERS' ASSOCIATION BOARD ROOM,
165 Broadway, New York City

Meeting called to order by Chairman Thompson, at 11 A. M., a quorum being present.

Hedley, Frank, being recalled for further examination, testified as follows:

Mr. Colby examining:

Q. I think I requested you yesterday, Mr. Hedley, to produce if you will, your contract of employment with the Interborough Rapid Transit Company. Have you been able to find it? A. I told you at that time that I didn't know whether I was under contract or not. I find that I am not. I have got no contract for employment at the present time.

Q. What was the last contract of employment that you entered into? A. The last contract of employment I entered into was in 1909.

Q. That contract you are able to produce? A. Yes, sir.

Q. Does it contain a definition of the duties that pertain to your employment? A. In a broad sense, yes, sir.

Q. Will you let me have it at two o'clock? A. I have it now. I have it in my pocket. I had to get it from the secretary of the company's file. I don't know where mine is. I don't know where it has gone.

Q. In your answer to the Committee's letter of January 13th you say with reference to the Prepayment Car Sales Company that " I made a contract with the Prepayment Car Sales Company." I think I asked you for that contract also. A. No, I don't recall that you did. You may have but I have no memorandum of that.

Q. Will you produce that? A. I have no memorandum of that, sir, but I will produce it, certainly.

Q. You further say that " Under the license of sales of patents that I have made I have always reserved the right that this company," referring to the New York Railways Company, " to use

the patent." This statement I assume applies to the Prepayment
Car Sales Company? A. Yes, sir.

Q. Has the Prepayment Car Sales Company instituted a suit
against the New York Railways Company over the matter of royalties? A. No, I don't think they have. I haven't heard of such
a suit. I believe the Pay-as-you-enter Car Company have a
suit against the receivers of the New York Railways Company, I
mean the New York City Railways Company.

Q. That is the only litigation that you know of? A. That's
all I know of, sir. I have had nothing whatever to do with that.

Q. You never have had any dealings with the Pay-as-you-enter
Car Company? A. No, sir.

Q. Either directly or indirectly? A. No, sir.

Chairman Thompson.— Do they handle any of your patents?

Mr. Hedley.— No, sir.

Q. That is a suit for royalties is it? A. That is as I understand it, that's only hearsay; as I understand it it is a suit for
royalties for the pay-as-you-enter cars that were furnished to the
Street Car Company during the time that the company was in
the hands of a receiver.

Q. What is the relation between the Pay-as-you-enter Car Company and the Prepayment Car Sales Company, any? A. I don't
know, sir.

Q. Will you give the benefit of your impression as to that? A.
I understand that the Prepayment Car Sales Company obtained
the selling rights of the patents owned by the Pay-as-you-enter Car
Company. That is my understanding.

Q. The Pay-as-you-enter Car Company is the major or parent
company? A. I believe it is.

Q. And the Prepayment Car Sales Company is a selling agent
of the Pay-as-you-enter Car Company? A. That is my understanding.

Q. Your dealings have been only with the Prepayment Car
Sales Company? A. That is correct.

Q. What patented devices have you sold to the Pay-as-you-enter
Car Company? A. None.

Q. And what device have you turned over to the Prepayment
Company? A. They have the right to and manufacture and sell

to any companies the low level cars, the double-deck cars, and two
or three minor patents with the low level and double-deck car that
are essential to that character of a car.

Q. The low level car is sometimes called a stepless car, isn't it?
A. Yes, sir. These contracts always carry with them a clause that
the railway company by which I am employed reserves the right
to buy them anywhere they please without payment of royalties
to anyone, and they do so.

Q. You claim to be the inventor of the stepless car? A. Mr.
Doyle and myself are the inventors.

The Chairman.— That is different than the low level car?

Mr. Colby.— Same thing, he has testified.

Q. Is that an undisputed claim? A. It has been awarded by
the patent office, and I have never heard anyone dispute it; be
on dangerous ground if they do.

Q. Do you know Mr. Jones, of Pittsburgh? A. I have heard
of him, and I know him, I have met the gentleman.

Q. Do you know of him in relation to the stepless or low level
car? A. Only what I have heard. I do not know anything
directly from him.

Q. Do you know that he claims to be the inventor of the stepless
car? A. I have heard that he claims to be the inventor, yes.

Q. Patents are rather casually granted in the first instance, are
they not? A. Why, I would not say so, no.

Q. I mean to say you, as a very active inventor, know that the
grant of letters patent is not regarded even by the patent office as
in any sense conclusive on the claim made on the patent? A.
Why, I don't feel that way about it. I know they make a careful
search and if they find anything that they think looks like what
you have got, they always have a stiff argument with you about it.

Q. You know the statute contains elaborate provisions for the
testing of patents that may have been granted by the government?
A. Oh, I know that they are frequently contested. I don't know
what the statute says.

Q. The reopening of the whole question of the patentee or the
inventor's claim is amply provided for, isn't it? A. That I don't
know. I know patents are often contested.

Q. Did you ever own any stock in the Prepayment Car Sales Company? A. No, sir.

Q. Or in the Pay-as-you-enter Car Company? A. No, sir.

Q. There are two pay-as-you-enter car companies, are there not? A. I don't know that there are. On my list that I sent to the accountant of this Commission, that is the complete list of everything I own.

Q. How much stock did you ever own in the Computing Tabulating and Recording Company? A. I own nineteen thousand dollars' worth of bonds and I own 187 shares of the common stock.

Q. You still own that? A. I still own that, yes, sir. And I paid for it in cash, the same rate as the other investors paid for it.

Q. What was that rate? A. I paid $25,000 for the whole thing.

Q. For the 19,000 bonds and the 187 shares of the stock? A. Yes, sir. That is the same rate, if I understand it, everyone else paid.

Q. That is the company that manufactures the coasting clock? A. They do manufacture the coasting clock, yes, sir.

Q. And sell it? A. No. They don't sell it. If I understand it, the Railway Improvement Company still have the exclusive right to sell. They would sell it, however, to the Interborough, if we wanted any. We can buy it anywhere we like.

Q. The Computing, Recording and Tabulating Company would sell to the Interborough? A. Oh, yes.

Q. Did you ever hold any official relation other than bondholder and stockholder in that company? A. No, sir. The bonds and the stock were put on the market, and I think it was Flint & Company I bought my bonds and stock from. They put them on the market and I got a circular and bought it, and I paid for them the same as anybody else.

Q. How long were you connected with the Railway Improvement Company prior to becoming its president? A. I was its president from the start.

Q. You were its organizer? A. Yes, sir, one of its organizers. I retained that position because I was going to keep it perfectly straight, so that the companies employing me would not buy anything from that company, and they never did.

Q. The companies, however, buy the coasting clock? A. Not from the Railway Improvement Company; no, sir. Direct from the manufacturer.

Q. The Computing, Tabulating and Recording Company was not its sole manufacturer? A. Yes, the sole manufacturer of the coasting clock; the sole manufacturer of the coasting clock.

Q. But you say the Railway Improvement Company was its selling agent? A. That is right.

Q. It is admitted that the Interborough has bought something like thirteen or fourteen hundred of those clocks? A. Yes, we have bought — I have the correct figure in my pocket.

Q. Thank you. A. I find that yesterday I overstated that. I told you yesterday more clocks than we are using, and I told you yesterday that my compensation was greater than it really is.

Q. I would be glad to have you correct any error in your testimony. A. I find that on the subway we have 372 clocks; on the elevated we have 735. That is a total of 1107.

Q. Have you contracted for additional clocks? A. Subway and elevated?

Q. Yes. A. No, sir.

Q. Have you any arrangement that all your cars are to be equipped with these clocks? A. No, sir.

Q. Have you stopped buying these clocks? A. No, sir. I shall recommend that they be purchased for our new cars, because they are not expensive apparatuses, and as I testified yesterday, those that we have now are saving annually to the railroad company over $600,000 a year, and for which the board of directors passed a special resolution which awards me a total of $4,151.25 per year. That is not —

(Flashlight picture taken)

Mr. Colby.— Who is the subject of all this bombardment? You?

Mr. Quackenbush.— Not I.

By Mr. Colby:

Q. Did I interrupt you? A. No, sir, you couldn't interrupt me.

Q. I might succeed measurably if I set out to do it. However,

I don't desire to. A. I just said, Mr. Colby, that the railroad
company out of this device is saving over six hundred thousand
dollars a year, and for which the board of directors recognize by
passing a resolution awarding me a payment of $4,151.25 per
year.

Q. You said — A. I don't think that is a very large proportion.

Q. You said that several times, and I would be tempted to
test my powers of interruption if you say it again. Allow me —
A. Yes, sir; I am very glad it is understood.

Q. How could the Interborough acquire these clocks if the
Computing, Tabulating and Recording Company is its sole manufacturer and the Railway Improvement Company is its selling
agent, and the selling agent was denied permission to sell it?
A. Well, that is not so. The Interborough Rapid Transit Company can buy these clocks from the Computing, Tabulating and
Recording Company. We can buy them for anybody else that
can manufacture them for us.

Q. Who in fact do they buy them from? A. They buy them
from the International Time Recorder Company, who later is the
Computing, Tabulating and Recording Company.

Q. Now, let us get that clear. That ought to be within our
combined power. What is the relation of the International Time
Recording Company to the Computing, Tabulating and Recording Company? A. If I understand it, the International Time
Recording Company was a company doing business by itself. Then
several other companies got together and formed a new company
and called it the Computing, Tabulating and Recording Company.

Q. Which I now understood from your answer a moment ago
is the sole manufacturer of the coasting clock? A. They have
been the sole manufacturer thus far, but they are not necessarily
the sole manufacturer. The Interborough have the right to buy
them from any person, but I am sure they can buy them cheaper
from the Computing, Tabulating and Recording Company than
they can get them from anyone else.

Q. I am content to rest my question with the fact that the
only manufacturer is the Computing, Tabulating and Recording
Company, understanding that in the future other manufacturers

may appear in the field, but they are not indicated now, are they, these other companies? A. They are the only people who manufacture a complete machine.

Q. Allow me. And the only people from which the Interborough has been able to obtain the coasting clocks which it has installed upon its equipment? A. That is correct; but if I explain. The General Electric Company or the Westinghouse Company, and I think may be some other companies, have made the electrical parts of these clocks; those electrical parts are made in Schenectady or Pittsburgh, and sent to the works of the Computing, Tabulating and Recording Company and assembled by them.

Q. I am not particularly interested in the mechanical details of the manufacturing. The point I want correct, and which I assume now I understand, is that this company, the Computing, Recording & Tabulating Company, is the maker and the vendor of these clocks? A. No. They are the maker. They can vend them to the Interborough, but the vending of them to any other company other than the Interborough, if I understand it right, has got to be done by the Railway Improvement Company. At least, that was the condition when I was conversant with the Railway Improvement Company.

Q. Well, what becomes of this distinction that you have been at some pains to establish between your willingness that the Computing, Tabulating & Recording Company here should sell your clocks to the Interborough, and your disinclination that the Railway Improvement Company should sell any of your devices to the Interborough? A. Well, because I practically owned the Railway Improvement Company at one time.

Q. But you are a very substantial owner of the securities of the Computing, Tabulating & Recording Company? A. No, I don't think I am a substantial owner.

Q. You don't think 187 shares and 19,000 of bonds is a substantial holder? A. No, I don't think so.

Q. I am going to excuse you after this question in order that I may call Mr. Pizzini, who tells me that he intends to leave for Chicago on Thursday to attend some convention, and that he then purposes continuing on to the Pacific Coast. A. Well, if I can get away, I intend to leave for Chicago on Thursday too.

Q. Well, we will see what we can do. I want you at 2 o'clock. I want to ask you this question: This Rapid Transit Subway Construction Company, of which you are the vice-president and general manager —— A. The vice-president.

Q. You are vice-president. That is the original Subway Company, isn't it? A. Yes, it is the original Subway Company; built the original subway.

Q. Were you identified with the company from its inception? A. No, sir.

Q. When did you become identified with it? A. Oh, I have had charge of the work in the Subway Construction Company for — since about 1907; about eight years, I should say.

Q. How much stock do you own in that company? A. None at all.

Q. Never have owned it? A. No. I put on my list all the stock I owned.

Q. In the last two years. You never had any financial interest in that company? A. No, sir.

Q. I would like to excuse Mr. Hedley — just a moment — will you have prepared, please, Mr. Hedley, and be prepared to testify from it, a statement of your total income from this list of patents, which I will go into at two o'clock?

Chairman Thompson.— On the income from each patent?

Q. Yes. A. From the Railroad Companies I am employed by?

Chairman Thompson.— No; all companies.

Mr. Hedley.— I can't do it.

Chairman Thompson.—Why?

Mr. Hedley.—Why, in the first place I don't know. It would take a longer time than until two o'clock for me to get it.

Chairman Thompson.— Do the best you can by two o'clock. We don't mean —

Mr. Colby.—We want that information.

The Chairman.— Tomorrow?

Mr. Hedley.—You can have most all the information you

want, sir. It is going to take me time to get it up. I don't keep any books.

By Mr. Colby:

Q. You don't keep any record of your income from this — the twenty-five or thirty patents? A. No. I know in a general way what it is, and I take — get a statement once in a while.

Q. From whom? A. From whoever has a right to build from my patents. I got a statement from one of them this morning.

Chairman Thompson.—Well, we will get at it the best we can.

Mr. Hedley.— I couldn't possibly do it.

By Mr. Colby:

Q. Mr. Hedley, do I understand you to say that from a list of patents here of thirty or more, many of which are in use by thirty or forty railroads? A. No, I didn't say that. I said some of them.

Q. Some of them. Thirty or forty railroads — A. I guess more than that, too.

Q. You preserve no memoranda of receipts of the royalties from such patents? A. No.

Q. You testified that some of the railroads, such as the Hudson McAdoo Tunnel and the Southern Pacific have paid you as much as $15 per car for the installation of one device? A. I said ten dollars, the Hudson.

Q. The Southern Pacific, the anti-climber — A. I said to the best of my recollection the Southern Pacific did pay $15.

Q. I think you also said it was equipped on many hundreds of their cars? A. I believe it is.

Q. Therefore it must be a very substantial income even for a man as large as you are. A. Well, it has been an income that I have appreciated, but after I have got it, made use of it, I don't bother my head about what has gone behind.

Q. Many of these patents you don't own yourself, but jointly? A. I know what has taken place every year, and Mr. Doyle gets the same statement I do from the people we have disposed of —

Q. Possibly Mr. Doyle has preserved a record of his receipts. A. He may have.

Q. In dividing — A. You are asking how much I got out of
these things, going back — some of them are very old, ten or
fifteen years.

Chairman Thompson.—About the last three years.

Mr. Hedley.— The last three years. Well, that is an easier
matter. I may have papers for the last three years, memorandum
of statements. If I have, I will dig them up for you as soon as
possible.

By Mr. Colby:

Q. I want a complete statement, Mr. Hedley, as far as you
can possibly compile it. A. I will give it to you that way, sir, as
complete — there won't be anything in it but what are facts, and
all the facts will be in.

Chairman Thompson.—We don't assume that. You have been
very decent about giving all the information we have asked, and
your company has.

Mr. Hedley.— Well, sir, I have got an open book, and the cards
are on the table all the time. You or anybody else that has the
right to can see them.

Chairman Thompson.— Mr. Quackenbush has been here with an
open face every time he came.

Mr. Quackenbush.—They just drew me up here. I haven't done
anything.

Mr. Chairman, Mr. Colby made a suggestion about the order
of proof here, and I stated to the Chairman before Mr. Colby
came, the reason that it would be desirable to have Mr. Doyle
called, just because he has been away from the shop so long. While
I don't want to interfere with the convenience of Mr. Pizzini, I
think Mr. Colby will realize that we are running a railroad that is
very important — if you could call Mr. Doyle now —

Mr. Colby.— I don't think I can call Mr. Doyle at the moment.
I should like to accommodate you.

Mr. Quackenbush.— Then I ask the Chairman to excuse Mr.
Doyle.

Mr. Colby.— I think Mr. Doyle might go back to the shop on agreement that he can respond to a half-hour summons.

Mr. Quackenbush.— Yes.

By Mr. Colby:

Q. Mr. Hedley, will you also bring me at 2 o'clock the minute book of the company, of its executive committee, containing resolutions in which these special awards have been made? A. I have got copies of them in my pocket, sir. You asked me for that before. And I have them with me, sir.

Q. Oh, yes. Let me have them. I assume they are under the seal of the secretary?

Mr. Quackenbush.— I will see that they are.

Mr. Hedley.— No, they are not. Just prepared in my office. There are some other figures you asked me for.

Mr. Colby.— Yes, thank you.

Mr. Hedley.— You asked for the capitalization of the Subway Construction Company. That is on the top of the memorandum there, too.

Mr. Colby.— Mr. Pizzini.

The Chairman.— Mr. Hedley, you are excused until 2 o'clock.

PIZZINI, ANDREW J., being first duly sworn, testified as follows:

By Mr. Colby:

Q. Your full name is Andrew J. Pizzini? A. Yes.

Q. And where do you reside? A. Hotel Ansonia.

Q. How long have you resided in New York? A. About seven and a half years.

Q. What is your business? A. Electrical railway supplies.

Q. Are you connected with any firm or corporation? A. Vice-president of the Railway Improvement Company.

Q. Are you connected with any other corporation? A. Wendell & McDuffy Company, vice-president.

4

Q. What is the Wendell & McDuffy Company? A. Railway equipment and supplies.

Q. Are you an officer of either of those companies? A. I am vice-president of the Wendell & McDuffy Company.

Q. Did I understand you to say what office you held in the Railway Improvement Company? A. Yes, vice-president.

Q. Are you connected with any other firm or corporation? A. As an officer, no.

Q. As a director? A. No. In New York?

Q. Yes. A. Not in New York city.

Q. Not in New York State?

The Chairman.— In New Jersey?

The Witness.— I am connected in the west. Not anything in New Jersey, no.

The Chairman.— And you are not connected with any one in New Jersey or Connecticut that do business in New York?

The Witness.— I am connected with a company in Arizona.

Chairman Thompson.— Well, that is a good ways away.

By Mr. Colby:

Q. Who is the president of the Railway Improvement Company? A. G. W. Fairchild.

Q. When did you — how long have you known Mr. Frank Hedley, who has just left the stand? A. About eight years — pardon me, I will correct that. About — from 1910; from about July, 1910.

Q. That was about the time the Railway Improvement Company was organized, wasn't it? A. Yes.

Q. When did you first become interested in railway equipment? A. I was employed by Mr. Hedley to work for the Railway Improvement Company.

Q. In July, 1910? A. Yes, sir.

Q. The company was then an infant company, wasn't it, just getting under way? A. It was incorporated in August, I think, about the 1st of August, 1910.

Q. Yes? A. Yes.

Q. In what capacity were you employed? A. As vice-president in charge of sales, managing the company.

Q. Had you had previous experience in that line? A. I had previous experience in the clock business.

Q. Clock business? A. Yes.

Q. Coaster clocks or eight-day clocks? A. Working for the International Time Recording Company that make all different types of clocks for factory purposes and recording.

Q. In what capacity were you employed by the International Time Recording Company? A. In the sales department, New York office.

Q. On a salary? A. On a commission. They pay — no salaries are paid.

Q. On what basis were you employed by Mr. Hedley for the Railway Improvement Company? A. On the same basis.

Q. Commission on sales? A. Commission on sales.

Q. In other words, although the vice-president, you were a salesman? You were employed because of your record and ability as a salesman? That is obvious. Are you still acting as a salesman for the Railway Improvement Company? A. Yes.

Q. That is your side of the work? A. I was employed to run the company. Mr. Hedley did not take any active part in the managing of the company. My duties were to run the company and to make reports to him of the results of my operation.

Q. When did you become a stockholder in the Railway Improvement Company? A. I took an option on Mr. Hedley's and Mr. Doyle's holdings of their stock on the 15th of December, 1914, just prior to my leaving for the west, and when I returned from the west I closed the option and bought their stock.

Q. You were not a stockholder until you closed that option? A. No.

Q. You were, however, an officer of the company? A. Yes.

Q. You had had only a nominal or qualifying interest, I assume — A. Had only a commission on the goods I sold.

Q. The point of my question is, how could you be an officer and director of the company without owning stock in it? A. I don't know.

Q. You were, however, an officer and director, and did own no stock in it? A. Yes, sir.

Chairman Thompson.— How about this Wendell, McDuffy? A. Same thing.

The Witness.— The Wendell & McDuffy Company? I bought an interest in it from Jack Wendell, who has since died.

Chairman Thompson.— When you first began with it?

The Witness.— No; I bought that interest, I think, about four years ago.

Chairman Thompson.— You had that when you went into the company?

Mr. Pizzini.— No.

Chairman Thompson.— Had no interest in that when you went in?

The Witness.— I don't understand your question.

Chairman Thompson.— In this improvement company, you went as vice-president, without owning any stock at all?

The Witness.— I was employed really to run the company.

Chairman Thompson.— I asked you if it was the same way with the Wendell & McDuffy Company.

The Witness.— I simply made an investment with the Wendell & McDuffy Company.

Chairman Thompson.— Before you were employed as vice-president?

The Witness.— I was working for the Railway Improvement Company when I made my investment in the Wendell & McDuffy Company.

By Mr. Colby:

Q. In other words, you made no investment in the Railway Improvement Company at the time? A. I did not.

Q. Do you know who the stockholders were of the Railway Improvement Company? A. At the time of my employment, I do.

Q. Who? A. Mr. Fairchild; Mr. McDuffy.

Q. How much does Mr. Fairchild own? A. He owned ten thousand dollars.

Q. How much did Mr. McDuffy own? A. I think he owned five.

Q. How was the other stock issued? A. Mr. Doyle. I think he owned about $12,500 — $13,000 worth, Doyle. Mr. Hedley, $13,000 worth. The balance of the stock I don't know who positively owned it. I think Mr. McDuffy secured the subscription, but I think it was had by the Pay-as-you-enter Car Company, $10,000.

Chairman Thompson.— The thing was incorporated for $50,000?

The Witness.— For $100,000. And $51,000 worth of stock was issued. Twenty-five in cash was paid into the treasury and $26,000 in stock was given to Mr. Hedley and Mr. Doyle in payment for their patents.

Chairman Thompson.— Did you buy their patents?

The Witness.— I was only employed by the company.

Chairman Thompson.— Did the company buy them?

The Witness.— The company gave them stock.

Chairman Thompson.— You said for their patents.

The Witness.— I will make that clear.

Chairman Thompson.— I think it is clear, but I don't think you have got any license to sit on the stand and say it was done for the patents, because Mr. Hedley testified he did not turn over the patents or even a license.

The Witness.— He turned over an assignment to the Improvement Company, for the right to sell, but the Interborough Company exempted the right to sell to the Interborough exempted.

Chairman Thompson.— The company did not get any interest in the patent?

The Witness.— I don't know what they got. I was giving you the best of my knowledge on the subject.

By Mr. Colby:

Q. The remainder of the stock was not at that time issued?   A. It has never been issued.

Q. Fifty-one thousand has been issued?   A. $51,000 issued.

Q. And the $26,000 of stock, issued not for money, but for some interest in the Hedley-Doyle patents, practically represented control of the company?   A. It did represent control of the company.

Q. And the only money was put up by Mr. Fairchild, who put up $10,000, Mr. McDuffy, who put up $5,000, and the Pay-as-you-enter Car Company, who put up $10,000, and it was on that $25,000 of actual funds in the way of capital that you started out on the business?   A. Right.

Q. I see. What was your age at this time, at the time of your first employment by the Pay-as-you-enter Company?   A. I was born in 1879. I was employed in 1910.

Chairman Thompson.— Thirty-one.

Q. A young man. Did you draw considerable income from the company?   A. No, the income for the first year, I don't remember — I think it was about between three and four thousand dollars. It got larger each year.

Q. Until it reached what figure?   A. I think I have made as high as $15,000 in one year.

Q. That was the last year?   A. That was —

Q. I mean that was —   A. 19—

Q. 15?   A. 1915 was probably our best year.

Q. Had you any other source of income?   A. Yes, sir.

Q. From invested funds?   A. Yes.

Q. Was this the greater part of your income, or only a —   A. The greater part.

Q. I mean what you derived from this Improvement company was the greater part of your income?   A. Yes.

Q. It was that you lived upon?   A. Yes.

Q. The company has never paid any dividend, I think Mr. Hedley testified?   A. The company paid a dividend last year and this year. Since I have owned the company it has paid two dividends, since I owned the stock I bought from Mr. Hedley and Mr. Doyle.

Q. What dividend did it pay last year? A. Twenty per cent.

Q. On $100,000? A. On $51,000.

Q. On its issued stock? A. Yes.

Q. When was that dividend paid? A. Paid in March.

Q. Nineteen hundred and fifteen? A. 1915.

Q. When was the second dividend paid? A. About a week ago.

Q. January, 1916? A. 1916.

Q. How much was paid then? A. Ten per cent.

Q. So that in less than a twelve-month it has paid dividends aggregating 30 per cent? A. Yes.

Q. Has it any surplus or undivided profits? A. About five thousand dollars surplus.

Q. What are its total assets irrespective of the value of these patents? A. The book accounts, tools and machinery, notes receivable and accounts receivable, cash.

Q. What do they total? A. I will be glad to give you a statement of the company.

Q. You haven't it in mind? Bring it, please. A. I will be glad to give you a statement — just a week old.

Q. You say that you obtained an option from Mr. Hedley on his stock in December, 1913. Is that option in writing? A. Yes, sir.

Q. Have you a copy of it? A. Yes, sir. I have a copy of the — the option is not signed by Mr. Hedley. It was a meeting which we held in Mr. Hedley's office, between Mr. Doyle, Mr. Hedley and myself, prior to my starting West, and when I got back to my office I wrote a letter and confirmed my understanding of the option, and sent a copy to him and sent a copy to Mr. Doyle, and I have a copy of my own.

Q. Have you a copy of the letter? A. Well, I would like to give you a copy. It is the only copy I have. I prefer to have it copied and give you a copy.

Q. Certainly. (Counsel takes letter from witness.)

Mr. Colby.— I will offer this in evidence.

Chairman Thompson.— Read it in.

Mr. Colby.— I will read it into the record.

Q. This is a true copy of the letter you sent to Mr. Hedley?
A. It is the original copy made by and initialed by me at the time it was made.

Mr. Colby.— "December 15, 1914. Mr. Frank Hedley and Mr. J. S. Doyle: Dear F. H. and J. S. D.: Here is a copy of the 60-days' option including stock and contract of the Railway Improvement Company. I thought I had better write this out the way I understand it and send it to you, so that there can be no mistake in case I am able to put over the deal. It is going to be a pretty hard thing to put over, but I am going to try my best. Very truly yours, A. P."

The Witness.— A. J. P.

By Mr. Colby:

Q. A. J. P. You signed it your initial. You say this conversation or conference that you had with F. H. and J. S. D. took place in the office of F. H. and J. S. D.? A. Took place in Mr. Hedley's office in this building.

Q. Was J. S. D. there? A. Yes.

Q. Who sent for you? A. What is that?

Q. Who sent for you to come to their office? A. No one. I went unsolicited. I was anxious to buy this stock, and I had been trying to get it for some time, and I went to Mr. Hedley's office to try and persuade him to let me buy it from him.

Q. Is that quite the fact? A. Absolutely the fact, sir, as I remember it.

Q. The terms of this letter don't indicate an anxiety on your part to purchase. A. That letter would give you probably an erroneous idea of the part that was hard. I had to raise $25,000 in cash to pay for that stock, and it was a very difficult matter to raise $25,000 in cash at that date, for me to do it.

Q. This is clearly the letter of a man who had been asked to do something, and he was doubtful of his power to do it. A. It might sound like that. It was a letter of a man trying very hard to get the stock, and the terms of payment were very difficult for him to meet them.

Q. What were the terms of payment? A. Twenty-five thousand dollars to be paid in cash for 260 shares of the stock.

Q. Cash down? A. Cash down.

Q. That is at variance with Mr. Hedley's testimony given yesterday as to the terms of this sale. A. That was not the terms of the sale. That was the terms of the payment he gave me. When I got back I could not raise but $10,000 in cash. And I paid him $10,000 and got him to wait for the other fifteen, which I afterwards paid him.

Q. How long did he wait? A. Until January this year.

Q. Did you give him a note? A. I gave him a note for one-half the amount and Mr. Doyle a note for one-half the amount.

Q. And what was the date of that note? A. I don't know. Probably the date of it at the time I got back from Arizona.

Q. What were the terms? A. I think it was the date of the contract of sale, the date of the time that I bought the stock from him.

Q. What were the terms of the notes? A. They were one year each.

Q. Payable one year after date? A. Yes.

Q. Where did you get the ten thousand? A. I borrowed it in the West.

Q. Have you repaid it? A. Yes.

Q. Is the stock — was the stock given as security for this loan? A. No. Pardon me, which loan?

Q. Evidenced by the notes, that is to say, the extension of the payment. A. The stock was held as security by Mr. Hedley and Mr. Doyle until I paid the second payment.

Q. And when was the stock delivered, on what date? A. It was delivered about a week prior to our annual meeting, when I paid the amount and got the stock in my possession.

Q. What was the date of your annual meeting? A. I think our annual meeting was last Tuesday, the 25th of —

Chairman Thompson.— January.

The Witness.— January. I was not sure that Tuesday was the 25th. I think that was the date.

Q. That would be right, wouldn't it, the 25th. In other words, this sale was actually consummated by the delivery of the certificates, last Tuesday, January 25, 1916? A. Well, I think the sale was consummated when I paid my first ten thousand dollars. I got the stock in my possession a week prior to our annual meeting.

Q. The stock was delivered to you on January 25; in other words, last Tuesday? A. No, I didn't say that.

Q. I understood you— A. I said the annual meeting was on the 25th, and I paid for the stock and got delivery of it about a week prior.

Q. About January 18? A. Eighteen.

Q. I don't want to mix you up. Are those certificates in your possession now? A. Yes.

Q. In the same condition in which they were delivered to you? A. They are.

Q. They stand in the name of Mr. Doyle and Mr. Hedley? A. No. They stand in my name.

Q. Then you have had them transferred? A. They were transferred at the time the $10,000 was paid, and the proper stamps were affixed to them and endorsed by me, in blank, and put up as collateral for the deferred payment.

Q. Were the stamps affixed previously or subsequently? A. Affixed at the time of the sale.

Q. You then endorsed this certificate back to Mr. Hedley as security for the note? A. More as collateral payment for my note given them at the time I paid the ten thousand dollars in cash, and promised to pay the remaining fifteen.

Q. What prompted you as a salesman, practically without any interest in the company, to go up to the artful gentlemen and ask them to deliver over to you on credit control of this company which they had organized? A. What prompted me to buy the company, you mean?

Q. I say what prompted you, who were up to the moment you undertook to put this deal over, according to your own words, what prompted you at that time, merely a salesman, practically, an employee of the company, without any interest in it, to go to the chief men in the company and ask them to deliver control of the company to you on a year's credit? A. I had been trying to purchase the Railway Improvement Company for over a year and I had been trying to persuade Mr. Hedley and Mr. Doyle to sell the company to me. I considered it a very good investment and I wanted to control the company I was employed by and working for.

Chairman Thompson.— Did you expect to do it without any money?

The Witness.— I didn't expect to do it without any money. I paid $10,000 in cash.

Chairman Thompson.— You had to go to Arizona to get it?

Mr. Pizzini.— That is all right.

Chairman Thompson.— It took a year —

The Witness.— I was not broke —

Chairman Thompson.— You said you wanted to get this company a year before you went to Arizona. You didn't have the money —

The Witness.— I didn't expect to buy it without money. I expected to have to pay for it.

Chairman Thompson.—Sure.

By Mr. Colby:

Q. You state here in your letter: " It is going to be a pretty hard thing to put over, but I am going to try my best." Did they ask you to try your best? A. Mr. Hedley was very reluctant to sell.

Q. Well, what pressure did you bring to bear on him to sell? A. No pressure at all. I tried to get him to sell it to me. I thought I was the logical one to own the company. I helped to establish it and I was running it, and I wanted to own it.

Q. Why were you the logical one to own it? A. I was really managing the company from the day it was incorporated, and I had run the company all those years, and I also felt that I created the company, or the business of the company.

Q. Why wasn't Mr. Hedley the logical man to own the company? He had organized it, and the subject matter with which the company was making all of its earnings were Mr. Hedley's and Mr. Doyle's patents. Did you feel that the logic pointed rather to you as the owner than to F. H. and J. S. D.? A. Yes, I thought it did.

Q. Did you mention that view to Mr. Hedley and Mr. Doyle? A. I mentioned to them that I thought I was the logical one to own the company.

Q. Did they say they thought it was a little fresh on your part? A. Mr. Doyle thought I was the logical one. I think Mr. Hedley thought so later.

Q. Mr. Hedley demurred a little? A. He was not anxious to sell the company to me or anyone else.

Q. If a man is not anxious to sell, why should he sell on such terms, taking a consideration of 40 per cent of the cash, and a year's credit to pay the remainder? A. I think the terms were very fair. I paid interest on the deferred payment, and I had a ten thousand dollar equity in the collateral. I don't think those terms were unfair. I think they were very nearly equivalent to getting the cash.

Q. They were unusual? A. No.

Q. Did you ever buy control of any other company on such terms? A. No.

Q. Did you ever hear of any company being bought on such terms? A. I cannot cite a case at present.

Q. What is your standard for thinking that is fair and usual? A. I have no standard for thinking so, except what is my own judgment in the matter.

Mr. Colby.— I understand that you wish —

Chairman Thompson.— I want to get away at quarter after 12. I have another matter I would like to take up, if it don't interfere with the examination.

Mr. Colby.— Shall we adjourn to 2 o'clock?

Chairman Thompson.— If there is no objection, we will suspend now until 2 o'clock. All witnesses are directed to appear at 2 o'clock.

Whereupon (at 12:10 P. M.), an adjournment was taken to 2 o'clock P. M. of the same date.

AFTERNOON SESSION

Meeting called to order by Chairman Thompson at 2 p. m., a quorum being present.

PIZZINI, J. W., being recalled, testified as follows:

Examination by Mr. Colby:

Q. Was the letter, of which you hand me a carbon copy and apparently dated December 15, 1914, actually written on that day? A. It was.

Q. What was the stock that you represented in that letter as included together, I mean the contract which you represented in that letter as included together with the stock in the option? Let me simplify that question. What is the contract you refer to in your letter of December 15, 1914? A. The contract that Mr. Hedley and Mr. Doyle had with the Railway Improvement Company when they assigned exclusive selling rights of their patents to the Railway Improvement Company and excluded the Interborough Rapid Transit Company.

Q. You have that contract, I believe? A. Why, no, I haven't it.

Q. Well Mr. Hedley have you that contract?

Mr. Hedley.— Yes, sir. I have a contract of that kind.

Q. Have you it with you? A. No, sir. I haven't been asked to bring that yet. I wasn't asked to bring the contract with the Prepayment Car Sales Company. I will bring you the contract if you wish it with the Railway Improvement Company.

Q. Would it trouble you too much to send down for that contract now or would it be too much trouble?

Mr. Hedley.— A. I will go and get it. I think I know where I can put my hand on it. At least I will make an effort.

Q. When did you conceive the idea of buying the control of this company of which you are salesman? A. I wouldn't want to give you the exact date, or rather I couldn't give you the exact date but I think about the first part of 1914 or the latter part of 1913.

Q. And you went to see Mr. Hedley and Mr. Doyle on the subject? A. I used to see them almost every week and I discussed it with them on several occasions.

Q. What occasion did you have to see them every week? A. I used to have lunch with Mr. Hedley at the Railroad Club. Whenever I lunched with him at the club I used to discuss with him how I was progressing with the Railroad Improvement Company.

Q. Do I understand you to say you lunched with Mr. Hedley nearly every day? A. No, I said I lunched at the Railroad Club nearly every day.

Q. Did I understand you to say then that you saw him every week? A. About once a week.

Q. And on all these occasions you discussed the affairs of the Railway Improvement Company? A. I did, a great many of them.

Q. How was this question of your buying Mr. Hedley's stock approached? A. I don't know just how it was approached. I simply told him I would like to get an option on his stock and buy it and own the company.

Q. What did he say? A. He used to tell me that he didn't want to sell it.

Q. How did you take the matter up with Mr. Doyle? A. About the same way I used to take it up with Mr. Hedley.

Q. What did Doyle say? A. Doyle did not appear particular whether he sold it or not. He didn't seem to be adverse to selling it or was he adverse to holding it.

Q. You apparently had the money at that time to buy the stock? A. I didn't have the actual cash but I had means of procuring money on property that I own.

Q. Where did you borrow the ten thousand dollars with which the payment was made? A. I borrowed it in the West. If you wish to know exactly from whom I got it I will be glad to tell you.

Q. I am not trying to pry into your personal affairs, I simply want to know the facts. A. I gave Mr. Hedley and Mr. Doyle a draft on the man I borrowed from, and that draft was paid.

Q. You gave them five thousand dollars apiece? A. Yes, sir.

Q. And where did you get the sixteen thousand dollars with which you completed the purchase? A. I sold some securities.

Q. And you are now the owner of that stock? A. I am.

Q. What relation of a business character have the Railway

Improvement Company with the Interborough Rapid Transit Company? A. We have none. Mr. Hedley would not permit us to have any business relations with them as long as he was in charge of the company.

Q. You never sold anything to the Interborough Rapid Transit Company? A. No, sir, not a dollar's worth of anything.

Q. Did you buy cars from manufacturers? A. I never bought a car in my life nor my company nor the Railway Improvement Company.

Q. What did you sell? A. Coasting clocks, anti-climbers and sanitary straps.

Q. You never sold any of these things to the Interborough Rapid Transit Company? A. Not one dollar's worth.

Q. Where did you buy your coasting clocks? A. From the International Time Recording Company.

Q. Did you buy only from them? A. Yes.

Q. Where did you buy the sanitary straps? A. I bought them from several manufacturers. We handle five types of sanitary straps, one type is made, the steel type, is made by the Standard Steel Welds Company of Cleveland, Ohio. Another type of strap is made by the Celluloid Company of America. You know the work on these devices is done in this way. The straps are manufactured by certain companies, the machine work and riveting is done by machine companies, etc.

Q. You paid Mr. Hedley and Mr. Doyle royalties on these devices? A. No royalties on sanitary straps. Mr. Doyle and Mr. Hedley do not own the patents on any of the sanitary straps that we handle except what is known as number five.

Q. Do you pay any royalties on any of these devices? A. On the anti-climber we pay a royalty to Mr. Hedley and on the coasting clock we pay royalties to Mr. Doyle and Mr. Hedley combined, but we did not pay any royalty while Mr. Hedley was president of the company, only since he sold out his ownership.

Q. Then the payment of royalties has begun? A. It has.

Q. How much do you pay Mr. Hedley on account of royalties? A. I couldn't tell you to my mind.

Q. Have you any idea? A. I should say about ten thousand dollars, probably more.

Q. For a period of several years? A. Yes, sir.

Q. Probably how much more have you paid than that? A. I can give you the exact amount.

Q. How much did you pay in royalties on the coasting clock? A. I will furnish you that information also.

Q. Please do. Can you approximately tell me? A. You mean Mr. Hedley alone?

Q. Hedley and Doyle on this coasting clock. Your contract is one that has been running since January last year, is it not? A. Why, I imagine we paid about one thousand dollars.

Q. Did Mr. Hedley and Mr. Doyle derive any income from the Railway Improvement Company until they had resigned and sold their stocks? A. Not that I know of.

Q. Are you able to testify to that? A. I am to my best knowledge. They didn't get a cent until I bought their stock.

Q. Is your knowledge complete? A. I think it is. I run the company.

Q. What is the Wendell, McDuffy Company? A. The Wendell, McDuffy Company is a concern that represents various corporations, various manufacturers, in different parts of the country, and sells the New York agents or in some cases the Eastern agents or general sales agents that represent the manufacturer. In some cases it is the Eastern agents and in other cases it is the general sales agents.

Q. Are you interested in the Wendell, McDuffy Company? A. I own one-fourth of it.

Q. Are you a director? A. Yes.

Q. Do you hold any other office? A. Vice-president.

Q. Where is its office? A. 61 Broadway.

Q. Does it share offices with the Railway Improvement Company? A. It does.

Q. Who is its president? A. Mr. R. L. McDuffy.

Q. What companies is the Wendell and McDuffy Company agent of? A. St. Louis Car Company, Consolidated Car Fender Company, The Russel Car and Snow Plow Company, The DuPont Fabricated Company, the Upson Company. Those are companies that come to mind. I cannot tell you more than that.

Q. Is there any relation between the Railway Improvement

Company and the Wendell, McDuffy Company? A. Absolutely none other than the fact that I own stock in both companies.

Q. Is Mr. McDuffy a stockholder of the Railway Improvement Company? A. He is.

Q. Does the Wendell, McDuffy Company sell to the Interborough Rapid Transit Company? A. I think they do.

Q. Don't you know they do? A. I don't know. I know they have sold them.

Q. Do they sell cars as agents of the St. Louis Car Company to the Interborough Rapid Transit Company? A. I think they do. I am quite sure.

Q. Can you tell how large a number of cars the St. Louis Car Company, the Wendell and McDuffy Company have sold to the Interborough Rapid Transit Company? A. From my own knowledge I cannot tell you exactly. I can make a guess if you like.

Q. Will you give me an approximate estimate? A. I can do that.

Q. Can you give me the absolute number by reference to your books? A. Yes, sir, I think that is possible. I think they sold 175 cars and I think they lost a great deal of money on the sale.

Q. When did they sell these cars? A. I do not know exactly. I know that they sold these cars at a ridiculously low price and that they lost a lot of money on it.

Q. In other words you lost some anticipated profits? A. No, the McDuffy Company have a contract for selling the cars with these manufacturing companies and they get a fixed commission for this service.

Q. And I suppose this commission is as much as 10 per cent. A. Absolutely not.

Q. Do you know Mr. George Kobing of the St. Louis Company? A. I know him.

Q. You have met him frequently? A. About a half dozen times in my life.

Q. Has the McDuffy Company ever made any payment to Mr. Kobing? A. I don't think Mr. Kobing is connected with the St. Louis Car Company in any way. However, I am not certain. I don't think he is.

Q. Has the McDuffy Company ever paid any sums personally to Mr. Kobing? A. To my knowledge, no.

Q. Now, Mr. Pizzini, I want a statement of all moneys paid by the Railway Improvement Company and the Wendell, Mc-Duffy Company to Mr. Frank Hedley and Mr. James S. Doyle? A. The Wendell, McDuffy Company have never paid Mr. Doyle or Mr. Hedley, one penny, in fact I know they haven't since I have been connected with them. I will give you a complete statement of all moneys paid by the Railway Improvement Company to Mr. Hedley and Mr. Doyle since its incorporation.

Q. Have you any agreement or understanding with Mr. Doyle as to their right to repurchase this stock at any time? A. None whatever.

Q. Nor the Railway Improvement Company? A. No, sir, it is not for sale.

Q. Did Mr. Hedley and Mr. Doyle know when they gave you this very generous option on their stock that the stock was soon to pay a dividend? A. I don't know if they did or not. They had access to the books and could tell about the financial basis of the company.

Q. Did you never discuss the earnings and resources of the company? A. Yes, I think they knew they were going to pay a dividend.

Q. Did you bring a copy of the company's statement? A. Yes, sir, I did. (Witness delivers copy of statement of the Railway Improvement Company to Mr. Colby, Counsel.)

Q. Have you any interest in any other company in which Mr. Hedley is also interested? A. I own stocks of the Computing Tabulating Recording Company. He just testified that he owned stock in that company.

Q. Any other companies? A. I own stock in the Gun Hill Realty Company.

Q. What is that? That's a real estate holding company? A. I believe it is.

Q. Where is it incorporated? A. I think in the State.

Q. Is there anyone else interested in that company except you, Mr. Hedley, Mr. Cutler or Mr. Fairchild? A. What companies do you refer to.

Q. Why I mean who is the third man. A. Why there is Mr. McDuffy, Mr. Fairchild, Mr. Doyle, and Mr. Hedley, that is in . the Gun Hill Realty Company.

Q. Well, that is what I am talking about. Who are the directors of that company? A. I don't know.

Q. Are you a director? A. I don't think I am.

Q. Are you an officer? A. No.

Q. What real estate do you own? A. I bought a piece of real estate about five years ago and we afterwards incorporated it into a company and issued stock for it so as to be able to take care of the assessments that were levied against it.

Q. Well tell me about that? A. Well, it runs on the corner of Gun Hill and White Plains road. I think they purchased from the Crowfoot Estate.

Q. What is the total investment of the company therein? A. You can get that best and more accurate from the books. I think it is about three hundred thousand dollars.

Q. Who is interested in that company? A. Mr. Hedley invited me to subscribe for a part of the stock of the company. I don't know who is interested in the company besides myself from my own knowledge. I think the American Railroad Company or one of the members of their company are members.

Q. You can find out all this information by looking at the books, can you not? A. I think I can. I am very certain of the fact that it was a very unprofitable investment for me. I thought it would be a very profitable one, but it has since proven otherwise.

Q. That's along the lines of the proposed new subway route, is it not? A. It is along the subway route, yes, sir.

Q. It was bought before the routes were finally determined or when the routes were in course of discussion, is that not so? A. It was bought five or six years ago. I do not know when the routes were decided upon.

Q. Well, there's a station on the subway on or about your property, is there not? A. Yes.

Q. What is the name of that station? A. I don't know.

Q. Where is the proposed location of the station? A. I think it is on Gun Hill road. It is a prominent crosstown road. The New York Central own some of the other lines out there.

Q. Have stations on that same road? A. I don't know.

Q. Isn't it a fact that you bought this land with the idea of anticipating the erection of the station on the subway? A. The Gun Hill Realty Company were the owners of this land.

Q. But were you not impressed with the probability of the construction of a station on this subway? A. I was imbued with the idea that a subway might run out there at some time.

Q. By Mr. Hedley? A. Yes, sir.

Q. Well you know that he runs the subway? A. Well, Mr. Hedley has something to do with it, I know that.

Q. How much stock do you own in this corporation? A. One-eighth.

Q. And what interest has Mr. Hedley in the land? A. I think one-fourth.

Q. Is this land improved now? A. I think it's much more valuable now than when we bought it. I would like to sell my interest for what I paid for it without charging interest on it during the time of ownership.

Q. Are you possibly in the frame of mind to buy control of the Gun Hill Realty Company also? A. I am not.

Q. Well, what did Mr. Hedley say to you when he asked you to take an interest in this company? A. He said it was very cheap and that we would probably make money on increased valuation.

Q. What was this increased valuation supposed to arise from? A. I don't know. Probably it was to be from the increased valuation of Bronx property and the increased facility for transportation.

Q. From every cause except the location of the subway route through this land and the installation of the subway? A. I don't think Mr. Hedley knew or anyone else knew where the location of the subway would be.

Q. You would credit Mr. Hedley with having fairly accurate impressions on that subject, would you not? A. I don't know that he had the determination of that subject. I thought it was determined by the Public Service Commission or someone in the city's authority.

Q. You just took it because Hedley asked you to take it? A. I did it because he had excellent judgment of real estate values.

Q. Do you know of any other real estate operations that Mr. Hedley had previous to this transfer? A. No.

Q. What were the basis of your impression as to his judgment in matters of Bronx real estate? A. The basis was that I thought he knew the property values and I thought he was an excellent judge of them.

Q. Why was he an excellent judge? A. Well, a man who has studied these conditions as well as he has and understands them as well as he does.

Q. You mean the railway companies? A. I mean general business conditions in the community.

Q. Now, Mr. Pizzini, didn't Mr. Hedley tell you that this land would be located along the present subway extension? A. He did not. He never mentioned it to me.

Q. Didn't he tell you that he had reason to believe that a station would be erected there? A. Absolutely not.

Q. Wasn't there a great question as to where the station was to be located? A. I know nothing about that, sir.

Q. The question of the Rapid Transit facilities through this property was not up at the time that you paid this draft? A. I don't believe you will think so if you will look at the property. I don't think the question of the stations or the routes were up at that time.

Q. Up where? A. Up before the city authorities or whoever it comes up before.

Q. Well, who else is interested in this company? A. I think Mr. Boynton is interested in the concern.

Q. What Boynton? A. I don't know what Boynton. I think he is connected with the American Real Estate Company. I am not certain whether Mr. Day is a member, but you can find out I think by the officers of the company or the owners.

Q. By the way, what assessment have you paid? A. I think my original investment was ten thousand dollars and I think the assessment has been about as much as the original amount paid in.

Q. Now, Mr. Pizzini, did he say, " Pizzini, come along, this is a good thing; come along and take an interest?" A. I think Mr. Hedley, if I recall the conversation correctly, told me that it would be a good investment.

Q. Why a good investment? A. On account of the increased value of the land and on account of the price being very low.

Q. How extensive is this plot of ground? A. I think it is about twenty acres.

Q. Are streets laid through it? A. That is what has caused the assessment, but I don't think they have been built.

Q. Just where has this new subway station been built? A. I don't know. I don't know just where it is. I believe it is just beyond Gun Hill road.

Q. Is that an express station? A. I don't know.

Q. You don't believe that this station is going to depreciate the value of your lots? A. I should think it would increase the value of any property.

Q. Are you prepared to say here as a witness, whether or not the question of this land or route of the subway was discussed by you or Mr. Hedley? A. I am not prepared to say that it was or wasn't. I don't think it ever was.

Q. Never alluded to it in any way? A. No, I don't think it was.

Q. Did he seem to regard that as a very profitable investment on your part? A. I don't know.

Q. Well, what did he say? A. Well, he said that it was a nice piece of property and could be bought very cheaply.

Q. Are you selling the lots? A. I wish we could.

Q. Have you an option on any of them for sale? A. I don't think so. I think the plans are to sell out.

Q. What was the last time you discussed this with Mr. Hedley? A. You mean the question of this land? I think I discussed the matter with him about two weeks ago, about when we were going to sell it.

Q. Well, did you ask him about the progress of the subway work out there? A. I didn't have to, because I have ridden out and seen the progress over there myself.

Q. Is Mr. Doyle interested in that land? A. I don't think so. No.

Q. What is the capital of the Wendell, McDuffy Company, capital stock? A. I think it's five thousand dollars.

Q. And you and Mr. McDuffy are the only interested men? A. I am not interested in it at all. Mr. McDuffy is the interested man in the company.

Q. What is the relation of the Wendell, McDuffy Company to the Prepayment Car Sales Company? A. I don't think there is any relation. I don't know.

Q. Isn't Mr. McDuffy a director? A. I think Mr. McDuffy is a director but that does not make them related very closely to the Wendell, McDuffy Company.

Q. Where is the office of the Gun Hill Realty Company? A. I think it is in Mr. Hedley's office, 165 Broadway. I am not certain about that. I have not paid much attention to it. I am not an officer or director of the company.

Q. When did you cease to be an officer? A. I don't think I ever was. They may have used my name, but I don't think I was ever an officer or director.

Q. Well the directory gives you as vice-president? A. I am not the vice-president.

Q. Well, doesn't it seem rather queer that the directory should carry you as vice-president if you are not? A. Well, I am not the vice-president.

Q. Who is president? A. I don't know. I think Mr. Hedley is.

Q. Well, the directory gives Mr. Hedley as a vice-president? A. Well, the directory is not infallible.

Q. Well, this same directory gives that office on Broadway as your office? A. It is not my office. Never has been my office.

Q. The directory is a very reliable instrument in this case. A. Well, as I said before the directory is not infallible and in this particular instance it is wrong. I think the company's charter will show its president, that's a matter of record.

Q. Well, I am simply asking where the office is. Isn't it at room 2224 at No. 61 Broadway? A. It is not, and I take oath of it.

Q. Do you know Mr. Otis Kepler? A. I have met him twice.

Q. Do you recognize his name in the personnel of the Gun Hill Realty Company? A. Yes, he is interested in that company.

Q. Do you know what his interest is in it? A. I think his interest is one-fourth.

Q. Did you ask him to go into it? A. No, sir.

Q. Did you ever know that he was interested in the company? A. Never knew it until about two years after I had been in the company and I found out that he was also interested. I would rather say that I met him about a year after I was interested in the company.

Chairman Thompson.— Who is this Mr. Day? What is his name?

Mr. Pizzini.— Joseph P. Day. The iron work is up on the station but the station is not yet completed.

Q. It is not completed yet? A. No.

Q. How much does the company pay for that property? What was the original purchase price of the whole property? A. I think the original purchase price was two hundred thousand dollars.

Q. Who did you buy it of? A. I don't know, I think from the Croker estate.

Q. Wasn't it from Day? A. I don't know.

Q. Has the Wendell, McDuffy Company sold any of the products of the Consolidated Fender Company to the New York Railways or the Interborough Rapid Transit Company? A. I don't think the Interborough Rapid Transit Company uses any of their products. I am quite sure of that.

Q. Well, do the New York Railways Company use any of it? A. Why, I think they have used what they call the " H. B." lifeguard which is an approved device of the Public Service Commission here.

Q. That is the Hedley device? A. It is not. That is what they call the H.B. device, an acknowledged efficient device and licensed in this country and it is equipped on every car in the United States nearly.

Q. Now, Mr. Pizzini, I will excuse you until to-morrow morning, requesting, however, that you bring an accurate statement of the sales of the Railway Improvement Company coasting clock, sanitary straps and anti-climbers, also a statement of all the moneys paid to J. S. Doyle and Mr. Frank Hedley. A. I never paid a cent to the Railway Improvement Company in my life. I can take oath to that.

Q. I want also a statement of the sales of the Wendell and McDuffy Company to the New York Railways Company and to the Interborough Rapid Transit Company for any of the concerns of which it is sales agent. A. You want a statement of sales between these corporations and the New York Transit Companies?

Q. Well, do they do business on a shoestring? A. They have been in business for eighteen years. Now you want a list of the sales of the coasting clock, the anti-climbers, and the sanitary straphangers and the amount of our sales of these three things.

Q. The amount paid to Mr. Hedley and Mr. Doyle also. A. You say the moneys paid to Mr. Hedley and Mr. Doyle, and you ask for a statement of the sales of the Railway Improvement Company of coasting clocks, you mean the amount of the money or the Railway Companies to whom we sold them to?

Q. Both. A. And sanitary straphangers?

Q. Yes, sir. I mean the three devices which I understand are manufactured by the Railway Improvement Company. By the way, is that all you handle? A. That's all we handle. For how long a period of time do you wish this statement, since I have been connected with the Wendell, McDuffy Company?

Q. I want it for a period from 1910 to February 1915. A. I don't think I was connected with the company then.

Q. Well, you are now. You can make it to January 1st, 1916. I notice in your statement that twenty-five thousand dollars of the stock of the Railway Improvement Company is in the treasury of the company? A. I don't understand how that could be. It should have been forty-nine thousand dollars. They issued and held in the treasury twenty-five thousand dollars.

Q. Where does that come from? A. Why, it was never sent out from the treasury.

Q. You say it was never sent out from the treasury? A. Certainly it was. I can explain that by stating that in the contract with Mr. Hedley and Mr. Doyle together with the Railway Improvement Company they specified that if any assignments of their patents and so forth were made they were to receive the controlling stock of the company. I think Mr. Hedley can let you have a more accurate idea on the subject than I can.

Mr. Hedley.— I have a young man now in charge of that who is looking up the papers. He will bring them down in a few minutes if he can find it.

Q. We will excuse you now, Mr. Pizzini, until to-morrow morning, February 2, at 11 a. m. A. I presume Mr. McDuffy can also be excused until that time.

Q. Yes, Mr. Duffy may also be excused until to-morrow morning at 11 o'clock.

FRANK HEDLEY, recalled.

By Mr. Colby:

Q. Mr. Hedley, I am indebted to you for the production of a copy of your agreement of employment with the Interborough Rapid Transit Company, dated May 3, 1909, and covering a period of five years from July 1, 1909, to June 30, 1914. You have no later contract of employment? A. No, sir.

Q. What is your view of the terms of your present employment? A. Why, each year the board of directors under the by-laws has to appoint officers, and I was appointed for this year by resolution of the board of directors appointing me vice-president and general manager in charge of operation, maintenance and construction.

Q. Is your theory that your employment is simply a continuation of the employment evidenced in this contract and that the provisions of this contract apply to your present relations to the company except as to the compensation and the dates? A. No; my duties have been enlarged since that contract was executed, and I have had more to look after, and perhaps I might say I have greater responsibility.

Q. This contract describes you, however, as vice-president and general manager, and by its terms the company employs you in the capacity or position of vice-president and general manager of its railroads. That is the nature and true statement of your present employment, isn't it? A. Of the subway and elevated since that contract was made, I am appointed to the same position on the New York railways. That is not mentioned in there at all. That contract was made in 1909.

Q. But as your duties have enlarged, they have not changed in character. You are still the vice-president and general manager, but of somewhat expanded interests as compared with the interest defined in this agreement. That is true, isn't it? A. That is my view of it, yes.

Q. The agreement to faithfully perform the duties of vice-president and general manager in conformity with such instructions as may be given from time to time by the executive officers and board of directors of the company, would apply to your present employment, would it not? A. Yes, sir, and has been fully carried out on my part.

Q. And to perform such duties to the best of your skill and ability? A. Yes, sir.

Q. That would apply to your present employment? A. And I have returned that service.

Q. This contract provides for a compensation of $30,000 per annum. In place of that, doubtless in recognition of the larger interests confided to you, your salary is now $50,000? A. That is correct.

Q. And in this contract you agree to accept $30,000 in full compensation for the services that you were to render as vice-president and general manager, and I suppose the same agreement on your part would apply to your present employment, that you agree to accept $50,000 per annum in full compensation for your services as vice-president and general manager? A. Well, there is no agreement on my part. I am employed and appointed for the year by the board of directors. I don't sign anything.

Q. Well, isn't that clearly an implied covenant inherent in your relationship with the company and necessarily involved in your employment with the company, to accept a stipulated compensation in full for your services? A. Yes.

Q. You have not any reservation on that subject in your mind to the effect that $50,000 is payment on account of the services? A. No, sir.

Q. It is taken in complete recompense? A. It is taken in full for my services, but if I do anything special that they want to recognize, and it saves the company large sums of money or the lives of people and they want to give me money for it, I will take it, and I do.

Q. I see that you do. Is it not a duty — hasn't the Interborough expressly undertaken in connection with the leasing and operation of the subway lines to see that it adopts and avails itself of every improvement, convenience or safety appliance that is necessary to keep its operation up to the highest practicable point? A. Yes, sir. We do everything that human ingenuity —

Q. No. I asked you is that a definitely undertaken obligation, expressly undertaken by the Interborough Rapid Transit Company? A. Well, that is the way I would act, and that is what I am doing.

Q. Do you know that it is a fact that the company has definitely agreed to do that, bound itself to do that in terms? A. Why, I assume that it is an obligation that the company accepts when it accepts a franchise to build and operate or lease and operate a railroad. That is the way it should be operated, and that is the way the Interborough operate all its properties.

Q. Your attention has never been called to any express agreement on the part of the company to do so? A. No, only with such language as is contained in the last contracts that we executed?

Q. You definitely engaged to do that in the last contracts that you executed? A. Yes, sir. Perhaps not in the exact language, but in spirit that is what the contract means.

Q. I would like to just impress your mind as to that. Mr. Quackenbush, you know where that is, don't you? You know where that covenant is, under operation?

Mr. Quackenbush.— I will get it for you. Go ahead with your other questions.

Mr. Colby.— I just want to get the language. I think he may recall.

By Mr. Colby:

Q. Isn't it a part of your duty as general manager and vice-president to do all that you can to help the company to fulfill and perform that covenant? A. Why certainly, and I do that.

Q. To keep the shops up to their highest efficiency and see that the experience of the company is recorded in improvements of their devices, their appliances and mode of operation? A. Yes, sir, and I have done so.

Q. Is it not a fact that many of these devices are simply those improvements which experience suggests and which are the result of operation and observation of operations? A. Why, certainly; I keep a very close touch on that, and where I see any improvements can be made I make the improvements and patent them, and the company has the full right to use them. If I didn't do it someone else would and then the company would have to pay toll for it.

Q. You mean you are protecting the company by patenting these devices? A. To a tremendous extent, yes sir.

Chairman Thompson.— What would happen if the company discharged you? What would you do with your patents?

The Witness.— Why, the patents I have now I would keep them going the same as they are now.

Chairman Thompson.— Take them along with you, wouldn't you?

Mr. Hedley.— No.

Chairman Thompson.— Could?

Mr. Hedley.— Well, I wouldn't do that.

Chairman Thompson.— I know, but you could.

Mr. Hedley.— I don't know whether I could or not. If I should leave the company's employ, I would consider that whether I had to legally or not, that such patents as I developed when in the employ of the company, I would give them the free right to use those patents during the life of the patents.

Chairman Thompson.— You think when you get $10 a car or $7.50 a car a year, why, that is a free right to use it?

Mr. Hedley.— I give them the free right to use it. The $10 a car that you refer to, or $7.50 a machine that you refer to, has been awarded me as recognition of special work.

Chairman Thompson.— I see you regard that as free? You regard that as an exercise of the free right to use?

Mr. Hedley.— I give them a free right. If they see fit to give me the money after I give them a free right, why I accept it.

By Mr. Colby:

Q. Have you a statement of your receipts from these patented devices, Mr. Hedley? A. I think I have, sir. (Witness produces papers.) In the hurried way in which this had to be prepared,

it all goes back as far as 1913 up to date, and I notice there is
one item back in 1912 here, and there is one item February 1,
1916, for which I received a check this morning.

(Papers handed to counsel.)

Chairman Thompson.— While the room is as crowded as it is, I
will have to make and enforce a smoking rule. It is — I am not
objecting to smoking particularly, but we are crowded so that I
cannot permit any smoking. Now.

By Mr. Colby:

Q. Have you the contract with the Prepayment Car Company?
A. Yes, sir. (Witness produces paper.) During the lunch hour
I had that contract copied. This is a certified copy of it, sir.

Q. Thank you. (Paper handed to counsel.) This statement
of your receipts from the various patented devices is admittedly
incomplete, Mr. Hedley, isn't it? A. Why, I would not say it is
admittedly incomplete. It is all I could dig up in the meantime,
and I don't know whether there is any more or not. If there is,
why I would be glad to give it to you. That was prepared very
hurriedly.

Q. My only thought was that it only shows the returns for a
limited period on six of the thirty patented devices which are contained in your summary of patents? A. Yes, sir.

Q. So I assume it is incomplete and I also notice. A. Well,
I don't think it is incomplete.

Q. — that the dates do not extend back to the dates when these
patents were completed. For instance —

Mr. Quackenbush.— You only asked for three years, Mr. Colby.

Mr. Colby.— Well, I say incomplete —

Mr. Quackenbush.— I thought you misunderstood, because I did
not want a misunderstanding. The Chairman said for the last
three years.

Chairman Thompson.— It was changed after that.

Mr. Colby — I want the complete statement of it. I am not
intending to impute —

Mr. Quackenbush.— I see you are not. There is evidently a misunderstanding.

By Mr. Colby:

Q. For instance, this coasting time device, which has been apparently a good source of revenue to you, was patented in 1909, and there are no records of receipts prior to 1913 here. I would like that statement completed. A. I will get it for you, sir. I told the young man to prepare that, to make it starting in 1913. That is what I understood the Chairman wanted for the last three years. If I had gone back to 1909, I certainly could not have had it prepared by this time.

Q. Are these amounts the amounts that you personally have received? A. That is correct, sir.

Q. For instance, the stepless car and auxiliary appliances, I understand, is a joint device of yourself and Mr. Doyle, isn't it? A. That is correct, sir.

Q. And you, since September, 1913, according to this memorandum, have received $11,000? A. I have, sir.

Q. And Mr. Doyle a like sum, I assume? A. Yes, sir.

Q. The automatic train line couplings, is that a joint device of yourself and Mr. Doyle? A. Yes, sir.

Q. I notice that from May 14, 1912, to February 1 of this year, your share from this patent has been $8,620? A. That is correct, sir.

Q. Mr. Doyle has no doubt received a like amount? A. Exactly the same.

Q. The coasting time recorder, as I recall it, is your own personal device? A. No, sir. That is jointly owned by Mr. Doyle and myself.

Q. Your share since April 13, up to October — from April, 1913 to October, 1915, from the Manhattan Elevated and the subway lines exclusively amounts to $12,363.75; is that right? A. That is correct, sir.

Q. Has Mr. Doyle drawn a like amount from both the Manhattan and subways in that period. A. Yes, sir.

Q. The anti-climber device, is that a Hedley or a Hedley and Doyle? A. No, that is a Hedley device.

Q. This statement gives me the return from November 28, 1913, to January 21, 1916, and shows that you have received $2,790 from the Interborough Rapid Transit Company on this account; is that right? A. That is correct.

Q. From September 29, 1915, to December 14, 1915, a period of two months and a half, I see that you received from the Railway Improvement Company on account of the coasting time recorders, $482.50? A. That is correct.

Q. And Doyle a like amount, I assume? A. Yes, sir.

Q. I have the returns of your receipts from the Railway Improvement Company on the anti-climber device from November 30, 1912, to October 7, 1915, amounting to $14,827.53? A. That is correct.

Chairman Thompson.— Doyle the same amount?

Q. No. This is exclusively Mr. Hedley's, as I understand it. Is that right? A. That is correct. That is from railroads other than the railroads that I am employed by. That is used very extensively all over the country.

Q. You carry those back for three years from the 1st of February, 1916? A. Correct.

Mr. Quackenbush.— We tried to get in three calendar years; and where it ran over, to make it up to date, Mr. Hedley put them in.

Q. Will you please take what time is necessary for the full compilation of these returns, and when you have it finished, within a day or two, will you give it to us? A. Will you tell me definitely how many years you want me to go back and tell you how much money I have made out of patents? A. I have been making it out of them for twenty years.

Q. I will state the question. Only to patents that you have made while an employee as general manager and vice-president of the New York Railways Company and the Interborough Rapid Transit Company? A. All right, sir.

Q. I understand that this summary or list of patents as it is called, is a complete list of your patents? A. Yes, sir; that is as complete as we have been able to prepare it in the time that we have had. I would not swear it is absolutely complete, but I think it is.

Q. As I run down the dates of applications for patents, I see none of a date anterior to your employment by the Interborough? A. The young man that made them up probably did not have those, but there are some that antedated my employment by the Interborough.

Q. In other words, this list of some thirty patents all seem to have been applied for and granted within the period of your employment? A. Yes, sir.

Q. By the Interborough? A. I believe that is true.

Q. And the New York Railways Company. I will read them: Automatic Control and Sanding Device. Let me ask you briefly a question simply to identify these devices. What is that, as simply stated as possible? A. That is a device for automatically feeding sand onto the rails at any time that the wheels may slip.

Q. That is a Hedley and Doyle invention? A. Yes, sir.

Q. Governing device, fluid pressure. What is that? A. That is a load governing device for maintaining a fixed percentage of braking on a car or railway train without regard as to whether the car is loaded or not.

Q. The stepless street car. That, I think, requires no description. The double-deck street car. Those are both Hedley-Doyle devices, are they? A. That is correct.

Mr. Qackenbush.— I understand, Mr. Colby, that that Pittsburgh Jones' car has steps on it, that you asked about this morning.

Mr. Colby.— I see.

Mr. Quackenbush.— So that that won't give you the trouble with him.

By Mr. Colby:

Q. Coasting record device? A. That is a device for registering a period of time that a motorman or a driver of a train of cars or a single car makes when he is traveling over the road, registering and printing at the end of his run the total number of minutes and seconds that he has coasted.

5

Chairman Thompson.— That was described yesterday.

Mr. Hedley.— Not using any power for either accelerating or decelerating.

Chairman Thompson.— That was fully described yesterday.

By Mr. Colby:

Q. Of the five devices I have already alluded to, are all in use by either the Interborough or the New York Railways Company? A. May I have the other copy of that I gave you, Mr. Colby; I gave you two copies.

Q. I only recall having seen one, but I will give it to you. A. And that is the only two copies I have.

Q. Let us get along with that one, because I seem to have only that one.   A. The automatic control for sanding device, we did equip one car with that.   I don't know that we ever put any more on.   I don't remember.   The governing device for fluid pressure, one equipment was made of that.   The stepless cars, there were 175 cars.   The double-deck cars, there was one.   The coasting record device, I testified yesterday the number of machines that we put on.

Q. Exactly.   I will resume the reading of them.   What is the current registering mechanism?   A. That is a mechanism that is very much similar to the coasting record device.   We are not using that.

Q. That is not used by the City Railways or the Interborough? A. No, sir, but the same instrument can be used for the current input time as we are using coasting time.

Q. What is the conductor's collection counter?   A. The conductor's collection counter is that system of receiving fares that you see in the low-level cars.

Q. That is in use on the surface lines?   A. On the 175 low-level cars and on one of the double-deck cars.

Q. The conductor's valve and emergency switch; what is that? A. That is a device for street railway work that performs the same functions as the conductor's valve on a steam railroad performs, except that this special conductor's valve is manipulated electrically.

Q. Is that in use on the city lines? A. On some of our cars it is, sir.

Q. That is on the surface lines? A. Yes, sir.

Q. The electrical heating system. Is that in use on the New York City Railways? A. We put it on to one car, I don't recall whether we have ever put it on any others or not.

Q. That is not the heating system generally used on the surface lines? A. It is the same heating system, but this is a system for regulating it.

Q. You consider it better than the —— A. Why, it looks very attractive, and if it can be worked in practice, it would be better.

Q. It is not, however, in general use yet? A. It is not fully developed yet, no.

Q. How many cars is it on now? A. I think it is only on one.

Q. I pass to the electric railway car heating system, which seems to be somewhat different from what you have just discussed. What is that? A. That is a secondary patent to the one you have just mentioned before.

Q. And the same answer applies to the extent of its use? A. Yes, sir.

Q. Air control system, what is that? A. That is a system of control that does not permit the motorman to start the car if the doors are open.

Q. Is that in general use? A. Yes, sir. It is on the low-level cars.

Q. Auxiliary control device is the next patent specified. A. That is a secondary patent to the one previously mentioned.

Q. And the same answer applies to the extent of its use? A. Yes, sir.

Q. The next patent is called the stepless car truck? A. That is a special design truck that is absolutely essential in order that a low-level car could be operated.

Q. And that is in extensive use on the surface lines? A. On all the low-level cars.

Q. Life-guard attachment for cars is the next specified patent. A. That is on one car.

Q. What is the nature of that device? A. That is a device that is gotten up for the purpose of further safeguarding the lives of pedestrians on the street.

Q. Do you consider it meritorious? A. Yes; it has some very meritorious features, but I am not sure that it can be used.

Q. Why hasn't it been more extensively tried or used if its aim is to prevent injuries, fatal accidents? A. Well, that is its aim, and if the vehicles that are passing about the streets would give it a chance, why it would be safer than the cars are now running; but it is necessarily a device that has to stick out beyond the end of a car.

Q. The next patent is a life fender and wheel guard. A. That is a secondary patent to the one I have just described.

Q. And not in extensive use yet? A. No, sir.

Q. There is another patent called life-fender and wheel guard. I call your attention to the dates of those, Mr. Hedley. (Shows paper to witness.) Three separate and distinct devices under the same name. A. Yes, three devices that are all leading up to the same thing, with the same end in view. It is a secondary patent to the other two previously mentioned.

Q. The next is a safety platform mechanism. What is that? A. That is the safety platform mechanism that we are installing at Fourteenth street in the subway.

Q. And that is not installed at any other point on the subway? A. No, sir.

Q. Automatic platform mechanism. What is that? A. That is a secondary patent to the one I have just mentioned.

Q. Automatic control mechanism platforms. What is that? A. That is another secondary patent to the previous two mentioned.

Q. Are any of the last three patents I have mentioned the descriptions of the platform which sometimes juts out from the cars as they come to a station where the fixed platform is circular, to bridge the interval between the step and the platform? A. No, sir, it is the reverse. The extended platform comes out from the station platform and not from the car platform.

Q. Something like that is installed at the Fourteenth street station of the —— A. That is what this is.

Q. That is called the safety platform mechanism or the automatic platform mechanism? A. Those three patents are a part of that mechanism that you see there, sir.

Q. What is the support or platform that shoots out from underneath the car platform? A. That is a steel construction with tongues on it that slide in under the fixed tongues that are on the station platform, thus (indicating).

Q. Is that one of your patents, too? A. They are all my patents.

Q. I have not seen that specified. A. That is what we are talking about, those three.

Q. The electrical coupling mechanism. What is that? A. That is a mechanical and electrical device for coupling cars together automatically without the use of any so-called jumpers or connections, and without the necessity of a man getting in between the cars.

Q. The next is the combined electrical coupling. A. That is a secondary patent to the one I have just mentioned.

Q. There is a further patent described as the combined electrical coupling, applied for on a different date, a year later. A. Same general device.

Q. And a similarly described device, applied for a year later, combined electrical coupling? A. Yes, sir.

Q. The next is a street sweeping machine. What is that? A. That is a specially designed street sweeper, to sweep the streets, snow, dirt, or anything, principally snow, that it sweeps the railroad tracks, and two feet outside of the railroad tracks, and has a swinging boom, with a brush on it, that sweeps the street about ten feet wide outside of the railroad tracks, the idea being that if we could get a sweeper that would sweep our own railroad tracks, at the same time sweeping a sufficient space in the street outside of the railroad tracks for vehicle traffic to run on, we could then run our cars better than we can now.

Q. Is that in use by the City Railways? A. We built one, used by City Railways, and has done some good work.

Q. Then there is another street sweeping machine which, I suppose, is a secondary patent? A. Yes, sir.

Q. And then I come to street sweeping apparatus? A. Another one of the same class.

Q. Not distinct machines or devices, but secondary patents in connection with the idea; is that right? A. That is right, sir.

Q. Then I come to the anti-climber, which I need not dwell upon, which is your personal device? A. Yes, sir.

Q. All those I have read down to anti-climber, are joint devices, jointly owned devices of yourself and Mr. Doyle? A. That is correct, sir.

Q. The next is buffer and anti-climber construction. What is that? A. That is a secondary patent to the anti-climber.

Q. I take it you did not invent that? A. Why, it was this way: That was a casting device through which the inventor put a pin, and that pin was a coupling pin. He got the patent confined to that coupling pin. He could not do anything with it without using my anti-climber. And I bought the patent of him.

Q. The man who invented that was Mr. Philip W. Roberts, according to your statement? A. Yes, sir.

Q. And you bought his idea from him and incorporated it in your anti-climber, combined it with the anti-climber? A. I bought the patent. I did not consider it of any value, but I wanted to get it out of the way.

Q. The next is a contact mechanism. What is that? A. Why, that is a specially designed mechanical apparatus for collecting the power from the third rail for running a car or train of cars over one or more different railroads where the location of the trolley rail varies in its location from the running rail.

Q. That seems to be, according to your statement, owned by yourself, Mr. Doyle and a gentleman named Wallestadt. It that right? A. Yes, sir.

Q. Did you and Mr. Doyle acquire the invention from Mr. Wallestadt? A. No, sir. The way that happened was this: We were endeavoring to get some kind of a mechanism that would perform the functions that I have just described. The problem had been worked on for a couple of years, and it was determined by our then consulting engineers that it could not be done. I said "I don't agree with you." And I made some sketches on it. Mr. Doyle came down to the office. I went over it with him. And I said, "Do you see any reason why this cannot be done? Now, I have got to be shown. I think you can do it this way." Well, we talked over it and he made some more suggestions. I said, "You take that back to Wallestadt," and Wallestadt was an engineer in the car department at that time, "and tell him that I am satisfied that can be done. He has got to work it out in that way." He did so, and when I made the application for the patent I put Wall-estadt's name on it, too, because he had assisted.

Q. Thank you. Will you look at this list and tell me how many of those 30 patented devices are now in use by the surface, elevated or subway lines? A. You mean in large numbers, or just as one or two, just one?

Chairman Thompson.— Just answer the question.

Q. In use. In use to any —

Chairman Thompson.— The question was perfectly intelligible. Just answer the question.

Mr. Hedley.— In use.

Q. Yes. A. They are all in use on either the subway, the elevated or the street cars, one or more of each, with one exception. And that exception is the electric coupling mechanism, and the three allied patents that go with it. All the others are in use. This one I have just referred to will be put in use. All of the patents I paid for personally, and paid the government fees and attorneys' fees.

Q. Your reiteration of that statement forces me to also repeat my reminder to you that you did not pay for the labor, shop, expenditures, or material. A. No, I did not.

Q. And when you say you paid for them, you paid the relatively small fees of patent attorneys for filing your application and getting the certificate issued by the Government therefor, and the small nominal Government fees on patent applications? A. Yes, sir; I stipulated what I paid for.

Q. Will you look at this list once more and tell me from how many of those devices you are deriving an income from the street car lines, the elevated or the subway lines? A. Why, nothing from the street car lines; no income whatever.

The Chairman.— The question is, Mr. Hedley, how many you are receiving an income from, either from the subway, elevated or the surface lines. If you want to explain any answer you make afterwards, the Chair will permit you to, but I would like to have you answer the question.

Mr. Hedley.— I am receiving an income from two of them on the subway and elevated, and none of them from the street cars.

Chairman Thompson.— How many — the question is how many of those thirty — whatever there is — are you receiving any income from, from either of the three sources?

Mr. Hedley.— Two.

Chairman Thompson.— Two. That is all. The rest you are not receiving any income from any source?

Mr. Hedley.— From the railroad companies.

By Mr. Colby:

Q. From how many have you received compensation in lump sum, from the surface, elevated or subway lines? A. From only two of them.

Q. From how many are you receiving an income from users other than the elevated, surface and subway lines of the city? A. I receive an income from eleven of these patents and allied patents, from sources outside of the railroad companies that employ me.

Q. And of that you will give me a statement in a day or two, as soon as you can compile it? Do you know the Tintic Company or Tintic Improvement Company? Did you ever hear of it? A. No, sir.

Q. You don't recognize it as the name of a railway supply company? A. No, sir. Will you say the name again?

Q. Tintic. T-i-n-t-i-c. A. Never heard of it.

Chairman Thompson.— Anything like it?

Mr. Hedley.— No, sir.

By Mr. Colby:

Q. What is the extent of your holdings in the stock or securities of the Interborough Rapid Transit Company? A. Why, I own 50 shares of the original Interborough Rapid Transit Company's stock. I own twenty or thirty thousand dollars — no, hold on — I own $40,000 of the 4½ per cent Interborough-Met. bonds. I own 200 shares of the Elevated Railway. All of which I paid for; bought them on the market.

Q. What is your interest — what is the extent of your holdings of the stock and securities of the Manhattan Railway Company? A. I own 200 shares.

Mr. Quackenbush.— That is a duplication.

Mr. Hedley.— I said 200 shares.

Q. Oh, that is the old Elevated? A. 200 shares of Manhattan Railway Company stock, that is.

Q. What is the extent of your holdings in the securities or stock of the Interborough-Metropolitan Company? A. I don't own any Interborough-Metropolitan stock.

Q. It was mentioned by mistake, I suppose, in this letter to the Committee? A. Well, it is the Interborough-Metropolitan 4½ per cent bonds I had in mind.

Q. None of the stock? A. None of the stock.

Q. Four and one-half per cent bonds? A. Yes, sir.

Q. What holdings have you in the 145th Street Crosstown Railroad Company? A. I hold a voting certificate; that is all.

Q. What is that? A. Personally I don't own anything.

Q. What is that? A. Why, qualifying shares.

Q. Oh, I see.

Mr. Quackenbush.— That company has no franchise.

Q. What about the holdings in the Fort George and Eleventh Avenue Railway Company? A. Qualifying shares.

Q. Twenty-third Street Railroad Company? A. Qualifying shares.

Q. New York & Queens County Railway Company? A. Qualifying shares.

Q. New York Railways Company? A. I don't own anything in the New York Railways Company.

Q. I see it stated. I suppose I may regard that an inadvertence or inaccuracy? A. The New York Railways Company?

Q. The New York Railways Company? A. Oh, I did own some New York Railway bonds.

Q. At the time this letter was written A. I don't know. I sold them and made some money on them.

Q. Recently? A. Yes, sir.

Q. What does the Interborough do with its surplus power? A. Why, we sell some of it.

Q. Whom do you sell it to? A. We sell it to the Queens County trolley lines, and we sell it to the New York Railways lines.

Q. What do you do with the power you don't sell? A. We use up what we want of it, and don't do anything with the rest of it.

Q. It goes to waste, in other words? A. No, we don't manufacture it. We may have the capacity there, but we don't turn it out.

Q. What power capacity has the Interborough beyond its operating requirements? A. Well, its operating requirements are fluctuating so much now it is hard to keep up with the game. We are putting in new units now.

Q. There are certain hours of every day when, of course, a great amount of power is necessary to carry the traffic, is not that true? A. Yes, sir.

Q. And the plant and equipment which can generate that power can keep on generating that power during portions of the day when the power is not needed by the railroad, is not that true? A. It could do it, but we don't run it during those hours. We only run the units when it is necessary to consume their output.

Q. There is, however, some surplus power which you dispose of as you have testified? A. Yes, sir.

Q. What amount of power do you sell to the Queens County trolley lines? A. Oh, I suppose — well, I cannot tell you, sir, what the daily power is. It has a peak of about 9,000 kilowatts.

Q. That is what you sell to the Queens County trolley lines? A. Yes, sir.

Q. You sell them enough power to operate their system, is that right? A. Not entirely. No, sir. They buy power from other people.

Q. Have you made an estimate of the total power capacity of the Interborough Railroad, its present plant? A. Yes.

Q. Through 24 hours? A. Yes. We don't specify it that way. The capacity of a plant is always based on its kilowatts hour production. For instance, we have got in the 74th street house three units that are capable of turning out 30,000 kilowatts each. We have got one unit that will carry about 8,500 kilowatts, and we have got five units that will carry 7,500 kilowatts. Now we can deliver that constantly if we run them all.

Q. What is your estimate of the surplus power possibilities of the Interborough plant and equipment in dollars and cents in value? A. Well, I have not made one.

Q. It is a very substantial value, is it not? A. Oh, if we could find a market for it and could run our units 24 hours a day, it is a very substantial value.

Q. It runs into the millions, doesn't it? A. Oh, yes, it would.

Q. And during the whole period of the existence of this elaborate and costly plant and equipment, there has been this potential value which you have not been able to realize upon? A. Yes, we cannot use it.

Q. There have been negotiations looking to the acquisition of this surplus power with your company, have there not, in the past? A. Yes. It has been talked of.

Q. Only to that extent? Only to the extent your answer would suggest — just talked of? A. Well, no contracts have been executed. Tentative drafts have been made of what could be done, but it never has been done.

Q. Haven't very elaborate and careful contracts been drawn on that subject providing for the sale of power at very large figures to the Interborough? A. No, I would not say careful and elaborate contracts.

Q. In other words, you are familiar with a contract, are you not? A. Oh, yes. I am familiar with a contract that was drafted, it seems to me, a couple of years ago.

Q. Did you take part in the discussion looking to that —— A. Certainly.

Q. Looking to that contract? A. Yes.

Q. Who else took part in those discussions? A. Why, Mr. Theodore P. Shonts, of course, the president of the company; he is the chief.

Q. Some lawyers? A. Mr. Andrew Freedman, who is now dead, and Mr. Samuel Untermyer, and that is all I had a talk with.

Q. There were a number of conferences, were there? A. Why, I think I had two conferences with Mr. Untermyer.

Q. Well, what was that negotiation? A. Why, that negotiation was started with a view of making our machinery earn money during the hours of the day when we do not need it for our own purposes.

Q. There is a fixed ratio of cost of production of power and if you once had the plant, the expenditure for the production of the power is a relatively small percentage of the value of the power; that is true, isn't it? A. Yes, that is true. It depends.

Q. In other words, there is a very important asset of the Interborough Company in its surplus power? A. Oh, yes; I think so.

Q. What was the price discussed for the surplus power in this negotiation that I have alluded to? A. Why, I started in at a cent and a tenth a kilowatt.

Q. Can you translate that into United States? A. Well, if you were trained in the art, sir, you would understand. That is the way we think of it. A cent and a tenth per kilowatt hour.

Q. Have you not the figure in dollars and cents?

Chairman Thompson.— That would be pretty nearly $70 a horse power, if it would run all the while?

Mr. Hedley.— Pretty nearly right.

Q. How many million dollars was it proposed to pay to the Interborough Company? A. Not any fixed sum of money, as I recall. Whatever they used, they were to pay a cent and a tenth per kilowatt flat.

Q. How large a transaction did you think you were discussing? A. I thought we would be able to make a couple of million dollars a year.

Q. Two million to two and a half million? A. Yes, with the possible chance of more.

Q. Did that fall through because of some arrangement between the Interborough and the Edison Company? A. Not that I ever heard. I don't know of any.

Q. Has the Interborough any understanding with the Edison Company. A. No, sir; not that I ever heard of.

Q. Is there any of those mute and implicit recognitions of

sphere of influence between these two companies? A. Not that I know of. If it is, it is about me.

Q. The transaction failed, however? A. It was never executed.

Q. Have you mentioned the names of all the gentlemen who took part in those negotiations that you recall? A. All the gentlemen outside of the railroad companies' men. Of course, the superintendent of motor power, Mr. H. D. Stott was — he prepared a great many figures for me. I don't think he attended any of the conferences.

Q. So that up to date, with this great potential asset of surplus power, the Interborough Company has not succeeded in realizing anything in the way of income except for these relatively unimportant sales to the Queens County lines and the New York Railways lines? A. No, sir; haven't been able to find any way they could do it and have some one take it.

Q. They have received more than one offer for their surplus power, haven't they? A. Only one that I know of. I never heard of but one.

Q. Was that negotiation conducted chiefly and almost entirely by Mr. Shonts and —— A. Why ——

Q. —— and Mr. Freedman? A. He, of course, was conducting the negotiations, yes. How far he went with it beyond what I know of, I don't know. I have told you about all I know about that.

Q. Yes.

Mr. Colby.— It seems to be fifteen minutes after your adjournment period.

Chairman Thompson.— Of course, these sales to these other railroads, they would take their power at the same time of the day you took yours, wouldn't they?

Mr. Hedley.— We have got, in order to be safe with this tremendous carload, we have got to have large surplus power; so that with one or two units laid down ——

Mr. Colby.— Surplus means surplus; means power you don't need.

Chairman Thompson.— Well, that surplus, when you are not using it, it would be worth a couple of million dollars a year to somebody. A cent and a tenth per kilowatt is fairly cheap?

Mr. Hedley.— No.

Chairman Thompson.— A cent and a tenth. The Edison Company get more than that.

Mr. Hedley.— I started high enough, you know.

Chairman Thompson.— The Edison Company get more than that, don't they?

Mr. Hedley.— Yes. Well, we had a 50 per cent profit in it at that basis.

Chairman Thompson.— Well, we will take it up again later. We will suspend now until 11 o'clock tomorrow morning. All witnesses are directed to appear tomorrow morning at 11 o'clock.

Whereupon (at 4:15 o'clock P. M.) the Committee adjourned to meet February 2, 1916, 11 o'clock A. M., at the same place.

FEBRUARY 2, 1916

NEW YORK COUNTY LAWYERS' ASSOCIATION BOARD ROOM,
165 Broadway, New York City

Meeting called to order by Chairman Thompson, at 11 A. M., a quorum being present.

Mr. Colby examining.

HEDLEY, FRANK, being recalled, testified as follows:

Q. Mr. Hedley, have you been able since our hearing yesterday to compile any of the figures and data that I asked you for? A. Yes, sir,. I have some of it and the balance, I think, will be here in a few minutes.

Q. Well, suppose you let me have what you have got. Is it in shape to file with me? A. I think it is, sir. You asked me yesterday to compile a list of returns on patents while in the employ of the company. The list is complete in so far as the coasting time recorders are concerned for moneys that I have received since

July 31, 1911, up to and including the present time. That is the list, sir. (Witness delivers copy of above list to counsel.) (Witness, continuing.) If it is satisfactory, Mr. Chairman, I would like to add to the list that I filed with you yesterday another patent that was omitted from that list. Having checked it up I find that there was one that was not put on the list there. It is on the hand straps. Mr. Chairman, I wish also, providing it is in order, to make another addition to my testimony of yesterday when I stated that there are so many of these patents used on the Interborough Rapid Transit Company and stating that the electric couplers were not yet used. There are, however, twelve cars that are equipped with the electric couplers. Another addition that I wish to make is as to the subscribers to the original stock of the Railway Improvement Company. I find that the Pay-as-you-enter Car Company subscribed $10,000 of that stock. That was at the time when I was employed by the elevated and the subway, where we did not use any material or cars that were purchased from the Pay-as-you-enter Car Company. The other part of the list of patent returns coming to me has not yet been completed but will be here in a few minutes.

Mr. Colby.— I will excuse Mr. Hedley until this data is complete so that we can introduce it without doing it in a fragmentary way.

Chairman Thompson.— Before the next witness is sworn I want to give you this letter, Mr. Colby, from the Public Service Commission in relation to power matters. The letter is written by Mr. Commissioner Strauss. Perhaps you want it on the record.

YOUNG, GEORGE W., being duly sworn, testified as follows:

Mr. Colby examining:

Q. Mr. Young, you were for many years a director of the Interborough Rapid Transit Company, were you not? A. 'I was.

Q. What was the period of your relation with the Interborough Rapid Transit Company, I mean, when did it begin? A. It began with the organization of the company. I was an incorporator of the Interborough Rapid Transit Company and a director, and a director of the Rapid Transit Construction Company.

Q. Up to what time did you continue to be a director of the Interborough Rapid Transit Company? A. Until the annual election in September, 1913.

Q. Some of your co-directors of the Interborough Rapid Transit Company have given testimony before this Committee in connection with the making of a certain contract for the third tracking extension and elevated lines. I believe that Mr. William A. Reed has testified before the Committee and I think Mr. J. P. Morgan has also given testimony on the subject. Were you a member of the Board at the time this subject of third tracking and extension came up for discussion? A. I was a member of the board when it was discussed, yes, sir. I was not a member of the board when the contract was passed. Mr. Morgan never was a member of the board to my knowledge.

Q. Well, I may be in error in associating him with the contract. I recall, however, reading the testimony that he has given relating to this subject.

Chairman Thompson.— Yes, Mr. Morgan has appeared before this Committee and my recollection of the affair is that this matter came up in the Spring of 1913. At that time Mr. Morgan was the underwriter of certain bonds and his interest was on account of the fact that he had underwritten the bonds.

Q. Mr. Young, you were regular in the attendance at the meetings of the board, were you not? A. Fairly so. I attended the meetings as far as I could consistent with my other business, I was fairly attentive.

Q. Do you recall when the subject of a contract for the third-tracking or extensions of the elevated line was mentioned to the board? Do you recall that matter? A. Very distinctly, yes, sir.

Q. As near as you can, will you please fix the time? A. The latter part of June, 1913.

Q. Was it at a regular meeting of the board? A. No, sir.

Q. Was it at some special meetings? A. Yes, sir.

Q. Did you receive a notice stating that, the usual written notice, that a special meeting had been called for the purpose of considering the proposed contracts of this kind? A. No, sir.

Q. What were the circumstances under which the meeting was

convened? A. I was summoned on the telephone in the afternoon to attend a special meeting of the board and asked to be present; that a matter of importance was to be brought up.

Q. You mean that you were summoned on the telephone on the same day of the meeting? A. In the afternoon.

Q. And the meeting was to be held instantly or very promptly thereafter? A. Sometime after 3 o'clock.

Q. Did you know at the time your attendance was sought for this meeting just what the meeting was for? A. No, I didn't.

Q. Where was the meeting held? A. In the regular board room in the company's office.

Q. There was a full attendance of the board? A. I think there was.

Q. Can you recall the names of the members who were present or some of them? A. Mr. Shonts was there. Mr. Berwind, John Pierce, Mr. Friedman, Mr. Reed, Mr. Sullivan and Mr. Lane and myself. I don't think Mr. Vanderbilt or Mr. Belmont were present.

Q. Was counsel to the company present? A. He was at some stage of the proceedings, yes, sir. Mr. Quackenbush, I think, was there. I don't know whether he was there at the time the meeting convened, but I think he was there at some stage of the proceedings.

Q. What Mr. Sullivan is that? A. I think his full name is Frank D. C. Sullivan.

Q. Is the Mr. Lane you refer to the late Gardinier M. Lane? A. Yes, sir.

Q. Of the Lee, Higginson Company of Boston and New York, they are bankers? A. Yes, sir.

Q. How was the subject of the meeting brought before the attention of the board? A. Brought by the president, Mr. Shonts.

Q. Do you recall any statement that he made at the time? A. Yes, I do.

Q. What did he say? A. Well, as nearly as I can recall he said that he had been arranging to go to Europe for some time on advice of his doctor and that he did not feel like going away and leaving the question of third tracking and the extension of the elevated unsettled. That he had consulted with the heads of his departments very fully on the subject and that they all felt that a contract of such importance could not be very well let in the usual way of asking for bids.

Q. How should it have been let if not to the lowest bidder after advertisement according to the statement of the president? A. In his judgment it needed a man, not one who was a construction engineer, but a man who had experience and reputation as an operating man and that the only man that he felt that he could recommend to the board who would fill the bill was a Mr. Stevens, who had been associated with him in the Panama work.

Q. What is the full name, if you recall it? A. I think John S. Stevens.

Q. Are those papers and documents the documents and papers mentioned in the subpoena that was served upon you, Mr. Young, all of them? A. I have all of them that I have been able to obtain. I didn't receive your subpoena until yesterday afternoon and I haven't been in my office and I have here such as has been gathered together by my secretary in the time allotted. I think they are all that I have.

Q. Now, referring to the question of the modes of awarding this contract, was it customary in the Interborough Rapid Transit Company for contracts for such work as the extension and third tracking of the elevated, I mean for such important contract work, should be given to the lowest bidder after public advertising. A. I don't know whether we advertise publicly or not. I think, as a general rule, important contracts were submitted to various contractors and prices obtained.

Q. You mean bids were invited? A. That is my impression, sir.

Q. This is a matter that would come more directly to the immediate attention of the executive committee at first hand and then they in turn, after the contracts were formulated and bids received, would report to the board with recommendations would they not? A. I think that would be the general way, sir.

Q. General practice? A. I think that is so.

Q. The method proposed by Mr. Shonts, according to your testimony, was a rather sharp deviation from that usual method, was it not? A. He explained the reasons for it, sir.

Q. What reason did he assign for it? A. On account of the

necessity of keeping the trains in operation. We had to operate our trains and at the same time go on with the construction to keep up the work and at the same time complete the work as laid out by the Public Service Commission.

Q. He said in other words according to his statement that Mr. Stevens was just the man for this necessary and difficult work? A. That's the impression I received from his remarks.

Q. What then was said or done after this explanation had been made? A. A general discussion of the matter, some questions asked and some answers given. It was a general discussion.

Q. Did Mr. Shonts assume that his proposals would be favorably regarded by the board? A. He would have very good reason to think that all recommendations of his would be well considered by the board, Mr. Colby.

Q. Were the details of the contract set forth in his explanatory statements? A. No, sir. The question then came up as to what the board felt would be a fair commission, percentage on the work and there was some discussion between myself and Mr. Pierce as to what it should be. I think it has varied anywhere from twenty per cent to five per cent.

Q. Mr. Pierce was the first in the practical work of construction? A. Yes, practical contractor. I think the amount was to a certain extent tacitly agreed to as a fair remuneration or assumed to be a fair remuneration; I think it was ten per cent.

Q. Do you mean tacitly agreed by the board or tacitly assumed by the president? A. It was the amount mentioned. There was no action taken on it.

Q. Was any copy of the contract or of the proposed contract produced at this time or, exhibited to or submitted to the board? A. It was after some questions had been asked as to the extent of it and how long it would take and it was finally submitted, yes, sir.

Q. The work to be done by Mr. Stevens was, as I understand it, chiefly supervisory and directive, is that right? A. Entirely so. He was to have entire charge of that work in conjunction with our own heads of our departments. That's my understanding of it, Mr. Colby.

Q. What was the amount of expenditure involved in this proposed work, Mr. Young? A. Something in excess of twenty millions. That included equipment, I think, however.

Q. And this percentage was computed upon that aggregate cost or aggregate sum? A. Yes, he got ten per cent of everything. He was to get ten per cent on all expenditures.

Q. You mean everything he expended in connection with the discharge or performance of the work he was called on to do in accordance with the terms of the contract as advocated by Mr. Shonts? A. That's my recollection, sir. Mr. Shonts generally outlined the contracts. It was read finally.

Q. It was finally read in full to the board? A. Yes.

Q. Was it an executed contract? A. No.

Q. It was in readiness for execution? A. It was a draft of contract, sir.

Q. Voluminous and complete? A. Seemingly very.

Q. Who had prepared the agreement, do you know? A. My recollection is that it was prepared with Mr. Quackenbush in conjunction with Mr. Stevens and his counsel. That's my memory of it.

Q. Did some member of the board request that the contract be read in full at this meeting? A. Mr. Reed moved that it be read.

Q. Mr. William A. Reed moved finally that the contract be read? A. Yes.

Q. He was dissatisfied with this general discussion and allusions to its contents and asked that it be read in full, is that so? A. Why, we were having a general discussion, an informal discussion, and then the contract was read. He asked for the reading of the contract so that he could make up his mind whether he was satisfied or dissatisfied.

Q. Well, didn't the board after the contract had been read to it express its opinion concerning it? A. Mr. Reed did.

Q. Do you recall any of the significance, provisions or material matters of the contract? You say it provided that he was to get ten per cent on every expenditure. Is that substantially correct? A. We provided the offices and everything connected with the offices.

Q. Do you mean the Interborough Rapid Transit Company undertook to pay for Mr. Stevens' offices? A. Yes, anything that was required in carrying out this contract. In other words the working equipments, whatever was required to carry out this contract.

Q. Well, he did do something. Didn't he give a bond for the faithful performance of his contract or wasn't he asked to give a bond? A. We paid for the bond.

Q. He didn't get any commission on the premium of the bond? A. That's the only exception in the matter.

Q. It would have been a little hard to have found justification for paying commission on the premium of a bond. What was the period of time that the completion of this contract was estimated to require? A. About two years.

Q. And Mr. Stevens was to receive ten per cent upon the twenty million dollar expenditure for services earned within two years? A. Whatever the amount of his disbursements was he was to receive ten per cent if we made the contract.

Q. That would be in rough figures about two million dollars for supervision and management, sir? A. Ten per cent of twenty million dollars is two million, Mr. Colby.

Q. That's a million dollars a year? A. It seems to so figure.

Chairman Thompson.— That's more even than Mr. Hedley gets.

Mr. Hedley.— Just a little, but not as much as I am worth.

Q. Taking a year of three hundred working days, that would be about three thousand dollars a day for his supervisory work. Isn't that about what it would have amounted to? A. It might have amounted to more.

Q. Of course, if the cost was exceeding twenty million? A. Yes. On your basis, Mr. Colby, it would be three thousand three hundred and thirty-three dollars and thirty-three and one-third cents.

Q. What was the comments by the board; was there any comment by any member of the board after the reading of this contract? A. I think there was more silence than comment, Mr. Colby, and Mr. Reed moved that the contract be not entered into.

Q. Mr. W. A. Reed. A. Yes.

Q. Was a motion put? A. I don't think so, sir.

Q. Was any formal action taken after the president's statement and the reading of this contract? A. Not at that meeting, sir.

Q. Were there any further remarks of the board? A. None that I can clearly recall. I think there was a sort of general discussion, but I cannot recall anything specific that was said. There was some discussion as to whether or not our own people under the charge of Mr. Hedley couldn't do it quite as effectively and efficiently as Mr. Stevens.

Q. There was some feeling that he could? A. Yes, I think there was.

Q. I gather from the fact after the reading of contract and the prompt motion of Mr. Reed that it be not entered into, that its provisions were recognized as being quite extraordinary? A. I couldn't answer what impression it left in the mind of anybody except myself.

Q. Did not the commission purpose to be paid to Mr. Stevens seem to you to be a rather extraordinary compensation, not to say excessive commission? A. I didn't like the contract and I would not have voted for it.

Q. Did anybody except Mr. Reed express himself on the subject? A. Mr. Lane did. I don't recall anything specific that was said on the part of individuals except that the contract was not entered into.

Q. As I understand it it involved a commission of 10 per cent to Mr. Stevens over the cost of his office furniture and fixtures and so forth? A. That would be my interpretation of the contract, sir.

Q. Was there any discussion after the contract was read? A. Nothing that I can specifically recall, Mr. Colby. I think the meeting thereupon adjourned, sir, and Mr. Reed and Mr. Lane left and some of the rest of us remained. I think after the meeting we called up, somebody called up Mr. Reed and tried to see if we could not get a meeting that night.

Q. Do you recall who it was that called up Mr. Lane? A. I couldn't state specifically.

Q. Did you have a meeting that night to resume the consideration of it? A. No.

Q. What became of this special meeting? A. It was adjourned.

Q. Was any attempt made after this manifestation of animosity towards the contract to justify it or to defend it by anyone? A. None that I recall.

Q. Did the Board take up any other matters at this special meeting? A. No, sir; not that I recall.

Q. Did the contract come up for discussion at any subsequent meeting? A. Next day, regular meeting.

Q. The following day was the day of the regular meeting? A. To my recollection, it was, sir.

Q. But Mr. Shonts had thought to have it in private, at a special meeting, hurriedly called on the day prior to the date of the regular meeting. That is correct, isn't it? A. I didn't say so.

Q. No, but it follows from what you have said that this special meeting was called on the day prior to the regular meeting? A. It was.

Q. Was the contract acted upon at the regular meeting? A. There was action taken.

Q. What was the action? A. I moved that a special committee of five be appointed to consider the contract and report to the full Board.

Q. Was that motion carried, Mr. Young? A. Yes.

Q. Do you recall who composed that special committee to consider this contract? A. Yes.

Q. Will you please name them? A. Mr. Berwind, Mr. Friedman, Mr. Lane, Mr. Reed, and I think Mr. Sullivan. I am not positive about Sullivan, but I think Mr. Sullivan was also a member of that committee.

Q. It was your idea that the contract should be gone into fully and acted upon only after a full understanding of its provisions and after a report of the said committee? A. Yes, sir, that was my idea.

Q. Mr. Young, did you have any talk with Mr. Reed and Mr. Lane who seem to have joined in opposition to these commissions or did they have any talks at other meetings or other times with you at which it was specially referred to? A. Once or twice.

Q. Well, did you ever have any meeting or any talk with Mr. Lane or Mr. Reed about this contract? A. Why we would talk

about it going to and from the meeting. We would generally
agree that we would never vote for that contract. I had more
talks with Mr. Lane than I did with Mr. Reed although I conferred with him from time to time about it.

Q. Well, did you leave the meeting with Mr. Lane and Mr.
Reed, or did they leave alone and join you later and you joined
them later. Of course, I assume that you had some meetings
about so an important matter as this. A. I had one or two meeting with them.

Q. This Committee was appointed, I mean the sub-committee,
at a regular meeting, held the following day after the special
meeting? Do I understand you correctly? A. That's my recollection, sir.

Q. Tell me what conversation you had either with Mr. Lane
or Mr. Reed subsequent to that meeting or subsequent to any later
meeting. I suppose the board met every week? A. Yes, sir, I
think every Wednesday.

Q. Did you have any talk with Mr. Lane or Mr Reed subsequent to the latter meeting? A. Yes, later in Mr. Reed's office,
once or twice. Mr. Reed I think was going to Europe or going
away and he asked me to write to Mr. Lane and tell him about
that. I remember one time he asked me to enclose some newspaper
clippings. I don't recall exactly what it was. There are a few
other little matters perhaps that he may have spoken to me about
but that's the only conversation I remember with Mr. Reed.

Q. In other words you felt, Mr. Young, that this contract
should not be passed upon except upon full discussion and approval
by the full board? A. That was my idea when I moved to have
this committee appointed.

Q. Did you have any talks with Mr. Lane himself? A. Yes, I
had a number of conversations with Mr. Lane.

Q. Where would they be held? A. At the board meeting. I
had several at his office at 43 Exchange place.

Q. Did anything of any particular note or significance occur
at any of these conversations? I mean did Mr. Lane express
himself in emphatic objection to this contract? A. Most emphatic, yes.

Q. Well, was anything done or said to — on the minutes of

the company, to record your attitude or that of Mr. Lane or Mr.
Reed on this contract? A. There never was any specific action
taken on that contract that I recall, apart from what I have stated
to you, when the motion was made to refer it to this committee
of five.

Q. Can you recall anything further of significance that was
said or done or written by anyone of you three on this subject?
I think you testified you had some correspondence? A. Yes, I
had correspondence with Mr. Lane on the subject.

Q. I think that the subpoena required you to produce any correspondence you had with your directors on this subject, Mr.
Young. Are you able to produce copies of any letters you have
written to Mr. Reed or Mr. Lane on this subject? A. I only
found two in my book. If you wish to see those, sir, I suppose
you have got the right to.

Q. The right of this Committee has been pretty generally conceded and is now unquestioned, I think.

Chairman Thompson.— Last few days it has not been.   A.
Well, I am not committing myself as to that.

Mr. Quackenbush.— So far as the Interborough is concerned,
there never has been any objection, Mr. Chairman, on the part
of any action taken —

Chairman Thompson.— Not the Chairman of the Committee.

Mr. Quackenbush.— I know of none. The Chairman has not
been advised about — those in authority at the Interborough —

Chairman Thompson.— We are not going to enter into political
discussions.

Mr. Quackenbush.— I did not assume you were.

By Mr. Colby:

Q. I am asking you only for letters written with explicit reference to this matter of the contract, the proposed contract? A.
I can assure you those are the only ones I will show you, sir.
Those are the only two that I recall, Mr. Colby. (Witness hands
letter copy book to counsel.)

Mr. Colby.— Mr. Young produces, in response to the Committee's subpoena, a copy of a letter dated July 22, 1913, addressed to Gardiner M. Lane, care of Lee Higginson & Company, Boston, Massachusetts. I will read the letter.

Chairman Thompson.— Read it into the record.

Mr. Colby.— Take this letter please, stenographer, just as I read it:

"July 22, 1913. My dear Lane: I saw Mr. Reed (William A.) for a few moments today, and promised him to drop you a line calling your attention to enclosed articles which appeared in the New York morning papers. He depends on you and me to watch over the situation during his absence, and I will be pleased to see you any time you are in New York relative to the same. I expect to be in town during the summer and be able to attend the regular meetings. In case my plans are changed, I will advise you. Sincerely yours, G. W. Young."

Q. This letter was sent to Mr. Lane, the letter which I have read from your letter-press copy book was sent to Mr. Lane? A. Yes, sir.

Q. Your words, "watch over the situation" referred to what? A. Contract for the extension.

Q. And third-tracking of the Elevated, this contract as to which you have been giving testimony?

Mr. Colby.— Mr. Young produces in response to the Committee's subpoena a letter — press-copy of a further letter to Mr. Gardiner M. Lane, dated September 19, 1913.

The Chairman.— Read it into the record.

Mr. Colby.— I read it into the record. "September 19, 1913. My dear Mr. Lane: I promised to send you the statement which I had dictated after the special meeting called for the purpose of passing the Stevens contract. I enclose same for your files, and would be pleased to receive for our mutual protection a copy of your memorandum in return. Please consider this communication absolutely confidential. Yours very truly, G. W. Young."

I should have noted that each of these letters appears to have been endorsed " personal."

By Mr. Colby:

Q. Mr. Young, you refer in your letter of September 19, 1913, to a memorandum or statement which you dictated after the special meeting called for the purpose of passing on the Stevens contract, and you also refer to a copy of a memorandum apparently prepared on the same subject by Mr. Gardiner M. Lane. Did you and Mr. Lane dictate your impressions or your recollection of what was said and done at the special and subsequent meetings of the board on the subject of the Stevens contract? A. We did, but not in — not by agreement. It was just a happen-so.

Q. You mean that you each by similar impulse and without knowledge that the other was doing it, prepared a memorandum of your impressions and recollections of what took place at these meetings? A. That is what occurred, Mr. Colby.

Q. Did you — when did you ascertain that Mr. Lane had also prepared a memorandum of his impressions of that meeting? A. Oh, after — after one of our meetings Lane asked me to go down to his office, and I went down with him — 43 Exchange place. And I went into his private room and he read me a memorandum, and gave it to me to read, of what had occurred, and it struck me as rather peculiar, because I had done the same thing, and I told Lane that, and he asked me for a copy of mine.

Q. Ah! And then you wrote him this letter in which you enclosed a copy of yours? A. No, I didn't, because he asked me for that in July, and repeated the request once or twice, and I think I finally sent it to him in September.

Q. In other words — Mr. Lane read to you his memorandum to see if the statements therein contained accorded — the statements it contained of his fresh and contemporaneous recollection accorded with your own recollection? A. That was his idea, sir.

Q. He read the memorandum to you, his memorandum to you? A. He read it, and then I read it.

Q. He gave it to you to read after he read it? A. He did.

Q. And this, I understand, was at the office of Lee Higginson & Company, 43 Exchange place? A. Yes, sir.

Q. You have testified that he made several requests for you to send him a copy of your memorandum, and that you finally did? A. I finally did, yes, sir.

Q. On the date of this letter, namely, September 19, 1913?
A. Correct.

Q. You requested in that letter that he send you also a copy of
his memorandum and he did so? A. He had agreed to, but he
didn't, no.

Q. Well, did he reply to this letter of September 19th? A.
Yes.

Q. Have you preserved the letter you received from him? A.
I have.

Q. I ask you to produce it, as it was embraced in the subpoena.
A. (No response.)

Mr. Colby.— Senator Thompson, I think it is clearly the right
of this Committee to have the production of that letter.

Chairman Thompson.— No question about it.

Mr. Young.— Don't you think it would be fair for me to have
a chance to confer with my own counsel before I show that letter?

Mr. Colby.— You are asking my opinion, Mr. Young. I tell
you in all candor, I think there is no occasion to hesitate. I think
it is clearly your duty, and I ask the Chairman to direct you, to
produce the letter. It is embraced in the subpoena.

Chairman Thompson.— I don't want to be harsh with the witness, but there is no question but that this correspondence is perfectly pertinent, and it would become the duty of the Chair to
direct you to produce it. Of course, I possibly appreciate your
position, but we have not played any favorites.

Mr. Young.— It is not a case of a question of whether it is pertinent to your inquiry. It is a question of my rights in the
matter, and protection of others outside of myself. There is nothing in the letter that I am ashamed of in any shape or form.

Chairman Thompson.— I think you had better produce it. It
is a public matter, and your duty to the public requires you to
produce it, if you have it.

Mr. Young.—Well, if I was as clear on that as you are, Mr.
Chairman, I would not hesitate.

Mr. Colby.— You have heard the statements of the Interborough's counsel that they have not questioned the power of the Committee at any point, and are prepared — have complied with every request, and are prepared to continue.

Mr. Young.— I have great respect for Mr. Quackenbush, but it does not happen at this moment that Mr. Quackenbush is my counsel.

Chairman Thompson.— I think I will direct you, Mr. Witness, to produce that letter. Have you it with you?

Mr. Young.— I have.

Chairman Thompson.— Then I direct you — the Committee, and I as Chairman of the Committee, direct you to produce the letter.

(No response.)

Mr. Colby.— There is no question of your duty, Mr. Young, to produce that letter. Here is the letter you wrote to Mr. Lane, and I ask you for his reply.

Mr. Young.— It might be a case of even mistaken duty makes a man hesitate sometimes, you know, Mr. Colby.

Chairman Thompson.— I think you better produce the letter, Mr. Young. You will have to produce it in the end anyway, and you might as well do it now and have it done with. It only makes the Committee trouble, and the public trouble, and your motives might be misconstrued, and the only course we will take is one of whatever powers the Committee has. We direct you to produce it.

(No response.)

Mr. Young.— I would like to have an opportunity to call my counsel on the 'phone, Mr. Colby.

Mr. Colby.—We will take a recess.

Chairman Thompson.—A recess of five minutes.

Mr. Colby.— Ten minutes.

Chairman Thompson.— That will be flexible, until you get through talking on the telephone.

(A recess was taken from 12:25 to 12:35 p. m.)

Chairman Thompson.— The Committee will come to order.

(The witness produces letter in question.)

By Mr. Colby:

Q. Is this the reply to the letter of September 19th to Mr. Lane that you received from Mr. Lane, Mr. Young? A. It is.

Mr. Colby.— Mr. Young produces a letter with an enclosure, dated New York, October 1, 1913, from Mr. Gardiner M. Lane.

(Counsel confers with Chairman.)

Chairman Thompson.— Yes, I think you had better read that into the record.

By Mr. Colby:

Q. Mr. Young, I hand you a letter which you have produced in answer to the Chairman's direction and under the Committee's subpoena, and I ask you if that is a letter you received on or shortly after its date from Mr. Gardiner M. Lane? A. It is, sir.

Q. Do you know Mr. Lane's signature? A. I do, very well.

Q. The letter clearly bears Mr. Gardiner M. Lane's signature? A. Absolutely, sir.

Mr. Colby.— I will read this letter in the record, Senator Thompson. It is on the letter paper of Lee Higginson & Company of Boston, New York and Chicago, and the letterhead also bears the name " Higginson & Company, London." The letter is dated 43 Exchange place, New York, October 1, 1913, is marked " personal " and is addressed to Mr. George W. Young, 59 Cedar street, New York city.

" My dear Mr. Young: I was sorry to have no opportunity this morning to speak to you about your personal letter of September 19th. On thinking the matter over pretty carefully it seems to me much better that I should not have the memorandum sent me in your letter. This is a very delicate matter, and while it seems to me wise that each of us who is conversant with the affair should preserve his own statement, yet I think he should not have the responsibility of keeping the statement of others. Death, for example, might cause these statements to come into the possession of others than those to whom they were originally entrusted, and in that way they might even become public. We who stood together know the understanding of one another, and if we each preserve for ourselves the notes made we shall all be in a position to act together in case of need. While the matter was undecided, it was well for each of us to know just what the other's understanding of the situation was. For this reason I showed you my memorandum which you read. I have now read yours, but return it to you for the reasons I have stated above. Of one thing in your additional memorandum I am a little doubtful. It is my recollection that I drafted my memorandum about the 30th of June and that your visit to my office was in the morning of July 1st. I have no recollection of your being in this office on the 25th. I have, of course, made no copy of your memorandum. I hope you will agree with me that the conclusion I have reached is a wise one. I cannot tell you how sorry I am, for personal reasons, that you are no longer one of the directors of the Interborough. Very truly yours, Gardiner M. Lane."

I think that probably Mr. Young will want to keep a copy of this letter. I mean, we can have copies made.

Chairman Thompson.— Better have copies made and give back the original. I think you had better read this memorandum.

By Mr. Colby:

Q. Mr. Young, this paper which I hand you, and which was contained in the envelope containing Mr. Lane's letter, I ask you if this is the enclosure to which Mr. Lane refers in the letter I have just read? A. It is, yes.

Q. This is your memorandum of what took place in the meetings? A. It is a copy of it.

Q. A copy that you preserved and sent to Mr. Lane in your letter of September 19, 1913? A. I originally wrote it in longhand and —

Q. And then had it typed? A. Then I dictated it to my stenographer later on.

Q. And this is the memorandum that you sent in your letter of September 19th? A. That is, yes.

Chairman Thompson.— That is the memorandum, the specific one.

Mr. Young.— That is the specific one.

Q. And this is the specific enclosure contained in Mr. Lane's letter to you of October 1st? A. Yes.

Mr. Colby.— Do you wish me to read this, Senator?

Chairman Thompson.— Yes.

Mr. Colby.— Mr. Lane, before I read, Mr. Lane speaks of a second memorandum. Is it contained in this paper?

Chairman Thompson.— Yes.

Mr. Young.— It is attached to it.

Chairman Thompson.—Attached to it.

Mr. Colby.— " On Tuesday afternoon, June 24, I was called up on the telephone from the Interborough office and advised that there was a very important special meeting to be held that afternoon at 3:30, and it was necessary I should attend. I accordingly went to the office of the Interborough Company where there was present Messrs. Shonts, Berwind, Freedman, Sullivan, Reed, Gardiner M. Lane, Pierce; Mr. Quackenbush, counsel; Mr. Pepperman, assistant to the President; and myself. Mr. Shonts stated that he had decided upon the advice of his physician to sail for Europe the following day, but before going he felt that it was essential that the question of contract for the third-tracking and extension of the Elevated should be disposed of; that the work was of such a nature that it could not be handled in the ordinary way of calling for estimates; that it was absolutely necessary that the work should be placed in charge of some competent engineer in whom he had confidence, who was not only capable from a construction standpoint but also from an operative standpoint; that after a most careful consideration of the entire question, and consultation with his associate officers, he had concluded that the best and, in fact, the only party that he would care to place in such a responsible position, would be his friend, Mr. Stevens; that he had known Mr. Stevens for a number of years, and had been associated with him in work on the Panama canal, and was confident that the work, if entrusted to him, would be efficiently and faithfully performed; that this being the final judgment of himself and associates, the question for the Board to determine was what commission was fair and proper to be allowed Mr. Stevens on the contract. In response to an inquiry as to whether or not Mr. Stevens had the organization to take hold of this contract, and in direct answer to the question as to what organization he did have, Mr. Shonts replied that Mr. Stevens' organization was in his head, and to give an idea of how he was considered by outside parties, he stated that at present he was receiving $1,500 a day from the B. & O. for expert engineering advice. Mr. Shonts was then asked what the total amount of the contract would be, and stated something in the neighborhood of $20,000,000, and that the performing of the contract would take two years. His attention was called to the fact that this would be paying Mr. Stevens at the rate of about $3,000 a day. Whereupon, at the request of Mr. Reed, the contract proposed to be made with Mr. Stevens was read by Mr. Quackenbush, who stated that he, Mr. Quackenbush, had drawn the contract in consultation with Mr. Stevens and his attorney. The contract as prepared by Mr. Quackenbush, when read, disclosed the fact that all expenditures in connection with the work, including office expenses, and so forth, were to be paid by the Interborough, including premium on indemnity bond and cost of plant, upon all of which payments, except the premium on indemnity bond, Mr. Stevens was to receive ten per cent commission. Mr. Stevens was also to have the right to sub-contract. Upon conclusion of the reading of the contract Mr. Reed moved that this contract be not entered into. This motion was not put, and after some further discussion Mr. Reed and Mr. Gardiner M. Lane retired from the meeting. Mr. Shonts subsequently called Mr. Reed upon the telephone and endeavored to arrange for another meeting some time that evening. This was found impossible, as Mr. Lane could not be reached. Upon the following day, which was the regular meeting day of the Interborough, the matter was again brought up for discussion, and

6

Mr. Young moved that the entire question be referred to a committee of five for investigation, the committee to report back to the full board before any action should be taken in connection with the work involved. This committee was appointed by Mr. Shonts and consisted of Mr. Berwind, Mr. Freedman, Mr. Sullivan, Mr. Reed and Mr. Lane."

"Additional memorandum referring to proposed Stevens contract. Upon leaving the meeting of the Interborough Board today, Mr. Lane requested me to go around to his office with him. On reaching the office we proceeded to Mr. Lane's private room, and Mr. Lane showed me a memorandum which he had drawn up stating what had taken place at the special meeting on Tuesday. This memorandum in addition went on to state that following the special meeting Mr. Shonts had taken him aside and stated that he wanted him, Mr. Lane, to understand the reason for entering into such a contract with Mr. Stevens; that neither himself nor Mr. Stevens nor Mr. Freedman was to receive any benefit from this contract, but that in connection with the securing of contract which had been closed between the City of Greater New York and the Interborough, Mr. Shonts had found it necessary to make certain commitments and incur certain obligations, and that it was by means of the Stevens contract that he expected to meet and pay these commitments and obligations. Mr. Lane's memorandum further stated that upon learning these facts, Mr. Lane had gone to the office of J. P. Morgan & Company and advised Mr. J. P. Morgan, Jr., of exactly what had transpired at the meeting referred to in his memorandum, and of the statement which had been made to him by Mr. Shonts."

Mr. Colby.— Where is that letter from Mr. Lane? Let me have that.

Chairman Thompson.— It is very near one o'clock, Mr. Colby. We suspend at once.

Mr. Colby.— I just want to ask one question.

Mr. Young.— Can't you finish with me?

Mr. Colby.— No, Mr. Young. I won't wait for that letter. I want to ask this one question.

Chairman Thompson.—All right.

By Mr. Colby:

Q. In the letter from Mr. Lane, which I read, Mr. Young, in which he returned this memorandum to you after reading, he referred to only one matter that was not in his opinion exactly in accord with his own recollection, and that was as to the date of one of these meetings; is not that true? A. Mr. Lane was correct as to that, sir.

Q. The only matter to which he took exception was a matter of a date? A. That is all; that is all.

Mr. Colby.— The phrase that I have in mind, Mr. Chairman, is this: " I have now read yours," meaning Mr. Young's memorandum which I have just read, " But return it to you for the reasons I have stated above. Of one thing in your additional memorandum I am a little doubtful. It is my recollection that I drafted my memorandum about the 30th of June, and that your visit to my office was in the morning of July 1st." That was the only thing —

Chairman Thompson.— Yes. That memorandum appeared to be in pencil.

Mr. Young.— This memorandum was taken by my stenographer from a memorandum —

Chairman Thompson.— Probably Mr. Lane struck that out.

Mr. Young.— I don't know.

Chairman Thompson.— We will suspend now until 2:30 o'clock. All witnesses are excused until 2:30 except those that have been excused to 11 to-morrow.

Mr. Young.— You want me?

Chairman Thompson.— You will need Mr. Young back at 2:30?

Mr. Colby.— Yes. I had intended to examine you further, Mr. Young.

Whereupon (at 1 o'clock P. M.) an adjournment was taken to 2:30 P. M. of the same day.

AFTERNOON SESSION.

Meeting called to order by Chairman Thompson at 2:30 p. m., quorum being present.

Chairman Thompson.— Mr. Chairman, I will announce that Mr. Young requested that he might be excused on account of not feeling very well. It seems that he has been sick, and he came here this morning because the Committee subpœnaed him. It was quite compelling, and he asked if he could not be excused, and under the circumstances he has been excused until to-morrow morning at 11 o'clock.

Mr. Colby.— Will Mr. Pizzini please take the stand?

A. J. Pizzini, recalled, testified as follows:

Mr. Colby.— Mr. Chairman, Mr. Pizzini has explained to me that he wishes to leave for Chicago to-morrow. At the present time he does not intend to return until about the first of March. He says, however, that he is prepared to return if desired by the Committee at any time on a telegraphic summons to return immediately.

Chairman Thompson.— What do you mean? How far are you going to be gone?

Mr. Pizzini.— I am going to San Francisco. I am going on a business trip that I have been in the habit of making every spring. I want to say, however, Mr. Chairman, that you may have full access to my office and access to any of my papers, contracts, bills, or anything you want that is there.

Chairman Thompson.— Where do you keep your bank account?

Mr. Pizzini.— Mechanics and Metals National Bank.

Chairman Thompson.— Will you give our accountant access to your books?

Mr. Pizzini.—Absolutely, yes.

Chairman Thompson.— Is that the only bank with which you do business?

Mr. Pizzini.— I have a personal account in the Mechanics and Metals Bank, and one in the Lincoln Bank.

Chairman Thompson.— Where does the Railway Improvement Company do their banking business?

Mr. Pizzini.— In the Mechanics and Metals National Bank.

By Mr. Colby:

Q. Do all the companies that you are interested in bank at the Mechanics and Metals Bank Company? A. I don't know where all the companies I am interested in do their banking business. I have stock in a good many companies.

Q. I mean companies in which you are a director or officer? A. Well, I think they do business in the Mechanics and Metals National Bank. I don't know of any others.

Q. Where does the Gun Hill Realty Company do their business? A. I don't know.

Q. How urgent or essential is it that you should absent yourself at this particular time? A. It is a business trip and a matter of personal business out there in the west. I have been trying to take my family out there for some time. It means personally quite a little to me. If you want any testimony at any time I will come back and I will answer any question in detail, or if you want any information I will give it to you while I am away. You may have access to my office and if any of the contracts, papers or anything else is of any service to you, you are very welcome to them.

Q. You consider that you should go now, and that it would be very disadvantageous to you to postpone your trip? A. I do.

Q. Will you return if summoned? A. Yes, sir. It will take four days to get back, but I will return immediately upon the receipt of a telegraphic summons. You can have anything in the world that you want from my office, in fact, I will leave the key with you. I haven't anything in the world that I want to conceal at all.

Q. Of course, Mr. Pizzini, you recognize, do you not, that you are still under our jurisdiction? A. Yes. There is nothing in the world that I have any objection you might inquire about,

Chairman Thompson.— It wouldn't make any difference whether you had or not. We have the right to ask it or take it. I notice that we get nothing down here that we are not entitled to, except possibly politeness. We get considerable of that.

Mr. Colby.— I personally, Mr. Chairman, am convinced of the good faith of Mr. Pizzini's request, and of the absolute necessity of his trip.

Chairman Thompson.— Of course March first will get us close to the extension of our time. I doubt now, however, whether if we ask for another extension, that it would be denied.

Mr. Colby.— Would it be possible, Mr. Pizzini, for you to fix a date a little earlier than March first? In other words, could you shorten your trip?

Mr. Pizzini.— I will telegraph you either on the 20th or the 21st, and if you wish me to come back sooner, I will do so.

Chairman Thompson.— Let me suggest that on the 15th of February you telegraph to Mr. Colby.

Mr. Pizzini.— I will not leave here until Monday night. I might say also that this trip is something that I have planned on for about two months.

Mr. Colby.— I might say that we are contemplating and have already entered into a very comprehensive examination into these various co-corporations with which Mr. Pizzini has been identified, and I do not desire at the moment to pursue his examination further. But I may wish to examine him very closely about the Wendell, McDuffie Company.

Mr. Pizzini.— I might say to you, Mr. Colby, if you will permit, that I have absolutely nothing to do with them whatever, and am really a silent partner with Mr. McDuffie. I am principally interested — in fact, my time is devoted to the Railway Improvement Company.

Chairman Thompson.— What day does the first of March fall on?

Mr. Pizzini.— Shall I telegraph to Mr. Thompson or Mr. Colby?

Chairman Thompson.— You may telegraph to Mr. Colby. If you should telegraph to him, he will tell me about it, and if you telegraph to me, I will surely tell him about it.

Mr. Colby.— The understanding is that Mr. Pizzini leaves under the express understanding that he return if asked for, and will return immediately, and will be here by March 1st, anyway. I think that will be all, Mr. Pizzini.

Mr. Pizzini.— I thank you very much.

Mr. McDuffie, being duly sworn, testified as follows:

Mr. Colby.— Mr. McDuffie is under subpoena, Mr. Chairman, and I wish him sworn. I wish also to say that Mr. McDuffie is obliged to go to Boston to-night, and will return on Friday, and I move that he be excused until Friday.

Chairman Thompson.— You may, therefore, be excused until Friday at 11 o'clock.

Mr. McDuffie, being sworn, testified as follows:

Mr. Frank Hedley, being recalled, testified as follows:

By Mr. Colby:

Q. Mr. Hedley, are you prepared to file with the Committee a statement of the receipts from your various patents? A. Yes.

Q. Will you please do so? A. The paper I have in my hand shows a complete list of payments received by me on my patents from the Interborough Rapid Transit Company for coasting time recorders, starting from July 31, 1911, up to and including October 8, 1915. (Witness delivers copy of above-referred to list to Mr. Colby.)

Mr. Hedley.— Mr. Chairman, when I handed you yesterday the list of patents that either Mr. Doyle or myself owned individually or jointly, so far as mine alone and Mr. Doyle's are concerned, or mine alone individually, I find that I omitted one patent, namely the patent for the hand strap.

Chairman Thompson.— That went into the record this morning.

By Mr. Colby:

Q. These additional receipts plus what you have already testified to, constitute a complete statement, do they? Or have you additional? A. I have additional on anti-climbers. I hold in my hand a complete statement of payments made to me by the Interborough Rapid Transit Company in accordance with resolutions passed by the board of directors awarding me sums of money for the use of the anti-climber patent; one sheet shows all the money received by me from the subway division, and the second shows the same information from the elevated division. The payments commence in January, 1909, showing all the payments from that time up to and including the present time, that have been made to me. (Witness delivers the above statement to Mr. Colby.) I think that is all you asked me to furnish, Mr. Colby.

Q. No, it is not, Mr. Hedley. I want the detailed receipts by you from all sources of royalties or sums otherwise paid for patents taken out by you individually or jointly with you and Mr. Doyle while you have been the vice-president and general manager of the New York Railways Company, the Interborough Rapid Transit Company, and the Subway Rapid Transit Construction Company. A. I have given you all the sums of money paid to me by the railroads on which I am employed, but I have not given you the sums of money that I have received from other railroads for the use of these patents.

Q. That is what I want and what I requested. A. I did not so understand it, sir.

Q. Will you have it prepared, then? A. Yes.

Q. Thank you. Will you? A. Yes, sir.

Q. Do I understand, Mr. Hedley, that these sums are additional to the sums that were set forth on your memorandum yesterday? A. No, sir. They are the total sums since I came in the employ of the company that I have received for patents that I have taken out since I entered the employ of the company.

Q. And it appears from this memorandum that you received, you have received from the subway division of the Interborough

Rapid Transit Company on the anti-climber device, a total of $14,540? A. Yes, sir, that is the amount. I own that patent outright.

Q. And from the Manhattan Division, that is to say, the elevated, you received on the same device, namely the anti-climber device, the sum of $18,490? A. That is correct, sir.

Q. For the coasting time recorder, it appears from the memorandum filed by you that you personally have received $20,576.25. Is that correct? A. That is correct, sir.

Q. Has Mr. J. S. Doyle received an equal amount? A. Yes, sir.

Q. In other words, $20,576.25 to Mr. J. S. Doyle also upon this coasting time recorder? A. Yes, sir. From 1911 to date.

Q. From July 31, 1911, to date? A. That is correct, sir.

Q. And you will let me have the additional data of your receipts from these patented devices that I have asked for at the next session? A. Yes, sir. If I understand that correctly, you want that since I came in the employ of the Interborough Rapid Transit Company the last time? I was employed by the Interborough in 1884.

Q. I mean since you have been vice-president and general manager of these railroad companies. I want your total receipts on account of royalties or sales, the list of which you have been good enough to furnish the Committee. A. I think you want more than that, Mr. Colby, if you will pardon me. I think what you intend to ask for, you pardon me for making this explanation, but I think what you want to know is how much money I have collected from outside parties, outside of the total I have given you since I have entered the Interborough Rapid Transit Company employment.

Q. That is correct. Can you get it for me? A. Yes, sir, I will secure it for you.

Q. May I ask you one further question, Mr. Hedley? Who is in charge of the minute books of the Interborough Rapid Transit Company? A. Why, the secretary.

Q. And the secretary is also in charge of the minute books of the Executive Committee? A. Yes.

Q. The Committee desires an examination of these books.

Chairman Thompson.— They have already been before the Committee.

Mr. Colby.—And we can examine them at the offices of the company?

Mr. Hedley.— Oh, yes.

Chairman Thompson.— We will now adjourn until to-morrow morning at 11 o'clock. All witnesses are directed to appear at that time who have not been otherwise excused.

The meeting thereupon adjourned until 11 o'clock A. M., February 3, 1916.

FEBRUARY 3, 1916.

NEW YORK COUNTY LAWYERS' ASSOCIATION BOARD ROOM,
165 Broadway, New York City

The Committee was called to order pursuant to adjournment, Chairman Thompson presiding.

Quorum present.

Chairman Thompson.— The Committee will come to order.

Mr. Colby.— Mr. Chairman, as I understood the program of the Committee, it was that Mr. Young's examination would be resumed this morning. Mr. Young's counsel, Mr. Connell, is here and has stated to me that Mr. Young is ill and will be unable to appear.

Mr. Connell.— I was talking on the 'phone with Mr. Yo this morning, and he stated that he was not able to get up and rise from his bed, and he stated that he expected to have a doctor's certificate, and that he would send it down immediately to the Committee. I have not yet received the doctor's certificate, although I was telephoned but a few minutes ago it was on its way.

Chairman Thompson.— Is it a good doctor?

Mr. Connell.— I will have to leave that to Mr. Colby.

Mr. Colby.— I have not any desire to interrogate the medical profession. I know Mr. Connell very well, and his statement, I think, can be accepted without question. We shall have to postpone Mr. Young's examination for the present.

Mr. Connell.— I expect to have the certificate in a minute, and I think that will resolve all doubt.

Chairman Thompson.— We will excuse Mr. Young until to-morrow, then.

Mr. Colby.— I should say certainly until to-morrow. Mr. Young stated to me yesterday he was convalescing from a severe attack of grippe, which kept him indoors for a good while, and I think it was apparent that he was not feeling in the very best of shape yesterday.

Chairman Thompson.— Mr. Young will be excused until to-morrow morning at eleven o'clock.

Hedley, Frank, recalled for further examination.

By Mr. Colby:

Q. Are we in a position this morning to put upon the record the total of receipts from the patented devices taken out by you; I mean invented by you or by you and Mr. Doyle jointly? A. Those are all on the file. You have before you now already submitted a complete list of all the patents taken out by myself or Mr. Doyle since 1903.

Q. With that supplemental patent that you mentioned in your testimony yesterday? A. With the one put in yesterday, that is all.

Q. Can you give us a brief and compact statement of the total income derived by you from those patents? A. Yes, sir. If you will take the statements that I gave to you yesterday.

Q. They are here. A. And you will consider that all the statements that I have given to you previous to that time are included in the statements that I gave you yesterday, and the additional statements that I will give you to-day, will include every dollar that I have received from any source whatever for patents that I own or jointly own with Mr. Doyle since I entered the service of this company in 1903.

Q. Now, let us have the figures.   A. The St. Louis Car Company paid to me as royalty on a patent railway car truck on February 16, 1907, $100.   In the month of May —

Q. May I interrupt you?   I am not particularly desirous of consuming the time by a recital of the items of your statement. If you can, with complete justice to any interest that you yourself have in presenting this in any particular form, give me the sub-totals and then the final total, and I think it will do, if you in addition file the statement; I do not want to encourage you to go into more detail than we really desire.   A. I am ready and willing to go into detail as far as this Committee desire me to. The details are shown, however, on the three sheets that I now have in my hand.   The total revenue on those three sheets that I have received from any and all patents outside of the railroad companies that employ me in the twelve years, have amounted to $50,756.70.   The last item on the third sheet of the three that I have in my hand, is a payment that was made to me by the Interborough Rapid Transit Company in October, 1903, of $5,000 for a sleet scraper, that I patented before I entered the service of the Company.

Q. Is that $5,000 included in the $50,000?   A. No, sir.

Q. Is it included in the receipts that you have already submitted statements of to me?   A. Not of the statements yesterday, and that is the reason I put it in to-day.   Yesterday's statement and to-day's statements are entirely complete with that $5,000 in there.   I now hand you the statement, sir.

(Witness hands statement to Mr. Colby.)

Assemblyman Burr presiding.

Q. I see no mention on this statement of the Southern Pacific railroad, or the New York, New Haven and Hartford railroad, or the Hudson McAdoo tunnel; I assume their purchases have been made through such agency companies, I might describe them, as the Railway Improvement Company?   A. No, sir; the New Haven railroad have never paid me any royalties.   The Hudson and Manhattan Railroad Company have.   That seems to be omitted here, Mr. Colby. Permit me to say, however, as I told you, I do not run any commercial system of books, and my entire papers are open to this Committee. I invite your accountant to go through everything I have got. He can examine all of my papers. He can have my bank books, and he can have my check books.

Q. But, Mr. Hedley, it is fair to assume that you are very familiar with the transaction, even if you have not preserved a record of them, and can readily from such data as you have in your possession compile a statement, and more readily than we can from a situation entirely strange to us? A. That certainly has been missed. I testified the other day I did receive royalties from them, and I did.

Q. I do not recall exactly the companies you mentioned, and it will take some moments, and I won't waste the time now to turn back in the record to that place, but I think I recall your saying the Southern Pacific Company had installed the anti-climber upon three or four hundred of its cars, and I think you said the Pennsylvania was using that device. A. There is a statement of that that was filed by my representative from the Railway Improvement Company, and that is correct.

Q. I do not recall it.

Mr. Quackenbush — I remember seeing it, about the Southern Pacific.

Mr. Colby.— The only statements of income I have from these memoranda, Mr. Quackenbush.

Mr. Quackenbush.— I do not question that, but I recall seeing that, and Mr. Hedley had a statement of it here.

Q. I will accept your suggestion, and we will place at your disposal one of the committee's accountants so we can feel we have cleaned up the matter and disposed of it, and get the total receipts. From the figures you have filed with the Committee, as I compute, it is $109,362.95. A. That is right, and I totaled it since I entered this room.

Q. Is that correct? A. That is correct, with the one item that does not appear to be in these totals that you now call my attention to, namely the Hudson Manhattan.

Q. Before I excuse you to put Mr. Doyle on the stand, will you tell me what the Interborough Consolidated Company is? A. The Interborough Consolidated Company is a company that was recently formed that has issued securities and, in a way, if I understand it, control the Interborough to a certain extent. I think Mr. Colby that if you will ask the secretary of the company or some other party he will be able to describe that to you better than I.

Mr. Quackenbush.— Shall I tell you?

Mr. Colby.— Yes.

Mr. Quackenbush.— The Interborough Consolidated Corporation is a successor of the Metropolitan Interborough Company and by consolidation accomplished the elimination from that company of the losses through the acquisition of the Metropolitan Street Railway Company, the idea being to write down the assets to the present value of them. The common stock has no par value. I assume that is what you want, and it is a holding company.

Mr. Colby.— Has the Interborough Metropolitan been dissolved?

Mr. Quackenbush.— It has, under the statute, which in my opinion automatically extinguished the Interborough Metropolitan.

Mr. Colby.— Swallowed and absorbed?

Mr. Quackenbush.— Exactly.

Q. Do you know the names of the officers of the Interborough Consolidated Company? A. No, sir; Mr. Shonts is President.

Q. You are not an officer? A. No, sir.

Q. Do you know the Secretary of the company? A. I believe Mr. Fisher is Secretary.

Mr. Quackenbush.— We filed that list with the Committee.

Mr. Colby.— We will excuse you for the time being, and will assist you in the compilation of those figures at any time convenient to you.

Mr. Hedley.— May I make a statement for the record, that I think will perhaps clear up some of this situation in figures?

Mr. Colby.— Is it long?

Mr. Hedley.— No, sir; very short.

Mr. Colby.— You may address your statement to the Chairman.

Assemblyman Burr.— I think that is proper.

Mr. Hedley.— The statement I handed you yesterday together with the one I handed you today contained these figures, from the subway anti-climber account I received $14,540; the elevated anti-climber account I received $18,490; the subway and elevated together coasting time recorders I received $20,576.25. I received $5,000 from the Interborough Rapid Transit Company for the use of a patent scraper that I patented before I entered the employ of the company. I have received a total from all outside sources from patents that I own or that I own jointly with Mr. Doyle, all of those figures being from 1903 up to date, the total of $50,756.70 from outside parties other than those who employed me. That is a total of $109,362.95, or at the rate of $9,113.58 per year for the last twelve years. That, however, does not include the one item that you now call my attention to, namely, the moneys the Hudson & Manhattan paid to me for royalties on anti-climbers, and that I would be glad to give you.

Q. Does it include the Southern Pacific? A. My recollection is it does. I am not sure whether the Southern Pacific did buy direct from me or from the Railway Improvement Company. I think it was from the Railway Improvement Company, and is included in the figures I gave you under the Railway Improvement Company.

Q. I understood you to say a moment ago the New York, New Haven and Hartford Company had not paid you any royalties? A. No, sir.

Q. Although they use some of your devices? A. No sir; they do not. The New York Central are using my devices, and they are contained in the list I handed you this morning, through the American Locomotive Company. The American Locomotive Company made those devices for the New York Central and the American Locomotive Company paid me.

Q. With the exception of the Hudson and McAdoo, and the

possible exception of the Southern Pacific, it is complete? A. Yes, sir; it is my full belief I have given you every dollar I have made outside of my salary, out of my patents, since 1903, with the exception of the Manhattan Railway Company.

Q. Did you receive during your employment by the New York Transit companies any bonuses or gratuity of any kind, or in any manner? A. No, sir; I did not. I have given you the total revenues from all sources that have come to me.

Q. Did you receive any stock or security allotments in any of the reorganizations that have taken place? A. No, sir.

Mr. Colby.— We will excuse you, for the time being

DOYLE, JAMES S., being first duly sworn, testified as follows:

By Mr. Colby:

Q. Your full name? A. James S. Doyle.

Q. Where do you reside? A. Mount Vernon.

Q. Are you employed by any of the New York Transit lines? A. Yes, sir; New York Interborough and the New York City Railway.

Q. You mean the Interborough Rapid Transit Company? A. Yes, sir.

Q. And the New York Railways Company? A. Yes, sir.

Q. In what capacity are you employed? A. Superintendent of car equipment.

Q. Do you fill that position in each company? A. Yes, sir.

Q. What salary do you receive from the Interborough? A. $3,333 — no, $6,333. My salary is divided three ways, one-third to the Manhattan, one-third to the Subway, and one-third to the New York Railways, a total of ten thousand dollars a year.

Q. You did not mention the Manhattan Elevated as one of the employer companies, did you? A. That is under the Interborough.

Q. You receive a total salary of ten thousand dollars per annum? A. Yes, sir.

Q. And it is apportioned among these three railway companies, is that right? A. Yes, sir.

Q. Or, rather, the Interborough pays $6,666, I take it, and the street surface railways, the New York Railway Companies, pay you the other third; that is correct, isn't it? A. Yes, sir.

Q. Where are you stationed? A. Ninety-eighth street and Third avenue.

Q. What is that, an office or shop? A. That is both; the general office building and also general shop. It is the old Manhattan Elevated Railway shop.

Q. The title of your position is Superintendent of Car Equipment? A. Yes, sir.

Q. What are your duties in that capacity? A. Everything pertaining to the construction and operation of electric traction equipment, from ordinary design to original design and operation.

Q. From ordinary design to original design? A. Yes, sir.

Q. And operation and equipment? A. Operation of the equipment. In other words, we design and make, or rather, we design and see that everything is properly made that is used on the entire system.

Q. Are there various gradations of design running between ordinary design and original design; you used the phrase " from ordinary design to original design," as if there were many intermediates. A. Just about as much as in the scale of development of the automobile. I have been in this business ever since it began.

Q. What business? A. Since the beginning of electric traction. I worked on the first electric traction road ever operated in Chicago, and I have had to do with the development of the electric motor since its infancy and helped in the development of electric traction since its beginning.

Q. You are an inventor? A. A man of ordinary common sense, filling a necessity in railway operation. It is ordinary railroad common sense, in railroad work. Some call it an inventor.

Q. I gathered from a statement of your duties that you are employed to supervise, devise and design, and see that they are kept at the high state of efficiency and up with the progress of the art of electric railroading, as it is moving along. A. We help in the progress of the art. We were the first railroad to use the heat-treated axles.

Q. Did you and Hedley patent the idea? A. No, sir; never got a cent out of it, and didn't patent it.

Q. Why didn't you patent that? A. Never thought of it. If we thought of patenting all the things we got up, I don't know how many patents we would have. I never thought of it.

Q. How long have you been employed by the Interborough and New York Railways Company? A. Fifteen years, starting with the Manhattan before the Interborough was built — before the subway was 'built. I was brought from Chicago to equip the Manhattan electrically, and the subway was constructed later, and that was included, and Mr. Hedley came along, and the Interborough was incorporated.

Q. You came on from Chicago as a very young man, didn't you? A. Yes, sir.

Q. How old were you when you came? A. About twenty-seven or twenty-eight. I am now forty-four.

Q. What was your position in Chicago when you were brought on here? A. Master mechanic, or superintendent of car equipment of the Metropolitan West Side Elevated.

Q. Were you master mechanic, or superintendent of car equipment? A. Master mechanic it is commonly called.

Q. As I understand the position usually described as master mechanic, it is a rather measly paid, but very useful and hard working position in a shop, isn't it? A. It is an enjoyable position.

Q. It is an important and useful workman's position, isn't it? A. Just as useful as you are a mind to make it.

Q. What were you getting there? A. One hundred and fifty dollars a month, I think I got there.

Q. And you were brought on to New York? A. Yes, sir.

Q. At an advance in salary? A. Yes, sir. I think I got $3,000 a year.

Q. How has your salary grown until to-day it amounts to $10,000? A. I am doing the work of three predecessors who got more than $11,000 a year. I am getting less than my three predecessors.

Q. When were you put upon your present basis? A. I do not remember the exact year. It was two or three years ago, 1913, I think. I do not remember the exact date, three or four years ago.

Q. You are thoroughly familiar with the subjects of accounts in the shops of the Interborough, are you not? A. Yes, sir.

Q. How many shops are there? A. We have two general repair shops, one at 98th street takes care of the general repairs, and a shop at 148th street, and one at 225th street, and that is an inspection and repair shop, and one at Bronx Park, and one at 179th street and Third avenue, inspection and repair shop, 148th street inspection repair shop.

Q. Any more? A. There is the New York Railways scattered all over town.

Q. How many men are employed in your shops? A. It varies. We have five or six thousand people at times, and depends on the amount of construction work we do. At the present time we are constructing and equipping 478 steel cars that are being built at Pullman. They are being equipped at the Highbridge yard of the New York Central, and at the construction yard 129th street, and that makes an additional force, and the force varies from three to five thousand men.

Q. Never under three and seldom over five? A. That is about right.

Q. Each shop has a foreman? A. Yes, sir, reporting to a general foreman. Each shop has a general foreman reporting direct to me.

Q. Have you a system of keeping costs accurately and apportioning costs to each line of work? A. Yes, sir.

Q. What department are those data kept in? A. We originate them and of course report them to the Auditing Department.

Q. And the Auditing Department has in its records a complete detailed statement of the costs apportioned to every species of work? A. Yes, sir, every penny spent.

Q. In other words if you were pursuing experimenting in connection with a truck for the stepless car, every expenditure made in connection with the promotion of that device would be carefully reported and carefully referred to the appropriate account and that record preserved, is that right? A. Yes, sir.

Q. So you can tell with reference to every device, how much money the Interborough or the New York Railways Company has expended in bringing it up to the stage of development at which it may be at the moment, is that right? A. Sure.

Q. Are you employed because of your knowledge of electrical

traction devices, your mastery of the art of electrical traction; is that the theory of your employment? A. No, sir; I imagine I am employed because my life's work has been in electrical traction railroad work. I am an electrical traction railroad man and master mechanic.

Q. And you say your duties extend out over the whole range of design, from ordinary design to original design? A. Yes, sir. May I add a word there?

Q. Certainly. A. Yes, sir, because I started in the infancy of electric traction, when there was not much of anything in an electric motor or power house, and it was finally worked out as we went along.

Q. Do you do any buying? A. No, sir.

Q. Are any of the company's purchases made through you as an agent or intermediary? A. No, sir.

Q. Are there any things the Interborough or New York Railway Company purchases billed to you in the first instance? A. No, sir.

Q. The Pullman Palace Car Company is not consigning or billing or selling to you personally, as a mere convenience? A. No, sir.

Q. And never has? A. No, sir, no company has, and we have nothing to do with the buying or purchasing department.

Q. Nor have you ever had any interest by way of commissions or participation in any purchases, large or small? A. No, sir.

Q. You are quite clear on that? A. Indeed, I am.

Q. When you say material and devices, you are not attempting to limit it to any specific questions of purchase; you mean all purchases? A. All purchases, yes, sir.

Q. Are you familiar with the list of patented devices that have been submitted to the Committee by Mr. Hedley, as patented, or invented rather than patented, by you and him jointly? In a general way, yes, sir; I have not looked over the list very carefully.

Q. I remember that upon that list is specified the double-decked car and the low-level car? A. Yes, sir.

Chairman Thompson.— You say you never have been interested in any purchase?

Mr. Doyle.— Well, that is my memory, as he put the question to me. I had nothing to do with the purchases at all.

Q. And do you know what the governing device fluid pressure is? A. In connection with what?

Q. I don't know, I am asking you. A. There are all sorts of devices of that kind. Do you mean in reference to the low-level car?

Q. I ask you what is the governing device fluid pressure; I am testing your familiarity with the business? A. Governing device fluid pressume; it would imply that a liquid is used to register pressures.

Q. You are not fully cognizant of its exact character? A. I think I am.

Q. You are the patentee of this device? A. I don't know what your are talking about, in a general way. Are you referring to the double-deck patent? I presume it is the double-deck patent, and it has to do with registering the load on a low-level car or a double-deck car so as to increase the braking power with an increased load, and provide also a means for increasing the electric power used in the motors. I think that is the thing you are referring to.

Q. What does it look like? A. I do not remember exactly. It is a long time since I saw it, but the purpose of the thing is a connection between the car body —

Q. What does it look like? A. Why —

Q. Is it animal, vegetable or mineral? A. I do not remember the detail of what it looks like. It is a pneumatic mechanical device for the purpose I have stated.

Q. Is it big or little? A. It doesn't weigh more than fifty or sixty pounds.

Q. Where is it attached? A. On the truck, and registers the weight of the car as the passengers get into the car, and changes the relation between the car body and the truck.

Q. Would you know it if you saw it? A. I certainly would.

Q. Did you invent it? A. I originated the idea and I directed the working out of the detail.

Q. Who did you give your directions to to work out the detail?
A. Why, in that particular case one of my assistants.   I think
the man's name is Rodney Kerns, one of my assistants.

Q. Employed by the Interborough?   A. Yes, sir.

Q. The work was done in the Interborough shops?   A. I think
so.   It was only one device, yes, sir.

Q. When did you patent that device?   A. Why, I think an
application was made —

Q. When did you invent that device?   A. The idea was originated shortly after we put the low-level car on, and that was made
in January of 1912 or 1913, 1912.   The double-deck car was
built in the same summer, and it was between January, 1912, and
September of 1912, somewheres along in there.

Q. Whom did you employ to take out the letters patent on that
device?   A. I do not know whether it was Darby or Wright.   I
do not remember which.

Q. You employed Darby or Wright?   A. Either one or the
other, I think so, I think it was, yes.   That is as I remember it.
I am not certain.

Q. Did you pay the fees for obtaining the patent?   A. I think
that was included in the fees Mr. Hedley paid for the combination
of the double-deck car.

Q. Did you personally pay anything?   A. Not for that, as I
recall it.

Q. What did Mr. Hedley have to do with this invention, if you
originated it?   A. That part of the combination of the double-
deck car — I do not claim to originate it altogether.   These things
are talked over and considered, just as you and the Senator talk
over your case, and the main points of your conference are consolidated, and a device developed along those lines.   That is the
general plan.

Q. How do you know I talk over this case with the Senator?
A. I imagine you would.   I think two heads are better than one.

Q. Are you imagining that is the course you adopted with Mr.
Hedley?   A. No, sir, but I have my imagination about what you
are doing.   I know what I am doing.

Q. I am not calling for any application of your imagination, but
I want to emphasize your recollection.   A. I am trying to make my
point clear, how two people can work on one subject.

Q. You are a very busy man and so is Mr. Hedley; how much time do you spend together on these devices and inventions? A. Whatever is necessary to perform our duties and perform our work. It varies. Sometimes I do not see Mr. Hedley for a week or so and other times if my work is directly related to the things I have to do with him I can see him every other day.

Q. Does he come up to the shop? A. Infrequently. I generally go to his place.

Q. Where does he work on the models and inventions? A. Mr. Hedley?

Q. Yes. A. I don't know what he does in that respect, but if you will let me cite —

Q. Answer my question. A. I do not know what Mr. Hedley does when he is off. All I know about my connection with him is when I meet him in the office and we talk over the work.

Q. Have you ever seen him at the drawing-bench with a tool or any machinery? A. No, sir.

Q. Has he ever spent any time in the shop testing or observing the operations of any of the new devices? A. Yes, sir, he would very frequently come up to the shop and look at the models we are making, for instance, the model for the stepless car, he came up a number of times and spent an hour or two looking over the model as we constructed it, and changed it. It was built of two by fours and paper, and his judgment and assistance in that was very valuable.

Q. Do you claim you or he invented the double-deck car? A. Can I explain the whole problem?

Q. I ask you a question. A. Co-operatively we worked it together, and I had some ideas on it and he had some others, and the objectionable parts of both of our ideas were eliminated, and the best were used.

Q. And you feel that you and Hedley are the true joint inventors of the double-deck car? A. Of the stepless double-deck car. It is the car without steps, on the lower level. There was never a car built without steps of any kind anywhere before. This car has no steps at all.

Q. Your thought is that the idea of a double-deck and also of a low level car, while both of those ideas alone are not novel, their combination constitutes a novelty? A. Only where there are no steps. Otherwise they are not anything.

Q. Do you mean to say you and Hedley invented low-levelness? A. Without steps — the lowest level, because we had no steps. The floor of that car is closer to the street than any other car built. It has a single step of twelve inches. Other cars have two or three steps of twelve inches each. It is a single step from the street.

Q. As I understand it, Mr. Doyle, you come nearer the street level than any other vehicles, is that right? A. Yes, sir.

Q. If you can achieve the street level, will you patent the street level? A. Not patent it, but use such a device. It is making a railroad run right and safe, and the purpose of that low-level car was to prevent people falling in getting on and off cars, and I want to say it has been accomplished, and there never has been a person injured getting on and off a low-level car, and it means more to the people than to Mr. Hedley or I and the Rapid Transit Company, and it is the safest device ever originated in that respect.

Q. The low-level car has been in operation all over the world? A. Yes, but not as low as this. This is the lowest-down car ever. Steps are the main source of trouble. In analyzing the New York Railways, we found more than 30 per cent. of the liabilities of the company of about $700,000 a year from accidents, was due to people falling off and on cars, on the steps, and we decided steps were bad, and we dispensed with them and arranged the cars so the doors could not be opened when the car was moving, and the foolish people could not precipitate themselves out in the street and kill themselves.

Chairman Thompson.— Is your total accident liability included in the $700,000 a year?

Mr. Doyle.— Of the accidents on the streets, $700,000 or $800,-000; something like that. We analyzed the cause of the troubles and we worked up this low-level car with the safety device to correct them.

Q. Aren't you employed to make the rolling stock of your companies better? A. Yes, sir, we do that.

Q. When you depressed the level you were doing what you were employed for, weren't you? A. Yes, sir, as a professor in college.

He works up a treatise on education for the purpose of that school and if the treatise, he thinks other schools want it, he owes it to the world at large to sell his knowledge, if other people want to use it, I do not see why we should deprive the public from its use of the low-level car if they want it.

Q. What is a current register mechanism? A. On the double-deck car?

Q. What is the current register mechanism? A. There is a million different kinds. Be specific.

Chairman Thompson.— When Mr. Colby asks you a question you answer it, or say you cannot, and you appeal to the Chair, and if there are a million angles we will divide them up, and do not argue it.

Q. You never had anything to do with any device called the current registering mechanism? A. The coasting climber?

Q. You know what a current registering mechanism is, do you? A. There are various kinds —

Q. Do you know anything which is described as a current registering mechanism? A. No, sir, I don't. I was going to say there are watt meters and there are ampere meters. The watt meter registers the amount of current used.

Q. That is a well known device, isn't it? A. Yes, sir, a common device used in electrical work.

Q. That is w-a-t-t, watt, isn't it? A. Yes, sir, w-a-t-t.

Q. Who makes that? A. I guess all the electrical companies do. The Weston Instrument Company are near Newark, and the Westinghouse Company make them, and the General Electric Company, and all the foreign electric manufacturing companies, I think.

Q. And what other names of those devices are there? A. The Sanger watt meter.

Q. I suppose there are many kinds of electric heating systems, too, aren't there? A. Yes, sir, for heating cars?

Q. Yes. A. There are different manufacturers, but they are all somewhat similar. They are all similar.

Q. And all about equally meritorious? A. Practically.

Q. Have you any particular preference for one as against another? A. No, sir.

Q. It can be obtained, can it, a standard electric heating system can be obtained of almost any electrical dealer? A. Yes, sir,

Q. What would you understand by an electric coupling mechanism? A. It is a device to improve and mechanically safeguard the electric connections between electric traction cars. For instance, the present arrangement provides for a suspension of the hanging between the ends of electric cars of a great number of copper wires, forty or fifty or sixty, covered with patent fabrics, and because of being covered with fabrics or rags they fail frequently, and that affects the reliability of the operation of the train, and also in a system like the Subway causes fire and smoke. The purpose of the electric coupler is to mechanically assemble all of these circuits.

Q. Has that subject ever interested you except as you have observed it in the course of your employment as superintendent of car equipment? A. It has been a problem electric traction men have been trying to solve for the last fifteen or twenty years.

Q. Have you ever concentrated your thought upon that? A. Yes, sir, many times.

Q. With any particular result? A. Yes, Mr. Hedley and I worked on the electric coupler for some time, and started an original work that finally resulted in a pretty fair development that is still continuing.

Q. You have not brought it to the point of a patent yet? A. Application has been made for the original ideas of the patent, and the fundamentals of an electric coupler of that particular kind.

Q. Has the patent been actually granted? A. The original patents, I believe, have been granted, as my memory serves me. I am not positive on that. I would have to look up my correspondence to see.

Q. What is a combined electric coupler? A. That has the draw-bars of a peculiar kind. They are locked, and in the draw-bars are the air circuits and in the same steel casting are all the electric circuits necessary for the operation of the train. Shall I describe what it is?

Q. I do not care to have you go unnecessarily into it. A. What it will accomplish, as brief as possible, the present coupling device between cars necessitates men climbing in and out uncoupling the air hose on steam railroads, and on air hose, and electric devices, and that endangers the lives of the men. This is arranged so the motorman in the cab does it by taking hold of a handle, and uncouples everything. Likewise, when a train is in motion, if desired to uncouple the train the man moves a handle and the uncoupling is made.

Q. Did you originate any device of that kind? A. Mr. Hedley and I worked out the original idea and the original model.

Q. Did you know you were the patentee of the current registering mechanism? A. I have a great many patents, some of which do not amount to much, I have patented.

Q. Do you mean to say this registering mechanism which you describe as a common mechanical device which you say can be purchased anywhere, did you know you were listed as a joint patentee with Mr. Hedley? A. I did not recognize it by that name. I have not worked on any patented ideas — or rather, I have not participated in any patented ideas I have not worked on. I think anybody that knows me will agree upon that.

Q. This governing fluid pressure device, that is one of Mr. Hedley's own inventions, is it? A. I do not recognize it by that name. To answer your question correctly, I would have to see the print or know what it means.

Q. Or possibly talk with Mr. Hedley? A. I don't think so. If you show me what it is, I will tell you all about it.

Q. Do you not recognize that as one of Mr. Hedley's inventions? A. Not just the way you mention it.

Q. Do your employees, any one of the three to five or six thousand employees, bring you ideas sometimes? A. They have never given me an original idea, for the very simple reason they are not in the work to see the necessity. It happens to be my job. When I see a necessity I have to help fill that, and the average man has not that opportunity, and he is confined to his particular detail position, and my work is general. Anything necessary in my department I am the one to analyze it.

Chairman Thompson.— Do you make all the employees walk home and back?

Mr. Doyle.— No, sir.

Chairman Thompson.— What do they do? Use taxicabs?

Mr. Doyle.— No, sir. The company furnishes them a pass, and they ride on the railroad.

Chairman Thompson.— Then why haven't they an opportunity
to see what the railroad needs?

Mr. Doyle.— It is not part of their business to summarize the
daily or weekly operations. It is my business to do that. Every
failure I have a record of it, and it is up to me.

Q. Why do you take Hedley in on the inventions of yours? A.
He is one of the best railway men I have ever met, and many times
invented devices that would beat the stuffing out of me.

Q. Mr. Shonts is a very good railway man, isn't he? A. I report to Mr. Hedley, and he is my superior officer.

Q. I suppose you have an understanding that anything that is
made you and he will patent together; is that right? A. No, sir;
no such understanding at all.

Q. How many years have you been taking out joint patents with
Mr. Hedley? A. I couldn't say. I suppose five years — let's see,
this is 1916; six or seven years, perhaps. He has taken out many
patents alone I have nothing to do with.

Q. How many? A. I don't know. He has the anti-climber,
and it is one of the most valuable patents I know of.

Q. That is one? A. Yes, sir, and the sleet scraper. I tried to
design a sleet scraper and I failed completely. The Manhattan
Elevated shut down completely for fifteen hours, and he designed,
and it has never shut down since.

Q. How many patents have you and Mr. Hedley taken out
jointly? A. I couldn't say. I would have to look the list over.

Q. Well, guess. A. It is just a guess, may be five or six or
eight or ten, something like that.

Q. You say he is your superior officer; is that the reason you
divide with him on the results of your original work? A. No, sir.
You asked me why I did not go to Mr. Shonts, and I said I reported
to Mr. Hedley. I do not come in contact with Mr. Shonts. He is
my superior officer.

Q. Do you consider the double-deck, low-level car a success?
A. The low-level, in so far as preventing boarding and alighting
accidents, is a success, because we have not had any such accidents.

Q. Is it popular? A. Well, I should say it was popular.

Q. It is described in New York newspapers as a diabolic con-
traption. A. That is only one man, and his opinion does not rule

the world. He makes the point the car is overcrowded. If the traffic were normal, taken care of as will be when the dual system is going —

Q. You say as it will be when the dual system is going —

Chairman Thompson.— Do you mean everybody has a seat?

Mr. Doyle.— No, sir. I don't think — I am not a transportation man. The travel will be greatly reduced when all the lines are completed, and at that time the objections to the cars that occurs from overcrowding will be very greatly reduced. That is the main objection made is that it is crowded.

Q. Your superior officer said the other day the straps and the people hanging from them were absolutely essential to the solvency of your railroad and the success of your operation, as I understood him. A. I am in the mechanical department, and if he said that I respect his opinion.

Q. If he said that it goes with you? A. Yes, sir, I have a great respect for his judgment and opinion and have known him a great many years.

Q. How much money have you received from the Interborough on patents that you have taken individually? A. I guess you have the record there, joined with Mr. Hedley.

Q. How much have you received in total from the Interborough? A. The money I have received from the Interborough is the royalty on the coasting recorder, I should say, in the main. The record that you asked Mr. Hedley —

Q. Are you testifying from the memorandum prepared by yourself? A. No, sir, it is the same thing Mr. Hedley submitted.

Q. Where did you get it? A. I got a copy the other day in Mr. Hedley's office.

Q. What day? A. I think it was Monday or Tuesday, or one of the days I was down here, perhaps Tuesday. It was after this subject came up. I have been here every day, and hadn't a chance to go to 98th street.

Q. You keep your own record of your receipts, don't you? A. No. sir, not a detailed record.

Q. You are dependent upon Mr. Hedley's record? A. No, sir.

Q. For the receipts from the joint patents? A. No, sir.

Q. Do you keep a record? A. No, sir, I do not.

Q. For the record, you are dependent upon somebody else's record, aren't you? A. No, sir, I should say this —

Q. Answer my question; you have your record which you testify you do not keep there, and if it is anybody's record it is somebody else's? A. I do not know whether anybody keeps records of my doings or not. I will answer what I do.

Q. Listen to me; if there is a matter of record, you have got to go to some record of it, haven't you? A. Yes, sir.

Q. You have testified you don't keep any record, haven't you? A. Yes, sir.

Q. If a matter of record comes along that is of importance to you to know, you have to go to your record somewhere, if you are going to get it at all, haven't you? A. Yes, sir.

Q. What record is there of the receipts of yours and Hedley's joint patents, except in Mr. Hedley's possession, if it is not in yours? A. In the auditing department of the Interborough Rapid Transit Company, for one place.

Q. Is that the only place where there is a record? A. I think so, yes, sir; as far as the Interborough Rapid Transit Company is concerned, that is the proper place for it.

Q. You have no record yourself of your receipts? A. No, sir, I don't keep it in the sense I think you mean. I can go through my records and make a record of what my income is, but I do not keep it up to date.

Q. What amount have you received from the companies of which you are an employee on account of the royalties for patents taken out by you jointly or individually? A. I receive the $4,100 per year from the royalty on the coasting recorder, and I think that is all I got from the Interborough.

Q. That is all you received? A. That is all I think of, for the moment, from the Interborough Rapid Transit Company.

Q. I am not disposed to object to your testifying from memorandum made by Mr. Hadley, although it is clearly, as your counsel will advise you, irregular; if you have a memorandum which you yourself have prepared, and if that memorandum refreshes your knowledge, you can testify from that and refresh your knowledge, but it is a most unusual thing for you to testify of knowledge on matters that you are puzzling out of a memorandum prepared by Mr. Hedley, and I wish you would lay that memorandum aside and give me the benefit of your best recollection on these important matters.

Mr. Quackenbush.— I call your attention to the fact that Mr. Doyle was not requested by any subpoena to produce these things.

Mr. Colby.— I am not taking exception to the minute accuracy, but I am trying to get his recollection on a matter personal to himself.

Mr. Quackenbush.— I think you are overlooking the fact Mr. Doyle is paid directly by the Interborough.

Mr. Colby.— I had rather Mr. Doyle would testify.

Mr. Quackenbush.— I will have nothing further to say. I thought you wanted to be fair.

Mr. Colby.— I certainly think I have exhibited that disposition. I do not want you in the course of a discussion as to the form of the inquiry to run rapidly over some facts as to which my witness seems to be at a loss.

Mr. Quackenbush.— I do not intend to do that, and I do not think you should say that. I call your attention to the fact it is perfectly apparent I have not talked with him or had him prepare notes.

Q. Well, Mr. Doyle— A. May I have a word?

Q. Certainly, sir. A. I referred to this paper, as you subpoenaed me to be here last Monday at 11 o'clock, and I have been here in attendance every day except out in a snowstorm, and I haven't had a chance to go to my office and get a list, and I will be glad to get it.

Q. Tell me approximately what you have obtained from the Interborough on your patents? A. The only thing I recall is the royalty of a little over four thousand dollars a year on the coasting recorder. That is approximately correct.

Q. How has this money been paid to you? A. It has been paid in the regular way, the same as my salary has been paid. It has been paid by check, and I think it comes directly from the Treasurer's office in the regular form, the same as I receive my monthly check.

Q. The only moneys that you have received on account of patents are in that form? A. From the Interborough Rapid Transit Company.

Q. What is your total income from patents approximately? A. I have not figured it out, and I haven't had an opportunity since you subpoenaed me.

Q. Have you any impression on the subject? A. Why, yes. Over what period of time?

Q. Since you have been an employee of the company? A. Fifteen years.

Q. The company has not been in existence fifteen years. Since you have been the superintendent of car equipment of the Interborough? A. I guess that is about twelve years, something like that.

Q. How much have you taken out of you patents? A. Roughly speaking, I should say it might run maybe a couple of thousand dollars a year; not more than that.

Chairman Thompson.—Are you underpaid?

Mr. Doyle.— I stated a moment ago I was receiving a thousand and some odd dollars less than my three predecessors.

Chairman Thompson.— You feel like Mr. Hedley, that you are underpaid too?

Mr. Doyle.— No, sir; I never worried very much about my pay. I think I earn what I get.

Chairman Thompson.— You think you get all you ought to have?

Mr. Doyle.— I never give it very much consideration. I never asked for a raise.

Q. The only device that you are jointly interested in with Mr. Hedley is what; the only device which the Interborough uses which you and Mr. Hedley are joint patentees of is what. A. The only device they use?

Q. Let me put the question a little more broadly; how many devices are you interested in with Mr. Hedley which are now in use by the Interborough? A. I would have to think that over and guess some, I suppose.

Q. Aren't you superintendent of car equipment? A. Yes, sir.

Q. Aren't you the joint patentee of these devices? A. Yes, sir.

Q. How much reflection is necessary for you to determine how many of your devices are in use on railroads of which you are the car equipment superintendent? A. You want an exact answer, and I would have to stop to think for a second or two. We are interested in the coasting time recorder. I would much prefer to take my list and go over it and be sure of my answer.

Q. I want to know whether you as the joint patentee with the general manager and vice-president of the company of a certain device cannot tell me how many of your devices are on the Interborough Railway? A. There is not very many. I will be glad to look them up and give you the list.

Q. In other words, you cannot tell without consulting the record? A. Yes, sir; I would have to have a little time.

Q. Would you say offhand it was as many as ten? A. I should say it was not ten. One device may have half a dozen — of complete devices, I would say no.

Q. You are jointly interested with Mr. Hedley in the coasting time recorder, are you? A. Yes, sir.

Q. You don't know how much you have received from the Interborough on royalties for that device, do you? A. I could estimate, I think, if I thought it over. I don't know the exact year, but it must have been 1911 or 1910, or somewheres about there; it was $4,000 a year, and six years roughly, and if that is so, it would be maybe $24,000.

Chairman Thompson.— I thought you said you only got $2,000 out of all of them a year?

Mr. Doyle.— For the average for twelve years. I asked him how long he wanted the average for, and he said with the Interborough Company, and taking the average for the twelve years it has been that. It is only the recent three or four years I have got that income.

Q. How much did you get from the Manhattan Elevated for the coasting time recorders? A. They were not in existence at that time.

Q. How long has the coasting time recorder been in existence?

7

A. I think somewheres about 1910 or 1911. I don't know the exact date, but somewheres in that neighborhood.

Q. You do not know the exact period for which you have been deriving an income as patentee of these devices? A. No, sir. I can get it.

Q. How much have you received as patentee of these devices from the railroads by which you are employed? A. Just the amount I said.

Q. State it again; I am asking you particularly in reference to this particular device. A. This device, as I recall it, pays a royalty of $4,100 and some odd dollars a year.

Q. I ask you how much have you received as co-patentee with Mr. Hedley for the use of your coasting time recorder? A. That is what I am trying to answer.

Q. Can you answer it; can you give me an approximate idea of the sum of money you have thus far received on the coasting time recorder? A. Roughly, I thought I did. I thought it was a matter of five or six years, say five years, and perhaps for five years $20,000. That is roughly guessing. I am not sure of my date. I would have to look up my records.

Q. Where do you keep your bank account? A. I have several bank accounts. I have a bank account at the Metal & Mechanics. I have savings bank accounts; three or four accounts.

Q. Are you a stockholder in the American Brake Shoe & Manufacturing Company? A. Not at the present time. In 1912 I bought fifty shares on margin expecting the value would go up, and the value did not go up, and the next year, 1913, I bought them outright and held them until 1914 when they went up to 58, I think, and I made 24 or 25 points and I sold them.

Q. Who are your stock brokers? A. Warner & Company.

Q. What is their address? A. On Wall street; I don't know their number.

Q. Are you a stockholder in the Agasote Company? A. No, sir.

Q. How long will it take you to produce before the Committee your bank books for the period from June 30, 1911, to January 1st this year? A. I don't know, I would have to — 1911? I don't know. I would be glad to get them as soon as possible.

Q. Will you have them sent down this afternoon so the Committee's accountant can make a brief examination of them? A. I will have to get them myself. They are in a box of which I have the key.

Q. Showing your deposits and receipts? A. Yes, sir.

Q. Check books and canceled checks? A. I haven't kept any canceled checks. I have destroyed them. I merely have my book.

Q. You have destroyed all of your canceled checks? A. Yes, sir.

Chairman Thompson.— How lately? A. Up until this last month. I have always destroyed them, and I have no occasion to keep canceled checks.

Chairman Thompson.— When did you destroy the last ones?

Mr. Doyle.— I don't know; I think a month ago. I always destroy them each month.

Q. You destroy your canceled checks each week? A. No, sir: every month.

Q. Do you preserve your check stubs? A. No, sir, I have no check stubs; merely a single check, without any stub on it. The checks are merely for household operating expenses usually.

Q. Let me understand you; you keep no check book? A. I have a check book. I make the check out, but I have no stubs, and never had.

Q. You keep a bank pass-book? A. Yes, sir.

Q. When do you have your account balanced? A. At the end of the month they submit a sheet and checks, and I check up my sheet against the checks and get my balance.

Q. How do you know what you have at the bank from day to day? A. I don't, not from day to day. It does not vary that much.

Q. You wait until the expiration of the month and the bank acquaints you with the fact you are to the good or overdrawn, or whatever the fact may be? A. Yes, sir. My business is not of such volume. I simply check —

Q. You are in receipt of $5,000 or so for twelve years or a lesser period of years — four or five thousand dollars for the last few years from one patent alone, and good salaries, one of $6,666 from one company and $3,500 from another, and I consider you at least, from the standpoint of untrained minds, are in receipt of a rather substantial income. Suppose the bank makes a mistake, you are absolutely dependent upon their accuracy, aren't you? A. I check up my balance sheet against my checks each month.

Q. And then you destroy the checks? A. Yes, sir. Why should I keep them?

Q. What I want to understand is have you a check book on which the payee and the purpose and the dates of your checks are noted, or haven't you? A. I have not.

Q. I understand also that you destroy your checks, the canceled or paid checks, every month? A. Yes, sir.

Q. Do you keep any other record of your receipts and expenditures? A. No, sir, no other record. I will explain to the accountant just what it is.

Q. Have you a check register? A. I have a check book in which the amount of money put in the bank is registered. Is that what you mean?

Q. Are you an officer or director of any company? A. No, sir.

Q. You have had a long business experience and admittedly, on your statement, you have dealt with business men and been a corporation employee; what has suggested to you the advisability or propriety of conducting your not inconsiderable operations in this recordless fashion? A. I do not consider it recordless. Each month I compare my checks with my sheets. I destroy the checks because they are of no use to me.

Chairman Thompson.— Did you ever have trouble over a bill because you did not have a receipt?

Mr. Doyle.— No, sir.

Chairman Thompson.— Don't you know every business man keeps a receipt for six years until it outlaws?

Mr. Doyle.— No, sir, I don't. My operations are household operations.

Chairman Thompson.— You destroy them every month?

Mr. Doyle.— Yes.

Chairman Thompson.—And isn't it safer to destroy them?

Mr. Doyle.— I don't think so. I have never had that in mind at all.

Chairman Thompson.— We will suspend until 2:15 o'clock P. M.

Whereupon (at 1:10 o'clock P. M.) a recess was taken to 2:15 o'clock P. M.

AFTERNOON SESSION.

Meeting called to order by Senator Lawson, acting as Chairman, at 2:15 P. M., a quorum being present.

Mr. Colby.— Is Mr. Doyle present?

Mr. Quackenbush.— No, Mr. Doyle is looking up some records which you requested. I think he will be here very shortly. And, Mr. Chairman, I wish to state that there is a witness subpoenaed here by the name of Barbett. Mr. Barbett has a jury notice which requires his presence for next Monday. Of course that is not until Monday, but I thought I would give you ample notice.

Mr. Colby.— Then I think I will put Mr. Barbett on the stand and dispose of him.

HARRY J. BARBETT, being duly sworn, testified as follows:

Examination by Mr. Colby:

Q. Will you state your full name? A. Harry J. Barbett.

Q. Are you employed by the New York railways or the Interborough Rapid Transit Company? A. By the Interborough Rapid Transit Company.

Q. Only? A. Yes. I work on the New York Railways.

Q. Do I understand you to say that you are employed by both companies? A. Yes, sir.

Q. Where do you work? A. Well, at all the shops and barns of both companies.

Q. What is your position? A. Head of the efficiency department.

Q. What is the character of that department? State it briefly. A. Consisting of the efficiency shop methods through the introduction of piecework.

Q. You are the head of the department? A. Yes, sir.

Q. How many men are embraced within the department? A. Seventeen, including myself.

Q. Are these seventeen men concentrated at one shop or distributed amongst the various shops? A. Amongst the various shops.

Q. In each shop I assume doing particularly the work of the efficiency department? A. Yes.

Q. What do they do? A. Make observations and collect data.

Q. What do they do with that data? A. Submit it to me.

Q. What do you do with it? A. I go over it, go over it with them, making piecework practice.

Q. What do you mean by piecework? A. Well, we establish a price on any article or any job in the shop.

Q. You are not selling articles? A. Oh, no.

Q. You establish a price for your own guidance for the company's information? A. For the men to work at.

Q. Just what do you mean for the men to work at? A. Well, a man gets, say a dollar for doing a certain job. That is a piecework price, whatever that job happens to be.

Q. That's merely with reference to fixing a price for your employees? A. For the job employees?

Q. For the shop employees? A. Yes.

Q. Is every bit of work that is done in the shop under the eye and to some extent the regulation of the efficiency department? A. Oh, no. This is a mechanical work.

Q. Do you pursue your observations with reference to the experimental or development work conducted in your shops? A. No.

Q. That is something that lies outside of the efficiency department? A. Yes.

Q. Does anybody observe the work of experimentation so far as it involved the use of any materials and expenditures of any funds? A. Not to my knowledge. If they do I don't know them.

Q. This work of experimentation and development goes on in your shops, does it not? A. Just what do you mean by experimentation and development?

Q. Well, experimenting work, experiments and experimenting with a view to improving devices, making improvements, making tests. A. There is a testing department.

Q. Where is the testing department? A. Why, I believe there is a test made on all operations.

Q. That is one, as I understand you, to test the practical efficiency of mechanical parts that are in progress or in cars (interruption by witness). A. I don't mean testing in that sense.

Q. It has been testified here that continuously and for a period, a long period of years, various numbers of men have been employed, I mean Interborough Rapid Transit Company and New York Railway Company's employees, have been engaged in experimenting with a view to improving devices in use on the railway, such as couplers, trucks, door openers, quite a long list of such devices, where does that work go on? A. I couldn't tell you that, sir. That doesn't come under me.

Q. You mean it doesn't come under any official? A. It doesn't come under my jurisdiction.

Q. Whose jurisdiction does it come under? A. I couldn't tell you.

Q. Does it not within your knowledge? A. It does not.

Q. Although you are the head of the efficiency department? A. Yes.

Q. And your business is to observe and collect data, yet you know nothing whatever about such work as that? A. No.

Q. You wouldn't be able to tell me whether it goes on or does not go on? A. No, I would not.

Q. Do you frequently come in contact with Mr. Doyle? A. Not so frequently, no.

Q. How often do you see him and in what connection? A. If there is any correspondence to be answered I go up to see him.

Q. Does Mr. Doyle do any work in the shops? A. If you mean working around the shops mechanically, no, I couldn't say.

Q. Are you familiar with the patented devices used by either the Interborough Rapid Transit Company or New York Railways Company? A. No, sir, I am not.

Q. Does the efficiency department do anything except fix the price of piecework, that is, to determine the price that it will pay these workmen? A. That's all.

Q. Is that the true scope of an efficiency department? A. In this case it is.

Q. Is that all the efficiency department that the Interborough Rapid Transit Company or the New York Railways Company maintain? A. It's the only one I know of.

Q. What does it do with reference to efficiency? A. With piece-work prices we make we are called an efficiency shop method.

Q. That's the sole element of efficiency with which you concern yourself? A. Yes.

Q. Have you anything to do with the efficiency of your machinery? A. Why, we sometimes make a new jig, take hold of a certain piece of work, recommend the manufacture of the jig. We do that.

Q. Do you observe or collect any data with reference to the efficiency of your power plant? A. No.

Q. Or your engines? A. No.

Q. Your installation of power or transmission of it? A. No.

Mr. Quackenbush.— Mr. Colby, I know you don't want to take this question up without my having called your attention to the fact that the power matters is entirely foreign to this proposition. It is an entirely different matter.

Mr. Colby.— Well, I know nothing about a true scope of an efficiency department and I wish to inquire of this witness about it.

Mr. Quackenbush.— Well, I assume you want me to call your attention to the facts, that I don't think you want to have anything like that on the record.

Mr. Colby.— I am just trying to ascertain what efficiency means as used to describe Mr. Barbett's department.

Mr. Quackenbush.—And if you limit it to his department, then there will be no question about the power matter.

Q. I understand, Mr. Barbett, you to say that you are the head of the efficiency department of the Interborough Rapid Transit Company? A. Yes, sir, car equipment.

Q. Of the department of car equipment only? A. That's all.

Q. There are other efficiency departments, are there? A. Not to my knowledge.

Q. Is there any efficiency department that has anything to do with any other department than car equipment in the Interborough Rapid Transit Company? A. Not that I know of.

Q. Your work carries you into all the shops of the company?
A. Yes.

Q. And brings you into touch with Mr. Hedley, the general manager of the company? A. No, sir.

Q. But with Mr. Doyle? A. Mr. Doyle is my superior.

Q. Do you test the efficiency of car tracks? A. No, sir.

Q. Do you test the efficiency of car brakes? A. No, sir.

Q. Do you test the efficiency of any of these devices for the control of heat, power or regulation as applied to cars? A. No.

Q. Do you test the efficiency of any of these devices for opening and closing doors? A. No.

Q. Isn't " efficiency department " a rather high-sounding form for what you actually do? A. Well, that was the form they gave it.

Q. That is all, Mr. Barbett.

WORTHA G. STRAIT, being duly sworn, testified as follows:

By Mr. Colby:

Q. Where do you reside, Mr. Strait? A. Mt. Hope, N. Y.

Q. With what companies are you connected? A. Interborough Rapid Transit Company and the New York Railways Company.

Q. In what capacity? A. Chief clerk in the car equipment department.

Mr. Quackenbush.— Let me interrupt, if you please. When your process server was at the shop, I think you had subpoenaed — called for some sort of a statistician, or something of that sort; at least, we didn't have a party there answering that description, so we had Mr. Barbett come here.

By Mr. Colby:

Q. You are chief clerk, then? A. Yes.

Q. What are your duties? A. I have the general charge of the accounting, statistical and general clerk's work on cars.

Q. Do you know anything about the cost of material or the cost of labor in connection with the experimental and development work conducted by Mr. Hedley and by Mr. Doyle? A. In a general way I do. Do you want statistics as to such cost? We keep a record of all costs and we have a record of this.

Q. I wish you would produce those records. To what account are such costs referred?

Senator Lawson (acting Chairman).— The Chairman will direct you, Mr. Strait, to produce these accounts asked for by counsel; bring them here to-morrow.

Mr. Strait.—All right, sir. Well, I don't remember anything definitely, except that I remember definitely about the matter of a low level car. That had a special accounting number, in charging that on the book, that I remember of.

Q. I hand you a list of devices patented by Mr. Hedley and Mr. Doyle, or by Mr. Hedley alone, and ask you to run over them, look over them rapidly and tell me if you recall any accounts of cost in connection with work on any of these devices? A. The first two I don't recall any experimental work. In regard to the stepless car, I remember that there was a model of that car constructed in the shop.

Q. More than one, or only one? A. One model.

Q. A small sized model? A. I think it was about half size, something like that.

Q. How long did the construction of that model take? A. One week, perhaps.

Q. How many men employed in its construction? A. I cannot recall the maximum number; three or four, perhaps.

Q. Is that all the work on that model that you recall having been done in the shop? A. Well, after that week there may have been a man occasionally to make changes. I think the record will show definitely the expenditure.

Q. Will you run your eye further down that list? A. Double-deck car. The same model was altered to show the double deck, the model to which I have previously referred.

Q. You mean to say the model of the low-level car was constructed in a week? A. I hardly figure it was longer than that. I think it was in its first form. I might say that probably during a period of three or four weeks there were slight alterations made from time to time, according to my recollection of it.

Q. Cast your eye further down the list and answer as to names that strike you as familiar. A. Current registering mechanism. I recall no experimental work in connection with that. Conductor's collection counter.

Q. Does your work bring you into familiarity with the work that is done in all the shops, in connection with car equipment? A. My work, yes, extends to all the shops of the car equipment department.

Q. I won't ask you further questions, if you will bring me information directed to be produced by the Chairman. A. Yes.

Q. You understand what it is? A. How far back am I to go on this?

Q. I want you to go back to the date upon which the anticlimber was patented, 1906 — December 10. A. I think, Mr. Colby, although I probably could — it would assist me if I had the dates of those patents, and a list of those things, in locating what I am to find.

Q. I will supply you with that readily, see that it is sent you. What is your address, Mr. Strait? A. Ninety-eighth street and Third avenue.

Mr. Colby.— I will excuse you now, Mr. Strait.

JOSEPH A. McCARTNEY, called as a witness, being first duly sworn, testified as follows:

By Mr. Colby:

Q. Will you give us your full name, please? A. Joseph A. McCartney.

Q. You reside where? A. 2280 Bathgate avenue.

Q. In Brooklyn, isn't it? A. Bronx.

Chairman Lawson.— That is the Bronx.

Q. What is your position with the Interborough and the New York Railways Company? A. Superintendent of the electrical department of the Interborough, car equipment.

Q. Superintendent of the record? A. Of the electrical department, car equipment, of the Interborough.

Q. What are your duties? A. I have charge of the electrical repair shops and the inspection plants.

Q. Are you familiar with the so-called Hedley or Doyle devices and patents? A. Some of them.

Q. Do you know anything at all about the work of their development or their perfection in the shops of the Interborough? A. Some of them.

Q. You would probably be dependent upon the records mentioned by Chief Clerk Strait as to the amount of time, labor and materials or — A. Yes, sir.

Q. — other elements of cost? A. Yes, sir.

Q. Attributable to this work? A. Yes, sir.

Q. And could add nothing to that? A. No, sir, nothing that I know of now, that I can recollect just at the present time.

Q. I don't think of anything further to ask you at the moment.

Chairman Lawson.— Just a moment. Have you any knowledge at all of the experiments carried on that Mr. Strait is in charge of, in the accounts?

Mr. McCartney.— Yes, sir.

Chairman Lawson.—Any of the details?

Mr. McCartney.— Some of them.

By Mr. Colby:

Q. Mention which one? A. Why, on the coasting clock was one of them; and on parts of the double-deck car and stepless car.

Q. In other words, the employees of the shop were from time to time busy on that work?

Mr. Colby.— I think we can get this information more systematically and briefly from the statements reproduced by Mr. Strait. I recognize that Mr. McCartney could no doubt discuss these matters with some informing result, but I thought, to shorten time, we had better take a more comprehensive statement from a man whose work brings him officially in contact with it more closely.

Chairman Lawson.— We will excuse you.

Mr. Colby.— Is there any other foreman here? Mr. Hume.

JOHN W. HUME, called as a witness, being first duly sworn, testified as follows:

By Mr. Colby:

Q. What is your position, Mr. Hume? A. General foreman of construction of the car equipment department.

Q. General foreman? A. Yes, sir.

Q. Have you general charge of all the shops? A. Of the construction shops.

Q. All the shops are construction shops except the repair shops, are they not? A. Well, we have one construction shop at 129th street, and then we are carrying on some construction work in the Highbridge yard of the New York Central Railroad.

Q. Have you a system of recording the costs of the work done in the various branches of the shops? A. That work is done at Ninety-eighth street.

Q. By whom? A. By the cost department down there.

Q. The cost department? A. Yes, sir.

Q. And so it comes under the cost department and not the efficiency department? A. It comes under Mr. Strait.

Q. Under Mr. Strait? A. Yes, sir.

Q. All those costs are preserved, their references to proper accounts are shown in the records in Mr. Strait's keeping; is that correct? A. That is what I understand.

Q. You personally have no knowledge on those subjects? A. No, sir.

Mr. Colby.— We will excuse you.

McCLELLAN EBRIGHT, called as a witness, being first duly sworn, testified as follows:

By Mr. Colby:

Q. Mr. Ebright, what is your position in the New York Railways and Interborough? A. Assistant superintendent of the mechanical department, car equipment, located at Forty-eighth street subway shop.

Q. You heard the questions I asked Mr. Hume a moment ago? A. Yes, sir.

Q. You have no personal knowledge of costs or distribution of accounts of expenditures in connection with different classes of work? A. No, sir.

Mr. Colby.— I think the Committee's process server was a little too — shall I say meticulous, in going through your shops?

Mr. Ebright.— That is what I thought.

Mr. Quackenbush.— We have had them here three or four days.

Mr. Colby.— I am sorry. If I had known that I might have interrupted the proceedings and put them on. Mr. Marx.

MAX MARX (128 Broadway), called as a witness, being first
duly sworn, testified as follows:

By Mr. Colby:

Q. Mr. Marx, you are Max Marx, the important and well known
real estate dealer? A. I don't know whether I am important. I
may be well known.

Q. You are a real estate operator, are you not? A. I am, yes,
sir.

Q. And I am asking you a perfunctory question when I am asking you if you are an extensive buyer and seller of real estate in
New York city? A. I am.

Q. Have you had any real estate transactions recently with the
Interborough Rapid Transit Company? A. Not recently. It is
about five years now, I think.

Q. You sold them some land, I believe, on the line of the proposed dual system? A. Yes, it was supposed to be the land for
their terminal facilities.

Q. Will you describe briefly the location of this land? A. That
land extended from about 238th street and White Plains road, on
the east side of White Plains road, about 400 feet along White
Plains road, and then eastward to Baychester avenue, and some
parts of it were across Baychester avenue.

Q. What was the area of this land? A. Containing between
thirty-five and forty acres of land.

Q. Was it improved? A. Well, there was some houses on it,
some detached residences.

Q. Of good character or of the poorer sort? A. Very good
character of land.

Q. Was this land all sold to the Interborough Rapid Transit
Company? A. I understood it was a direct sale to the Interborough Railroad Company.

Q. About what street running north would this land be situated
on? A. Between 277th and 278th, I presume.

Q. Who were the brokers in this transaction? A. J. Clarence
Davies.

Q. What was the consideration you received? A. I think it was
around $300,000 or $325,000, something in that neighborhood.

Q. On what terms was this land sold to the Interborough Rapid

Transit Company? A. I believe we owed on the property, first mortgage, around $130,000. I believe they paid me about $75,000 or $80,000 in cash and gave me a second mortgage for around a hundred. I don't remember the exact amounts without referring to the book.

Q. Will you refresh your mind as to those amounts, and send to Chairman Thompson of the Committee a brief memorandum of the consideration received by you and how it was paid? A. Yes, sir.

Q. Who searched the title? A. The Title Guarantee & Trust Company acted for the Interborough. I was not present at the closing of the title at all.

Q. And the Interborough gave you a second mortgage as a consideration? A. I think that second mortgage was made by some dummy, if I recollect.

Q. Do you recall his name? A. I can if I refer to our memorandum in the office.

Q. Please give me in summary form, as you understand — A. We can give you the whole statement.

Q. — the statement of that transaction? A. Yes.

Q. Thank you for coming. A. You want to know when it was paid off and everything, the second mortgage?

Q. Yes. I want to know the consideration, the name of the purchaser, the date of the sale, and the terms. A. Yes, sir, I can give you all that, because we keep all our papers.

Q. And give me a fairly accurate description, so that I can recognize it on the maps. A. You can have our old contract if you want.

Q. Thank you. A. Shall we get a receipt for it?

Chairman Lawson.— Oh, yes.

Mr. Colby.—And what is more, you may get the contract back.

Mr. Marx.—Are you through with me?

Chairman Lawson.—All through. Thank you, Mr. Marx.

Mr. Colby.— Will you call Mr. Calvin Tomkins to the stand, please?

Chairman Lawson.— Is Mr. Calvin Tomkins here?

CALVIN TOMKINS (30 Church street, business address;
Wyoming apartment, residence), called as a witness, being
first duly sworn, testified as follows:

By Mr. Colby:

Q. Mr. Tomkins, you have stated your address? A. I have.

Q. What is your business? A. Manufacturer of builders' supplies, building materials, broken stone, plaster of paris.

Q. You were formerly the Commissioner of Docks of the City
of New York, were you not? A. I was.

Q. And I happen to know, and merely ask you to assent to the
fact that you are connected officially and otherwise with various
civic organizations, and are well known in such? A. To a certain
extent.

Q. Some time ago, Mr. Tomkins, bids were invited to supply
ballast for the subway construction, which your company examined,
and decided to submit proposals on? A. We did.

Q. What was about the date of that invitation for proposals?
A. My letter will show, I think, that I gave you. I have forgotten
the date of it. (Counsel hands letter to witness.) It was about
the latter part of August, 1915, the proposals were dated August
4, 1915.

Q. Do you recall how much stone ballast was covered in the
advertisement? A. I think it was most of the ballast required in
the new subway, but I don't remember the yardage.

Q. Did you make a bid? A. We did.

Q. Do you recall whether any other companies bid? A. Yes,
other companies bid on it as well.

Q. You made a bid in your own name, I believe? A. May have
been my name, or Tomkins Crushed Stone Company. It is immaterial, as I am the agent of the company.

Q. I see in the calendar of the Board of Estimate and Apportionment of October 8, 1915, that the bid made by you is described
only by your own name. A. Then it was in my own name.

Q. What other companies bid on this job? A. I think the —
I am not sure, but I think the Upper Hudson Company bid on it.

Q. The Upper Hudson Stone Company? A. Yes.

Q. And do you recall the name of any other bidder? A. Well,
the Trap Rock companies bid on it, but I don't recollect under
what name it went in.

Q. Do you recall whether the Haverstraw Crushed Stone Company made a bid? A. I think they did. I was in Nova Scotia the time the bid was made.

Mr. Colby.— I will read into the record, Mr. Chairman, an extract from the calendar of the Board of Estimate and Apportionment for October 19, 1915 — October 8, 1915. This is subject or matter No. 65 on the Board of Estimate's calendar for that day.

"Report of the Comptroller."—I may say first that this was the statement of the matter that came up before the Board of Estimate for its consideration and action on that date.

"Report of the Comptroller recommending (1) that the Board consent to a proposed contract to be entered into between The City of New York, acting by the Public Service Commission for the First District, and The Upper Hudson Stone Company for a supply of ballast, Portion A, Order No. 3, for use in the construction of rapid transit railroads at an estimated cost of $228,010; (2) that the Board prescribe the limit of $228,010 to the amount of bonds to be made available to meet the city's obligations under the contract, and (3) that it direct the Comptroller to issue bonds to said amount, the same to be charged against the authorization of $28,200,000 for Contract No. 3.

"On August 4, 1915, the Public Service Commission opened three bids for the supply of this ballast. The amounts of the bids were as follows:

Calvin Tomkins	$141,912 00
Upper Hudson Stone Company	230,440 00
Haverstraw Crushed Stone Company	260,850 00."

I am still reading from the calendar of the Board of Estimate.

"The low bid was rejected by the Commission because, in the opinion of its chief engineer, the material to be furnished was unsatisfactory, and no award was made to the next bidder because this bid had been declared informal by counsel to the Commission.

"The specifications for ballast were met by the samples submitted by Calvin Tomkins, with the exception that the material proposed to be furnished was not from a quarry meeting with the approval of the engineer of the Commission, which approval was withheld because, in his opinion, based on reports submitted to him by engineers employed by the Commission, the material was softer than required and was not sufficiently uniform in quality.

" The crushing stress requirement of 12,000 pounds per square inch specified in the contract was more than met, the Tomkins Cove limestone tested in 1-inch cubes having withstood a crushing stress of 28,120 pounds. The Upper Hudson Stone Company's limestone withstood a crushing stress of 37,080.

" The contract was readvertised. On the readvertisement the specifications were changed in a number of particulars; the requirement for crushing strength was increased from 12,000 to 29,000 pounds per square inch.

" The previous low bidder submitted no bid on the readvertisement and the price of his next higher competitor on the previous opening, the Upper Hudson Stone Company, was reduced 1 per cent per cubic yard, that is 166,000 cubic yards at 97 cents and 77,000 cubic yards at 87 cents, or a total of $228,010 as against the rejected bid of Calvin Tomkins upon the first advertising of $141,912.

" On October 1, 1915 (Cal. No. 79), this matter was laid over for one week, under Rule 19, and the Chief Engineer of the Board was instructed to report at this meeting on the necessity of increasing the crushing stress.

" Report of the Chief Engineer concurring in the Comptroller's recommendation that the Board consent to the award of the proposed contract."

Q. That is a substantially accurate statement as far as it goes? A. I think it is.

Q. I understand, Mr. Tomkins, that in the invitation or proposals for this great quantity of stone or rock ballast the crushing stress requirement was stated at 12,000 pounds, is that right? A. That is right.

Q. And the crushing stress of the limestone that you were prepared to supply was tested and found to be 28,120 pounds? A. That is right.

Q. In other words, nearly two and a half times the crushing requirement specified in the invitation for bids? A. Correct.

Q. Is that correct? A. That is correct.

Q. Your bid was then about $90,000 under that of the next lowest bidder? A. The combined bids were about $119,000 lower than the next lower bidder, as we computed it at that time.

Q. Yes. A. Our combined bids.

Q. There for some reason or other has been a readvertisement of this matter and under altered specifications; is that true? A. That is true.

Q. And the crushing stress was raised from the invitation, from 12,000 pounds to 29,000? A. Just a little above 28,000.

(Chairman Thompson resumes the chair.)

Q. In other words, just a few hundred pounds above your test? A. Yes.

Q. Notwithstanding that the Public Service and its engineer had only required a crushing strength or requirement of 12,000 pounds in its first advertisement? Is that correct? A. That is correct.

Q. And then the Upper Hudson Valley Stone Company, or the Upper Hudson Stone Company, bid again, is that right? A. Correct.

Q. And they lowered their bid about — well, about $2,000 — still about $115,000 or $116,000 in excess of your bid? A. Yes.

Q. Well, can you — there was considerable discussion of this matter in the meeting of the Board of Estimate and Apportionment before action was taken, was there not? A. Well, we discussed it. I discussed it with several members — with Mr. McAneny and I think some other members of the Board. I am not sure. I protested against it, and wrote a letter to every member of the Board, so as to bring formal protest before them, copy of which letter I hand you. This is the letter. (Witness hands letter to counsel.)

Mr. Colby.— I will read into the record a copy of a letter produced by Mr. Tomkins, dated August 20, 1915, and addressed to the Acting Mayor and Chairman of the Board of Estimate and Apportionment, New York City: " Sir: I write to protest against the award of Portion C, Public Service Commission contract, for the supply of ballast, Order No. 3. Under the proposals submitted to the Public Service Commission August 4, 1915, my bids on Portions A and C of 58.4 cents to 59.4 cents, respectively, were approximately $119,000 lower than the next lowest bidder, and the material offered under this proposal was far in excess of the requirements of the advertised specifications. Yours respectfully, Calvin Tomkins."

Q. Mr. Tomkins, is 12,000 pounds per square inch more than the requisite crushing strength that stone should possess for this purpose? A. In my judgment it is. The ties would not stand any more than that.

Q. Do you know whether stone of less crushing strength has been used extensively in subway construction? A. I cannot say that. I know our stone has been used for the last twenty years on the West Shore Railroad for ballast and is regarded by them as good as any material they can get.

Q. Well, this specification was drawn presumably by the engineer of the Public Service Commission? A. I presume so, by the engineer or by the consulting engineers of the Public Service Commission; Mills & Gibbs, I believe, drew that.

Q. And when they fixed 12,000 per square inch as the specification that all bidders must meet, they were specifying a liberal stressing requirement and were well within the limits that cautious supervision might suggest? A. In my judgment they were. At any rate, that is the practice of the West Shore Railroad, and of the Long Island Railroad, to whom we have sold material for ballast.

Q. Did you ever hear of a requirement of a crushing stress for stone ballast for track construction amounting to 29,000 pounds? A. No.

Q. And after this specification had been changed, and proposals had been resolicited or invited the second time, they jacked up the crushing stress just above the crushing stress of your stone? A. What our stone tested.

Q. What your stone tested? A. That is so.

Q. In other words, your stone tested 28,000 pounds where only 12,000 was required in the first advertising? A. Yes.

Q. And they put it just a few hundred pounds over your maximum test? A. That is correct.

Q. And of course you could not bid under the terms of the second invitation, could you? A. We did not think it safe to do so, especially after feeling the engineering department was not with us. We thought it was not a safe thing to bid.

Chairman Thompson.— The engineering department of the Public Service Commission?

Mr. Tomkins.— The engineering — the engineers and consulting engineers of the Public Service Commission.

Chairman Thompson.— Who were the consulting engineers?

Mr. Tomkins.— Mills & Gibb or Mills & Gibbs, I believe, are the consulting engineers.

Q. And the Upper Hudson Stone Company practically repeated its bid under these highly favorable conditions? A. They slightly lowered their bid.

Q. Lowered $230,000 to $228,000? A. I believe those are the figures.

Q. And went into the second bidding under a specification that excluded at the threshold the only competing bidder whose bid was lower than theirs in the first advertising? A. Virtually.

Chairman Thompson.— Have you any knowledge that their stone actually met with this increased pressage power?

Mr. Tomkins.— I cannot tell. The stone is a good stone.

Chairman Thompson.— You have no knowledge it did meet with the new test required?

Mr. Tomkins.— I have no reason to think it did not. I think the test was fair.

By Mr. Colby:

Q. Do you happen to know whether any director of the Rapid Transit Company is a director of the Upper Hudson Stone Company? A. Not that I know of.

Q. Can you think of anything to add to this transaction as it has been stated, that you recall? A. Nothing except we were very glad to be out of the contract. It was the lowest bid we ever made for broken stone, to my knowledge, in New York city in thirty years, and we were glad to be relieved of the contract. We have sold stone at higher prices since.

Q. I think that is all, Mr. Tomkins. Thank you very much.
A. Thank you.

Mr. Colby.— Has Mr. Doyle returned yet?

Mr. Quackenbush.— Mr. Hedley is here, if you want to complete one or two of those items.

FRANK HEDLEY, recalled, further testified:

By Mr. Colby:

Q. Simply about that question of the Hudson and McAdoo tunnel, wasn't it? A. I have gone over my papers and the anti-climbers were put on the Hudson-Manhattan cars at a time when a firm by the name of Al. Whipple had the selling right for the anti-climbers, and I cannot find that I was ever paid for that. I have no record of having received the money. I don't think I did. I know that in that case I told him that he could keep that money in the business, in his business, and soon after that he failed and went out of business, and I have no record of ever getting the money. If the accountant of this Commission can help me find out whether I did or not, I would be glad to have him go over all my papers and find out for me. I don't believe I ever did get it.

Q. I have nothing to ask you at the moment, Mr. Hedley.

Mr. Hedley.— In relation to the Southern Pacific.

Q. You were uncertain about that? A. Yes, sir, I was uncertain about that. I find that the Southern Pacific, from my papers, have used some coasting clocks. They have a very large number, though, I understand, under order, which order, however, has been received since I severed my connection with the Railway Improvement Company, so those figures will be shown on the Railway Improvement Company's figures that you have or are about to get, as you asked Mr. Pizzini to produce. What impressed my mind so forcefully with the Southern Pacific, that they had used some of my patents, was the fact that I had received a check that morning which I have in my pocket for royalties on another one of the devices that I patented, namely, the electric couplers. I have that check in my pocket now. I have not yet had time to put it in the bank.

Q. On this phase of the inquiry, I don't desire to ask you any further questions at the moment.

Mr. Colby.— Mr. Chairman, the next witness that I have is in connection with this crushed rock ballast incident, and I desire to read a somewhat extensive extract from the discussion in the Board of Estimate and Apportionment, and from the record of the proceedings before the Board of Estimate and Apportionment prior to the award of that contract. It will be somewhat lengthy, and it is so near the closing time, and the conditions in this room are so unbearable, I suggest that we take a recess now at six minutes of four, rather than open up on that matter only for a few moments. Let me say, Mr. Chairman, and call the attention of the Committee to the fact, that I suppose that there are nearly seventy-five or a hundred men sitting in this very cramped room which, so far as I can perceive, has apparently no external ventilation whatever. The only ventilation I can see is the transom that opens in a narrow hall.

Acting Chairman Burr.— I think, Mr. Colby, we will be out of here before Monday.

Mr. Colby.— It is an atmosphere in which I cannot exist with any feeling of —

Mr. Hedley.— I know it would never pass the inspection of the Health Department.

Mr. Colby.— And I think this Committee should really, in justice to itself, to say nothing of witnesses or counsel, who are entitled to no consideration, get some more livable quarters.

Acting Chairman Burr.— We will have better quarters. We are not to be here long. How long a recess do you want?

Mr. Colby.— I suggest we adjourn for the day.

Acting Chairman Burr.— Until to-morrow morning at 11 o'clock.

Whereupon, at 3:54 o'clock P. M., the Committee adjourned to meet February 4, 1916, 11 o'clock A M.

FEBRUARY 4, 1916

NEW YORK COUNTY LAWYERS' ASSOCIATION BOARD ROOM,
165 BROADWAY, NEW YORK CITY

The Committee was called to order pursuant to adjournment, Chairman Thompson presiding.

Quorum present.

Mr. Colby.— I would like to have Mr. Fisher take the stand a moment.

HORACE M. FISHER, being recalled for further examination, testified as follows:

By Mr. Colby:

Q. Mr. Fisher, you have been examined, I believe, before, have you? A. Yes, sir.

Q. Are you the Secretary of the Interborough Rapid Transit Company? A. Yes, sir.

Q. Are you an officer of the Interborough Consolidated Company? A. Yes, sir.

Q. What office? A. Secretary.

Q. Are you secretary of any other of the New York transit lines? A. Yes, sir, the Rapid Transit Subway Construction, New York & Queens, and the Subway Realty Company.

Q. Is that a complete list? A. You are referring to the Interborough System?

Q. The Interborough or the New York Railways. A. And the New York Railways.

Q. That is a complete list, is it? A. Yes, sir, except some of the subsidiary lines of the New York Railways system, which are included in the New York Railways.

Q. How many of such subsidiary lines do you occupy a position as officer with? A. Probably three or four.

Q. Do you hold any other office in the traction system of New York? A. No, sir.

Q. Are you a director in any of these companies? A. Yes, sir, in the Interborough and the Interborough Consolidated.

Q. As secretary of the Interborough Rapid Transit Company and of these other companies, are you the custodian of the minute books of the boards of directors? A. Yes, sir.

Mr. Colby.— At a former hearing, Mr. Chairman, the statement was made by you that you desired the minute books of the Interborough Rapid Transit Company.

Chairman Thompson.— Mr. Fisher had them here once before. and I think he will produce them.

Mr. Fisher.— I will bring them down again, if you desire.

Q. What we wish are the minute books from the date of the Public Service Commission, which was July 1, 1907? A. Yes. sir.

(Witness excused to secure the books requested.)

(An elastic recess was taken pending the production of the books.)

AFTER RECESS

Examination by Mr. Colby (resumed):

Q. Mr. Fisher, you produced the books containing minutes of the meetings of the board of directors of the Interborough Rapid Transit Company from 1907 to date? A. Yes, sir.

Q. And they are here? A. Yes, sir.

Chairman Thompson.— That also includes the meetings of the executive board?

Mr. Fisher.— Yes, sir.

Chairman Thompson.— And whatever special meetings may have been held?

Mr. Fisher.— Yes, sir.

Q. Have you been secretary of the company for the period covered by these books? A. Yes, sir.

Q. You have personally recorded the proceedings of the board of directors; in other words, have yourself kept the books? A. Yes, sir.

Q. Are these minute books indexed? A. Yes, sir.

Q. So you can readily refer to the dates and the records by topic? A. Yes, sir.

Q. Indexed under the names of directors? A. Indexed under the names, subjects, and cross-indexed. At least they are supposed to be.

Q. Do they contain a record of all extras, awards, bonuses and gratuities voted by the board to any members of the board or to the officers of the company? A. They do.

Q. Is that subject indexed? A. Yes, sir.

Q. Under what heading? A. That depends on the subject. If it is for extra services probably indexed under services, and might be indexed under name also, and if bonus probably under bonus.

Chairman Thompson.— Have you anything under commitments?

Mr. Fisher.— Not that I recollect.

Q. Will you let me see the index under bonus? A. What year, sir?

Q. Well, I will take the year 1913.

(Witness produces book and opens to the index.)

Q. I see nothing about bonus there. A. I guess there were no bonuses then.

Q. In 1913? A. No, sir.

Q. Extra compensation, is that an index heading? A. It probably would be under services.

Q. I see two entries under services. Will you please state what they are? A. Services of Richard Reid Rogers.

Q. How do you spell Reid? A. R-e-i-d.

Q. Read the full entry there. A. I am getting to that. Payment of $50,000 for extra compensation in connection with subway and elevated extensions and financing. The second entry, services of Theodore P. Shonts, President. Committee appointed regarding extra compensation in connection with subway and elevated extensions and financing.

Chairman Thompson.— How much is that?

Mr. Fisher.— The index does not give it.

Q. What is the page of the latter entry? A. 133 and 150.

Q. You have referred me to the minutes of a regular meeting of the board of directors of the Interborough Rapid Transit Company held at the company's offices on May 14, 1913; there seems to have been, and I will read from the minute book into the record the following members of the board in attendance at the meeting: Edward J. Berwynd, H. M. Fisher, Andrew Freedman, W. Leon Pepperman, William A. Read, F. De C. Sullivan, Cornelius Vanderbilt, George W. Young. Mr. Edward J. Berwynd in the chair. It appears that the president of the company did not preside, nor was he present. Although this is a regular meeting, the only business which according to the record was transacted was the passage of a resolution approving the minutes of the regular meeting of the executive committee held May 7, 1913, and the regular meeting of the board held on the same day. Then follows the following resolution, which I now read into the record: " In view of the extra and successful services rendered by the president in connection with the financial needs of the company and the negotiations recently concluded with the city for new subway and elevated extensions, extending over a period of about four years, it was, on motion duly seconded, resolved that a committee of three members of the board, consisting of Messrs. Edward J. Berwynd, Andrew Freedman and Cornelius Vanderbilt, be, and they hereby are, appointed to consider said extra services and report back to the board." I note that upon the minutes of the board there appears to have been no mover of this resolution, nor any record of a seconder, nor any record of any discussion; do you know who offered that resolution? A. No, sir, I don't.

Q. Was it customary to note the name of a proposer of a resolution? A. It is not customary.

Chairman Thompson.— Why not?

Mr. Fisher.— No special reason for it and no necessity for it.

Chairman Thompson.— Don't you think there would be a good necessity to know in this case who proposed that resolution?

Mr. Fisher.— I don't think so.

Q. Then following the resolution is the statement: " There being no further business, on motion, duly seconded, the meeting adjourned," and the minutes bear your signature, do they not, Mr. Fisher ? A. Correct.

Q. So that appears to have been the only subject taken up and discussed or considered at that regular meeting of the board ? A. Yes, sir.

Q. Now, I notice that the Committee, consisting of Messrs. Berwynd, Freedman and Vanderbilt, were appointed to not only consider said extra services but to report back to the board. Did they report back to the board ? A. They did, yes, sir.

Q. And would their report be found at a subsequent meeting here referred to on the index under services, referred to at page 150 ? A. I presume so.

Chairman Thompson.— Haven't you any recollection who offered that resolution ?

Mr. Fisher.—No, sir.

Chairman Thompson.— Was the resolution already prepared when the meeting commenced ?

Mr. Fisher.— It was not.

Chairman Thompson.— Who wrote it ?

Mr. Fisher.— I did.

Chairman Thompson.— Who told you to write it ?

Mr. Fisher.— I wrote it, following my duty as secretary.

Chairman Thompson.— Did you offer it ?

Mr. Fisher.— I did not.

Chairman Thompson.— Did you write it before the meeting commenced or afterwards ?

Mr. Fisher.— Afterwards.

Chairman Thompson.— Don't you remember who asked you to write it ?

Mr. Fisher.— No one asked me to write it.

Chairman Thompson.— It was an action taken by the board, and the subject appears on the minutes; wasn't there a slip of paper offered with this resolution on ?

Mr. Fisher.— No, sir.

Chairman Thompson.— Somebody said it and you wrote it in the books?

Mr. Fisher.— The resolution is stated, and that is the subject by some one, and moved and passed. I did not use the exact wording perhaps.

Chairman Thompson.— There is no written slip or paper accompanying the resolution?

Mr. Fisher.— I couldn't say. I usually write the main part of the resolution on my calendar.

Chairman Thompson.— Written out after the man offered it, whoever he was?

Mr. Fisher.— Yes, sir.

Chairman Thompson.— You don't recollect who he was?

Mr. Fisher.— No, sir.

Chairman Thompson.— What is your best recollection on the subject, as to who it was?

Mr. Fisher.— I have none at all.

Examination by Mr. Colby, resumed:

Q. I call your attention to the record of a special meeting of the board of directors appearing at page 150 of the minute-book of the year 1913. Is the record appearing on that page and the following page, 151, the official minutes of the meeting of the board of directors held on the day mentioned, June 4, 1913? A. Yes, sir.

Q. You were present at the meeting? A. Yes, sir.

Q. Did you act as a secretary? A. Yes, sir.

Q. You kept and transcribed the minutes? A. Yes, sir.

Q. That is your signature thereto as secretary? A. Yes, sir.

Mr. Colby.— The minutes to which the Committee's attention is called appear to be the minutes of a special meeting of the board of directors of the Interborough Rapid Transit Company held at the company's offices in New York, Wednesday, June 4, 1913, pursuant to notice given in accordance with the by-laws. I read from the official minutes and request that what I read be noted in the record.

Chairman Thompson.— Take it.

Mr. Colby.— There were present at this meeting Mr. Edward J. Berwynd, Andrew Freedman, H. M. Fisher, W. Leon Pepperman, William A. Read, F. De C. Sullivan, Cornelius Vanderbilt and George W. Young. Mr. Edward J. Berwynd was in the chair. I now read verbatim from the minute book: " The chairman submitted a report of the special committee appointed by the board of directors on May 14, 1913, to consider the extra services rendered by the president dated June 4, 1913, and after discussion it was decided that whereas Theodore P. Shonts in negotiating and securing for the company the contract for the extension of its subway system recently made with the City of New York and in connection with arranging for the financing of such contract has rendered services of an extraordinary character and of great value to the company, in the judgment of this board such services in the interest of efficient administration, should be properly recognized by an increase in salary or otherwise; whereupon, it was, on motion, duly seconded, resolved that in recognition of and in compensation for the extraordinary and efficient services rendered by Theodore P. Shonts, as aforesaid, he be paid the sum of $125,000. There being no further business, on motion the meeting adjourned."

Q. That resolution was passed? A. Yes, sir.

Q. I see no one's name mentioned as the proposer of the resolution or a seconder; do you recall the name of a proposer or seconder? A. No, sir.

Q. Do you recall whether the resolution was the subject of any discussion? A. I do not at this time.

Q. Where is the report which the Committee appointed by the board at this special meeting of May 14th delivered? A. Their report was a verbal one and their conclusions are incorporated in those minutes.

Q. They made no report except a verbal report? A. No, sir.

Q. Do you recall who made the verbal report? A. Will you read the names of those present, please?

Q. Berwynd, Freedman, Fisher, Pepperman, Read, Sullivan, Vanderbilt and Young. A I think the report was made by Mr. Berwind.

Q. Do you recall what he said? A. No, sir, I don't, except in a general line with what the resolution says.

Q. Did he state what the extraordinary character of the services rendered by the president of the company was? A. He might have. I don't recollect.

Q. Would you say there was any such statement of the extraordinary services rendered by the president made? A. I wouldn't say there was or was not.

Chairman Thompson.—The question is, not what you would say, but what is the fact about it?

Mr. Fisher.— That is the reason I won't make a statement, because I don't remember the facts.

Chairman Thompson.— Do you know the fact, or don't you recollect it, is what we want?

Mr. Fisher.— I have said I don't recollect there of any particular discussion. There was a discussion, but it was very general.

Q. Was it also very brief? A. Reasonably so.

Q. How long was taken at the board meeting in the making of this report, its receipt and consideration and the proposal and adoption of this resolution? A. Probably half an hour.

Q. I notice that there is a rather unusual notation on the first page of the minutes of this meeting, of this special meeting of June 4, 1913; the word "approved" is contained in the minutes opposite the enumeration of the directors present. A. Yes, sir.

Q. And underneath appear to be the autographic signatures of two men; what are those names? A. August Belmont and Gardiner M. Lane.

Q. What is the meaning of that entry? A. They asked to be permitted to approve of the minutes, because they couldn't be present at the meeting.

Q. You say they asked to be allowed to approve the minutes? A. Yes, sir.

Q. How do you know that; did they ask you? A. They asked me to be permitted to approve the minutes. You can put it in the nature of a request, if you wish, that is practically what it was.

Q. You mean you requested them to approve the minutes? A. No, sir.

Q. Was it suggested to you that you get their approval? A. No, sir.

Q. Tell me about that; that is quite unusual; does it occur at any other point in your minute book? A. Yes, sir; in quite a number of instances.

Q. Similar to this? A. Not on similar subjects.

Q. Explain that; it strikes me as interesting. A. They simply asked at a subsequent meeting what action was taken at that meeting. As I recollect it now, the subject came up when the minutes were read, and they simply asked to be permitted to approve those minutes, and I brought them the original minutes and they approved them in that shape.

Q. I turn to the next meeting, to the minutes of the next meeting; at the next regular meeting of the board, I do not see anything in the minutes to the effect that the minutes of this special meeting at which the extra compensation was voted to Mr. Shonts, were even read. A. Let me see the minutes.

Q. Furthermore, it does not seem that Mr. Lane was even present at the next regular meeting.

(Mr. Colby hands minutes to the witness.)

A. You are right; that was an oversight.

Q. Can you find any subsequent minutes or the minutes of any subsequent meeting in which there is any record of the minutes of this special meeting ever having been read or discussed or alluded to? A. These minutes were read at the following meeting, and these minutes should have read " Minutes of the regular meeting and of the special meeting were read and approved." Through some oversight the minutes of the special meeting were left out.

Chairman Thompson.— That is the time Mr. Belmont and Mr. Lane came to you and asked to have their approval noted?

Mr. Fisher.— I cannot say whether that time or subsequently.

Chairman Thompson.— I thought you said a little while ago it was at the time the minutes were read at a subsequent meeting they asked to put their names in there.

Mr. Fisher.— That is what I thought.

Chairman Thompson.— You said the minutes were read at the next meeting?

Mr. Fisher.— Yes, sir; they were.

Chairman Thompson.— You said at the time the minutes were read the men came to you and asked to approve the previous minutes. Mr. Fisher, was Mr. Belmont present at the subsequent meeting?

Chairman Thompson.— Can you answer the question, without referring to the minutes; Mr. Belmont was not present at the meeting when you say the minutes were read, and neither was Mr. Lane.

Mr. Fisher.— Probably they brought it up at some subsequent meeting.

Chairman Thompson.— Do you want to convey to the Committee that Mr. Belmont and Mr. Lane were overjoyed when they heard Mr. Shonts had a bonus of $125,000, and they wanted to put their names on the books?

Mr. Fisher.— No, sir. They heard the minutes read and asked to approve of the minutes.

Chairman Thompson.— Weren't they asked to approve the minutes?

Mr. Fisher.—No, sir.

Chairman Thompson.— If your memory would only carry an average load we would get along all right.

Mr. Fisher.— I think it carries sufficiently for my purposes.

Chairman Thompson.— I think it peaks sometimes.

Mr. Quackenbush.— That remark is hardly warrantable.

8

Chairman Thompson.— I won't take it back. I think Mr. Fisher remembers more than he voices.

Chairman Thompson.— You do not have many meetings where you vote a man $125,000 extra, do you?

Mr. Fisher.— That meeting is not much different than others.

Chairman Thompson.— If you had a meeting every little while where you voted $125,000 out of the company I would not be surprised you did not remember it.

Mr. Fisher.— I do not remember the particular time they came and requested to approve the minutes. I do recollect the circumstance they asked to approve them, and they were not requested to do it.

Q. I call you attention to the minutes of the subsequent regular meeting of the board, and among the names of the directors there present I do not see the name of Mr. Lane mentioned there as present at all. A. It is not there.

Q. So Mr. Lane was not present at the next regular meeting of the board, nor in fact was he present at the special meeting at which the extra compensation was voted? A. No, sir, and your chairman stated Mr. Belmont was not present, and the minutes show he was.

Q. I ask you this, why was a special meeting of the board of directors held in the afternoon of June 4, 1913, to consider only this question of extra compensation for the company's president when there was a regular meeting of the board held on the same day only a few hours previously, to wit, at 11 o'clock, at which it appears that Mr. August Belmont was present? A. As near as I can recollect, the Committee was not ready to report, and if my memory serves me right Mr. Berwind asked me to call the special meeting for the afternoon.

Q. Was the money paid to Mr. Shonts? A. I don't know.

Q. Who is the proper officer to ask that question of? A. The treasurer.

Mr. Colby.— Will you have the treasurer here so I can examine him at this session on that point?

Mr. Quackenbush.— Yes, sir.

Q. Was there any additional compensation ever voted to Mr. Shonts in connection with this subject? A. As near as I can recollect the intention was to vote him —

Q. Wait a minute; I asked you a question, was any additional compensation on this subject, namely, this extraordinary services in connection with the negotiations of the subway and elevated contracts with the city, was any additional compensation under this heading ever voted to Mr. Shonts? A. I think there was $25,000.

Q. At what date was that done? A. I couldn't tell you. The minute books will show.

Q. Was it subsequent to this action of 1913? A. I couldn't say whether before or after.

Q. Will you look at the succeeding minute book; I see no other entry opposite Mr. Shonts' name in reference to services in the year 1913 book, except the two entries we have just had reference to? A. Yes, sir, I will examine the record. The last resolution, bottom of page 113.

Mr. Colby.— The witness produces the minute book of the year 1914 and opens the same to the minutes of a regular meeting of the board of the Interborough Rapid Transit Company held on April 22, 1914, and calls attention to the following resolution appearing at page 113 of the 1914 minutes: I read verbatim from the minutes, and ask that the following be noted on the Committee's record: " The chairman brought up the subject of the report and the oral recommendation of the special committee that Mr. Theodore P. Shonts be allowed $150,000 for special services rendered in connection with the subway and elevated contracts, and on motion, duly seconded, it was resolved that Mr. Theodore P. Shonts be paid $25,000 additional in conformance with the oral recommendation of the special committee appointed by the board of directors on May 14, 1913, to consider the value of the extraordinary services rendered by Mr. Shonts in connection with the negotiations and securing for the company the contracts for the extension of its subway system and elevated lines. Mr. Shonts did not vote on above resolution."

Q. I ask you as the secretary of the company if the resolution I have just read from the minutes of the regular meeting held on April 22, 1914, was passed by the board? A. It was.

Q. At the meeting on that date? A. Yes, sir.

Q. There appear to have been present the following directors at this meeting: " Mr. Edward R. Bacon, Mr. August Belmont, Mr. H. M. Fisher, Mr. Andrew Friedman, Edwin S. Marston, W. Leon Pepperman, Theodore P. Shonts, F. De C. Sullivan, Cornelius Vanderbilt; Mr. Belmont in the chair."

Q. I call your attention to a discrepancy between the record of the meeting of May 14, 1913, and this record that I have just read. It now appears that the special committee of the board to recommend for the board's guidance on the subject of an additional allowance to Mr. Shonts recommended $150,000, and the entry in the minutes of 1913 stated that the board recommended $125,000; I am right, am I not? A. Yes, sir.

Q. Do you mean to say that your minutes of the former meeting were incorrect? A. As I recollect the circumstances, it was contended by someone, and I think it was Mr. Friedman, that the extra compensation voted at the previous meeting was not sufficient and it should be made more. I think —

Q. Will you allow me to interrupt you? A. Certainly.

Q. You say Mr. Friedman, the late Mr. Friedman, brought the subject up, as you testified? A. Yes, sir.

Q. When did he do that? A. At the meeting.

Q. At this meeting on April 22, 1914? A. The second meeting, yes, sir.

Q. This meeting that I am reading from? A. Yes, sir.

Q. What did he say? A. As near as I can recollect, he said that he thought he should be voted a sum of $200,000 or $225,000.

Q. Instead of $125,000? A. Yes, sir, instead of $125,000, and following the general discussion the board decided to vote him $25,000 additional.

Q. On Mr. Friedman's suggestion? A. Yes, sir.

Q. Did Mr. Friedman say the special committee had had a further meeting? A. He did not make any mention of that fact.

Q. Mr. Friedman was only one of the three members of this special committee? A. Yes, sir.

Q. The other members were Mr. Berwind, and Mr. Vanderbilt; did he say he had conferred with his colleagues on this special committee? A. I think he did say he did.

Q. There was no further report of the committee as such? A. No, sir.

Q. Mr. Friedman was not the chairman of this special committee? A. No, sir.

Q. Mr. Friedman did not make the original report in favor of the $125,000, did he? A. I don't think he did.

Chairman Thompson.— I am sorry I criticised you before, but that is the way I like to have your questions answered. I think you mean to be fair, and I do not mean to be unduly harsh about the thing at all, and I know you mean to tell us all the facts about it.

Mr. Fisher.—I do, certainly.

Mr. Quackenbush.— I am glad you said that, Senator. I think you have said the handsome thing. I thought you were mistaken in what you said before.

Q. Did Mr. Friedman offer the resolution as to the additional $25,000 compensation at the 1914 meeting? A. I think I could safely say he did in that case.

Q. I notice another discrepancy between the resolution passed at the 1913 meeting and this resolution at the 1914 meeting; there is no mention in the latter resolution of any extraordinary services by Mr. Shonts, but only of special services? A. Inasmuch as I wrote both the resolutions, I had in mind I had already stated that in the previous resolution.

Q. There is also no mention in the latter resolution of anything except the subway and elevated contracts as to services? A. That may be so. That same reply would apply there.

Q. At the earlier meeting there was also an allusion to extraordinary services in connection with the subway and elevated contracts, but also a reference to his extraordinary services in connection with the financing of said contracts? A. I endeavored to make the resolution cover all the points which arose in the discussion at the meeting, at the first and second meetings both, and having stated it at the first resolution I did not think it necessary in the second.

Q. In other words, the discussion that preceded the passage of the second resolution at the latter meeting referred only to his

service in the subway and elevated contracts, and your form of
resolution made no further reference, is that correct? A. No, sir,
I wouldn't say that was exactly correct. The first resolution covered, as I stated, all the discussion, and the second resolution was
made shorter, simply intended to cover points probably not covered
by the first, but the two resolutions should be taken together and
read as one.

Q. And the amount was not so big? A. The amount should be
read as one. If you do that you get the correct facts.

Q. How do you account for what I consider to be a material
discrepancy, that the report of the special committee made to this
special meeting of the board held after the committee's appointment for the purpose of receiving the report which the committee
was directed to make to the full board recommended only $125,000
while here you speak of the report as being for the payment of
$150,000; Mr. Friedman's suggestion could not alter the fact the
committee had already reported in favor of $125,000, could it?
A. No, sir.

Q. And if the committee had reported in favor of paying Mr.
Shonts $125,000 as an extra bonus or extra compensation they had
not also reported in favor of paying him $150,000, had they? A.
in writing the second resolution, after the second discussion I
gained the impression from the discussion it was their intention
to pay him $150,000 instead of $125,000, and I wrote the resolution accordingly.

Q. Although the report of the prior meeting was acted upon and
no further report of the committee had been made, you recited in
the minutes of the latter meeting the committee had in effect reported in favor of $150,000? A. Yes, sir, that is the impression
I had gained and tried to convey by the resolution.

Q. That awakens in my mind a very earnest train of thought,
because I should hate to believe that your minutes were kept in
that very temperamental manner; in other words the committee
made a report to one effect or didn't, and if the acts of the special
committees of the board or of its officers are to be recorded, not in
the form in which those acts were performed, or their recommendations made, but in the form in which your mind thought they
probably intended to act or intended the recommendations to be

made, it casts a serious imputation upon this minute book and
upon this whole series of minutes; therefore I return to the question and ask you to answer me in the affirmative or negative
whether this special committee appointed by the board in 1913
ever made a report that Mr. Shonts should be allowed $150,000?
A. The report —

Q. I ask you to answer in the affirmative or negative? A. Yes,
sir, they did.

Q. When did they make that report? A. At the second meeting.

Q. You mean in 1913? A. 1914.

Q. But Mr. Berwind, the chairman of this special committee,
was not present at the special meeting on April 22, 1914? A. That
may be so.

Q. I ask you to look at the record of those present and tell me
if Mr. Berwind, the chairman of this special committee, was
present at the 1914 meeting? A. He was not.

Q. Do you wish to qualify the answer you just made to the
effect the committee made a report? A. I do not.

Q. Who made a report? A. I think I have already answered
that question, Mr. Friedman, the second time.

Q. You did not say Mr. Friedman made a report? A. That
is what I meant, if I didn't say it.

Q. You said there was some informal discussion and Mr. Friedman expressed his opinion Mr. Shonts should have received a
greater compensation than voted to him in 1913? A. And he
suggested that be put down as a report of the committee, I think.
I think that committee had some informal meeting of which no
record was taken.

Q. What basis have you for that assertion? A. Only I saw
them come in and meet, and I judge they met on that subject.
I was not present.

Q. You don't know of any formal or informal meeting? A.
No, sir, not myself.

Q. Mr. Friedman said he thought he should receive $200,000
or $225,000, and he presumably expressed his opinion at a meet-
ing of this committee? A. I presume so.

Q. But the committee apparently were not influenced by his
opinion, or at least were not willing to adopt it? A. I don't know.

Q. Wasn't that apparent, from the fact they refused to recommend $200,000 or $225,000? A. He might not have made that suggestion at that time.

Q. He said later he had the belief he should receive a sum at least as large as $200,000, did he not? A. Yes, sir, at the second meeting.

Q. Mr. Friedman, Mr. Cornelius Vanderbilt and Mr. Berwind were members of this special committee? A. Yes, sir.

Q. And they recommended $125,000 to Mr. Shonts? A. At the first meeting, yes, sir.

Q. And you know of no subsequent meetings held of the committee? A. I don't know of any meetings held by the committee.

Q. The chairman of the committee was not present at the second meeting? A. No, sir, he was not.

Q. And the only member who addressed the board on the question at all that you heard was the late Mr. Friedman? A. He made the suggestion, according to my recollection.

Q. How long does a special committee exist? A. It usually runs out at the end of the year, unless otherwise stated in the minutes.

Q. That is a special standing committee, you mean? A. Yes, sir, or —

Q. I mean this, how long does a special committee appointed at a regular meeting of the board to report at a subsequent meeting, how long does that committee exist? A. Until the purpose for which they have been appointed has been disposed of, unless sooner discharged.

Q. So this committee appointed by the board to consider the question of extra compensation and report, you would assume expired the moment its function was performed and the moment its report was made? A. I would assume so, but evidently it was not.

Q. That is the practice of your company? A. Yes, sir, that is the practice.

Q. Otherwise you would accumulate a number of superfluous and dead committees? A. That is the practice of our company.

Q. It would be hard if that was not the practice for you to enumerate the special committees of your board? A. That is the practice of our company.

Q. What salary was Mr. Shonts as president receiving in 1912?
A. I don't know; I couldn't say.

Q. Who knows that? A. The treasurer.

Q. I would like to have you step aside and allow the treasurer to take the stand for a few moments to make my record complete. A. Yes, sir.

Mr. Quackenbush.— He is not here yet, but he can be called immediately, if you wish. He will be right here. I have called him.

Q. These are indexed under extra services, are they not; not services but extra services? A. They might be indexed several ways. I do not index them.

Q. The reason I ask you is because I do not see the entries of April 22, 1914, referred to in the index under the subject of services. A. I noticed that same thing, and it was indexed under the name of Mr. Shonts, you will see, but not under services, for some reason.

Q. So if I were to examine this book to see what allowances were made by way of extra recompense to other officers, I might have to look under the names of different officers? A. You might have, or under the head of extra services, or services for honorarium.

Q. The allowance to the president by way of extra compensation was not the only allowance made under that heading, was it? A. It was not; no, sir.

Q. While we are waiting for the treasurer, let me ask you a question or two; tell me what other officers received at any time within your recollection honorarium or extra allowance for special services? A. Mr. Rogers, whom you already know of, and Mr. Gaynor, the auditor.

Q. What is his full name? A. E. F. J. Gaynor.

Q. Do you recall any others? A. No, sir, I do not. I think those are all.

Chairman Thompson.— How much did Gaynor get?

Mr. Fisher.— Ten thousand dollars.

Chairman Thompson.— They forgot the secretary, didn't they?

Mr. Fisher.— Yes, sir.

Q. You have produced the minute book for the year 1913, and there appears under the heading of services in the index a payment of $50,000 to R. R. Rogers for extra services in connection with subway and elevated extensions, and so forth? A. Yes, sir.

Q. Do you recall a resolution authorizing such payment was authorized by a meeting of the board held in 1913? A. I am not positive, without looking at the minutes.

Q. The index refers to page 214, and I hand you the minute book and ask you to refer to page 214. A. Yes, sir.

Mr. Colby.— I read from the minutes of the meeting, of the regular meeting of the board held on September 17, 1913, the following resolution: " The president stated that all legal matters in and about the contracts for the construction and the equipment of the new subways and elevated lines with the city of New York prior to March 19th had been conducted by Mr. Richard Reid Rogers, counsel for the company; that the work was long continued and exacting and had been performed in conjunction with his other duties in a highly satisfactory manner and without the employment of associate counsel, thus resulting in a large saving to the company. He laid before the board the consideration of an amount to be allowed Mr. Rogers for his extra services in connection with said contracts, whereupon, upon motion duly made and seconded, it was resolved, that the sum of $50,000 be paid Mr. Rogers for his services in connection with the contract for the construction and equipment of the new subways and elevated lines, the same to be charged to the proper construction account."

Q. Was that resolution as recited in the minutes passed? A. Yes, sir.

Q. You were present as secretary? A. Yes, sir.

Q. You drew the entries? A. Yes, sir.

Q. I have read it correctly? A. Yes, sir.

Chairman Thompson.— Did you have an improper construction account?

Mr. Fisher.— No, sir, but we have a number of construction accounts. In charging to the proper account it would be charged to the proper construction account.

Q. How many construction accounts have you? A. I do not know. You will have to call the auditor for that.

Q. How do you know you have a number? A. I imagine so, because we have a number of pieces of work.

Q. Each piece of work has a construction account? A. I imagine that is the way he keeps his books. I couldn't tell you.

Q. Do you mean one for the excavation? A. No, sir, one for elevated improvements and one for subway construction, and probably one for equipment, and that wouldn't be construction.

Q. Under what heading would you think extra legal services most easily fell, subway construction, elevated or equipment? A. Probably one or both. I left that to his discretion, as you see by the minutes. He knew more about it than I did.

Q. Do you know whether these amounts were actually paid or not? A. No, sir, I don't.

Q. Where does the Gaynor allowance appear? A. I think in the 1912 minutes.

Q. You do not know to what account the allowances to the president of the company were charged? A. No, sir, you will have to ask the auditor.

Q. Probably some construction account? A. I could not tell you and I wouldn't want to hazard a guess.

Chairman Thompson.—All witnesses may be excused until 2:30 o'clock, and the witnesses subpoenaed for 2 o'clock are directed to appear at 2:30.

JOHN H. CAMPBELL, being first duly sworn, testified as follows:

Examined by Mr. Colby:

Q. Mr. Campbell, where do you reside? A. 118 East Seventy-eighth street, New York city.

Q. You have stated your full name to the stenographer? A. Yes, sir.

Q. Are you the treasurer of the Interborough Rapid Transit Company? A. Yes, sir.

Q. And of any other companies engaged in the transportation field in New York? A. Yes, sir.

Q. Which other companies? A. Interborough Consolidated, New York Railways, New York & Queens Company, Thirty-fourth Street, Central Crosstown, 145th Street, and two or three others.

Q. As treasurer of the Interborough, you are the disbursing officer, at least you know of the actual disbursements made by the company? A. Yes, sir.

Q. You are in immediate charge of its bank accounts and of its funds? A. Yes, sir.

Q. Testimony has been given this morning by the secretary of the company of certain resolutions passed at the meetings of the board of directors held in 1913 and 1914 awarding the president of the company in recognition of extraordinary services in connection with the subway and elevated contracts additional compensation? A. Yes, sir.

Q. In one instance the sum of $125,000 was voted to him? A. Yes, sir.

Q. And a little later, there being a feeling that that sum was insufficient, an addition was made to it of $25,000 and a special resolution passed? A. Yes, sir.

Q. Will you tell me if the amounts I have mentioned were actually paid to Mr. Shonts? A. I have sent for the vouchers. They are up in the voucher room, and I expect to have them down in a few minutes.

Q. Do your records of disbursements show the moneys were sent to him? A. Yes, sir.

Q. In all $150,000? A. I am not positive about the $150,000. I have so much to take care of I do not want to swear positively until I see the vouchers.

Q. You have your double record? A. Yes, sir, I have a cash book.

Q. And what you refer to as a voucher is a sort of confirmatory bit of evidence showing the receipt? A. No, sir, it is the finality. It shows the receipt and what appropriated for, and if directed by a resolution, the resolution is attached. The cash book shows I charged it and the vouchers show who got it.

Chairman Thompson.— You always paid out everything charged?

Mr. Campbell.—Absolutely everything.

Q. Your own books of expenditures show that you remitted or paid to Mr. Shonts in obedience to a resolution $125,000 upon one occasion and later $25,000? A. That is my recollection, but I would have to bring the cash books down and show you.

Q. What was Mr. Shonts' salary in 1912? A. $75,000 in 1912.

Q. What was his salary in 1913? A. $100,000; I think the change came in August, 1912.

Q. His salary since then has been at the rate of $100,000? A. Yes, sir. This is a voucher connected with another, and Mr. Quackenbush asked me to take it down, in reference to Mr. Rogers.

Q. Are you ready to testify as to the $50,000 to Mr. Rogers? A. Yes, sir.

Chairman Thompson.— We will by unanimous consent take a recess until 2:30.

Mr. Colby.— I ask to have these books left here for examination during the recess, and a representative of the Interborough can remain with them if desired.

Mr. Quackenbush.— It seems to me there is a question of propriety for the Legislature of this State to consider, as to whether Mr. Colby or any of the accountants are to have access to our books to go through them generally. We have nothing to conceal from this Committee and anything, as I have said, will be produced by our officers so far as I have any control over them, but I do protest against Mr. Dawson having the right to roam at pleasure through our books.

Mr. Colby.— Mr. Dawson was associated with Mr. Justice Hughes throughout the insurance inquiry, and Mr. Dawson knows perfectly well what he wants, and the limits of his instructions and my requests, and I distinctly repudiate the intimation here that there is any interest actuating Mr. Dawson's request for access to those books except to develop just such data as produced this morning and were produced by Mr. Dawson as the result of a very few moments' survey.

Mr. Quackenbush.— Mr. Dawson came and said he wanted the information about salaries, and I told the secretary to get them and he got them. and there wasn't any inquisitorial work of Mr. Dawson needed, and I do not want him examining them generally, or Mr. Colby either, and let us get this understood.

Chairman Thompson.— Of course I know you would be glad to have me go through the books, but so many things people are evidently glad to have me do, and the limitations of humanity are such I cannot do them all. I do not want Mr. Dawson roaming through your books generally, but that is the same attitude that has been taken by the secretary of the Public Service Commission time and time again. If we could ask specifically for certain information we always got it, but we got nothing more, and an investigating committee, if it knew what the information was exactly would not have any office to perform. We have got to investigate into these particular subjects. I want Mr. Dawson to have the opportunity, or some one that I have confidence in, and I have in him, and I think you have, to find out by actual original inspection from us what bonuses there are, and not putting us in a position of saying to the secretary whatever you throw open that is all we can see.

Mr. Quackenbush.— I get your point exactly. I do not question your right at any time. I am talking about propriety.

Chairman Thompson.— I guarantee there won't be any information taken except upon a subject proper to our inquiry, and it will not be done, and whenever and wherever the books are looked into by Mr. Dawson you should have a representative of your company present and any time that representative thinks Mr. Dawson is looking for something outside of this inquiry, close the books and come back to this Committee with it and we will take it up.

Mr. Quackenbush.— That is satisfactory.

Chairman Thompson.— We will now take a recess until 2:30 o'clock P. M.

Whereupon, at 1:15 o'clock P. M., a recess was taken until 2:30 o'clock P. M.

AFTERNOON SESSION.

The Committee was called to order by Chairman Thompson at 3:20 P. M.

Mr. Colby.— Is Mr. Nelson here?

(No response.)

Mr. Colby.— Is Mr. Mason of the Gillespie Company here?

Senator Thompson.— Is there any one here representing the company?

(No response.)

Mr. Colby.— Mr. Campbell, will you take the stand?

JOHN H. CAMPBELL, recalled.

Chairman Thompson.— I want to make this statement on the record. Mr. Gillespie — a subpoena was issued for him. Mr. Gillespie, it appears, left town within a few days. Mr. Mason, the clerk or secretary, or somebody, was subpoenaed at 2 o'clock. He had an attorney here to represent him, saying that some lawyer they wanted to consult had left town, and they wanted until Monday. We declined to give until Monday, so then since recess they said that we could have access to the books. It then turned out that they had given us access to a part of the books and not all of the books. We are now waiting to see whether they will arrange it to have access to all the books. That is all there is in the Gillespie matter. The attorney is Mr. Gurath. I didn't know his name. So that's why I didn't mention it.

By Mr. Colby:

Q. Have you been supplied with the vouchers you wanted this morning? A. Yes, I have them.

Q. Will you let me have them? Thank you. A. I am sorry I kept you waiting a little while. I was waiting for those vouchers.

Chairman Thompson.— Don't worry about that.

Mr. Campbell.— I ain't worrying, but I only want to evade the impression that I was not trying to hurry; that is all.

Chairman Thompson.— Well, don't worry about that. If everybody else would be as nice as you are, I would recommend that all these people hire Mr. Quackenbush for a lawyer.

Mr. Campbell.— That is very good. I think he is deserving. Perhaps he will get an increase in salary.

Chairman Thompson.— I am going to look into that,

Mr. Campbell (to Mr. Quackenbush).— He says he is going to recommend it. I expect witness fees for this.

Mr. Colby.— I hope you don't meditate creating increased salaries faster than I can make a record of them.

Mr. Campbell.— That I don't premeditate what?

Mr. Colby.— I hope Mr. Hedley is not premeditating an increase of salaries faster than I can make a record of them.

Mr. Campbell.— He is entitled to more, if he can get it. He is worth it.

Mr. Colby.— That seems to be the impression of all the officers and employees of the Interborough, that they are sadly underpaid, and are entitled to a great deal more than they are receiving.

Mr. Campbell.— Well, you look them over and see.

Assemblyman Burr.— The greatest lot of boosters I ever heard of.

Chairman Thompson.— The investigation will now take another angle. Proceed, Mr. Colby.

Mr. Colby.— Mr. Campbell, the treasurer, produces, Mr. Chairman, canceled check of the Interborough Rapid Transit Company, dated June 5, 1913, for $125,000, to the order of T. P. Shonts, signed by J. H. Campbell, treasurer, and countersigned by W. Leon Pepperman, assistant to the president, the check being drawn upon the Guaranty Trust Company of New York, numbered 0406, bearing apparently the endorsement of T. P. Shonts, and no other endorsement, and not indicating —

Chairman Thompson.— All it needed, wasn't it?

Mr. Colby.— not indicating through what collecting bank or otherwise it had been paid. It apparently could have been paid only by presentation to the Guaranty Trust Comany of New York, and the payment by the Trust Company of cash to the payee.

Mr. Campbell.— I think the number on there, through the perforation, shows the Guaranty Trust Company's number, don't it?

By Mr. Colby:

Q. I will ask Mr. Campbell. How was that check collected?
A. How was that check collected?

Q. Yes. A. The voucher shows it was sent to Shonts, and he signed a voucher for it.

Q. How was the check itself put through? A. (Witness looking at perforation on check.) "Paid 6-5-13"—I think that was probably presented to the bank. There is no clearing house stamp on it. That is probably the —

Chairman Thompson.— " E ", it says.

Assemblyman Burr.— Paid June 6, 1915.

Chairman Thompson.—'13.

Assemblyman Burr.— 1913.

Mr. Colby.— I will ask that a copy of this check be taken as a part of the record.

Chairman Thompson.— Very well.

Copy of original check was supplied by Mr. Quackenbush, on a regular check form. Copy of check follows:

" $125,000.00   No. 0406.

INTERBOROUGH RAPID TRANSIT CO.

New York, June 5, 1913.

Pay to T. P. Shonts........................OR ORDER
One Hundred & Twenty Five Thousand and 0/100......Dollars

(Signed)   J. H. CAMPBELL,
                                          Treasurer.

Countersigned:
(Signed)   W. LEON PEPPERMAN,
                             Assistant to President.

To
    GUARANTY TRUST COMPANY OF NEW YORK,
          NEW YORK CITY."

(On the back of the check): " T. P. Shonts."
(Perforation as follows): " Paid x6-5 13 E."

Mr. Colby.— Mr. Campbell presents me, in connection with the check just described, one of the Interborough Rapid Transit Company's vouchers. It is voucher No. 116,894, dated June 5, 1913, the date of the check. It is endorsed — I mean, it is entitled, " To T. P. Shonts ", and under the heading of " distribution " I find these endorsements upon the voucher — under " distribution ": " Other suspense ", and second, " proposed subway routes." The contents of the voucher are as follows:

INTERBOROUGH RAPID TRANSIT COMPANY.

To   T. P. Shonts   Dr.

1913

June 5,   For services rendered. In accordance with
Resolution of the Board of Directors dated June
, 4th, 1913, certified copy of which is hereto attached $125,000 00

Examined and found correct,
    (Sgd)   E. F. J. Gaynor,"— is that?

Mr. Campbell.— That is the auditor, yes.

Mr. Colby.— " E. F. J. Gaynor, Auditor." There is a further notation. "Approved for Payment, (Sgd) W. Leon Pepperman, Assistant to President."

There follows a receipt for this sum of money reading — it is a part of the voucher, and reads as follows:

" NEW YORK, June 5th, 1913.
Received from the INTERBOROUGH RAPID TRANSIT CO. One Hundred Twenty-five Thousand and 00/100 Dollars, for payment in full of the above account."

This receipt is signed " T. P. Shonts."

Annexed to the voucher is a certificate by Mr. H. M. Fisher, the secretary of the Interborough Rapid Transit Company, in the usual form of the resolutions — or, I should say, singular, the resolution adopted by the board of directors on June 4, 1913, upon the coming in of the report of the " special committee appointed by the board of directors on May 14, 1913, to consider "— I am still reading — " the extra services rendered by the president."

I think this should go into the records of the Committee.

The certificate referred to is as follows:

" INTERBOROUGH RAPID TRANSIT COMPANY.

" Transcript from Minutes of Special

Meeting of the BOARD OF DIRECTORS held on Wednesday, June 4th, 1913, at 2:30 o'clock P. M.

" ' The Chairman submitted a report of the special committee appointed by the Board of Directors on May 14th, 1913, to consider the extra services rendered by the President, dated June 4th, 1913, and after discussion it was decided that;

" WHEREAS, Theodore P. Shonts, in negotiating and securing for the Company the contract for the extension of its subway system recently made with the City of New York, and in connection with arranging for the financing of such contract, has rendered services of an extraordinary character and of great value to the Company, and in the judgment of the Board such services, in the interests of efficient administration, should be properly recognized by an increase in salary or otherwise; whereupon, it was

" On Motion, duly seconded,

" RESOLVED: That in recognition of and in compensation for the extraordinary and efficient services rendered by Theodore P. Shonts as aforesaid, he be paid the sum of One Hundred and Twenty-five Thousand Dollars ($125,000).'

" I hereby certify that the above is a true copy of resolution from minutes of Special Meeting of the BOARD
(SEAL) OF DIRECTORS of the INTERBOROUGH RAPID TRANSIT COMPANY, held on Wednesday, June 4th, 1913, at 2:30 o'clock P. M.

(Signed) H. M. FISHER,
Secretary."

Mr. Colby.— Mr. Campbell, the company's treasurer, produces a further voucher, for $25,000, and also check of the company for $25,000, to the order of Theodore P. Shonts —

Chairman Thompson.— Now —

Mr. Colby.— which is referred to in the voucher.

Chairman Thompson.— In reference to allowing the stenographer to copy these in the record and get the originals back, what about — shall we trust the stenographer to take these? I am perfectly satisfied to trust her with them.

Mr. Campbell.— I want a receipt.

Mr. Quackenbush.— I will have a copy of them made for you on the forms, in the official way.

Chairman Thompson.— She will have to certify as to the minutes. He wants it copied and wants to get the original back.

Mr. Campbell.— Give me a receipt.

Mr. Quackenbush.—All right; if that is satisfactory. I thought we could make copies on these blanks, and things of that sort.

Chairman Thompson.—All right. That would be the better way, I think.

Mr. Colby.— Yes, and then compare them.

Mr. Campbell.— You will make a copy?

Mr. Quackenbush.— Yes.

Mr. Colby.—And compare them. You produce the originals where they can be produced.

Chairman Thompson.— Before we adjourn this afternoon?

Mr. Campbell.— Sure.

Mr. Quackenbush.— Yes.

Mr. Campbell (to Mr. Quackenbush).— Send your boy.

Mr. Colby.— The second check produced by the treasurer, Mr. Campbell, is as follows: It is dated April 22, 1914. It is drawn on the National Bank of Commerce in New York. No. 16,882. It reads as follows:

"New York, Apr. 22, 1914.

PAY Theodore P. Shonts.....................OR ORDER
Twenty five thousand 00/100...................DOLLARS

Signed "J. H. Campbell, Treasurer."   Countersigned "W. Leon Pepperman, Assistant to President."

It is endorsed: "Pay to Farmers Loan & Trust Company for deposit to credit of Theodore P. Shonts."

It contains the routine banking endorsements incident to the collection of the check, as follows:

Mr. Campbell.— Yes.

Mr. Colby.—"Pay the National City Bank of New York or order, the Farmers' Loan & Trust Company, Augustus V. Healy, vice-president and secretary."

Then the same obscure endorsement, "Received payment through the New York Clearing House," and the guarantee of prior endorsements by the National City Bank of New York.

Mr. Campbell.— Yes.

Mr. Colby.—Accompanying this check, Mr. Campbell, the treasurer of the company, hands me the company's voucher No. 127,001. It reads, "April 22, 1914. For special services rendered in connection with the negotiations and securing for the Company of the contracts for the extension of its subway system and elevated lines, in accordance with resolution of the Board of Directors of April 22, 1914, $25,000."

Appended to the voucher, and constituting a part of it, is a receipt under date of April 27, acknowledging by T. P. Shonts of the payment of $25,000 "in full of the above account."

The voucher bears the endorsements of Mr. E. J. F.

Mr. Campbell.— E. F. J.

Mr. Colby.—E. F. J. Gaynor, auditor, certifies the voucher is examined and found correct. And it is approved for payment by W. Leon Pepperman.

And there is annexed to the voucher the certified transcripts of the minutes of the regular meeting of the board held on April 22, 1914, the check and voucher being both dated on the date on which the meeting of the board was held and the payment authorized.

It sets forth the resolution, which we have already read into the minutes at the morning session.

There is also annexed to the voucher a letter from Mr. H. M. Fisher, the secretary, to Mr. E. F. J. Gaynor, auditor, in which Mr. Fisher says, under date of April 22, 1914, " Enclosed I send you certified copy of resolution adopted at to-day's meeting of the Board of Directors of this Company with respect to special compensation for Mr. Theo. P. Shonts, President, in connection with the recent contracts for subway and elevated extensions. Please make voucher in favor of Mr. Shonts for the amount stated in the resolution, and oblige,   Yours very truly,

(Signed)   H. M. FISHER,
Secretary."

Also attached to the voucher is a page entitled " Distribution." Under the word " Distribution " are the following words: " Other suspense. Proposed subway routes."

By Mr. Colby:

Q. Have you also, Mr. Campbell, the voucher relating to the extra payment of $50,000 to Richard Reid Rogers? A. That is it, there. Isn't it there?

Chairman Thompson.— What does that mean, that "distribution "? What does that mean?

Mr. Campbell.— An account in the auditor's office. That you will have to get him for that. I have nothing to do with that, about the naming of an account in his office.

Chairman Thompson.— Is that the account to which this was charged?

Mr. Campbell.— No, the distribution — he first says " Distribution? "

Chairman Thompson.— Yes.

Mr. Campbell.— That is the name by which the different accounts would be charged under, I presume. Under that is " other suspense," or something, isn't it? .

Chairman Thompson.— Yes.

Mr. Campbell.— That is the title of the account, probably, it was charged against.

Chairman Thompson.— That is what that is for?

Mr. Campbell.— " Distribution " is on all our vouchers.

Chairman Thompson.— I see it is printed on there.

Mr. Campbell.— For instance, if something is purchased that ought to be paid for out of different accounts —

Chairman Thompson.— When it says " distribution " printed in red, and " other suspense."

Mr. Campbell.— That would be the title of the account.

Chairman Thompson.— In a rubber stamp, then " proposed subway routes," that means this was charged in the account, under the account of " Proposed Subway Routes? "

Mr. Campbell.— That I don't know. You will have to get the auditor.

Senator Lawson.— Mr. Campbell, what do you understand by suspense accounts?

Mr. Campbell.— That, I don't know what he means, other than he has an account in his ledger for suspense account.

Senator Lawson.— What do you understand is commonly understood by suspense accounts in New York business houses?

Mr. Campbell.— What do I understand.

Senator Lawson.— Yes.

Mr. Campbell.— That I don't know. Different houses might have different titles for that — suspense account, or whatever they might be.

Senator Lawson — There are trade customs —

Mr. Campbell.— What?

Senator Lawson.— I say they apply these different appellations to different —

Mr. Campell.— That might be.

Senator Lawson.— Has it ever come to your attention that the suspense account is termed promotion account?

Mr. Campbell.— No, never has. I have never had any dealings with any promoters.

Senator Lawson.— That is all.

Mr. Colby.— I offer this check, and the voucher accompanying it, as a part of the Committee's record, and ask that it be set forth in full on the Committee's record.

Chairman Thompson.— Yes. I will ask Mr. Quackenbush to get this copied.

Mr. Quackenbush.— All right.

(The check referred to is as follows):

" $25,000.00   No. 16882.

INTERBOROUGH RAPID TRANSIT CO.

NEW YORK, *Apr.* 22, 1914.

PAY Theodore P. Shonts........................or order
Twenty-five Thousand 00/100..................DOLLARS

TO THE NATIONAL BANK OF COMMERCE
1–23   In New York.   (Signed)   J. H. Campbell.
                                                  Treasurer.

Countersigned
          (Signed)   W. Leon Pepperman,
                          Assistant to President."

(Endorsements on back of check as follows):

" Pay THE NATIONAL CITY BANK
of New York, or order
THE FARMERS LOAN & TRUST COMPANY
Augustus V. Healy,
                          Vice-Pres. & Secy."

" Received Payment through the
New York Clearing House
          APR 23 1914
Prior Endorsements Guaranteed
THE NATIONAL CITY BANK OF NEW YORK
                          Kavanagh, Cashier."

Perforation
Paid

" Pay to FARMERS LOAN AND TRUST COMPANY FOR DETROIT,

To Credit of..

(Signed) Theodore P. Shonts.

(Perforation on check as follows): " Not over twenty-five thous. $25000."

(The voucher referred to is as follows):

" INTERBOROUGH RAPID TRANSIT COMPANY

Voucher No. 127001

To Theodore P. Shonts,

Address No. 165 Broadway, New York City.

Month April 1914 Paid Apr 22, 1914.

1914

April 22. For special services rendered in connection with the negotiations and
securing for the Company of the contracts for the extension of its subway system and elevated lines, in
accordance with resolution of the
Board of Directors of April 22, 1914 $25,000 00."

" PAID

APR. 27, 1914

INTERBOROUGH

RAPID TRANSIT CO.

,   (Sgd.) H. T. B.

Examined and Found Correct ($25,000.00).

(Sgd.) E. F. J. Gaynor, Auditor.

Approved for Payment

(Sgd.) W· Leon Pepperman,

Ass't to President.

NEW YORK, *Apr.* 27, 1914.

Received from the INTERBOROUGH RAPID TRANSIT CO.

Twenty-five thousand and 00/100...................Dollars

for payment in full of the above account.

(Sgd.) T. P. Shonts."

(On the reverse of the sheet appears the following):

" Distribution

Other Suspense

Proposed Subway Routes."

(Letter accompanying voucher is as follows):

" INTERBOROUGH RAPID TRANSIT COMPANY

" April 22nd, 1914.

" Mr. E. F. J. GAYNOR, *Auditor:*

" Dear Sir:— Enclosed I send you certified copy of resolution adopted at to-day's meeting of the board of directors of this company with respect to special compensation for Mr. Theo. P. Shonts, president, in connection with the recent contracts for subway and elevated extension. Please make voucher in favor of Mr. Shonts for the amount stated in the resolution, and oblige,

" Yours very truly,

"(Signed)   H. M. FISHER,

" Secretary."

Mr. Colby.— Mr. Campbell, the treasurer of the company, produces a further check for $50,000 drawn by the treasurer of the Interborough Rapid Transit Company, countersigned by H. M. Fisher, Secretary, dated September 26, 1913, and reads as follows: " Pay Richard Reid Rogers or order fifty thousand dollars." The check is numbered 67,713, and is drawn on the National Park Bank of New York. It bears the following endorsements: " Pay to the order of Guaranty Trust Company of N. Y., Richard Reid Rogers," and the further endorsement, " Received payment through New York Clearing House, September 26th, 1913. Guaranty Trust Company of New York."

The voucher is as follows:

" September 26th " — " Interborough Rapid Transit Company to Richard Reid Rogers, Dr. September 26, 1913. For extra services in connection with the contracts for the construction and equipment of the new subways and elevated lines, etc., in accordance with resolution of the Board of Directors of September 17, 1913. $50,000."

It bears the following notations: " Examined and found correct, E. F. J. Gaynor, Auditor. Approved for payment, H. M. Fisher, Secretary."

There is also a receipt from Mr. Rogers, which constitutes a part of the voucher, reading as follows: " New York, September 26, 1913. Received from the Interborough Rapid Transit Company, $50,000 for payment in full of the above account."

Attached to the — or, marked on the back of the voucher, under the head of " Distribution," I find the following words: " Other suspense," on one line; second line, " Proposed subway routes," and in lead pencil, " Prior determination." The voucher is numbered 120079. Attached to it is the certified transcript from the regular meeting of the board of directors, held on Wednesday, September 17, 1913, setting forth the explanatory statement of the president and the resolution thereafter passed by the board at its meeting held on that date, the resolution being apparently in strict accord with the resolution read at this morning's session.

There is also attached to the voucher a letter from H. M. Fisher, secretary, addressed to Theo. P. Shonts, president, enclosing the copy of resolution which I have just referred to, authorizing this payment to Mr. Rogers, the general counsel of the company, and saying, " For extra services in connection with the contracts for the construction and equipment of the new subways and elevated lines."

I offer this paid and cancelled check for $50,000, together with the company's voucher, produced by Mr. Campbell, in connection with the check, as a part of the Committee's record, and ask that it be noted thereon.

(The check referred to is as follows):

" $50,000.00   No. 67713

" INTERBOROUGH RAPID TRANSIT CO.

" New York, Sep. 26, 1913.

" Pay Richard Reid Rogers.....................or order
fifty thousand ....dollars.

" To THE NATIONAL PARK BANK
            OF NEW YORK.

                    " (Signed)   J. H. CAMPBELL,
                                         " Treasurer.

            " Countersigned,
                    " (Signed)   H. M. FISHER,
                                         " Secretary."

(The following endorsements appear on the back of the check):
" Pay to the order of Guaranty Trust Co. of N. Y.
" (Signed)   RICHARD REID ROGERS.
Perforation:
    N. P. B.
    Paid.
" Received payment through New York Clearing House Sept.
26, 1913, — m., Guaranty Trust Co. of New York."

(Letter enclosing voucher is as follows):
    " INTERBOROUGH RAPID TRANSIT COMPANY.
                              " Sept. 25, 1913.
" Theo. P. Shonts, Esq., President:
    " Dear Sir: — I send you herewith certified copy of resolution
adopted by the Board of Directors on September 17th, 1913, authorizing payment to Mr. Richard Reid Rogers, General Counsel,
for extra services in connection with the contracts for the construction and equipment of the new subways and elevated lines,
etc.
                    " Yours very truly,
                        " (Signed)   H. M. FISHER,
                                          " Secretary.
" Copy to J. H. C.
    E. F. J. G."

The resolution referred to in above letter is as follows:

Transcript from minutes of regular meeting of the board of
directors, held on Wednesday, ——— 17, 1913.

    " INTERBOROUGH RAPID TRANSIT COMPANY.

" The President stated that all legal matters in and about the
contracts for the construction and equipment of the new subways
and elevated lines of the City of New York, prior to March 19th,
ultimo, had been conducted by Mr. Richard Reid Rogers, counsel
for the company; that the work was long continued and exacting
and had been performed, in conjunction with his other duties,
in a highly satisfactory manner and without the employment of
associated counsel, thus resulting in a large saving to the company.
He laid before the Board the consideration of an amount to be

allowed Mr. Rogers for his extra services in connection with said contracts. Whereupon,

"On motion, duly seconded, it was

"Resolved, That the sum of fifty thousand dollars ($50,000) be paid Mr. Rogers for his services in connection with the contracts for the construction and equipment of the new subways and elevated lines, the same to be charged to the proper construction accounts."

"I hereby certify that the above is a true copy of resolution from minutes of regular meeting of the Board of Directors of the Interborough Rapid Transit Company, held on Wednesday, September 17, 1913.

"(Signed)   H. M. FISHER,
                "Secretary."

The voucher is as follows:

"INTERBOROUGH RAPID TRANSIT COMPANY.

"To Richard Reid Rogers, Dr.

"1913.

"Sept. 26th. For extra services in connection with the contracts for the construction and equipment of the new subways and elevated lines, etc., in accordance with resolution of the Board of Directors of September 17th, 1913...........$50,000.00

(Sgd.) H.T.B.

"Examined and found correct.

(Sgd.) E. F. J. Gaynor,
        Auditor.

"New York, Sept. 26, 1913.

"Received from the

"INTERBOROUGH RAPID TRANSIT CO.

"Fifty thousand and 00/100 Dollars for payment in full of the above account.

(Sgd.) RICHD. REID ROGERS.

"Approved for payment,
    (Sgd.) H. M. Fisher,
    Secretary.

"INTERBOROUGH RAPID TRANSIT COMPANY.
Voucher No. 120079
To Richard Reid Rogers,
Address No. 165 Broadway, New York City,
$50,000.
Paid Sep. 26, 1913.
. ... Division .... Ave. Line.
" Distribution
Other suspense.
Proposed Subway Routes.
(In lead pencil:) Prior Determination.
" Paid
Sep. 26, 1913
INTERBOROUGH
RAPID TRANSIT CO."

By Mr. Colby:

Q. Mr. Campbell, I notice that the payment of $125,000 —

Mr. Colby.— Will you let me have the two Shonts vouchers
just a moment, Mr. Quackenbush? I will hand them right back
to you.

By Mr. Colby:

Q. I notice, Mr. Campbell, that the — directing your attention
to the vouchers for $125,000 and $25,000 respectively, being payments to Mr. Shonts, that the earlier voucher contains Mr. Shonts'
receipt for payment in full of the above account, which, according
to the voucher and the certified resolution, which is affixed to it,
were services of an extraordinary character, in securing for the
company the extension of its subway system recently made with
the City of New York, and in connection with arranging for the
financing of such contract. That is true, isn't it? (Counsel
hands papers to witness.) A. Yes, sir.

Q. And yet, apparently, a few months later, in April, 1914, a
further sum was paid by the company, of $25,000, on account of
the same services, notwithstanding Mr. Shonts' receipt in acknowledgment of $125,000 as full payment for such services? A.
You don't understand that on all vouchers the receipt in full is
printed on there. That is for the payment of that amount of

Q. And for the reason and for the account stated in that voucher, is it not? A. It does not so state. It says, " Received for payment in full." ·

Q. It says "Received for payment in full of the above account "? A. That is exactly what is in the voucher, the amount of the voucher. You will find every voucher the same way.

Q. Now the voucher says for services rendered. A. Yes, sir.

Q. In accordance with the resolution of the board, dated June 4? A. Yes.

Q. 1913? A. Well, you will find —

Q. Just allow me. I will give you ample opportunity. Certified copy of which is hereto attached. The certified copy hereto attached contains the resolution as follows: " Whereas, Theodore P. Shonts, in negotiating and securing for the company the contract for the extension of its subway system recently made with the City of New York, and in connection with arranging for the financing of such contract, has rendered services of an extraordinary character and of great value to the company, and in the judgment of this board such services in the interests of efficient administration should be properly recognized by an increase in salary or otherwise, whereupon it was, on motion, duly seconded, resolved, that in recognition of and in compensation for the extraordinary and efficient services rendered by Mr. Shonts ", etc., " he be paid the sum of $125,000 " ? A. Yes.

Q. Now, I ask you isn't this voucher — doesn't this voucher represent not only the payment of $125,000, but the liquidation of such payment of the obligation — A. It does not.

Q. — recited in and set forth in the voucher? A. It does not.

Chairman Thompson.— In other words " in full of account " —

Mr. Campbell.— The recital on that voucher is on the very voucher.

Chairman Thompson.— I see, and don't mean anything?

Mr. Campbell.— It means nothing. It calls simply for what is in the voucher.

By Mr. Colby:

Q. Why do you affix the description of the services or a statement of the account? A. That statement of the services is put in by the auditor, I presume, but in my receipts I exact a receipt for the amount of the voucher in full. I care nothing about what is put in the body of the voucher.

Q. Then this receipt by Mr. Shonts in which he acknowledges this sum of $125,000 in full of the above account, is not an acknowledgment in full of the above account? A. It is an acknowledgment of the amount of money that he received from me —

Q. He does not say " Received "— A.— and what that voucher calls for.

Q. He does not say " Receipt is hereby acknowledged of $125,-000 " ? A. What does the receipt say? Will the counsel please read the receipt?

Q. I will read it entirely. " Received from the Interborough Rapid Transit Company $125,000 for payment in full of the above account " ? A. Exactly.

Q. Well, what is the above account? A. That is the title — that is the name that the voucher — that the auditor puts in that voucher.

Q. What name? A. But that is not the name of the account. You will find on every voucher I have that every payment I make, I accept the full payment for the amount of money that I pay.

Q. Well, what was paid in full, if it was not the account set forth in this voucher? A. $125,000 paid, and for which I received a receipt in full of the amount of that voucher.

Q. In other words, your interpretation of the meaning of this voucher is that it should read " Received $125,000 in payment of $125,000 " ? A. Absolutely. My receipts —

Q. And that is all it amounts to? A. $125,000, exactly.

Chairman Thompson.— With a concern like that, with so many men working for it who are underpaid, you could hardly conclude that at any time, with any language, you had settled with them.

Mr. Campbell.— What do you mean?

Chairman Thompson.— You have several people working for you who are underpaid, and they realize it, and I presume the rest of you do. Now, it would not hardly, knowing that, be just to those men to at any time conclude them by a payment, that they should not some time receive something more for the same services ?

Mr. Campbell.— 1 don't think that calls for an answer. I am a smart fellow, but I can't see that.

By Mr. Colby:

Q. Suppose, Mr. Campbell, you were paying a coal bill? A. Yes, sir.

Q. And the bill was annexed to the voucher? A. Yes, sir.

Q. And it was sent to you with these approvals and directions for payment, and you made a check for the amount of the voucher? A. Yes, sir.

Q. And the coal bill said, "June 5, 1913, to goods, wares and merchandise, consisting of bituminous coal sold and delivered by John Smith to the Interborough Rapid Transit Company, $25,000, and then you gave the coal dealer a check for $25,000, and he said, "For payment in full of the above account"? A. That would be an entirely different proposition, because in the first place, his bill would be attached to the voucher, and a recital of that might not be in the voucher, but just the endorsement on the voucher, and then it would be in full of that bill, whatever bill was attached to that voucher, and not something that was to come or something that had passed.

Q. In other words, you think the president of the company preserves his right to, we will say, ask for more, as, in fact, he did? A. I cannot answer that question.

Q. It is a matter of record, by not sending a bill to the company for $125,000; is that right? A. I cannot answer that.

Q. Why can't you? A. Because I am not qualified to speak for Mr. Shonts.

Q. You are not speaking for Mr. Shonts. You are speaking for yourself. I am trying to find out what your theory is of the meaning and significance of these vouchers which you are so careful to preserve and so reluctant to relinquish? A. On the contrary, I excused myself to the chairman for the delay.

Q. I don't mean in the sense of unwilling. You don't want them to go out of your custody, and quite naturally.

Chairman Thompson.— The treasurer has been quite diligent in getting us what we asked for.

By Mr. Colby:

Q. What is your theory, as to what Mr. Shonts should have done to have rendered this voucher, to use the Chairman's words — as conclusive against a renewal of his claim, or enlargement of it? A. I cannot speak for Mr. Shonts. I would like to say that in all our vouchers — and I want it distinctly plain, as plain as I can make it, that the receipt in full is in full for the account as — called for — the amount of money I pay out.

Q. And for the purpose stated in the voucher? A. I cannot say that.

Q. Or for the purpose, as far as it is stated in the voucher? A. As far as it is stated in the voucher; that might do.

Assemblyman Burr.— You mean for the amount claimed?

Mr. Campbell.— I mean for the amount that is in the voucher.

Assemblyman Burr.— The amount he claims there.

Mr. Campbell.— Exactly. Exactly. He don't make any claim. That is directed, ordered by the Board of Directors.

Chairman Thompson.— Now, Mr. Campbell —

Mr. Campbell.— Yes, sir.

Chairman Thompson.— Suppose, along when I go up to the hotel, some fellow throws me down on the track, and a train comes along and hits me a bump, and I sue your road, and they settle with me for $150?

Mr. Campbell.— Yes, sir.

Chairman Thompson.— I take your voucher?

Mr. Campbell.— Yes, sir.

Chairman Thompson.— $150. Now, when I sign that in full of account, is that just because I receive $150, or is that the full compensation you will ever let me have for that injury? A. That is an entirely different matter. In the first place —

Chairman Thompson.— Let us just settle this matter. Perhaps it is different. Would that be in full; if I signed one of those vouchers, could I ever recover more for that injury, do you think?

Mr. Campbell.— That I don't know.

Chairman Thompson.—-What is your idea about it?

Mr. Campbell.— My idea — I would get a receipt for what I paid you.

Chairman Thompson.— If I sign a voucher for $150 on that blank, in full of account, could I ever recover $25 or $50 more.

Mr. Campbell.—You could if you knew the lawyers, probably; but you couldn't get anything from me.

Chairman Thompson.— That would be concluded in your shop, anyway?

Mr. Campbell.— I have got to see everything that comes in my place.

Mr. Quackenbush.— We would take a general release. That is the way we would do. That would not be in a voucher.

Chairman Thompson.— I am not going to get down in there, anyway.

Mr. Campbell.— Well, I would treat you right.

Chairman Thompson.—You want this to go into the record, too.

Senator Lawson.—You didn't hear that. The treasurer says he will treat you right.

Chairman Thompson.—Well, I won't volunteer.

By Mr. Colby:

Q. Well, whatever the effect of a receipt in full for the above account may be, the sum of $25,000 was subsequently paid to the president for substantially the same purpose you recite in the voucher accompanying the $125,000 payment; that is true, isn't it? A. Made out a check for $25,000 on the direction of the Board of Directors. What their idea of what it was for, I don't know.

Q. Except so far as it is stated in the voucher?

Mr. Colby.—I would like the minute-book. Is Mr. Fisher in the room? Let me just ask this question.

Mr. Campbell.— I thought you wanted to ask me about Queens county.

Mr. Colby.—I do not believe I will pursue your examination any more at the moment.

Mr. Campbell.—You excuse me now?

Mr. Colby.—Yes.

Mr. Campbell.—When to? You can send for me. I will be on tap.

Chairman Thompson.—You don't intend to go away?

Mr. Campbell.— I will be upstairs.

Chairman Thompson.—We will send for you.

Mr. Campbell.— I will be there any time. You are turning those over to Mr. Quackenbush (referring to checks and vouchers).

Chairman Thompson.— Mr. Quackenbush will look after that.

Mr. Colby.— I would like the minutes of the year 1913. Is Mr. Fisher in the room?

H. M. FISHER, recalled.

By Mr. Colby:

Q. Mr. Fisher — A. Yes, sir.

Q. I want the proposed contract that was — Mr. Fisher, you have produced the minute-book for the year 1913? A. Yes, sir.

Q. I turn to page 158, where I see the minutes of a special meeting of the Board at which I find this entered: "Contract for the construction of the elevated railway, third tracks and extensions was discussed, but no action taken." What contract was that that was referred to? A. It was contract No. 3 — known as contract No. 3, which covers the new subways and the elevated third tracks and elevated extensions.

Q. Was that a proposed contract with John Stevens? A. No, sir, with the city. That is, I presume — without reference to the minutes, I am not sure.

Q. This was a contract for the construction (Counsel shows minute-book to witness)? A. Will you let me look back in the minutes to see why that special meeting was held?

Q. I will let you. A. I would have to see that.

(Witness returns minute-book to counsel.)

The Witness.— That is a contract for constructing the elevated extensions, as it says there, but without refreshing my memory, I could not just say which contract is under discussion.

Q. Just which of what contracts? A. For the construction of the elevated extensions. It may have been a tentative contract or form of contract, to be submitted to the Public Service Commission for approval. It may have no reference to the Stevens' contract at all, and until I looked into my records further and saw what contract I have reference to there, I could not identify the particular contract.

Chairman Thompson.—Just for a minute, open one of those windows.

By Mr. Colby:

Q. Do you keep some other record of the company's proceedings besides the minute-book? A. Only the correspondence and the contract records. That is, the files of the original contract. We keep a file of the original contracts.

Q. Are you familiar with the tentative contract or the proposed contract with John Stevens for the construction of the Elevated railway? A. Third tracks and extensions. I know of it, but I am not familiar with it.

Q. In your possession? A. No, sir, I don't think so.

Q. In the company's possession? A. Presumably a copy of it is.

Q. Who has it? A. It would probably be in the president's office.

Q. Has it ever been in your possession? A. No, sir.

Q. Have you seen it? A. I saw it in the board room, but I did not read it.

Q. You heard the discussion about it? A. I heard some discussion about it; yes, sir.

Q. Do you recall its provisions, or some of them, or its more significant provisions? A. Only in a very general way, but it was a contract providing for the construction of the third tracks and the elevated extensions on a percentage basis. The percentage was not stated.

Q. Was not stated where? A. In the contract.

Q. Was it stated in the meeting? A. There were various percentages discussed in the meeting, running from five to fifteen.

Q. What — was any recommendation made as to a proper per cent? A. No, sir.

Chairman Thompson.— Who wanted to give fifteen?

Mr. Fisher.— I could not tell you; simply a general discussion.

Chairman Thompson.— Somebody wanted to give fifteen?

Mr. Fisher.— Not that I recollect. There was a general discussion as to the proper percentage to be paid to the contractor, with general supervisory powers of that nature. Some were of the opinion that he should have a certain percentage, and others were of the opinion he should have a different percentage. They did not arrive at any final conclusion.

By Mr. Colby:

Q. I want that tentative contract with John F. Stevens. It was discussed at that meeting? A. It can be produced.

Q. How long would it take you to get it? A. Probably a very few minutes.

Mr. Quackenbush.— I will see that you get that.

Mr. Fisher.— Right away?

Mr. Colby.— I would like it right away.

Chairman Thompson.— Five minutes?

Mr. Quackenbush.— My boy is gone to get it.

Mr. Colby.— If you will send someone for it, I will continue with the witness.

Mr. Quackenbush.— I will do that.

By Mr. Colby:

Q. I call your attention to page 158 of the minute book for the year 1913, and ask if it contains a record of the proceedings of the board of directors at a special meeting held on June 24, 1913? A. Yes, sir.

Q. This is signed by you as secretary, this page? A. Yes, sir.

Mr. Colby.— I will read into the record a few extracts from the minutes of this meeting. "A special meeting of the board of directors of the Interborough Rapid Transit Company was held at the office of the company, No. 165 Broadway, on Tuesday, June 24, 1913, at 3.30 o'clock p. m., pursuant to notice," etc. "There were present Messrs. Berwind, Fisher, Freedman, Gardiner M. Lane, Pepperman, Pierce, Read, Shonts, F. De C. Sullivan, and Young. Messrs. James L. Quackenbush and Frank Hedley were also present. Mr. Shonts in the Chair." The entire record — the minutes of the meeting consist of only this brief sentence: "The contract for the construction of the elevated railway third tracks and extension was discussed but no action taken."

Chairman Thompson.— That is already in the record, I think.

Mr. Colby.— No. That was stated in the memorandum read on —

Chairman Thompson.— I think we took that last October.

Mr. Quackenbush.— Got a certified copy of that.

Mr. Colby.— I didn't know that. I am not as cognizant of the record as I might be.

By Mr. Colby:

Q. I call your attention to page 160, at which appears the minutes of a regular meeting of the board of directors of the Interborough Company, held on June 25, 1913. Are the pages beginning at 160, and following, the record of the proceedings of that regular meeting of the board of directors? A. Yes, sir.

Q. You were present as secretary? A. Yes, sir.

Mr. Quackenbush.— That has already been in the record. That was all gone into last October.

Mr. Colby.— I propose to take just a little time on this.

Mr. Quackenbush.— I am trying to help you, and there is no use of your saying anything of that kind. The Chairman knows perfectly well why I say that.

Chairman Thompson.— There is no question of that. You see, Mr. Colby has not been in the case very long.

Mr. Quackenbush.— I am not trying to balk anything. There is no occasion to say he is going to take a little time. I know he will take the time of everybody here until next fall. I have not any objections to its going in.

Mr. Colby.— Why, I said I proposed to take a little time on this meeting.

Mr. Quackenbush.— Exactly.

Mr. Colby.— Why so hot, my hasty man?

Mr. Quackenbush.— Because the reply which you made was not in keeping with my intentions. I was trying to tell you, as the Chairman told you a moment ago, that the other resolution you have, it has already been gone into by Senator Lewis with as much care as you are now proceeding to do. And your record is there. If you want to go on and ask Fisher if he was somewhere and if that was done and repeat what Senator Lewis did, I am perfectly willing.

Mr. Colby.— That is good. Now, that is good.

Mr. Quackenbush.— The era of good feeling being again restored.—

Chairman Thompson.— The Committee will decide in favor of Mr. Quackenbush on the question of politeness, and in favor of Mr. Colby on the question of time.

Mr. Colby.— I wish to have entered in connection with the inquiry I am pursuing, that at the meeting of June, held on June 25, 1913, that "the matter of the contract for the construction of the elevated third track and extensions was again brought up by the president, and on motion, duly seconded, it

was resolved that the president appoint a committee to consider
and study the subject and to report their conclusions back to the
board.   The president thereupon appointed as such committee
Messrs. Berwind, Read, Gardiner M. Lane, F. De C. Sullivan,
and Andrew Freedman."

By Mr. Colby:

Q. Did this special committee ever report? A. No, sir.

Q. I find on the following page, a record kept by you as secretary, of a meeting of the special committee, whose names I have
just read, which was held on Monday, June 30, 1913, Mr. Berwind apparently being the chairman of that special committee.
The full record in the minutes of that special committee is this
sentence: "The matter of entering into a contract for the construction of the third tracks and extensions of the Manhattan
Railway Company was discussed, but no action taken." That is
a correct statement of the proceedings of the special committee?
A. Yes, sir.

Q. I notice that among those present at the meeting of the
special committee are its members as appointed by the president,
and that Mr. Shonts was also present, though not a member of the
Committee; is that correct? A. If it is stated there, it is correct.

Q. I ask you to testify on the point after referring to the
minutes (shows minutes to witness). A. Yes, sir, that is correct.

Q. That is correct? On the following page there seems to be
a further record of the meeting of this special committee appointed June 25. This further meeting was held on July 1,
1913, at 2 o'clock p. m., and according to the minute book there
were present Messrs. Berwind, Freedman, Read, Lane, Sullivan,
and again, although not a member of the Committee, Mr. Shonts
was present.   Is that correct, that Mr. Shonts was present (showing minute book to witness? A. That is correct.

Q. The only — the minutes consist only of this sentence:
"The matter of entering into a contract for the construction of
the third tracks and extensions of the Manhattan Railway Company was discussed, but no action taken." Was any other meeting of this special committee held, that you know of? A. Not
unless it is recorded there.

Q. With your familiarity with the minute book, will you take it and tell me if there were any subsequent meetings (counsel hands minute-book to witness)? A. There were no further meetings.

Q. Did the special committee ever make a report? A. Not to my recollection; no, sir. I am not positive.

Q. Was it ever discharged? A. No, sir.

Q. Did it just evaporate? A. That is all.

Q. Was the subject simply dropped? A. It was dropped, yes, sir.

Mr. Colby.— Let me have the minute book of 1914.

(The required book is handed to counsel.)

(Senator Towner in the Chair.)

Mr. Colby.— Has the proposed contract with Mr. Stevens yet come?

Mr. Quackenbush.— I have it here. I wanted to look at it before I give it to you.

Mr. Colby.— Oh certainly, Mr. Quackenbush. Where is Senator Thompson, Mr. Chairman?

Acting Chairman Towner.— He just stepped out. I don't know whether he expects to return or not. I don't think he does this afternoon. He may be in one of the side rooms.

Mr. Colby.— Mr. Chairman, I am going to suggest an adjournment until to-morrow morning, at 11 o'clock, in a few moments, and it might be in order to announce that witnesses subpoenaed for to-day or any prior day, and in attendance, will not be required until to-morrow morning at 11.

Acting Chairman Towner.— A recess will be taken, or an adjournment, until to-morrow morning.

Mr. Colby.— Not at this point. I have one other question. You might announce the witnesses in attendance will be excused until to-morrow at 11.

Acting Chairman Towner.—Witnesses are excused until 11 o'clock to-morrow.

Mr. Colby.— Have you the contract?

Mr. Quackenbush.— I believe that that is a correct copy, and if I find there is any error about it, I will let you know.

(Senator Thompson returns to Committee room.)

Mr. Colby.— Mr. Quackenbush, I really want the contract that was submitted at the meeting in June, 1913.

Mr. Quackenbush.— That is the identical one.

Mr. Colby.— If this is the document, and you state that to be so, I will assume it to be so.

Mr. Quackenbush.— It was because I wanted to be able to make that statement that I looked at it.

Mr. Colby.— This is not a copy. This is —

Mr. Quackenbush.— That is the one I had in my hands at the meeting of the Board.

Mr. Colby.— The witness, upon request produces a paper, stating that it is the proposed contract with John F. Stevens, discussed at the meetings in June and July, 1913.

Mr. Fisher.— I am willing to say so.

Mr. Colby.—Will you look at this paper, which Mr. Quackenbush hands you, and tell me if that is the proposed agreement with Mr. John F. Stevens for the third tracking, and extension?

Mr. Fisher.— The draft of agreement was never in my possession.

By Mr. Colby:

Q. Do you recall it was in that form? A. Yes, it was in this form.

Q. Unbound?

Senator Thompson.— I suggest we adjourn until tomorrow at 11, but we don't intend, I understand, to take any proof tomorrow. Being Saturday, we will try and take a half holiday.

Acting Chairman Towner.— Before we adjourn, I want to ask the witness one question. Have you in your office anything that would indicate to you the final liquidation for service rendered, an account liquidated for services rendered? Have you any way of ascertaining when the final service has been paid for?

Mr. Fisher.— You are referring now to —

Acting Chairman Towner.— Any service; legal service or otherwise.

Mr. Fisher.— That would not be kept in my office. That would be kept in the office of either the Auditor or the Treasurer, or both, for services, or itemized accounts, sent to him with voucher.

Senator Towner.— You would have no evidence of that in your office?

Mr. Fisher.— No, sir.

(Chairman Thompson resumes the Chair.)

Mr. Colby.— Mark that, will you, this contract, this Stevens contract?

(Contract referred to was marked Exhibit No. 1 of February 4, 1916, but was returned to Mr. Quackenbush.)

Mr. Quackenbush.— I think I have copies of it, but I was going to suggest —

Mr. Colby.— This will do.

Mr. Quackenbush.— I want that myself. I will have the copy compared and let you have it in a very few minutes.

Mr. Colby.— You want to take this away with you?

Mr. Quackenbush.— Yes.

Chairman Thompson.— You can furnish that, and your man, Mr. Dawson, will still continue on your books, and then, with that understanding, we will suspend until tomorrow at 11 o'clock.

The so-called Stevens contract referred to is as follows:

"1. This contract is made between the Interborough Rapid Transit Company, hereinafter called the Company, and Jno. F. Stevens, of the City of New York, hereinafter called the contractor.

"2. The Company is the lessee and operator of the elevated railroads of the Manhattan Railway Company in the City of New York. On March 19, 1913, the Public Service Commission delivered to the Manhattan Railway Company, and that Company accepted, a certificate for the construction and operation of additional tracks on Second avenue, Third avenue and Ninth avenue. The original of that certificate is on file with the Commission and is made a part of this Contract, so far as it may be applicable.

"3. On the same date, the Commission delivered to the Interborough Rapid Transit Company, and the Company accepted, a certificate for the construction and operation of the Webster Avenue Line, the Eighth Avenue and One Hundred and Sixty-second Street Connection, the Queensboro Bridge Line and the West Farms Subway Connection. The original of that certificate is on file with the Commission and is also made a part of this Contract, so far as it may be applicable.

"4. This Contract is intended to be a sub-contract for the performance by the Contractor of all of the obligations as to construction and equipment imposed upon the Company by the acceptance of the two certificates just referred to, with the exception of certain things hereafter stated which the Company will do itself, or engage others to do.

"5. The Contractor hereby undertakes the performance of all such construction and equipment obligations and agrees to do all work and furnish all labor, tools, machinery, plant and materials necessary therefore, in strict accordance with the terms and conditions of the two certificates and to the satisfaction of the Chief Engineer of the Company where the work pertains to the Engineering Department; of the Superintendent of Motive Power of the Company where the work pertains to the Department of the Superintendent of Motive Power; of the Superintendent of Car Equipment of the Company where the work pertains to the Department of the Superintendent of Car Equipment, and in accordance with the specifications hereto annexed and the drawings herein referred to, which are hereby made a part of this Contract, for the actual cost and expense incurred, plus   per cent.   Said drawings bear the general title "Interborough Rapid Transit Company," and are specified and identified in Schedule A annexed hereto. The Contractor shall also do such other work and furnish such other materials as may be required by the Chief Engineer, or either Superintendent, as the case may be, upon the same terms and conditions.

" 6. The Company, in consideration of such performance, will pay to the Contractor the full actual costs and expenses thereby incurred by the Contractor, and, except as hereinafter provided, in addition thereto a sum equal to   per cent. of such actual costs and expenses as compensation to the Contractor for his services and also for all obligations and risks herein assumed by the Contractor, hereinafter called the Contractor's percentage.

" 7. The actual costs and expenses shall include:

"(a) The sums actually and necessarily paid by the Contractor for superintendence, rents, licenses and permits, office management and expenses; engineering, legal expenses and administration;

"(b) The sums actually and necessarily paid by the Contractor for such insurance or indemnity bonds as the Company may prescribe or as the Contractor may otherwise deem proper; no Contractor's percentage shall be allowed on such sums;

"(c) Expenditures necessarily incurred in defending and discharging claim for damages to persons or property arising from negligence, or otherwise, by the Company, the Contractor, or whomsoever done; or at the option of the Company, the Contractor will turn over to the Law Department of the Company all such claims and suits for adjustment, litigation or payment by the Company; no Contractor's percentage shall be allowed on expenditures in payment of claims or judgments for injuries to persons or property.

" 8. On or about the first day of each month, the Chief Engineer, the Superintendent of Motive Power and the

Superintendent of Car Equipment shall make an estimate in writing, such as, in the opinion of the said Chief Engineer, or of either of said Superintendents, as the case may be, shall be just and fair, of the actual costs and expenses incurred for the work done and materials delivered, pertaining respectively to the Engineering Department, Department of Superintendent of Motive Power and the Department of Superintendent of Car Equipment, to the end of the preceding calendar month, or since the last monthly estimate. The Chief Engineer, or either Superintendent, as the case may be, shall also make an estimate in writing, such as, in the opinion of any of them, shall be just and fair, of the actual costs and expenses incurred by the Contractor for materials procured by him and in his possession in The City of New York, or in the possession of the car builders, although not yet delivered to the Company, provided that such materials be set apart and marked and identified as the property of the Company.

" 9. On or about the fifteenth day of each month ninety per centum of the amount appearing due by such estimates, together with the Contractor's percentage thereof, shall be paid to the Contractor in cash at the office of the Company upon delivery of receipts satisfactory to the Company.

" 10. Whenever, in the opinion of the Chief Engineer, or either Superintendent, as the case may be, the Contractor shall have completely performed a substantial and conveniently separable portion of this Contract, the Chief Engineer, or either Superintendent, as the case may be, shall, prepare an intermediate estimate as to such separable portion showing from actual measurement the whole amount of work done and materials furnished as to such portion and the actual costs and expenses thereof according to the terms of this contract. At the expiration of thirty days after the delivery of such intermediate estimate as to any such substantial portion, the Company shall pay to the Contractor the amount of such costs and expenses, plus the Contractor's percentage then remaining unpaid as to such substantial portion, *provided* that as to all other portions remaining unperformed, progress satisfactory to the Chief Engineer, or either Superintendent, as the case may be, shall have been made by the Contractor.

" 11. Whenever, in the opinion of the Chief Engineer, or either Superintendent, as the case may be, the Contractor shall have completely performed this Contract, the Chief Engineer and the respective Superintendents shall prepare a final statement or estimate showing from actual measurements the whole amount of work done and materials furnished by the Contractor and the actual costs and expenses thereof, plus the Contractor's percentage to the Contractor. At the expiration of thirty days after the delivery of such final estimates, the Company shall pay to the Contractor in cash the amount remaining after deducting from the amount stated in such final estimates all such sums as shall theretofore have been paid to the Contractor under any of the provisions of this Contract, and also any sum or all sums of money as by the terms hereof the Company is or may be authorized to reserve or retain. All prior monthly or intermediate estimates or other certificates upon which partial or other payments may have been made (being merely estimates) shall be subject to correction in the final estimates.

" 12. The acceptance by the Contractor of the last or final payment shall be and operate as a release to the Company from all claim and liability to the Contractor for anything done or furnished for, or relating to, the work, or for any act or neglect of the Company or the Chief Engineer or either Superintendent, as the case may be, or of any person relating or affecting the work.

" 13. It is understood that this Contract must be performed without seriously interfering with the normal and usual operations of the railroads and the power house, substations, shops, terminals and other places and appliances of the Company, and therefore it is expressly agreed that, as to all matters, the Contractor and his subordinates will cooperate and confer, and comply with the directions of the Chief Engineer, Superintendent of Motive Power and the Superintendent of Car Equipment with regard to all matters pertaining to their respective departments so that the Company and the Contractor shall have the benefit at all times of the technical and practical knowledge and skill of those representatives of the Company, and their respective assistants. This provision shall apply as well to the acquisition of equipment and the labor and materials for equipment, and the labor and materials for construction, as to all work of construction and of equipment, and the time, manner and methods of the performance of each and every part thereof.

" 14. The Company may, whenever it deems it advisable, establish a system of accounts, vouchers and pay-rolls to be used by the Contractor in connection with this Contract, and may, from time to time, prescribe and alter the form and manner in which they shall be kept. The Company shall at all times have access to all such accounts and other records for inspection and examination, so that the actual costs and expenses can, at all times, be promptly and accurately determined and the property identified.

" 15. No payment, credit, compensation, or concession, of whatsoever character, having in any way to do with the actual costs and expenses of the Contractor under this Contract, shall be determined to be a part of such costs and expenses, unless the Contractor, before making such payment, credit, compensation or concession, shall forthwith file with the Company a duplicate voucher, credit slip or other original evidence thereof, for audit by the Auditor of the Company and approval for payment by the President of the Company, or by some person by the president thereunto duly authorized.

" 16. The Company may object to any expenditure either made or proposed, as unreasonable or improper, and thereupon such expenditures shall not be estimated by the Chief Engineer, or either Superintendent, as the case may be, as a part of the actual costs and expenses; but the disputed items shall be held in suspense and submitted to adjudication either by arbitration or in the courts.

" 17. The Contractor shall not assign this Contract without first having obtained the consent in writing of the Company, and without such consent no such assignment shall be recognized by, or be binding upon the Company; but nothing herein contained shall be deemed to affect the right of his personal representatives to complete the same in case of his death.   The Contractor shall (except in such cases where permission to do otherwise is expressly granted from time to time in writing by the Company through its President or a Vice-President) before entering into any contract, agreement or undertaking having to do with the construction or equipment of the railroads, submit the same to the President or a Vice-President for his approval, and he may, as a condition of approval, require the insertion of such terms and conditions therein as may be deemed necessary.   The Company may further require the Contractor, before entering into any agreement having to do with the construction or equipment of the railroads, to ask for proposals upon forms of contracts satisfactory to the Company in a specific manner and for a specified time.

" 18. This Contract contemplates the most thorough and minute inspection by the Company and its Chief Engineer, or either Superintendent, as the case may be, and by their representatives or subordinates, of all work and materials (and of the manufacture or preparation of such materials) entering into both construction and equipment, and the Contractor shall at all times give to the Company and its officers, to the Chief Engineer and his duly authorized assistants and subordinates; to the Superintendent of Motive Power and his duly authorized assistants and subordinates; to the Superintendent of Car Equipment and his duly authorized assistants and subordinates, and to any person designated by the President or a Vice-President of the Company, all facilities, whether necessary or convenient, for inspecting the materials to be furnished and the work to be done in and about the construction and equipment under this Contract, and such representatives of the Company shall be admitted at any time summarily and without delay, to any part of the work or to the inspection of materials at any place or stage of their manufacture, preparation, shipment or delivery. But it is expressly agreed however, that no omission on the part of the Company, or its Chief Engineer, or either Superintendent, as the case may be, or any other representative thereof, to point out any errors, variations or defects, shall give the Contractor any right or claim against the Company, or in any way relieve the Contractor from his obligation to do the work and furnish the materials according to the terms of this Contract.

" 19. The Contractor also agrees strictly and fully and freely to comply with every provision of the two certificates in respect to inspection and supervision by the Public Service Commission to the extent that such provisions have to do with the performance of this Contract.

" 20. Simultaneously with the execution of this Contract, and before the same shall be or become binding upon the Company, the Contractor shall deliver to the Company a bond in the form attached hereto and made a part hereof, executed by the Contractor and a surety or sureties, approved by the Company in the sum of One Million Dollars ($1,000,000.00) as security for the faithful performance of this Contract by the Contractor.

" 21. In addition, and as further security, the Company may retain ten per centum (10%) of the amounts certified from time to time to be due on each preliminary estimate until said ten per centum (10%) shall have been paid in full upon an intermediate estimate, or a final estimate, as hereinbefore provided.

" 22. The Company reserves the right to change the location, and to alter in any way it may deem necessary, the drawings aforesaid, in part or altogether, at any time during the progress of the work, without constituting grounds for any claim by the Contractor for payment or allowance for damages or extra services, or loss of profit other than payment of the actual costs and expenses for work done and materials furnished, plus the Contractor's percentage.

" 23. Any directions or explanations given by the Chief Engineer or either Superintendent, as the case may be, to the Contractor, or his agents, employees or subcontractors, to complete or give proper effect to the plans and specifications, shall be deemed a part of said specifications and of this Contract; but all such directions shall be in writing and a copy thereof duly delivered to the Contractor at his office immediately thereafter.

" 24. All materials furnished and work done not in accordance with said plans and specifications shall, on demand of the Chief Engineer, or either Superintendent, as the case may be, be removed by the Contractor, (unless erected or furnished by direction of the Company) at the expense of the Contractor, and other materials shall be furnished and work done in place thereof which shall be in accordance with said plans and specifications, the Company reserving the right to continue to use the rejected parts in service until new parts have been furnished, and such alterations shall be without cost to the Company.

" 25. To prevent disputes and litigations, the Chief Engineer, or either Superintendent, as the case may be, shall, in all cases, determine the amount, quality, acceptability and fitness of the several kinds of work and materials which are to be paid for under this Contract, except as to the expenditures objected to by the Company as in paragraph 15 provided; shall determine all questions in relation to the work and the construction thereof, and shall, in all cases, determine every question which may arise relative to the fulfillment of this Contract on the part of the Contractor. Such determination and estimate shall be final and conclusive upon the Contractor, and shall be a condition precedent to the right of the Contractor to receive any money under this Contract.

" 26. During the progress of the work, it will be necessary for other contractors and persons to do work in or about the construction or equipment upon, or adjacent to, some portion of the railroad embraced within this Contract. The Contractor shall afford to such other contractors or persons such facilities as the Chief Engineer, or either Superintendent, as the case may be, may require. Any difference or conflict which may arise between the Contractor and other contractors of the Company in regard to their work shall be adjusted and determined by the Chief Engineer, or either Superintendent, as the case may be.

"27. The Company may pay the amount of any liens upon or growing out of any of the work done or materials furnished hereunder, and may deduct the amounts so paid from the amount then or thereafter falling due to the Contractor, and the Contractor hereby undertakes to indemnify and save harmless the Company from and against all loss, damage or expense arising from such liens.

"28. Time is of the essence of this Contract. The Contractor shall begin the performance of the work and the furnishing of materials in such portions or sub-divisions, and in such quantities, when and as directed by notice in writing by the Chief Engineer, or either Superintendent, as the case may be. At the time of such notice the Chief Engineer, or either Superintendent, as the case may be, may issue additional or supplemental specifications to the specifications hereto annexed, which additional or supplemental specifications shall be deemed to be a part of this Contract. The Chief Engineer, or either Superintendent, as the case may be, shall specify in such notice or in such additional or supplemental specification, the date when the work or materials therein specified to be done or furnished, shall be completely done or furnished. The Contractor will carry on the work with such force and number of shifts and in such manner and order as may be directed by the Chief Engineer, or either Superintendent, as the case may be.

"29. In the computation of the time occupied by the Contractor in completing the performance of the work, or furnishing the materials specified in such notice or such additional or supplemental specifications, the length of time, during which the work or any part thereof has been delayed by any act or omission of the Company, or by interference by public authority, or by injunction for which the Contractor is in no way responsible, or other causes beyond the reasonable control of the Contractor, shall be allowed to the Contractor and the time for completion shall be extended by the

Company by the amount of the time of such delay; provided, however, that no period of such delay shall be deemed to begin until written notice thereof shall be given by the Contractor to the Company.

" 30. The Company shall be accorded the right, if it so desires, to intervene or become a party to any suit or proceeding in which an injunction shall be obtained, and to move to dissolve the same or otherwise, as the Company may deem proper. If necessary the attorney or counsel of the Company shall be authorized by the Contractor to appear, for that purpose, as attorney or counsel for the Contractor.

" 31. The Company reserves the right of temporarily suspending the execution of the whole or any part of the work herein contracted to be done at such times and for such periods as the Chief Engineer, or either Superintendent, as the case may be, may deem necessary, and it shall be the duty of the Contractor during such period of suspension to maintain and preserve the plant and the work theretofore completed in proper and safe condition and to provide and furnish all labor and materials necessary therefor. The actual costs and expenses, plus the Contractor's percentage as hereinbefore defined, of such maintenance and preservation shall be paid to the Contractor, but no additional percentage or other compensation shall be paid because of such suspension.

" 32. The permitting of the Contractor to continue the performance of work, or the furnishing of material, or any part thereof, after the time specified in such notice or additional or supplemental specifications for completion, or after the date to which the time of completion may have been extended, or the making of partial payments to the Contractor after any such periods, shall in no wise operate as a waiver on the part of the Company of the right to terminate the employment of the Contractor or to invoke any other of the remedies herein provided in case of abandonment or delay, nor shall any such permission or payment be deemed a waiver or forfeiture by the Company of any claim for damages or expenses arising from such non-completion within the time or times specified.

" 33· In case the Contractor shall fail to complete the performance of work or the furnishing of materials specified in such notice or additional or supplemental specifications, in accordance with the specifications and to the satisfaction of the Chief Engineer, and either Superintendent, as the case may be, within the time specified therefor, the Contractor shall and will pay to the Company the sum of 1/100 ot one per ccent. of the estimated cost of the particular portion as to which he shall be in default, for each and every day the time consumed in said performance and completion may exceed the time allowed for that purpose, which said sum, in view of the difficulty of ascertaining the exact damage which the Company will suffer by reason of delay in such performance or completion, is hereby agreed upon, fixed and determined by the parties hereto as the liquidated damages that the Company will suffer by reason of said delay and default, and not as a penalty; and the Company shall and may deduct and retain the amount or amounts of such liquidated damages out of the moneys which may be due or become due to the Contractor under this Contract.

" 34. Should the Contractor at any time refuse or neglect to supply a sufficiency of properly skilled workmen or of materials of the proper quality, or fail in any respect to prosecute the work with such diligence as will, in the opinion of the Chief Engineer, or either Superintendent, as the case may be, insure its completion within the time herein stipulated, or fail in the performance of any of the agreements herein contained, the Company shall be at liberty, after ten days' written notice to the Contractor, to provide any such labor or materials, and to deduct the cost thereof from any money then due or thereafter to become due to the Contractor under this Contract; and if the Chief Engineer, or either Superintendent, as the case may be, shall certify that such refusal, neglect or failure is sufficient ground for such action, the Company shall also be at liberty to terminate the employment of the Contractor for said work and to enter upon the premises and take possession for the purpose of completing the work comprehended under this Contract, of all materials, plant, tools and appliances thereon, and to employ any other person or persons to perform said work, and to provide the materials therefor; and in case of such termination, the Contractor shall not be entitled to receive any further payment under this Contract until said work shall be wholly completed, at which time, if the unpaid balance of the amount to be paid under this Contract shall exceed the expense incurred by the Company in completing the work, such excess shall be paid by the Company to the Contractor; but if such expenses shall exceed such unpaid balance, the Contractor shall pay the difference to the Company; and the certificate of the Chief Engineer, or either Superintendent, as the case may be, of the cost of furnishing the materials and completing the work, shall be conclusive upon the parties.

" 35. In case of the bankruptcy, insolvent assignment or failure of the Contractor before this Contract is completed on his part, the Company may, in addition to all other rights and remedies herein or by law provided, elect to take possession of the unfinished work of this Contract, or any part thereof, and the materials required therefor, and to have the same completed and delivered at the expense of the Contractor or his assignees.

" 36. All risk of loss or damage not caused or contributed by the Company, to the work or to any part thereof, or to any of the materials, tools, machinery, plant or other things used in doing the work, ordinary wear and tear excepted, is assumed by the Contractor, and any such loss or damage shall be made good by him at his own cost, and the construction shall be carried forward by him in accordance with this Contract without additional cost to the Company by reason of such loss or damage, unless the same shall be caused by the act of God, the public enemy, riots, or the malicious or criminal acts of others.

" 37. It is expressly agreed, however, that the Contractor shall not be discharged or relieved from any obligations and liabilities hereunder by the employment of a subcontractor. The provisions of this Contract shall apply to such subcontractor, its agents and employees, in all respects, and all acts and negligence of the subcontractor, its agents and employees, shall be deemed to be those of the Contractor.

" 38. The tools, machinery and plant to be used, installed and operated by the Contractor shall be of the best kind and sufficient for the work to be done; but if at any time the Chief Engineer, or either Superintendent, as the case may be, shall deem such tools, machinery and plant insufficient, or methods of operation faulty, either for performing the work in the manner or time required by the Contract and specifications, or for the security of persons or property, he may order them changed or discontinued, and the Contractor shall comply immediately.

" 39. The Chief Engineer, or either Superintendent, as the case may be, may order the discharge of any employee of the Contractor for inefficiency or for conduct which in the opinion of the Chief Engineer, or either Superintendent, as the case may be, is prejudicial to the interests of the Company, and the employee shall not again be employed on the work. Sub-contractors and their employees shall be considered as employees of the Contractor.

" 40. The Contractor shall obtain all licenses and permits necessary for the prosecution of the work, and observe and comply with all laws of the United States, of the State of New York, and all local ordinances or regulations in any manner regulating or affecting the labor or materials involved in the performance of this Contract and shall protect the Company from any penalties incurred in consequence of violation or neglect thereof by the Contractor or by anyone in the employ of the Contractor.

" 41. In the event of any doubt as to the meaning of any portion or portions of the specifications or contract drawings, or the text of this Contract, the same shall be interpreted as calling for the best construction, both as to materials and workmanship, capable of being supplied or applied under existing local conditions, irrespective of any provisions herein contained as to the inspection of the said work and materials.

" 42. The specifications and other provisions of this Contract and the drawings are intended to be explanatory of each

other. Should, however, any discrepancy appear or any
misunderstanding arise as to the import of anything contained in either, the explanation of the Chief Engineer, or
either Superintendent, as the case may be, if in writing, shall
be final and conclusive.

" 43. If any inconsistency or conflict shall exist between
any part of this Contract and said specifications, the provi
sions of this Contract shall prevail.

" 44. In the absence of the Contractor, the Chief Engineer, or either Superintendent, as the case may be, shall
have authority to give such instructions as he may deem immediately necessary to the superintendent or foreman in
charge at the point where such instructions are given, and the
same shall be obeyed as though issued to and by the Contractor; but all such directions shall be in writing, and a
copy thereof duly delivered to the Contractor at his office
immediately thereafter.

" 45· All written notices to the Contractor herein provided for shall be given by mailing or delivering the same,
addressed to the Contractor at his principal office in The City
of New York, State of New York. Proof of sending same by
registered mail shall be sufficient for all purposes. The provisions of this paragraph shall also apply to all notices to be
given to the Contractor or to the surety or sureties of the Contractor under or in connection with the surety bond given or
required in accordance with this Contract.

" 46. The Company reserves the right at its option to execute with its own organization, or to engage others to execute,
such portions of the work as it may deem advisable because of
its or their greater familiarity therewith, or as a matter of
convenience in connection with its ordinary other business.
In general, such expected work will be changes in founda-
tions, signalling, power house appliances and electrical matters, including car wiring and such similar things of a technical nature as may best be done in that manner; the cost
of all which excepted work is estimated to be a sum not exceeding two million dollars. But the Contractor agrees to
leave all such questions to the judgment of the Company,

acting by its Chief Engineer, or either of its Superintendents, as the case may be.

" 47. This Contract, except for temporary occupation by the Contractor, does not include the procurement of real estate or easements, or rights, titles and interests in real estate for the construction of the railroads or their operation; nor matters pertaining to franchises or consents incidental thereto.

" 48. The provisions of the certificates as to arbitrations shall be followed by the Company and the Contractor in the adjustment of disputes so far as those provisions may be workable under this Contract.

" 49. Under the completion of any part of the work, the Contractor shall, on demand of the Chief Engineer, or either Superintendent, as the case may be, remove therefrom or turn over to the Company, as directed, the plant, tools, machinery, appliances and materials then remaining on hand which have been paid for by the Company as part of the Contractor's actual cost and expenses, or such portions thereof, as the Chief Engineer, or either Superintendent, as the case may be, may deem necessary so as not to impede the execution of the remaining work by the Contractor or others. Upon the final completion of the entire work and its acceptance by the Chief Engineer, or either Superintendent, as the case may be, the Contractor shall remove from the Company's property all the plant, tools, machinery and appliances then remaining on hand and leave the premises free from rubbish and waste materials and in a clean and finished condition, and the Contractor shall turn over to the Company all the plant, tools, machinery, appliances and materials, wherever located, then remaining on hand which have been paid for by the Company as part of the Contractor's actual cost and expenses. If any such articles shall be sold or disposed of by the Contractor before the final completion of the work, the proceeds shall be credited by the Contractor upon his monthly estimates as equivalent to cash payments by the Company; but no such articles shall be sold or disposed of by the Contractor without first procuring the approval of the Company.

"STATE OF NEW YORK, ⎫
  "COUNTY OF NEW YORK, ⎬ ss.:

"On this ...... day of ...., 1913, before me personally came Theodore P. Shonts, to me known, who, being by me duly sworn, did depose and say that he resides in The City of New York, State of New York; that he is the President of Interborough Rapid Transit Company, the corporation described in, and which executed the above instrument; that he knows the seal of said corporation; that the seal affixed to said instrument is such corporate seal; that it was so affixed by authority of the board of directors of said corporation; and that he signed his name thereto by like authority."

———

"STATE OF NEW YORK, ⎫
  "COUNTY OF NEW YORK, ⎬ ss.:

"On this ...... day of ...., 1913, before me personally came Frank Hedley, to me known, who, being by me duly sworn, did depose and say that he resides in the City of Yonkers, State of New York; that he is the Vice-President of Interborough Rapid Transit Company, the corporation described in, and which executed the above instrument; that he knows the seal of said corporation; that the seal affixed to said instrument is such corporate seal; that it was so affixed by authority of the board of directors of said corporation; and that he signed his name thereto by like authority."

———

"STATE OF NEW YORK, ⎫
  "COUNTY OF NEW YORK, ⎬ ss.:

"On this ...... day of ...., 1913, before me personally came John F. Stevens, to me known and known to me to be the individual described in and who executed the foregoing instrument, and he thereupon acknowledged to me that he executed the same."

"Know all men by these presents that we, John F. Stevens, as principal, and ...., as surety, are held

and firmly bound unto Interborough Rapid Transit Company
a corporation created and existing under the laws of New
York, in the sum of One Million Dollars ($1,000,000) law-
ful money of the United States of America, to be paid to the
said Interborough Rapid Transit Company, its successors or
assigns, for which payment, well and truly to be made, we
bind ourselves and our respective heirs, executors, administrators, successors and assigns, jointly and severally, firmly
by these presents.

"Sealed with our seals, dated this ..... day of ....,
1913.

"Whereas, the above bounded principal, by an instrument
in writing under his hand and seal, bearing even date with
these presents, has contracted with the said Interborough
Rapid Transit Company to do certain work and furnish certain materials on the conditions and for the considerations in
the said instrument mentioned and contained, a copy of which
instrument is hereto annexed.

"Now, therefore, the condition of the above obligation is
such that if the above bounden John F. Stevens, his heirs,
executors, administrators, successors, or assigns, shall well
and truly and in a good, sufficient and workmanlike manner
perform said Contract and each and every provision therein
contained on his part to be done and performed, and complete the same in accordance with the covenants, terms and
stipulations therein stipulated and contained, and in each
and every respect comply with the conditions and covenants
in said contract contained, then this obligation to be void,
otherwise to remain in full force and virtue.

"Signed, sealed and delivered
        in the presence of
                    ....(L. s.) "

"STATE OF NEW YORK,⎫
    "COUNTY OF NEW YORK, ⎰ ss.:

"On this ..... day of ...., in the year one
thousand nine hundred and thirteen (1913), before me per-

sonally came John F. Stevens, to me known and known to me to be the individual described in and who executed the foregoing instrument and he thereupon acknowledged to me that he executed the same.

....
Notary Public."

" STATE OF NEW YORK,⎫
  " COUNTY OF NEW YORK, ⎬ ss.:

" On this ...... day of ...., in the year one thousand nine hundred and thirteen (1913), before me personally came .... to me known, who, being by me duly sworn, did depose and say, that he resides in .... that he is .... of .... the corporation described in and which executed the above instrument; that he knows the seal of the said corporation; that the seal affixed to said instrument is such corporate seal; that it was so affixed by order of the Board of Directors of said corporation and that he signed his name thereto by like order.

....
Notary Public."

Chairman Thompson.— We will excuse witnesses until Monday morning. Now, what are you going to do with these books to-night?

Mr. Quackenbush.— We will have to put them in our vaults, of course.

Mr. Colby.— We will work right here.

Mr. Quackenbush.— You could come up to our office. You will have better air.

Mr. Colby.— This air will be all right.

Chairman Thompson.— Is there anything more?

Mr. Colby.— Nothing.

Chairman Thompson.—All witnesses are excused until Monday morning at 11 o'clock. The Committee will be adjourned until to-morrow morning at 11 o'clock, same place.

Whereupon (at 4:35 o'clock P. M.) the Committee adjourned to meet Saturday, February 5, 1916, at 11 o'clock A. M. at the same place.

FEBRUARY 5, 1916

NEW YORK COUNTY LAWYERS ASSOCIATION BOARD ROOM, 165 BROADWAY, NEW YORK CITY.

The Committee was called to order, pursuant to adjournment, Chairman Thompson presiding.

Chairman Thompson.— Subpoenas are directed to be issued for the books and papers of Andrew Freedman and directed to his executors, Messrs. Untermyer and Oakman, and the Guaranty Trust Company.

There being nothing else to come before the Committee at this time, we will suspend until Monday morning at eleven o'clock at the same place.

Whereupon, at 1 o'clock P. M., an adjournment was taken to 11 o'clock A. M., February 7, 1916, at the same place.

FEBRUARY 7, 1916

NEW YORK COUNTY LAWYERS ASSOCIATION BOARD ROOM, 165 BROADWAY, NEW YORK CITY.

The Committee was called to order, by Chairman Thompson, at 11 A. M., quorum being present.

Mr. Colby.— Mr. Chairman, Mr. Shonts is under subpoena to appear here this morning, and I understand that Mr. Stanchfield is here in his behalf.

Mr. Stanchfield.— I desire to say, Mr. Chairman, what is probably more than a motion. It is of course merely a suggestion and generally speaking it is to this effect. I assume from the information that was handed to me that this Committee in its investigation into the affairs of the Interborough Rapid Transit Company and its deals with the Public Service Commission was actuated by a desire to obtain information with reference to perhaps future legislation. Now running back quite a number of years, perhaps fifteen years ago, and from that time until this in the building of the entire subway system, Mr. Delancey Nicoll has represented as counsel the various railway corporations engaged in these enterprises. Mr. Nicoll will not be here until next week, as he is returning from a trip abroad. For the purpose of assisting the Committee, if for no other purpose, it would be extremely valuable to have the personal presence and assistance of Mr. Nicoll. My suggestion is, or motion, if it should be made in that form, that the examination of either Mr. Shonts or the directors of the Interborough Rapid Transit Company with reference to contracts running back over a period of years be deferred until the return of Mr. Nicoll.

Mr. Colby.— I might say, Mr. Chairman, that the suggestion came to me informally prior to the hearing to-day that the examination of Mr. Shonts be deferred until Mr. Nicoll's return.

Mr. Stanchfield.— He sailed last week and in the ordinary course of events, barring storms and submarines, he is expected to be here next Monday.

Chairman Thompson.— You realize of course, Mr. Stanchfield, the Committee I think want to be courteous. We don't want to make any technical demands and still time passes and we are very anxious to conclude our work as soon as properly possible, and while we have allowed witnesses to have counsel before the Committee and I raised no question about it, yet it is not right to be represented by counsel and if we adopted that rule we would probably get through with this investigation some time about 1920. I don't know that Mr. Nicoll has any particular information which he is at liberty to divulge to this Committee, and I don't like the idea of a witness, when he is subpoenaed, not appearing before this Committee. I think when a witness is subpoenaed before this Committee that he should come.

Mr. Stanchfield.— It's only a question of coming down here and telling what the facts are and that should be easy to tell. Mr. Shonts can be here in a very short time if you desire his presence. I am sure Mr. Shonts is ready and willing to testify to any matter that might be a proper subject of inquiry.

Chairman Thompson.— Surely Mr. Nicoll isn't the only lawyer in New York that is able to advise the Interborough Rapid Transit Company.

Mr. Stanchfield.— Mr. Nicoll is the only lawyer in New York who has been connected as legal adviser to Mr. Shonts and the directors of the Interborough Rapid Transit Company for certainly fifteen years. At any rate, Mr. Chairman, I ask that Mr. Shonts be excused until the return of Mr. Nicoll.

Chairman Thompson.— Now I don't want to do anything that would be considered unfair or discourteous but as I say, time is passing and if we allowed every witness to have this sort of delay our investigation would not be completed until 1920 or later. However, I desire to extend any reasonable courtesy.

Mr. Stanchfield.— I might state, Mr. Chairman, that I was extended one of your courtesies with the result that my client was subsequently indicted. But that is merely a little passing unpleasantness.

Chairman Thompson.— Well, I am not going to enforce the rule about witnesses this time because it happens to be the president of the Interborough Rapid Transit Company. I will, however, enforce it regarding the next witness that comes along. I will enforce it because this Committee cannot delay in its inquiry.

Mr. Stanchfield.— I trust I may not be the next one that comes along. Then I am to assume, Mr. Chairman, that it is satisfactory for Mr. Shonts to appear before the Committee upon the return of Mr. Nicoll, which I understand will be next week, Monday or Tuesday.

Mr. Colby.— What about the legality of the subpoena?

Mr. Stanchfield.— I will have Mr. Shonts here without fail. I will produce Mr. Shonts.

10

Chairman Thompson.— Well, then, so that we will give the ship time to get in and Mr. Delancey Nicoll time in which to have a few talks about this matter some time after he gets in, we will excuse Mr. Shonts until Tuesday morning the 15th at eleven o'clock and I want to have it thoroughly understood that if Mr. Nicoll don't arrive by that time he must get somebody else. He must be here.

Mr. Stanchfield.— It stands then until Tuesday, February 14th, at eleven o'clock, Mr. Chairman.

Chairman Thompson.— Yes, sir.

Mr. H. M. Fisher, being recalled, testified as follows:

Mr. Fisher.— Mr. Chairman, I would like to ask permission to correct some of my testimony given the other day as I had no chance to refresh my memory after a lapse of about five years, and while the testimony which I gave was correct in the main, yet there were a few facts which I desire to correct.

Chairman Thompson.— That will be all right. There is one thing I notice by the morning papers, that Mr. Prendergast, city comptroller, desires to talk to this Committee. Now the Committee have been here six months or more for that very purpose and we are continuing here for the same purpose and along the lines of our inquiry if the comptroller of the city of New York has got anything that will be of assistance to this Committee, I am very sure we will be glad to have it and we will welcome it, and for fear that Mr. Prendergast might change his mind about this I direct that a subpoena be issued returnable Friday morning to Mr. Prendergast.

Mr. Fisher (continuing).— My files show that memorandum was prepared and transmitted to Mr. Freedman, Mr. Berwind, and Mr. Vanderbilt on May 27, 1913. Subsequent to the date of the special meeting held at 2:30 in the afternoon there was a meeting of the Committee called at 2 o'clock. I was not present at that meeting and therefore made no minute of it.

By Mr. Colby:

Q. You mean the special meeting or the regular meeting? A. The special meeting. I would like to say that my records show that I asked Mr. Berwind and Mr. Lane to sign that memorandum and that was borne out by the fact that on my calendar I find minutes to be approved by Mr. Berwind and Mr. Lane. My records show that Mr. Berwind approved the minutes at the next meeting but that Mr. Lane did not approve the minutes until at a subsequent meeting. That is also borne out by the minutes because Mr. Lane was not present at the next meeting.

Q. Have you a memorandum of the special services? A. Yes, sir. Do you wish it?

Q. Yes, I would like to look at it. This memorandum, Mr. Fisher, is in the form of a committee report dated June 4th. What was done on May 14th? A. That was the date the Committee was appointed, on May 14th.

Q. The memorandum that you made for the information as to Mr. Shonts' services was dated May 27th? A. Yes.

Q. Is this the memorandum? (Memorandum examined by witness.) A. Yes.

Q. And it was prepared therefore in the form of a report and bearing the date of June 14th, 1913? A. Yes.

Q. Although prepared and submitted to the Committee on May 27th? A. Yes.

Q. 1913? A. Yes.

Q. I see that your memorandum begins as follows: " New York, June 4th, 1913," the report stating that " This Committee had been appointed at the request of the directors to suggest some suitable acknowledgment of the services rendered by the president in bringing to a successful conclusion the contract with the city for the construction and operation of the new subway and elevated extensions whereby he had secured for the company a long lease of profitable operation of the road and new lines, and for the city numerous subway extensions so vital to its development." In other words, without reading at the moment, you intended that the information which you supplied to the Committee should be in a form so that they could avail themselves of your memorandum and incidentally sign a report recommending the award of a considerable bonus? A. That is correct.

Q. Who asked you to prepare the report in that form? A. I don't just remember who asked me to make it in that form. They simply asked me to prepare a memorandum. I had it in that form so as to save them trouble.

Q. I will examine this memorandum and reserve the right at a later date to further question you about it. Who suggested to you that you get Mr. Berwind and Mr. Lane to approve the minutes of the special meeting awarding Mr. Shonts this bonus? A. There was no suggestion made to that effect. That was done of my own accord.

Q. I suppose due notice as prescribed in your by-laws was given of this meeting? A. Yes.

Q. You didn't deem the presence of Mr. Berwind and Mr. Lane essential to the proceeding of the special Committee? A. No, sir.

Q. Was there any thought in your mind that possibly they might take exception to this action? A. No, sir. This matter had been discussed quite thoroughly in an informal way. I simply asked them to approve the minutes in order to make the record complete.

Q. Do you recall any instance under which similar approval of the minutes had been asked? A. I don't recall at the present time.

Q. Do you recall any instance? A. I don't recall at the present time.

Q. How was this $125,000 charged on the books of the company? A. That I couldn't tell you. You will have to ask the auditor about that.

Q. Was it in fact paid by the Interborough Rapid Transit Company? A. Yes.

Q. Did it figure in any particular or special fund? A. I wouldn't like to answer that. I couldn't answer it correctly and I prefer not to hazard a guess.

Q. Who could most readily answer the question? A. Probably Mr. Rogers.

Q. Has he anything to do with the books of record of the company? A. No, sir, but I think he and the auditor discussed the various charges and they probably understand better than anyone else. I mean they discussed them with the Commission.

Q. You mean the Public Service Commission? A. Yes.

Q. Am I to understand that this payment of $125,000 to Mr. Shonts was ever discussed with the Public Service Commission? A. That I couldn't say.

Q. Was any statement containing this payment to Mr. Shonts ever submitted to the Public Service Commission? A. That I couldn't tell you. That was handled entirely by the auditor.

Q. By the auditor? A. Yes.

Q. I turn to the company's voucher for the payment of $50,000 to Mr. Richard R. Rogers and I see at the meeting of the board of directors on Wednesday, September 17, 1913, that this payment was authorized and that the payment was made "For all legal matters in and about the contract for the construction and equipment of the new subway and elevated lines of the city of New York prior to March 19th last which had been conducted by Mr. Rogers, counsel for the company. That the work of subway construction had been conducted in conjunction with his advice in a highly satisfactory manner and without the employment of associate counsel, thus resulting in a large saving to the company." Were there no associated counsel engaged and paid by the Interborough Rapid Transit Company in connection with the dual subway contracts? A. Not any to my recollection except I think Mr. Stetson was employed to pass upon the legality and the trust indenture covering the issue of $300,000,000 of bonds.

Q. He was employed by the company to examine the trust indenture of securing the bonds? A. I wouldn't say he was employed by the company. I rather think he was employed by the bankers to examine it and the expense paid by the company.

Q. By the bankers, whom do you refer to? A. I refer to the bankers who agreed to take the bonds, J. P. Morgan & Co.

Q. Have you Mr. Stetson's bill and voucher of the amount paid him for that service? A. The auditor has it in his record.

Q. Can you produce it? A. Yes.

Q. You haven't it with you? A. No, sir.

Q. Will you produce it at two o'clock A. Yes.

Q. Were any other payments made except to Mr. Stetson in connection with the dual contracts to outside counsel? A. Not that I can remember at the present moment. I have asked the auditor to prepare a memorandum of all such payments. It should be ready by tomorrow.

Q. When will it be ready? A. I think perhaps I can get that tomorrow or later today.

Q. I would like to see the minute book for 1913 a moment. (Witness produces minute book.) I refer to you Mr. Fisher, the minutes of the regular meeting of the Board of Directors of the Interborough Rapid Transit Company on June 25, 1915. I call your attention to page 163 thereof. Do you see there resolutions and references to the matters referred to in my questions? A. Yes, sir.

Q. Does that refresh your recollection as to the matter stated there? A. Yes. That covers the payment to Francis L. Stetson for professional services in connection with the Public Service Commission contract number three, and the preparation of mortgage to the Equitable Trust Company of New York dated March 20, 1913, amounting to $50,079. It also covers bill of Nicoll, Anable, Lindsay & Fuller for professional services rendered from April 1, 1912 to June 1, 1913, which according to my recollection are miscellaneous services and not connected with any special work relating to contract number three, although I may be mistaken.

Q. Do you recall whether any further sums were paid to Mr. Nicoll in the year 1913? A. I couldn't tell you without looking at the record.

Q. I notice that the bill of Mr. Stetson and Mr. George A. Gardiner according to the minutes from which you have just read was referred to the President of the company with power. What does that mean with power? A. I think the idea was that he might obtain a reduction and they simply gave him power to act.

Q. I notice that the bill of Mr. Nicoll amounting to $42,292 was approved and ordered paid. Have you a distinct recollection as to what the bill of Nicoll, Anable, Lindsay & Fuller was for, that is to say what services were included in it? A. I have not. Where special services were rendered I usually specified in the minutes. The fact I didn't do it in this case makes me think it was for ordinary miscellaneous services.

Q. I see that the matter of the payment of one of these bills was again referred to at the regular meeting of the board on July 2, 1913. I call your attention to the minutes of the regular meeting held on that day. (Counsel exhibits minute book to witness.)

Q. You were present at the meeting, Mr. Fisher? A. Yes, sir.

Q. You signed the minutes? A. Yes.

Q. What report did the President make in relation to the bill of Mr. Stetson? A. He stated that he had seen J. P. Morgan regarding the matter and that Mr. Morgan was of the opinion that the charge was a reasonable one and should be paid. The bill was thereafter approved and ordered paid.

Q. Why did he see Mr. Morgan? A. That I cannot say. He was given authority to act with power with a view to getting a reduction.

Q. Was Mr. Morgan a director of the company? A. No.

Q. Was he an official of the company? A. No.

Q. Do you mean to say Mr. Fisher, that the Interborough Rapid Transit Company referred this matter to a gentleman not a member of the board for determination? A. No, sir. They referred it to their President.

Q. Then do you mean to say that the President with the acquiescence of the board consulted an outsider as to what the company should do in this matter? A. Not with the acquiescence of the board. He took his own means of endeavoring to secure a reduction in the bill.

Q. Was it habitual or customary to refer matters to Mr. Morgan before the board acted on them? A. No, sir.

Q. Or to guide the board in its action? A. No.

Q. Was that customary on the part of the President? A. No.

Q. There was nothing unusual in this case then? A. I think Mr. Stetson had a great deal to do with the preparation of the mortgage and Mr. Morgan agreed to take the bonds under that mortgage and it would seem quite natural Mr. Shonts should consult with him with respect to Mr. Stetson's bill.

Q. Was this account eventually charged? A. I presume it was. I have here the original voucher which I think will give you all the information on the subject. (Witness produces Interborough Rapid Transit Company's voucher No. 117623 dated June 23, 1913, for amount as per attached bill, $50,079.75. The bill attached is a bill of the Interborough Rapid Transit Company to Mr. Stetson dated June 23, 1913 and reads as follows: " For professional services and advice, self and George H. Gardiner

first in connection with the Public Service Commissions and Board
of Estimate and Apportionment concerning new contracts for subways and extensions of elevated railways and second in connection with preparation of new mortgage; services being rendered
and charged against you pursuant to your contract with J. P.
Morgan & Company and amount of charge having been approved
by Mr. J. P. Morgan and President Shonts. The bill is for
$50,000, the disbursements amounting to $79.75, making the total
of the bill $50,079.75. The bill is endorsed and approved by
Theodore P. Shonts, president, and payment is acknowledged. I
find on the back of the voucher under the heading of " Distribution " the following endorsements "Amortization, discount and
expense, $8,245.13, other expense $37,362, proposed subway route
$21,967.49, proposed subway equipment, $8,701.35, Interborough
Rapid Transit Company extension $5,451.19, improvement and
Manhattan division power plant $1,241.97." These last four
items make the total of the amount.

Q. How was this apportionment arrived at? A. That I cannot
say. They have a method of doing it under the Public Service
Commission system of accounting.

Q. Have you the voucher of the Nicoll bill? A. No, sir. Do
you want that?

Q. Have you that? A. No, sir, I have not. I can get it for you.

Q. Can you tell me the names of other lawyers who were associated with outside attorneys, that is associate counsel that were
employed at or about this date? A. No, sir. I could not.
Although it was quite possible that we may have a bill from the
Equitable Trust Company who are the trust company in this
matter.

Q. Do you recall the attorneys who examined this instrument?
A. No, I do not.

Mr. Quackenbush.— It was Mr. Davis. If you want me to
refresh Mr. Fisher's recollection regarding the others, I will be
glad to do so. I remember Judge O'Brien was retained to argue
a case in the Appellate Division and I think Mr. Grout was also
retained.

Q. I would like a statement of these matters. I notice in the
minutes of 1912, a meeting of the board of directors held on

October 9, 1912, at which two bills were submitted to the board and apparently approved and ordered paid, one to Hays, Hershfield and Wolf for $37,809.90 and another to Guggenheimer, Untermyer & Marshall amounting to $25,817.22. Are you able by reference to the minutes to refresh your mind sufficiently to testify to the payment of these amounts to these gentlemen? A. Yes, sir.

Q. Do these bills relate to the Dual subway contract or to any matter growing out of them? A. Yes.

Q. What service did Messrs. Hays, Hershfield and Wolf render for which they were paid $37,809.90 by this company? A. For professional services and expenses in determining the validity of the proposed extension of the subway system and the terms of operation thereof by the Interborough Rapid Transit Company and the terms of operation thereof by the Interborough Rapid Transit Company in connection with suits of the Admiral Realty Company vs. Gaynor and the City of New York.

Q. And what was the service rendered by Guggenheimer, Untermyer & Marshall? A. The same.

Q. In connection with the same suit? A. Yes.

Q. Did they represent the Interborough Rapid Transit Company, or did their firm represent the Interborough Rapid Transit Company? A. I think they did, in view of the fact that we paid their expenses but I am not familiar with it.

Q. Are you familiar with that action? A. Not very.

Q. Do you know who these firms represented in that action? A. The Interborough Rapid Transit Company, I imagine.

Q. The Interborough Rapid Transit Company? A. Yes.

Q. Have you other bills and other vouchers too? A. Yes.

Q. Can you produce them? A. Yes.

Q. Is this the case you refer to that is recorded in volume 206 in New York Court of Appeals at page 210 in which the Admiral Realty Company is the appellant and the City of New York and others are the respondents. This case was argued in June 1912, and decided on June 29, 1912? A. That's the case.

Q. I see that the Interborough Rapid Transit Company which is one of the parties respondents in that action, was represented by Mr. R. R. Rogers and Alfred E. Mudge. I see no mention in that case that Messrs. Guggenheimer, Untermyer & Marshall represented the Interborough Rapid Transit Company? A. No, I presume they were associate counsel.

Q. I see no reference in the report of the case in the Court of Appeals report that Messrs. Hays, Hershfield & Wolf represented the Interborough Rapid Transit Company? A. I presume the same would apply in that case.

Q. That they were associate counsel to the Interborough Rapid Transit Company? A. That is my recollection.

Q. Was the Interborough Rapid Transit Company interested in the prosecution or in the defense of that action? A. You will have to ask the counsel to the Interborough Rapid Transit Company about that.

Q. It appears to be an action to enjoin the execution of the Dual Subway Contract? A. It was.

Q. And the Interborough Rapid Transit Company was resisting that injunction? A. Yes.

Q. I see the Brooklyn Rapid Transit Company was represented by counsel in that case, Mr. Charles A. Collin and Mr. George D. Yoeman? A. I think the companies joined together in securing a decision in this case.

Q. I observe that Messrs. Hays, Hershfeld & Wolf represented the plaintiff in that action in which the Admiral Realty Company were endeavoring to enjoin the execution of the Dual Subway Contract; is that true? A. It's possible.

Q. That these attorneys who have received in one instance 37,000 odd dollars for services in this action and in another instance $25,000 from the Interborough Rapid Transit Company didn't so far as the records indicate represent the Interborough Rapid Transit Company at all, that on the contrary they represented the plaintiff.

Chairman Thompson.— Did the Interborough Rapid Transit Company pay them?

Mr. Fisher.— Yes.

Chairman Thompson.—And probably paid them within a very short time after this action was decided?

Mr. Fisher.— The Interborough Rapid Transit Company usually pays its bills promptly.

Q. Can you explain these two payments, one to Guggenheimer, Untermyer & Marshall and the other to Hays, Hershfield & Wolf? A. Not without looking up the record. I think we have our attorney here. I think he may be able to explain it without trouble.

Chairman Thompson.— I think he should explain it. If there is any explanation of it, I should think it should be explained to the Bar Association.

Mr. Colby.— If you desire, Mr. Chairman, and Mr. Quackenbush is willing to explain that, I suppose we may have that explanation when we convene this afternoon.

Chairman Thompson.— I am frank to say that if it appears to be true I think it is a matter that should be taken up with the Bar Association.

A. As I remember it it was simply a suit brought to secure a decision on the validity of this construction and operation and I presume our attorneys can explain it.

Chairman Thompson.— As a lawyer, I think that is really serious on the face of it, in relation to the propriety of the question of professional ethics.

Mr. Colby.— I would suggest that before the passing of any inferences on the subject, we pursue our inquiry and Mr. Fisher, if he will, will present at 2 o'clock the bills received by these firms. I would like a statement of all counsel fees paid by the Interborough Rapid Transit Company to outside counsel from January 1, 1906, and I don't care to have that from you in any particular form, simply the items and particulars and I would like that, if possible, by 2.30, and also the vouchers if you can get them readily, Mr. Secretary.

A. I will see that they are furnished.

Q. You don't know of any other amount of payments to Guggenheimer, Untermyer & Marshall and to Hays, Hershfield & Wolf, do you? A. No, sir. The voucher will explain that.

Q. Upon the consummation of the Dual Contract, Mr. Fisher, how were the bonds of the Interborough Rapid Transit Company issued? A. Just what do you mean by that? Why there was a contract between the Interborough Rapid Transit Company and the bankers relating to the issuance of the bonds. There was an exchange of letters as to the sale of the bonds.

Q. And no contract other than the writing of the letters? A. That's all.

Q. And the letters specified in what amount the bonds should be issued and in what amount the proceeds thereof from the bankers should be paid? A. Yes.

Q. Will you produce those letters? A. I will.

Q. Can you describe the process? A. Of any statement contained in the letters, yes, sir. The bonds were sold to J. P. Morgan & Company at 93½.

Q. In other words the entire issue of bonds was sold to J. P. Morgan & Company at that figure? A. Yes, sir. The first fifty million were to be taken for refunding purposes at once. Thirty million, I think, were to be taken for construction purposes and thirty million each year following until the last year, 1916, thirty-two million. Those are approximate figures and should total one hundred and sixty million.

Q. And what rate of interest do these bonds carry? A. Five per cent.

Q. And the moment the bonds were issued the interest begins to run against the Interborough Rapid Transit Company? A. No, sir. The interest runs against the Construction Fund.

Q. Do I understand you to say that fifty million were refunded, were repaid to the bankers at once? A. Approximately fifty million.

Q. What were refunded with the proceeds of this fifty millions of bonds? A. Proposed issue of five per cent. bonds and notes aggregating approximately forty-five million dollars or thereabouts.

Q. The discrepancy between the fifty million dollars and the outstanding five per cent. bonds and notes being accounted for how? A. A part of it is accounted for on reduction of the five per cent. bonds and various other expenses which I cannot state with accuracy at the present time.

Q. Will you have a statement of that transaction prepared? A. I will, yes, sir.

Q. At what price were these bonds issued to the bankers? A. At 93½.

Q. That's what the Interborough Rapid Transit Company realizes? A. Yes.

Q. At what price were the bonds issued subsequent to the public? A. They were sold at various prices. The last price that I remember they were sold at was 99½.

Q. Were they ever sold for less than 99? A. Yes, I think some of them were sold at 96.

Q. There was a syndicate formed in connection with these bonds was there not? A. I understand there was, yes.

Q. Composed of Lee, Higgins & Company, Kissell, Kinnicutt & Company and Harris Forbes & Company? A. I think that is correct.

Q. In other words, as I understand the bonds were issued by the Interborough Rapid Transit Company to J. P. Morgan & Company? A. Yes.

Q. And those bankers in turn delivered the bonds to the syndicate consisting of these three banking houses? A. Yes.

Q. And these banking houses have sold these bonds at an average price at around 99½? A. Yes.

Q. How are the proceeds of these bonds paid to the company? A. The proceeds were credited to various accounts, some to the subway construction account, to the subway equipment account and elevated extensions account, elevated third track and the power account and general.

Q. Do you call on the bankers for given sums of money as the proceeds of the bonds or do they call upon you from time to time? A. They called upon us in accordance with our agreement.

Q. As set forth in those letters? A. Yes.

Q. And then you turn the bonds over to them? A. Yes.

Q. Did you receive at the time the full proceeds of the bonds? A. Yes, sir, all the proceeds were credited to our account.

Q. To your account with them? A. Yes, sir. We had a special account for this transaction with J. P. Morgan & Company and the proceeds were credited to that account.

Q. And then drawn out by you as required? A. Yes.

Q. Will you please prepare also a statement of current monthly

balances of J. P. Morgan & Company of all accounts? A. Yes,
I will.

Chairman Thompson.—We will now take a recess until 2:30
p. m.

_____

AFTERNOON SESSION.

The Committee was called to order at 2:55 p. m., Chairman
Thompson presiding.

Chairman Thompson.—While we are waiting for Mr. Colby, I
will save a little time. Just as a matter of interest as to the way
correspondence is carried on, and the great publicity that was
given to the files of the Public Service Commission, the Secretary's
department, and sort of a slam on it, I will put in the record a
copy of a letter written to the Public Service Commission, and a
copy of the reply by the Secretary.

The letter is:

"INSPECTION OF RECORDS.

"*September* 22, 1915.

"*Public Service Commission,* 154 *Nassau Street, New York
City:*

"DEAR SIRS:— On Tuesday, September 21, I appeared
at your offices and requested to see the file of ' Informal Complaint No. 12567.' Parenthetically, I might say that I am
the complainant thereof, in behalf of the Brooklyn Civic
Committee. I was informed, to my surprise, that I could
not obtain access thereto, unless permission was given by the
Secretary or a Commissioner.

"I thought that the question of seeing documents in your
office had been settled once and for all time last summer. On
May 29th, 1915, I submitted a brief to your Commission,
wherein I established my right to see the file of ' Informal
Complaint No. 9349,' and any other file in your possession.
Our Committee has never been given a definite answer as to
whether we could, without molestation, see complaint files in
your office. Commissioner Williams has, however, personally
assured the writer that he could peruse any file upon application to him.

" The Brooklyn Civic Committee has many complaints filed with your Commission. The members of our transit committee oftentimes find it necessary to inspect the file of a complaint, made by this organization. There will be no end of trouble and annoyance if we should be forced to make personal application to some one higher up every time we want to see a file. We are sick and tired of these regulations, which seem to have been promulgated to discourage persons who have made a meritorious complaint and wish to prosecute it to a finish. We also deny that your Commission has the right to make such an arbitrary regulation. (See my brief of May 29th, 1915.)

" We want to have an unequivocal answer whether or not in the future we can see a file upon application to the person in charge thereof.

" Truly yours,
" LEO KENNETH MAYER,
"Chairman."

In answer to that, Mr. Mayer, September 24, 1915, received this reply:

" STATE OF NEW YORK
PUBLIC SERVICE COMMISSION
FOR THE FIRST DISTRICT
Tribune Building, 154 Nassau street

Edward E. McCall, Chairman George S. Coleman
J. Sergeant Cram Counsel
George V. S. Williams Travis H. Whitney
Robert C. Wood Secretary
William Hayward .
Commissioners

Telephone 4150 Beekman

NEW YORK, *September* 24, 1915.

Mr. Leo Kenneth Mayer, Chairman, Brooklyn Civic Committee, 1307 Putnam avenue, Brooklyn, New York.

Dear Sir: No.

Truly yours,
TRAVIS H. WHITNEY,
Secretary."

Now, by that I understand that the question in this letter, as to whether they can, without molestation, see complaint files, is answered in the negative. They must be molested. And they cannot, in the future, see files upon application to the person in charge. I think Mr. Whitney should explain.

H. M. FISHER, recalled.

Mr. Colby.—When you are ready to resume, Mr. Fisher; not until then.

Chairman Thompson.— I want an explanation on the record about this thing. This is all I have, and I put in my own personal opinion. I think one of the biggest things about the Public Service Commission is it was established for the purpose of allowing one person to come in and have their rights adjusted by the arm of government, and have them adjusted at once. And because there happens to be just one, and he happens not to have on as good clothes as somebody else, I don't think he is entitled to a letter of this kind, I don't care who he is.

By Mr. Colby:

Q. Mr. Fisher, what are you ready to let me have of the matters that I wanted, statements, and so forth?

Chairman Thompson.— This—I want to say this, too, so far as there is any question of politics in this. This matter was brought to the attention of the Committee by Assembly Burr.

A. I am ready to let you have correspondence of J. P. Morgan & Company, covering, and our agreement with them, to take $170,000,000 of bonds, which was subsequently reduced. The first letter is dated —

Chairman Thompson.— I can't allow any smoking.

The Witness (Continuing:) — June 3, 1913, which was subsequently reduced to one hundred and sixty million, six hundred and fifty-eight, by letter of December 31, 1915, together with letter from Messrs. Morgan & Company, showing the amount of interest they will show us on the proceeds and sale of bonds deposited with them.

Q. Yes, Mr. Fisher? A. I also have a statement of bonds issued and delivered to Morgan & Company, and bonds issued and delivered to the trustee. They were delivered to Morgan & Company as of this date, $148,658,000, and delivered to the trustee, certificate, $154,531,000, the difference of $5,873,000, referred to therein are subject to the order of the treasurer — are with the trustee, subject to the order of the treasurer. This statement also shows a distribution of this amount between the subway construction account, Manhattan third tracking account, Manhattan power-house account, elevated extension account, and the refunding.

Q. Anything further, Mr. Fisher? A. Yes, sir, there is a memorandum showing the total amount of bonds delivered to Morgan & Company, $148,658,000, and the amount of cash proceeds realized therefrom, $138,995,230, and the amounts credited to each of the separate accounts I just enumerated. I have a statement here of the cash balances with Morgan & Company, on general account, subway construction account, Manhattan third tracking account, Manhattan power-house account, and elevated extension account. In connection with that, so as to make your records complete, I have here note of the Public Service Commission which gives the amounts of bonds authorized for each of the accounts referred to in those statements. The statements of vouchers and payments of counsel fees from 1906 to date, I am sorry to say we have not yet had time to prepare, but I have a number of vouchers here, selected at random, which I will be glad to give you and among those is the vouchers of Guggenheimer, Untermyer & Marshall and Hays, Hershfield & Wolf, in the Admiral Realty Case?

Q. You are still at work on that? A. Yes, sir. I think that is all the papers you asked for.

Q. Mr. Fisher, I doubtless did not make myself clear this morning as to the statement of balances with J. P. Morgan & Company, that the Committee wished. We want the statement of current monthly balances on these various accounts, such as subway contribution account, general account, Manhattan third tracking account, Manhattan power-house account, elevated extension account, as well as any other accounts, from month to month, from the date of the inauguration of the contract between the company and Morgan & Company, evidenced by the letters which you have filed with the Committee. I assume that will take some little time to compile, at your convenience. A. I will have it for you to-morrow morning.

Chairman Thompson.— Mr. Quackenbush, will you send for those original checks, the one for $125,000 and $25,000 — the original checks?

Mr. Colby.— The witness produces the bills of Hays, Hershfield & Wolf, and Guggenheimer, Untermyer & Marshall, each dated October 3, covering as alleged therein professional services rendered in determining the validity of the proposed extensions of the subway system and the terms of operations thereof by the Interborough Rapid Transit Company, in connection with suits of Admiral Realty Company vs. Gaynor (Action No. 1), and Admiral Realty Company vs. City of New York (Action No. 2), from Supreme Court to and including Court of Appeals, as per memoranda, $35,000. The disbursements of Hays, Hershfield & Wolf, added thereto, amounting to $2,809.90, and their bill aggregating $37,809.90.

The witness further presents a bill of Guggenheimer, Untermyer & Marshall, made out to Hays, Hershfield & Wolf reading as follows: " To counsel and services from July, 1911, to July, 1912, in the following matters: Admiral Realty Company vs. Gaynor, et al., revising complaint and affidavits on motion for a temporary injunction, application to Judge Giegerich for temporary injunction, and procuring order to show cause. Argument of motion for injunction at a special term held by Mr. Justice Ford. Preparation of brief at Special Term. Consultations with regard to appeal to the Appellate Division. Preparation of brief on such appeal, and argument of the appeal at the Appellate Division.

Then, in the case of the Admiral Realty Company vs. The City of New York, et al., conferences with counsel for the Public Service Commission, with regard to the preparation of complaint in a suit to test the constitutionality of the proposed contracts between the City of New York, the Interborough Rapid Transit Company and the Brooklyn Rapid Transit Company for the construction of the new subways. Revising the complaint. Preparation of brief on argument of the demurrer interposed by the several defendants. Arguments of the issues of law on the demurrers at a Special Term held by Mr. Justice Blackmar. Revision brief for the Appellate Division of the Second Department, and argument of the appeal in that court. Preparation of brief for the Court of Appeals, and argument of the appeal in that court, $25,000. With $318.72 added, making the total of Messrs. Guggenheimer, Untermyer & Marshall, $25,318.72. The bill of Messrs. Hays, Hershfield & Wolf is rendered to the Interborough Rapid Transit Company, and includes a statement of their services and charge as read, and the bill of Guggenheimer, Untermyer & Marshall, with their charge as read. Hays, Hershfield & Wolf rendering a bill to the Interborough Rapid Transit Company for the combined services of the two firms, amounting to $63,128.82.

Q. I turn to the minute book of the board of directors, where the proceedings of the regular meeting of the board that occurred on October 9, 1912, are set forth. I ask you, Mr. Fisher, as secretary of the company, whether resolutions were passed at that meeting authorizing the payment of the bills that I have just mentioned (showing minute book to witness)? A. Yes.

Q. I read from the minute book: " The president submitted for the consideration of the board bills of Messrs. Hays, Hershfield & Wolf for $37,809.90; and Messrs. Guggenheimer, Untermyer & Marshall, for $25,318.72, for professional services and expenses in determining the validity of the proposed extension of the subway system, and the terms of operation thereof by the Interborough Rapid Transit Company in connection with suits of Admiral Realty Company vs. Gaynor and The City of New York. Whereupon, on motion duly seconded, it was resolved that the bills of Messrs. Hays, Hershfield & Wolf, for $37,809.90, and Guggenheimer, Untermyer & Marshall, for $25,318.72, for professional services and expenses in the suits above referred to, be and the same hereby are approved, and the president authorized to pay the same."

Was there any discussion at that meeting so far as you recall, of the services rendered and of the propriety of these charges? A. Not beyond the usual questions that are asked on matters of that kind, whether it was a proper charge, and properly payable by the company, which were all answered in the affirmative.

Q. There was no reference of the matter to the president to see— A. No, sir.

Q. — if they were proper or — A. No, sir.

Q. — would be reduced? What is the Admiral Realty Company? A. That I could not say.

Q. Are Messrs. Hays, Hershfield & — you say you could not say. Do you mean you do not know? A. Beyond a realty company in this city, I don't know.

Q. You don't know where their office is? A. Downtown somewhere, I could not tell you.

Q. You don't know what their business is? A. I suppose it is real estate business.

Q. You don't know what particular branch of the business of real estate it is? A. No, sir.

Q. Do you know of any connection between the Realty Company and the Interborough Rapid Transit Company? A. There is none that I know of.

Q. Do you know who employed Messrs. Hays, Hershfield & Wolf to institute this action? A. I do not.

Q. Or Guggenheimer, Untermyer & Marshall? A. No, sir. I assume they were employed by the Admiral Realty Company.

Q. Well, if they were hired by the Admiral Realty Company, why is the Interborough paying the Admiral Realty Company's lawyers? A. The Interborough, of course, was interested in that suit, to the extent of knowing that the dual contract was valid, and that they would not issue any bonds and have them outstanding, and have the Court of Appeals or the Court decide later on that the contract was invalid.

Q. Did the Interborough Rapid Transit Company pay any other bills in this litigation? A. There probably were some other small bills. I think there was another small bill of $5,000, in a case somewhat — a case connected with that — to Morgan J. O'Brien. I have the voucher for that (shows voucher to counsel).

Q. Well, Judge O'Brien renders this bill to the Interborough Rapid Transit Company for services as counsel to the Interborough Rapid Transit Company? A. Yes, sir.

Q. There is a distinction between a bill rendered by counsel for the company to the company and these bills of Guggenheimer, Untermyer & Marshall and Hays, Hershfield & Wolf, who were representing apparently an adverse litigant. I can understand the rendition of Judge O'Brien's bill to the Interborough Company, because apparently he was employed by it. But these two bills, aggregating $63,000, seem to be the bills of your adversaries' counsel. A. You can understand also the Interborough's interest in the case, I presume.

Q. Well, interest in the sense in which a spectator is interested, or an observer is interested, or do you mean interest in the sense in which one has an interest in the subject matter? A. In knowing that the contracts could be legally entered into.

Q. Did they simply thankfully reward these attorneys for their services in bringing an action against them? A. I shouldn't say very thankfully. I know they rewarded them.

Q. Does the Interborough bestow on attorneys for the opposite side, if the case is interesting to them, payments of such magnitude as this, ordinarily? A. Have you your own case in mind, for example?

Q. Well, I confess I have not for the moment. A. I am not aware that they do.

Q. In other words, do they go to the attorney for the plaintiff in a case in which they are defendants, and say "Your work interests us very much. Won't you send your bills to us, and we will pay them, our interest is so great in your work?" What is the explanation of this, Mr. Fisher? A. I think the explanation is very simple. I have already told you that the Interborough was interested to the extent of seeing these contracts were valid and they could legally issue their bonds against them.

Q. And so they procured a collusive suit to be brought by themselves? A. I am not saying that. I don't know who it was started by, or whose authority, or anything about it, beyond what I have told you.

Q. Am I to understand this litigation was posed, cast and performed as if it were a production for the edification of the public and the harassment of various judges before whom these arguments were had, from the special term up to the Court of Appeals? A. You can put your own construction on it.

Q. I am not endeavoring to put my own construction on it yet. What I am endeavoring is to get a statement of the facts, Mr. Fisher. A. I have given it to you, so far as I know them.

Q. Who knows who employed Guggenheimer, Untermyer & Marshall and Hays, Hershfield & Wolf to sue the Interborough Rapid Transit Company, or to bring these actions against the Mayor and the City of New York, for the Admiral Realty Company? A. I think that suit — the Admiral Realty Company probably could tell you.

Q. Do you know whether the Interborough employed these lawyers to bring this action? A. I don't think they did; no, sir.

Q. But in the course of the action their services became so interesting to the Interborough that the Interborough decided to give $63,000? A. In the course of the action, the Interborough was brought into the case.

Q. I see in the minute book that the president submitted the bills to the board. Did he make any recommendations as to their payment? A. I should imagine he did. He usually does, when he submits bills for approval.

Q. Did you pay your own counsel any special fee in this matter? A. Not unless it was Mr. Nicoll, who I think was associated in some manner with the case.

Q. Let us see who Mr. Nicoll represented in this case. I guess your recollection is a little in error on that point, Mr. Fisher. I don't see Mr. Nicoll's name among the counsel.

Chairman Thompson.— You are not a lawyer, Mr. Fisher?

Mr. Fisher.— No, sir.

Chairman Thompson.— Mr. Fisher could hardly know about these matters in a legal way.

Q. I see in the report of this case in the Court of Appeals that the attorneys for the Admiral Realty Company asserted and maintained that the proposed contracts for the operation of the subways about to be constructed by the City of New York, and the provisions of chapter 226 of the Laws of 1912, intended to authorize their execution, violate section 10 of Article VIII of the New

York Constitution. And there is a citation of a number of cases on that point. They also contended, according to the official report that the provisions of the Rapid Transit Act, so far as they authorized the Public Service Commission for the First District to grant franchises to railroad companies to lay down tracks, are also in violation of Article III, section 18 of the Constitution. Were you interested in seeing these contentions prevail? A. Not particularly.

Q. Do you ordinarily — I am asking you as to the practice of the Company — does the Interborough Rapid Transit Company pay such amounts as $60,000 and more to have the attorneys come into court to assert that the Interborough's course is in violation of the Constitution in several particulars? A. I think in a case where a $300 mortgage is contemplated —

Mr. Quackenbush.— Three hundred million.

The Witness.— Three hundred million dollar mortgage is contemplated, that it is worth that amount to know whether the contract which it is proposed to enter into is legal or not. I think it was worth that amount to the Interborough.

Q. Was anything — I see no mention in this case to the effect that this was a one-sided litigation in which the Interborough was paying counsel on both sides of the proposition. Was that stated at any time to any Court? A. I don't think so. I don't think you could get a very fair decision if that was stated.

Q. You mean you think the Court could throw the case out of court if that was known? I am inclined to agree with you, but I am not certain on that point. I see in the statement of disbursements which the Interborough Rapid Transit Company paid, that they paid costs to the Corporation Counsel, that they paid costs to George Coleman, that they paid two other bills of costs and disbursements, amounting to $600 irrespective of the form — although this attack upon the contracts had failed the Interborough is paying costs as if they were the defeated litigant. A. The City of New York and the Public Service Commission were equally interested with us, to know whether that contract was legal or not.

Q. But the City of New York and you prevailed, and won your case, and yet you are paying costs as of a defeated litigant; and

these costs are of a substantial amount. Did the city know this
was a prearranged and collusive case? A. I am not aware of
that.

Q. The Admiral Realty Company won either way, didn't it?
A. Probably.

Q. And these substantial payments to these distinguished
counsel would have been very substantial payments, had they conducted a real and arduous and serious litigation, wouldn't they?
A. I imagine that was pretty serious, entailed a good deal of
work.

Q. You don't recall any serious and earnest litigation in which
the counsel of your company were really trying to defend you
and to assert some valuable right, on which the attorneys were
paid on any more handsome scale than this, do you? A. Not at
present.

Q. I read from the endorsement on the memorandum — on the
voucher. Voucher No. 109942, that the amount paid Messrs.
Hays, Hershfield & Wolf, which, although not stated, I assume is
the aggregate of their bill and Guggenheimer, Untermyer &
Marshall's bill, namely, $63,000— $63,128.62, when it came to
distribution, was charged to " other suspense," and also to " proposed subway routes;" is that correct (shows voucher to witness)?
A. Yes, sir.

Mr. Colby.— I would like copies of that made (referring to
voucher No. 109942).

Mr. Fisher.— Can I get copies of these (to Mr. Quackenbush)?

Chairman Thompson.— Will somebody ask Senator Lawson to
step back here a minute?

Mr. Colby.— Let me just run over these other vouchers. I
think I won't use those until I have the complete statement
(witness hands vouchers to counsel).

Mr. Colby.— The witness produces —

Mr. Quackenbush.— Mr. Colby, had you finished your questions about that voucher?

Mr. Colby.— About the Guggenheimer, Untermyer & Marshall
vouchers? Yes. Would you like to make an explanation of that
matter?

Mr. Quackenbush.— If you will permit me, I will say it in the way that might be a little different from your characterization.

Mr. Colby.— Well, just a moment. Just a moment. I am anxious for an explanation, and would like to have it made on the record, and authoritatively, and I will ask the witness to step down, and ask you to take the stand.

Mr. Quackenbush.— I am willing to have anything I say go on the record.

Mr. Colby.— Just a second. This point is not so immaterial as I think you imagine.

Mr. Quackenbush.— I don't think it is immaterial at all. I propose, if the Chairman will permit me, to make a statement — a question of privilege.

Mr. Colby.— My suggestion is that the witness take the stand and tell us what he —

Mr. Quackenbush.— Just a moment. I have no objection to taking the stand any time the Chairman wishes me to.

Chairman Thompson.— All right. make your statement, and then we will see.

Mr. Quackenbush.— I have no personal knowledge of this transaction, but at noon I waited until Mr. Rogers had got back from court, and called his attention to the situation, and Mr. Rogers stated to me —

Chairman Thompson.— I think Mr. Rogers — you have no personal knowledge of it?

Mr. Quackenbush.— Mr. Rogers would be glad to come here at any time. I am not going to say what he said. I think I know the rules of evidence pretty well. Mr. Rogers will be glad to come here and explain the matter any time. He is detained in court.

Chairman Thompson.— That is fair.

Mr. Quackenbush.— I don't think that would require my being sworn.

Mr. Colby.— You are quite right, Mr. Quackenbush.

Chairman Thompson.— I am going to state right now that we have not caught Mr. Quackenbush in anything bad yet.

Mr. Quackenbush.— Not yet.

Mr. Colby.— I offer that voucher of the payments to Guggenheimer, Untermyer & Marshall and to Hays, Hershfield & Wolf, with the accompanying papers as produced by the witness in evidence. Will you direct that they be put in the record as evidence?

Chairman Thompson.— Yes. It will be extended in the record in full.

Voucher and attached papers follow:

INTERBOROUGH RAPID TRANSIT COMPANY,
To Hays, Hershfield & Wolf, Dr.,
Counsellors-at-Law.

Telephone " Cortlandt 301."
Rector, 791.   115 Broadway.

NEW YORK, *October* 3, 1912.

To professional services rendered in determining the validity of the proposed extensions of the subway system and the terms of operation thereof by the Interborough Rapid Transit Company, in connection with suits of Admiral Realty Co. vs. Gaynor (Action No. 1) and Admiral Realty Co. vs. City of New York (Action No. 2)— from Supreme Court to and including Court of Appeals, as per memoranda....... $35,000 00
Disbursements, as per memorandum annexed 2,809 90
                                                    $37,809 90

Bill of Guggenheimer, Untermyer & Marshall $25,000 00
Their disbursements 318 72
                                                    25,318 72

Total $63,128 62

MESSRS. HAYS, HERSHFIELD & WOLF,
To Guggenheimer, Untermyer & Marshall,
Counsellors-at-Law, 37 Wall street. ·

NEW YORK, *October* 3, 1912.

To counsel and services from July, 1911, to July, 1912, in the following matters:

Admiral Realty Co. v. Gaynor et al.

Revising complaint and affidavits on motion for a temporary injunction; application to Judge Giegerich for temporary injunction and procuring order to show cause; argument of motion for injunction at a Special Term held by Mr. Justice Ford; preparation of brief at Special Term; consultations with regard to appeal to the Appellate Division; preparation of brief on such appeal, and argument of the appeal at the Appellate Division.

Admiral Realty Co. v. City of New York, et al.

Conferences with counsel for the Public Service Commission with regard to the preparation of complaint in a suit to test the constitutionality of the proposed contracts between the City of New York, the Interborough Rapid Transit Company and the Brooklyn Rapid Transit Company for the construction of the new subways; revising the complaint; preparation of brief on argument of the demurrers interposed by the several defendants; argument of the issues of law on the demurrers at a Special Term held by Mr. Justice Blackmar; revision of brief for the Appellate Division of the Second Department, and argument of the appeal in that Court; preparation of brief for the Court of Appeals, and argument of the appeal in that court............ $25,000 00

Disbursements:

Traveling expenses of Mr. Marshall, from Saranac Lake and return...	$20	00
Carfares, telegrams, etc..........	12	27
Typewriting, copies of papers, etc..	120	00
Copy of opinion................	2	50
Printing brief in Gaynor Case.....	163	95

                                                    318 72

                                              $25,318 72

INTERBOROUGH RAPID TRANSIT COMPANY,
To Hays, Hershfield & Wolf, Dr.,
Counsellors-At-Law,
Telephone " Cortlandt 301."   115 Broadway

NEW YORK, *September 25, 1912.*

To professional services rendered in determining
the validity of the proposed extension of the subway system and the terms of operation thereof by
the Interborough Rapid Transit Company, in
connection with suits of Admiral Realty Co. vs.
Gaynor (Action No. 1) and Admiral Realty Co.
vs. City of New York (Action No. 2) — from
Supreme Court to and including Court of
Appeals, as per memoranda................ $35,000 00
Disbursements as per memorandum annexed......   2,809 90
                                                _____
                                                 $37,809 90

INTERBOROUGH RAPID TRANSIT COMPANY,
To Hays, Hershfield & Wolf, Dr.,
Counsellors-At-Law,
Telephone " Cortlandt 301 "   115 Broadway.

NEW YORK, *July* 8, 1912.

Actual disbursements:

1911.

July	27	Copies of contract................	$9 00
Aug.	1	Law Reporting Co................	1 50
	26	Subway plans	31 00
Sept.	8	Fidelity bond	10 00
	12	Fidelity bond	15 00
	16	Contract maps	15 00
Oct.	25	Filing note of issue..............	3 00
	28	Additional maps	2 50
	28	Additional maps	15 00
Nov.	14	Press of Fremont Payne..........	296 85
Dec.	1	Opinion	2 50
	29	Certified copy of order............	65

1912.

Jan.	23	A. R. Watson, Corporation Counsel, costs	$27	04
		George S. Coleman, costs..........	83	58
		James Lynch	5	18
March	14	Stern & Wolf, ext. Penn. authorities..	15	00
		Fidelity bond	10	00
	18	Appeal Printing Co...............	65	35
		Appeal Printing Co...............	98	30
May	9	Maurice Deutsch, civil engineer.....	150	00
June	4	Costs, A. R. Watson, Corp. Counsel..	75	50
	15	Fidelity bond	10	00
		Incidental disbursements, long distance telephones, copies opinions and other innumerable items	100	83
		Evening Post — printing case.......	769	87
		Evening Post — printing brief......	220	30
		Evening Post — printing appeal.....	17	40
		Evening Post — printing brief......	159	55
		Two bills of costs and disbursements to be hereafter taxed, estimated....	600	00

$2,809 90

Interborough Rapid Transit Company.

Transcript from Minutes of Regular Meeting of the Board of Directors, held on Wednesday, October 9, 1912.

" The President submitted for the consideration of the Board bills of Messrs. Hays, Hershfield & Wolf for $37,-809.90 and Messrs. Guggenheimer, Untermyer & Marshall for $25,318.72 for professional services and expenses in determining the validity of the proposed extension of the Subway System and the terms of operation thereof by the Interborough Rapid Transit Company in connection with suits of Admiral Realty Company vs. Gaynor and the City of New York. Whereupon,

On motion, duly seconded, it was

Resolved: That the bills of Messrs. Hays, Hershfield & Wolf for $37,809.90 and Messrs. Guggenheimer, Untermyer & Marshall for $25,318.72 for professional services and expenses in the suits above referred to be, and the same hereby are, approved, and the President authorized to pay the same."

> I hereby certify that the above is a true copy of resolution from Minutes of Regular Meeting of the Board of Directors of the Interborough Rapid Transit Co., held on Wednesday, October 9, 1912.
>
> (Signed)   H. M. FISHER,
> *Secretary.*

(SEAL)

Telephone " Rector 791 "
Hays, Hershfield & Wolf, Counsellors-at-Law.   No. 115 Broadway
Daniel P. Hays,
A. Hershfield
Ralph Wolf
Edwin D. Hays
S. P. Friedman

NEW YORK, *Oct.* 21, 1912.

Interborough Rapid Transit Co.,
    Mr. Campbell,

Dear Sir.— The bearer, E. D. Hays, of our office, is authorized to receive check and receipt in our firm name for bill heretofore rendered you, which includes bill of Messrs. Guggenheimer, Untermyer & Marshall.

> Yours truly,
> (Signed)   Hays, Hershfield & Wolf.

Oct. 17, 1912.

E. F. J. Gaynor for voucher as per Resolution of Board of Directors, I. R. T. Co. of Oct. 9, 1912, copy of which was sent you.   (Signed)   W. L. P.

INTERBOROUGH RAPID TRANSIT COMPANY,
    To Hays, Hershfield & Wolf, Dr.

1912.

Oct.   17th.   For professional services rendered in determining the
                validity of the proposed extensions of the Subway
                system and the terms of operation thereof, as per
                bill attached, $63,128.62

H. T. B.

NEW YORK, *Oct.* 21st, 1912.

Examined and found correct,   Received from the Inter-
(signed) E. F. J. Gaynor,   borough Rapid Transit Co.
                    Auditor.   Sixty-three thousand one hun-
Approved for payment,   dred twenty-eight and 62/100
(signed) W. Leon Pepperman, ... Dollars
    Assistant to President.   For payment in full of the
                                     above account.
                                        (signed)   Hays,   Hershfield
                                                               & Wolf.
                                     Per Edwin D. Hays.

Q. The witness produces another voucher, numbered 92402,
apparently indicating a payment to Edward M. Grout. I hand
you this voucher and ask you what that payment was for (handing voucher to witness)? A. For professional services in connection with subway matters.

Q. Is there any specification upon Mr. Grout's bill as to what
the services are? A. Here is another bill. That is the retainer,
and this is the balance of his bill. Perhaps that might give you
a little further explanation.

Q. The witness produces a further voucher numbered 110613,
for the payment of $7500 to Edward M. Grout, on December 5,
1912. The former payment is apparently under date of July 7,
1911. Seven thousand five hundred dollars is additional to the
prior payment. And affixed to the later voucher is a letter from
Mr. Rogers, general manager of the company, addressed to the
Auditor, advising the Auditor that 'Mr. Grout's claim was for
$15,000 additional to the ten first paid him, but that Mr. Rogers
has been able to arrange, through a third party, a compromise of
the claim, by the payment of $7500. There is no statement, Mr.

Fisher, that I can discover on either voucher or the papers annexed to it, as to what the services rendered by Mr. Grout were, or in what connection they were rendered. Can you enlighten me, after examination of the papers? A. I cannot. Not beyond the fact they were personal conferences with the President in connection with subway matters, the new subway matters.

Q. Are these bills annexed to the vouchers the only bills received by the Interborough from Mr. Grout? A. Yes, sir.

Q. One bill says, "June 23, 1911. The Interborough Rapid Transit Company to Edward M. Grout, Debtor, To retainer, $10,000." Was any bill with a greater degree of specification ever delivered to the company? A. No, sir.

Q. Annexed to the later voucher is a bill from Mr. Grout to the Interborough Rapid Transit Company, which says "to professional services, $15,000." The voucher dated December 5, 1912, contains an acknowledgment of Mr. Grout's receipt or $7500, in full payment of the above account, confirming Mr. Rogers' statement in his letter that he had arranged a compromise. There is no statement on either voucher or the purposes of these services or what the bills cover? A. No, sir.

Q. Let me see the earlier one, please. (Witness hands voucher to counsel.)

Q. The earlier voucher, numbered 92402, for $10,000, contains the following notations, under the head of "distribution." "Other suspense" and "proposed subway routes." The subsequent voucher, dated December 5, 1912, for $7500 — this is voucher No. 110613 — contains, under "distribution" the same notations; that is to say, "other suspense", and "proposed subway routes." This term, or this account, described as "other suspense", recurs on most of these vouchers; can you tell me what it is? A. No, sir, I could not.

Q. Would you infer that there is an account on the books of the company entitled "other suspense"? A. I could not say.

Q. Would you infer that? A. I seldom infer when I don't know anything about it.

Q. You don't know anything about it.

Mr. Quackenbush.— Mr. Gaynor is here now, if you want an explanation.

Q. Do you know whether these are names of accounts? A. I presume they are. I can only guess at it. I am not familiar with that.

Q. It was customary under " distribution " to indicate the names of the accounts? I gather that from other vouchers where the amounts are apportioned, and referred to different accounts? A. (No answer.)

Mr. Colby.— I offer the two vouchers containing recital of payments to Edward M. Grout, which I have so fully read in evidence.

Chairman Thompson.— Received. You can mark them, to-day's exhibits 1, 2, 3 and 4.

Q. I understand, Mr. Fisher, that when the Interborough Interborough Rapid Transit Company's bonds, under the contract with J. P. Morgan & Company, were delivered to the bankers, in other words, to Morgan & Company, the proceeds of the bonds were not delivered to the Interborough Rapid Transit Company but were placed to its credit, or rather, more exactly, to the credit of its accounts with J. P. Morgan & Company; is that correct? A. That is correct, but it amounted to the same thing. They were there subject to our checks.

Q. But to be precise, when you delivered $30,000,000 of bonds per year, as you were called upon to do, you did not receive 93½ per cent. of $30,000,000 in the form of warrant or check? A. Placed to our credit.

Q. And you drew as your occasions required? A. Yes.

Q. The result of that method was a very considerable amount of cash in Morgan & Company's possession belonging to the Interborough Rapid Transit Company? A. Yes, sir.

Q. Running into millions? A. Yes, sir.

Q. And into many millions, even, from an Interborough Point of view? A. Quite right.

Q. You have drawn off for me, at my request this morning, a statement of your balances with J. P. Morgan & Company at the close of business Saturday, February 5, 1916, I believe? A. Yes, sir.

Q. And is this memorandum which you hand me a correct statement of the amount of those balances? A. Yes, sir.

Q. I ask you how much the Interborough Rapid Transit Company on that date had to its credit at J. P. Morgan & Company's, on general acount (hands paper to witness)? A. $5,489,000.62.

Q. I think you are in error. A. $5,000, I should have said. I am used to dealing in millions. Excuse me.

Q. Never mind, Mr. Fisher. We will simply carry the discrepancy to "other suspense." How much of a balance did the Interborough Rapid Transit Company have on February 5th, with J. P. Morgan & Company on account of subway contribution? A. About forty-four millions.

Q. Will you read the exact figures from your memorandum? A. $44,166,721.83.

Q. How much on Manhattan third-tracking account? A. $54,943.33.

Q. And how much on elevated extension account? A. $6,857,646.27.

Q. In other words, as I hurriedly foot up those — the amount of those accounts, it was considerably in excess of fifty million dollars? A. Yes, sir.

Q. Now, J. P. Morgan & Company have already received the bonds of the Interborough Rapid Transit Company covering these amounts, have they not? A. Yes, sir.

Q. And the Interborough Rapid Transit Company is earning and paying interest on all bonds delivered to J. P. Morgan & Company, is it not? A. It is not paying interest from earnings. We will put it that way.

Q. Well, they are paying interest at the rate stipulated in the bonds? A. Yes, sir.

Q. And that rate is 5 per cent.? A. Yes, sir.

Q. What rate of interest are you getting from J. P. Morgan & Company on those amounts? A. Two and one-half per cent.

Chairman Thompson.— Fifty-fifty.

Q. In other words, as an indirect or inherent result in the arrangement existing between the Interborough Rapid Transit Company and J. P. Morgan & Company, J. P. Morgan & Company is deriving 2½ per cent. profit on their money in your possession? A. I should not say so.

Q. As the result of the operation of your mutual accounts? A. No, sir.

Q. How can you — A. I imagine not. I am not positive, but I imagine not.

Q. I mean to say there is a difference between what you are paying 5 per cent. and interest, on your bonds, and what you are receiving on the idle proceeds of the bonds that lie at Morgan's, of 2½? A. We are not paying that interest to J. P. Morgan. We are paying that to the bondholders.

Q. How large an amount of your bonds are at present in the possession of J. P. Morgan & Company? A. That I could not say. We delivered the bonds to them, and how many they have sold I don't know. I imagine they have sold them nearly all.

Q. They have had from time to time during the operation of this contract large amounts? A. They call them large amounts. How long they hold them I could not tell you.

Q. Is there any stipulation in your contract with J. P. Morgan & Company, or any private understanding, that these large balances shall remain in the possession of J. P. Morgan & Company at 2½ per cent.? A. They have agreed to allow us 2½ per cent. while they remain there. They only remain there so long as we don't need them elsewhere.

Q. Have you ever said, or have the Interborough said, to J. P. Morgan, that "We don't need to issue bonds now. We have all the money we need, and if we do we will have 2½ per cent."— A. We made a contract with Morgan to issue, as stipulated (answer not heard by stenographer). They did so, and we delivered them without question. They naturally want to take advantage of any bond market in disposing of them.

Q. Two and one-half per cent. is rather of a low rate on money in Wall street? A. No, sir, it is not unusually low.

Q. You can't get money for 2½ per cent.? A. Perhaps I have not the collateral.

Q. I mean the Interborough Rapid Transit Company cannot get money for 2½ per cent.? A. The Interborough Rapid Transit Company can borrow money as cheap as anybody.

Q. Two and one-half per cent.? A. That I don't know.

Q. How much is the Interborough Rapid Transit Company really paying for the money it gets on the bonds? Nominally they pay 5 per cent. on par. In reality they are getting only 93½ per cent. Say they are paying 5 per cent. on par, what per cent. is that on 93½ ?   A. Five and three-eighths.

Q. I want a statement of the current balances by the month ? A. I have a memorandum of that.

Q. I will resume that inquiry when you are equipped to answer the questions. I call your attention to page 236 of the minute book of the Interborough Rapid Transit Company for 1911. There appears there a record of the meeting of the board of directors held on November 29, 1911. Is this record beginning at page 236, the minutes of the company, of a regular meeting of the Board held on that day ?   A. Yes, sir.

Q. I read from the minutes of a regular meeting of the Board of Directors held on November 29, 1911:

"The President laid before the Board a claim of Messrs. J. P. Morgan & Company for services as bankers during the past few years in connection with the negotiations of the Interborough Rapid Transit Company with the authorities of the City of New York on the subway and elevated extensions and improvements, and also a claim of Messrs. J. P. Morgan & Company on behalf of themselves and their syndicate associates, for commitments, for money approximating thirty million dollars, to cover elevated extensions and improvements, and $7,500 to cover subway extensions and improvements. In order to enable the Interborough Rapid Transit Company to effect a contract with the City authorities. The President further stated that as a result of conferences with Messrs. J. P. Morgan & Company, they had agreed to accept $250,000 to cover their personal services, and $250,000 to cover the services and commitments of their syndicate associates, the latter sum, however, to be deducted from any commissions which the syndicate associates might become entitled to if an agreement should be entered into with the City for the construction of subway extensions or elevated extensions prior to March 1st, 1912, all terms of such advances to be the subject of future agreement between the Interborough Rapid Transit Company and Messrs. J. P. Morgan & Company. Whereupon," the minutes continue,

"upon consideration, it was duly resolved that the claim of
Messrs. J. P. Morgan & Company for personal services be
adjusted at the sum of $250,000, to be paid Messrs. J. P.
Morgan & Company personally; and that the claim of Messrs.
Morgan & Company, on behalf of their financial associates,
for financial commitments, be adjusted at the further sum of
$250,000, to be paid them on account of their syndicate asso-
ciates, the latter sum, however, to be credited upon any commissions or profits that may go to the syndicate associates
for further services or commitments in event an agreement
should be entered into between the Interborough Company
and the City of New York for the construction of elevated
or subway extensions and improvements, prior to March 1st,
1912, all terms of such advances to be the subject of future
agreement between the Interborough Rapid Transit and
Messrs. J. P. Morgan & Company, and that vouchers of the
company be made out and delivered to Messrs. J. P. Morgan
& Company in conformity with this resolution."

Chairman Thompson.— Is there anywhere in these books a
definition of what the word "commitment" means?

Mr. Colby.— We are hopeful —

Mr. Fisher.— Pretty good definition right there.

By Mr. Colby:

Q. Have you a voucher of this payment of $500,000 to J. P.
Morgan & Company? A. I presume we have; yes, sir. I am
quite sure we have, because no payments are made without
vouchers.

Q. Am I correct in assuming that pursuant to this resolution,
the sum of $500,000 was paid to J. P. Morgan & Company? A.
Yes, sir.

Q. I see that the sum that was to be paid to Messrs. Morgan &
Company on behalf of their syndicate associates might be deducted
from the commissions eventually received by the syndicate
associates; that is right? A. That is right.

Q. But the $250,000 that was paid to J. P. Morgan & Company
personally was not subject to any application on subsequent commissions? A. No, sir.

Q. The date of this meeting was November 29, 1911? A. Yes, sir.

Q. When were the dual contracts entered into? A. Signed, you mean?

Q. Yes. A. March 19, 1913.

Q. Something over a year later? A. Yes, sir.

Q. About fifteen months later I would say? A. Yes, sir.

Q. The Interborough Rapid Transit Company began paying out money on account of these dual contracts pretty early in the game, didn't it. A. I believe that speaks for itself.

Q. Now, why was this $500,000 paid to Messrs. J. P. Morgan & Company fifteen months before the dual contract was signed? A. The Interborough were on the verge of signing — negotiating a contract with the city for about two years. They could not close the contract committing themselves to an obligation of practically one hundred or one hundred and twenty-five million dollars without having the money in sight. Their arrangements with the bankers were the bankers should furnish the money. The bankers in turn, I presume, had formed a syndicate to take these bonds. This syndicate, of course, could not make commitments elsewhere so long as they were committed to the bankers, Morgan & Company, to take these bonds when offered. Naturally their losses were more or less severe on that account. And that is the service for which this amount of money was paid. In other words, keeping themselves in readiness for a period of about two years to furnish the Interborough on demand with one hundred million dollars of cash.

Chairman Thompson.— In other words, they charge for money down here according to the peak of the load?

Mr. Fisher.— Yes, sir; I think you might say they do. And legal expenses on a peak, too.

Chairman Thompson.— Yes.

By Mr. Colby:

Q. Mr. Fisher, this is a very interesting phase of this important transaction, and I would like to pursue it closely and question further. In other words, Morgan & Company were paid for their services in holding themselves in readiness to do something; is that right? A. Not exactly. You might put it more aptly, if you said Morgan & Company were paid for their services in holding one hundred million dollars ready to be delivered to the Interborough on demand.

Q. Do you understand they held it in cash? A. I do not understand they actually held the cash. But if they obligated themselves, as they had agreed to do any time we signed the contract, to furnish this hundred million dollars, they would have to know where to go and get the money.

Chairman Thompson.— Where is that obligation? Have you got it?

Mr. Fisher.— No, sir. I don't think we have any written obligation.

Chairman Thompson.— Was there ever a written obligation?

Mr. Fisher.— There might have been letters between the President's office and the bankers, of which I have no knowledge.

Chairman Thompson.— Well, then, how was there an obligation? A man's word to lend money isn't any good.

Mr. Fisher.— I should say Morgan & Company's is.

Chairman Thompson.— You think, it would be enforced in court?

Mr. Fisher.— I don't know. I don't think they would let it come to that point.

By Mr. Colby:

Q. This obligation to furnish money could not be a very serious or burdensome obligation if the process finally hit upon builds up, as is apparently the case, a balance of over $50,000,000 of your money in the hands of J. P. Morgan & Company. It can't be very burdensome if that is the operation and true effect of the obligation. A. That is the effect of the obligation at the present time, while we have a very good bond market. If you had received a statement of that kind probably a year or two ago, you would have found the balance very much smaller.

Q. The balance has fluctuated from time to time? A. Yes, sir.

Q. That has always been important and considerable, has it not? A. Yes, sir; but it was very low, as I say, during the money stringency, if you want to call it that.

Q. But it might be cut in half, and still be in excess of $25,000,000? A. It has been very much below that.

Q. And as I understand it, Morgan & Company are only called upon to pay you 93½ per cent. of thirty millions per year? A. Yes, sir.

Q. So that the balance might be half of what it is now down toward the conclusion of this operation, and still be equal to the entire obligation of Morgan & Company in any given month; is that not true? A. Yes, sir.

Q. In order not to take this important subject up in a fragmentary way, Mr. Fisher, I will resume your examination when you have the statement of the monthly current balances which I assume without great effort can be produced to-morrow morning, can it not? A. Yes, sir. I would like to make a correction in my testimony. I find that I actually have the contracts here between Morgan & Company and ourselves, agreeing to furnish this money. This contract or letter is dated September 15, 1910, and it covers all of the matters about which I just explained. I have not read it myself since that time, and it passed out of my memory. (Hands papers to Chairman Thompson.)

Q. Mr. Fisher, you will produce the Morgan voucher to-morrow, will you? A. Yes, sir.

Q. And also the statement of current balances? A. Yes, sir.

Q. Also the complete statement of legal expenses of Interborough Rapid Transit, Interborough-Met., and the other companies? A. Yes, sir.

Mr. Fisher.— Have you finished with me?

Mr. Colby.— Finished, thank you very much. You will be here at 11 o'clock to-morrow?

Chairman Thompson.—All witnesses are excused until to-morrow morning at 11 o'clock.

Whereupon (at 4:05 o'clock P. M.), an adjournment was taken until Tuesday, February 8, 1916, at 11 o'clock A. M.

FEBRUARY 8, 1916

New York County Lawyers' Association
Rooms, 165 Broadway, New York City.

Meeting called to order by Chairman Thompson at 11 A. M., February 8, 1916, pursuant to adjournment, a quorum being present.

H. M. Fisher, being recalled, testified as follows:

Mr. Colby.— Mr. Chairman, there are various inferences on these accounts paid to outside counsel which suggest to me the propriety of introducing these vouchers and calling the Committee's attention to the services covered by them so as to show that the minutes of the company directing that a bonus be paid to Mr. Rogers on the ground that his services which defeated the employment of outside counsel is to a very large extent inaccurate, I think I am justified in saying misleading. Furthermore the bonus which the evidence shows amounted to $150,000 paid to the company's president decidedly is extraordinary, and under the circumstances, Mr. Chairman, I think it is necessary that the record should contain and that the Committee should receive a statement of the kind of services rendered along identical lines that have been rendered by outside counsel to the company, and that we should put that in evidence. I might say, further, Mr. Chairman, that in introducing these vouchers for payment to outside counsel, I read the terms of the resolution under which the Rogers bonus was paid. It seems to expressly recite that it is a guarantee of a payment of $50,000 for Mr. Rogers' services which in effect relieves the company of the necessity of employing outside counsel.

Q. Mr. Fisher, the Interborough Rapid Transit Company has regular attorneys of its own under permanent or rather fixed engagements from year to year, has it not? A. Yes, sir.

Q. The general attorney of the company is Mr. Quackenbush? A. Yes.

Q. Mr. Quackenbush has a large suite of offices that are part of the offices in this building occupied by the Interborough Rapid Transit Company? A. Yes.

Q. He employs many attorneys and assistants, does he not? A. Yes.

Q. Mr. Quackenbush is in charge of what I may correctly describe as the legal department of the Interborough Rapid Transit Company, is he not? A. Yes.

Q. Do you know how many men or how many persons are employed in the legal department? A. I couldn't say.

Q. Can you testify to this approximately? A. I wouldn't like to; no sir.

Chairman Thompson.— Will Mr. Quackenbush have any objection to informing the witness?

Mr. Quackenbush.— I cannot tell you offhand, Mr. Chairman, the exact number of employes in the legal department, but I can have a list prepared.

By Mr. Colby:

Q. Could you testify from recollection about the number of lawyers?

Mr. Quackenbush.— The attorneys are paid for by all of the companies, and their services are distributed, for instance, among the Interborough Rapid Transit Company, the New York Railways and the Third Avenue system. I should think there were about sixty lawyers.

By Chairman Thompson:

Q. That is your department? A. Yes.

By Mr. Colby:

Q. And a considerable number of clerks, stenographers, process servers, I presume? A. Yes, sir, so that I think in a general way the force I am in charge of runs up at the present time to something over 200 persons.

Q. That is the recognized law department of the railway company? A. Yes, sir.

Q. What is the average cost per annum to the department?

Mr. Quackenbush.— I wouldn't like to state that from memory, but I will be glad to have a statement prepared and submitted to you.

Chairman Thompson.— At the rates we have established for legal talent Mr. Quackenbush's salary should be fixed by this Committee at $500,000 a year.

Mr. Quackenbush.— I am quite willing it should be done.

By Mr. Colby:

Q. I didn't know but what you could tell me about what the cost of the legal department was per annum.

Mr. Quackenbush.— I would not care to state that from recollection, but I will have a statement of it for you.

By Mr. Colby:

Q. I asked you for some data yesterday, Mr. Fisher. A. You asked me for some original vouchers and here they are (witness delivers vouchers to Mr. Colby).

Q. Did I not ask for some other records. I think I asked you for some other records also, Mr. Fisher. A. A statement of the monthly balances of J. P. Morgan & Company. I have that.

Q. Have you a statement of the amount paid to counsel I asked for yesterday? A. A statement of counsel will be down in a few minutes.

Q. And you are at work on the memorandum as to financing? A. Yes, sir.

Q. I asked you yesterday also for the vouchers covering the payment or commiting of $500,000 to J. P. Morgan & Company by the Interborough Rapid Transit Company for their services as bankers either for themselves or the syndicate which they represented, that is the statement of the amount paid to J. P. Morgan & Company for their own services as bankers and also for their services as bankers representing a syndicate. Have you produced the two vouchers in question? A. I have. (Witness delivers two vouchers referred to by Mr. Colby.)

Q. I have here voucher No. 97,767 representing payment of $250,000 to the firm of J. P. Morgan & Company. The voucher is dated November 29, 1911. It appears from the terms as stated in the voucher that it is an amount to cover commitments to Messrs. J. P. Morgan & Company and to their syndicate associates for money approximating $30,000,000 to cover elevated extensions and improvements and $75,000,000 to cover subway extensions and improvements. The voucher then goes on to recite that this amount to be credited upon any commission or profits that may go to Messrs. J. P. Morgan & Company or their syndicate associates for further service and commitment in the event of an agreement being entered into between the Interborough Rapid Transit Company and the City of New York for the construction of elevated or subway extensions and improvements prior to March 1, 1912. Then there is a statement which reads that the payment is in accordance with the resolution of the board of directors of November 29, 1911, and annexed to the voucher is a certified transcript of the minutes, setting forth the resolution which was read yesterday. The payment of this sum of $150,000 is acknowledged by J. P. Morgan & Company, under date of December 1, 1911. There is a notation on the voucher to the effect that the amount of this voucher is distributed 31/105 to the Interborough Rapid Transit Company, Manhattan improvement and 74/105 proposed subway routes. Under distribution it appears on the bottom of the voucher that there was carried through the Interborough Rapid Transit Company, Manhattan improvement miscellaneous $71,428.57 and that there was charged or referred to other suspense and proposed subway routes $178,571.43. I offer this voucher in evidence.

Chairman Thompson.— Received and copy will be sent to us for our records. Can you have a copy made for us, Mr. Fisher?

Mr. Fisher.— Yes, sir.

(Voucher No. 97,767 was thereupon offered in evidence and received.)

Mr. Colby.— The second voucher produced by the witness is Interborough Rapid Transit Company voucher No. 97,768. It sets forth a payment of $250,000 to J. P. Morgan & Company under date of November 29, 1911, for services as bankers during the past two years in connection with the negotiations of the Interborough Rapid Transit Company with the City of New York for subway and elevated extensions and improvements. It shows that this sum is acknowledged by Messrs. J. P. Morgan &

Company, on December 1, 1911, and there is annexed to the
voucher a certified transcript of the minutes setting forth the
resolution of the board adopted on November 29, 1911, under
the authority of which the payment was made.

Mr. Fisher.— Yes.

Chairman Thompson.— Should not that first voucher which
you have read into the record, Mr. Colby, be for $250,000 instead
of $150,000?

Mr. Colby.— Yes, that is correct and should appear so on the
record. This latter voucher contains this endorsement under the
heading distribution. " To Interborough Rapid Transit Company, Manhattan improvement, $71,428.57. To other suspense,
proposed subway routes, $178,571.43."

Q. These two separate payments of $250,000 to J. P. Morgan
& Company seem to have been contributed in practically the same
way, Mr. Fisher? A. I understand so.

Q. That is correct, is it? A. Yes.

Q. Do you know how the distribution was determined? A.
No, sir. That was determined by the auditor.

Q. You don't know what the standard of distribution or what
the theory of distribution was? A. No.

Q. Now this payment of $250,000 to J. P. Morgan & Com-
pany was for services as bankers during the past two years, that
is to say for the two years prior to 1911. I call your attention
to that in the voucher. Do you know what service Morgan &
Company rendered from 1909 to 1911? A. I think that is
pretty fully explained in the resolution you examined.

Q. Will you just take the resolution and see if you can answer
it I am calling attention to the payment on account of services
for the two years prior to 1911. A. The service consisted of
holding themselves in readiness to furnish as stated in the resolution $30,000,000 to cover elevated extensions and improvements
and $75,000,000 to cover subway extensions and improvements on
demand of the Interborough Rapid Transit Company.

Q. Do you understand that J. P. Morgan & Company held any
given number of million dollars in hand during the two years

prior to 1911, set aside for this fund? A. Not necessarily so,
but they obligated themselves to furnish the money on demand.

Q. Well the contract however, was not signed until ten months
had elapsed after November, 1911? A. That was for proposed
contracts or probable contracts which the company hoped to enter
into with the city and for which negotiations were had.

Q. Did Morgan & Company receive any pay for their services
as bankers in holding themselves in readiness, as appears by the
payment of this $250,000 in accordance with the voucher, and
the time when the contracts were actually signed? A. No.

Q. Well that is rather queer, isn't it Mr. Fisher? That period
as I have before called your attention, Mr. Fisher, amounted to
fifteen months and so they received practically $500,000 for hold-
ing themselves in readiness to receive some more. A. That is
covered by the agreement to take the bonds at a price. They
would receive payment for that service from the commissions that
they got on the sale of the bonds.

Q. You mean for the state of preparedness in which presumably
they held themselves for the fifteen months that elapsed after that
payment? A. For their agreement to furnish the money we
wanted.

Q. Did J. P. Morgan & Company make any agreement to hold
themselves in readiness to meet your financial requirements?
A. They had agreed to do so.

Q. In what form was that made? A. In the form of a letter
in 1910.

Q. But the period covered by their bill for services embraces
1909. Did they make any agreement in 1909 to hold themselves
in readiness to meet your requirements? A. There was no
previous agreement to the 1910 agreement.

Q. Have you the 1910 agreement? A. Yes.

Q. The original of it? A. I can get it in a few minutes.

Q. I wish you would send for it. A. I will send for it at once.

Q. What is your understanding of the syndicate referred to
in the second bill of $250,000 paid to J. P. Morgan & Company?
A. My understanding is that Morgan & Company had formed a
syndicate to take any bonds we might issue and advance the money.

Q. Do you know what the term commitment means in the Morgan voucher? A. I couldn't say in what relation they used it.

Q. Well, what does it mean in the resolution of your Board?. A. It means that they have committed themselves to the Interborough Rapid Transit Company to furnish this money when wanted.

Q. Their syndicate associates, I believe, you testified were three firms of bankers here? A. Yes.

Q. That was the Lee, Higgins & Company, Kissell, Kinnicutt & Company and Harris, Forbes & Company? A. That is correct.

Q. Is it your understanding that this $250,000 was divided among the various members of the syndicate? A. No. I have no knowledge on that subject whatever.

Q. Was any statement made that the members of the syndicate were entitled to some compensation for something or other? A. That was a matter known entirely by Morgan & Company. It wouldn't come within our knowledge.

Q. That somewhat elaborate reference to a syndicate may have been merely the terminology that Morgan & Company employed in asking the Interborough Rapid Transit Company the amount represented by that payment? A. Not necessarily so. It is customary to organize a syndicate to take a bond issue.

Q. Was there a statement in the board meeting at which you were present, Mr. Secretary, to the effect that Morgan & Company wanted $500,000? A. Nothing beyond what you see in the resolution.

Q. The point which I am directing your thoughts to Mr. Fisher, is this, was there any statements that Morgan & Company must have $500,000, any discussion of these two separate amounts of $250,000? A. No. It was understood that they had incurred this expense in holding themselves in readiness during a period of two or three years while we were negotiating with the city for subway and elevated extensions to furnish the money on demand to the company.

Q. You say that they had incurred this expense. You say the Morgan Company had incurred this expense in the matter of two or three years. One of the Morgan & Company vouchers expressly says for services as bankers. A. I couldn't say how that is described.

Q. Well, now, Mr. Fisher, I am referring to the $500,000 as

a whole. I am quite correct, I know, as I read the voucher for the payment of the $250,000 which I show to you that it states that it is for services as bankers? A. Yes.

Q. What is the meaning of this reference in one of the vouchers to the effect that this amount to be credited upon any commission or profits that may go to Messrs. J. P. Morgan & Company or to their syndicate for further services and commitment. A. That means that any commission which they would receive on the sale of the bonds within the time specified would be credited to that account.

Q. Well, what commission did they receive from the sale of the bonds? A. They did not receive any commissions on the sale of the bonds. They bought the bonds outright at a price of 93½.

Q. So that I am to understand that there never were any commissions upon which the amounts of these vouchers could be credited? A. That was a subsequent transaction. This transaction was a closed one in 1912. It was subsequently carried out in 1913.

Q. So that the provision in the resolution of the board which also appears in this voucher, that the amount of the payment to Morgan & Company were to be credited upon commission or profits that might go to Morgan & Company, expired by limitation on March 1, 1912? A. Except that Mr. Shonts succeeded in securing an extension of that time until April 1st.

Q. 1912? A. Yes. As we had hoped to close the contract with the city in the meantime.

Q. But at any rate upon the expiration of four months after the receipt of this money, Morgan & Company's title to it became absolute and freed of any obligation to credit against the subsequent commission? A. Yes.

Q. Wasn't that a pretty short time in view of the state of the negotiations at the time of these payments? A. That was for a payment from the beginning of negotiations in 1909 or 1910, covering a period of two or three years during which they held themselves in readiness.

Q. Do you recall exactly the state of the negotiations on December 1, 1911? A. No, sir. I do not without reference to the record.

Q. Do you know whether the negotiations looked as though an agreement was going to be reached at that time? A. The negotiations with the city looked as though an agreement might be reached at any time during the entire period.

Q. Why, if Morgan & Company received this $500,000 for holding themselves ready to do this business, which appeared at the moment to have been exceedingly profitable to them, why did they include the statement that the payment should only be chargeable against commission provided it was done prior to March 1st? A. That was fixed afterwards. There was a period of time there during which it looked as if the company would not be able to make any terms with the city and it was during that time that this period was fixed.

Q. So, Mr. Fisher, this elaborate statement in the resolution as well as in the voucher about the amount of these payments being credited upon any commission or profits that may be subsequently received is already inoperative and has no present significance? A. No.

Q. It is not operative at the present time? A. No, sir.

Q. And this payment of $500,000 to Morgan & Company for their services and that of their three banking firm associates had become an absolute payment? A. An absolute payment, yes, sir.

Chairman Thompson.— Who is this syndicate?

Mr. Colby.— That is already on the record, Mr. Chairman. It is Lee, Higgins & Company; Kissell, Kinnicutt & Company, and Forbes & Company.

Mr. Fisher.— I would like to note that there is nothing in the record to show that these three firms compose the syndicate under that original proposition which you are speaking of.

Q. Don't these three firms compose the present syndicate. That is the syndicate that had disposed of the bonds? A. Yes.

Q. Lee, Higgins & Company are sometimes referred to as the Boston Correspondents of J. P. Morgan & Company, are they not? A. That I cannot say.

Q. Have you ever heard that? A. Yes, sir, I have.

Q. Is any member of the firm of J. P. Morgan & Company a member of the Lee, Higgins & Company of Boston? A. Not to my knowledge.

Q. Or *vice versa*? A. Not to my knowledge.

Q. Have you the contract with Morgan & Company that they were holding themselves in readiness? A. I have, sir. (Witness produces contract and delivers same to Mr. Colby.)

Q. The services rendered by J. P. Morgan & Company during the two years prior to 1911 were pursuant to the contract set forth in the letter you have produced dated September 15, 1910, is that correct? A. That is my understanding at the present time.

Q. There is no record in the Company's files of any contract with J. P. Morgan & Company relating to this service, made at the time they are alleged to have begun is there? A. No, sir.

Q. This is the only letter there is on the subject? A. Yes. I would like to add to my statement that there were daily conferences between President Shonts and Mr. Morgan and his firm and there may be some correspondence in the President's file relating to that of which I have no knowledge.

Mr. Colby.— I will read into the record the letter written on the letter head of J. P. Morgan & Company, dated New York, September 15, 1910, and addressed to Mr. Theodore P. Shonts, President, Interborough Rapid Transit Company, 165 Broadway, New York.

" Dear Sir.— We beg to confirm as follows the substance of our conversation of yesterday relative to a plan for financing the Interborough Rapid Transit Company.

" 1. The basis of the plan will be a new First and Refunding Mortgage securing an authorized issue of $150,000,000, fifty year 5 per cent. coupon and registered form bonds in 1960, interest payable semi-annually. The mortgage will contain provisions for an annual sinking fund, not exceeding 1 per cent. of the total amount outstanding, and other provisions satisfactory to us and will be a general lien on all the company's properties and rights. The present mortgage of the Interborough Company dated November 1, 1907, is to be closed against issue of bonds thereunder, except as required by the convertible clauses of the notes due May 1, 1911, and except bonds for an additional amount at par sufficient to reimburse the company for capital expenditures heretofore made out of earnings (the bonds heretofore issued as collateral, except as so required, to be cancelled).

" 2. During the month of November, 1910, the Interborough Company will issue its 6 per cent. two and one-half year notes for the principal amount of $30,000,000 secured by $37,500,000 par value of the new bonds due 1960 above mentioned, the interest on such notes to be payable quarterly or semi-annually as may be agreed between us, and the notes to be redeemable at par, at the election of the Interborough Company, either at the end of the first year or on any interest date thereafter, the Interborough Company to give at least thirty days' prior notice of its election to redeem.

" 3. During the month of November, 1910, J. P. Morgan & Company, will purchase from the Interborough Company and the latter will sell to J. P. Morgan & Co., the $30,000,000 of notes above mentioned at 97, the proceeds to be credited to the Interborough Company on the books of J. P. Morgan & Co., who will allow the Interborough Company interest at the rate of 3 per cent. per annum on the daily credit balances, with the understanding, however, that the Interborough Company will not withdraw the same except as and when required from time to time in meeting its payments on construction and equipment; and we understand that this will mean substantially as follows:

During the first	quarter after deposit, not exceeding..	$1,500,000
During the second	quarter after deposit, not exceeding..	1,900,000
During the third	quarter after deposit, not exceeding..	2,450,000
During the fourth	quarter after deposit, not exceeding..	2,800,000
During the fifth	quarter after deposit, not exceeding..	3,500,000
During the sixth	quarter after deposit, not exceeding..	4,200,000
During the seventh	quarter after deposit, not exceeding..	5,900,000
During the eighth	quarter after deposit, not exceeding..	6,900,000

" 4. Referring to the Interborough Company's notes aggregating about $22,000,000 due May 1, 1911, which contain clauses under which the notes may be converted into the present Interborough Mortgage 5's: On or before May 1, 1911, the Interborough Company, at its election, may issue

a second series of its 6 per cent. notes to the principal amount
of $22,000,000 or less (and at its election to a principal
amount sufficient to produce $22,000,000 net) maturing at
the same time as the above mentioned series of $30,000,000
secured by $27,500,000 par value, or a proportionate larger
or smaller amount, of the new bonds due 1960, the interest
on such notes to be payable and the notes to contain redemption clauses as in the case of the above mentioned $30,000,000
series. On May 1st, J. P. Morgan & Co., will purchase and
the Interborough Company will sell to J. P. Morgan & Co.,
at 97, such notes as the Interborough Company shall have
elected to issue under this clause 4, the proceeds, so far as
needed, to be used by the Interborough Company in paying
the convertible notes maturing May 1, 1911, which shall not
have been converted into the present Interborough 5's, and
the proceeds so far as not needed to pay such convertible
notes, to be deposited with J. P. Morgan & Co., and to be
withdrawn only as and when required by the Interborough
Company in meeting payments on account of improvements,
equipment or construction; and with that understanding,
J. P. Morgan & Co., will allow the Interborough Company
interest at the rate of 3 per cent. per annum on the Interborough Company's daily credit balance. At least sixty days
prior to May 1, 1911, the Interborough Company will give
J. P. Morgan & Co. written notice of the amount of the
second series of notes which the Interborough Company will issue. In consideration of J. P. Morgan & Co.'s
commitment (necessarily made at a date in advance of
the final approval of a plan and while the amounts involved
are wholly uncertain) to purchase, if required, the total
authorized series of such notes, without any corresponding
obligation on the part of the Interborough Company, on
May 1, 1911, will pay to J. P. Morgan & Co., in cash, three
per cent. on the entire portion of such total authorized series
which shall not then have been issued.

" 5. The Interborough Company agrees to provide the
funds for the retirement of the above mentioned notes aggregating $52,000,000, or thereabouts, by a sale through J. P.

Morgan & Co., of the new bonds due 1960; and the latter agree to offer such new bonds for sale, for account of the Interborough Company, the offer to be made at any time within the above mentioned two and one-half years when in the judgment of J. P. Morgan & Co., it shall be desirable to make the offer, and at a price satisfactory to the Interborough Company, the proceeds of the sale of such bonds to be credited to the Interborough Company on the books of J. P. Morgan & Co., and to be used only in the payment of such notes. For the services rendered and to be rendered under this article by J. P. Morgan & Co., they shall be entitled to receive and the Interborough Company shall pay a commission equal to three per cent. of the par amount of the bonds offered by them. Such commission of three per cent. shall be exclusive of all expenses attending the offer and in view of the commitment of J. P. Morgan & Co., to offer the entire amount of the new bonds, shall be payable by the Interborough Company to J. P. Morgan & Co., partly in advance as follows: Three hundred thousand dollars being 1 per cent on $30,000,000, payable in November, 1910, when the first series of notes are issued; $220,000 being one per cent on $22,000,000, payable on or before May 1, 1911; and the remainder of 2 per cent on the total amount shall be payable as and when the bonds shall be sold.

" 6. The papers and corporate proceeding are to be satisfactory in form to counsel for J. P. Morgan & Co., and all expenses in that connection are to be paid by the Interborough Company.

" Please confirm.

" Very truly yours,

" (Signed)   J. P. MORGAN & CO."

Q. There seems to be a notation signed by the Interborough Rapid Transit Company which I assume is the acceptance of this proposition? A. Yes.

" New York, September 23, 1910.

" P. S.—Agreed to and accepted to be put into effect if the franchise for elevated extensions and improvements shall be granted by the Public Service Commission and by the board of estimate and apportionment and the issue and disposition of notes and of bonds and the proceeds thereof, as above proposed, shall have been approved and authorized by the Public Service Commission.

" (Signed)

"INTERBOROUGH RAPID TRANSIT CO.

"By T. P. SHONTS,

" *President.*"

Q. It was so signed and executed? A. Yes.

Q. This is the contract, Mr. Fisher, which sets forth the services that J. P. Morgan & Company rendered for the $500,000 paid them in accordance with the two vouchers examined by me this morning? A. Yes.

Q. Did this contract fall upon the expiration of the period up to March 1st, and extended to April 1st when the two contracts were not signed at that time? A. Yes.

Q. Was nothing done in this contract except the payment of $500,000 to J. P. Morgan & Company? A. No, sir.

Q. No notes were redeemed? A. No, sir.

Q. No notes refunded under this contract? A. I don't think so.

Q. No bonds were retired? A. Not to my knowledge.

Q. Did Morgan & Company subsequently act as the bankers in the refunding and retiring of this issue of notes mentioned in this letter? A. Yes.

Q. And in effect they subsequently undertook all the obligations set forth in this letter? A. Yes.

Q. Were they the same or in modified terms? A. On different terms.

Q. Was that upon another contract? A. Yes, sir.

Q. Can you produce the contract? A. Yes, sir.

Q. You have a copy of that contract in your possession? A. I think it is here.

Q. Can I ask you for the original letters setting up this contract? A. Yes. The contract consists of a series of letters. (Witness looks through file and delivers letter to Mr. Colby.)

Q. This is a letter of April 9, 1912? A. Yes.

Q. From J. P. Morgan & Company to the president of the Interborough Rapid Transit Company? A. Yes.

Q. Have you a copy of that letter? 'A. No, sir.

Mr. Colby.— I will read the letter of J. P. Morgan & Company addressed to Mr. Theodore P. Shonts, president of the Interborough Rapid Transit Company.

" J. P. MORGAN & COMPANY

" Wall street, corner Broad, New York

" NEW YORK, *April 9, 1912.*

" T. P. SHONTS, ESQ., *President, Interborough Rapid Transit Company, No.* 165 *Broadway, New York City:*

" DEAR SIR.—As the negotiations of the Interborough Rapid Transit Company with the city authorities appear to be approaching completion, we take this opportunity of setting forth the agreement between your company and ourselves relative to the financing of your company to enable it to carry out its agreement with the city.

" We understand that the amount of money required by your company will be approximately as follows:

For refunding its present debt............	$50,656,950
For construction of new subways..........	56,000,000
For Manhattan Railway improvements, about.	30,000,000
For equipment of new subways............	21,000,000
	$157,656,950

" In order to procure this money, we understand that the Interborough Rapid Transit Company proposes to authorize and issue new first mortgage 5 per cent. fifty-three-year bonds to an aggregate amount of about $170,000,000. The bonds are to be called the Interborough Rapid Transit Company first mortgage 5 per cent. gold bonds of 1912, and shall be secured by a first mortgage on all the property, leasehold and freehold, of the Interborough Rapid Transit Company. The mortgage securing these bonds will contain provisions satisfactory to us, for the issue of such additional amount of bonds in excess of the $170,000,000 thereof above mentioned as may be needed to provide the money for extensions and improvements which may be authorized by the city, and agreed to by your company, during the period of your company's lease.

" The mortgage is also to provide for a sinking fund of one per cent. on the total amount of bonds issued, such sinking fund to begin five years from completion of the new subways, not more than ten years from the date of the bonds. The proceeds of the sinking fund are to be invested in bonds of this issue, which may be drawn for the sinking fund at 110, or bought in the market at a lower price.

" The amount of money required being estimated at $157,656,950, we are to buy from your company, and your company is to sell to us, at the price of 93½ and accrued interest, such an amount of said Interborough Rapid Transit Company first mortgage five per cent gold bonds of 1912 as may required to produce the sum needed, not exceeding in all $170,000,000 par value of the said bonds.

" The bonds are to be taken and paid for by us during a period of four years beginning July 1, 1912. It is understood with you that the bonds will be delivered and paid for as follows:

	Bonds.
During the year from July 1, 1912 to June 30, 1913	$78,000,000
During the year from July 1, 1913 to June 30, 1914	30,000,000
During the year from July 1, 1914 to June 30, 1915	30,000,000
During the year from July 1, 1915 to June 30, 1916, not more than.............	32,000,000
	$170,000,000

and it is also understood that all or any part of each year's instalment of bonds may be taken by us at any time during that year, at our option.

"It is understood with you, as part of this transaction, that the moneys received by your company from the sale of these bonds shall be deposited with us as bankers, to be checked against as required to enable your company to carry out its contract with the city, and that during the time such moneys are on deposit with us we shall allow your company such rate of interest as may be agreed upon between us from time to time.

"It is our intention to form a syndicate to take these bonds, in which syndicate we ourselves shall have a share, and it is agreed that the syndicate will divide equally with your company any amount received on the sale of the bonds in excess of an average price of par and accrued interest.

"It is fully understood that the entire transaction above outlined depends upon the legality and constitutionality of the contract between the city and your company being confirmed by the courts, and that no action under this agreement is to be taken on either side until all parties are satisfied as to the legal enforceability of such contract and of the bonds hereinabove mentioned.

"It is further understood that, should the confirmation of the courts, above referred to, be delayed, the four years during which we are to take the bonds contracted for shall begin and shall terminate at a date later than that above set forth as in our opinion shall be reasonable, necessary and convenient.

"The terms of the bonds and of the mortgage are to be satisfactory to our counsel (whose charges are to be borne by your company).

"We shall be glad of your confirmation of the terms of this letter, if it accords with your understanding of the arrangement.

"Yours very truly,
"(Signed)   J. P. MORGAN & CO."

Chairman Thompson.— We will now take a recess until 2:30 P. M.

AFTERNOON SESSION

The Committee was called to order at 3:02 o'clock P. M., Chairman Thompson presiding.

H. M. FISHER, recalled.

Mr. Colby.— Mr. Fisher, I am ready when you are.

Mr. Fisher.— All right, sir.

By Mr. Colby:

Q. I would like to turn once more to the letter of April 9, written by Morgan & Company. This letter of April 9, 1912, from J. P. Morgan & Company, is the basis of the present contract between the Interborough Rapid Transit Company and the firm of Morgan & Company, for the issuance on the one hand, and the acquisition on the other, of the bonds of the Interborough Rapid Transit Company. Is that right? A. No, sir. That is an entirely different basis. I think you will find in that contract they agreed to take the bonds and sell them on commission, which accounts for their being willing to apply some of that fund, which we paid them, on those commissions in case they sold the bonds under that agreement.

Q. I am referring to this letter of April 9, 1912. You have that in mind? A. No, I have the 1910 contract in mind. I beg your pardon; I am wrong.

Q. I will ask the stenographer, if you think it is necessary, to repeat the question, unless you have it in mind. A. I have it in mind. The letter of April 9, 1912, that is the basis of the present contract; yes, sir.

Q. This letter called for a reply, and I suppose a reply was sent, Mr. Fisher? A. Yes, sir.

Q. Is it here. A. I presume so.

(The witness produces a copy of a letter to J. P. Morgan & Company dated April 12, 1912.)

Q. This is the letter which the Interborough Rapid Transit Company, through its president, wrote in reply to the Morgan letter, is it. A. I could not say without seeing the letter.

(Counsel hands paper to witness.)

Mr. Fisher.— Yes, sir.

Q. I will read this short letter in the record. "April 12, 1912. Gentlemen: Your letter of April 9, 1912, accords with our understanding of the arrangement for the sale to you by the Interborough Rapid Transit Company of approximately $170,000,000 of bonds as therein outlined. I hereby on behalf of the Interborough Rapid Transit Company confirm such sum, according to the terms of your letter, such confirmation being especially athorized by resolution of the board of directors of the Interborough Rapid Transit Company, of which I enclose a copy." (Signed) — this is a blank, president. Must have been signed by Mr. Shonts, president? A. T. P. Shonts.

Q. The resolution referred to adopted by the board of directors must have been adopted at a meeting held between April 9 and April 12, 1912; is that right? A. What resolution are you referring to?

Q. Mr. Shonts says in his letter confirming the sale according to the terms of the Morgan letter, " Such confirmation be authorized by resolution of the board of directors "— A. Yes, sir.

Q. —" of which I enclose a copy," says he. But I don't see the copy in the vouchers. I suppose I can find it readily in the minute book A. Yes, sir.

Q. The former contract between the Interborough Rapid Transit Company and Morgan & Company, under which $500,000 was paid to Morgan, expired on March 1, 1912, did it not? A. April the 1st.

Q. But under the terms of the earlier contract, March 1st is extended — A. Extended —

Q. — until April 1, 1912? A. Yes, sir.

Q. And upon April 1st, the period fixed by the former contract, expiring on that date, the matter was resumed by Morgan & Company only eight days later, April 9th; that is right, isn't it? A. If it happens to be in the same year. I am not sure. I have not got that. Will you turn to the other contract and see if that expired in 1912 or 1911? I am not sure.

Q. What would be the date of that? A. That is the first — the letter tied with the red ribbon. I think it is right here. This would be it.

Q. Let me see the Morgan voucher a minute. I have a copy of that Morgan voucher.

Mr. Quackenbush.— It is being copied. It cannot be here and there both at the same time.

Mr. Colby.— I will have to reserve that question.

Mr. Quackenbush.— Shall I send for it?

Mr. Colby.— No. I will reserve it.

Mr. Dawson.— It is in the minutes. It is 1912.

Mr. Colby.— I am quite certain it is 1912.

Mr. Fisher.— May I look at that voucher?

Mr. Colby.— Mr. Dawson calls my attention to the minutes of the board of directors held April 3, 1912.

Mr. Fisher.— Yes, sir.

Mr. Colby.— In which there is a reference to the subject of my question. I find this entry in the minutes: "The president referred to minutes of this board, dated March 6, 1912, and stated that he had secured a further extension of three weeks from April 1, 1912."

Mr. Dawson.— Extended beyond the date of the other contract, you see.

By Mr. Colby:

Q. During which further period the payment of $50,000 for commitments of syndicate associates of Messrs. J. P. Morgan & Company, in connection with the negotiations with the city, would apply to any commissions which the bankers may be entitled to receive, etc.? A. That is right.

Q. So it was the same year? A. Yes, sir.

Q. And yet this letter gives some clew to the state of the negotiations between the Interborough and the City at that time. You remember I asked you this question this morning, and your memory did not serve you. Mr. Morgan — J. P. Morgan & Company, however, say "as the negotiations of the Interborough Rapid

Transit Company with the city authorities appear to be approaching completion, we take this opportunity of setting forth the agreement between your company and ours?" A. The negotiations with the city approached completion quite a number of times during 1912, but were never completed.

Q. But Messrs. Morgan & Company also took the opportunity to foreclose their possession of this $250,000 against any liability to deduction against commissions earned. That is the point, Mr. Fisher.

Chairman Thompson.— I had a query in my mind that came to me. The Board of Estimate passed this thing in May, 1912. Now, they had all that time, and you never got these till March 19, 1912. What was the hold-up?

Mr. Fisher.— There were negotiations with the Public Service Commission and the Board of Estimate. There were several times that they were on the verge of closing when something intervened to prevent.

Chairman Thompson.— Who was it that — who on the Public Service Commission held back?

Mr. Fisher.— That I could not tell you. I would have to go over that — the record is so voluminous, and the negotiations interrupted so often, that I will have to go and make a chronological statement of events.

Chairman Thompson.— I see. All right, Mr. Fisher.

By Mr. Colby:

Q. We have given Mr. Fisher a good deal to prepare. I wish you would make a note of that, Mr. Fisher, to prepare at your first opportunity. A. All right, sir.

Q. Morgan & Company further say in their letter of April 9th: "It is our intention to form a syndicate to take these bonds, in which syndicate we ourselves shall have a share." They don't say they have formed a syndicate, do they? A. No, sir.

Q. They don't say, "We have made any commitments with members of a syndicate," do they? A. No, sir.

Q. They further say it is agreed that the syndicate will divide equally with your company any amount received on the sale of the bonds in excess of an average of par and accrued interest? A. Yes, sir.

Q. Has that average ever been attained in any sale of bonds? A. Not yet, no sir.

Q. So that this agreement to divide is inoperative as yet? A. As yet, yes.

Chairman Thompson.— That is like the city getting a profit out of it, is it?

Mr. Fisher.— The city is more liable to get a profit out of the contract than we are out of the sale of bonds.

Chairman Thompson.—And neither one of you has got any yet?

Mr. Fisher.— No.

By Mr. Colby:

Q. The syndicate price, as I recall, was 96½? A. I don't know what —

Q. The price to the syndicate. A. I don't know what the price to the syndicate was — 96 or 96½, but I have not that.

Q. In other words, the proposal to divide was to divide equally with your company any profits after the syndicate had realized the difference between par and 96 or 96½, whichever the price of the syndicate might be? A. Yes, sir.

Chairman Thompson.— You ought to.

Mr. Fisher.— I think so myself.

Q. Then follows this sentence: " It is further understood that the entire transaction above outlined depends upon the legality and constitutionality of the contract between the city and your company being confirmed by the courts?" You understand that this suggestion was the source of the Admiral Realty Company action? A. That I could not say.

Q. You don't know whether this suggestion has any relation to the institution of the Admiral Realty Company action to enjoin — A. I don't.

Q. — the execution of the contracts as unconstitutional? A. I don't.

Q. I see also this sentence, that "the four years during which Morgan & Company are to take the bonds may begin and may terminate at a date later than that set forth in the letter, so much later as in their opinion shall be reasonable, necessary and convenient." What does that mean? In other words, is there any definite agreement on Morgan & Company's part to take — to begin taking these bonds at any future date? A. I think you will find in some of the subsequent letters, after the agreement had been made with the city and signed, that there is a letter agreeing to take the bonds on certain dates.

Q. This sounds a little like Colonel "Cyarter's" promissory note, "as soon as possible after date, for value received, I promise to pay as much as is convenient." A. That is quite plausible, though, in view of the fact the contract had not been signed with the City. Still in the negotiations — and as events proved, it was not signed for a year after.

Q. As a man of long experience in corporation and business affairs, generally, you would consider that reservation an exceedingly amiable and gentle provision in any contract of this kind, wouldn't you? A. I have no comment to make on that, sir.

Q. Messrs. Morgan & Company required of the Interborough, as a part of the contract, as I read the letter, that the proceeds of all bonds turned over by the Interborough remain on deposit with Morgan & Company until drawn out by the company for some of the purposes authorized in the bond? A. Yes, sir.

Q. There was also a stipulation that Morgan & Company's counsel should pass on the mortgage? A. Yes, sir.

Q. And upon the form of the bonds? A. Yes, sir.

Q. But that the Interborough should pay the fees for such? A. Yes, sir.

Q. The witness has produced a statement of monthly balances of the Interborough Rapid Transit Company with J. P. Morgan & Company from April 21, 1913, to February 1, 1916. Is this a correct statement of the current balances between these dates. Mr. Fisher? A. Yes, sir.

Q. On this statement are listed the following accounts: Subway contribution; third track; power-house; elevated extension; redemption account; note account; Interborough Rapid Transit

Company. I take it the last account is your current account? A. General account.

Q. General account. Under subway contribution account I notice that the balances vary from $15,000,000 to $44,000,000. That is correct, isn't it? A. Yes, sir.

Q. The third track account shows balances varying from $200 — oh, varying from $24,000, which seems to be the lowest, to as much as $223,000 — no, to as much as $2,231,000, which seems to be the largest amount. Mr. Dawson has computed the equivalent of these fluctuating balances, and has stated for our guidance their yearly equivalent, that is to say, the equivalent of such an amount as on deposit for a year would be equivalent to these fluctuating amounts. For the subway contribution account, he figures that the balances are the equivalent of $68,000,000 for a year. For the third track, he computes that the equivalent would be $1,016,000 for a year. The power-house account also shows some fluctuation, one item being — one month showing as little as $44,000, but most of the months being larger, one as much as $1,550,000. Mr. Dawson computes the power-house balances as equivalent to a year's balance of $1,235,000. The elevated extension account fluctuates between three-quarters of a million to as much as $2,285,000. Mr. Dawson computes these balances as equivalent to a daily balance of $3,795,000. The redemption account is apparently a less important account, although it has had in it as much as $1,400,000 at one time. Mr. Dawson computes these balances as equivalent to a yearly balance of $233,750. The note account amounts to as much as a million and a half — oh no, more than that, one time as much $15,000,000. Mr. Dawson calculates this account in yearly equivalent to be $2,500,034. The Interborough Rapid Transit Company's general account shows some fluctuations, amounting at times to maybe $3,000,000, and at times declining to a little over $200,000, or even less than that. Mr. Dawson computes the balances in the general account on the basis of a yearly equivalent at $1,709,721. The total balances on the basis of the calculation of Mr. Dawson is $78,604,307.61. Will you please make a note of this further request, Mr. Fisher, to let me have a statement of the interest credited or received by the company from Morgan & Company on these various deposit balances? A. Yes, sir.

Chairman Thompson.— What did you finally agree on? What was the rate finally agreed upon for interest?

Mr. Fisher.— Two and a half.

Chairman Thompson.— Two and a half.

By Mr. Colby:

Q. Mr. Dawson figures that the interest on these balances computed on the yearly equivalent basis at 2½ per cent. amounts to $1,965,107.69. Now, the Interborough paid the counsel fees of Messrs. Morgan & Company in this transaction. What did they pay the trustee of the bonds? A. They paid the trustee of the bonds the usual charge for certifying bonds, which is fifty cents per bond.

Q. How much would that amount to? A. Eighty thousand dollars on $160,000,000 issue.

Q. Were there any other expenses in connection with the bond issues? A. Yes, sir; there were printing and other incidentals.

Q. Were there any fees to the counsel of the Guaranty Trust Company? A. I think there were. I think the counsel of the Guaranty Trust Company made a charge for examining the trust deed.

Q. Even though it had been approved and prepared, in fact, by Morgan & Company's counsel? A. No trust company will act as trustee without having their own lawyers examine the deed of trust first.

Q. Do you recall who the lawyers were who examined the deed of trust on behalf of the trustee? A. I think Stimson made the charge, if I am not mistaken.

Q. Do you recall its amount? A. About $15,000, as near as I recollect. I would have to confirm that.

Chairman Thompson.— I want to welcome the presence of ex-Senators Ormrod and Monroe.

Mr. Colby.— Pursuing — Mr. Chairman, pursuing the subject of outside counsel, and referring again for the purpose of showing my primary intention in pursuing this line of evidence a little further, to the minute adopted by the Board on awarding its counsel, Mr. Rogers, the bonus of $50,000, namely, that his ser-

vices had obviated the employment of outside counsel, I am handed
by the witness voucher No. 105,235.

Chairman Thompson.— That is, you thought that when you
found that Mr. Rogers had been paid $50,000, he had done all
this work, and now you are disappointed that you don't find that
is so?

Mr. Colby.— But the ground assigned for payment of bonus to
Mr. Rogers was that he had made it unnecessary — at least, obviated the employment of outside counsel.

Chairman Thompson.— I see.

Mr. Colby.—At least to some extent. To what extent, it is also
inferable from the amounts payable to outside counsel in this
matter.

Chairman Thompson.— He is probably entitled to some consideration for having to get along with all these outside counsel.

By Mr. Colby:

Q. The witness hands me voucher of the Interborough Rapid
Transit Company, numbered 105,235. Will you look at this
voucher, Mr. Fisher, and tell me what payment it represents? A.
It is a payment to Nicoll, Anable, Lindsay & Fuller, for professional services from April 1, 1910, to April 1, 1912, consisting
of conferences with the president, officers and directors, attending
meetings of the executive committee and directors, and advice
and opinion upon matters affecting the interests of the company,
including —he mentions among those matters, some of the principal ones. Matters relating to new subways and the various negotiations representing the same. The legality and constitutionality
of the various features of the proposed plans. Necessary legislation, etc. Advice as to various legislative matters during the sessions of 1911 and 1912. Examination of advertising contracts,
and advice and opinion with respect to the right to terminate same.
Numerous conferences and consultations and advice with respect
to the Longacre Electric Light & Power Company. Services in
the following actions.

Q. Those are accident damage actions — quite a number of
them? A. Accident damages arising out of the Murray Hill

explosion, out of the construction of the subway covered by contract No. 1.

Q. Personal injury cases? A. Most of them; yes, sir.

Q. Injuries to person and property, I suppose, combined? A. Mostly personal injuries, and other miscellaneous accidents.

Mr. Colby.— I call Mr. Fisher's attention to the fact that the minutes expressly recite with reference to the payment of this bonus to Mr. Rogers, not only as he performed his — that all legal matters — let me give this to you exactly. In the minutes of September 17, 1913, I find this reference to Mr. Rogers: " The President stated that all legal matters in and about the contracts for the construction and equipment of the new subways and elevated lines of the City of New York, prior to March 9th, ultimo, had been conducted by Mr. Richard Reid Rogers; that the work was long, continuous and exacting, and had been performed in conjunction with his other duties in a highly satisfactory manner, and without the employment of associate counsel, thus resulting in large saving to the company." And it was upon such statement that the motion was apparently based authorizing the payment of this bonus.

Chairman Thompson.— Evidently some error about that.

By Mr. Colby:

Q. Have you stated the amount of the payment evidenced by this voucher to Messrs. Nicoll, Anable, Lindsay and Fuller? A. No, sir; I did not.

Q. And what was the amount of the payment it represents? A. $53,172.33.

Mr. Colby.— I offer this voucher in evidence, in which Messrs. Nicoll, Anable, Lindsay & Fuller acknowledged the receipt on July 2, 1912, of $53,172.38. This amount is according to the voucher distributed among the following accounts, as appears on the voucher: Collection account, Rapid Transit Subway Construction Company, $22,863.73; other suspense of proposed subway route, $10,000; general law expenses, $20,308.55; and under the bills rendered, the services which are charged for include all matters relating to new subways, and various negotiations respecting the same.

By Mr. Colby:

Q. Will you give me a copy of that? A. Yes, sir.

(Copy of voucher not handed to the stenographer.)

By Mr. Colby:

Q. The witness further produces voucher of the Interborough Rapid Transit Company, numbered 118,187. Will you look at this voucher, and tell me what payment it evidences, and to whom? A. That is to Nicoll, Anable, Lindsay & Fuller, for $43,292, for professional services from April 1, 1912, to June 1, 1913.

Mr. Colby.— This voucher acknowledges the receipt of the payment of $43,292, and the amount is distributed, according to the notations on the voucher, as follows: One-quarter, namely, $10,000, with $1,698.36 disbursement, is charged to the various suits against McDonald; one-half is charged to the new subway contracts and elevated certificates, amounting — the charge to this account amounting to $220,259.61; the remaining one-quarter is charged to general law expenses. I offer that in evidence.

Chairman Thompson.— Mark it the next exhibit.

(Stenographer not in receipt of voucher.)

By Mr. Colby:

Q. The witness produces a further voucher, numbered 129,261, of the Interborough Rapid Transit Company. Will you tell me what payment and to whom this voucher sets forth? A. Nicoll, Anable, Lindsay & Fuller, dated June 10, 1914, for professional services rendered from June 1, 1913, to June 1, 1914, $36,516.48.

Q. Did this bill cover in large measure services in connection with the new subway contract? A. I think the services are fully explained on the bill.

Q. Will you look at the bill and answer that question, please, Mr. Fisher? (Counsel hands paper to witness.) A. Yes, sir. It covers conferences and consultations with the president, members of the executive committee, and other officers and directors, and advice and opinions upon matters affecting the interests of the company, including questions arising under the new subway contracts, the elevated extensions, and third tracks; examination of bills and advice respecting matters of proposed legislation; advertising contracts; C. H. Venner's assault on the credit of the company and its securities. That is counsel's language. Services under the following actions — and there follows a number of accidents.

Q. I don't suppose he meant assault and battery on your securities? I find under the heading of "distribution" that this payment of $36,516 was distributed as follows: Collection account, $15,716.48; rapid transit subway construction, general law expenses, $20,800, this being in turn subdivided into two equal amounts, one charged to the Manhattan division, $10,400, and an identical amount to the subway division.

Chairman Thompson.— This will be the next exhibit. Just mark them as exhibits.

(Stenographer not in receipt of copy of voucher.)

By Mr. Colby:

Q. The witness produces voucher No. 141,200, of the Interborough Rapid Transit Company. Will you tell me what payment and to whom this voucher evidences? A. The same parties. Covering personal services rendered from June 1, 1914, to June 1, 1915, amounting to $25,345.25.

Q. To whom was that amount paid? A. Nicoll, Anable, Lindsay & Fuller. The results of conferences and consultations of the president, members of the executive committee and other officers and directors, and advice and opinions upon matters affecting the interests of the company, and especially upon the following matters: New subway contracts, elevated extensions, third trackings, and advertising contracts; attacks by C. H. Venner upon the credit of the company and its securities; attacks by the New York American and other newspapers on account of accidents happening on the elevated and subway. Investigations of the Public Service Commission by legislative committee, and all the matters connected therewith.

Chairman Thompson.— When is that dated?

Mr. Fisher.— It was not your committee. "Examination of bills and advice respecting matters of proposed legislation. Services in the following actions," and there follows a number of accident cases.

By Mr. Colby:

Q. What attack did the company sustain as a result of the accidents on the elevated and the subway? A. I am not prepared to say. I don't know exactly what he was referring to.

Q. It says, "Attacks by the New York American and other newspapers on account of accidents happening on the elevated and subway." Was Mr. Delancy Nicoll or his firm going to punish the newspapers for anything they had done to the Interborough Rapid Transit Company? A. I could not say.

Q. Was he going to shut off criticisms or comments on account of such occurrences on the elevated and subways? A. You will have to ask Mr. Nicoll.

Q. What do you suppose he did for which he was paid, including some other services, this amount of $25,000? A. My supposition would not be of any value there, Mr. Counsel.

Q. Was he paid, do you suppose, to hold the hands of your officers and soothe their fears under criticism? A. We have no officers of that kind.

Q. Well, passing to the next item of his service: "Investigation of the Public Service Commission by legislative committee, and all matters connected therewith — all matters connected therewith."

Chairman Thompson.— What is the date of that?

Mr. Colby.— June 1, 1915.

Chairman Thompson.— I am afraid that does mean us.

Mr. Fisher.— Probably it does.

Chairman Thompson.— How much did he get for that, that part of it? Was it charged to "suspense"?

Mr. Fisher.— Charged to experience, I guess.

Q. Under "distribution" of this payment I find collection account, $10,345.25. This seems to be a collection account in connection with the Rapid Transit Subway Construction Company.

Do you know how newspaper criticism of an accident on the elevated railroad can find its way into the cost of construction of the Rapid Transit Subway tunnels? A. I think you will find, if you look at his bills, that also covers settlements of accidents of the Construction Company, and is probably made for that purpose.

Q. Well, there seem to be six subdivisions into which this bill is divided: First, the new subway contracts and elevated extensions, third tracking, advertising contracts; and then the attacks by C. H. Venner upon the credit of the company; then subdivisions 3 and 4 are the attacks by the newspapers on account of accidents; and, four is the investigation of the Public Service Commission by the legislative committee. Why should the Interborough Rapid Transit Company be hiring outside counsel in an investigation of the Public Service Commission by a joint legislative committee of the Senate and Assembly?

Chairman Thompson.— You don't remember that investigation prior to June 1st, they attacked the Interborough in any way, do you?

Mr. Fisher.— Not that I am aware of.

Chairman Thompson.— Well, not that I was, either. And I was Chairman of the Committee all the time they were here.

Mr. Fisher.— I will call your attention to the fact that is a statement by counsel.

Mr. Colby.— I thoroughly appreciate any fact that you know, you are stating with freedom and with manifest accuracy and fullness. I am simply bringing out these points in the bill. I don't know that anybody could explain them, and your inability to explain them is nothing that I think reflects upon you, nor may I add, is it anything that surprises me.

Chairman Thompson.— Mr. Fisher is just the secretary.

Mr. Colby.— Possibly someone else can venture an explanation, and we may see then what that explanation is. I offer that in evidence.

(Copy of voucher referred to not received by stenographer.)

Chairman Thompson.— I hope I will be forgiven for having an idea that there are some folks around the Interborough that are honest, but I rather look at the counsel that draws a fair fee, but really does the work and has a department — I understand Mr. Quackenbush gets about $40,000 or $45,000 a year, and is satisfied with it.

Mr. Quackenbush.— Mr. Chairman, if my compensation is of any interest to anybody, I might say that from all sources I return to the Federal Government as my compensation the sum you have mentioned, but the Interborough and several other companies go to make that up.

Chairman Thompson.— I would not have made that remark if I had thought about the income tax things.   I did not think about that.

Mr. Colby.— Mr. Quackenbush, have you had an opportunity to give me a statement of the total cost of the legal department?

Mr. Quackenbush.— I have the aggregate of the payrolls.

Mr. Colby.— Could you state that?

Mr. Quackenbush.— I have asked to have them take off from that a list of the attorneys, which I think is what you want.

Mr. Colby.— I am not particularly desirous at the moment of going into the details of the attorneys, if you could tell me what is the approximate aggregate per annum of the cost of the legal department of the Interborough Rapid Transit Company as distinguished from the outside attorneys who have been so freely employed.

Mr. Quackenbush.— I labor under this difficulty about that, at the moment; that the payrolls of the Interborough are divided into four subdivisions.   There is one payroll that covers the litigation with reference to the easements on the Interborough-Elevated system; one that covers miscellaneous general business; one covers the trial of the accident cases; another one that covers the expenses of the claim department in connection with accident cases.   And I have those bills.   Now, upon each of those payrolls are several attorneys, and also clerks and stenographers and investigators, etc., and the totals show the entire expense of all of these character of employees. If you want that, I can give you that now.

Mr. Colby.— I would appreciate it.

Mr. Quackenbush.— And I have only as a sample, the January payrolls, which are fairly typical. They don't vary much. The January payroll for easements division, that is the new work in connection with the elevated railroad extensions, $10,763.66; miscellaneous law, $3,457.66; the trial of accident cases, $4,534; the claim department, the accident cases, $3,826.67, making the total $22,581.99.

Mr. Colby.— That is the total monthly expenses, including all salaries?

Mr. Quackenbush.— Yes, all kinds.

Mr. Colby.— For the month of January this year?

Mr. Quackenbush.— For the month of January this year, yes, sir.

Mr. Colby.— And that is an average month, and the annual expense could be arrived at by a simple calculation?

Mr. Quackenbush.— That would be a fair statement of it, I should say, for the last two or three years.

Mr. Colby.— Yes.

Chairman Thompson.— You have charge of that whole department?

Mr. Quackenbush.— Oh, yes.

Chairman Thompson.— What do you get, forty or forty-five?

Mr. Quackenbush.— My compensation from the Interborough Rapid Transit Company is $36,000 a year, which is divided on the books into an allotment for the accident business, another for the handling of the easement litigation, and everything connected with it; another for the general law expenses. Speaking from memory, the amount for the general law expenses, I think, is $600 a month; for the accident, $650; for the easement litigation, covers all this new work, $500 a month.

Chairman Thompson.— What is the total amount?

Mr. Quackenbush.— From the Interborough it is $1,750 a month. On the New York Railways —

Chairman Thompson.— I don't care for the details, unless you care to put them in.

Mr. Quackenbush.— We might as well have it. There is no mystery about it. Very glad to have the thing in. My compensation from the New York Railways is $1,150 a month, which is divided about equally between the accident business and the general law expenses. My compensation from the Third Avenue system, and this is entirely outside of the Interborough and New York Railways, is $6,600 a year. From two roads and the Long Island system, $2,400 a year. So that my aggregate income for all professional activities for the railroads of New York city is $36,000 a year from the Interborough and New York Railways, distributed as I have said; $2,400 from the two Long Island roads, in which the Long Island Railroad Companies have an interest; $6,600 from the Third Avenue system, which makes a total of $45,000. I might add, as long as my matters are the subject of inquiry, that I came here from Buffalo twelve years ago, and my compensation was $25,000 a year. That was to cover only my reorganization of the trial department of the New York City Railways Company. At various times I took charge, after 1904, of the claim department of that company, subsequently of the field department; then when the merger between the surface lines and the Interborough took place, I took charge of the entire accident business of the Interborough; and then, upon the retirement of Mr. Charles A. Gardiner and Mr. Alfred Gardiner from the Interborough, I took charge of the general law business of the Interborough; and upon the retirement of Mr. Veeder from the Queens County lines, I took charge of all the business of the company. Upon the retirement of vice-president Gennon of the New York City Railways Company, I took his duties in connection with the claim department; upon retirement of Alfred Skid as

vice-president of the Elevated Railway, in connection with the
land damage litigation, and I have also, since the retirement of
Mr. Wickersham as general counsel of the Interborough, and Mr.
Cravath as general counsel of the surface system, and Mr. Davies
as general counsel for the Manhattan Elevated, taken over very
largely the work performed by them. For these services, which
I have mentioned, during the last twelve years, my compensation
has been increased from $25,000 in the beginning, to the amount
of $45,000 at the present time. During about eight years of that
time I was paid by the receivers of the surface lines who asked me
to continue to take charge of their litigation during that period,
when I represented them, as well as the companies not in the hands
of the receivers. My salary has each month been deposited in my
bank account, and I have drawn against it by checks, all of which
is available for the examination of the world at any time, an
account of my returns to the income tax, and all things considered,
I am quite satisfied.

Chairman Thompson.— Mr. Quackenbush having received this
amount of money and performed all the work these companies had
to do, counsel better look up these other matters and see what those
men really did for the money they got.

Mr. Quackenbush.— Well, that is not altogether accurate, Mr.
Chairman. I don't want to be put in a position of having claimed
anything beyond what I have done. But I don't like, either, to
have any notion get out that I have been paid in any excessive
amount at any time.

Chairman Thompson.— The Committee don't have. I can say
that, can't I?

Mr. Quackenbush.— I have no grievance against anybody —

Chairman Thompson.— It is important only as a matter of
comparison with these other matters, that is all.

Mr. Colby.— Let me ask you this, Mr. Quackenbush: From
what you have stated as to the January expenses of the legal
department, it would appear that the annual expenses of this great
legal department, with its many lawyers and some 200 employes,
is about $270,000. It that correct?

Mr. Quackenbush.— That is the Interborough part of it, you know. When I told you the entire number, that meant the entire thing, the total payroll of the law department, of which I am in charge, for January, $49,118.49.

Mr. Colby.— The $22,581 was the Interborough alone?

Mr. Quackenbush.— For the Interborough alone. The others are the New York Railways and New York & Queens County.

Mr. Colby.— And the Manhattan Elevated?

Mr. Quackenbush.— Oh, no, that is —

Mr. Colby.— The total of the legal department, we will say — the total of the ordinary legal expenses of the Interborough would be about $270,000 per annum?

Mr. Quackenbush.— That is, payroll.

Mr. Colby.— Payroll?

Mr. Quackenbush.— Yes, sir.

Mr. Colby.— That includes salaries?

Mr. Quackenbush.— Yes.

Mr. Colby.— Of chiefs as well as subordinates?

Mr. Quackenbush.— Yes.

Mr. Colby.— The other expenses are the usual expenses of a law office, an apportionment of rent and other things?

Mr. Quackenbush.— Yes, but that is not included.

Mr. Colby.— No, does that include Mr. Rogers' pay?

Mr. Quackenbush.— No. I am giving you the law department of which am the head. Mr. Rogers reports directly to the president and directors. I also report directly to the president and directors.

Mr. Colby.— I am trying to arrive at a fair statement of the total paid to the legal staff of the Interborough Rapid Transit Company.

Mr. Quackenbush.— Aside from Mr. Rogers' salary.

Mr. Colby.— Mr. Rogers' salary, I believe it appeared on one of the minutes, is $30,000 per annum?

Mr. Quackenbush.— Yes. That is also distributed among the different companies.

Mr. Colby.— Yes. So that it would bring, we will say, the total paid to the legal staff of the Interborough permanent legal staff, to something in excess of $285,000 per annum.

Mr. Quackenbush.— Between $275,000 and $300,000 per year.

Mr. Colby.— Yes. Now, the monthly expense of the New York Railways — that is the surface lines?

Mr. Quackenbush.— Yes.

Mr. Colby.— Is another item, another matter entirely?

Mr. Quackenbush.— Yes.

Mr. Colby.— While this is not strictly germane to the point of my inquiry at the moment, suppose — you have the figures there — you state that.

Mr. Quackenbush.— Without giving the subdivisions of them, the aggregate of the New York Railways for January was $23,430.50.

Mr. Colby.— That was for the month of January?

Mr. Quackenbush.—Yes. Of course you will note that the New York Railways Company, a surface company, has a much larger volume of accident business than the elevated and subway.

Mr. Colby.—And the New York & Queens County is small?

Mr. Quackenbush.— $2,106. Now, Mr. Colby, if this is to be pursued further, I ought to say at this time these are all the amounts that appear on the payrolls of the several companies, but at the end of each month charges are made backward and forward as the attention of individuals shall have been given, or has been given to companies other than the ones upon which he appears on the payroll. For instance, if there should be a large volume of business of the Interborough, I would shift it to certain men from the New York Railways. Those are taken up. Accounts are kept. So that the payrolls would not always check with the auditor's books. But that — the cost is there.

Mr. Colby.—Yes; and it is a fair statement that the average payroll, annual payroll of the Interborough legal staff is about $300,000 — make it a little less.

Mr. Quackenbush.—Always, if you use the term " legal staff ' to cover something besides lawyers, because much of it is made up of —

Mr. Colby.— Investigators, clerks.

Mr. Quackenbush.— People of that sort. I will give you a statement of the attorneys. In fact, I have already given it. It is with Mr. Morris. It is only a matter of compiling. As to the New York Railways, there is charged from that payroll to the Third Avenue system its proportional part of the work done by this staff for that company. I think that covers it.

Mr. Colby.— Mr. Fisher, I asked you some time ago, a few moments ago, as to the amount paid by the Guaranty Trust Company for counsel fees in connection with the subway mortgage.

Mr. Quackenbush.— Mr. Colby, before you go further — you have given your receipt for these Nicoll vouchers. If you don't mind, I will have my boy take it to the Auditor and there get the receipt.

Mr. Colby.—All right.

Examination of Mr. Fisher, resumed.

By Mr. Colby:

Q. You were unable to recall the exact amount paid to the counsel of the trustee named in the mortgage. Possibly your statement there will refresh your recollection. A. I stated $15,000. I find it is $16,500.

Q. Yes. And the attorneys who represented the trustee were who? A. Winthrop & Stimson.

Q. Have you the vouchers of Mr. Towns, or Hatch & Sheehan's here?

Mr. Quackenbush.— Towns, you say (hands copy of voucher to counsel).

By Mr. Colby:

Q. Mr. Fisher, I have a copy of the voucher produced yesterday, number 102,038, of the Interborough Rapid Transit Company. Will you tell me what payment and to whom that voucher sets forth? A. It was to Mirabeau L. Towns, 149 Broadway, for professional services rendered, $5,000. The date of the bill is March 25, 1912. There are no details.

Q. And yet, under "distribution" I see that this payment is charged to "other suspense," and "proposed subway routes." Was the bill of Mirabeau L. Towns for $5,000 ever rendered in more detailed form than the bill annexed to the voucher? A. No, sir.

Mr. Quackenbush.— There is the receipt, Mr. Colby.

Mr. Colby.— Thank you.

By Mr. Colby:

Q. This is the bill of March 25, 1912, Interborough Rapid Transit Company to Mirabeau L. Towns. It says, "In full for professional services rendered to date, $5,000." The voucher acknowledges the receipt of the payment of this amount. Do you know what Mr. Towns did with reference to the proposed Subway routes? A. I do not, sir.

Q. You know nothing whatever as to the scope or extent of his service? A. No, sir.

Q. Who would be likely to know, what officer of the company should I question on that point? A. I suppose either the attorneys or the president could tell you.

Q. Yes.

Mr. Colby.— I offer this voucher in evidence. The original was produced yesterday.

Chairman Thompson.—What is it?

Mr. Colby.— The voucher representing a payment to Mirabeau L. Towns of $5,000.

Chairman Thompson.— This is a copy?

Mr. Fisher.—Yes, sir.

Chairman Thompson.—What did he do for this?

Mr. Colby.— I have covered that. The witness says he has no idea.

Chairman Thompson.— Oh!

Mr Colby.— He knows nothing as to the extent or character.

Chairman Thompson.— It is another exhibit. Mark it as an exhibit.

(Document referred to is copy of voucher No. 102038, and is marked Exhibit 1 of February 8, 1916, V. E. V.)

By Mr. Colby:

Q. I would like a statement of the Company's treasurer of the total amount paid to outside counsel in connection with the negotiations resulting in the subway contracts, and in connection with the closing of these contracts, and in connection with the issuance of the bonds and the making of the mortgage to secure the same. I suppose the auditor is the man to make that statement? A. Yes, sir.

Q. You are making a memorandum of these matters I am requesting? A. Yes, sir.

Q. Because I am relying on the stenographer's minutes.

Mr. Quackenbush.— There are some more (handing vouchers to counsel).

Mr. Colby.— Thank you.

I call attention of the Committee to the fact that the payment of $2,500 to Morgan J. O'Brien, was in connection with the Hopper injunction case, the bill of Judge O'Brien is rendered to the Interborough Rapid Transit Company and is for services to the Interborough Rapid Transit Company in the Hopper injunction case, against the execution of the subway contracts. In accordance with the resolution of June 2, 1913, and recites the payment to him was receipted by him, of $2,500.

Chairman Thompson.— I never thought of asking this before, but which side did he represent?

Mr. Colby.— He represented the Interborough Rapid Transit Company.

Chairman Thompson.—All right.

Mr. Colby.—Which was apparently an adverse party to the injunction sought by Hopper. I think John J. Hopper was the plaintiff in one of the actions which were embraced and consolidated, I believe, with the Admiral Realty Company case and argued before the Court of Appeals at the same time. That is the voucher for $2,500. There was another payment of $2,500 to Judge O'Brien, if I am not incorrectly informed —

Mr. Quackenbush.— I think that Judge O'Brien was paid $2,500 by the Brooklyn Rapid Transit Company, and $2,500 by the Interborough, so, if you have a return of $5,000, that is probably what you have in your mind.

Mr. Colby.— Somewhere I have seen that. The matter is fully set forth, Mr. Quackenbush, in the resolution of the Board annexed to the O'Brien voucher, and appears there. Your recollection is right. Twenty-five hundred dollars was paid by the Brooklyn Rapid Transit Company, $2,500 by the Interborough Company, and the authorization of the payment of the $2,500 by the Interborough recited the agreement of President Williams of the Brooklyn Rapid Transit Company to pay an equal amount for services in that suit.

Senator, if you wish to adjourn, I am ready now. This is a good point.

Chairman Thompson.— Have the stenographer mark them as exhibits.

(Copy of voucher No. 117,890, to Morgan J. O'Brien, $2,500, marked Exhibit No. 2, February 8, 1916, V. E. V.)

(Copy of voucher No. 117,623, Interborough Rapid Transit Company to Francis Lynde Stetson, $50,079.75, is marked Exhibit No. 3 of February 8, 1916, V. E. V.)

(Copy of voucher No. 110,613, Interborough Rapid Transit

Company to Edward M. Grout, $7,500, is marked Exhibit No. 4 of February 8, 1916, V. E. V.)

(Copy of voucher No. 92,402, Interborough Rapid Transit Company to Edward M. Grout, $10,000, is marked Exhibit No. 5 of February 8, 1916, V. E. V.)

Chairman Thompson.—We will suspend now until to-morrow morning at 11 o'clock, at the same place.

(Whereupon, at 4:25 o'clock P. M., an adjournment was taken to Wednesday, February 9, 1916, at 11 o'clock A. M., at the same place.)

FEBRUARY 9, 1916

NEW YORK COUNTY LAWYERS' ASSOCIATION BOARD ROOM
165 Broadway, New York City

Meeting called to order by Chairman Thompson at 11:50 A. M.

Chairman Thompson.— The Chair has been delayed because of the fact that the custodian of Mr. Freedman's books have not given our expert accountant access to certain papers that he wants.

Mr. Quackenbush.— I don't think I heard that statement.

Chairman Thompson.— It doesn't refer to your matter. The Guaranty Trust Company are interfering with out expert account. You may proceed, Mr. Colby, whenever you are ready.

Mr. Quackenbush.— So that I may get through with my contribution to this matter I have now a statement taken from the payroll of attorneys as far as I know, and the amount of the attorneys' salaries for January was $24,176.66 out of the total of $48,118.49, and I imagine that roughly it run about in that same ratio in other months. That is to say, the attorneys are about 50 per cent. of the payroll. I should imagine it would run in January a trifle over that. It is $24,976.66 out of $48,118.49, which is probably 51 or 52 per cent. and it will average about that. I should imagine it is a fair distribution of it. I find that my memory was correct in relation to the number of lawyers — that the number is sixty and that means that the attorneys will aggregate about $300,000 a year.

By Mr. Colby:

Q. That's for the Interborough Rapid Transit Company? A. For the whole system. There is a distribution there which, as I understand it, is subject to a variation back and forth as the work varies each month. The figures that I have given you is an average of the distribution under normal conditions.

Q. May I ask you just one further question, Mr. Quackenbush?

Mr. Quackenbush.— Certainly; I shall be glad to answer any question, Mr. Colby.

Q. I think you stated yesterday that it was a monthly total of $48,100 per month. A. That is the total payroll of the law department of all the companies I have to do with and includes not only lawyers, but stenographers, clerks, investigators, adjusters and process servers, every character of employ that is in the law department.

Q. And this total of $24,976 is the January amount paid, and what you state the average monthly payment for merely the lawyers? A. Yes.

Q. Have you in mind the total cost of your department for maintenance and operation, including the payroll? A. Meaning by that such items as stationery, rental, etc.?

Q. Yes. A. I have no data on that. The auditor can give you that.

Q. What counsel are under annual or permanent retainer? A. The only counsel who are under permanent retainer are Francis L. Wallman, in accident cases; Mr. Fred Moses, who tries accident cases; Mr. John Graham, who tries accident cases in the Long Island counties only, and Mr. Lemuel E. Quigg, who tries accident cases and does general work also.

Q. And Mr. Rogers? A. Mr. Rogers is under salary and reports directly to the president.

Q. Are there any other attorneys acting in similar relation to that of Mr. Rogers? A. No. The organized law department consists of Mr. Rogers as general counsel, reporting directly to the president and myself as general attorney and reporting direct to the president and associated with me the lawyers whose names are on that list and the clerical force and the force that I have mentioned to you.

Q. The names of Mr. Wellman and Mr. Quigg and the other two attorneys whom you mentioned as under annual retainers in connection with certain employments, etc., they are not on this list? A. No.

Q. But to get the cost of the legal department of the company it would be necessary to throw into the total the amount of their annual retainers? A. Yes. That I have filed with Mr. Lawrence.

Q. Could you tell me the aggregate of these retainers? A. Mr. Wellman's retainer or minimum is at present $7,500 a year, and then a sliding scale depending upon the volume of business and it runs up some fifteen to twenty thousand dollars a year, including the $7,500. Mr. Moses is paid entirely on a per diem per case basis. He averages ten to twelve thousand dollars a year. Mr. Graham is paid by the case. We have very little business in Long Island these days, so his compensation would not exceed a few thousand dollars. Mr. Quigg is paid quarterly $5,000 — $20,000 a year.

Q. Nothing else? A. No.

Q. So that it would amount to possibly an additional — say $50,000 — to the aggregate cost, is that not correct? A. In round numbers that is correct; not exceeding that.

Mr. H. M. FISHER, being recalled, testified as follows:

Mr. Colby examining:

Q. Mr. Fisher, I asked you yesterday if you would be kind enough to prepare a tabulation showing the total payment by the Interborough Rapid Transit Company to what we have come to describe as outside counsel.

Chairman Thompson.— These men don't report to you, Mr. Quackenbush, as I understand it.

Mr. Quackenbush.— No, they do not.

Chairman Thompson.— Are they employed for their whole time?

Mr. Quackenbush.— No, for special services.

By Mr. Colby:

Q. Will the stenographer please repeat my question. Question repeated as follows: Mr. Fisher, I asked you yesterday if you would be kind enough to prepare a tabulation showing the total payment by the Interborough Rapid Transit Company to what we have come to describe as outside counsel? In connection with contract number 3, that is to say contracts having to do with the construction of the new subway. Have you prepared such a statement? A. Yes.

Q. Is the statement you hand me the statement you have prepared? A. Yes.

Q. Mr. Chairman, I will, with your leave, offer this in evidence and ask that it be put on the record. The details of this statement have been fully covered in the testimony already given.

Chairman Thompson.— We will accept the statement. Statement received and marked Exhibit No. 1.

INTERBOROUGH RAPID TRANSIT COMPANY

Memorandum of Payments to Outside Counsel in connection with Contract No. 3 and the Allied Certificates and the First and Refunding Mortgage.

Hays, Hershfield & Wolf —

Admiral Realty Company matter:

Services	$35,000 00	
Disbursements	2,809 90	
		$37,809 90

Guggenheimer, Untermyer & Marshall —

Admiral Realty Company matter:

Services	$25,000 00	
Disbursements	318 72	
		25,318 72
Mirabeau L. Towns — professional services		5,000 00
Edward M. Grout — professional services		17,500 00

Francis Lynde Stetson —

Professional services in connection with negotiations concerning new contracts and
in connection with preparation of mortgage:

Services	$50,000 00	
Disbursements	79 75	
		$50,079 75

John F. Dillon —

Professional services rendered the Manhattan
Railway Company in the matter of third
tracking the Elevated Lines and the exten-
sions thereof 5,000 00

Julien T. Davies —

Professional services rendered the Manhattan
Railway Company in the matter of third
tracking the Elevated Lines and the exten-
sions thereof 10,000 00

Morgan J. O'Brien —

Services in the Hopper injunction 2,500 00

Nicoll, Anable, Lindsay & Fuller —

Proportion of services for the two years ended April 1, 1912	$10,000 00	
Proportion of services for the period from April 1, 1912 to June 1, 1913 . . . $20,000 00		
Proportion of disbursements	269 61	
	20,269 61	
		30,269 61

Total $183,477 98

AUDITOR'S OFFICE,

NEW YORK, *February* 9, 1916.

Mr. Colby.— It shows payment to nine separate individuals or firms of lawyers and shows an aggregate payment in this one specific connection of $183,477.98.

A. I might say, Mr. Colby, with your permission that these payments to various counsels are not all of them under the control of the company. These payments made to counsel are not all under the control of the Interborough Rapid Transit Company. For example, the payment to Francis L. Stetson for professional services in connection with the mortgage amounting to $50,079.75 should be deducted as should also the payment to Mr. J. P. Davies for services in connection with the Manhattan third track and elevated extensions, amounting to $10,000, as well as the payment to Hays, Hershfield & Wolf, Guggenheimer, Untermyer & Marshall and Morgan J. O'Brien, amounting to $37,809.90, $25,318.72 and $2,500, respectively, which were special services for the purpose of ascertaining the validity of the subway contract.

Q. We will exclude reference for the moment to Mr. Stetson's bill. Were any of these other payments charged to some account having to do with subway construction or with contract number 3? A. Yes.

Q. Then why should they be deducted from this statement? A. Because I understand the point you are trying to get at is the amount of counsel fees employed, counsel employed to aid Mr. Rogers in the preparation of the contract and mortgage and in negotiation of the contract. None of these parties were employed in any such capacity.

Q. None of them were employed in the negotiation of the contract? A. No.

Q. I would like Mr. Stenson's voucher on that point because you are clearly in error there, Mr. Fisher? A. No, sir; they were employed to examine the mortgage for the Guarantee Trust Company.

Chairman Thompson.— This mortgage had been made by your lawyers and then been passed on by Mr. Stetson?

Mr. Fisher.— Passed on by Mr. Stetson for J. P. Morgan & Company.

Chairman Thompson.— Do you think he could have added or deducted from any advice that your attorneys might have given on that subject?

Mr. Fisher.— The trustees require that the mortgage be passed upon by their own lawyers. It was in that way that the services of Mr. Stetson were rendered.

Mr. Colby (continuing):

Q. Mr. Stetson's bill, I believe, also included conferences in connection with the contract. To what extent I could not say. I don't like to make any references to the statements contained in that bill without having it before me. I have a very definite recollection, however, that it included services in connection with the negotiations of the subway contract, including a special mention of reference before the Board of Estimate. Am I not correct, Mr. Quackenbush?

Mr. Quackenbush.— Yes.

(Answer by witness).— A. As services for the Interborough Rapid Transit Company employed in examining the indenture for J. P. Morgan & Company.

Q. He does not say that. A. At any rate, deducting these amounts would reduce this bill very materially.

Q. Of course deducting half of these amounts would reduce the bill by half, and deducting three-fourths would still further reduce it. The question is should these deductions be made. In the payments to the attorneys who represented ostensibly the Admiral Realty Company, were not their services in procuring an opinion of the Court as to the validity of the contracts of as much value to the company as were, well say, Mr. Rogers' bonus, as to some features of the contract? A. Yes, but they were not employed in negotiating the contract.

Q. Let me see the minutes in reference to Mr. Rogers' bonuses. Can you refer to that, do you think? (Minute book is handed to counsel, who reads as follows): The statement in the Company's minutes of the Board meeting held on September 17 in relation to the granting of the Rogers bonus was apparently made by the President himself. The minutes say this — "The president stated that the legal matters in and about the contract for the construction and equipment of the new subway and elevated lines prior to March 19th had been conducted by Mr. Rogers, that the work was long continued and exacting and had been furnished in conjunction with his other duties in a very satisfactory manner and without the employment of associate counsel." So that the statement on which the resolution was passed boiled down is this: The President stated that the legal matters in and about the contract had been performed in a satisfactory manner without the employment of outside counsel. So I think you will agree with me, to use a mild word, it is an inaccurate statement of the facts? A. I think he meant to convey the matters relating to the negotiations, the making of the contract.

Q. He does not say that. A. That would be my interpretation of that resolution.

Chairman Thompson.—What date is that?

Mr. Colby.— September 17, 1913.

Q. Well, interpretations differ. The statement is all legal matters in and about the contract. I am willing that your interpretation of that as meaning only matters affected or concerned in the negotiations looking to the making of the contract should stand as the statement of your thought in the matter. In other words, only matters controlled by the Interborough Rapid Transit Company.

Q. You said that the employment of Hays, Hershfield & Wolf and the employment of Guggenheimer, Untermyer & Marshall was a matter out of the control of the company? A. Yes.

Q. How did that come about? A. I don't understand that they were employed by the company, although they were paid by the company.

Q. Now, Mr. Fisher, you have handed me a statement in compliance with the Chairman's request of the payment made to outside counsel by the Interborough Rapid Transit Company for a period of nine years ending December 1, 1915. This is not a

complete statement of all outside counsel employed by the transit
lines, but only by the Interborough Rapid Transit Company; is
that right? A. No, sir; that is a statement, as I understand it,
paid all counsel, and it is apportioned among the various
companies.

Q. I think possibly you are in error there. It does not include
anything about the payments to counsel for the Consolidated Company or the Interborough–Metropolitan Company. A. I think
the statement is complete.

Q. Possibly I may not have made my point clear. That statement as I interpret it includes only counsel employed by the
Interborough Rapid Transit Company irrespective of the payments made to them? A. Yes.

Q. There was other counsel employed by these other companies
direct? A. Yes.

Q. And it is a statement of these expenditures that is in course
of preparation? A. That is correct, sir.

Q. Before leaving the question of the propriety of including
the payments set forth on the statement you have submitted this
morning, the payments to outside counsel on the new subway
contracts, before leaving the question of the propriety of excluding
the Stetson payment, the voucher of that payment was handed
to me, and I call your attention, Mr. Fisher, to the fact that the
statement of services there is under two heads, first, and I am
reading, "in connection with negotiations with Public Service
Commission and Board of Estimate Committee, concerning new
contracts for subway and extensions of elevated railroad?" A.
Yes.

Q. So that the interpretation I gave it on that point is correct,
is it not? A. Yes, sir. A portion of that bill would be chargeable
to that.

Q. But not all? A. Not all. The point I was trying to make
was that if outside counsel had been employed to negotiate this
contract and they had charged the company at the rate at which
outside counsel usually charged that the bill would have been
about a million dollars.

Chairman Thompson.— That is quite interesting. Then that
charge of a million dollars was commuted in the payment of a
fifty thousand dollar bonus to Mr. Rogers?

Mr. Fisher.— Quite likely.

Chairman Thompson.— Then you figure that by giving a bonus of $50,000 to Mr. Rogers the company may have saved eight or nine hundred thousand dollars?

Mr. Fisher.— They made quite a considerable saving.

Chairman Thompson.— I was looking at it from the other way, that the way other outside counsel charged here it would be just the same as though the company had given Mr. Rogers a million dollars? A. That is one way to put it, if you arrive at the same result.

Q. In other words, you are not impressed after looking at the bills you see, not impressed that the value of the services were as valuable as the amount of that bill? A. I wouldn't like to say that. I mean to say that the outside services employed in negotiating this contract were not excessive.

Chairman Thompson.— This is a mighty good town for a lawyer to live in.

By Mr. Colby:

Q. This voluminous statement of outside counsel employed by the Interborough Rapid Transit Company contains the names of some sixty-six individuals and firms whom the company has more or less continually or regularly employed during the period covered by the statement. I am postponing the footing of the amount until the data on this subject is completed on the statement which you promised me at 2 o'clock. I am able, however, at the moment, to direct your attention to a sample of the points on which the Committee would like a little more light. What has the firm of Breed, Abbott & Morgan done for the company? A. I understand we are represented at Albany by Mr. Morgan.

Q. Of that firm? A. Yes.

Q. There seems to be a record here of annual payments to Mr. Morgan's firm for a period of at least four or five years back. A Yes.

Q. And, also, some additional disbursements, not of large amount? A. Yes.

Q. The aggregate of the retainer and of the disbursements not exceeding, except in one instance, $11,000.

Chairman Thompson.— I can give you some information on that point. Whenever there is a bill before the Committee on Public Service in the Senate, of which I happen to be Chairman, Mr. Morgan generally, if he favored the passage of the bill or objected to it, would ask for a hearing on the bill. I presume last year he asked for ten, perhaps fifteen hearings, on different bills. Mr. Dawson was also there in reference to a bill on Eleventh avenue. Mr. Morgan appears regularly before the various committees.

Mr. Quackenbush.— And his bills are regularly certified and placed on file at Albany. He is the supervisor of current legislation at Albany in the employ of the Interborough Rapid Transit Company.

Chairman Thompson.— Yes, acting in their interest.

Mr. Quackenbush.— It don't think that is hardly a fair statement, Mr. Chairman.

Chairman Thompson.— Mr. Morgan appears in the open and has hearings before the Committee, which everybody is entitled to do.

Mr. Quackenbush.— May I add something? I think in fairness to Mr. Morgan I should say this: That some years ago a statute was passed requiring that all appearances in respect to legislation be made by filing a notice of appearance with the Secretary of State to be followed within thirty days after the close of the session with the filing of a statement of —

Chairman Thompson (interrupting).— I think we understand all about that, Mr. Quackenbush. He is a lobbyist, as we call it.

Mr. Quackenbush.— I don't just like that characterization. The theory was that there would be created a parliamentary bar, as there is in London, and Mr. Morgan during all these years has registered, and I regret the use of the term lobbyist.

Chairman Thompson.— Yet unfortunately they do that.

Mr. Quackenbush.— The theory was that attorneys before the Legislature of this State would be raised in dignity so that any lawyer might go there and appear as he appears in court, and any appearance that has been made in respect to legislation by Mr. Morgan has been made in that way.

Chairman Thompson.— I draw my distinction, as long as we are indulging in the question of politics. Where a man appears before a legislative committee on any pending legislation and advances his side of the bill I think that is proper. Where a man appears clandestinely before a committee or a member of it or a member of the Legislature or either, then I think that is improper.

Mr. Quackenbush.— I agree with you thoroughly, Mr. Chairman.

By Mr. Colby:

Q. I see, Mr. Fisher, that there is a record of payments to Messrs. Breed, Abbott and Morgan as follows: Period of the Constitutional Convention, $2,750. Do you know what that payment represents ? A. I do not.

Q. It is manifest, however, that the company hired these attorneys to do some work in connection with the supervision or watching or reporting upon the proceedings of the Constitutional Convention ? A. That I could not say.

Q. Did the company have any salaried attorney who was a member of that convention ? A. No, sir.

Q. Wasn't Mr. Lemuel E. Quigg a member of that convention ? A. I don't think so.

Mr. Quackenbush.— Of course, Mr. Colby, I would like to have it understood in reference to that answer —

Mr. Colby.— Of course I understand the witness is simply uninformed.

Mr. Quackenbush.— There is no doubt that Mr. Quigg was a member of the Constitutional Convention and the question was whether he was a salaried employee.

By Mr. Colby:

Q. What is the sum paid to Mr. Quigg annually, according to

your memorandum, by the Interborough Rapid Transit Company?
A. $20,000.

Q. Did he in any year receive more? I call your attention to
1910. A. Yes, sir, in 1910 he received $30,000, but in 1908 and
1909 I think he received ten thousand dollars and eight thousand
dollars, respectively, and I understand a portion of that year were
added to 1910, bringing that amount up to $30,000.

Q. That is in addition to his disbursements, which I observe are
trifling amounts? A. Yes.

Q. What is Mr. Quigg's department, or what is his specific
duty? A. Trial lawyer.

Q. That exclusively? A. General matters besides.

Q. You cannot make your answer more explicit than your last
statement, can you, on that point? A. No, sir, I couldn't.

Q. In what office of the company or under the direction of what
official of the company are his services rendered in the main?
A. To the general attorney.

Q. Does he confer with the President? A. Not to my
knowledge.

Q. Mr. Dawson has had the amounts set forth on this statement paid to outside attorneys for the period mentioned footea
up in the aggregate $805,250.07, and for the period covered by
the statement averaged annually $89,372.23. I assume I may
correctly state that tabulation, the result of that tabulation, in the
record, and in connection with the complete data which I am
advised we will later have, and that will make a complete footing
of the matter. A. I think it would be fair to state in connection
with that amount that it is mostly for a trial lawyer's accident
cases. I may be wrong. A large portion of it is for accident
cases. I would like to add to my last statement that in addition
to accident cases this covers land damage cases and patent cases
for the company.

Q. Where are the patent cases referred to, Mr. Fisher? (Witness examines statement and indicates to council the data
required.)

Q. Were the payments to Mr. F. E. Darby in connection with
the Hedley and Doyle patents? A. That is not my understanding.

Q. Do you know what these considerable payments to Mr. Darby on patent cases were for? A. Only in a general way. I think it was in connection with patents on machinery and other things that we purchased in connection with the operation of our lines.

Q. I see another item of expenditure for services in legislative matters of 1915, payment to Messrs. Hun & Parker. Had they anything to do with the Constitutional Convention or any questions presented there? A. That I do not know.

Q. I call your attention to the memorandum handed me which seems to refer that payment to Hun & Parker specifically to the Constitutional Convention. That is correct? A. Yes.

Q. Mr. Fisher, I dare say that this is an oversight on your part, but I call your attention to the fact that on the memorandum of services of Hun & Parker, on the original, it is described "Account legislative matters in 1915," while the other statement makes different mention of the kind of service rendered. I do not wish to impugn your testimony at all, Mr. Fisher, but I would like to have the discrepancy explained. A. That is quite correct. That was a duplicate statement made from the original, and there may be some slight corrections to be made.

Q. Do you wish to make any other corrections? Any that you wish to make, Mr. Fisher, you are at libery to do so. I do not wish to impugn your testimony at all. A. I think that there are a few minor corrections to be made, and I think you had better use the original instead of the duplicate statement.

Q. Did the company pay Mr. Lemuel E. Quigg his monthly installments on account of his annual retainer during his attendance at the Constitutional Convention? A. That I could not say. I have no other information beyond what is down on this statement.

Q. There is no information on your books of any fact which leads you to believe, to suppose, that they did not pay him? A. None whatever.

Q. Are there any other payments other than I have mentioned which are references to service in connection with the Constitutional Convention of 1915? A. That I cannot say.

Mr. Colby.— Mr. Fisher, the Chairman requests that you step aside for just a moment as I understand that Mr. Sabin, the president of the Guaranty Trust Company is here. Is Mr. Sabin, Mr.

Charles H. Sabin in the room. (No answer.) Is any representative of the Guaranty Trust Company in the room? (At this point Mr. Charles H. Sabin appeared before the Committee.)

SABIN, CHARLES H., being duly sworn, testified as follows:

By Chairman Thompson:

Q. Mr. Sabin, a subpoena has been served upon you and Guaranty Trust Company of which I am advised you are president and also upon the Guaranty Trust Company as executor of the will of Andrew Freedman, late deceased, requiring the production of certain books, papers, documents, and letters in the possession of the Guaranty Trust Company. Are you familiar with that subject? A. I just received one.

Q. Mr. Morse reports that the Guaranty Trust Company have refused him access to a portion of these papers. I want to know whether that is correct. A. My understanding is that Mr. Morse has been given access to such papers as we have seen, and in any way, relevant to this case.

Q. Now, Mr. Sabin, that matter, that question has been thrashed out by very eminent people and the other day by Mr. Colby and Mr. Quackenbush. This is an investigating Committee of the Legislature and we have got to be given access rather than delegate to anybody the decision of what is and what is not of interest to the investigation of this Committee, that is, what is or what is not proper to be investigated or inspected. In other words we can be given an ordinary right of investigation into these documents. A. You mean his private papers?

Q. We mean investigation to ascertain whether there is among these private papers anything that bears upon the subject of our inquiry and the decision is not for anybody but this Committee and the Legislature of the State to what is and what is not the subject of our inquiry.

Thomas Garrett, Jr.— Mr. Chairman I appear here for Mr. Sabin and I wish to state that a subpoena *duces tecum* was served upon Mr. Sutton, a trust officer of the Guaranty Trust Company. Pursuant to that subpoena Mr. Sutton by arrangement with Mr. Sabin allowed Mr. Morse, the accountant for this Committee, I believe, to examine all Mr. Freedman's books of accounts, all his vouchers, return vouchers from the bank and all his office books. The subpoena called for all papers in possession of the executor which were relevant to the conduct or the proceedings of Mr. Freedman as a director of the Public Service Corporation.

Mr. Colby.— I think you are slightly in error in that Mr. Garrett.

Mr. Garrett.— Pardon me, I saw the subpoena this morning. It said Public Service Corporation since 1906. Now after that was over I was told this morning Mr. Morse desired to go through all the papers in possession of the Guaranty Trust Company at a storage warehouse and after consulting with the attorneys for the other executor, one of the other executors, Mr. Untermyer, we came to the conclusion that a miscellaneous investigation into the private affairs of Mr. Freedman was not justified under that subpoena and we were not in position to grant it. We are prepared to give any information regarding the contents of these papers and will produce any papers wanted upon your subpoena in connection with the affairs of Mr. Freedman or in connection with this particular matter or whatever is relevant.

Chairman Thompson.— This Committee is not going to delegate its power of investigation to the Guaranty Trust Company.

Mr. Garrett.— I don't ask that, Mr. Chairman, and we will aid your Committee in whatever way we can.

By Mr. Colby:

Q. Have you the subpoena with you, Mr. Garrett? A. I have not. The subpoena I believe was handed to Mr. Sutton and Mr. Sutton believes he handed it over to Guggenheimer, Untermyer & Marshall.

Q. I am anxious to see that. I am inquisitive as to the contents of that subpoena. My own recollection, Mr. Chairman, as to the language of the subpoena is that it called for the production of all records and all papers in any way appertaining to Mr. Freedman's relations of any time whatsoever with any Public Service Corporation for the period mentioned in the subpoena.

13

Chairman Thompson.— I might say that we are not going to take up and expose in any way, nor do we want to go through any papers that don't refer to this investigation and have an important bearing on it. We are not going to expose private matters. We have never done it.

Mr. Garrett.— We are willing to obey the subpoena of this Committee and never shall try to avoid it.

By Mr. Colby:

Q. Is it your contention Mr. Garrett, that the subpoena is not broad enough? A. My contention is that subpoena does not justify the accountant in your employ going through these private papers.

Q. Do you mean to say that the subpoena is not specifically or suitably drawn? A. I am not instructing the Committee on this point.

Chairman Thompson.— I will just state that point over again. You mean to say that we have no right to send a private accountant to your papers to go through them, we don't claim that. We have a right to require you to bring these papers before this Committee and lay them on the desk. As a matter of convenience in subpœnaing papers from various people to be delivered to this Committee and with the idea in mind that many of those papers might be private and might not refer to the subjects of our investigation or to be of any value to it, we have sent our private accountant to the office or offices of the people under subpoena merely as a matter of accommodation.

Mr. Garrett.— I am not here to avoid anything. We are perfectly willing to do anything that is right. We have have no interest in trying to avoid the production of papers.

Chairman Thompson.— If you would rather bring the things up here, bring them here. I am sure that Mr. Morse would not make any indiscriminate investigation of your books.

By Mr. Colby:

Q. In other words, Mr. Garrett, you want to give us whatever you personally consider relevant to our inquiry? A. I will give every book of account which was in our possession.

Q. Those boxes are also in your legal possession because you are the executor. A. There are no boxes there. There is some private correspondence there which we consider the private affairs of Mr. Freedman.

Q. Why I understand there are four boxes over there, isn't that so? A. It is my understanding that there are four boxes of papers, cancelled papers at the Manhattan Storage. We don't know what is in them, and we do not feel that we have the right to subject them to the inspection of anybody, the private affairs of Mr. Freedman, unless we are joined in making such consent by other co-executors. Here is another point, Mr. Samuel Untermyer is in Florida and we have had no communication with him whatsoever.

Q. I cannot imagine a better man for you to consult as to the proper standing and rights and powers of this Committee than Mr. Untermyer.

Q. Mr. Sabin has so far as I know, and I believe endeavored to cooperate with this Committee. I think it is rather unfortunate and is also to be regretted that this question should be put in the position of resisting the Committee because I am certain on a very little dispassionate discussion that Mr. Sabin will recognize that this Committee will judge as to the relevancy of the matters of inquiry and irksome or distasteful as it is to inspect papers which you suspect of being private in character, you must remember that this inspection is by the Legislature. It has to pursue a very important inquiry and it should be the judge of the relevancy or character of the material which it seeks. Certainly it would defeat the entire purpose of this investigation if every witness should be permitted to pass upon the materiality of the question that was asked him or the relevancy or the propriety of the documentary evidence that he is asked to produce. I think you will find that its powers are very broad. As I recall its resolution it is broad enough to obtain these papers. The methods of this Committee as described is intended to extend every consideration to the Guaranty Trust Company and as an expression of the Committee's confidence in the desire of the Guaranty Trust Company and of its officers to meet the Committee with candor, I say to you with perfect sincerity that you are inviting a little contest which will cause the Trust Company's position and that of these co-executors to be most interesting. It is a resistance that is not based upon facts and I might further observe that we have too much that is highly pertinent, particularly relevant to this inquiry to spend and waste any time in crowding discussions into the record over a matter of this kind.

Mr. Sabin.— There are two other executors besides ourselves and it would not take long to communicate with Mr. Untermyer.

Q. And with the other executors? A. I think we could do that promptly.

Q. Is Mr. Oakman in town? A. I don't know where he is. He was a day or two ago.

Chairman Thompson.— We are very fair about these matters but it does seem that there are an awful lot of people on the ocean, in Florida and in California and we cannot afford to waste any more time.

Mr. Colby.— May I make this suggestion to you. Of course the law is that each executor owes all the duty that his co-executor owes and that each acts with full power in any matter pertaining to the estate, but Mr. Sabin is a banker, a layman, and I think that these questions are difficult and confusing to him, simply because they are unfamiliar and it seems to me that possibly the best solution would be to give Mr. Sabin a couple of hours to consult counsel and communicate with Mr. Untermyer and Mr. Oakman.

Chairman Thompson.— I think Mr. Oakman should appear also. To make sure that he does I direct that a subpoena be issued for Mr. Oakman this afternoon.

By Mr. Colby:

Q. Mr. Sabin, I hardly need to ask for your assurance but with it I shall be entirely content that of course there will be no attempt to deceive as to the location of the depositories A. I promise you that, Mr. Colby.

Chairman Thompson.— We will now suspend until 2.30 p. m.

Whereupon an adjournment was taken.

AFTERNOON SESSION

The committee was called to order at 3:10 o'clock P. M., Chairman Thompson presiding.

Mr. Colby.— Mr. Chairman, Mr. Fisher advises me that some of the materials which we hoped to have at 2 o'clock are still in course of preparation and may not be completed until this evening.

Chairman Thompson.— All right.

Mr. Colby.— I will therefore turn aside from the subjects of my examination this morning, and take up some other matters that I consider of importance, pending the completion of the data requested.

Chairman Thompson.— The Committee has grown to have great confidence in matters which counsel considers important.

Mr. Colby.— Mr. Quackenbush, I would like to have Mr. Gaynor present about ten minutes of four, to ask a few questions, with a view to defining some materials I want him to furnish, if that is agreeable and convenient.

Mr. Quackenbush.— All right, sir.

By Mr. Colby:

Q. Mr. Fisher, I asked you to give me a statement of the number of bonds of the Interborough Rapid Transit Company issued under their first and refunding mortgage, up to date, that have been sold. A. Yes, sir.

Q. Is this the statement in compliance with that request, which you file? A. Yes, sir.

Mr. Colby.— The witness hands me a statement entitled " Issue and sale of Interborough Rapid Transit Company first and refunding mortgage five per cent. bonds to date."

(Document referred to is received in evidence and marked Exhibit No. 2, February 9, 1916, V. E. V.)

By Mr. Colby:

Q. The date is February 4, 1916. What is the total amount of the first and refunding mortgage 5 per cent. bonds authorized by the Public Service Commission to be issued by your company? A. $160,957,000.

Q. $160,957,000. What is the total amount of bonds delivered by you to the Guaranty Trust Company and certified by it? A. $154,531,000.

Q. Leaving a balance of authorized bonds of what amount? A. $5,873,000.

Q. It says $6,000,000. A. (referring to Exhibit No. 2) That is right. $6,426,000.

Q. Are those bonds in the possession of the Interborough Company? A. They are subject to — you mean the difference between —

Q. The amount authorized and the amount delivered to and certified by the trustee. A. Yes, sir.

Q. You have, in other words, $6,426,000 of those bonds still in your possession? A. Yes, sir.

Q. Out of the total issue of $160,000,000? A. Yes, sir.

Q. How many of the bonds already issued and certified have been sold? A. $148,658,000.

Q. On your statement it appears that those bonds are sold to J. P. Morgan & Company. A. Yes, sir.

Q. There would appear, therefore, to be a balance of bonds already issued and certified, but still unsold? A. Yes, sir.

Q. That balance amounts to how much? A. That is $5,873,000.

Q. And where are those certified bonds? A. Those are on deposit with the Guaranty Trust Company, subject to the order of the treasurer.

Q. And are subject also to delivery to J. P. Morgan & Company as the latter call for them? A. That is correct.

Q. The latter having the right to call for the bonds which it contracts to take in any given year? A. Yes, sir.

Q. At any time within the year? A. Yes, sir.

Q. And your impression is that those bonds are still uncalled for by J. P. Morgan & Company? A. Yes, sir.

Q. Can you tell me what is the amount of the proceeds of the sale of bonds that has passed to the Interborough Rapid Transit Company? I don't believe it appears there. A. I don't think I have that figure. It is very — you can figure it out — $148,658,000, on the basis of 93½, and that will give you the amount.

Mr. Dawson.— I will figure that.

Chairman Thompson.— Is accrued interest in there? Has that been taken into account?

Mr. Fisher.— No, sir.

Chairman Thompson.— That will make a difference in the figures?

Mr. Fisher.— That will make a difference in the figures. I don't know what the interest charges are.

Mr. Dawson.— $138,995,230.

(Counsel hands paper with figures to witness.)

By Mr. Colby:

Q. The proceeds of the bond sale would be 93½ per cent. of the par value of the bonds sold? A. Yes, sir.

Q. Through Morgan & Company? A. Yes, sir.

Q. And that would amount, according to the calculation in your hands, to what figure? A. $138,995,230.

Q. Has this amount either been received by the Interborough Rapid Transit Company or placed to its credit? A. Yes, sir.

Q. And of that $138,000,000, I understood you to testify at a previous session that something over fifty million dollars is now on deposit with J. P. Morgan & Company? A. Yes, sir.

Q. So that, speaking roughly, and not taking the time to make an accurate calculation, the actual amount received by the Interborough Rapid Transit Company thus far — that is to say, spent by it — A. Yes, sir.

Q. — is the difference between $138,000,000 and this large amount on deposit with Morgan & Company? A. Yes, sir.

Q. Which would be something in excess of eighty millions? A. Yes, sir.

Q. And in that eighty millions are included many charges except for payments on the actual work on construction and equipment, are there not? A. There are some included. I could not say how many.

Q. Would Mr. Gaynor be the one? A. He could tell. We are limited by the contract to 3 per cent. to cover extraordinary charges. Mr. Gaynor could give you that more in detail than I can.

Q. Three per cent. to cover extraordinary charges. What are they, speaking to the extent of your knowledge? A. I would not like to enumerate on them —   .

Q. So far as you can, simply for our guidance. A. I would prefer that you get them accurately from the accountant.

Chairman Thompson.— Who got the 3 per cent.?

Mr. Fisher.— That is deductable. We can deduct — we are allowed 3 per cent. for the expense of issuing the mortgage, expenses connected with issuing the mortgage and contract.

By Mr. Colby:

Q. Three per cent. on one hundred and sixty millions? A. No, sir; upon eighty millions. That is subway contributions, not upon the Manhattan Elevated.

Q. Upon eighty millions of the one hundred and sixty millions? A. Yes, sir.

Q. You are allowed 3 per cent. to cover the expense in connection with the issuance of the $160,000,000, and of the mortgage — and the making of the mortgage to secure it? A. Yes, sir. The city allows us to deduct that sum. That is more than accounted for, I might say, by the discount on the bonds.

Q. In other words, your allowance of 3 per cent. is practically swept away by the discount at which the bonds are issued? A. Yes, sir. Anything in excess of that the Interborough must take care of itself out of its own surplus.

Q. Or issuing additional bonds? A. No. Out of its own surplus.

Q. So this 3 per cent. for expenses did not avail you anything, owing to the discount at which the bonds were sold? A. No, sir.

Q. And the expenses which the 3 per cent. was designed to cover had to be met out of the surplus of the company? A. Yes, sir.

Q. Do you know, in general, the aggregate of such expense? A. I could not tell you; no, sir.

Q. But Mr. Gaynor can, I see? A. He can; yes, sir.

Q. Now are the directions given to the Interborough company by Morgan & Company for the issuance of the excessive installments of these bonds given? A. He simply calls upon the president for a certain amount of bonds at a certain date; within the provisions of his contract, of course.

Q. How practically has that worked out? Has it called for bonds — in what amounts, ordinarily? A. All the way from five up to twenty millions.

Q. The more bonds it calls for in advance of your cash requirements, the larger the deposit, the balance with Morgan & Company becomes? A. Yes, sir.

Q. And the larger is the differential of interest against the Interborough company? A. Yes, sir.

Q. In view of the fact that your balances to-day amount to between fifty and sixty millions with Morgan & Company, have any representations been made to Morgan & Company as to the resultant hardship and loss to the Interborough company of having so many bonds outstanding and so large an amount of cash on deposit? A. Not that I know of. I am only speaking for myself, understand.

Chairman Thompson. It costs a million and a quarter a year to carry fifty millions, don't it?

Mr. Fisher.— About that.

Mr. Colby.—A little in excess of that. The bonds — reckoning the price at which the bonds were sold by the Interborough, and remembering the bonds bear 5 per cent. on par, it has been testified that the actual interest paid by the Interborough is five and three-eighths, and the interest on the deposit balances with Morgan

& Company is 2½, so it lacks but an eight of a per cent. of 3 per cent. against the company.

Chairman Thompson.—A million and a half a year, at that rate.

Mr. Fisher.— I would like to explain here in connection with that large balance with Morgan & Company, that the apportionment of the bonds to be taken each year was arranged after conferences with the Public Service Commission, and was based upon the time in which it was expected to complete the new subways and elevated extensions.

Chairman Thompson.—When was that time?

Mr. Fisher.— Prior to the signing of the contract, I think. Mr. Shonts had the contract.

Chairman Thompson.—Was it an open conference?

Mr. Fisher.—Yes, sir.

Chairman Thompson.— Before an open meeting of the Public Service Commission?

Mr. Fisher.— There was nothing secret about it. Whether it was before an open meeting or not I don't know.

Chairman Thompson.—A public meeting?

Mr. Fisher.— It might have been an informal meeting, or before a public meeting. Anyway, it had the approval of the Public Service Commission. That was based upon completing the subway in four years, beginning with 1913, and I have stated in the contract, the lease was to become effective January 1, 1917. Of course there has been considerable delay so far with the tunnels under the river, I understand, and that will probably bring the completion of the tunnel over to the middle of summer in 1918. Had the original plan been carried out, you can readily see these balances would not have been so large, because payments would have been made out much more rapidly.

By Mr. Colby:

Mr. Fisher, has the Interborough any financial reason or motive for postponing the date of operation of the new subways? A. Absolutely none.

Q. What is the effect upon interest, credits or debits, from the postponement of the actual operation? A. The interest charges, of course, are charged against construction, until such time as the different sections are put into operation. In other words, the Interborough would not have to pay interest on any bonds issued to construct any sections of the subway until those sections were actually placed in operation.

Q. Now, let me see if I understand you there. The Interborough immediately begins the payment of interest on its bonds as soon as issued. A. Yes, but it is charged to construction account; it is not charged to earnings.

Q. The interest is charged to construction? A. Yes, sir.

Q. And this interest amounts up, as long as operation is postponed, on only one side of the ledger, doesn't it? Correct.

Q. In other words —

Chairman Thompson.— The fact of it is, this million and a half is practically paid by the city?

Mr. Fisher.—You can issue bonds for it.

Chairman Thompson.— I know, but the city has got to pay it.

Mr. Fisher.— It is part of the construction charge.

Chairman Thompson.— I say the city has to pay it.

Mr. Fisher.— Not the city any more than the company. If bonds are issued, the interest on the bonds would come out, of course, before any division of the profits by the city.

By Mr. Colby:

Q. Let me see — just read the question.

(The question was read by the stenographer as follows):

" Q. And this interest mounts up, as long as operation is postponed, on only one side of the ledger, doesn't it? "

Q. I mean, there are no offsets to the mounting interest charges, as long as operation has not started? A. No, sir; there are not.

Q. And there are no receipts from income or operation to carry this interest? A. No, sir.

Q. And this rising interest charge becomes an increased charge against construction, doesn't it? A. Yes, sir.

Q. Well, now, the city undertook to — I mean to say, the company undertook to expend a fixed and stated amount on construction, and no more, didn't it? A. Yes, sir.

Q. That amount was $58,000,000, wasn't it? A. Yes, sir.

Q. Did that include 3 per cent., we will say, for expenses in connection with the mortgage and the issuance of bonds? A. Fifty-eight million dollars had to be produced in cash.

Q. Well, was this 3 per cent. charged against the construction? A. No, you would have to issue bonds on the basis of 93½ to produce that money.

Q. These interest charges are carried to construction, you testified? A. Yes, sir. In other words, we are contributing cash, not contributing bonds.

Q. Well, the larger the amount that is paid for interest charges, the less amount you have to pay or expend on construction, haven't you? A. Yes, sir, that is one way of putting it.

Q. Isn't that a perfectly accurate way of putting it, Mr. Fisher? A. Yes, sir.

Q. And if there is any deficit in the money available for construction purposes, it has got to be supplied from some source, hasn't it? A. It must.

Q. That is supplied by the city, isn't it? A. Yes, sir.

Q. So that on these excessive interest charges, and on all losses arising from interest, it is the city that is holding the bag, isn't it? A. Yes, sir.

Q. And the loss of interest resulting from the difference between the rate of interest prescribed in the bonds, and what you are receiving from Morgan & Company, is in turn charged to construction, and in turn borne by the city, isn't it? A. Yes, sir.

Q. Is there any limit to which the city is obligated to make good and sustain, singly and alone, the burden of these improvidences and extravagances? A. It is limited by the completion of construction, and placing the subway in operation.

Q. In other words, your obligation for construction is fixed at $58,000,000? A. Yes, sir.

Q. And if you spend ten, fifteen or twenty millions of that money for things that are only theoretically items of construction, the actual cost of construction has got to be made up, under the terms of the contract, by the city of New York? A. Yes, sir.

Q. Now, I suppose there are some very fluctuating items under engineering and superintendence, are there not? A. Not necessarily fluctuating, I don't think.

Q. Let me say indeterminate. A. Naturally, the longer the completion of the work is postponed the more those items will mount up.

Q. Has that something to do in connection with other reasons which I have seen loudly urged for the failure to connect up the Lexington Avenue subway at 42nd street? A. That I could not say. The Lexington Avenue subway at 42nd street is not yet completed. It would be a physical impossibility to connect it up. I think you have in mind —

Q. Is the fact that the Interborough does not financially suffer through the postponement of operation, but on the contrary profits through these mounting interest charges, the real reason why operation on the Lexington subway seems to be so indefinitely postponed? A. Absolutely not.

Q. I suppose the reason is what I have heard urged by the company, and seen in the papers, that there is some difficulty about the East River tunnel? A. The Interborough is not constructing the East River tunnel.

Q. But there is some relation between the East River tunnel and its general comprehensive scheme of operation, is there not? A. The tunnel is a part of the main contract.

Chairman Thompson.— The Public Service —

Q. What is the reason? A. There are no delays —

Mr. Colby.— I didn't want to cut you off, Mr. Chairman. I was just pursuing the line because of my interest in it.

Chairman Thompson.— Let him make his answer.

Mr. Fisher.— I didn't want to interrupt. You go ahead.

Chairman Thompson.— I am going to be Chairman now, so I am going to make you go ahead, just to show my authority.

Mr. Fisher.— I was going to say that there have been no delays that I know of in any of the construction under the supervision of the Interborough; that is, under construction being done by the Interborough Rapid Transit Subway Construction Company, the total amount of this stock is owned by the Interborough Rapid Transit Company, and I don't understand any charges have been made against the Rapid Transit Company or the Interborough Rapid Transit Company, of delays.

Chairman Thompson.— Does the Public Service Commission understand the fact that this interest is finally chargeable in the way you just demonstrated here in the last few minutes.

Mr. Fisher.— Certainly ought to, and I presume they do.

Chairman Thompson.— They have not performed the opening of the Lexington Avenue route?

Mr. Fisher.— I understand there is some talk to that effect.

By Mr. Colby:

Q. I will leave this very interesting question briefly, but I will return to it. I have asked you, Mr. Fisher, to produce a statement of the interest received by the company or credited to it on various amounts on deposit to your credit with J. P. Morgan & Company. A. Yes, sir.

Q. The witness hands me a statement simply entitled "Recapitulation." Annexed to it are detailed statements of the interest on daily balances with J. P. Morgan & Company, on the following accounts: Subway contribution account, on which the interest is 2½ per cent., and I may say for brevity, that the rate of interest on all the accounts that I shall read appears to be 2½ per cent. except on general account, on which the interest is but 2 per cent. The accounts of which details are supplied me are the following: Subway contribution account, which I have mentioned; Manhattan third-tracking account; Manhattan power-house account; elevated extension account; redemption account; note account; general account; special account. I call the Committee's attention to the fact that we put in evidence yesterday a statement of the credit balances in each of those accounts, so it is not necessary to refer to that again to-day. The total of interest received by the Interborough, according to this statement, signed by J. H. Campbell, its treasurer, up to February 9, 1916, is $1,829,089.47? A. Yes, sir.

Q. That is correct. In this connection —

Chairman Thompson.— The loss in interest, then, must have been more than two million dollars. It would be the difference between 2½ and 5⅜, wouldn't it?

Mr. Fisher.— Yes, that is right.

Mr. Colby.— I offer in evidence —

Chairman Thompson.— Who keeps this? Who gets this? This difference between 2½ and 5⅜?

Mr. Fisher.— The bondholders.

Mr. Dawson. — They get the whole five and three-eighths.

By Mr. Colby:

Q. The bondholders get five per cent. in such fraction as is represented by the actual price at which they purchase the bonds. Speaking generally, they get the price — they get the interest stipulated on the bonds? A. Yes, sir.

Q. The interest that is lost to the Interborough is the interest between five and three-eighths per cent., which the Interborough pays — A. Yes, sir.

Q. — and two or two and one-half per cent., as the case may be, on the current balances of these seven accounts with J. P. Morgan & Company? A. Two and one-half per cent. The general account there is current account, and that interest fluctuates, of course, with the rate of call money.

Chairman Thompson.—Well, now, you pay to these bondholders five and three-eighths on 93. Now, you have received this $1,800,-000. Now, up to the time when they begin operation — this new construction — you say the interest on these bonds to which this five and three-eighths is charged — is paid by the City. In that event, do you turn to the City this $1,800,000?

Mr. Fisher.—Yes, they get the credit. The account gets the credit, which is just the same.

Chairman Thompson.— Or your share?

Mr. Fisher.— No. It is credited to construction account, the interest.

By Mr. Colby:

Q. In other words, as I was developing, the fact, as I understand it, the loss of interest on these seven current accounts with J. P. Morgan & Company is the difference between five and three-eights and two and one-half per cent — A. Yes, sir.

Q. — or two per cent.? A. Yes, sir, about two per cent.

Q. Computed upon the amount of those balances? A. Yes, sir.

Q. Which today are between fifty and sixty million? A. Yes, sir.

Q. And in view of the fact that the interest on current account, stated by your treasurer, is today two per cent., and may even be lower, if the rate for call money is lower — A. In most cases I think it is lower. I think that is a very good rate for money today.

Q. You have received less than two per cent. on current account? A. Yes, sir.

Q. I would probably be quite accurate if I said the interest loss on these accounts would equal three per cent.; in other words, if the rate was two and seven-eighths per cent., if the rate was fixed at two and one-half per cent., your loss would be two and seven-eighths, and considering that on the current account the interest rate is sometimes under two, and fluctuates, usually downward, I might say that three per cent. was a fair statement of the average loss of interest on those current accounts? A. I do not see where that makes an additional loss. I should say we are getting remarkably good interest there, considering the interest paid on deposit at the present time.

Q. It may be very good compared to what other financial institutions are paying on general deposit, but what I am directing your attention to is there is a loss of three per cent. to you, computed to-day upon the sum of between fifty and sixty million dollars, which I understand to be the fact. That is substantially accurate, is it not? A. Well, I would not like to say without figuring it out myself.

Q. Well, it is at least the difference between five and three-eighths and two and one-half that you have testified to? A. Yes, that difference.

Q. And that is two and seven-ninths, and what I am trying to call attention to is that that is an inadequate statement of entire loss, because on current account you are not getting two and one-half but only two, and sometimes less? A. That would make a more favorable instead of a worse statement. The general account has nothing to do with those construction accounts. Those are all current operating balances, and it does not lessen the rate of interest that we get on the total construction accounts.

Q. And that loss, at any rate, would be two and seven-eighths per cent? A. Yes, put it that way.

Q. And does the interest that you receive go into the construction account? A. The City is credited with that interest.

Q. Not the excess they are called upon to pay? A. Yes, sir.

Q. Their obligation is, in the first instance, to pay any deficiency on construction? A. Yes, sir.

Q. In other words, the picture is this: You and the City each agree to expend about the same amount of money on this work of construction, to wit, about fifty-eight million dollars; is that right? A. Ours is fifty-eight million, and theirs about sixty-six million, as I remember.

Q. Yes. And it was assumed that with the exception of the authorized deductions, that money would be expended on construction, wasn't it? A. Yes, sir.

Chairman Thompson.— It cost the City as much to issue those bonds as it did you to issue yours?

Mr. Fisher.— That I could not tell you.

By Mr. Colby:

Q. Are these — is the $500,000 paid to J. P. Morgan & Company carried to the cost of construction? A. No, sir.

Q. Where does that item finally nestle? A. Out of the Interborough surplus, I believe. It is one of the items that comes out of that three per cent. It does not come inside.

Chairman Thompson.— What does that mean —" proposed subway routes?" Oh, we will find that from the Auditor, some day.

Mr. Fisher.—Yes, he can explain those items.

Mr. Colby.— I offer in evidence the statement of the monthly
balances of the Interborough Rapid Transit Company with J. P.
Morgan & Company from April 21, 1913, to February 1, 1916.

(Statement of monthly balances referred to is received in evidence and marked Exhibit No. 3, February 9, 1916, V. E. V.)

Mr. Colby.— I further offer in evidence the statement of interest receipts, to which I have just made reference, together with
the recapitulation .sheet, showing the total amount of interest
received.

(Document referred to, comprising nine pages, is received and
marked Exhibit No. 4, February 9, 1916, V. E. V.)

By Mr. Colby:

Q. I would like, for the purpose of cleaning up the record, to
ask you a question about the report of the special committee, or
the report you prepared for the special committee, recommending
the payment to Mr. Shonts of a bonus. Was that report ever
signed by the Committee? A. No, sir.

Q. By the special committee or by any member of it? A. No,
sir.

Q. It was delivered to the committee? A. Yes, sir.

Q. Did the committee mention any refusal — any ground for
their refusal to sign the report? A. No, sir. I will say that one
member of the Committee said he would like to make some corrections in the phraseology, after which he would sign the report.

Q. Who was that? A. That was Mr. Freedman.

Q. Did he make those corrections? A. No, sir, he never did,
not that I know of.

Q. Did the verbal report which the committee made, according
to testimony already given, mention any specific sum to be
awarded Mr. Shonts? Or did it merely say a substantial increase
of salary, or otherwise? A. I don't think it mentioned any specific sum. There were discussions of sums ranging from $100,000
to $225,000 or $250,000. It was decided at that time to give
him $125,000, leaving for a future date to decide whether that
amount would be increased, and how much.

Q. There was nothing in any minute as to leaving anything to
a future date for decision? A. No, sir. The minutes only cover
the amount actually voted.

Q. Are you testifying from your recollection as to what was said? A. I am testifying from my recollection as to what was written.

Q. Well, I will call your attention to the fact there was nothing written that suggested that this was a payment of so much for the time being, and that the payment of an additional sum was left to the future. A. No, sir, there was nothing written on that subject.

Q. So you — it is not quite accurate to say you are testifying from what was written? A. I meant written in the minutes of that particular meeting.

Q. There is nothing in the minutes of that particular meeting referring to a payment of an additional sum at a later date? A. I think I answered that there was nothing in writing showing that they intended to pay an additional sum at a later period, and that my minutes dealt with the sum voted at that particular meeting.

Q. I see. So it was the board of directors which really determined upon the payment of this amount, wasn't it? A. Yes, sir.

Q. The special committee making no recommendation on the subject? A. I would not like to say positively whether they made a recommendation or not. I don't recollect that any specific recommendation was made.

Q. Isn't it a fact that the recommendation of the committee was to give Mr. Shonts a year's salary? A. There was some mention made of that in the discussion.

Q. Was that the exact recommendation that was made by the special committee? A. No, sir, That simply came out of the discussion.

Q. Isn't it a fact that the first recommendation on the subject of the bonus to Mr. Rogers was something other than the $50,000 that was finally voted him? A. I think so; yes, sir.

Q. What was the actual recommendation as to the award to Mr. Rogers? A. The actual recommendation, when it was finally made to the Board, was $50,000. There was, however, in the earlier discussion, some — something was said about $30,000. I cannot recollect what it was, or who brought the matter up.

Q. Was there any vote to award Mr. Rogers any sum other than $50,000? A. No, sir.

Q. Isn't it a fact that the recommendation was to award Mr. Rogers $40,000? A. No, sir. That never came up. It was $30,000 originally, and was afterwards changed to $50,000.

Mr. Colby.— I see that Mr. Gaynor is in the room. You expect to have a report in a little while, I assume, on the production of the Freedman books?

Chairman Thompson.— I expect Mr. Sabin and Mr. Oakman here at 4 o'clock.

Mr. Colby.— I have five minutes to devote, in the meantime, to preliminary questions of Mr. Gaynor, and I would suggest that Mr. Fisher be excused, with the request to be available at 11 o'clock tomorrow morning.

Chairman Thompson.— Very well.

Mr. Colby.— I assume that we can have that material you have been at work on so diligently, at that time?

Mr. Fisher.— I will try to have it all for you, if you don't keep Mr. Gaynor too long.

GAYNOR, EDWARD J. F., called as a witness, being first duly sworn, testified as follows:

Examination by Mr. Colby:

Q. Mr. Gaynor, where do you reside? A. One hundred and fifty-one West 88th street.

Q. What position do you occupy with the Interborough Rapid Transit Company? A. Auditor.

Q. Do you occupy the same position with any other companies? A. Yes, sir.

Q. Specify them? A. The Interborough Consolidated Corporation, the New York Railways, the New York & Queens County Railway Company, the Broadway and Seventh Avenue Railway Company, the 42nd and Grand Street Ferry Railroad Company, the Subway Realty Company, the Rapid Transit Subway Construction Company and Brooklyn & North River Railroad Company, and possibly one or two more.

Q. I assume you are busy, ordinarily. You are the general

auditor of the transit lines affiliated with the Interborough? A.
Yes, sir.

Q. Consolidated Company? A. Yes, sir.

Q. The surface lines with the exception of one or two lines that
are not a part of the Interborough system? A. With the exception of Third Avenue.

Q. Are you auditor of the Elevated? A. Yes, sir.

Q. The Elevated, the Subway and the Surface lines, speaking
generally? A. Excepting the Third Avenue.

Q. Operating in New York, with the exception of the Third
Avenue? A. Yes, sir.

Q. How long have you occupied that — these positions? A.
I have been auditor of the. Interborough since April 1st, 1903; of
the other companies at various dates from that time to this. Prior
to April 1, 1903, I was auditor of the Manhattan Railway Company, then operating the elevated lines, which position I held
since April 1, 1881.

Q. You are an expert accountant, are you not? I am not asking you to state anything that would be embarrassing, but that is
your profession, isn't it? A. Yes, sir.

Q. You are familiar with the books of account of all these companies? A. I am.

Q. You are the head of the accounting department of these
companies, are you not? A. Yes, sir.

Q. That is an extensive department? A. Yes, sir, it is.

Q. How many assistant auditors have you under you? A. One
for the Interborough Rapid Transit and its directly associated
lines; one for the New York Railways Company and its associated lines —

Q. Will you mention the names of the men in each one of
these? A. The assistant auditor of the Interborough Company's
lines, Henry H. Berry; assistant auditor of the New York Railways and Associated lines, Frank Samuelson; and the assistant
auditor of the New York & Queens County, Miss I. M. Tritt.

Q. How many employees are their in the auditing department
under you? A. Approximately 200.

Q. And your salary? A. $15,000.

Q. Are you entirely familiar with the negotiations between the company and the city, and also with the bankers, preceding the making of the so-called dual subway contracts? A. In a measure.

Q. You are entirely familiar with some phases of the negotiations? A. I am.

Q. And the phases of the negotiations and the subsequent operation of the agreements have to do, I assume, particularly with the record of receipts and expenditures, is that correct? A. Largely so, yes sir.

Q. With what other aspects of this important subject are you familiar? A. Why, when you refer to the steps leading up to the contract, and the receipts and expenditures incident to the contract itself, and the allied certificates, you cover the ground generally pretty well.

Q. Yes. For instance, you know about the payment of $500,000 to J. P. Morgan & Company? A. I do.

Q. You know on what theory it was paid? A. Yes, sir.

Q. You know from what fund it was paid? A. I do.

Q. And you know to what accounts the amount was charged? A. I do.

Q. From what fund was it paid, this $500,000? A. From the general fund of the Interborough Rapid Transit Company.

Q. To what accounts was the amount charged? A. Other suspense account.

Q. Entirely to other suspense account? A. Yes, sir.

Q. What is " other suspense " account? A. It is an account laid down for our guidance by the Public Service Commission in the uniform system of accounts promulgated about January 1, 1909.

Q. And what items are properly charged to " other suspense " account? A. In the language of the Commission, any expenditure which cannot be permanently classified at the time it is made can be carried in other suspense account, pending its determination.

Q. Now, there are a great many items carried by you in other suspense account, are there not? A. Yes, sir.

Q. Eventually those items will require final reference or classification, will they not? A. Yes, sir.

Q. Can you produce to the Committee this account? A. Other suspense account?

Q. Yes, sir. A. If you wish it.

Chairman Thompson.— That means that is charged to — other suspense means you have not made up your mind as yet which account these items shall be subsequently charged to?

Mr. Gaynor.— That is correct.

By Mr. Colby:

Q. Are there any other accounts in which such items are carried, pending final reference or classification? A. No, sir.

Q. What other suspense accounts are there than "other suspense"? A. None.

Q. Where did the Interborough carry the items which now are carried in other suspense accounts, prior to the promulgation by the Public Service Commission of this direction? A. They had no items that could be considered parallel to these items which you are considering.

Q. Tell me in a general way, fully, however, as you can, what items have been charged by you in other suspense account; I mean items of what character? A. Generally speaking, the preliminary expenditures made incident to, leading up to and connected with, more or less directly, the contract No. 3 and the allied certificates.

Q. Can you testify from your knowledge what is the aggregate of the amount of the items now carried in other suspense account? A. I should say about $600,000.

Q. Where is the bonus paid to the president of the company, amounting to $125,000 carried? A. The total bonus paid, $150,000 —

Q. There were two payments, I am aware. A. Yes, sir; and the $125,000 was apportioned between contract No. 3 and the allied certificates in the ratio of the amounts of money which we expected to expend upon those three contracts.

Q. In other words, they were charged to construction account? A. They were, yes sir.

Q. The entire amount was charged to construction account? A. Yes, sir.

Q. It has been testified to this afternoon that the obligation of the Interborough on account of construction, it is agreed, should not exceed $58,000,000. Is that correct? A. That is correct.

Q. And if the amount available for the work of construction should not be adequate for the completion of construction work, that the difference is to be made up by the city; is that correct? A. That is correct.

Q. There is no question but that there will be a difference to be made up by the city on account of construction, is there? A. Of course, that is a subject that any of us might differ with respect to. It depends very largely upon whether or not the work is completed along the lines of the general plans, the original plans.

Q. How much money has been expended on account of construction, of this $58,000,000? A. By the company?

Q. Yes. A. Well, its construction expenditures must be considered, I take it, in connection with its commitments under the construction contracts.

Q. I understand you, and I think that is correct. A. So that its disbursements, plus its commitments and interest charges, would approximate at this time, say, fifty-five million dollars.

Q. What percentage of the construction work undertaken to be done is represented by this fifty-five million? A. Well, it varies according to the different sections. Some of the sections are as much as 70 or 75 per cent. completed. Others have been let but very, very recently, and the work performed there may not exceed ten per cent., fifteen or twenty per cent.

Q. This $55,000,000 represents the cost of work done — A. And to be done.

Q. And to be done? A. Yes, sir.

Q. Does it include 100 per cent of all the construction work to be done? A. That the Interborough Company is liable for.

Chairman Thompson.— That was not his question.

Mr. Colby.— Just read the question.

(The question was read by the stenographer as follows: " Does it include 100 per cent. of all the construction work to be done? ")

A. The fifty-five million dollars covers the expenditures which the Interborough Rapid Transit Company will finally and event-

ually make under the construction contracts now in progress, plus
the interest, taxes, and other incidental payments of that description, until the work is finished.

Q. What amount of construction did the Interborough undertake to complete? A. About $37,000,000 of direct construction
contracts.

Q. Then, do I understand you to say that the appropriation for
construction amounted to $58,000,000, although the actual amount
of construction undertaken was only $37,000,000? A. Read that
question, please?

(The question was read by the stenographer as follows: " Then
do I understand you to say that the appropriation for construction
amounted to $58,000,000, although the actual amount of construc-
tion undertaken was only $37,000,000? ")

A. No; what I mean to say is that the company stands prepared
to pay for construction work, as described in contract No. 3, an
amount equal to $58,000,000.

Q. How much does the city contribute to the construction work
defined in contract No. 3? A. Something over $60,000,000.

Q. Suppose the amount — the combined amount of your contribution and the city is not adequate to the completion of the
construction work and the payment of all cost; the city has to pay
the deficiency, hasn't it? A. It has.

Chairman Thompson.— That is all in.

Q. Well, is there a defined amount of construction work which
the company is to complete? A. There is a defined amount which
the company is to contribute under specific contracts which have
been awarded by the city for construction work.

Q. And then it ceases contributing after reaching that amount?
A. Yes, sir.

Q. And then the city goes on paying? A. Yes, sir.

Q. And the bonus to the president of the company is a part of
the city's contribution? A. No, sir.

Q. To the construction account? A. No, sir.

Q. It is charged to construction, isn't it? A. It is.

Q. And if a controversy arose between the city and the company
as to whether or not it had paid the full amount of the contribu-

tion to construction which it has agreed to pay, this portion of the — this amount paid to Mr. Shonts, which is carried to construction account, would be treated by you as a credit on your obligation, wouldn't it? A. It is so carried.

Q. As a credit on your mutual undertaking with the city? A. Yes, sir. That is to say, the proposition which I have heretofore described in the ratio of substantially eighty to one hundred million, eight to twenty million.

Q. But it is carried and charged to construction accounts? A. Yes, sir.

Q. But to two different construction accounts? A. Three.

Chairman Thompson.— And what he wants to know is, there is not going to be enough of the $58,000,000 to complete all the construction that is going to be had under this contract.

Mr. Gaynor.— I don't know that.

Chairman Thompson.— What is your opinion?

Mr. Gaynor.— That is an engineering question.

Chairman Thompson.— Haven't you an opinion on the subject?

Mr. Gaynor.— A general opinion, but not an opinion I would like to express under oath.

Chairman Thompson.— I would like to have you express it.

Mr. Colby.— Of course, the oath does not alter the fact it is an opinion.

Mr. Gaynor.— I will answer in this way, so far as my knowledge goes. The $116,000,000 originally contemplated as being necessary on the part of both the city and the company, was determined upon engineering studies of the cost of the various sections of the subway now in process of construction. In many instances the contract has been let at less than the engineers' estimates underlying those large sums which I have mentioned. For that reason, there is a possibility that the amounts heretofore assumed by both the city and the company may finish the work as planned at the time the contract was made.

Chairman Thompson.— I was asking you what your opinion was. Now, there is quite an accumulation of interest that goes in here.

Mr. Gaynor.— That all forms part of the cost, was allowed for by the engineers, and while your interest may cost more or less than estimated, your materials and labor may cost more or less.

Chairman Thompson.— There is no question the interest is going to cost more than estimated.

Mr. Gaynor.— No.

Chairman Thompson.— Not a bit of question. What is your opinion? Do you think this work can be constructed within the $58,000,000, or must you have more?

Mr. Gaynor.— Well, that — unfortunately, I cannot answer that question as you put it, for the reason that it assumes a joint obligation for the completion of the whole enterprise, whereas the contract itself provides that $116,000,000 is the cost, the estimated cost, and the contracts were based upon that estimate.

Chairman Thompson.— Well, what is your opinion as to whether this money will build those contracts that are estimated?

Mr. Gaynor.— It will come pretty near doing it.

By Mr. Colby:

Q. But you are not worrying, Mr. Gaynor, because the city will make up the deficit, anyway? A. Yes, sir; that is provided by the contract.

Q. And possibly that has been a clarifying reflection when it has come to charging to the proper account such payments as $150,000 to the president. A. Had no bearing on it whatever.

Q. You mean did not operate in your mind in determining? A. Not at all.

Chairman Thompson.— It don't alter the fact it would be charged that way.

Mr. Gaynor.— But it makes some difference as to my mental operation.

Chairman Thompson.— So far as you are concerned.

Mr. Colby.— May I ask a question?

Chairman Thompson.— I want to ask one just here, if you will let me, one I was asked to ask. Is $58,000,000 the extreme limit to be expended by the Interborough? Suppose eventually three or five million of interest should be added to the $58,000,000? Would the city get the benefit of it?

Mr. Gaynor.— Fifty-eight million dollars is the limit of expenditure on the part of the Interborough for the work which is designed by the contract No. 3.

Chairman Thompson.—And whatever interest you receive don't increase that $58,000,000 that you are liable for?

Mr. Gaynor.—Are you referring to the interest we receive on bank balances?

Chairman Thompson.— Or any other.

Mr. Gaynor.— The interest we receive on bank balances operates in favor of the contract, to the extent that as the interest is earned upon such bank balances, you thereby automatically increase the amount available for construction, and diminish the amount required for interest.

Mr. Colby.— That is a somewhat complicated matter which I wish to go into a little more fully with you, Mr. Gaynor, but not at this point.

By Mr. Colby:

Q. Was a certain amount of bonds set aside for expenses other than construction or equipment? A. A certain amount of bonds set aside for expenses other than construction work?

Q. Yes. A. Yes, sir.

Q. In other words, for certain actual expenditures made that were in the nature of contingent — A. No, sir; nothing of that kind, but there are certain other bonds set aside for redemption purposes.

Q. Only redemption purposes? A. That is right.

Q. What? A. Cancelling bonds of the Interborough Company prior to the making of this contract.

Q. I suppose we may have access to your accounts, and you will help us find our way through their intricate windings? A. Yes, sir, in every way that I can.

Q. We would like to avail ourselves of that willingness. A. You can count on my help in every matter that I can help you with.

Mr. Colby.— We will adjourn your examination until — we will let you know.

(To Mr. Quackenbush): In the meantime, we may want to take up the matter with him.

Mr. Quackenbush.— That is all right.

Chairman Thompson.— I understand Mr. Sabin and Mr. Oakman are present.

C. H. SABIN, recalled.

Mr. Thomas Garrett, Jr.— Mr. Colby, Mr. Chairman: Mr. Sabin is here, and on his behalf I will read the following statement.

Chairman Thompson.— Let me see it.

(Mr. Garrett hands copy of typewritten statement to Chairman Thompson.)

Chairman Thompson.— No, I won't let you make that statement. You can swear to anything under oath, but I cannot allow you to make statements on our record not under oath.

Mr. Garrett.— Well, I shall give it to Mr. Sabin to read. He is under oath.

Chairman Thompson.— Mr. Sabin will answer such questions as are propounded to him by counsel.

Mr. Garrett.— I shall give this statement, of course, to the press.

Chairman Thompson.— I don't care what you do with it.

Mr. Colby.— Do you wish me to examine the witness?

Chairman Thompson.— It is up to you. You can do as you like.

By Mr. Colby:

Q. Mr. Sabin, I am directed by the Chairman to ask you briefly a question or two as to your attitude towards this Joint Legislative Committee and toward its practice. I understand that a subpoena of this Committee has been served upon you as executor of the estate of the late Andrew Freedman. You are the president of the Guaranty Trust Company of this city? A. I am.

Q. The Guaranty Trust Company is an executor of the estate of the late Andrew Freedman? A. One of them.

Q. Who are the other two executors? A. Mr. Samuel Untermyer and Mr. Oakman.

Q. This was a subpoena requiring you to produce before the Committee all the books and papers, records — I have not the exact phraseology of the —

Mr. Garrett.— It is not directed to Mr. Sabin at all. It is another subpoena with which we complied. Mr. Sabin's was merely to appear here.

Chairman Thompson.— No, no.

Q. A subpoena was served upon the Guaranty Trust Company, wasn't it, Mr. Sabin, requiring it to appear before this Committee and to bring — and to have with it the ledgers, cash-books, check-books, or check-stubs, cancelled checks, bank-books, day-books, journals, voucher, registers, vouchers of all kinds, and letters, copies of letters, memoranda, of the late Andrew Freedman, and comprised in his estate and effects, containing any entries of or reference to, or in any wise relating to his duties and activities as an officer or director of any public utility corporation in the State of New York, together with all papers, documents, and records, in any way pertaining thereto, from January 1, 1906, to date. That was served upon your company, was it not? A. You have it there, and read it. I did not read it. No doubt that is correct.

Q. This is the only subpoena we issued? A. Yes.

Q. I think you recall my telephoning you and advising you

that the subpoena was ready for issuance, and asking you to permit us to serve it upon some officer of the company which would make the service legal? A. Yes, I remember.

Q. Are you prepared to produce the various papers called for in the subpoena? A. My understanding is they have been produced to your representative.

Mr. Colby.— We have not them here. Our representative has been afforded access, I understand, to some of the papers, and denied access to others. The Committee desires compliance with the subpoena. Are the papers here?

Mr. Garrett.— I think we are ready to supply anything asked for in the subpoena.

Chairman Thompson.— Very well. Then produce it at once before the Committee.

Mr. Garrett.— We have not been able to gather together those papers, as a said — the papers asked for in that general language, and we shall produce everything as soon as we can find them, everything for which you ask.

Chairman Thompson.— Just a minute, sir. You are hereby directed, Mr. Sabin, to produce before this Committee to-morrow morning at 11 o'clock, all the papers mentioned in the subpoena served upon the Guaranty Trust Company. You may be excused.

Mr. Garrett.— I shall make this statement to the Committee now, the statement that we shall produce everything which we can find at that time.

Chairman Thompson.— We want no statement.

Mr. Garrett.— That comes within the four walls of the subpoena, and nothing further in the —

Chairman Thompson.— We won't hear you further. You need not take it down. That last statement of counsel you can expunge from the record. We are glad to have met you, and hope you will come again.

Mr. Garrett.— We will be here.

Mr. Charles H. Russell.— We are in no danger, Mr. Colby. You are going beyond your powers.

OAKMAN, WALTER G., called as a witness, being first duly sworn, testifies as follows:

Chairman Thompson.— Have you in your possession any papers or books or documents or letters or memoranda which relate in any way to the Public Service Commission or the public service corporations of this city, or their officers or directors?

Mr. Oakman.— In this relation as an executor of the—

Chairman Thompson.— Either personally or as executor?

Mr. Oakman.— I simply am a director of several of the corporations, and have their reports.

Chairman Thompson.— Will you produce those papers that relate to either the Public Service Commission or the officers of the the Public Service Commission or the public service corporations or the directors thereof, included in this district, before this Committee to-morrow morning at 11 o'clock?

Mr. Oakman.— But, Mr. Chairman, I have not any papers of anything other than this, simply copies of published reports sent out from time to time.

Chairman Thompson.— I don't care about them, but other papers.

Mr. Oakman.— I have no others.

Chairman Thompson.— That in any way relate to public service corporations or commissions?

Mr. Oakman.— No.

Chairman Thompson.— Well, you were subpoenaed personally, I think, Mr. Oakman.

Mr. Oakman.— I don't know whether I was or not. I have the subpoena here.

Chairman Thompson.— You may be excused until to-morrow morning at 11 o'clock, and you are directed to appear before the Committee at that time, at this place.

Witnesses, unless otherwise excused, are directed to appear to-morrow morning at 11 o'clock. We will suspend now until to-morrow morning at 11 o'clock.

Whereupon (at 4:27 o'clock P. M.) an adjournment was taken to Thursday, February 10, 1916, at 11 o'clock A. M.

FEBRUARY 10, 1916

NEW YORK COUNTY LAWYERS' ASSOCIATION BOARD ROOM,
165 Broadway, New York City.

The Committee was called to order, pursuant to adjournment, Chairman Thompson presiding.

Quorum present.

Chairman Thompson.— The Committee will come to order.

Mr. Colby.— Mr. Chairman, my attention has been called this morning to the appearance in one of the evening newspapers of a letter written by Mr. Gillespie, accompanied by what purports to be a fac simile reproduction of a check to the order of Mr. Quigg. I feel that it is my privilege, and I also feel that it is a duty I owe myself and my associate, Mr. Dawson, to state that neither he or I had any knowledge of the existence of the letter or of the check until both letter and check were published in the afternoon newspaper. We regret exceedingly the premature unconsidered disclosure of these documents. I may say further that we recognize that the informal, not to say irregular, way in which these documents found their way into public notice, involves what we cannot deny to be a reflection under which we are resting, upon the Committee and upon Counsel and upon everyone connected with it. It is not denied that the books of T. A. Gillespie & Company are at this moment under inspection and under examination on behalf of this Committee, and I wish merely to add that the continuance of myself and Mr. Dawson as the servants of this Committee and as modest contributors toward the completion of what we regard as its important work is conditioned upon assur-

14

ances that we trust and have received that no possible recurrence of such an incident as this can happen. The work of collateral and supplemental investigation on behalf of the Committee from this point on will be under the charge and absolute direction of Mr. Dawson, whose position at the bar and whose position in this community I need not myself call attention to. It is above suspicion or reproach, and speaking as in a subordinate relation of counsel to this Committee, I sincerely trust with the disavowals that shall be made and the explanation that will be made this morning that this most regrettable and unconsidered incident will not be permitted to qualify or retard in any way the progress of this Committee toward the realization of the great ends which it has in view and which are animating its labors.

Chairman Thompson.— In behalf of the Committee, or rather in behalf of the Chairman of the Committee, I will say that I do not know that I expect an investigation to proceed without some mistakes being made somewhere, and I want to acknowledge, as far as Mr. Colby's statement goes, that he or Mr. Dawson did not know anything about this until this morning, and it is correct they did not, and in the course of the work of the organization of this Committee you should have known that. The Chair is to blame for this matter, and I decline to put the blame or responsibility on anybody else, either a member of the Committee or person connected with the Committee. I am to blame for it entirely, if there is any blame about it, and there is not any disposition to go into anybody's books or papers, or anything else, and publish anything on the side at all, and I do not intend to do it, and I have absolute confidence in our counsel and Mr. Dawson, and he is acting as an assistant counsel and actuary, and Mr. Dawson is not an expert account. I have great confidence in Mr. Dawson, and I desire to have this work done through him. Of course the responsibility of the Chairman of this Committee will continue, and it has got where we do not know what tomorrow brings forth in this investigation, and never have, and probably never will, and as it comes along we simply try to do the best we can and make the best investigation our human limitations will permit, and will try and continue in the same old way, and I want to again reiterate my confidence in counsel and confidence in assistant counsel and to say to them publicly that this matter, in so far as it disturbs them or anyone else, that the Chair takes the absolute blame for it all, wherever there is blame, and we will continue, and I trust hereafter any matters that come up such arrangements will be made that the counsel will know about them as soon as the Chairman does.

Mr. Dawson.— Mr. Chairman, I accept the very heavy responsibility which devolves upon me under the appointment which you have so kindly and generously made accompanied with words so flattering, and I fear so undeserved, with much reluctance. It is not at all infrequent that the word actuary is confused with that of an accountant, and I was particularly careful when invited to join your investigation to make it clear that I was not a public accountant by profession. It is the duty of insurance actuaries to make themselves thoroughly familiar with accounts and to be in position to audit accounts of insurance companies which are frequently complicated, as a part of their work, and it is only in that way that I have any special familiarity with it. In coming into the work I had no notion in the world, as you know, that this very heavy responsibility would, especially under circumstances like these, devolve upon me, but I have every confidence in the integrity of the Chairman of this Committee and absolute confidence in the integrity and ability of the Chief Counsel of this Committee, and I shall be very glad to do what I can to deserve the confidence which you have reposed in me.

Chairman Thompson.— I want to say this, I do not know that I have ever shrank from any responsibility that happened to come my way. This matter that became public I wish that it had not ever happened to come at all before the Committee or before anybody concerned, and if I have any duty I am going to perform it, and as these investigations bring things up, I do not care who it hits, if they get in the way they will have to be hit. I cannot help but now beg indulgence for the very human idea of reluctance, and I am frank to say that I am reluctant and I am sorry that this thing had to be published at all.

Mr. Colby.— I believe the President of the Guaranty Trust Company is present, as well as counsel, in obedience to the Committee's subpoena, and that they have some papers and documents ready for delivery to the Committee, in compliance with the subpoena.

Mr. Garrett.—Yes, sir.

Mr. Colby.— Well, leave them with the Committee and we will examine them.

Mr. Garrett.— Mr. Dawson is to examine them, is he?

Mr. Colby.—Yes, sir.

Mr. Garrett.— I put them in the custody of Mr. Dawson.

Chairman Thompson.— The counsel of the Committee is Mr. Colby. Put them in custody of Mr. Colby. We are not going into details in regard to the organization of our Committee at all.

(Mr. Garrett hands the papers and documents over to Mr. Colby, as requested.)

Mr. Garrett.— Mr. Sabin's attendance is not required until further notice?

Chairman Thompson.— No, sir.

Mr. Colby.— Mr. Chairman, I call your attention to the fact that Mr. Walter G. Oakman is in attendance under the subpoena. Is there anything you wish of him?

Chairman Thompson.— I would like to talk with Mr. Oakman a few minutes.

Senator Towner, presiding.

FISHER, HORACE M., being recalled for further examination, testified as follows:

Examination by Mr. Colby:

Q. Mr. Fisher, while we are waiting for some material which you have sent for, I will take up this phase of the subject; The Interborough Metropolitan Company was a holding company and possibly is still a holding cocmpany? A. Yes, sir.

Q. About when was it incorporated? A. In the early part of 1906, in March, I think.

Q. In March, 1906? A. Yes, sir.

Q. And what was it intended to hold? A. To hold securities of other companies, to advance moneys for the construction of transportation lines, and so on.

Q. Do you mean to say of the subway? A. No, sir, of the —

Q. That was then building? A. No, sir, not of the subway specially.

Q. Not of the subway specially? A. No, it was supposed simply to aid in the construction of transportation lines in general.

Q. To aid in the construction of Interborough or allied transportation lines? A. Yes, sir.

Q. It was not going into the business generally of constructing transit lines? A. No, sir, but aid subsidiary companies in construction and extension of their lines.

Q. In other words it was conceived and created as a part of the general scheme of maintenance and direction and operation of the transit lines in New York? A. Yes, sir.

Q. Were its directors substantially the directors of the Interborough Rapid Transit Company? A. No, sir.

Q. Many of the Interborough Rapid Transit Company directors were its directors, however? A. Yes, sir.

Q. In other words, there were many common directors? A. Yes, sir.

Q. Were there some men who were officers of both companies, other than as directors? A. Yes, sir.

Q. You have a very remarkable and assistful memory that I am constantly relying upon more, and can you recall the names of the common officers of the companies? A. They have changed quite a number of times since the organization.

Q. At the time of its incorporation; will that memorandum help you? (Colby hands memorandum to the witness.) A. These are the officers at the present time. I take it you do not want the present officers.

Q. My question had in view the original officers; if you can only tell me the present officers, let me have that? A. The present officers, chairman of the board, is August Belmont; president, Theodore P. Shonts; assistant to the president, W. Leon Pepperman; vice-president, duties to be assigned, H. H. Vreeland; vice-president to sign securities, E. Mora Davison; vice-president, G. W. Ross; secretary, H. M. Fisher; treasurer, J. H. Campbell; general counsel, Richard Reid Rogers; general attorney, James L. Quackenbush; auditor, E. F. J. Gaynor.

Q. Are those the officers of the Interborough Metropolitan or the Interborough Rapid Transit Company? A. Interborough Consolidated Corporation, formerly Interborough Metropolitan Company. (Witness hands memorandum back to Mr. Colby.)

Q. So that the officers are practically the same of the Interborough Consolidated Corporation and the Interborough Rapid Transit Company? A. Yes, sir.

Q. Is Mr. August Belmont chairman of the board of the Interborough Rapid Transit Company? A. Yes, sir.

Q. And he holds the same position in the Consolidated Corporation? A. Yes, sir.

Q. What is the capital of the Interborough Consolidated? A. Its bonds, 4½ per cent. collateral trust bonds —

Q. I mean the capital stock? A. Common stock 932,626 shares, without par value; preferred stock, 6 per cent. preferred stock, 457,405 shares, par value $100 each. Do you want the bonded indebtedness?

Q. Yes. A. 4½ per cent. collateral trust bonds, 1956, $67,825,000; ten year notes, 1925, $2,500,000.

Q. The Interborough Consolidated Corporation was formed recently, was it not? A. Yes, sir.

Q. When? A. June 1, 1915.

Q. And I understand you to say that it is the successor of the Interborough Metropolitan? A. Yes, sir.

Q. And took over the holdings and assets, speaking generally of the Interborough Metropolitan? A. Yes, sir.

Q. Now, the Interborough Metropolitan from its incorporation in the early part of 1906 acquired what stock of the local transit companies? A. The stock of the Interborough Rapid Transit Company, Metropolitan Street Railway Company, and Metropolitan Securities Company.

Q. It was what I may describe as the nuptial knot of the subways and the surface lines in New York; is that a fair figure of speech? A. I guess that will answer as well as any other.

Q. It was the outgrowth of the negotiations that culminated in that year between Mr. Belmont of the Interborough and Mr. Ryan and his associates as the chief owners of the surface lines; is that correct? A. Yes, sir.

Q. What was the capital of the Interborough Metropolitan? A. $35,000,000 — I beg your pardon; I was thinking of the Interborough Rapid Transit. The capital of the Interborough Metropolitan Company was the same as the capital of the Interborough Consolidated Corporation, with the exception the common stock carried a par value of $100 a share.

Q. In other words, the Interborough Metropolitan had a capital stock of $93,262,000? A. Yes, sir.

Q. What was the preferred stock? A. Preferred stock was the same as the Interborough Consolidated, $45,740,000.

Q. Did it have any bonds, the Interborough Metropolitan? A. $67,625,000.

Q. In other words, the new company formed in June, 1915, called the Interborough Consolidated, and the predecessor company, the Interborough Metropolitan, had the same number of shares of preferred stock and the same number of shares of common stock, speaking approximately? A. Yes, sir.

Q. And the same outstanding bond issue? A. Yes, sir.

Q. What was the necessity or occasion for the formation of the Interborough Consolidated Company? A. Primarily for the purpose of inaugurating the payment of dividends.

Q. On its preferred or common stock? A. Preferred stock.

Q. Had the Interborough Metropolitan made no payments of dividends? A. Only in the early period, about a year and a half, I think, after the organization.

Q. What dividends did the Interborough Metropolitan pay? A. 5 per cent.

Q. How many years did you pay them? A. About a year and a half, I think; I am not sure.

Q. They made, in other words, one annual and possibly a half-year payment of dividends? A. Yes, sir.

Q. And discontinued payment as early as 1908? A. Discontinued payment of dividends in July, 1907.

Q. In other words, only a few weeks more than a year after its incorporation? A. Yes, sir. The next dividend would have been due October 1st.

Q. And, with the exception of that dividend paid by the Interborough Metropolitan, am I to understand the Interborough Rapid Transit Company, notwithstanding the great development of its traffic and extension of its lines, has paid no other or later dividends on its stock? A. Yes, sir; the Interborough Rapid Transit Company has continued to pay dividends on its stock from the beginning.

Q. But its stock is held by the Interborough Metropolitan? A. Yes, sir.

Q. And it paid that dividend into the Interborough Metropolitan Company? A. Yes, sir.

Q. And no stockholder of the Interborough Metropolitan ever got a dividend? A. No, sir.

Q. Since 1907? A. No, sir.

Q. Not even the holders of the preferred stock of the Interborough Metropolitan got any dividend after 1907, in July? A. Correct.

Q. In other words, the dividends — I mean to say, in other words, the great and increasing earnings of the Interborough subway operations have been paid into the holding company and have apparently encountered some quicksand? A. No, sir.

Q. At least they have not any longer constituted dividends after touching the Interborough Metropolitan Company? A. They were put to good uses.

Q. They were put to good uses? A. Yes, sir.

Q. You mean paying the interest on bonds? A. Yes, sir, they were used to pay the interest on the 4½ per cent. bonds.

Q. On the $67,625,000 outstanding bonds of the Interborough Metropolitan? A. Yes, sir, and I might add, so as to clear up the entire situation, that the Interborough Metropolitan made a loan, I cannot tell you now in what year, of $15,000,000 of which approximately $8,500,000 was paid in, and the balance of the moneys received from the Interborough Company dividends went to reduce that loan, to pay off that loan, rather.

Q. You mean the Interborough borrowed $50,000,000? A.

$15,000,000. They did not borrow $15,000,000. They authorized it, and only borrowed $8,500,000.

Q. About what time, as near as you can fix it? A. 1907 or 1908, I am not sure which.

Q. Who did they borrow that from? A. These figures are very simple, and I have them upstairs, but I have no preparation and I cannot remember the dates.

Q. I do not want to pursue the thing if you are not clear to answer; I will have it understood my questions are of somewhat of a general purport, and you can answer approximately subject to confirmation, if we deem it important. A. All right, sir.

Q. Who was this money borrowed from? A. It was — I don't remember exactly how that transaction was carried out. I would have to refresh my memory by referring to the correspondence.

Q. Explain to me the purpose of the passage of the Interborough Metropolitan into the Interborough Consolidated Corporation? A. As I stated, it was for the purpose of inaugurating the payment of dividends on the preferred stock of the Interborough Metropolitan Company, now the preferred stock of the Interborough Consolidated Corporation.

Q. Why could not the Interborough Metropolitan pay dividends on the preferred stock if of the same amount and the same property? A. Because its liabilities were in excess of its assets. In other words, they had a liability of approximately $135,000,000 and an asset of approximately $50,000,000.

Q. And what did you do in the reorganization toward the reduction of your liabilities? A. Took the par value off of the common stock.

Q. What were the assets then, what were the assets of the Interborough made up of, speaking generally? A. You mean the Interborough Metropolitan?

Q. The Interborough Metropolitan? A. The stock of the Interborough Rapid Transit Company, the stock of the New York Railways Company and the stock of the Metropolitan Securities Company and a substantial interest in the stock of the New York Transportation Company, and miscellaneous securities.

Q. Have you the last balance sheet of the Interborough Metropolitan prior to the formation of the Interborough Consolidated? A. Yes, sir, but not in my possession here.

Q. Was the stock of the New York Railways Company of any value in your opinion? A. Yes, sir.

Q. About what value? A. I should place a value of about forty dollars per share on the stock at the present time. Understand, that is a subject of fluctuation.

Q. It pays no dividend? A. No, sir.

Q. And it has not paid any dividend for years? A. It has not paid any dividend since its organization in 1912. It was organized in 1912, and it has never paid a dividend.

Q. What is the aggregate of its stock? A. It is about seventeen million and a half.

Q. Par value? A. Yes, sir.

Q. Which you reckon as worth forty dollars a share, which would be forty per cent. of that amount? A. Yes, sir.

Q. In other words, about $7,000,000? A. Yes, sir.

Q. Has the Metropolitan securities stock any value? A. No, sir.

Q. That is absolutely valueless? A. Absolutely valueless.

Q. What do you consider the value of the stock of the Interborough Rapid Transit Company? A. $325 per share.

Q. And what is the total of that stock, as an asset of the Interborough Metropolitan Company; what was it? A. 319,728 shares, I think is what the Interborough Consolidated owns, of a total issue of 350,000 shares.

Q. In other words, as an asset, the stock of the Interborough Rapid Transit Company in the possession of either the Interborough Metropolitan or the new corporation the Interborough Consolidated is worth about $32,000,000? A. You said worth. You mean the par value?

Q. Yes, the par value would be about $32,000,000 and it is worth 3¼ times that, according to your price? A. It is a little different than that. Let me see the statement you have there, and I think I can give the figures accurate from that. I have that here.

Mr. Quackenbush.— Mr. Colby, you have all of this information in the black covered book that was turned over to Mr. Dawson and it will save time if you have that here.

Mr. Colby.— That does not seem to be here, but I will have it here at 2 o'clock. A. That is approximately correct, but I would like to confirm it later.

Q. In other words, speaking approximately, for the purpose of the moment, the value of the Interborough Rapid Transit's stock in the hands of the Interborough Consolidated is about one hundred, or one hundred and two or one hundred and three million dollars? A. Yes, sir, somewhere along there.

Q. So that with the wiping off of the par value of the Interborough Metropolitan common stock, you have brought that balance sheet to the point where the payment of a dividend is possible on the preferred stock? A. Correct.

Q. In other words, the formation of the Interborough Consolidated marks the recognition by the present manager of the Interborough Rapid Transit Company that the so called merger of the Interborough Rapid Transit Company with the surface lines in March, 1906, was of no value to the Interborough Rapid Transit Company whatever? A. I wouldn't care to answer that question.

Q. In other words, the only value which survives out of that merger is the Interborough Rapid Transit Company's stock with a possible qualification of a theoretical value of forty dollars a share to the stock of the surface railways which concededly have paid no dividend for years? A. Plus its interest in the New York Transportation Company.

Chairman Thompson presiding.

Q. What did the surface lines receive at the time of the merger into the Interborough Metropolitan as a consideration of turning over their stocks and securities to the Interborough Metropolitan? A. That is also set out in the papers you have. It was one share of preferred stock and fifty-five dollars in common. I think that is correct, for one share of stock of the Metropolitan Street Railway.

Q. The Metropolitan Street Railway stock has practically evaporated, so far as value is concerned, and its former owners still hold the share of preferred stock and of common stock of the

Interborough Metropolitan? A. It was given to them, whether they still hold it or not I couldn't say.

Q. It is not recalled? A. No, sir.

Q. And it is to pay dividends upon such preferred stock the drastic reorganization of the Interborough Metropolitan has been accomplished? A. To pay dividends on the Interborough Consolidated preferred; yes, sir.

Q. In other words, the subways are still under the obligations they contracted at the time of their merger with the surface lines, and the consideration passing to the surface lines has disappeared as an asset in the Interborough company's chest? A. With the exception of the New York Railway's, which it still holds.

Q. And the Interborough Rapid Transit Company, or to speak colloquially, the subway, is trying to disburden itself of some of this one-sided obligation in order that it may pay dividends upon the stock which it issued to the owners of the Metropolitan Street Railway companies? A. I do not understand it is trying to disburden itself in any way.

Q. Concededly it has charged off in this reorganization $95 out of every hundred of the value of the common stock, or at least of the par value of the common stock, of the Interborough Metropolitan? A. Yes, sir.

Q. And that common stock is nearly one hundred millions? A. That is correct.

Q. And of the obligations which the Interborough Metropolitan issued, not to say assumed, but issued, this reorganization is the charging off of ninety-five millions in round numbers, or at least approximately ninety? A. Not quite as much as that. You are not very far out of the way.

Q. We will go into these figures a little more accurately later? A. Yes, sir.

Chairman Thompson.—We will suspend, now, and in the meantime if there is any information given out it will be given through the Chairman of the Committee. We will suspend until 2:30 o'clock.

Whereupon, at 1:05 o'clock P. M. a recess was taken until 2:30 P. M.

AFTERNOON SESSION

The Committee was called to order at 2:52 o'clock P. M., Senator Towner in the chair.

Chairman Towner.— The Committee will come to order.

H. M. FISHER, recalled.

By Mr. Colby:

Q. Mr. Fisher, will you please state the losses which have been incurred by the Interborough-Metropolitan Company which were the — one of the immediate occasions for its reorganization into the Interborough Consolidated? A. Perhaps I had better start from the beginning and say that the Interborough Consolidated corporation was formed for the purpose of adjusting our balance sheet and wiping out a very large deficit composed of losses incurred through the bankruptcy of the Metropolitan System and the Metropolitan Securities Company, aggregating in the total about — between eighty and ninety million dollars would be about as near as I can recollect.

Q. That was the amount of your losses? A. Yes, sir. They consisted of losses on the Metropolitan Street Railway stock and the stock of the Metropolitan Securities Company.

Q. When the Interborough-Metropolitan acquired the subways and the surface lines, did the Interborough Rapid Transit Company make certain guarantees to the holders of either the bonds or the stocks of the surface lines? A. The Interborough Rapid Transit Company did not; no, sir.

Q. Did it guarantee a dividend upon any of the stock or other securities of the surface lines? A. No, sir.

Q. Did it guarantee a dividend upon the Interborough-Metropolitan stock delivered to the stockholders of the securities of the surface lines? A. No, sir. The dividend that was paid originally on the Interborough-Metropolitan preferred stock was obtained from the Metropolitan Street Railway stock at that time, that income having ceased — dividends on the preferred stock of the Interborough-Metropolitan Company ceased at about the same time, so that the revenue for the payment of the dividends on the preferred stock was derived from the Metropolitan System originally.

Q. The acquisition of the surface lines through the medium of the Interborough-Metropolitan you have testified was in March, 1906? A. Yes, sir.

Q. When did the surface lines or the system of surface lines go into bankruptcy? A. In 1908, as near as I can remember.

Mr. Quackenbush.— No, that is a mistake.   September 24, 1907.

Q. September 24, 1907? A. Yes.

Q. What is this total of loss of between eighty and ninety millions made up of, speaking necessarily with some generality? A. It was a loss in the Metropolitan Street Railway stock and Metropolitan Securities Company approximately, and the losses incurred from loans to the — I am wrong — it is made up principally of the loss of the Metropolitan Street Railway and Metropolitan Securities Company stocks.

Q. Which has been acquired by this holding company, the Interborough-Metropolitan? A. Yes, sir.

Q. What did the Interborough Rapid Transit Company estimate the stock of the Metropolitan Street Railway Company to be worth at the time the holding company acquired it? A. I am not aware that any estimate was made — at least I have never seen any figures.

Q. It appears in one of the minute books, an estimate made by Mr. Skid? A. I was not aware that estimate was made as a basis for issuing securities, though. I think that was more of an estimate made on the earning powers of the property, and an estimate of future earnings. I have not seen that estimate since 1907, but that is my recollection.

Q. Did the estimate figure as a matter of persuasion or inducement to the Interborough in entering upon this disastrous transaction? A. I presume so, but I cannot say definitely.

Q. As a matter of fact, do you recall what Mr. Skid's estimate was of the value of the Metropolitan stock? A. I do not.

Q. You do not recall that he estimated it as worth $155 a share at that time? A. I don't know; no, sir.

Q. If your attention were called to such an estimate, you would be obliged to conclude it was very extravagant, wouldn't you? A. I think so.

Q. Why did the Interborough acquiesce in this arrangement? Why did it make this arrangement with the surface lines? A. That I could not say. That arrangement was made by my superiors, and I have no statement to make on it.

Q. Was there any element of compulsion or pressure exerted upon the Interborough Rapid Transit Company? A. I could not say, sir.

Q. Were there any attacks pending at the time upon the Interborough Rapid Transit Company, proceeding from the surface lines or other owners? A. I have no recollection of any attacks.

Q. Any threats of attack? A. No, sir.

Q. Any threat to build a competing system of subways? A. Oh yes, they were figuring on competing systems at the time.

Q. Who were commonly understood to be the controlling owners of the surface lines at that time? A. Mr. Ryan and his associates.

Q. And was this Interborough-Metropolitan Company the corporate name of the so-called Ryan-Belmont merger, you remember, with which we have all grown familiar? A. Yes, sir.

Q. Was the Interborough Rapid Transit Company at that time in quest of legislative aid or relief at Albany? A. No, sir; not to my knowledge.

Q. You don't recall that they were seeking some enabling statutes for the purpose of facilitating the completion of their subway system? A. That is quite possible.

Q. Did the subway line encounter some mysterious but formidable opposition in gaining that legislative relief? A. That I could not say, Mr. Counsel. I had nothing to do with the conduct of those negotiations.

Q. Did the Interborough — was the Interborough Rapid Transit Company keenly desirous of acquiring the surface lines? A. I could not say.

Q. This prompt collapse of the surface lines entailing this entire disappearance of its securities as elements of value to the

Interborough Rapid Transit Company, was it foreseen or dreamed of or suspected by the Interborough people? A. I don't think so.

Q. Is the Interborough Rapid Transit Company still making regular payments on account of stock or other guarantees in discharge of obligations contracted under this merger? A. Did I understand you to say the Interborough Rapid Transit Company?

Q. Yes. A. No.

Q. Is any company affiliated — is that true of any company affiliated with the Interborough Rapid Transit Company? A. Yes, sir.

Q. What company? A. I beg your pardon, I misunderstood your question.

Mr. Colby.— Read the question again.

The question was repeated by the stenographer as follows: " Is any company affiliated — is that true of any company affiliated with the Interborough Rapid Transit Company? "

Mr. Fisher.— No, the question preceding that.

(The preceding question was repeated by the stenographer as follows): " Is the Interborough Rapid Transit Company still making regular payments on account of stock or other guarantees in discharge of obligations contracted under this merger? " A. This same answer will apply to all other companies now owned or controlled by the Interborough Consolidated Corporation.

Q. Was the Interborough Rapid Transit Company compelled under the terms of this Interborough-Met. merger, to buy and pay for a certain amount of stock of the Metropolitan Securities Company? A. No, sir. The stock of the Interborough-Metropolitan Company was issued from the Metropolitan Securities Company.

Q. What do you consider the value of what the Interborough Rapid Transit Company parted with in this merger to be? A. I am not aware that it parted with any value. It still has the same value it had before, or would have had if it had not joined in the merger.

Q. Did I understand you to say the merger practically accomplished an equal division of its ownership, however? A. In accordance with the securities issued.

Q. And it was tantamount, practically, to an equal division of ownership, was it not? A. It was not an equal division; no sir.

Q. Indicate to be the basis on which the surface lines were merged with the subway line? A. The Interborough was given $200 in 4½ per cent. bonds, and $99 in and on the stock of the Interborough-Metropolitan Company, for one share of the — for $100, I should have said, of the Interborough Rapid Transit stock. The Metropolitan Securities Company was given $93.50 of common stock of the Interborough-Metropolitan Company for one share of — $100, I should have said, of stock of the Metropolitan Securities Company, $75 paid in. The Metropolitan Street Railway Company was given one share of the preferred stock of the Interborough-Metropolitan Company, and $55 of common stock for — I should not have said one share — I should have said $100 of preferred stock and $55 of common stock for $100 of the Metropolitan stock. I will give you that basis in a little better form — (witness takes book from Mr. Colby.) Now, if you will allow your stenographer to take it down, I will read it from the records and get it correct.

Mr. Colby.— Take it down, as Mr. Fisher makes the statement.

Mr. Fisher.— The Interborough Rapid Transit Company received $200 in bonds and $99 in common stock for $100 in stock of Interborough Rapid Transit Company. The Metropolitan Street Railway received $100 of preferred stock and $55 in common, for $100 of stock of the Metropolitan Street Railway Company. The Metropolitan Securities Company received $93.50 of common stock for $100 of stock of the Metropolitan Securities Company, $75 paid in.

By Mr. Colby:

Q. Now, everything is a loss there except the bonds which the Interborough Rapid Transit Company received, and the preferred stock which the Interborough-Metropolitan issued? A. Yes, sir.

Q. And it is for the purpose of paying a dividend upon this preferred stock that the Interborough Consolidated corporation has been formed? A. Not exactly for the purpose of paying a dividend, but for the purpose of adjusting its balance sheet, cleaning house, as it were, wiping out that deficit.

Q. For the purpose of shaking clear this loss of eighty or ninety million dollars? A. Yes, sir.

Q. And eliminating from your balance sheet the common stock of the Interborough-Metropolitan as a liability? A. No, sir. The common stock was not eliminated altogether as a liability. I believe the law requires the liability to be set up of $5 a share minimum.

Q. That does not mean that the stock is worth $5 a share? A. The stock is worth very much more than five dollars a share.

Q. Do you remember what you stated this morning? A. We are carrying it on our balance sheet at $5 a share.

Q. Having eliminated 95 per cent.? A. Having made its stock of no par value.

Q. When was this reorganization of the Interborough-Metropolitan begun? A. In June, 1915; June 1, 1915.

Q. Were committees appointed of its stockholders? A. Yes, sir.

Q. Both preferred and common? A. Yes, sir.

Q. Do you recall the names of the committee? A. I can give you the Chairman. That is a matter of record.

Q. Yes. A. I can get it for you in a very few minutes.

Q. The chairman of each committee. A. A. J. Hemphill, who is chairman of the — or Horace Harding — I don't know which.

Q. Some officers of the Interborough? A. That is a matter of record.

Q. Some officers of the Interborough constituting members of the Committee?

Mr. Fisher (to Mr. Quackenbush): Send up and get that.

By Mr. Colby:

Q. There were two committees? A. Yes, sir, common stockholders' committee, and the preferred stockholders' committee.

Q. And invitations were addressed to the shareholders to deposit their stock? A. Yes, sir.

Q. You recall who the depositors were of each committee? A. No. The committee asked the depositors to send in proxies. They were sent in to me.

Q. There was no deposit of stock at that time? A. Well, one of the committees asked that proxies be sent in to them, and they received some and turned them over.

Q. Subsequently the stock was sent in for exchange after the incorporation of the Interborough Consolidated? A. Yes, sir.

Q. And those exchanges have been effected? A. It has not all been exchanged.

Q. There are some loose ends, you mean, some inconsiderable amounts still? A. Well, the preferred, about 98 per cent. has been exchanged, and the common, probably 80 per cent., and is being exchanged as it comes in.

Q. I suppose each of these committees had counsel? A. Yes, sir.

Q. Do you recall who the counsel were? A. I think you will find the counsel appears on your record that I gave you this morning, if you will let me have that, the Interborough Consolidated sheet that I gave you, This one, the largest you have. (Witness takes sheet referred to.) The counsel was employed by Alexander J. Hemphill and Willard V. King.

Q. Willard V. King was chairman of the committee on— A. — common stock.

Q. — The exchange of the common stock? A. Yes, sir; and Mr. Hemphill of the preferred.

Q. Who paid the expenses of the reorganization? A. The Interborough Consolidated Corporation.

Q. Were these expenses chargeable against the Interborough Rapid Transit Company? A. No, sir.

Q. Not immediately or finally in any way? A. No, sir.

Q. Now, you have handed me, Mr. Fisher, statements on the dates and issues of notes by the Interborough Rapid Transit company, and the retirement thereof. There are here listed some five transactions which I would like to examine in conjunction with the minutes in relation thereto. I will ask you to turn to the minutes of the company showing the sale of 5 per cent. notes dated April 29, 1912, to J. P. Morgan & Company. (Minute book is handed to witness.) A. You want me to read this in the record?

Q. Let me see it a moment. I call your attention to one transaction which was authorized by the Board at its meeting on

April 7, 1912. I read from the minutes of the Board of Directors of the Interborough Rapid Transit Company: " The President stated that on April 29, 1912, there would be due and payable $15,000,000 of the company's notes, ten millions of which were 4½ per cent. notes issued April 29, 1911, due April 29, 1912; and five millions of which were 5 per cent. notes issued September 6, 1911, due April 29, 1912; and that subject to the approval to the Board, he had arranged with Messrs. J. P. Morgan & Company, bankers, through whom these notes were originally sold, to discount at the rate of 5 per cent. per annum, new notes of the company for the aggregate principal sum of $15,000,000, payable January 29, 1913, the proceeds to be applied towards the payment of the outstanding notes due April 29, 1912." What rate of interest did the new notes which were to be given to Morgan & Company for $15,000,000 carry? A. I could not say. There were quite a number — quite a number of shares of notes issued during the years from 1905 to 1912; the interest varied from 4½ to 6 per cent. I think it is shown on the statement. I could not identify any particular interest charge with any particular item without having the statement before me.

Q. What statement, Mr. Fisher? This statement that you prepared? A. Yes, sir. (Statement is handed to witness.) Now, I answer your question, 5 per cent.

Q. The notes bore interest at 5 per cent? A. Yes, sir.

Q. They were practically for a year? A. Yes, sir.

Q. Did Morgan & Company buy these notes at par? A. I think that is also stated there.

Q. It is stated that you realized $14,437,500 on the issuance of $15,000,000 of these notes. You mean to say these notes were simply discounted by Morgan &'Company at a different rate of interest? A. Yes, sir, that is my understanding.

Q. And your — did this amount remain on deposit with J. P. Morgan & Company for any length of time? A. I could not say without looking at the records. Probably not. As I recollect, it was a refunding issue.

Q. Will you just verify that at your convenience? A. Yes, sir.

Q. You told me you had not been able to verify the details of all of these matters. I want to find out what that accommodation cost the Interborough Rapid Transit Company. A. Yes, sir.

Q. What the true rate of interest was — that is to say, at which the notes, in terms — the rate of interest the notes in terms carried, and whether there is any addition to the discount price; what the bankers' commission was; what amount, if any, remained on deposit with the bankers at a lower rate of interest that the note carried? In other words, I want to see what this accommodation cost the Interborough Rapid Transit Company, and also what it netted the bankers, and without attempting to pursue this line of examination now, I will hand this statement back to you, Mr. Fisher, with the request that you let me have those. A. You wish that information with respect to all of those various issues?

Q. Transactions which I assume are all the note issues for the period covered by this statement. A. Yes, sir.

Q. You have handed me a capital memorandum of the Interborough Rapid Transit Company showing its capital stock and the amount of bonds, both the 5 per cent. gold bonds and the first mortgage 5 per cent. bonds, dated November 1, 1913, which are outstanding. Your capital stock, I see, is stated to have been partly issued in the acquisition of $6,000,000 of the capital stock of the Rapid Transit Subway Construction Company, which owned an undivided three-quarters interest in the lease of the subway contract between John B. McDonald and the city of New York, dated February 21, 1900, and I see that the amount of stock issued under this heading is $9,600,000; is that correct? A. Yes, sir.

Q. Of the six million dollars of the Rapid Transit Subway Construction Company's stock, how much had been paid in on that? A. Sixty dollars per share.

Q. In other words, $3,600,000? A. Correct.

Q. That was all the paid up value of the Rapid Transit Subway Construction Company stock? A. Yes, sir.

Q. And yet you issued for that $9,600,000? A. On the basis of $160 per share of Interborough Rapid Transit stock for $60 per share of Rapid Transit Subway Construction Company paid in.

Q. What was the justification of that? A. I suppose we could not get it any cheaper.

Q. And had $60 paid in on this Subway Construction Company stock become worth, in your opinion, $9,600,000? A. The $9,600,000 represents securities. It does not represent cash.

Q. But you could only issue your securities for cash or its equivalent? A. The cash value of that stock, as I remember it, at the time, was about $80 per share, which is just 50 per cent. of the amount stated there.

Q. Doesn't that $9,600,000 represent a profit to somebody of its securities? A. Only an apparent profit. They may have disposed of their holdings for, as I say — at the low price, which was about — $79 per share, I think, is the low for that stock.

Q. But the stock under the terms of your Interborough Consolidated merger is worth $325 a share, isn't it? A. If they held it, it is worth $325 to-day; yes, sir.

Q. Was it worth $160? A. No, sir.

Q. How much was it worth then? A. I think it was worth about $80 per share.

Q. What did the Interborough Rapid Transit Company represent at that time? A. The Interborough owned —

Q. What did it own? A. The Interborough Rapid Transit Company represented the operating company, formed to operate the new subway which was being constructed at that time.

Q. It had a capital of $35,000,000? A. Twenty-five millions, which was subsequently, in the same year, I think, increased ten millions, making it thirty-five million dollars.

Q. And yet I see $19,200,000 of that capitalization was issued at par? A. That was later on, I think.

Q. Two millions was issued for $110? A. Yes, sir; that was later on.

Q. And yet you say the $9,600,000 was only worth fifty? A. You are asking me to tell you from memory the value of that stock. I recollect it from the fact that the Murray Hill explosion occurred in that year, and at that time the stock was selling at seventy-nine and seven-eighths, which was the low point it reached.

Q. I see here issued in the acquisition of the remaining one-quarter interest in the subway lease, $2,500,000 of your stock. A. Yes, sir.

Q. Who owned that one-quarter? A. John B. McDonald and his associates.

Q. Who were his associates? A. I could not tell you.

Q. Was Mr. Freedman? A. I could only guess at that.

Q. I think it would be a very good guess. A. I prefer not to guess, though.

Q. You did not give Mr. John B. McDonald and his associates quite the same treatment as you gave the owners of the other three-quarters of the subway contract, did you? A. I could not say about that.

Q. Because if you paid $2,500,000 for one-quarter, and only nine — and at the same rate, presumably, seven and one-half million for three-quarters — but you gave the owners of the Subway Construction Company stock, $9,600,000? A. Well, they had paid something — $60 per share on their Rapid Transit Subway Construction stock. You would have to deduct that. Mr. McDonald received more proportionately for his than they did for theirs.

Q. So you gave them $3,600,000, to represent $3,600,000 of cash payments? A. Yes, sir; we gave them $9,600,000, to represent the $3,600,000 cash payment.

Q. There was a litigation before you arrived at a final settlement with McDonald, was there not? A. I think so.

Q. What did he claim? A. I could not say.

Q. Who knows? A. I don't know.

Q. You were secretary of the company at that time, were you not, Mr. Fisher. A. You give me that date, please.

Q. I should — oh no, apparently it was prior to your secretaryship. A. I think so. I became secretary in 1903.

Q. It was prior to your secretaryship. I see next here, issued in the acquisition of the shares of capital stock and bonds of the Pelham Park & City Island Companies, and also as compensation for the services of August Belmont & Company, in connection with the acquisition by your company of the fifty-year lease in the Subway, contained in the contract between John B. McDonald and the City of New York, and the securing of cash subscriptions to the stock of the company, etc., $1,500,000. What was that one million and a half issued for, the purchase of the Pelham Park

& City Island Railroad? A. No, sir. I think that is explained more fully in a memorandum which I gave your actuary yesterday.

Q. I am just trying to put the facts on the record. This stock is said to have been issued in the acquisition of the stock and bonds of the Pelham Park & City Island Railroad Company. A. That is wrong, sir.

Q. What was it issued for? A. It was issued principally for services and incidentally the Pelham Park & City Island Railroad was thrown in.

Q. In other words, the services for which this one million and a half was in reality issued was the real consideration for it? A. Yes, sir, practically so.

Q. And the purchase of the stock and bonds of the Pelham Park & City Island Railroad Company was a mere term or cover in which the payment of services was — shall I say, concealed? A. If you mean by that, that the payment of $350,000 was a term to cover that transaction, why, you are correct.

Q. I see nothing about $350,000. A. That is about what the Pelham Park & City Island Railroad cost, according to my recollection, cost the bankers, I mean, Belmont & Company.

Q. And the remainder of the one million and a half was to cover Mr. Belmont's services? A. Yes, sir.

Q. The emphasis in the statement is put upon the purchase of the stock and bonds of the Pelham Park & City Island Railroad Company, although that is the least considerable part of the consideration for the million and a half of stock which 1 am discussing? A. That is correct.

Q. Does the company own the Pelham Park & City Island Railroad Company now? A. Not at present, no, sir.

Q. Where is this railroad? A. It is up in the Bronx somewhere.

Q. What is its equipment? A. I couldn't say at the present time.

Q. Has it any? A. I couldn't say. We don't own the railroad at the present time.

Q. Did you own it for a number of years? A. Yes, sir.

Q. Did you operate it? A. Yes, sir.

Q. Did it have an operating income? A. A small one, yes, sir.

Q. Do you recall its income in any given year? A. No, sir, I don't.

Q. What was it, electric, horse railroad or steam railroad? A. Mule tramway, I should say.

Q. Mule tramway. How many mules did the railroad consist of? A. Probably a dozen or so.

Q. Were these mules looked over by your efficiency experts before acquisition? A. I couldn't say.

Q. Was there any charge off for deterioration or depreciation on mule car? A. Hardly.

Q. How many cars did this little railroad own? A. Roughly speaking, I think about a dozen.

Q. When you say "roughly speaking," you are not alluding to any of the characteristics of the travel on this Pelham Park & City Island Railroad? A. I would like to call your attention to the fact the road was purchased for its charter and not for its intrinsic value.

Q. In other words, you think its intrinsic value is almost negligible but its charter may have had some value? A. Yes, sir.

Q. It seems obvious and it must be to you, clearly, Mr. Fisher, that a mule tramway up in the Bronx was not valuable as such to the subway system in New York, or even to the surface lines in Manhattan; that is true, isn't it? A. Yes, sir.

Q. You say that this road was acquired for $350,000? A. That is what I understand it cost Belmont & Company.

Q. And when you disposed of it, whom did you dispose of it to? A. To the Third Avenue — to — I am wrong — to Mr. Frederick W. Whitridge.

Q. Did he like the mules? A. I could not say.

Q. Was it difficult to persuade Mr. Whitridge to become the purchaser of this mule tramway? A. I did not sell the property.

Q. How much did he give you for it? A. $40,000.

Q. And of this $1,500,000 which you stated as the inclusive consideration for this railroad, and for Mr. Belmont's services, services amount to about $1,150,000, in round figures; is that correct? A. I presume so.

Q. Was Mr. Belmont the chief owner of the Rapid Transit Subway Construction Company's stock at this time? A. I could not tell you how that stock was distributed.

Q. How had that stock — you don't know whether he was or not? A. I don't.

Q. I would like you to produce the records at that time, because I think you can; you are the secretary of the company now. How was this stock originally issued, this $9,600,000 that went to the Subway Construction Company? What I mean is, was it in the first instance issued directly to the Rapid Transit Subway Construction Company? A. No, sir; it was issued to the stockholders of the Rapid Transit Subway Construction Company.

Q. It was, in other words, an original issuance of your stock? A. Of the Interborough stock.

Q. Of the Interborough stock? A. Yes, sir.

Q. And presumably was issued for $9,600,000 of value, because you could not have issued your stock for less than par, could you? A. We could not at the present time.

Q. I mean you could not at that time. It has been the law of the State for many years. What you acquired for that $9,600,000 was undoubtedly represented on your records? A. It was undoubtedly worth $9,600,000.

Q. Now, does this $1,500,000 paid to Belmont and the owners of the Pelham Park Railway figure in the $35,000,000 which represents the total capitalization? A. Yes, sir.

Q. And does this profit of $6,600,000 — or this profit of $6,000,000 paid to the holders of the Subway Construction stock figure in that $35,000,000, as part of it? A. Yes, sir.

Q. How much of the $35,000,000 was issued for actual cash? A. I think that is shown on the statement. ·

Q. Would you say it appeared to be about $21,000,000? (Counsel hands statement to witness.) A. $21,400,000.

Q. In the new subway contracts, this $35,000,000 is treated as the basis of a calculation of what income the Interborough Rapid Transit Company shall receive under the subway operation, is it not? A. I think it is; yes, sir.

Q. And the total valuation of the subway lines, which, under your agreements with the city, the latter may some time acquire, is made up of this $35,000,000, among many other items, is it not? A. Yes, sir.

Q. What was the par value of the old bonds refunded by the

sale of $36,572,000 of new bonds which are mentioned next on this statement? A. Thirty-three million dollars and some odd hundred thousand. You have it on the bottom there.

Q. $33,959,000 is the redemption price of the old bonds, isn't it? A. Yes, sir.

Q. That is to say, that is all that the bondholders were entitled to, under the terms of their security? A. Yes, sir.

Q. How did it happen that it took you — that it required some $2,600,000 more than the redemption price in order to effect the redemption? A. If you will let me see the statement, I will tell you. (Counsel hands statement to witness.) Those bonds were redeemed at — $32,950,000 of bonds were redeemed at 105, with new bonds issued at 93½. The discount and premiums will account for the difference.

Q. These are some of the bonds that you recently sold to J. P. Morgan & Company from the new $160,000,000 issue? A. Yes, sir.

Mr. Colby.— Mr. Fisher, to-morrow I am going to ask you to go a little more in detail on those matters (handing to witness statement entitled " Memorandum showing dates and issues of notes and the retirement thereof ").

Mr. Chairman, the next subject that I wish to go into are the letters that have passed between the Interborough Rapid Transit Company and the firm of J. P. Morgan & Company, of which I have just concluded an analysis. The subject is an important one, and I could only cross its threshold in the time remaining this afternoon, and if it seems in the judgment of the Committee, you and your associate committeemen — I will suggest we do not enter upon that phase of the subject to-night.

Chairman Towner.— I assume they will defer to your judgment in the matter. I prefer to consult with the Chairman, Mr. Thompson.

Mr. Colby.— Suppose you do that.

Mr. Dawson.— He is coming in.

Mr. Colby.— We have some important matters to consider this afternoon.

(Senator Thompson takes the Chair.)

Chairman Thompson.— What's the matter; did the clock run down? Is there anything more?

Mr. Quackenbush.— Mr. Chairman and Mr. Colby: I think that Mr. Fisher has inadvertently made a statement this afternoon that should be corrected. If my memory is correct, the capitalization of the Interborough Rapid Transit Company plays no part whatever in the contract with the city, and I should like to have it understood that that may be subject to correction. I think Mr. Fisher, in his answer to your question that the capital —

Mr. Fisher.— Mr. Quackenbush is correct.

Mr. Colby.— I suppose it is also correct that there is an estimate of the earnings of the company made as an item in the calculation of what returns there shall be continued to be guaranteed by the city, and a certain rate is assumed to be the rate previously earned by the present subway on its existing capital.

Mr. Quackenbush.— That is the point I want to make, and I will verify it by reference to the contract, that the capital is not a measure there. It is a question of the average earnings of the two years preceding the making of the contract.

Mr. Colby.— But, as I understand it, Mr. Quackenbush, you have calculated that the existing earnings of the subway yield you a certain rate of return.

Mr. Quackenbush.— Not at all. It is a lump sum, $3,335,000. It has no relation to capital whatever. Mr. Dawson will confirm what I say.

Mr. Fisher.— I did not understand your question.

Chairman Thompson.— If it is so — Mr. Dawson says it is so.

Mr. Dawson.— It is the way it has been recorded.

Mr. Quackenbush.— No question about it.

Mr. Fisher.— You are correct, Mr. Quackenbush.

Mr. Quackenbush.— I know Mr. Fisher was speaking inadvertently because it was in the contract.

Mr. Fisher.— I misunderstood Mr. Colby's question. The contract is based on the two years' earnings — on the average of two years, 1910 and 1911.

Mr. Quackenbush.— This is in the interest of historical accuracy, that I make the suggestion, Mr. Chairman.

Chairman Thompson.— Well, for to-night we will leave it as it is, but if the fact changes by to-morrow, we will change it back again.

Mr. Quackenbush.— There is no doubt in my mind about the inaccuracy of Mr. Fisher's statement. We will give you an extract which will convince you of my statement, in the morning.

Chairman Thompson.— Is there anybody else with a grievance to-day? If so, let them air it.

Mr. Quackenbush.— I might say, Mr. Chairman, also in the interest of accuracy, as long as we are making corrections, I might say Mr. Fisher was also in error in stating that the power of the Pelham Park Road was mule power. It was horse power. They were not mules up there.

Mr. Fisher.— That is also in the interest of accuracy.

Chairman Thompson.— Perhaps Mr. Fisher was thinking of the time when they acquired the Panama Zone.

Mr. Quackenbush.— Well, I don't know about that. I don't think he was there.

Chairman Thompson.—Any other corrections?

(Vouchers referred to on the afternoon of February 8, 1916, but copies of which were not available to be marked as exhibits, were to-day handed to the stenographer, and were marked as follows):

Copy of voucher No. 105235, Interborough Rapid Transit Company to Nicoll, Anable, Lindsay & Fuller, $53,172.38, marked Exhibit No. 6 of February 8, 1916, V. E. V.

Copy of voucher No. 118187, Interborough Rapid Transit Company to Nicoll, Anable, Lindsey & Fuller, $43,292, marked Exhibit No. 7, February 8, 1916, V. E. V.

Copy of voucher No. 129261, Interborough Rapid Transit Company to Nicoll, Anable, Lindsay & Fuller, $36,516.48, marked Exhibit No. 8, February 8, 1916, V. E. V.

Copy of voucher No. 141200, Interborough Rapid Transit Company to Nicoll, Anable, Lindsay & Fuller, $25,345.25, marked Exhibit No. 9, of February 8, 1916, V. E. V.

Chairman Thompson.— Well, we will suspend now until tomorrow morning at 11 o'clock.

Whereupon, at 3:55 o'clock P. M., an adjournment was taken to Friday, February 11, 1916, at 11 o'clock A. M.

FEBRUARY 11, 1916

NEW YORK COUNTY LAWYERS ASSOCIATION BOARD ROOM,
165 Broadway, New York City

The Committee was called to order, pursuant to adjournment, Chairman Thompson presiding.

Quorum present.

Chairman Thompson.— The Committee will come to order.

Mr. Colby.— Mr. Chairman, as counsel to the Committee I received last evening a copy of a letter from Messrs. Cravath & Henderson, Attorneys for T. A. Gillespie Company and for Mr. Thomas A. Gillespie. It is a carbon copy of a letter which it is stated in the supplemental letter was sent to my office. I received this carbon copy at my house, and it is a somewhat voluminous letter that I think need not be introduced as a cumbrance to the record. I can tell you in a word its purport. Messrs. Cravath & Henderson refer to the publication of some letters written by Mr. Gillespie to his brother as in their opinion a breach of the stipulation under which they have submitted their books and papers to the inspection of the Committee's accountant, and follow with this significant statement of theirs to the effect that further submission of the books and papers will not be accorded to the Committee. I want to say that of course we cannot permit Messrs.

Cravath & Henderson to overplay this slip up and to create of it a diversion which can operate in any degree or manner to the protection of the Gillespie Company or to the frustration of the Committee's duty and legitimate desire to prosecute their examination of the affairs of the Gillespie Company fully and to the bottom. I think that this matter of the premature publication of those letters in so far as it involves any departure from the strictest proprieties of preliminary investigations has been to some extent exaggerated in its importance and significance. I think that this Committee needs no suggestion from any outside monitor, particularly when the suggestions proceed from counsel for parties whose books and papers we are in the course of examining. I think that what took place at the beginning of yesterday's session should be evidence of the most satisfactory character that the Committee is concerned as to the observance of every reasonable propriety and is quite competent to exercise an alert supervision and control of its own conduct, and that of its own motives. I think it was made very apparent by the impressive, and manful and possibly in my opinion exaggerated measure of responsibility which the Chairman so promptly took for the incident concerning which we all expressed regret.

Of course, Mr. Chairman, there is no favor being shown to this Committee in submitting books and papers which possibly contain material and informative notice to this Committee. There seems to be reflected in the letter of Cravath & Henderson an idea that we are dependent upon their grace and concession. I think it is due the Committee that counsel should promptly repudiate that idea, and call emphatic attention to the fact that this Committee is proceeding by virtue of the power lawfully given it by a Senate and Assembly of the State, and that we wish nothing outside of our powers and are quite content to rely upon our powers to obtain all we deem pertinent to our inquiry.

The examination of books and papers at the office of Messrs. Gillespie & Company is a concession on the part of this Committee for the purpose of not disrupting the business of Gillepsie & Company, and of not subpoenaing their officers to attendance before this Committee, and incidental loss of time in subjecting their papers to carriage between their office and the Committee rooms from day to day.

I think a complete and sufficient answer to this letter of Cravath & Henderson would be the service upon the T. A. Gillespie Company of a subpoena in which I will ask that the Chair direct the production before the Committee of all contracts, copies of contracts, maps, plans, specifications, books of accounts, time sheets, material records — I mean records of materials — requisitions, orders, bills of lading, checks, correspondence, inter-office communications, memoranda, records, costs data, bills, receipts, and all other books, papers, writings and memoranda of every type and character in connection with or in any respects relating to the Manhattan Elevated Railway improvement and the Manhattan Elevated Railway extension, or in relation to all their dealings with Terry & Tench, and Snare & Triest, in anywise connected with the foregoing matters, together with all letters and other communications received by you, and copies of letters written by you to the Interborough Rapid Transit Company, or any of its officers and employees, or from any of your officers and employees, in connection with the foregoing matters. I also suggest that Mr. Thomas Gillespie, who is in Florida, but whose return can be had, I am assured, on the request of this Committee, be requested to return to New York at once for the purpose of submitting to examination.

Chairman Thompson.— We also want his personal books and papers.

Mr. Colby.— Yes. I will supplement this suggestion by suggesting further that a similar subpoena covering all of these matters be served as soon as possible upon Mr. Thomas A. Gillespie personally, or upon any one in charge of that material.

Chairman Thompson.— I direct the issuance of that subpoena, and I want to say that this Committee's position is exactly the same as it has been since this investigation started. The Committee is authorized by the Legislature. We have such powers as our resolutions give us. We do not care to in any manner exceed those powers, and we are here to act by whatever power the Legislature has that it has delegated to us. We never have and we do not propose now to be under the slightest obligation whatever to any person who is subpoenaed to appear before this Committee or who has books, papers or documents that the Committee desires to inspect, and we decline to in anywise, through ourselves or any of our officers, to be under obligations to men subpoenaed or to their counsel, whoever they may be, for the production of any book, paper or document, before this committee. We do not want a thing that we have not the power to take, and I want that emphatic, and I want every corporation and every person who is likely to be a witness before this Committee, and every attorney who represents them to understand that absolutely, perfectly. We do not want anything we are not absolutely entitled to by virtue of the power of the Legislature which has been delegated to us. Therefore there can be no such thing as the co-operation of any attorney, Mr. Cravath or anybody else, with this Committee. The Committee realizes that we have not the power to send a man to another man's office and inspect his books and papers. We cannot subpoena books and papers to be produced before somebody who is not a member of the Committee, and we do not undertake to assume that power. We have allowed that to be done in several instances where it would be a convenience to the corporation, because it suits their convenience. Our powers are to require the production of those papers before this Committee, and that is the power we contend for, and if the Legislature has not that power it is time the Legislature understood it and we found it out, and if we have not sufficient power we will see whether we can get it.

So much for that phase of the situation. I make this statement with the complete accord of every member of the Committee and the counsel employed by the Committee.

In relation to the matters that came before the Committee yesterday, there is just a little human element by which you hesitate sometimes about a matter. I am glad that check and those letters were published. It simply shows, and shows nothing else, and nothing beyond the fact that men in such business can spend their idle time in framing up a public official. That is all it shows, and there is not a single thing about it that shows that a public official had the slightest thing to do with it. They can

15

write their letters among themselves, and draw their checks to
each other, and that does not affect the person mentioned in an
official capacity, and I want the public to understand that, so that
this matter, as I see it, and I think the Committee sees it, is not
a reflection upon the Governor of this State or any other public
official.

I have known of instances where men in Legislative bodies
have been asked by men how they were intending to vote upon a
subject, and upon being told the truth have gone out and tried
to trade upon that knowledge before the vote has been cast, and
numbers of public officers are exposed continually to that sort of
thing.

The letters themselves and the check itself are interesting, and
a matter entirely within the scope of the inquiry of this Com-
mitte, as affecting the men like the drawers of the check and the
recipient of the check, and nothing further.

Mr. Colby.— I have further to suggest to the Committee that
the records of the Constitutional Convention held last year
in so far as they contain a record of the measures introduced
looking to the broadening of the power of judicial review of findings or judgments of the Public Service Commission, and,
further, in so far as they look towards the diminution of the
power of removal of Public Service Commissioners and the con-
version of their office into a Constitutional office which would be
immune from such power of removal, I have to ask that all such
records be subpoenaed before this Committee, including the
record of the debates on those questions showing who participated,
the reports of all committees on those questions, and the record
of the votes of members of the convention on those questions, and
of the Committee.

Chairman Thompson.— I think that matter might be produced
without a subpoena, and the reason why is Mr. Ledyard P. Hale,
the counsel for the upstate Public Service Commission, was chairman of the committee on public utilities, I think, of the last Constitutional Convention, and we have power to ask Judge Hale to
appear before us, and perhaps he might think he was not entitled

to bring the records of the Constitutional Convention. Perhaps a subpoena would be as well.

Mr. Colby.— However, most easily the material can be obtained. I desire to trace the progress of the various proposals from introduction to the point of their incorporation in a proposed form in which a revised Constitution by a margin that could hardly be called narrow, failed of public adoption and approval.

Chairman Thompson.— The Committee agree with you, and if you will, prepare and issue such a subpoena, and I will have it done.

(Senator Towner presiding.)

HORACE M. FISHER, being recalled for further examination, testified as follows:

By Mr. Colby:

Q. Mr. Secretary, you hand me a file of letters? A. Yes, sir.

Q. Do these letters contain — does this file contain the letters received by the Interborough Rapid Transit Company, or its president, from the banking firm of J. P. Morgan & Co. and the letters addressed to said firm by your company or its officers touching the negotiations and the final agreements under which the new bonds of the Interborough Rapid Transit Company were issued and purchased by Morgan & Company? A. Yes.

Q. I understand that these letters ensued upon some formal and personal conferences between Mr. Shonts and Mr. J. P. Morgan? A. Yes.

Q. And when those conferences had progressed to a certain point it was deemed advisable that the matter should thereafter take the form of letters; is that correct? A. That is my understanding.

Q. I call your attention to a letter dated June 24, 1909, addressed to Mr. T. P. Shonts, President of the Interborough Rapid Transit Company, and apparently signed J. P. Morgan, Jr. Was such a letter received by your company from Mr. J. P. Morgan, Jr.? A. Yes, sir.

Q. And this is the letter? A. Yes, sir.

Mr. Colby.— I will read this letter, Mr. Chairman, into the record of the Committee.

(Mr. Colby reads the letter referred to, which is as follows):

"June 24, 1909.

" MY DEAR MR. SHONTS:

" I think it would be as well to put on paper the understanding arrived at as far as any understanding was arrived at this morning, between you and Mr. Belmont on the one side and J. P. Morgan & Co. on the other.

" It is understood that the Interborough Rapid Transit Company will apply to the Public Service Commission for authority to build further subways, substantially duplicating its present line, on the general basis as set forth in a letter from you to the Chairman of the Public Service Commission, dated June 11, 1909, of which you have given me a copy.

" You stated to me that this proposition came to J. P. Morgan & Co. entirely free from any other claim on it, that you had authority to deal with anyone you wished, and that you had dealt with no one else.

" I advised you that, in our opinion, the financing of the improvements and the extensions to the Manhattan Elevated Railway presented no difficulty, but that as far as regards the extensions to the Interborough subways were concerned, a plan would have to be devised by which the new money, which would be put into the extensions, could receive a reasonable share in the company, in addition to the mere interest on the bonds which had at first been contemplated.

" I also said that if such a plan could be found, and if it could be arranged that we should finance simply the Interborough Rapid Transit Company and had no relations with the Interborough Metropolitan Company in this connection, we were much interested in the business and would endeavor to formulate a plan which would be satisfactory to the public and creditable to all parties concerned in it, and that in our opinion the chances of a plan being found were sufficient for you to feel authorized to apply to the Public Service Service Commission for permission to make the extensions mentioned.

"I think this letter expresses the extent of the understanding arrived at between us, and if it agrees with your recollection I should be glad if you would confirm it.

"Yours very sincerely,

"J. P. MORGAN, JR.

"T. P. SHONTS, ESQ., President,
    "Interborough Rapid Transit Company,
        "165 Broadway, City."

Q. What in your opinion do Morgan & Company mean when they say that the proposition on Mr. Shonts' assurance came to them entirely free from any other claim on it? A. I am sure I don't know.

Q. They further say that they understand that Mr. Shonts had authority to deal with anyone he wishes. Do you know what that means? A. No, sir.

Q. It would appear, would it not, that the Board of Directors had left some matters pretty much to Mr. Shonts; you have no reason to question the accuracy of that statement in the Morgan letter, have you? A. I have not.

Q. They say that the financing and extensions to the Manhattan Elevated Railway presented no difficulty; what was the difference between financing the Manhattan Elevated extensions and the Interborough extensions, so far as difficulty is concerned? A. The Manhattan had a perpetual franchise, while the Subway only a lease, and I presume they thought it was easier to issue Manhattan bonds than additional subway bonds. The Manhattan mortgage I may say provides for extensions and for capitalizing those extensions at so much per mile, so they may have in mind the issuing of additional first mortgage bonds for that purpose.

Q. And although the Interborough Rapid Transit Company is the lessee of the Manhattan Elevated Railway, the latter has power in its own right to borrow money necessary for its extensions and betterments, has it not? A. Only under the provisions of the lease.

Q. But that power exists, if there — A. Not independent of the Interborough Company.

Q. The lessee can borrow for the Manhattan Elevated Railway Company as lessee? A. Yes, sir.

Q. And can subject the Manhattan Elevated property to the liens of any mortgage or other form of pledge which may be necessary to raise money for the Manhattan in accordance with the terms of the lease? A. In accordance with the terms of the mortgage, I suppose, and of the lease.

Q. Mr. Morgan says that the interest of his firm in the business — he says " We are very much interested in the business," and says the chances of a plan being found are sufficient for you (meaning Mr. Shonts) to feel authorized to apply to the Public Service Commission for permission to make the extensions mentioned; was Mr. Shonts deriving his authority in any measure from Mr. J. P. Morgan for his official acts as president of this company? A. No, sir; I don't understand that that letter intimates any such thing.

Q. And yet the letter would seem to me to go much beyond an intimation. Mr. Morgan says: " You may consider yourself authorized to apply to the Public Service Commission for permission to make the extensions mentioned? " A. In so far as our furnishing the money is concerned, that would be the interpretation I would put on it.

Q. Would you not also put the interpretation on the letter that Mr. Shonts requested Mr. Morgan's permission to apply on behalf of his company to the Public Service Commission for the necessary permit to make extensions? A. Only in so far as it related to his furnishing the money.

Q. I suppose Mr. Morgan replied to that letter, and I ask if the next letter in the file, which appears to be a carbon copy of a letter addressed to Mr. Morgan dated June 25, 1909, is a copy of a reply to Mr. Morgan? A. Yes, sir. You mean Mr. Shonts' reply?

Q. Yes, sir; I mean Mr. Shonts' reply to Mr. Morgan? A. Yes, sir.

Mr. Colby.— I will read the copy of Mr. Shonts' letter, dated June 25, 1909, to Mr. Morgan.

Mr. Colby reads the letter referred to, which is as follows:

Letter addressed to Mr. J. P. Morgan, Jr., care of J. P. Morgan & Company, New York City. June 25, 1909. (The letter is marked " Personal.")

" My dear Mr. Morgan:

" I have your letter of yesterday, setting forth your understanding, so far as an understanding has been reached, between J. P. Morgan & Company on the one hand, and Mr. Belmont and myself on the other, with respect to financing of certain extensions and improvements of this company.

" The understanding set forth by you in this letter entirely agrees with the understanding of Mr. Belmont and myself, except that you will remember in a previous conference between you and myself I stated that the Interborough Rapid Transit Company, as lessee of the Manhattan Company, has the right to call upon that company for corporate action in regard to such improvements of the Elevated system as we (the lessee) may decide upon. We further have the right, if we consider it advantageous, to finance these improvements ourselves, without asking the cooperation of the Manhattan Company. If, however, it is thought best to finance the Manhattan improvement through an additional issue of Manhattan stock or other form of Manhattan securities, the Manhattan Company will have to be consulted.

" In any event, under the lease of the Manhattan system, we are authorized to issue Manhattan bonds in a sum slightly in excess of five million dollars for general improvements, which issue of bonds was provided for in the lease in contemplation of the reduction of the fixed charges of the Manhattan Company by $200,000 per annum, at the date of the redemption of the 6 per cent bonds in 1908.

" The lease further provides for the issue of securities in the sum of $600,000 per mile, for any extensions of the Elevated, under the consolidated mortgage, with the terms of which I understand you are thoroughly familiar.

" Very truly yours,"

Q. When Mr. Shonts refers in this letter to the Manhattan improvements, he refers to the third-tracking of the Elevated and its extensions, does he not? A. Not necessarily. It includes all the improvements to the Manhattan as well as additional extensions.

Q. Is not the term " Manhattan improvements " used by the Gillespie Company to describe the third tracking and extension of the Manhattan lines? A. Yes, sir.

Q. On June 26, apparently, Mr. Morgan, Jr., again wrote to Mr. Shonts; is this the letter the president of your company received from Mr. Morgan? A. Yes, sir.

Mr. Colby read the letter referred to, being dated June 26, 1909, into the record, as follows:

" NEW YORK, *June* 26, 1909.

" MY DEAR MR. SHONTS:

" Thanks for your letter of yesterday, in answer to mine of the 24th instant.

" As I understand the position in regard to the Manhattan Elevated Company, whatever financing is done for that company will have to be done by, or through, the Interborough Rapid Transit Company, and certainly with its consent, and I presume that — in order to enable us to plan for the entire proposal — no scheme of financing would be undertaken except by some method which might seem right to the Interborough Rapid Transit Company and ourselves. What I particularly wish to guard against is the financing of the Manhattan Elevated Company by other parties at the same time, or nearly at the same time, that we are undertaking work of that character for the Interborough Rapid Transit Company.

" As your letter is not very specific on this point, I should be glad if you would confirm my understanding.

" Yours very sincerely,

" J. P. MORGAN, JR.

" T. P. SHONTS, ESQ., President,
" Interborough Rapid Transit Company,
" 165 Broadway, City."

Q. Mr. Morgan in his first letter, however, expressed his appreciation of the fact that the financing of the Manhattan Elevated presented no difficulty, did he not? A. Yes, sir.

Q. And what he particularly expressed his wish to guard against is the independent financing of the Manhattan Elevated by other parties than himself or his firm while undertaking the work of the same character for the Interborough Company. Did Mr. Morgan think it might interfere with his financing of the Interborough if the Manhattan Elevated exercised its concededly adequate power of independently financing itself? A. I couldn't say what Mr. Morgan thought.

Q. Is that the idea conveyed in his letter, to your mind? A. I presume so.

Q. There follows a letter dated June 29, 1909, addressed to Mr. J. P. Morgan, Jr. Is this a reply by your company's president to the letter of Morgan that I just read? A. Does it so state?

Q. The carbon copy is without a signature. A. I mean the date of the letter.

Q. June 29 and June 26. A. Yes, sir.

Q. This is Mr. Shonts' reply? A. Yes, sir.

Mr. Colby read into the record letter dated June 29, 1909. It is as follows:

"*June* 29, 1909.

"My dear Mr. Morgan:

"I have yours of the 26th, with respect to your understanding that whatever financing is done for the Manhattan Company will have to be done by or through the Interborough Company, and certainly with its consent.

"Under the terms of the lease:

"(a) The Interborough Company has the right to finance additions or improvements to the elevated lines without the co-operation or consent of the Manhattan Company, provided the Interborough Company does not call upon the Manhattan Company to insure any of its own securities;"—

Q. In that statement Mr. Shonts does not say the Interborough Company is under a duty to finance additions or improvements to the elevated, but says it has the right to finance additions or improvements; it would imply, does it not, the terms under which such financing might be done was of such advantage to the Interborough as to be looked upon as a right rather than as a duty to be imposed upon it by the lease? A. Not necessarily. It would be to the interest of both companies to get whatever moneys were required for improvements upon the best terms possible, and that was all Mr. Shonts was trying to do in that case.

(Mr. Colby continues reading of the letter as follows:)

"(b) The Manhattan Company, upon the request of the Interborough Company, must 'from time to time execute and deliver to the Interborough Company for issue for new mileage, and sale at not less than par, bonds secured by the general mortgage of the Manhattan Railway, the proceeds of which shall be used only in accordance with the terms of the mortgage,' i. e., at the rate of $600,000 per mile for new double track and $300,000 for single track.

"(c) The Manhattan Company covenants and agrees that it will on or after the 1st day of July, 1908, at the request of the Interborough, issue at the highest price obtainable, a new series of bonds bearing 4 per centum interest per annum, payable semi-annually, to the amount of $5,409,000, secured by mortgage covering, if deemed advisable by the Interborough, either a portion of the whole of its franchise rights, privileges and property, the proceeds of which shall be used only for one or more of the following purposes, viz.:

"For land damage claims or easements;

"For improvements on Manhattan Railway property.

"(d) Under Article 25 of the lease certain valuable parcels of real estate not needed for the operation of the road can be sold and the proceeds utilized for the same purpose as the bonds in the preceding section.

"Summed up, therefore, the Interborough may, by issuance of its own securities, finance extensions or additions to the Manhattan, without reference to the Manhattan; whereas the Manhattan cannot issue either of the two classes of securities above mentioned, or any securities, or create any indebtedness, except with the consent and approval of the Interborough Company.

" Therefore, your desire to particularly guard against the independent financing of the Manhattan by other parties at the same time, or nearly at the same time, that you are undertaking work of that character for the Interborough Company, is in all respects protected.

" Very truly yours,

"......................

" President.

" Mr. J. P. Morgan, Jr.,

" Broad and Wall Streets, New York City."

Q. Did the provisions of the Manhattan lease contain any protection to the Interborough for such obligations as the Interborough might incur for financing Manhattan extensions or additions? A. To a limited extent; yes, sir.

Q. Does Mr. Shonts mean in this letter that the Interborough would issue its own securities, liens only against Interborough property, and expend the proceeds of such securities for the benefit of the Manhattan property? A. No, sir; I suppose it would also be a lien against the property of the Manhattan, or rather our equity in the lease.

Q. But he says this power of the Interborough exists without reference to the Manhattan? A. That is to issue its own securities.

Q. He says the Interborough may by the issuance of its own securities finance extensions to the Manhattan, without reference to the Manhattan Company? A. The Interborough Company can issue securities for the improvement of the Manhattan Railway without reference.

Q. And those securities may constitute a lien upon the property of the Manhattan? A. No, sir; upon the Interborough's equity in that property, a lien upon it.

Q. In other words, the value of its lease? A. Yes, sir.

Q. But will not be liens upon the Manhattan property? A. No, sir.

Q. In other words, the suggestion that one company can, without the consent of the other, charge the latter with liens as to the creation of which it has no say, is not true? A. It does not mean that.

Q. And no such fact is contemplated in that regard? A. No, sir.

Q. The Manhattan reserves some power of independent action in the issuance of its securities, does it not? A. Yes, sir.

Q. That is subject to the consent and approval of the Interborough Company? A. Yes, sir.

Q. Notwithstanding the lease to the Interborough, it preserves its corporate organization, does it not? A. Yes, sir.

Q. Has its president and board? A. Yes, sir.

Q. And they meet with regularity? A. I couldn't say as to that.

Q. They transact business? A. Yes, sir.

Q. Has the Manhattan any income except what it receives from its lease to the Interborough? A. I don't think so; not that I am aware of.

Q. It has no operating business? A. No, sir.

Q. Which its board or president is charged with directing? A. No, sir.

Q. All the president or directors of the Manhattan are concerned with is the receipt of the periodic rental of their property from the Interborough and its application to the payment of debts and dividends; is that right? A. And to see that their property is properly maintained, in accordance with the terms of the lease.

Q. Does the Interborough pay the Manhattan shareholders directly a certain dividend? A. I think it is paid through the Manhattan; I am not sure.

Q. It is a guarantee of what per cent? A. Seven per cent.

Q. Do you consider that lease advantageous to the Interborough? A. I do.

Mr. Colby.— The next letter is a letter from J. P. Morgan & Company, dated September 15, 1910, which has already been read into the record, and I need not again read it. It outlines a plan for financing the Interborough Rapid Transit Company.

This plan in brief calls for the issuance of first refunding mortgage bonds to the amount of $150,000,000, and notes running two and one-half at six per cent. for $30,000,000, or in the alternative, $37,500,000 of bonds in November, 1910. Morgan & Company undertook to discount the notes and allow three per cent. on balances, provided withdrawals did not exceed $1,500,000 to $6,900,000 each month.

Mr. Colby.— This entire letter had best be copied into the record.

The letter referred to is dated September 15, 1910, and is as follows:

"New York, *September* 15, 1910.
" Theodore P. Shonts, President,
   Interborough Rapid Transit Company,
     165 Broadway, New York.

Dear Sir.—We beg to confirm as follows the substance of our conversation of yesterday relative to a plan for financing the Interborough Rapid Transit Company.

1. The basis of the plan will be a new first and refunding mortgage securing an authorized issue of $150,000,000, fifty-year five per cent. coupon and registered form bonds due in 1960, interest payable semi-annually. The mortgage will contain provisions for an unusual sinking fund, not exceeding one per cent. of the total amount outstanding, and other provisions satisfactory to us, and will be a general lien on all the company's properties and rights. The present mortgage of the Interborough Company dated November 1, 1907, is to be closed against the further issue of bonds thereunder, except as required by the convertible clauses of the notes due May 1, 1911, and except bonds for an additional amount at par sufficient to reimburse the company for capital expenditures heretofore made out of earnings (the bonds heretofore issued as collateral, except as so required, to be cancelled).

2. During the month of November, 1910, the Interborough Company will issue it six per cent. two and one-half year notes for the principal amount of $30,000,000 secured by $37,500,000 par value of the new bonds due 1960 above mentioned, the interest

on such notes to be payable quarterly or semi-annually as may
be agreed between us, and the notes to be redeemable at par, at the
election of the Interborough Company, either at the end of the first
year or on any interest date thereafter, the Interborough Company to give at least thirty days prior notice of its election to
redeem.

3. During the month of November, 1910, J. P. Morgan &
Company will purchase from the Interborough Company and the
latter will sell to J. P. Morgan & Company the $30,000,000 of
notes above mentioned at ninety-seven, the proceeds to be credited
to the Interborough Company, on the books of J. P. Morgan &
Company, who will allow the Interborough Company interest at
the rate of three per cent. per annum on the daily credit balances
with the understanding, however, that the Interborough Company
will not withdraw the same except as and when required from
time to time in meeting its payment on construction and equipment; and we understand that this will mean substantially as
follows:

During the first quarter after deposit, not exceeding $1,500,000.
During the second quarter after deposit, not exceeding
$1,900,000.
During the third quarter, after deposit, not exceeding
$2,450,000.
During the fourth quarter, after deposit, not exceeding
$2,800,000.
During the fifth quarter after deposit, not exceeding $3,500,000.
During the sixth quarter after deposit, not exceeding $4.200,000.
During the seventh quarter after deposit, not exceeding
$5,900,000.
During the eighth quarter after deposit, not exceeding
$6,900,000.

4. Referring to the Interborough Company's notes aggregating
about $22,000,000, due May 1, 1911, which contained clauses
under which the notes may be converted into the present Interborough mortgage 5's: On or before May 1, 1911, the Interborough Company, at its election, may issue a second series of its
six per cent. notes to the principal amount of $22,000,000 or less

(and at its election to a principal amount sufficient to produce $22,000,000 net) maturing at the same time as the above mentioned series of $30,000,000 secured by $27,500,000 par value, or a proportionate larger or smaller amount, of the new bonds due 1960, the interest on such notes to be payable and the notes to contain redemption clauses as in the case of the above mentioned $30,000,000 series. On May 1, 1911, J. P. Morgan & Company, will purchase and the Interborough Company will sell to J. P. Morgan & Company, at ninety-seven, such notes as the Interborough Company shall have elected to issue under this clause 4, the proceeds, so far as needed, to be used by the Interborough Company in paying the convertible notes maturing May 1, 1911, which shall not have been converted into the present Interborough 5's and the proceeds, so far as not needed to pay such convertible notes, to be deposited with J. P. Morgan & Company, and to be withdrawn only as and when required by the Interborough Company in meeting payment on account of improvements, equipment or construction; and with that understanding, J. P. Morgan & Company, will allow the Interborough Company interest at the rate of three per centum on the Interborough Company's daily credit balance. At least sixty days prior to May 1, 1911, the Interborough Company will give J. P. Morgan & Company, written notice of the amount of the second series of notes which the Interborough Company will issue. In consideration of J. P. Morgan & Company's commitment (necessarily made at a date in advance of the final approval of a plan and while the amounts involved are wholly uncertain), to purchase, if required, the total authorized series of such notes, without any corresponding obligation on the part of the Interborough Company to issue the same or any part thereof, the Interborough Company, on May 1, 1911, will pay to J. P. Morgan & Company, in cash, three per cent. on the entire portion of such total authorized series which shall not then have been issued.

5. The Interborough Company agrees to provide the funds for the retirement of the above mentioned notes aggregating $52,-000,000 or thereabouts, by a sale through J. P. Morgan & Company, of the new bonds due 1960; and the latter agree to offer such new bonds for sale, for account of the Interborough Company, the

offer to be made at any time within the above mentioned two and one-half years, when in the judgment of J. P. Morgan & Company, it shall be desirable to make the offer, and at a price satisfactory to the Interborough Company, the proceeds of the sale of such bonds to be credited to the Interborough Company on the books of J. P. Morgan & Company, and to be used only in the payment of such notes. For the services rendered and to be rendered under this article by J. P. Morgan & Company, they shall be entitled to receive and the Interborough Company shall pay a commission equal to three per cent. of the par amount of the bonds offered by them. Such commission of three per cent. shall be exclusive of all expenses attending the offer and in view of the committment of J. P. Morgan & Company, to offer the entire amount of the new bonds, shall be payable by the Interborough Company to J. P. Morgan & Company partly in advance as follows:

Three hundred thousand dollars being 1 per cent on $30,000,-000 payable in November, 1910, when the first series of notes are issued; $220,000, being 1 per cent on $22,000,000 payable on or before May 1, 1911; and the remainder of 2 per cent on the total amount shall be payable as and when the bonds shall be sold.

6. The papers and corporate proceedings are to be satisfactory in form to counsel for J. P. Morgan & Company, and all expenses in this connection are to be paid by the Interborough Company.

Please confirm.

Yours very truly,

J. P. MORGAN & CO.

NEW YORK, *September* 23, 1910.

Agreed to and accepted to be put into effect if the franchise for elevated extensions and improvements shall be granted by the Public Service Commission and by the Board of Estimate and Apportionment and the issue and disposition of notes and of bonds and the proceeds thereof, as above proposed, shall have been approved and authorized by the Public Service Commission.

INTERBOROUGH RAPID TRANSIT CO.

By T. P. SHONTS, *President.*"

Q. This, I understand, Mr. Fisher, was the Morgan proposal
with reference to the first subway plan? A. Yes, sir.

Q. And it was upon the proposals here contained that the first
of the two subway plans was constructed as to financing, is that
right? A. I would not like to say whether the first plan, but one
of the earlier. There were quite a number of plans between 1909
and 1913; probably fifty or more.

Q. I am referring to the two plans that came before the Board
of Estimate and Apportionment at different times, one failing
of adoption, and the other finally securing the necessary approval
of all parties? A. I could not say what particular plan was
referred to. Those plans were being modified and changed
constantly at that time.

Q. Am I not right in saying one plan failed of adoption in the
Board of Estimate? A. Yes, sir.

Q. It was pretty fully discussed and finally got in form for
official action? A. Yes, sir.

Q. Do you recall the date of that vote? A. No, sir, I don't.

Q. Is there any record in the room which would enable you to
fix that date? A. That first record I gave you I think would,
yes, sir. Our negotiations with the city began on April 24, 1907,
and they continued up to the time the final contract was signed.

Q. And that was in 1913? A. Yes, sir, 1913.

Mr. Quackenbush.— The date of the first plan failing of
adoption, I think, was July, 1911.

Mr. Fisher.— The negotiations were discontinued in the latter
part of 1911 and resumed by outside parties in October, 1911,
and it must have been prior to that.

Mr. Colby.— I think it was July, 1911.

Mr. Quackenbush.— There is no doubt about it.

Q. That failed in July, 1911? A. I think that is right.

Q. And those negotiations were resumed by outside parties in
about October? A. October, 1911, yes, sir.

Q. Meaning by outside parties, whom? A. It was taken up
by disinterested parties to see if they could not arrange terms
between the city and the Interborough, so as to get them together.

Q. Who were those parties? A. The Pennsylvania Railroad represented by its president, Mr. Samuel Rae, Mr. Seth Low and others. I don't remember them all.

. Q. I am interested to know who these disinterested parties are, Mr. Fisher. A. I have given you the principal ones.

Q. It was a considerable number of persons, was it not? A. I presume they brought others in from time to time. Negotiations were conducted by Mr. Shonts. Whatever negotiations each party had with the Interborough were conducted with Mr. Shonts.

Q. Mr. Shonts was directing these disinterested parties in their negotiations? A. No, sir.

Q. Was he conducting their own spontaneous negotiations as their spokesman and agent. A. No, sir.

Q. What do you mean when you say the negotiations were under his direction? A. I did not say under his directions. I said these parties came to Mr. Shonts when they desired to consult with the Interborough with respect to the negotiations.

(Chairman Thompson presiding.)

Q. In other words, the negotiations had crumpled up, and the Interborough and J. P. Morgan had abandoned the matter when the Pennsylvania Railroad, as a disinterested third party, came to the rescue of the negotiations; is that about right? A. I couldn't say that they had abandoned the matter.

Q. At any rate they were out of breath and were inactive? A. That is your own interpretation.

Q. I am trying to form a correct picture in my mind as to the situation, because, frankly, it is quite refreshing to find the Pennsylvania Railroad Company cast in the roll of the disinterested party in this drama. A. The Pennsylvania Railroad was very much interested in getting a subway connection with their station at Seventh avenue.

Q. And who, on behalf of the Pennsylvania Railroad, impersonated first aid to these halted negotiations. A. Mr. Rae and Mr. County. Mr. County, I think, was Mr. Rae's assistant.

Q. Mr. Rae is the president of the company? A. Yes, sir.

Q. And Mr. Seth Low? A. Yes, sir.

Q. And do you recall any other name? A. Not at the moment.

Q. There were other names? A. I think there were others in the negotiations, but I am not competent to say.

Mr. Quackenbush.— My recollection is gentlemen representing the Chamber of Commerce and the Merchants' Association, and in my mind at present as representing those bodies was Mr. Outerbridge, Mr. Claflin, and a number of citizens of that character, who felt a mistake had been made by the city in its conduct, and intervened, and with Mr. Rae and Mr. Low approached Mr. Shonts with an idea of seeing if something could not be done, and those negotiations continued from October well into the spring of 1912, when finally the fundamental thing of the final plans were agreed upon at conferences at which those gentlemen were participants. That is in brief the situation.

Mr. Colby.— There had been a complete collapse so far as an immediate fact, on the part of the Interborough, Morgan & Company and the city, to arrive at any agreement in July, 1911.

Mr. Quackenbush.— I would not say there was a collapse, but the Interborough had reached a conclusion that any further negotiations were fruitless for the time being. They had made offer after offer to the Public Service Commission, and had assumed that they had reached a meeting of the minds from time to time only to find that they had not, and I think that the feeling was the task was hopeless and the only thing to do was to go ahead and do the best we could with what we had.

Q. In other words, Mr. Fisher, the plan outlined by Morgan & Company in the letter of September 15, 1910, may be said without any distortion of the facts to have failed in July, 1911; I think that is a fair statement? A. Yes, sir.

Q. Was any record kept of the activities of these disinterested intermediaries? A. It is probably shown in the correspondence file, such correspondence as they may have had, that is.

Q. Who was President of the Merchants' Association, do you recall, at that time? A. I do not recall.

Q. Was it Mr. Breed, would you say? A. I don't think so.

Mr. Quackenbush.— He had nothing to do with it. Nobody connected with us, and it was an entirely outside interest.

Q. And it was not until the spring of 1912 that a new plan was forthcoming and the negotiations were renewed? A. Yes, sir.

Chairman Thompson.— Was this initiated by the Merchants' Association?

Mr. Colby.— No. The testimony is, on the subject of the intervention of negotiations, after apparently the failure of the first plan.

Chairman Thompson.— Who intervened?

Mr. Colby.— The Pennsylvania Railroad and Mr. Seth Low and Mr. Outerbridge, Eugene H. Outerbridge, in behalf of the Chamber of Commerce.

Q. The $500,000 payment to J. P. Morgan & Co.—

Mr. Quackenbush.— I would add, for the Chairman's information — I did not attempt, from memory, to make the statement comprehensive. There were in addition, it occurs to me, to these parties, numerous neighborhood associations throughout the line of the proposed lines who took considerable interest in it, in Brooklyn and the Bronx and various parts of the city.

Chairman Thompson.— Do you take any interest in the civic organizations; do you have your friends join them, or anything of that kind?

Mr. Quackenbush.— There has not been anything of that kind in many years. The last transactions of that kind were at the time the contest was on hand between the Metropolitan Street Railway Company and the Interborough. I wouldn't say there are no members in any of the associations, because we have among our people a good many people who take an active interest in their own neighborhoods.

Senator Lawson.— Did not the Interborough buy memberships in the Civic League in Brooklyn within a year?

Mr. Quackenbush.— Not to my knowledge.

Senator Lawson.— Do you remember it was published in the

paper that the Interborough bought twenty memberships and the
B. R. T. a like number?

Mr. Quackenbush.— I don't know anything about it, if it was.
I think what the Senator has in mind I may say with accuracy
has not been the case.

Q. The $500,000 payment to J. P. Morgan & Company was
for service alleged to have been rendered in connection with the
first proposal? A. Yes, sir.

Q. And yet that proposal was abandoned with the failure of
the plan of adoption by the Board of Estimate? A. Yes, sir.

Mr. Quackenbush.— I do not want to interrupt, but Senator
Lawson made a statement I would like to add a word about, and
in reply to the Chairman. As to any matters concerning any
such organization as embraced within the inquiry of the Chairman, and the suggestion of Senator Lawson, I state the fact to
be of my knowledge that anything of that sort we have, we have
our membership perfectly open, and it is a thing we are entitled
to have, and our company is the largest taxpayer in the city of
New York, and we have interests in many localities, and I have
no hesitation in saying I think it would be very important, if we
had the time and could have members in each one of these things
so we could meet the people in the neighborhood face to face and
have a correct understanding of things. In the sense the Chairman means, in getting up pro forma meetings, there is nothing
in it.

Chairman Thompson.— I want to express my gratification at
the way Mr. Quackenbush and ourselves agree on moral questions
here.

Senator Lawson.— There is no question in your mind that it
has been the policy of street railways in Greater New York to
participate through their employees in civic matters. I do not
mean in any but a legitimate manner.

Mr. Quackenbush.— Some years ago there was a great deal of
that, and that is what the Chairman has in mind, but I say, and
I am speaking — the author of the phrase is well known. I do

not want to take your time. I want to make it plain there has
not been any of the acceleration you speak of.

Mr. Colby.— The following letter in the file is one dated
November 18, 1910, from the firm of J. P. Morgan & Company,
addressed to the President of the Rapid Transit Company.

Q. Was such a letter bearing date November 18, 1910, received
by your company? A. Yes, sir.

Mr. Colby reads the letter dated November 18, 1910, referred
to, in the record. It is as follows:

" NEW YORK, November 18, 1910

" Theodore P. Shonts, Esq., President,
  " Interborough Rapid Transit Company,
  " 165 Broadway, New York City.

" Dear Sir:

" Referring to our letter to you of September 15, 1910,
and your endorsement dated September 23, 1910, on a duplicate thereof, in which our agreement with your company
relative to a plan for financing your company is stated and
confirmed. In view of the delay in negotiations between
your company and the city which renders improbable the
issue of $30,000,000 of notes during the present month, as
contemplated at the date of our letter and your endorsement,
we are willing to agree that the time in which such notes shall
be issued to your company and sold to and purchased by us,
be extended to and including January 31, 1911, it being
agreed, however, that the notes shall be delivered at the
earliest possible moment after the franchise is granted; our
agreement in other respects to remain unchanged.

" If satisfactory, please advise us, and our letters will be
treated as a modification of the agreement in the one respect
above mentioned.

" Very truly yours,
" J. P. MORGAN & CO."

Accepted by T. P. Shonts, President.

Mr. Colby.— I find at the foot and in pen, as follows: "Accepted by T. P. Shonts, President."

Q. I am struck by some phrases employed in that letter, Mr. Fisher; it apparently is an extension by J. P. Morgan given to the Interborough Rapid Transit Company in the matter of the issuance of a large obligation; they say, "We are willing to agree that the time in which such notes shall be issued by your company and purchased by us be extended"; it looks as though they had a right to exact the making and delivery of these notes to you, and that you were delinquent in respect to the making and issuance of those obligations; is that not apparent from the letter? A. I don't think so.

Q. Isn't that suggested by the sentences and phrases? A. No, sir.

Q. In other words, a man who extends the time for the doing of a certain act is a man who has the right to exact the doing of the act; that is true as a generalization, isn't it? A. Not always.

Q. I say generally. A debtor, for instance, does not notify his creditors as a rule that he has extended the time for the payment of his debts, does he; it is the creditor says to the debtor, "I extend your time for the discharge of the obligation of yours that I hold"; here are Morgan & Company extending your time to issue $30,000,000 of your obligations; what is the explanation of those singular phrases? A. Without going into the correspondence any further, I think it was simply extending the time of the refunding operations of the various issues we had outstanding preliminary to the main bond issue. Those extensions of course were necessary by reason of the fact the contract had not been closed, and I assume you will find in the correspondence there the time was further extended.

Q. It could not be possible, as I must insist, these phrases suggested that Morgan & Company had any say or control as to when this company should make its obligations or in what amount? A. I have no knowledge of their ever having tried to exercise any such control, except in so far as was covered by agreement.

Chairman Thompson.— Is this an answer to a letter from the company?

Mr. Colby.— This refers to the letter of September 15, 1910, which outlined the first plan and formulated by Morgan & Company, which was not successful before the Board of Estimate; and this letter is one of November 18, 1911, which refers to their letter of September 15, 1910.

Chairman Thompson.— This letter was not in answer to a request of the Interborough for extension?

Mr. Colby.— Not so far as the letter discloses.

Chairman Thompson.— Or any other prior letter discloses?

Mr. Colby.— No, sir.

Mr. Colby also read into the record a further letter dated November 18, 1910:

"New York, November 18, 1910.

"Theodore P. Shonts, Esq., President,
  "Interborough Rapid Transit Company,
  "165 Broadway, New York City.

  "Dear Sir:

  "Enclosed herewith please find a copy of the letter passed to-day.

"Yours very truly,

"J. P. MORGAN & CO."

Q. What does that mean, Mr. Fisher? A. What is the date of that letter?

Q. They are both dated November 18th. A. I couldn't say, unless he wanted a copy for the purpose of endorsing on the bottom. I couldn't say what it was, otherwise than possibly that.

Q. I assume the letter dated April 27, 1911, you will testify is the letter received by Mr. Shonts from J. P. Morgan & Company? A. Yes, sir.

Mr. Colby read into the record the letter referred to, which is dated April 27, 1911, and is as follows:

"New York, April 27th, 1911.

"Theodore P. Shonts, Esq., President,
"Interborough Rapid Transit Company.
"165 Broadway, New York City.

"Dear Sir:

"We confirm the arrangement recently entered into with your company, by which we are to purchase and your company is to sell to us, at par, $10,000,000 face value of your company's one year 4½ per cent. notes, dated April 29, 1911, interest payable semi-annually, both principal and interest to be payable semi-annually, both principal and interest to be payable at our office, and by which we are to receive a commission of 1 per cent. of the face value of the notes for our services in connection with the matter — the proceeds of the notes, less such commission, to be credited on our books to your company, which is to be allowed interest at the rate of 2 per cent. per annum on the average daily credit balance of its account.

"It is understood that the time limit mentioned in the agreement between us and your company shown by our letter to you of September 15, 1910, and your acceptance dated September 23, 1910, relating to a plan for financing your company, is extended until June 1, 1911' and is not to be affected by the above arrangement.

"Please acknowledge receipt of this letter, and your acknowledgment will be our agreement on the subject.

"Very truly yours,

"J. P. MORGAN & CO."

Q. Now, why did your company issue ten million dollars of its 4½ per cent. notes at this time? A. I presume they were issued for some refund purpose. I couldn't say without having the correspondence there and looking at the facts. I think you will find all of those details will be included in a memorandum which the auditor is now preparing.

Q. Would a stipulation be made with reference to such a transaction that a certain amount should remain on deposit with Morgan & Company at 2 per cent? A. It usually is. The bankers usually stipulate that the proceeds shall remain on deposit, to be checked out as required.

Q. But if this was a refunding transaction, the entire amount would be necessary to pay and retire some notes whose maturity was either very close to hand or rapidly approaching? A. Notes are not always presented at maturity, all of them. I mean to say, in a refunding operation you seldom find all the notes or bonds presented at one time for redemption.

Q. I will get the details of that transaction. A. Yes, sir.

Q. The commission of the Morgan house on that transaction was $100,000; is that right? A. It was one per cent; yes, sir.

Q. On the par value? A. Yes, sir.

Q. You do not know the period of those notes? A. I think you said one year notes.

Q. What was the advantage in a one year note for refunding purposes? A. Without having that statement before me, I could not tell you.

Chairman Thompson.—We will suspend now until 2:30 o'clock. I want to direct the counsel to have the Gillespie subpoena served and returnable at 4 o'clock to-day.

Whereupon, at 1:15 o'clock P. M., a recess was taken to 2:30 o'clock P. M.

AFTERNOON SESSION

The Committee was called to order at 2:50 o'clock P. M., Senator Towner in the Chair.

H. M. FISHER, recalled.

By Mr. Colby:

Q. Have you your file there, Mr. Fisher? A. (Witness hands file to counsel.)

Q. Were you able, in the short time at lunch, to find the details of that — of the note transaction mentioned in the letter of April

27? A. I didn't look for it because the statement is again prepared in the form that I don't think would answer your purpose.

Q. You think this all right, now? A. I don't think it will answer your purpose, so that I will have to prepare it myself between now and Monday, and I will do it.

Q. I will just make a note of that and go on. The next letter that I come across in the files — in the file — is apparently a reply by the president of the Interborough Rapid Transit Company to the Morgan letter of April 27. Is the copy that I hand you a copy of President Shonts' letter of April 28, 1911? A. Yes, sir.

Q. Sent to Morgan & Company? A. Yes, sir.

Q. I will read the letter of Mr. Shonts:

"April 28, 1911.

"Messrs. J. P. Morgan & Company, No. 23 Wall street, New York city.

"Dear Sirs.— I am in receipt of your letter of April 27, 1911, embracing the terms upon which you have purchased from the Interborough Rapid Transit Company the $10,000,000 face value of the company's 4½ per cent. notes, dated April 29, 1911. I beg to confirm the financial arrangement with your firm with respect to the said issue of notes as set forth in your letter. I further confirm the understanding that the general financial arrangements set forth in your letter to the Interborough Rapid Transit Company, dated September 23, 1911, is extended to June 1, 1912, and that the arrangement therein set forth is not affected by the notice you above refer to.

"Yours very truly,

. . . .

"President."

I don't find J. P. Morgan & Company's letter of September 23, 1910, Mr. Fisher. A. You have got the entire set of correspondence there, haven't you? It may be in that.

Mr. Quackenbush.— Isn't that the big letter with the red on it?

Mr. Colby.— That is September 15, 1910. I think I see the — I think I see this. Well, no. I would like you to ascertain if there is such a letter as the letter of September 23, 1910. It appears on the letter of September 15, 1910, that under that date the Interborough agreed to and accepted the offer of the proposals contained in the Morgan letter of September 15. It may be that addendum to the Morgan letter which Mr. Shonts refers to as under date of September 23, and yet he refers to a letter to the Interborough Rapid Transit Company of September 23.

Mr. Quackenbush.— I think the file is complete there.

Mr. Fisher.— No, that file is the contract file. It is not the complete file. If a letter has no reference to the arrangement with Mr. Morgan for furnishing the money, it would not be in the file.

Mr. Colby.— But this plainly has, I should say. We will look that up, Mr. Chairman.

Mr. Quackenbush.— September 23 —

Mr. Colby.— 1910. Morgan to the Interborough Company.

By Mr. Colby:

Q. There follows copy of a letter written apparently by the president of the company to Mr. Morgan, Jr. Is the copy of a letter — is this copy purporting to be under date of March 1, 1912, a copy of the letter sent by the president to Mr. Morgan, March 1, 1912? A. Yes, sir.

Q. I will read it:

"My dear Mr. Morgan.— Referring to the agreement between our company, yourself and syndicate associates, in which we agree to pay you $250,000 for financial commitments, which agreement was approved by our board November 29, 1911, on condition that an agreement should be entered into between the Interborough Company and the city for the construction of subway extensions and elevated improvements prior to March 1, 1912, I now beg leave to confirm our understanding of our talk this morning in which you very kindly consented to extend this date thirty days from to-day.

" Very truly yours,

. . . .

" President.

" To Mr. J. P. Morgan, Jr.
" 23 Wall street, New York city."

I have not seen any agreement in writing between the company and Mr. Morgan with reference to that $250,000, Mr. Fisher. A. I don't think there is anything but a letter from Mr. Morgan there. I think you have got a copy of it, probably. That file is all there is on the subject.

Q. And Mr. Shonts does not necessarily refer in this letter, in your opinion, to any written agreement on the subject? A. I did not understand it so.

Q. Wasn't it November 29, 1911, the date of the actual payment of this money? A. I think it was, yes, sir; the date of the resolution.

Q. That apparently is the fact? A. Yes, sir.

Q. And yet Mr. Shonts, referring on March 1, 1912, some five months later — four months later, at least — referring to the agreement between " our company, yourself and syndicate managers, in which we agree to pay you $250,000, I now beg leave to confirm my understanding of our talk this morning in which you very kindly consented to extend this date " ? A. I think you will find that — that refers to the extension of the date of the applying of the $250,000 on the commissions of any subsequent bond issue, not on the payment of the money.

Q. Mr. Shonts, in other words, was endeavoring to preserve the company's right to offset this amount — A. Yes, sir.

Q. — to the bankers' commissions as they might be earned? A. Yes, sir.

Q. And he got an extension from the bankers of thirty days before that payment should be deemed conclusive and irrevocable? A. Yes, sir, and I think three weeks' additional.

Q. On March 1, 1912, Messrs. Morgan & Company seemed to have addressed you a letter. They did, did they? A. Yes, sir.

Q. And is that the letter that was received (showing paper to witness)? A. Yes, sir.

Q. "*March* 1, 1912.

" To Theodore P. Shonts, *President.*

" Dear Sir.—We beg to acknowledge receipt of your favor of March 1st addressed to our Mr. Morgan, Jr., and note contents. It will be agreeable to us to accede to your request as therein expressed, to extend for thirty days, namely, to April 1, 1912, the period within which the payment of $250,-000 made by you on November 29, 1911, shall cover the commitments of our syndicate associates under an agreement which will be entered into by your company and the City of New York for the construction of subways," and so forth.

" Yours very truly,

"J. P. Morgan & Company."

And follows a further letter from J. P. Morgan & Company, dated March 29, 1912, which I assume the company duly received from Morgan & Company? A. Yes, sir.

Q. Which I will read:

" New York, *March* 29, 1912.

" T. P. Shonts, Esq., *President.*

" Dear Sir.—We beg to confirm our telephonic conversation this day, in the course of which it was agreed that we will extend the arrangement with you in regard to the $250,000 advanced for new commitments, for a further period of three weeks from April 1, 1912. Trusting that this will be satisfactory and that the agreement may be made before the end of this time, we are, dear sir,

" Yours very truly,

" J. P. Morgan & Company."

Now follows the letter of April 9. 1912, which has already been read, and quite fully commented upon, and I will simply offer that as a part of the file, so that the stenographer may preserve a copy of it. This is the letter, Mr. Chairman, in which J. P. Morgan & Company set forth a new financial plan, the financial plan contained in the letter of September 5, 1910, having, as you will recall, failed of approval and of adoption by the City authorities in July of 1911. In the meantime I expect that the efforts of the intermediaries, the disinterested intermediaries had borne fruit, and the matter was apparently resumed in the form of a revised proposal by the banking firm. I understand that there was no further extension after the expiration of the three weeks on April 1st in connection with the $250,000 paid to Mr. Morgan for commitments of his syndicate associates? A. That is correct.

Q. That was the final extension? A. Yes, sir.

Q. That payment became absolute upon the expiration of that final period of three weeks? A. Yes, sir.

Q. And yet, before that final expiration of three weeks had expired, we find Mr. Morgan writing Mr. Shonts: "As the negotiations of the Interborough Rapid Transit Company with the City authorities appear to be approaching completion, we take this opportunity of setting forth the agreement between your company and ourselves, relative to the finances of your company, to enable it to carry out its agreement with the City." That is true, isn't it? A. Yes, sir.

Q. And yet, although J. P. Morgan & Company had willingly granted extensions, first of a month and then of three weeks, then the negotiations took on this promising appearance, no further extensions were granted, although the new plan had been entered upon before the expiration of the final extension? A. The preliminaries, I think, had been entered upon. I don't think the final arrangements had been made.

Q. But that payment of $250,000 became absolute some ten or twelve days subsequent to the writing of this letter in which is recited the hopeful and promising aspiration of the negotiations? A. I understand so.

Q. This is the letter in which occurs the paragraph already read, to the effect that it is fully understood that the entire transaction above outlined depends upon the legality and constitutionality of the contract between the City and your company being confirmed by the courts, and that no action under this agreement is to be taken on either side until all parties are satisfied as to the legal enforceability of such contract? A. Yes, sir.

Mr. Colby.— You will take a copy of this, stenographer.

(Letter referred to is as follows):

"INTERBOROUGH RAPID TRANSIT COMPANY
"165 Broadway

"THEODORE P. SHONTS, *President and Chairman of Executive Committee.*

"NEW YORK, *Apr.* 9, 1912.

"GENTLEMEN.— The City of New York and the Interborough Rapid Transit Company have agreed upon a contract by which the City and the Interborough Rapid Transit Company shall build, and the Interborough Rapid Transit Company equip and operate, extensions to the present subway, particulars of which are fully set forth and described in the enclosed analysis of the proposal of the Interborough Rapid Transit Company to the city. The agreement has been entered into subject, on both sides, to the reservation that it shall be passed upon by the Courts before any action is taken under it, and all agreements suggested in this letter are to be taken subject to the same provision.

"The sum estimated to be required for the construction of the new subway is $112,000,000, of which sum the Interborough Rapid Transit Company agrees to contribute one-half. Should the construction cost exceed this amount, the city agrees to furnish the additional amount required.

"Under the terms of the contract, the Interborough Rapid Transit Company will modify its present leases, fixing the expiration of all its subway leases at 49 years from the completion of the new subways. The Company will be authorized to take annually during this period from the aggregate net earnings of the old and new subways the sum of $6,335,000, being the average amount of the net earnings during the last two years on the present subway; also the sum of $4,620,000, the equivalent of 5 per cent. interest, and one

per cent. sinking fund, on the investment by the Interborough Rapid Transit Company of $77,000,000 of new
money, viz.: $56,000,000, the company's contribution toward
the cost of construction, and $21,000,000, the estimated total
cost of equipping the new subways. These payments are to be
a first charge on such net earnings, and are to be cumulative.

" MANHATTAN RAILWAY COMPANY.   The Interborough
Rapid Transit Company is lessee of the Manhattan Railway
Company, which owns the elevated railways in New York
city and receives authority, under the agreement with the
city, to make extensions and additions, including third tracks
on the Second Avenue, Third Avenue and Ninth Avenue
elevated lines.

" The estimated cost of these extensions, additions and
equipment of same is approximately $30,000,000. The city
and the Interborough Rapid Transit Company agree to
divide equally the additional earnings produced by these
extensions beyond interest and sinking fund of the new
money invested. The average profits of the Manhattan Railway Company lease for the past two years have been approximately $1,500,000 per annum.

" The amounts required to be raised by the Interborough
Rapid Transit Company are as follows:

For refunding its present debt............	$50,656,950
For construction of new subway (Inter- borough Company's one-half)...........	56,000,000
For Manhattan Railway Improvements, about	30,000,000
For equipment of new subways...........	21,000,000
For other charges including discounts, about.	9,500,000
	$167,156,950

" In order to procure the necessary funds to carry out this
contract, and retire its present debt, the Interborough Rapid
Transit Company proposes to issue new first mortgage 5
per cent. fifty-three year gold bonds to the amount of about
$170,000,000. The mortgage securing these bonds will also

16

provide for the issue of such additional amounts of bonds as may be needed for extensions and improvements as may be authorized by the city and agreed to by the company during the period of the lease — as provided in the agreement.

"A sinking fund of 1 per cent will be provided for, to begin five years from the date of opening the new subways or in any event not more than ten years from the date of the bonds. Bonds may be drawn for the sinking fund at 110, or bought in the market at a lower price, and by the operation of the sinking fund, will be paid off during the term of the lease.

" Our company has agreed to sell to you and you have agreed to buy from it about $170,000,000 of these bonds to provide for the company's financial requirements for construction and equipment of the new subways, elevated extensions and improvements, and to refund the present debt of the company, the bonds to be taken and paid for as follows:

During the year from July 1, 1912 to June 30, 1913	$78,000,000
During the year from July 1, 1913 to June 30, 1914	30,000,000
During the year from July 1, 1914, to June 30, 1915	30,000,000
During the year from July 1, 1915, to June 30, 1916, not more than	32,000,000
	$170,000,000

"All or any part of such annual installment of bonds may be taken and paid for by you at any time during the year.

" Your company has further agreed that the syndicate which you will form to take these bonds will divide equally with this company any amount received on the sale of the bonds in excess of an average price of par and accrued interest.

" When the subways are completed, the Interborough Rapid Transit Company will have a prior claim on the net earnings of the properties, which claim will aggregate, $14,568,000.

" This is made up as follows:

Average annual earnings of present subway during the last two years..............	$6,335,000
Five per cent. interest and 1 per cent. annual sinking fund on $77,000,000, the amount of Interborough's new investment in subways	4,620,000
Interest and annual sinking fund on approximately $30,000,000 new capital invested in elevated railways	1,800,000
Profits from Manhattan Railway lease and other income which during the last two years have averaged annually...........	1,813,000

" During the past two years the average annual net earnings of the present properties including profits from the Manhattan Railway lease and other income have been, $8,148,000.

" Including the $56,000,000 of new money provided by the city there will be, when the new subways and elevated extensions are completed, a new investment in additional subways and elevated properties amounting to $163,000,000 and it is conservatively estimated that during the first four years' operation after the new subways are opened, the additional earnings from the new investment should average at least 3 per cent. thereon or, say (including Manhattan), $4,890,000 and that beginning with the fourth year the earnings should amount to at least 4½ per cent on the new investment, or say $6,927,500.

" Or, in other words, after the third year of the operation of the new subways, the aggregate annual net earnings of the properties should be at least $15,075,000

" The annual interest upon the total issue
of $170,000,000 of new bonds will be....... $8,500,000
and the annual sinking fund upon the same
which will not begin, however, until five years
after the enlarged system is put into operation,
will be 1,700,000

" During the construction period interest has been provided for as part of the cost of the work.

"As indicated above, when the new subways are open for
operation, the earnings of the property will show from the
start an ample margin above all fixed charges.

" Very truly yours,

" T. P. SHONTS,

" President.

" Messrs. J. P. Morgan & Company,
" 23 Wall street, New York city."

By Mr. Colby:

Q. There follows a letter apparently written by President
Shonts under the date of April 12, 1912. He wrote a letter to
Morgan & Company under that date of which that is a copy? A.
Yes, sir.

Q. I read:

" April 12, 1912.

" Gentlemen.—Your letter of April 9, 1912, accords with
our understanding of the arrangement for the sale to you by
the Interborough Rapid Transit Company of approximately
$170,000,000 of bonds as therein outlined. I hereby, on
behalf of the Interborough Rapid Transit Company, confirm
such sale according to the terms of your letter, such confirmation being especially authorized by resolution of the board of
directors of the Interborough Rapid Transit Company, of
which I enclose a copy."

Next in order in the file, but apparently dated on April 12 —
April 9, is a letter addressed to J. P. Morgan & Company by the
president of your company, containing some interesting estimates
of costs of building, earnings, estimated returns to the bankers,

estimated returns to the city. This is a letter written by Mr. Shonts to the bankers, under date of April 9, 1912? A. Yes, sir.

Q. I will read this letter:

"*April* 9, 1912.

"Gentlemen.— The City of New York and the Interborough Rapid Transit Company have agreed upon a contract by which the City and the Interborough Rapid Transit Company shall build, and the Interborough Rapid Transit Company equip and operate extensions to the present subway, particulars of which are fully set forth and described in the enclosed analysis of the proposal of the Interborough Rapid Transit Company to the City. The agreement has been entered into subject on both sides to the reservation that it shall be passed upon by the courts before any action is taken under it, and all agreements suggested in this letter are to be taken subject to the same provision."

I suppose that is a reference to the suit of the Admiral Realty Company, or, at least, that is the idea which was subsequently carried out by the suit of the Admiral Realty Company? A. I think it is possible. I don't think it had that suit in view, though.

Q. Not that particular name of the plaintiff, possibly, but some suit or proceeding of that kind?   A. Had some suit in view, yes, sir.

Q. In other words, an action which should test the validity of the proposed contracts? A. That is right.

Q. And apparently this was not only Mr. Morgan's stipulation as disclosed in his letter of the same date, but was an understanding or agreement to which the City was a party as well as Mr. Morgan, Mr. Shonts saying: "The agreement has been entered into subject on both sides to the reservation that it shall be passed upon by the courts before any action is taken under it"? A. I think the city was anxious to secure a decision, the same as Messrs. Morgan & Company and the Interborough.

Q. So that when this action reached the courts, there was really no agreement, much less a controversy?

(Senator Thompson takes the Chair.)

A. I understand it was properly contested. You are referring now to the Admiral Realty case?

Q. Yes —

Chairman Thompson.— Mr. Bordwell, what about that subpoena that you had on Mr. Gillespie?

Mr. Bordwell.— The subpoena was turned over to me to serve on Thomas H. Gillespie, vice-president of the T. A. Gillespie Company. I called there about 2:15. About five minutes ago they came out and asked me whom I wanted. I said: "Thomas H. Gillespie, Vice-president of T. A. Gillespie Company." They stated he had gone out to lunch and they did not know whether he would be back to-day or not. They would 'phone me about four o'clock — if I called up — whether I could get in touch with him or not.

Chairman Thompson.—Well, you can make a subpoena in blank and take a man with you and go down and find out the name of whoever is there in charge of the office, and subpoena him here forthwith, with these books and papers.

(Senator Towner takes the Chair.)

By Mr. Colby:

Q. The point I am trying to state with fairness upon the record seems to be clearly suggested in this letter, and I don't wish to say more than the letter says, but it is apparent that the agreement was subject to a reservation on both sides, that it had been even entered into subject to the validation of its terms and of its effect by a court action. And until that court action was had, there was not only no real controversy between the parties to this suit, but there was no agreement out of which a controversy could arise. Isn't that obvious? A. I don't see any connection between the letter which you refer to and the suit which I believe you have in mind. It was understood —

Q. Let me see if I cannot develop that connection. Mr. Morgan, in his letter of September 9 — of April 9, 1912, says: "It is fully understood that the entire transaction above outlined depends upon the legality and constitutionality of the contract between the City and your Company being confirmed by the courts, and that no action under this agreement is to be taken on either side until all parties are satisfied as to the legal enforceability of such contract and of the bonds hereinabove mentioned." That is the statement in the Morgan letter of that date ? A. Yes.

Q. On the same date, Mr. Shonts, writing Morgan & Company, goes further. He does not say, " No action shall be taken under the agreement until the courts have validated it." He says, " The agreement has been entered into subject on both sides to the reservation that it shall be passed upon by the courts before any action is taken under it "? A. Certainly.

Q. In other words, the agreement was a mere tentative agreement, the mere semblance of an agreement, the mere form as distinguished from the substance and fact of an agreement, until this court action ? A. It was understood that the court action was to be taken to test the validity of the contract and the mortgage.

Q. Had this court action not been taken, there would have been no agreement, would there ? A. Probably not.

Q. Until this action was prosecuted to final judgment, and a decree validating the provisions of the agreement, it was a nothing, wasn't it ? A. Correct.

Q. Although it was signed, sealed, and although it recited the agreement as of a certain date and the — A. It does not —

Q. Well, of course, I mean to say, that although it recited an agreement as having been entered into by the parties as of a certain date, and although the parties had thereunto set their hands and seals, it was purely prospective and tentative, dependent upon court action before it became operative as an agreement ? A. It does not state what steps were to be taken to secure this court action.

Q. No; that is quite true, Mr. Fisher; but it does say that the agreement has been entered into subject to the reservation on both sides that it shall be passed upon by the courts before any action is taken on it ? A. It is quite possible that when Mr. Shonts found the Admiral Realty had brought an action to test the validity of the contract, he thought that action would answer as well as any other, and that he took advantage of it. Have you thought of placing that construction upon the letter? A. I confess I had not, because it would be quite an extraordinary coincidence that an action to test the constitutionality of this important agreement should happen along by a street car, Mr. Shonts, with this very important stipulation with the banking house of Morgan & Company, and an agreement with the City of New York, should simply say: "This is in exact conformity with the mutual agreements of ourselves and our bankers and our board"? A. I don't think any doubt can be thrown on that action. I think that other parties intervened that could not be accused of being friendly.

Q. I am not accusing anyone of even friendliness. I am simply endeavoring to explore the facts. You don't know when the Admiral Realty Company action was brought? A. I don't.

Q. Or to whom the president refers as having assented on the part of the city to that proposition? A. I don't.

Q. You don't know whether the agreement was actually exchanged between the parties pending the completion of this legal test, do you? A. I saw no such agreement.

Q. You would hardly say that there was an actual controversy between the original parties to this suit as to the constitutionality of the Interborough's proposed agreement with the City? A. I prefer to let our legal force inform me on that point.

Q. Maybe I had better defer that question. I will continue the reading of Mr. Shonts' interesting letter of April 9:

"The sum estimated to be required for the construction of the new subway is $112,000,000, of which sum the Interborough Rapid Transit Company agrees to contribute one-half. Should the construction cost exceed this amount, the City agrees to furnish the additional amount required.

"Under the terms of the contract, the Interborough Rapid Transit Company will modify its present leases, fixing the expiration of all its subway leases at forty-nine years from the completion of the new subways. The Company will be authorized to take annually during this period from the aggregate net earnings of the old and new subways the sum of $6,335,000, being the average amount of the net earnings during the last two years on the present subway; also the sum of

$4,620,000, the equivalent of five per cent. interest, and one per cent. Sinking Fund, on the investment by the Interborough Rapid Transit Company of $77,000,000 of new money, viz.: $56,000,000, the Company's contribution toward the cost of construction, and $21,000,000, the estimated total cost of equipping the new subways. These payments are to be a first charge on such net earnings, and are to be cumulative."

In other words, Mr. Fisher, the Interborough not only carries such payments as the Shonts bonus into construction account, but it is entitled to five per cent. interest on that item and other similar items, and also a one per cent. contribution to a sinking fund, to ultimately extinguish those charges from the proceeds of operation, and in preference to any participation by the City; that is true, isn't it? A. Are you using that letter as a basis of your conclusions?

Q. I am using that statement there. A. That letter is based on the operations of the company after the subways are completed, and the operations begin.

Q. Well, it is a fact that Mr. Shonts states, in outlining the proposed arrangement and the arrangement that was made, to his bankers, not to the purchasers of the bonds, not to the citizens of New York, not to the members of his board of directors, but to the bankers, a serious to some extent, confidential and intimate representation of the basis under which the bankers' participation was invited? A. Nothing confidential about it.

Q. Good. A. If you get the contract, you will see the terms are laid down.

Q. Does the contract then provide that the company shall be entitled in addition to $6,335,000, to five per cent. interest and one per cent. sinking fund on its contribution towards the cost of construction? A. It certainly does.

Q. That is all I am bringing out. It has been already testified to the Shonts bonus, which I will take as a — as representative of a number of other debatable entries to construction account, has already reached construction account? A. You are now mixing the construction account with operating account.

Q. Mr. Gaynor testified that the Shonts bonus goes to construction account. A. Yes, sir. But we are not speaking of that bonus in this letter.

Q. I am speaking of bonus, but the letter speaks of construction account. A. That is the cost of construction, the amount of money we issued bonds for.

Q. In other words, there is the total of construction account. The Shonts bonus enters into construction account, and the company is entitled to five per cent. interest and one per cent. sinking fund — A. On the total amount of its bonds issued for construction purpose. That includes all items included in construction.

Q. We don't disagree. I will continue to read:

> " Manhattan Railway Company. The Interborough Rapid Transit Company is lessee of the Manhattan Railway Company, which owns the elevated railways in New York City, and receives authority, under the agreement with the City, to make extensions and additions, including third track on the Second avenue, Third avenue and Ninth avenue elevated lines. The estimated costs of these extensions, additions and equipment of same is approximately $30,000,000. The City and the Interborough Rapid Transit Company agree to divide equally the additional earnings produced by these extensions beyond interest and sinking fund on the new money invested. The average profits of the Manhattan Railway Company lease for the past two years have been approximately $1,500,000 per annum."

How are you going to compute the profits arising from these extensions? How are you going to estimate the additional earnings produced by these extensions? A. That you will have to ask the auditor.

(Senator Thompson takes the Chair.)

Q. There is not a prospect of very much division to the city on that aspect of the contract, is there, Mr. Fisher? A. I think there is a very good prospect.

Q. If the cost of the extensions and the additions is $30,000-000, and the additional earnings that are divisible with the city, are first subject to deduction for interest and sinking fund on the new money invested —

(Chairman Thompson and Mr. Colby confer together.)

By Mr. Colby:

Q. Now, the amounts required to be raised by the Interborough Rapid Transit Company are as follows:

For refunding the present debt................	$50,656,950
For construction of new subway (Interborough Company's one-half)	56,000,000
For Manhattan Railway improvements, about....	30,000,000
For equipment of new subways................	21,000,000
For other charges including discounts, about.....	9,500,000

The totals of the amounts required to be raised by the Interborough Rapid Transit Company, amounting to $167,156,950? A. That is approximately correct.

Mr. Colby.— Do you wish to interrupt this, Senator?

Chairman Thompson.— Go ahead. Well, I will read this letter in the record. I just received it in the mail from John C. Wilson.

" Washington, February 10, 1916 "— inasmuch as it comes from the largest stockholder in the Interborough Railroad, I thought I would not hold it:

" To the Thompson Legislative Committee, New York city.

" Gentleman.— I am, and have been for the last fifteen years the largest individual stockholder in the Interborough Rapid Transit Company, my holdings being about ten times as great as the combined holdings of all the directors.

" I have long believed that the directors have taken advantage "—

Mr. Colby.— There is no John C. Wilson?

Mr. Quackenbush.— He is a stockholder.

Mr. Colby.— The largest?

Mr. Quackenbush.— I would not say that.

Chairman Thompson.— I don't want any advantage taken over anybody. If you think it is a lunatic's letter, treat it accordingly. I just opened it.

(Questions by newspaper men.)

Mr. Quackenbush.— I don't assume this is going to take this character, quite. I don't think you mean that.

Chairman Thompson.— What?

Mr. Quackenbush.— That the secretary is going to answer questions from all the gentlemen in the room.

Chairman Thompson.— Mr. John C. Wilson writes the letter from the Cosmos Club, Washington, D. C., and I just received it.

Mr. Quackenbush.— I understand, perfectly.

Chairman Thompson.— If the statement is true that he is the largest stockholder individually, and owns ten times the amount of stock that all the directors combined own, why, it becomes important as an interest in this matter. I did not like to hold it over Sunday, that is all. We are going to adjourn in a half hour or so.

Mr. Colby.— It seems to me possibly that very material fact, if that is the fact, of which the letter's interest depends, might be well to ascertain.

Chairman Thompson.— Well, do you know Mr. Wilson?

Mr. Fisher.— Yes, sir.

Chairman Thompson.— Is he an intelligent citizen?

Mr. Fisher.— Yes, sir.

Chairman Thompson.— And this would not be regarded as a crank letter?

Mr. Fisher.— No; I would regard it as a letter from a chronic kicker.

Mr. Colby.— Do you know how much stock he owns?

Mr. Fisher.— 2,700 shares.

Mr. Colby.— Is there a larger interest than that?

Mr. Fisher.— I could not say what the other interests are. The total amount of stock outstanding is 11,872 shares.

Chairman Thompson.— Then, if you will come to order I can read the letter, and you can all have it.

"I am and have been for the last fifteen years, the largest individual stockholder in the Interborough R. T. Co. My holdings being about ten times as great as the combined holdings of all the directors.

"I have long believed that the directors have taken advantage of their position to make personal profits for themselves and their friends through the payment of unnecessary and excessive salaries, bonuses, commissions, &c., and I have endeavored to the best of my ability to expose and thwart them.

"I have opposed the making of contract No. 3 with the City because it involved an expense to the Co. in commissions, fees, &c., of about $13,000,000, with no possible advantage to the Co. & the possibility of enormous loss.

"I want to see the methods of the directors and other officers thoroughly exposed by your Committee & I ask leave to suggest the bringing out of the following facts:

"I. That the entire Board of Directors at the time of the stockholders meeting, in 1913, held 245 shares of stock & had held about that amount for some years previous. My share of the $150,000 bonus voted to Mr. Shonts without my knowledge or consent, amounted to $1,071.00. The share of all the Directors amounted to about one tenth of that sum; so in regard to the bonuses to Mr. Rogers and Mr. Gaynor.

"II. That altho' the Directors publish an annual report & hold an annual stock-holders' meeting, the reports contain no reference to the payments, which have been unearthed by your Committee. I have repeatedly tried by letters & by questions at the stock-holders' meetings to learn what salaries were being paid to the directors & officers; the information has always been refused. The evidence before your Committee gave me my first knowledge.

"III. In the balance sheet in the report for 1913 is an item:

"Unamortized debt, disc. & exp. (Contract No. 3), $1,042,795. I asked for an explanation of this item, showing what the money was paid for, who got it & whether any officer or director got any part of it. All explanation was refused.

"There is nowhere, in any of the annual reports, any reference to the enormous payments to lawyers brought out by your Committee.

"IV. In a letter dated 27 June, 1911, to the Public Service Commission and Board of Estimate and Apportionment, Theodore P. Shonts says, in answer to the city's offer: ' The margin of safety in our offer of May 9th was so narrow that the introduction of the Broadway Competitive Route reducing our estimated revenues by not less than $5,000,000 a year, would have made it impossible for us to carry that offer into effect.' Then, after giving some expert estimates of the probable increase in travel, he continues: ' This showing not only would defer forever the prospect of any dividend returns whatsoever to the Interborough Co., but would involve it in an actual deficit upon the bonds which it must assume as a fixed obligation.' The contract eventually made, and for obtaining which Mr. Shonts claimed and received a bonus of $150,000, Mr. Rogers $50,000 and many lawyers enormous fees, was subject to all the objections cited by Mr. Shonts. Besides these sums, the bonus paid for the redemption of the outstanding mortgage and the discount on 170,-000,000 of bonds amounted to $12,700,000. Did ever corporation buy trouble at such a price?

"V. Three separate actions have been commenced against August Belmont and other directors of the company: — one by Clarence Venner, one by Fred'k Ayer, and one by me, to compel them to account to the company for several millions, the value of stock issued to them, in contravention of the laws of New York, upon consideration so grossly inadequate as to amount to fraud. The Venner case, after many hearings and appeals, on technical points, was at last heard on the merits and decided against Venner. It is now pending in the Court of Appeals. These cases are in no sense attacks on the credit of the company or suits against the company, on the contrary they are suits on behalf of the company and are brought by stockholders because the directors naturally refused to bring suit against themselves. If successful no money would be payable to the plaintiffs, except their expenses. The accounting would be to the company.

"And yet Nicoll & Anable have claimed and received from the company fees for resisting these efforts to compel treacherous trustees to pay back to the company the money of which it has been deprived. Mr. Nichol appears to have been in the employ of the company since it was organized. On the scale of his fees, disclosed to you, he must have drawn from it hundreds of thousands greatly to the personal profit of the directors. The result to the company, which paid his fees, will appear from an examination of the following deals, made presumably under his legal advice:

" $1,500,000 of the company's stock paid to Belmont & Co. for certain securities, which a few months before had cost Belmont & Co. $270,000 (which were useless and worthless to the company) and for certain indefinite services of Belmont & Co., who were at that time being paid a large salary as financial agents of the parties in interest:

" $9,600,000 in stock paid to Belmont and other directors for the stock of the R. T. Subway Construction Co., which had cost them $3,600,000 and had not earned anything (the Interborough Co. afterwards paid up $2,400,000 on this stock and in nearly fourteen years has received one dividend of $900,000);

" $2,500,000 paid to McDonald, Belmont and other directors and their associates for the McDonald contract which had cost them nothing, and the value of which at that time was purely problematical;

" $7,000,000 invested at or near par in the purchase of

stocks and bonds of the New York & Queens Co. Ry. and in advances to that company, which at the time of the purchase was practically bankrupt, which has never paid a dividend and as far as I can ascertain, has never earned the interest on its bonds;

" $10,839,130 invested in the Belmont tunnel which was never operated and was finally sold to the city for $3,000,000 subject to a deduction of about $500,000 for taxes.

" There are other transactions in the past reflecting as little credit on the management; but as they are not connected with the contract between the City and the company, I will not trespass further on the patience of your committee.

" Respectfully,

" JOHN C. WILSON,

"Address: Cosmos Club, Washington."

Mr. Quackenbush.—You will note in that letter that Mr. Venner is a plaintiff in the actions against the company involving these very questions in his letter, and he also states that the Supreme Court has decided those questions against Mr. Venner, in favor of the company.

Chairman Thompson.— The only consideration I had here, of course, is it annoys and bothers counsel with the matters at issue. It came in a few minutes ago. It was important because it came from the largest individual stockholder. It was important because it came from a stockholder, and it is important to know that the Committee's progress so far under the way the matters have been proved here, has met with approbation up as high as the stockholders of the company.

Mr. Quackenbush.— The only thing that could be added would be that the subjects that the Committee are now investigating in this letter have also met with the approval of the Supreme Court of the State of New York in behalf of the Interborough.

Chairman Thompson.— Not wanting to have any more question about any papers, I wanted to get it in as quick as possible.

Mr. Fisher.— I would like to make a little explanation on his being the largest stockholder. He is the largest individual outstanding stockholder — that is, stock outstanding of course, you understand that the Interborough Consolidated Corporation owns 339,128 shares, against 11,872 shares outstanding. I just wanted to make that plain.

Mr. Colby.— It seems inconceivable that that holding is the largest holding, individual holding in the company. I think Mr. Fisher has made that clear. However, I will not — it cannot be gainsaid it is a substantial stockholding interest.

Mr. Quackenbush.— No question about it. Mr. Venner also has some considerable shares of stock.

Mr. Colby.— Well, now, shall I resume this estimate by the President of the Company —

Chairman Thompson.— For half or three-quarters of an hour.

(Senator Towner takes the Chair.)

Mr. Colby.— Yes. Of the earnings, the indicated earnings of the proposed new subways, the agreed mode of division, the amounts that would accrue to the bankers or to the company first, and the amounts that might at some future period accrue to the City of New York. Mr. Chairman, I had just concluded reading Mr. Shonts' estimates of the amounts to be raised by the Interborough Rapid Transit Company under this proposed new plan, and they aggregated $167,156,950.

Mr. Shonts continues:

> " In order to procure the necessary funds to carry out this contract, and retire its present Debt, the Interborough Rapid Transit Company proposes to issue new First Mortgage Five Per Cent. Fifty-three-Year Gold Bonds to the amount of about $170,000,000. The Mortgage securing these bonds will also provide for the issue of such additional amounts of bonds as may be needed for extensions and improvements as may be authorized by the City and agreed to by the Company during the period of the lease — as provided in the agreement.

"A Sinking Fund of One Per Cent. will be provided for, to begin five years from the date of opening the new subways or in any event not more than ten years from the date of the bonds. Bonds may be drawn for the Sinking Fund at 110, or bought in the market at a lower price, and by the operation of the Sinking Fund will be paid off during the term of the lease.

" Our Company has agreed to sell to you and you have agreed to buy from it about $170,000,000 of these bonds to provide for the Company's financial requirements for construction and equipment of the new subways, elevated extensions and improvements, and to refund the present debt of the Company, the bonds to be taken and paid for as follows:

During the year from July 1st, 1912 to June
   30th, 1913 .... $78,000,000
During the year from July 1st, 1913 to June
   30th, 1914 30,000,000
During the year from July 1st, 1914 to June
   30, 1915 30,000,000
During the year from July 1st, 1915 to June
   30th, 1916, not more than............. 32,000,000

                                 $170,000,000

"All or any part of such annual installment of bonds may be taken and paid for by you at any time during the year.

" Your Company has further agreed that the syndicate which you will form to take these bonds will divide equally with this Company any amount received on the sale of the bonds in excess of an average price of par and accrued interest.

" When the subways are completed, the Interborough Rapid Transit Company will have a prior claim on the net earnings of the properties, which claim will aggregate $14,568,000.

" This as made up as follows:

Average annual earnings of present subway
   during the last two years.............. $6,335,000

Five per cent. interest and 1 per cent. annual
sinking fund on $77,000,000, the amount of
the Interborough's new investment in
subways $4,620,000

Interest and annual sinking fund on approximately $30,000,000 new capital invested in
elevated railways   1,800,000

Profits for Manhattan Railway Lease and
other income which during the last two years
have averaged annually   1,813,000

During the past two years the average annual
net earnings of the present properties including profits from the Manhattan Railway
lease and other income have been $8,148,000

" Including the $56,000,000 of new money provided by
the City there will be, when the new subways and elevated
extensions are completed, a new investment in additional
subways and elevated properties amounting to $163,000,000,
and it is conservatively estimated that during the first four
years' operation after the new subways are opened, the additional earnings from the new investment should average at
least three per cent. thereon, or, say (including Manhattan)
$4,890,000, and that beginning with the fourth year, the earn-
ings should amount to at least 4¼ per cent. on the new investment or, say, $6,927,500. Or, in other words, after the third
year of the operation of the new subways, the aggregate
annual net earnings of the properties should be at least
$15,075,500. The annual interest upon the issue of
$170,000,000 of new bonds, will be $8,500,000, and the
annual sinking fund upon the same, which will not begin,
however, until five years after the enlarged system is put in
operation, will be $1,700,000. During the construction
period, interest has been provided for as part of the cost of
the work.

"As indicated above, when the new subways are open for
operation, the earnings of the property will show from the
start an ample margin above all fixed charges."

By Mr. Colby:

Q. By "fixed charges," the president of the company undoubtedly refers to interest upon the total issue of new bonds, did
he not? A. Yes, sir.

Q. That amounts to $8,500,000? A. Yes, sir.

Q. And that is the sum which he has in mind when he says,
when the new subways are opened for operation, the earnings will
show from the start an ample margin above all fixed charges? A.
Yes, sir.

Q. He also estimates — in fact, states to the firm of Morgan
& Company that when the subways are completed, the Interborough Rapid Transit Company will have a prior claim on the
net earnings of the properties which claim will aggregate $14,-
568,000? A. Correct.

Q. And not until the third year, after actual operation does
he estimate that the net earnings of the properties will equal, or
even by a small figure surpass this large amount which is a prior
claim in favor of the company on the net earnings of the companies? A. That is correct. His estimates are very conservative.

Q. In other words, this preferential, I suppose that is the name
you gave to $14,568,000? A. That is the name given to the
$6,335,000.

Q. Well, this claim as to which the company has a prior — I
mean this amount constituting the company's prior claim on net
earnings, to wit, $14,568,000, any failure of the earnings to
reach that figure in any given year results in an accumulation of
the difference, does it not? A. Yes, sir.

Q. So that, if the earnings the first year of operation consists
of the estimated average for the last two years of $6,335,000 in
the present system, and an estimated increase of $4,800,000 from
the new subways, the total will be about $11,000,000, will it not?
A. Yes, sir.

Q. And the difference between $11,000,000 and $14,568,000
will amount to some $3,500,000? A. Yes, sir.

Q. Which passes into accumulative prior lien or prior claim
in favor of the company upon the net earnings of the new subways? A. Yes, sir.

Q. And the second year, while you estimate that the earnings .

from the new subways will slightly increase, the combined earnings from the new subways and the agreed average of earnings for the past two years on the existing subway will equal the amount as to which the company has a preferred claim against the net earnings,— A. Yes, sir.

Q. Resulting again in another difference. So that it will be considerably over three years before even the estimated earnings of the properties will equal the amount of the preference claim which the company has in the net earnings of the enlarged subway system? A. Probably.

Q. Disregarding the fact that for the first years of operation, that the earnings will not equal the amount for which the city has a preferred claim — I mean, for which the company has a preferred claim — against the company's earnings,— disregarding those important facts, which, in view of the cumulative character of this preference, continually postpones the date when the earnings will equal the preference, much less show a surplus— I say, disregarding those annual deficits, and assuming that Mr. Shonts' estimates as to the aggregate earnings of the new subway at the end of the third year is fairly accurate $15,075,500, the city will get very little of that; that is true, isn't it? A. That is true.

Q. In other words, assuming that at the end of the fourth or fifth year, the earnings of the new subway are $15,075,000, there must first be deducted not only $14,568,000, but these additional deficits for the intervening years? A. Yes, sir.

Q. Disregarding these deficits from the intervening years, and let us take only the basic sum of $14,568,000, there would be only about a little over $400,000 difference; that is correct, isn't it? A. Yes, sir.

Q. And under the terms of the contract with the city, the Interborough Rapid Transit Company has a right to half of that, hasn't it? A. I don't think I understand that question.

Q. In other words, after the payment of this prior claim on earnings which the city has — A. Yes, sir.

Q. The remainder, if there is any remainder, of net earnings, is divided equally between the company and the city? A. After the deficit is paid up.

Q. Of course, I have eliminated from this discussion, for the purpose of showing the structural features of the contract, that deficit, which is a very important thing, because it is constantly being added to this cumulative preferential claim, and constantly postponing the time when the city will derive any participation in this at all.

Senator Lawson.— The deficit might run on for a dozen years.

Mr. Fisher.— Those figures are based on the deficit running out the third year; so that the fourth year of operation will show a profit applying to the payment of the previous year's deficit. When that deficit has been liquidated, the earnings are divided equally between the city — I am wrong there — I say when that deficit is liquidated, the city then gets interest on its bonds — 8.76 per cent, which is an equivalent amount which it is allowed on the Interborough on all of its money which it has invested. After that interest has been paid, then the profits are divided equally.

Q. In other words, how much of the $15,000,000 which is estimated to be the revenue at the end of the — at the fourth — beginning of the fourth year, would the city receive, in view of this preferential of $14,568,000 ?   A. Nothing at the end of the fourth year.   They would still be paying on the deficit at the end of the fourth year.   It would probably be the fifth year before the deficit was entirely liquidated and the city began receiving interest on the bonds.

Senator Lawson.— All those estimates are approximately ?

Mr. Fisher.— Yes, sir.

Senator Lawson.— There is no surety, guarantee that the profits might be sufficient to eliminate the deficits ?

Mr. Fisher.— Our estimates always have been very much overrun.   We make them conservative for our own guidance principally.

Senator Lawson.— There is no guarantee on the part of the Interborough that those deficits will be wiped out in four or five years ?

Mr. Fisher.— No, sir; they make no guarantee, of course.

Senator Lawson.— They might run for ten years?

Mr. Fisher.— It is not likely.

Assemblyman Burr.— Not based on those figures.

Senator Lawson.— Those figures are approximate.

Mr. Fisher.— Our estimates are based on a matter of forty year's experience. It has always proved they are conservative, and we figure the deficit would be wiped out at the end of the third year, and the city would begin to receive its interest on the money the fourth year.

(Discussion off the record, Messrs. Burr. Lawson and Fisher participating.)

By Mr. Colby:

Q. In other words, Mr. Fisher, the first deduction of earnings is $6,335,000, to the Interborough Company? A. Yes, sir.

Q. And then $4,620,000 for interest on the amount of the Interborough's new investment in the subways, including construction? A. Yes, sir.

Q. And then the interest and annual sinking fund on the Manhattan improvement? A. Yes, sir.

Q. Amounting to $1,800,000. And then the profits from the Manhattan Railway lease and other income? A. Yes.

Q. Now, it is stated here that during the past two years, the average annual net earnings of the present subway, including the profits from the Manhattan Railway lease, amount to $8,148,000? A. Yes, sir.

Q. By no means equal to these deductions which are already provided for in advance — I mean to these priorities in favor of the Interborough Company, which are provided for in advance; in other words, on the present basis — on the basis of your present income, the amount of your preferential claim on earnings is $6,500,000 in excess of your present income? A. No, sir. I think the figures are very plainly set out there.

Q. I thought so myself. I don't think I am in error. The income from the present properties, including the Manhattan

Railway lease, is $8,148,000, according to the President's letter. A. That is the net income, I assume.

Q. That is the net income, net earnings, net income? A. Yes, sir.

Q. And the only sources from which that income is going to receive additions is the earnings of the new subways? A. And the third tracking and extensions, elevated third tracking.

Q. Yes, the new — the additional lines. But the moment the subway in its entirety is ready for operation, you have got the income from your present properties, namely, $8,148,000, as the basis upon which you are going to build additional income as a result of the operation of the new lines; is that right? A. Yes, sir.

Q. But at that same time this cumulative preferential or preferred claim on all earnings begin to accumulate earnings from these deficits; that is true? A. The preference is only —

Q. I am using that term possibly differently from you. What I am describing is the $14,568,000. A. I don't catch your point, Mr. Colby. We have gone over that before. You are stating the facts differently, but you are arriving at the same conclusion.

Q. What I mean is that at the expiration of the first year of the subway operation, the company, despite the city's great investment, will receive, presumably, on account of net earnings, $8,148,000 plus $4,890,000; in other words, $13,000,000 and something more, and the city will receive nothing? A. That is correct.

Q. And at the end of the second year, according to Mr. Shonts' statement to his bankers, the company will receive something approximating $14,000,000 again, and the city will receive nothing? A. That is correct. We went all over this ground before.

Q. When? A. Just now. You arrived at a deficit the first three years of operation.

Q. I don't want to weary you or tire your patience. I want to get this thing clear beyond possibility of misunderstanding. A. I thought we had.

Q. And then at the end of the third year, what happens so far as the city is concerned? A. I don't understand that the city receives any return at the end of the third year. As I have explained, our estimates show there will be a deficit which will be cumulative for the first three years. This deficit will begin to be liquidated, if our estimates are correct, the fourth year, would probably be wiped out the fourth and fifth years. After that the city will begin receiving interest on its bonds. And after it has paid 8.76 per cent. on its bonds, the revenue will be divided, 50 per cent. between the city and the company.

Q. And in the meantime, during these years in which the city is receiving nothing, and you are receiving the various amounts climbing up toward the amount of your preference here of $14,-500,000, the city is paying interest on the amount of its contribution to the construction of these subways? A. Yes, sir.

Q. And that interest is mounting up? A. If I —

Q. And accumulating? A. It has been some time since I have read the contract, but I think that interest is taken care of largely first before the revenue is divided between the company — I mean the cumulative interest, before the revenue is divided.

Q. The Interborough has a cumulative preference, while the city has a cumulative deficit during the earlier years, at least, of this operation? A. Naturally, if we have a cumulative preference, and the city must —

Senator Lawson — But that is true?

Mr. Fisher.— He has stated it correctly.

Mr. Colby.— Mr. Chairman, I believe that — Mr. Fisher, that will be all for to-day. But I believe there is something further to take up. Mr. Fisher, I am sorry to try you, because you are very nice and patient about it.

Mr. Fisher.— Oh, that's all right.

(Senator Thompson resumes the Chair.)

Mr. Colby.— Mr. Chairman, permit me to introduce to you Mr. de Gersdorff, a member of the Bar, and well known as such.

Mr. de Gersdorff.— I appear here, Mr. Chairman, on behalf of Mr. Gillespie, of T. A. Gillespie & Company.

The Chairman.— Yes, but we subpoenaed Mr. Gillespie.

Mr. Colby.— He is here.

Mr. de Gersdorff.— He has been subpoenaed to produce a large number of documents which are being gotten together. He was subpoenaed, I think, about three o'clock, so that he has not got them with him, but they will be produced as soon as it is practicable to get them together. We propose to conform to the subpoena and produce the papers in his possession, and to submit him to examination in the regular way. It has been suggested that some method may be found to obviate the production of an enormous amount of papers before the Committee. It would take three or four truck-loads to bring them here. If it is agreeable to counsel and Committee, I will see if with Mr. Colby and Mr. Dawson, we can arrange some way that we can facilitate the examination of the papers. If not, we will have to bring them here.

Chairman Thompson.— There was so much talk about this, that I don't care — on behalf of the Committee, I don't care to enter into any agreements at all. I don't want you to produce anything before this Committee that we are not able to go and get. I don't want any favors from anybody.

Mr. de Gersdorff.— Perhaps I have not made myself clear. The papers which we have been called upon to produce, and which we will produce, are very voluminous; it will take probably three or four trucks to bring them here. Probably four-fifths of them have already been examined. It does not seem necessary to bring them all here again. We will do so, if the Chairman prefers. In talking with Mr. Colby, I thought if we could get together we might arrange some way by which the examination might be conducted with greater facility, and not loading up the room with all these papers which we would otherwise have to bring.

Chairman Thompson.— That is the same thing we have found so many times before, and the reason why the representative of the Committee has been sent where the books are — if that is done, it is generally more as a convenience to the people who own the books and papers than it is to us, because it would be much more convenient to have all the things brought to our hearing, than for us to go somewhere else. That can be arranged. If it can be arranged down there, if it can be arranged to have it done somewhere where you have a man, and go around and look over papers in your office, set apart a room, fix up a room, or something of that sort. It is all agreeable.

Mr. de Gersdorff.— Possibly that might do.

Chairman Thompson.— I think the Committee will be agreeable, so that you arrange it. But I don't want to adjourn the Committee unless I understand they can work to-morrow on it.

Mr. de Gersdorff.— Well, I cannot stipulate that, unless — I cannot stipulate that to-day. We are prepared to produce them here unless you can give us an opportunity to arrange with counsel to make some other arrangement.

Chairman Thompson.— Our Committee has got to work to-morrow, and I think it is better here.

Mr. de Gersdorff.— It will take hours to pack them up.

Chairman Thompson.— We will wait. We will keep in session then. You can get them up.

Mr. Colby.— I don't understand Mr. de Gersdorff to in any way assert any limitations upon the city's — suggest any limitations upon the Committee's subpoena or qualify in any way his announced willingness to obey the Committee's process. I might explain to you, Mr. de Gersdorff, that the Committee's efforts to facilitate witnesses by conducting necessary examinations under such circumstances as are usually — that is to say, involving the least disruption of papers, the least inconvenience of carriage and transportation, has been misconstrued by people who are really the beneficiaries of that on the part of the Committee, and instead of it being recognized as a favor by the Committee, it has been put forward as a condescension on the part of the witness. That is what the Chairman has in mind.

Mr. de Gersdorff.— I have not —

Mr. Colby.— I am simply saying that —

Mr. de Gersdorff.— I thought we had been trying to facilitate the Committee, and the result does not seem to have been very fortunate so far.

Chairman Thompson.— If you delay the matter over Sunday, you won't be facilitating the Committee a bit. We have a limited time. We want to get at it.

Mr. Colby.— Mr. de Gersdorff comes to the Committee to-day to say that he is in the course of unquestioning and unqualified obedience to the subpoena, and the books will be here shortly, which is, of course, right. That is what the subpoena called for. Now, all we want is the unfettered privilege of pursuing our material examinations into the records that are at Mr. Gillespie's office. I would suggest possibly the very correct and consistent way to leave the matter at the moment, Mr. Chairman, would be to allow this process of obedience and compliance with the subpoena to be carried on rapidly, as rapidly as may be, and in the meantime if Mr. de Gersdorff, who at present finds his authorization somewhat limited, and wishes to refer back, if he is able to assure us of that opportunity, which is all we want, to examine the books and complete the examination of the Gillespie matters, which is far progressed, I might say, why, that would be the practical solution of all questions.

Chairman Thompson.— I suggest that we take a little recess of four or five minutes, and you and Mr. de Gersdorff drop out and talk this over, so we can have the work done to-morrow. I don't want to lose to-morrow and Sunday. Our time is too limited. I like New York, but I want to get through.

(An elastic recess was taken.)

Chairman Thompson.— Come to order a minute, please. This telegram or cablegram, Mr. Smith — I will read it. I wish you would send it.

" Pierpont Morgan, care of Morgan, London.

" In view of important development during past several days relative to finances and other matters concerning subway construction, in which your testimony is most desirable to all concerned, can you give some more definite date as to your return, since Mr. Davison informs us that you will be absent from six weeks to possibly three months. George F. Thompson."

Mr. Smith, will you send that to-night as a week-end letter?

We will take an elastic recess.

(A recess is taken.)

Mr. de Gersdorff.— We have not been able to arrive at any satisfactory solution at the moment which would avoid the regular compliance with the subpoena as served. We are now engaged in trying to comply with that subpoena. We are getting the books all together, and they will all be here to-morrow morning. It is a physical impossibility to have them here to-night. They will be here to-morrow, unless in the meantime we can arrive at some other solution, but I don't know whether it will be possible or not. I will talk further with Mr. Colby.

Chairman Thompson.— Very well.

Mr. de Gersdorff.— At the moment, we cannot do it. And we will have them here at —

Chairman Thompson.— Counsel sits here to-morrow. You are not going to raise any question if the Committee is not here?

Mr. de Gersdorff.— Oh, no.

Chairman Thompson.— All witnesses except those in obedience to the Gillespie subpoenas are excused until Monday at 11 o'clock. We will suspend until Monday at 11 o'clock.

Whereupon, at 4:50 p. m., an adjournment was taken to Monday, February 14, 1916, at 11 o'clock a. m.

FEBRUARY 14, 1916

NEW YORK COUNTY LAWYERS ASSOCIATION ROOM,
165 Broadway, New York City

The Committee was called to order by Chairman Thompson, at
12:10 P. M., a quorum being present.

Mr. Colby.— Mr. Chairman, Mr. de Gersdorff, representing
T. A. Gillespie & Company is here, and I should report to you
that on Saturday during the Committee's recess, T. A. Gillespie
Company produced here a vast amount of books and papers and
we were prepared to undertake their examination.   Counsel for
the Gillespie Company, however, stated that they did not intend
to submit the books to general inspection but that they were and
would be produced in connection with examination of a witness,
and as called for in the course of such examination.   It was of
course impossible to act upon such examination owing to the fact
that the Committee was not in session and there was no power to
compel replies or to compel production of papers called for.   The
Gillespie Company took the books and papers back to their office
and Mr. de Gersdorff is here again this morning to renew his proffer of the books as called for in connection with the examination
of a witness.   Of course that would be a very laborious and long
process and would involve examination consuming endless time
and under ordinary conditions and directness of procedure would
be most impracticable.

Chairman Thompson.— Do I understand that Messrs. Gillespie
& Company want to advise this Committee as to how this investigation shall be made?

Mr. de Gersdorff.— Oh, no, not at all.

Chairman Thompson.— I think we can dispose of this matter
very readily.   I don't propose to waste any time with this proposition and in order to settle it now, I will appoint a sub-committee
consisting of Assemblyman Feinberg, Senator Lawson and Assemblyman Burr to examine these books.   You can produce these
books and papers before them in whatever manner they direct.

Mr. de Gersdorff.— May I be given an opportunity to state our
position?

Chairman Thompson.— No, sir.   Not unless you want to go under oath.

Mr. de Gersdorff.— Well, I am not a witness here.

Chairman Thompson.— I do not care to take any statement unless it is made under oath.

Mr. de Gersdorff.— Then I am not permitted to make a statement.

Chairman Thompson.— Not except under oath.   I don't care to have any general statements made here unless they are made under oath.

Mr. de Gersdorff.— Well, I simply wanted to state this however, and I think Mr. Colby will bear me out, and that is that the papers were produced and produced according to the subpoena. The reason why the books,— (interruption by Chairman Thompson).

Chairman Thompson.— You can produce them before this sub-committee and tell them all about it.   You can make any statement to them that you desire.

Mr. de Gersdorff.— Well, I would simply like to state Mr. Chairman,—

Chairman Thompson.— Now I don't care to hear any further statements.   The matter is disposed of.

Mr. de Gersdorff.— What hour are these records to be produced?

Chairman Thompson.— Eleven o'clock, to-morrow morning.

Mr. de Gersdorff.— In this room?

Chairman Thompson.— Whatever room the sub-committee see fit to sit.

Assemblyman Feinberg.—We will arrange that Mr. de Gersdorff.

Mr. de Gersdorff.— Do I understand that the subpoena continues?

Chairman Thompson.— Yes, sir.

Mr. de Gersdorff.— Because I shall decline to produce them except,— (interruption by Chairman Thompson.)

Chairman Thompson.— We don't care what you do. We don't want any favors from T. A. Gillespie Company or their lawyers or anybody connected with them. We simply want what we have a right to have. The proceeding is closed and I decline to hear anything further about it. You produce these records before the Committee and the sub-committee will take charge to-morrow morning.

Assemblyman Feinberg.— Do you want a conference with Mr. Dawson and the members of the sub-committee?

Mr. de Gersdorff.— I should like to have one. Now, Mr. Chairman, I would simply like to state the position of my clients.

Chairman Thompson.— I don't want to hear you any further. We have other matters of more importance than this.

Assemblyman Feinberg.— We will take that up with you Mr. de Gersdorff.

Mr. Colby.— Mr. Chairman, for the purpose of continuity and for real progress I wish to complete the introduction of the correspondence that passed between the Interborough Rapid Transit Company and the J. P. Morgan Company in relation to various matters.

Chairman Thompson.— Very well, Mr. Colby.

Mr. Colby.— I think we can make rapid progress with these letters. I think their importance justifies their introduction.

FISHER, H. M., recalled, testified as follows:

Examination by Mr. Colby:

Q. Mr. Fisher, in order to obviate the repetition of the questions I have been asking you upon the production of each one of these letters, I think I might ask if the file which you gave me is a complete file of the letters received by the Interborough Rapid Transit Company from J. P. Morgan & Company up to December

31, 1913, and also if it contains arranged in consecutive order the replies sent to Morgan & Company by the Interborough Rapid Transit Company or President? A. Yes, sir. That's supposed to be a complete file of letters pertaining to financial arrangements made between Morgan & Company and the Interborough Rapid Transit Company and replies made to their propositions.

Q. There are other letters that passed between the company and J. P. Morgan & Company? A. I presume so, and they would be in the President's file.

Q. Is no other file in your possession besides this? A. No.

Q. At the close of the last session I had introduced Mr. Shonts' letter to J. P. Morgan & Company dated April 9, 1912, containing his estimate of the preferential to Morgan & Company and the prospective income from the enlarged subway operation. What interest has the city in the operation of the Manhattan Elevated Company? A. It secures a division of the profits after a certain preferential is earned.

Q. So that the information contained in a public statement by the Comptroller to the effect that the city has no interest in the moneys expended in the third-tracking of the elevated and its extension is not exactly correct? A. I couldn't say on what terms the Comptroller bases his statement.

Q. You saw such a statement? A. I read something of the kind in the papers.

Q. In other words, although the company accomplishes the third-tracking with its own funds, is the money expended for the extension wholly the money of the Manhattan Elevated Company? A. It is money raised from the 5 per cent. refunding bond issue of $160,000,000, which was sold to Morgan & Company.

Q. And the city's participation in the income of the Manhattan Elevated is postponed in time and subservient in order to the receipt by the Interborough Rapid Transit Company, as the lessee of the Manhattan Elevated Company, to interest upon the cost of said third-tracking and extensions and also the sinking fund apportionment for the discharge of such cost. A. Yes.

Q. So that it would appear that Mr. Shonts is entirely correct in the theory at least in including as a part of the Interborough

17

Rapid Transit Company's preferential claim on the combined earnings, the interest and sinking fund charges on the so-called Manhattan improvement? A. Yes.

Q. The next letter I shall read into the record is Mr. Shonts' letter of April 15th addressed to J. P. Morgan & Company.

"NEW YORK, *April* 15th."

" Dear Sir:

" Referring to the correspondence exchanged between us under dates of April 9th and 12th relative to the sale to you of approximately $170,000,000 of the new 5 per cent bonds of the Interborough Rapid Transit Company, I write to confirm the understanding that the price at which the bonds are sold under the terms of the aforesaid correspondence includes item (3) allowed by the Public Service Commission, being brokerage charges of 3 per cent upon $77,000,000 to be furnished by you to defray this excess contribution toward the cost of construction and equipment of the new subway.

" Very truly, yours,

" (Signed)   T. P. SHONTS,
" *President.*

" To Messrs. J. P. Morgan & Co."

Upon this letter is the following endorsement.

" This accords with our understanding." and I assume that is the signature of J. P. Morgan & Company? A. Yes, sir.

Q. The letter is signed by J. P. Morgan & Company. What does this letter mean? A. It means that the city agreed to allow 3 per cent for their banker's commission, brokerage charges or other expenses connected with the securing of money and the issuance of the mortgage.

Q. Who received that 3 per cent? A. The company would receive that for its expenses connected with these transactions.

Q. The company would receive that? A. Yes.

Q. That would amount to nearly two and a half million dollars upon $77,000,000, would it not? A. About $2,300,000.

Q. Did the company receive that money? A. It was taken out in the discount in the bonds. In other words, the bonds were sold at 93½ per cent which was 6½ per cent less than par. Therefore whatever expense there was connected with this issue over and above the 3 per cent allowed by the city, the company paid out of its own funds.

Q. In other words the city agreed that you should sell the bonds at a discount of 3 per cent, is that true? A. No. They simply agreed to allow us 3 per cent on the cost of the money plus the expense of the mortgage.

Q. From what funds did this 3 per cent come, they allowed it to you you say. They allowed it out of what? A. Out of construction account. They allowed us to deduct 3 per cent. In other words the cost of the money would become part of the cost of construction and instead of allowing us to include the entire cost, which in this case would have amounted to 6½ per cent plus whatever the cost of the mortgage amounted to, they allowed us to include 3 per cent, the balance being payable by the Interborough Rapid Transit Company.

Q. Now before we go any further, let me understand clearly about this three per cent. Now, you were under an agreement with the city to contribute $58,000,000 to construction? A. Yes, sir.

Q. Was that $58,000,000 made subject to a credit in your favor of $2,300,000, being this 3 per cent? A. That was subject to a credit of 3 per cent, yes, sir.

Q. So co-incidentally with your agreement to supply $58,000,-000, you were allowed by the city $2,300,000 in the form of this 3 per cent allowance for brokerage? A. We were allowed that amount for the purpose of securing the money, yes, sir.

Q. And that brokerage charge in view of the supposed obligation to make good any deficiency over and above your contribution to construction is really a charge against the city, isn't it? A. I presume so.

Q. Now, you say the cost over and above that 3 per cent the Interborough Rapid Transit Company directly bore. Now what was that for? A. The cost of the mortgage, legal fees connected therewith, plus the difference between the 3 per cent allowed and the 6½ per cent which we paid for the money. In other words selling the bonds at 93½ per cent. instead of par.

Q. So that there would be charged 6 per cent upon the par value of the bonds sold for construction account? A. Yes, 3 per cent.

Q. And that 3½ per cent additional was paid for by the Interborough Rapid Transit Company? A. Yes.

Q. How was it paid for? A. Out of its own funds.

Q. Well, isn't it true that an additional issuance of bonds is provided for in order to defray such costs, to defray cost to be assumed by the Interborough Rapid Transit Company? A. In order to equalize the discount at which these bonds were sold.

Q. In other words you are permitted to sell additional bonds in order to make good the 3 per cent discount. A. No.

Q. Where did you get the additional 3½ per cent from? A. Out of surplus.

Q. And that additional 3½ is not charged to construction? A. That is not charged against the city in any way.

Q. To what account is it charged? A. To surplus.

Q. It isn't charged to equipment account contract No. 3? A. No.

Q. Nor to the construction equipment account, in relation to the Manhattan Elevated? A. No.

Q. Nor to construction and equipment account, in relation to the elevated extensions? A. No.

Q. Nor to power plant improvement? A. No.

Q. Nor to other suspense? A. No.

Q. Nor prior determination? A. No, sir, I don't think so.

Q. Are you able to testify whether any part of it is charged to prior determination? A. That I couldn't say. The auditor could give you that information.

Q. I now read the letter of April 16, 1912, addressed to Mr. Theodore P. Shonts, Esq.

" Dear Sir.— Confirming our conversation, we understand that you have sold to us subject to confirmation by your Board $15,000,000 of notes dated April 29, 1912, and due nine months from that date, which notes we are to discount for your company at the rate of five per cent. on the 28th

inst., crediting your company's account here with the proceeds. We should like to have the notes in denominations of
$5,000 for one half and $10,000 as to the other half.

" Yours very truly,

"(Signed)   J. P. MORGAN & COMPANY."

" NEW YORK, *April 22nd*, 1912.

" J. P. Morgan & Company,

" Gentlemen.— I beg to confirm the sale to you of
$15,000,000 worth of this company's notes dated April 29th,
1912, due in nine months and discounted by your company
at the rate of 5 per cent. per annum and I attach an extract
from the minutes of the Board of Directors of the Interborough Rapid Transit Company of April 17th approving
this transaction.

" Instructions have been given as requested by you to execute one half of the notes in the denomination of $5,000 and
one half in the denomination of $10,000.

" Yours very truly,

ˣ"(Signed)   . . . .

President."

" To Messrs. J. P. Morgan & Co."

" NEW YORK, *May* 3, 1912.

" Mr. Theodore P. Shonts, President, Interborough Rapid
Transit Company, New York City:

" Dear Sir.— Referring to our letter of April 9th and your
letter of April 12th in reply in regard to the financing of
the Interborough Rapid Transit Company's proposed contract
with the City, we beg to advise you that on the proposed
arrangement for financing as outlined in the letters referred
to, it is contemplated that the execution of the contracts with
the City shall be within a reasonable time.

" We understood from you that the decision has not yet
been arrived at and we are therefore obliged to give you notice
that unless said contract is agreed upon promptly it may very
likely be necessary for us to entirely revise the scope of the

financing. We are not willing to pledge ourselves to the investment of about $170,000,000 at any time in the future regardless of conditions.

"Accordingly unless we hear from you within the next few days, that the contract with the city has been closed, we shall be compelled to cancel the agreement set forth in the letters above referred to.

" Yours very truly,
"(Signed)   J. P. MORGAN & COMPANY."

On May 4th, Mr. Shonts in reply to this letter wrote Mr. J. P. Morgan, Jr., as follows:

" NEW YORK, May 4, 1912.

" My dear Mr. Morgan.— I beg to acknowledge receipt of your letter of yesterday formally notifying us that unless our proposition is accepted by the responsible city officials within a few days, you will be compelled to cancel the agreement with us to finance the improvement and I beg leave herewith to enclose copy of a letter I have to-day forwarded to President McAneny, Chairman of the Finance Committee of the Board of Estimate and Apportionment, which is self explanatory.

" Yours very truly,
"(Signed)   . . . .
President."

The letter to Mr. McAneny, of which a copy is enclosed, I shall also read. This letter was written by Mr. Shonts to Mr. McAneny.

" NEW YORK, May 4th, 1912.

" My dear Mr. McAneny.—As you are aware the Interborough Rapid Transit Company made arrangements with Messrs. J. P. Morgan & Company to finance the Interborough Rapid Transit Company's proposition for Rapid Transit improvements made to the Public Service Commission, February 27th, 1912, accepted by that Board March 13th, 1912, and referred to the Board of Estimate and Apportionment for its approval.

" Our agreement with the bankers was based upon our
understanding with the city officials that the proposition as
made was acceptable to the majority both of the Public Service Commission and the Board of Estimate and Apportionment and would be promptly acted upon and promptly
approved by both of these Boards.

" Owing to the delay on the part of the Committee, of
which you are Chairman, in making a report to the Board
of Estimate and Apportionment, action by that Board has
been delayed until now, under date of May 5th, 1912, our
bankers have notified us in writing that because of changed
conditions that if they do not hear from us in the next few
days that our proposition has been accepted by the responsible city authorities they will be compelled to cancel their
existing agreement with us to finance the proposed Rapid
Transit's improvements.

" I therefore trust that our proposal of February 27th,
1912, may receive the formal approval of the Board of Estimate and Apportionment at its next meeting.

" Very truly yours,

"(Signed) . . . .

President.

" To Hon. George McAneny."

Q. You don't know whether there was any conference between
the President and J. P. Morgan & Company as to putting a little
pressure on the city by the writing of such letters as that? A.
I do not.

Q. I will now read the letter from Mr. Shonts to J. P. Morgan
& Company dated May 24th, 1912.

" Gentlemen.— The City of New York and the Interborough Rapid Transit Company have agreed upon a contract
by which the City and the Interborough Rapid Transit Company shall build, and the Interborough Rapid Transit Company equip and operate, extensions to the present subway,
particulars of which are fully set forth and described in the
enclosed analysis of the proposal of the Interborough Rapid
Transit Company to the City. The agreement has been

entered into subject, on both sides, to the reservation that it shall be passed upon by the Courts before any action is taken under it."

The agreement suggested in this letter was to be taken subject to the same provision. In other words Mr. Fisher, Mr. Shonts again states that the agreement with the city, which he says in this letter of May 24, 1912, has been reached subject on both sides to the reservation that it shall be passed upon by the courts before any action is taken under it and the agreement suggested in this letter is to be taken subject to the same provision. My attention was called this morning to the particular statement of the Comptroller of the city in which he said that no such agreement was ever made by the city of New York or anyone on its behalf. I don't recall his exact language but that is about what he said. That is at variance with the statement that I have just read in Mr. Shonts' letter, is it not? A. I don't think Mr. Shonts commits the city in any way in that letter of being a party to any such arrangement.

Q. Of course, he is not acting for the city but he states that the city of New York and the Interborough Rapid Transit Company have agreed and that this agreement has been entered into subject on both sides to the reservation that it shall be passed upon by the city. However, Mr. Prendergast can profit by some education from the Thompson Committee as well as imparting information to the Thompson Committee. It seems that the two points which are disposed in this correspondence are directly at variance with Mr. Prendergast's statements and that he is in error.

Chairman Thompson.—I have read Mr. Prendergast's letter this morning. It was in the papers and I think if counsel will read it again he will readily find that there is nothing said in it. It is a very general affair and there are no details or any facts. I just want to say this, Mr. Colby, and that is that a man in Mr. Prendergast's position may be of a great deal of assistance to this Committee and really I wish he would. I wish he would come and give us whatever light there is for facts. We are not investigating Mr. Prendergast. We are investigating the Public Service

Commission and we are going back seven years. I wish he would say something.

Mr. Colby.— His observations might be a little more illuminating if they were a little more accurate.

> " The sum estimated to be required for the construction of the new subway is $112,000,000, of which sum the Interborough Rapid Transit Company agrees to contribute one-half. Should the construction cost exceed this amount, the City agrees to furnish the additional amount required."

Q. Let me ask you at this point, Mr. Fisher. This is of course a later letter than the one which I read on Friday, April 9th, and I assume proposes a slight revision in demands? A. Yes.

Q. And was written after Mr. Shonts, at Mr. Morgan's suggestion, had sent that little prod to Mr. McAneny and is the outline of the agreement which subsequently was brought into the contract, is that correct? A. Why that statement is your observation and not mine, Mr. Colby.

Q. Well, I am simply trying to hurry the matter along. Is that not correct? A. No, sir. You insinuate something about some arrangements between Mr. Morgan and Shonts about writing to a city officer. I know nothing about that.

Q. The letter set forth the stage of the negotiations to this date? A. Yes.

Q. And this was the contract, this is a sketch of the provisions of the larger features of the contract which Mr. Morgan was in a hurry to have executed? A. I presume so, yes, sir.

Q. I shall continue with the letter:

> " Under the terms of the contract, The Interborough Rapid Transit Company will modify its present leases, fixing expiration of all its subway leases at 49 years from the completion of the new subways. The Company will be authorized to take annually during this period from the aggregate net earnings of the old and new subways the sum of $6,335,000, being the average amount of the net earnings during the last two years on the present subway; also the sum of $4,620,000. the equivalent of five per cent. interest, and one per cent.

Sinking Fund, on the investment by the Interborough Rapid Transit Company of $77,000,000 of new money, viz., $56,000,000 the Company's contribution toward the cost of construction, and $21,000,000, the estimated total cost of equipping the new subways. These payments are to be a first charge on such net earnings, and are to be cumulative."

Q. There was a good deal of controversy at the time, was there not, as to what the average net earnings for the period of two years was? A. I think there was some, yes.

Q. Do you recall that Mayor Mitchel very actively and earnestly combatted the company's claims that its net earnings amounted to $6,335,000? A. I do not. If I remember correctly, I think the company combatted the claim, that it should in reality amount to more.

Q. Was there any provision with reference to your contribution as to equipment similar to the provisions with reference to construction, that any deficiency would be made up by the city on that item? A. That refers to the whole sum for construction and equipment.

Q. There was no specific reference made to equipment, that is, did the city have to make up any deficiency on that score? A. They were to have the city make up any deficiency on that score.

Q. And then the agreement was that the city would settle any deficiency that might result from construction or equipment and it applied to both construction and equipment? A. Yes, sir.

Q. Has there been any apportionment of interest to equipment as there has been to construction? A. I presume so, but I cannot say. Very little of the equipment has been purchased, consequently there would be no interest charges.

"The Interborough Rapid Transit Company is lessee of the Manhattan Railway Company, which owns the elevated railways in New York City, in the Boroughs of Manhattan and The Bronx, and receives authority, under the agreement with the City, to make extensions and additions, including third tracks on the Second Avenue, Third Avenue and Ninth Avenue elevated lines.

"The estimated cost of these extensions, additions, and equipment of same is approximately $30,000,000. The Interborough will be authorized to take annually from the net earnings of the old and new elevated lines, the Manhattan rental and the average profits derived from the Manhattan Railway Company lease for the past two years — approximately $1,500,000 per annum; also interest and 1% Sinking Fund on the new money invested in the elevated improvements; after which deductions, the remaining profits will be divided equally with the city.

"The amounts required to be raised by the Interborough Rapid Transit Company are as follows:

For refunding its present debt............	$50,656,950
For construction of new subway (Interborough Company's one-half)...............	56,000,000
For Manhattan Railway Improvements, about	30,000,000
For Equipment of new subways...........	21,000,000
For other charges including discounts, about.	9,500,000
	$167,156,950"

Q. What were the other charges, Mr. Fisher, including discount? A. I couldn't tell you. It includes discount. I don't know what else outside the expenses of the printing of the mortgage and the issuing of it.

Q. You cannot tell me in a word what J. P. Morgan & Company got on this transaction? A. No, sir, I couldn't.

Q. You cannot tell me what the Interborough Rapid Transit Company figured they had conceded to J. P. Morgan & Company by virtue of the assessment, interest, brokerage, commission, and so forth, on these transactions. A. They conceded nothing. It sold the bonds to J. P. Morgan & Company at the rate of 93½.

"In order to procure the necessary funds to carry out this contract, and retire its present debt, the Interborough Rapid Transit Company proposes to issue new first mortgage five per cent. fifty-three-year gold bonds to the amount of about $170,000,000. The mortgage securing these bonds will also provide for the issue of such additional amounts of bonds as may be needed for extensions and improvements as may be authorized by the city and agreed to by the company during the period of the lease — as provided in the agreement."

Q. What is the total amount of the authorized bond issue as provided in the mortgage? A. You mean authorized by the Interborough Rapid Transit Company?

Q. Yes. A. $300,000,000.

Q. Does the mortgage contain a provision for the issuance of additional bonds? A. For other purposes, yes, sir.

Q. Is there any limitation upon the amount of additional bonds the company may issue with the approval of the city? A. $300,000,000.

Q. Of which the company has issued about $170,000,000 or $165,000,000? A. Of which it has had authority from the Public Service Commission to issue about $163,000,000. It has actually issued $148,658,000.

Q. Out of an authorized issue as provided in the mortgage of $300,000,000? A. Yes.

Q. I notice that the mortgage, the term of the bonds is fifty-three years and the term of the lease is committed to forty-nine years. Does that mean that it was concluded that the construction and equipment of the new subway would take four years and that the leases should begin upon the completion of the subway? A. I presume that was the idea at the time.

"A cumulative sinking fund of one per cent. will be provided for, to begin five years from the date of opening the new subways or in any event not more than ten years from the date of the bonds. Bonds may be drawn for the sinking fund at 110, or bought in the market at a lower price, and by the operation of the sinking fund the whole issue will be amortized during the term of the lease. The company reserves the right to increase the sinking fund at any time."

Q. Does that mean that the company without the consent of the city can appropriate a larger amount of the joint earnings of the subways for the purpose of increasing the sinking fund? A. No, sir. I should not say it was. I should not think they could do that without the consent of the city.

Q. And yet it says the company reserves the right to increase the sinking fund at any time. That's very clear in the letter, isn't it, Mr. Fisher? A. That's what the letter states.

Q. And I suppose that cumulative sinking fund of one per cent. to begin five years from the date of opening of the new subways was calculated to add to the sinking fund to completely amortize them before their maturity? A. That is correct.

Q. I presume Mr. Shonts meant in writing this letter that that was the position of the company and the city taken together and not separately? A. I don't know.

Q. Of course it would be to the advantage possibly of the holders of these securities and to the interest of the bankers if the time for their redemption at the premium at which these bonds were bought, if they could be undisturbed or hastened? A. I don't see any special benefit.

Q. It might enhance the value of the bonds and possibly increase their salability, would it not? A. Perhaps.

Q. The reserved right of the company to increase the sinking fund at any time may have a very prejudicial effect upon the city's participation in these joint earnings, may it not? A. I don't think that is likely.

"Our company has agreed to sell to you and you have agreed to buy from it about $170,000,000 of these bonds to provide for the company's financial requirements for construction and equipment of the new subways, elevated extensions and improvements, and to refund the present debt of the company, the bonds to be taken and paid for as follows:

During the year from July 1, 1912, to June 30, 1913	$78,000,000
During the year from July 1, 1913, to June 30, 1914........................	30,000,000
During the year from July 1, 1914, to June 30, 1915........................	30,000,000
During the year from July 1, 1915, to June 30, 1916........................	32,000,000
	$170,000,000

"All or any part of such annual installment of bonds may be taken and paid for by you at any time during the year.

" You have further agreed that the syndicate which you will form to take these bonds will divide equally with this company any amount received on the sale of the bonds in excess of an average price of par and accrued interest after deducting all expenses."

Q. That agreement not divisioned what the syndicate is void of any yield so far to the company? A. Yes.

" When the subways are completed, the Interborough Rapid Transit Company will have a prior claim on the net earnings of the properties, which claim will aggregate $14,568,000.

" This is made up as follows:

Average annual earnings of present subway during the last two years..............	$6,335,000
Five per cent. interest and 1 per cent. annual sinking fund on $77,000,000, the amount of Interborough's new investment in subways.	4,620,000
Interest and annual sinking fund on approximately $30,000,000 new capital invested in elevated railways	1,800,000
Profits from Manhattan Railway lease and other income which during the last two years have averaged annually..........	1,813,000

During the past two years the average annual net earnings of the present properties, including profits from the Manhattan Railway lease and other income, have been....	$8,148,000
Including the $56,000,000 of new money provided by the city there will be, when the new subways and elevated extensions are completed, a new investment in additional subways and elevated properties amounting to.	163,000,000

It is estimated that the net earnings of the
completed property available for interest the
first five years will average.............. $13,038,000

Beginning with the fourth year the earnings
amount to 15,075,000

Against this amount will be a charge of...... 10,200,000

made up as follows:

The annual interest upon the total issue of
$170,000,000 of new bonds............ 8,500,000

And the annual sinking fund upon the same,
which will not begin, however, until five
years after the enlarged system is put in
operation 1,700,000

"Interest during the construction period has been provided for as part of the cost of the work.

"As indicated above, when the new subways are open for
operation, the earnings of the property will show from the
start an ample margin above all fixed charges.

"Very truly yours,
"(Signed)   T. P. SHONTS,
"*President.*"

"MESSRS. J. P. MORGAN & COMPANY,
"23 Wall street, N. Y. City."

Q. This letter, Mr. Fisher, is substantially in accordance with
the terms of the earlier letter of Mr. Shonts, dated April 9, 1912,
which was read at the last session. It contains a slight revision
of the figures relating to apportionment and deductions from the
joint earnings for the purpose of meeting that preferential and this
cumulative deficit and it shows upon the reduction of the negotiations in response to the Morgan letter suggesting haste and the
Shonts letter to McAneny suggests quick action. It shows also
upon the resumption of the negotiations an agreement was reached
again in substantial conformity with the first record.

Mr. Quackenbush.— That is not the final one.

Chairman Thompson.— We will now take a recess until
2:45 P. M.

AFTERNOON SESSION

The Committee was called to order at 3:15 o'clock p. m., Chairman Thompson presiding.

Horace M. Fisher, recalled.

By Mr. Colby:

Q. This letter of May 24, 1912, that I have just read, from Mr. Shonts to the bankers, was issued by J. P. Morgan & Company apparently in connection with their so-called syndicate agreement? A. Yes, sir.

Q. And the statements therein mentioned as to the preferential of the railroad company in the matter of income, the estimates of earnings, etc., were circulated widely, stating the merit of the security which was offered through the syndicate; is that right? A. I presume so.

Q. I see in the syndicate agreement it is stated as a fact that the company reserves the right to increase the payment to the sinking fund? A. That is correct.

Q. This syndicate agreement was printed and published by Morgan & Company subsequent to the making of the contracts for the dual subway? A. Yes, sir.

Q. What was the date of the contracts for the dual subway? A. March 19, 1913.

Q. And you have those contracts with you, Mr. Fisher? A. No, sir. (To an Interborough employee.) Have you got a copy? All right.

Mr. Colby.— I am going to offer this entire file in evidence, Mr. Chairman.

Chairman Thompson.— Very well.

Mr. Colby.— Alluding to only one or two matters specifically. The syndicate agreement is dated June 5, 1912.

(The file of letters referred to by Mr. Colby is the original file of the Interborough Rapid Transit Company, and was not given to the stenographer.)

By Mr. Colby:

Q. I call your attention particularly to a letter dated August 7 — or to a resolution of the Board of the Interborough, of August 7, 1912, and some letters on or about that date. Referring to the withdrawal by the Interborough Rapid Transit Company of $40,000,000 of bonds from the syndicate, what was the meaning of that transaction? A. I don't see how I can give you any better explanation than the resolution does.

Q. See if I can turn to that letter. I will read Mr. Shonts' letter of August 7, 1912, on this matter.

"To J. P. Morgan & Company.

"Referring to our contract with your firm for the sale of bonds of this company, I have given considerable thought to the conversation had with you relative to your suggestion that permission be given to participants to withdraw their bonds from sale. My understanding is that such withdrawals shall not be counted as sales by the syndicate, and therefore shall not be calculated in determining the amount which is to be divided without determination of the syndicate, and that the clause in regard to such division shall apply only to those bonds which are sold by the syndicate for account of the syndicate. It is my understanding that the amount of withdrawals contemplated aggregates $30,000,000 and possibly $40,000,000. And it is further understood that whatever withdrawals are made will not come upon the market again during the life of the syndicate. I see the force of your suggestion that if you are able to announce that a considerable number of the bonds have been sold privately, and therefore the amount of the bonds to be sold by the syndicate has been materially reduced, it will tend to improve the market value of the bonds remaining to be sold as to make it probable that the clause in the contract above referred to will be more profitable to us, as well as to the syndicate. I therefore suggest that if it is agreeable to you to modify our contract with you so as to permit this procedure, I should be glad to submit same to my Board, with recommendations."

To which Morgan & Company replied on the following day, addressing Mr. Shonts:

"Dear Sir: Referring to your letter of yesterday's date, we shall be very glad to modify the contract in the particular which is suggested by you. In regard to the amount of bonds to be withdrawn, we are unable to fix any figure as yet, but would suggest it would be well for you to get the agreement of the Board up to an amount of, say, $50,000,000. We shall notify you by some given date what is the total amount of withdrawals. Trusting that this will be satisfactory," etc.

What was done in carrying out the suggestions contained in these two letters? A. They were allowed to draw $40,000,000, as I understand.

Q. Who were allowed? A. Morgan & Company. In other words, that $40,000,000 — in other words, we were not to participate in the profits in excess of par with respect to that $40,000,000.

Q. In other words, Morgan & Company, syndicate, having taken the entire issue of bonds, Morgan & Company were, by these letters, and by the resolution referred to, permitted to withdraw from their own syndicate $40,000,000 of bonds? A. That is correct.

Q. Although they suggested $50,000,000 of bonds? A. Yes, sir.

Q. In other words, that gave to Morgan & Company the right to dispose of $40,000,000 worth of bonds, not to the syndicate for 96½, but for any price the bonds would realize? A. Privately, yes, sir.

Q. Privately. And in order to make that transaction possible — A. Yes.

Q. — the Interborough waived its right under the Morgan contract. A. Correct.

Q. — to participate equally in whatever is realized on the bonds over par; is that right? A. That is right.

Q. So that the measure of Morgan & Company's compensation this transaction could not be arrived at by simply assuming y sold the bonds to the syndicate at 96½? A. No, sir.

Q. You would have to know what they realized on this $40,-
000,000 or $50,000,000 withdrawn from the syndicate? A.
Yes, sir.

Q. Now, this 1 per cent paid into sinking fund is such an
amount as sustained during the life of the bonds would completely discharge the bonds, at their maturity? That is the
purpose of the clause? A. That is the purpose of the sinking
fund, yes, sir.

Q. And if under this reserved right of the company to pay
more than 1 per cent into sinking fund, the fund grew more than
was calculated, that redemption could be had at an earlier date?
A. Yes, sir.

Q. And under the terms of the bonds, they are redeemable at
110? A. Yes, sir.

Q. And there is not any doubt that the bonds are susceptible
to redemption at 110 under the operation of the sinking fund
clause? A. None at all.

Q. The only question is will the subsequent earnings be maintained for the next 53 years at their present rate? A. They
would have to be maintained at a sufficient rate to pay the interest
and the 1 per cent.

Q. Yes. But, according to Mr. Shonts' letter to Mr. Morgan,
the income from the present subways is more than sufficient to
pay all the fixed charges? A. Yes, sir.

Q. And fixed charges means interest and sinking fund? A.
And sinking fund, correct.

Q. So that it would be hard to imagine a better security than
this bond? A. I could not imagine one.

Q. What did the city realize on its bonds? I mean to say, at
what price were the city bonds sold? A. That I don't know.
If you — I do know that at the time we made this arrangement
with Morgan & Company, at the time we sold him this $170,-
000,000 of bonds at 93½, it was a little later, I think about nine
months later, the syndicate borrowed $100,000,000 from the same
source, and they paid 6 per cent for the money.

Mr. Quackenbush.— You mean the city?

Mr. Fisher.— The city. The city borrowed $100,000,000 from
the same source, and they paid 6 per cent for the money: And,

furthermore, there was an understanding that they were to deposit
that money with the various members of the syndicate, that they
were to receive 2 per cent interest as against our 2½ per cent.   I
simply cite that to show that we did not make such an unprofitable contract, after all.

By Mr. Colby:

Q. That $100,000,000 transaction was during the early weeks
of the war, when there was some question as to the necessity of
banking support for the maintenance of the city's credit?   A.
It was September, 1914.

Chairman Thompson.— Who negotiated that for the city?

Mr. Fisher.— I would not like to say.

Chairman Thompson.— I wish you would, if you know.

Mr. Fisher.— I don't know.

By Mr. Colby:

Q. It is fair to assume, the chief financial officer?   A. I could
not say.

Q. Do you know at what price the city sold its bonds for the
purpose of making its contribution to this dual contract?   A. At
various rates of interest, and I don't remember at the present time
just what they were.

Q. Was the rate of interest on their bonds over 4½?   A. I
would not like to say without checking it up.

Q. They sold them at a better price than 93½?   A. A slightly
better price, I think.

Q. And they paid a lower rate of interest than the Interborough is paying on its bonds?   A. Yes, sir.

Chairman Thompson.— Who is that?

Mr. Colby.— The city.

By Mr. Colby:

Q. Is there any provision in the city bonds for 1 per cent
amortization of sinking fund?

Chairman Thompson.— The city couldn't sell their bonds for
less than par, could they?

Mr. Fisher.— No, sir.

(The last question was read by the stenographer as follows: " Is there any provision in the city bonds for 1 per cent amortization of sinking fund ?")   A. I could not say; I presume there is, yes, sir, but I could not be positive.

Mr. Colby.— Now, let me see the contracts, will you please?

By Mr. Colby:

Q. I just want to come back to that question of the city's borrowing of the $100,000,000 in September, 1914. Isn't it true the city had a short-term obligation abroad at that time ?   A. I am not conducting the city's finances; I could not say. It was a three-year note which they borrowed the money on. I know they paid that rate of interest.

Q. It was at a time when international exchange was in a perturbed condition, was it not ?   A. I don't think international exchange was at that time in a perturbed condition. I think that came —

Q. There was great uncertainty —   A. — later on, in 1915.

Q. There was great uncertainty as to what the course of foreign exchange would be at that time?

Chairman Thompson.— What date?

Mr. Colby.— September, 1914.

Mr. Fisher.— I have not seen it referred to generally.

By Mr. Colby:

Q. You know that subsequently the rates on sterling exchange declined beyond any thing known in the history of finance?   A. That was in 1915.

Q. I mean, subsequently it was a progressive, successive decline, and that very unusual expedients and great international effort was necessary in order to maintain on some degree of stability the rates of foreign exchange? In other words, Mr. Fisher, my point is that the amount of money, the amount of interest which the city had to pay for this short-term emergency accommodation is hardly a fair basis of — is hardly a criterion as to the wisdom or the propriety of the rates paid by the Interborough on these 53-year bonds secured by the subway income. I don't think possibly you realize that the two transactions were so utterly diverse in character and purpose and intent, but it would be very difficult to draw any comparison between the two transactions. The redemption of these bonds at 110 is a real feature of the bonds? It is not just a nominal provision of the bonds? These bonds are going to be redeemed? A. Yes, sir.

Q. Under their terms after the lapse of a few years, they will be redeemed; they must be redeemed? A. They are only called for the sinking fund during the term of the mortgage.

Q. And the only way by which the call to the sinking fund can be met is either by redemption at 110 or by purchase in the open market, should the bonds be selling at lower than 110? A. Correct.

Q. And those purchases in the open market constitute the only calculably widely known demand for these bonds, and invariably work the price of the bonds upward? A. I should say so.

Q. So that when a banking house buys bonds with the sinking fund provision as certain as this, which are redeemable at 110, and pays only 93½ for them, it is a fair thing to assume that those bonds will be sold at some price approaching if not reaching 110 in the near future? A. They might sell at some price approaching 110 in the near future; yes, sir, but the bankers would not necessarily benefit from that.

Q. My point is simply this, that the waiver of your right to participate in the receipts of those bonds over par, was the waiver of a substantial right, when you consider the amount as to which the waiver operated, namely, $40,000,000? A. It did not prove to be.

Q. Not yet. A. No. One hundred and forty-eight million dollars of bonds have been sold, and there has been no participation so far.

Q. You have sold the bonds, however, greatly in excess of your actual present requirement? A. That we could not control.

Q. Because you had acquiesced in an agreement with Morgan to let them have them upon call? A. That agreement was based on the construction of the present subways over a period of four years from 1913.

Q. And whether Morgan gets the locked-up profit that is in these bonds up to 110, or somebody else, who is a member of their syndicate, the fact remains that you to the extent of 148 million dollars have parted with all your right or prospect of benefit from that appreciation in bonds? A. Yes, sir.

Chairman Thompson.— Have these bonds ever been quoted at 110?

Mr. Colby.— They would not be quoted at that.

By Mr. Colby:

Q. Now, Mr. Fisher, you are familiar with this contract, and you heard me read the letter of September 12, 1912 — I mean May 24, 1912, in which Mr. Shonts makes a representation to the bankers of the preferential, the average earnings, interest and sinking fund, all of which is prior in time and also in order to the city's participation in the subway earnings. Will you indicate to me what, if any, of those features are not embodied in this contract? In other words, does not this contract carry out fully the representations published by Morgan & Company, and which were stated to Morgan & Company by the present railroad? A. It is supposed to; yes, sir.

Q. Is there any discrepancy or deviation between this statement of priorities contained in the Shonts' letter, and in this contract? A. Would you mind enumerating the statement of priority, please? There is the preferential, and interest on the bonds, as I understand, and the preferential on the Manhattan.

Q. This is what Mr. Shonts says: "When the subways are completed, the Interborough Company will have a prior claim on the net earnings of the properties, which claim will aggregate $14,568,000. This is made up as follows: Average annual earnings of the present subway, $6,335,000." That is a preferential, isn't it? A. That is provided for in the contract.

Q. "Five per cent interest and one per cent annual sinking fund on the amount of Interborough's new investment in subways"? A. That is provided for.

Q. That amounts to $4,620,000. Interest and annual sinking fund on approximately $30,000,000 new capital invested in elevated railways? A. That is provided for.

Q. That amounts to $1,800,000. Are the profits from the Manhattan Railway lease which during the last two years have averaged

$1,813,000 provided for? A. To the extent of about a million and a half. Three hundred and odd thousand dollars represents miscellaneous income, not provided for in the contract. That is income from investments, rentals, real estate and so on.

Q. So it would be very unfair to characterize these letters and statements of the president to Morgan & Company as irresponsible representations of the money used prior to the contracts, and having no relations with the provisions of the contract? A. Based pretty generally on the provisions of the contract.

Chairman Thompson.— The city practically guarantees these bonds?

Mr. Fisher.— Well, it is a guarantee —

Mr. Colby.— The Comptroller sought to dismiss these figures set forth in the proceedings of the Committee on Friday, on the theory they antedated the contract by many years. As a matter of fact, the letter I read was a letter written only a few weeks prior to May 24, Mr. Chairman, 1912, and was followed by the letter of May 24, 1912, which is the basis of Morgan & Company's printed offer of the bonds to their syndicate members, and in accordance with the testimony of the witness, these priorities and these preferentials are explicitly and fully recognized in the contract itself.

Chairman Thompson.— But it is a fact the city practically guarantees these bonds. Isn't that so?

Mr. Fisher.— It operates as a practical guarantee, although not set forth in so many words.

Chairman Thompson.— But as I say, it is a practical guarantee by the city of the bonds?

Mr. Colby.— Will you have Mr. Gaynor here in a few minutes?

Mr. Quackenbush.— Yes, sir.

Mr. Fisher.— May I make a little explanation in connection with that sinking fund?

Mr. Colby.— I would like to hear anything you have got to say.

(Senator Lawson takes the Chair.)

Mr. Fisher.— The company in almost all mortgages of that kind reserves the right invariably to increase the sinking fund. I think it has done so in this instance. I think you will find it in the mortgage covering the $170,000,000. That means, of course, that the company, if it so desires, may invest in sinking fund bonds and may increase the sinking fund from sources other than the earnings of the company. By doing so, in this instance, it would not work hardship on the city. It would have no right to deduct any amount larger than one per cent from the earnings, because to the extent it did that, it would be taking away from the opportunity of the city to participate in the excess profits.

By Mr. Colby:

Q. Well, why should the company reserve its right to apply its own funds to the sinking fund? A. Well, it might have a sum of money — might come in possession of a sum of money realized from the sale of real estate or securities or other sources, and might — it would depend much on the price of the bonds — it might decide it would be better to increase the sinking fund and retire those bonds than to invest the money in other directions.

Q. But why, in outlining the agreement between J. P. Morgan & Company, was it necessary to say, as a feature of that agreement with the company, that the city reserves the right to increase the payments to the sinking fund? A. Because that is a feature usually accompanying the borrowing of a sum of money under mortgage of that sort, and it really makes the mortgage a little more valuable; makes the bonds a little more valuable for the investor.

Q. Your idea is this: That all the President had in mind was that the company might from funds of its own make donations to the sinking fund that would increase it and contribute to the celerity of the redemption of the bonds? A. And thereby call more bonds.

Q. And such increases to the sinking fund did not contemplate the application of anything beyond the one per cent out of the earnings of the dual system? A. You understand it correctly.

Q. While I am waiting for Mr. Gaynor, I am going to ask you a few questions about the Subway Realty Company. What is the Subway Realty Company? A. That is a company formed

at the time of the construction of the original subways, covered
by contracts Nos. 1 and 2, for the purpose of acquiring easements.

Q. Who constituted the Subway Realty Company? A. I don't
remember the original stockholders. I think the original stockholders were composed mostly of the original investors in the
Rapid Transit Subway Construction and Interborough stocks.

Q. Do you recall who the president of the company was? A.
I think the first president was August Belmont.

Q. Would this memorandum help you? A. Not at the present
time, no, sir; because —

Q. The officers have changed? A The officers have changed
since then.

Q. And the holders of the stock and the officers and directors
were Interborough Rapid Transit Company men? A. Yes, sir.

Q. Well, what was the capital of the company? A. $2,000,000.

Q. Was it paid in? A. Yes, sir.

Q. Cash? A. Yes, sir.

Q. What did it do with these easements it acquired? A. The
easements were turned over to the city. They were acquired under
the original contract.

Q. And what did the company receive for these easements from
the city? A. I could not tell you what it received in each instance.

Q. Well, speaking generally? A. I think it averaged generally
about the carrying charges of the property only. I think they
were turned over to the city at cost plus carrying charges.

Q. And that was to enable the company to acquire its routes?
A. No; to facilitate the construction of the line. They thought
they could acquire them and turn them over to the city at a better
advantage than the city could.

Q. Is Mr. Belmont still the president? A. Mr. Shonts is
president.

Q. Mr. Shonts is the president. Is this the owner of the Belmont hotel, this company? A. Yes, sir.

Q. How did it acquire the Belmont Hotel? A. It acquired an
easement of 42d street, which property could not be disposed of
to good advantage, and the hotel was therefore constructed as an
investment.

Q. At what cost? A. Approximately $6,000,000.

Q. Was this money raised and expended by the Subway Realty Company? A. Yes, sir; it was.

Senator Lawson.— You say the company acquired an easement. They did not build the hotel on an easement?

Mr. Fisher.— It acquired some additional property besides the property required for easement purposes.

Mr. Quackenbush.— I think you might explain that in full. They had to make the curve there, Senator, and in order to get the curve from Fourth avenue into 42d street they had to have more than an easement.

Senator Lawson.— Therefore acquired the fee, and thereafter built the hotel?

Mr. Quackenbush.— Yes, sir.

Mr. Fisher.— Yes, sir. I am sorry I did not make myself plainer.

Senator Lawson.— Has the Interborough any direct control of the operation of the Hotel Belmont?

Mr. Fisher.— No, sir, none at all. It is leased to what they call the August Belmont Hotel Company, until 1926, at a stipulated rental.

Senator Lawson.— In other words, this company, the holder of the easements, is kept separate from the Interborough?

Mr. Fisher.— Yes, sir.

Mr. Quackenbush.— As long as you are on that subject, so as not to have any misunderstanding: The Interborough subsequently acquired the stock.

Mr. Fisher.— We haven't got to that subject.

Senator Lawson.— That is the question I asked, whether the Interborough Company owned the Belmont Hotel. He said —

Mr. Fisher.— The Interborough does not own all the stock of the Subway Realty Company. The Interborough acquired the stock, part of it, at par, plus 5½ per cent. interest, from the time the investment was made.

Senator Lawson.— Does the Interborough own a majority of the stock ?

Mr. Fisher.— Yes, sir.

Senator Lawson.— Then it practically controls the Hotel Belmont ?

Mr. Fisher.— In that it controls through the Subway Realty Company.

Mr. Quackenbush.— I don't want you to misunderstand, Mr. Fisher. We filed a statement of that with Mr. Colby.

Senator Lawson.— That is the only question I want.

Mr. Fisher.— These companies operate separately, and I forget sometimes.

Senator Lawson.— Oh, I know. You have a great deal on your mind, I know.

Mr. Colby.— I have not followed these questions quite as closely as I would like.

 (Discussion off the record, of Mr. Colby and Senator Lawson.)

Senator Lawson.— It has since developed that the Interborough acquired a majority of the stock of this realty company and now actually controls the Hotel Belmont as part of the system of the Interborough.

By Mr. Colby:

Q. What amount — what is the total capital stock of the Subway Realty Company ? A. $2,000,000.

Q. And how much is owned by the Interborough Rapid Transit Company ? A. About $1,800,000.

Q. And the remaining shares are owned by Interborough men ? A. No, sir; the remaining shares are owned by J. P. Morgan & Company, and the Adams estate — the Weir estate, I should have said, the former president of the Adams Express Company.

Q. How much does J. P. Morgan & Company own?
A. Nearly all of the balance. Only a small portion is owned by
the Weir estate.

Q. So that it is the Interborough and J. P. Morgan & Company
who own the Belmont Hotel site? Has this easement passed into
a title? Does the Subway Realty Company own the land? A.
Yes, sir.

Q. Did the Interborough ever own the land there? A. Only
through its control of the Subway Realty Company.

Q. The Subway Realty Company acquired the site of the Belmont Hotel from the original — at least, from the former owners,
former individual owners? A. Yes, sir.

Q. What rights have the Interborough in that land? A. They
have no rights other than their ownership of their stock in the
Subway Realty Company.

Q. In other words, the railroad is run through land that belongs to someone other than the railroad company there? A.
Well, it belongs to a company controlled by the railroad.

Q. But technically —

Mr. Quackenbush.— Oh, I think that is wrong. You are asking him technical questions now. My understanding is that the
city, as the owner of the subway, has all of the rights, and that in
getting around that curve, as I said, when your attention was distracted, it was found that the easement would not be sufficient,
could not get an easement, or it would be so expensive that it was
thought better to buy the fee, and that the hotel was erected upon
the ownership of the fee subject to the easement of the right of
way of the railroad.

Mr. Colby.— I see.

Mr. Quackenbush.— I am quite sure that is correct. It took
place before my time, but I think that is correct.

Mr. Fisher.— You have stated it correctly.

By Mr. Colby:

Q. Then it was the Subway Realty Company that erected the
hotel? A. Yes, sir.

Q. And borrowed in large part the money necessary to erect it?
A. Yes, sir.

Q. And equipped it?   A. Yes, sir.

Q. Who is operating that hotel?   A. The August Belmont Hotel Company.

Q. How did they acquire the right to operate the hotel?   A. They leased it.

Q. From the Subway Realty Company?   A. Yes, sir.

Q. Was Mr. Belmont president of the Subway Realty Company at that time?   A. I don't think so.

Q. Was he a director?   A. No, sir.

Q. Or a stockholder?   A. No, sir; I don't think he was either.

Q. He had been, however?   A. He had been.

Q. He had been president?   A. Originally, yes, sir.

Q. A director and considerable stockholder?   A. I don't know to what extent.

(Senator Foley takes the Chair.)

By Mr. Colby:

Q. When was the lease made?   A. I could not give you that date without looking it up.

Q. Is it a twenty-year lease?   A. I don't know. Runs to 1926.

Q. Would any memoranda that you have in this little book refresh your mind?   A. I don't think so.

Q. Will you see if it will?   A. I will find out in just a second for you. No, it won't. (Witness looks in book.)   The lease is dated November 1, 1906, and it is a twenty-year lease. I got that from the records.

Q. The lease was dated November 1, 1906, and ran for twenty years?   A. Ran for twenty years.

Q. When was the subway Realty Company formed?   A. I think that is also —   (Refers to book.)   I think it was incorporated in 1901 or 1902.   (Witness referring to book.)   April 19, 1901.

Q. What are the terms as to rental of this property?   A. It is a stipulated sum.

Q. Per annum?   A. Per annum.

Q. What is the sum?   A. It is about $328,000, as near as I recollect. It is not down here.

Q. Is that a low or a high rental for that property? A. Well, as it proves at the present time, I think it is not a very high rental. I understand that it is — I see it is shown here; excuse me. The rental is $318,256.34 a year.

Q. Who pays the taxes? A. The August Belmont Hotel Company.

Q. And this — this rent is net to the Subway Realty Company, is it? A. Yes, sir.

Q. Have they any charges in connection with the maintenance or upkeep of the hotel? A. None at all.

Q. What do you estimate the value of that property at the present time to be? A. I don't think any estimate was ever made.

Q. At what is it assessed? A. That I could not tell you.

Q. Is there any provision in the lease for reappraisal or revaluation prior to 1926? A. No, sir.

Q. The August Belmont Hotel Company is simply a company formed for the purpose of operating the Belmont Hotel? A. Yes, sir.

Q. Has the Interborough any interest in the August Belmont Hotel Company? A. No, sir.

Mr. Quackenbush.— Mr. Gaynor is here, Mr. Colby.

Mr. Colby.— Yes. Mr. Gaynor, how long will it take you to produce the construction account under Contract No. 3, and the equipment account under Contract No. 3?

Mr. Gaynor.—As I promised, I will have those for you in the morning.

Mr. Colby.— I don't mean the memorandum drawn from the account, but I mean the original.

Mr. Gaynor.— I will have those in the morning.

Mr. Colby.— Can't you produce it here now?

Mr. Gaynor.— Well, in part, but not satisfactory.

Mr. Colby.— Let us see if it is not satisfactory.

By Mr. Colby:

Q. Before I leave this subject, Mr. Fisher, is the Belmont Hotel built in any part upon city property? A. I don't think so. I think that property was all acquired by the City Realty Company for that purpose.

Q. And was that the property, including any right of easement, partly acquired by the city or at the expenditure of city funds? A. No, sir. The easement, I think, was turned over to the city.

Q. The railroad, as I understand it, curves under the Belmont Hotel in part, doesn't it? A. Yes, under the northeast corner.

(Senator Thompson takes the Chair.)

Q. And if that is now a right of way or an easement owned by the city, the Belmont Hotel to that extent is built over land owned by the city, is it not? A. That is a legal question. I prefer not to answer it.

Chairman Thompson.— That is a technical thing the secretary is not familiar with.

Mr. Colby.—Are you (to Mr. Quackenbush)?

Mr. Quackenbush.— I will take your statement of the law on that.

Mr. Colby.— I am only trying to ascertain the facts.

Mr. Quackenbush.— The city, as I thought I had stated it, has a permanent right of way for the subway under the Belmont hotel. Now, just how much it goes under is an engineering matter, that I cannot say. But my understanding, and I believe it is correct — I will check it up and let you know the facts, if I am in error — was that in laying out the subway, as it made the curve from Fourth avenue into 42nd street, it was found necessary to get outside of the street line, and to acquire the easement for that curve under what is now the Hotel Belmont was found to be pretty expensive, and the people who were promoting the enterprise at that time thought they could save money by buying the fee, transferring the right of way to the city, and then erecting upon the site a hotel, and that is what I understand was done, so that the legal and technical situation is that there is carved out of the fee, the permanent right of way for the railroad. I think the same situation exists under the Times Square building at 42nd street and Broadway.

Mr. Colby.— Did the Subway Realty Company sell its right to the city?

Mr. Quackenbush.— I think it was conveyed. I think every easement that the —

Mr. Colby.— No doubt it was conveyed.

Mr. Quackenbush.— I don't know as to the price. As I said, that was before my time, and I will have to check those questions up.

Chairman Thompson.— The papers ought to state about it. There should be papers on file.

Mr. Quackenbush.— We have plenty of them. I will furnish the title search and everything else, if you want it.

Chairman Thompson.— That is the best way to get at it.

Mr. Fisher.— I am quite sure all of those easements were conveyed to the city at a price. I forget what it was now.

Chairman Thompson.— Does anyone know how much was paid for it and how much the city paid?

Mr. Fisher.— We can easily find out.

Mr. Quackenbush.— I will get you a statement of the whole transaction.

By Mr. Colby:

Q. How did this company acquire the Belmont Tunnel? A. Speaking now of the —

Q. Interborough Rapid Transit Company. A. It advanced the money for the construction of the tunnel.

Q. Did it acquire a contract from a man named Peirce? A. Yes, sir.

Q. What was his full name? A. John Peirce.

Q. What was the nature of the Peirce contract? A. I think

18

he was to purchase the franchise and stock and whatever other property the company owned.

Q. What company? A. The New York & Long Island Railroad Company, as it was known at that time, for a stipulated sum. And I believe you have a copy of that contract in your possession.

Mr. Colby.— Have we a copy of that contract?

Mr. Dawson.— There is, in the papers.

By Mr. Colby:

Q. What is the relation of this property — of this tunnel — to the Rapid Transit Subway system as projected by the new routes? A. It was a part of the new contract No. 3. The city purchased the tunnel.

Q. What did the city pay — I mean what did this company pay for the rights acquired from Peirce? A. About $350,000, as near as I can recollect.

Q. Did that — what right in the tunnel did that acquisition give to the company? A. That gave them the right to all property, including any construction that they had then performed at that time.

Chairman Thompson.— You mean —

Mr. Fisher.— Stock.

By Mr. Colby:

Q. It was an uncompleted tunnel, is that right? A. Yes, sir.

Chairman Thompson.— You mean the company purchased this for $350,000, don't you?

Mr. Fisher.— Yes, sir.

Chairman Thompson.— You said the city. I think it was a misstatement. I wanted to know what the city paid for it. You said $350,000.

Mr. Fisher.— The company, I should have said, not the city.

By Mr. Colby:

Q. What additional sums has the city paid — I mean, the company paid in connection with the acquisition of the tunnel? A.

Advanced money in connection with constructing the tunnel — approximately $10,000,000 and some odd hundred thousand dollars.

Q. The Interborough did? A. Yes, sir.

Q. How much of this money has been charged off? A. You would have to ask the auditor. That is a matter of bookkeeping.

Q. I want to excuse you for a moment, Mr. Fisher, and ask the auditor a few questions. A. Yes, sir.

Mr. Colby.— Thank you.

EDWARD J. F. GAYNOR, recalled.

By Mr. Colby:

Q. Mr. Gaynor, I know that you are in the course of — that there is in course of preparation under your direction a number of statements which I have requested of you, and it is not to depart from that orderly method of collecting and presenting that data that you are at work upon, but I want to ask you a few questions as to your general scheme of accounts, particularly with relation to the expenditures in connection with the dual subway contracts. While we are in a hurry, we don't want to put you under a sense of pressure in the preparation of material, and I know it takes time to prepare it. I may say, Mr. Chairman, I am promised Mr. Gaynor's statements as requested some time this evening.

Chairman Thompson.— Yes.

Mr. Colby.— He is busily at work on it, so I don't want to take a great deal of his time now.

By Mr. Colby:

Q. Under what accounts are the expenditures made by the Interborough Rapid Transit Company in connection with its part of the new subway construction entered? A. Under two accounts, one known as construction under contract No. 3; the other equipment, contract No. 3.

Q. There are other construction and equipment accounts in connection with the work which is now in progress, are there not? A. Yes, sir.

Q. What are they? A. Construction, Manhattan third tracking; equipment Manhattan third tracking; construction, elevated extensions; equipment, elevated extensions; power plant improvements.

Q. There are other accounts, however, in which certain items are carried, which have been expended in connection with the subway contract, are there not? A. Yes, sir.

Q. What is " other suspense? " A. That is the account, as I described the other day, into which items are carried prior to the determination of the final lodgment of the expenditure.

Q. Aren't construction items to some extent carried in this account? A. They were — certain construction items relating to contract No. 3, and to the elevated extension third tracking and improvement work were originally carried into " other suspense account " but have been carried into the appropriate construction account some time ago.

Q. There was also — there is also a considerable number of charges to " other suspense " which have not yet been finally distributed? A. Yes, sir.

Q. Or placed in their — A. Yes, sir.

Q. — ultimate account? There is another account called " prior determination," is there not? A. No. " Prior determination " is not an account, " prior determination " is an act of the Public Service Commission.

Q. I see on some of the vouchers which have appeared in evidence thus far, that the amounts paid are distributed under "proposed subway routes." What does that mean? A. They were distributed to " proposed subway routes " before contract No. 3 and the allied certificates became definitely fixed.

Q. I see. What items are carried to construction account, contract No. 3, speaking generally? A. All construction items.

Q. What do you consider construction items? A. The cost of building the new subways, so far as the Interborough is concerned, can be generally divided into two items: One, the cost of construction, the work which is in progress under the direction of the city officers; two, the work of equipping the new subway, a work which is in progress under the direction of the Interborough.

Q. Well, is it proper to charge interest to construction account?
A. It is.

Q. Not all interest? A. All interest that is properly lost in construction work.

Q. That ordinarily means the interest upon the amount expended in construction, before the construction is complete, doesn't it? A. No, sir. It means ordinarily the loss of interest involved in raising capital for any construction enterprise. And the loss of interest is a construction item until the road is open for operation.

Q. And whether that interest were lost in raising capital for the particular construction work under way or not, would it be a proper item to include in construction? A. It would.

Q. In other words, if we were undertaking a construction work which was to cost $56,000,000, and if that were the maximum of your obligation to contribute to that construction work, would you consider it proper to carry in that account a loss of interest in connection with the sale of $164,000,000 of bonds? A. No, sir.

Q. Have you got construction account, contract No. 3, here? A. Yes, sir. Some of it. Enough, I think, to answer the questions indicated by you.

Q. Can I see it? A. Yes, sir. (Witness hands transcript of construction account, contract No. 3, to counsel.)

Q. Of course, the amount actually expended for the prosecution of the work of construction presents no difficulty to any mind. That is clearly a proper charge to construction account A. I think so.

Q. Now, this is a statement of the account, without any attempt at detail. This is, in other words, a summary of some other account? A. That is a summary of the construction account, to December 31st, and also of the equipment account to December 31st. What do you call this, ledger account? A. That is a condensation of thousands of entries supporting the figures which you see there. It is generally described as cost of construction and cost of equipment under contract No. 3.

Q. There are two or three filtrations, as I might call them, of details from original entries on the most detailed record, until there appears on this, the most condensed record; that is true? A. Several thousand.

Q. You have a ledger account? This isn't it? This is a summary drawn from the ledger? A. It is a summary in harmony with the ledger account, but prepared from data distributed in thousands of sheets.

Q. Yes. A. Thousands of subdivisions.

Q. And then you have a sub-ledger account, haven't you? A. The sub-ledger is really the collation of these thousand items which I am referring to.

Q. And where are these manifold items first recorded? A. They are first recorded in the general ledger.

Q. And there is the sub-ledger? A. Yes, sir.

Q. And then the ledger? A. No. The sub-ledger really — there is a ledger and sub-ledger, if you term it so, and the sub-ledger, which you so describe, contains all of the detail which underlies these figures.

Q. Yes. So that going down the scale, it is this statement, and sub-ledger, ledger, and then the time sheets and material vouchers? A. The sub-ledger refers to the vouchers.

Q. This is an accurate statement, I assume, Mr. Gaynor? A. It is.

Q. There first appears here expenditures of contract No. 3. That is for the subway extensions, the new dual routes, isn't it? A. The new dual subways.

Q. There is the Seventh Avenue branch, the Lexington Avenue branch, the Eastern Parkway division, the Steinway Tunnel line, the White Plains road. The total expenditure thus far charged to this construction account seems to be $26,995,397.04? A. That is right.

Q. That was on December 31, 1915? A. That is right.

Q. Of that total, I find these entries: Debt discount, $809,-861.88; what is that? A. That is 3 per cent of the cost of construction to December 31, 1915.

Q. Why did you figure that 3 per cent? A. That was a condition of the contract.

Q. You have not paid that money? A. No, discount is never received, and therefore cannot be paid, but it is a recognition by the contract of that much of the cost of the construction work,

presented by a loss of capital between the par value of the bonds
l what you have to sell them for.

Q. You are crediting yourself with expenditure of $809,000 in effect, at least? A. Hardly that. You are entering to the cost of construction three per cent of the cost of the whole construction work which in effect is substantially three per cent of the discount, which to the Interborough Company is in its completeness 6½ per cent, the difference between par and 93½.

Q. Somebody gave you that amount of money, of credit, didn't they? A. No, sir.

Q. You didn't pay that? A. If you sell bonds for 93½ per cent, you don't receive the 6½ per cent; you receive the 93½ per cent, not the 6½ per cent. So that the 6½ per cent under ordinary conditions, would be an element in the total cost of whatever construction work was in progress under your plans. But under the contract with the city — or, if I will go a little further — under the contract with the city, we are allowed only 3 per cent of discount.

Q. Well, how do you connect up $809,861.88 with construction work? A. Because that is exactly 3 per cent of the total amount chargeable to construction work for the period ending December 31, 1915.

Q. What has that got to do with digging tunnels and building subways? A. You could not dig the tunnels or provide anything else for the dual subway, unless you first got the money to be prepared to meet those payrolls and supply bills. Now, the 3 per cent is one of the elements of cost of the construction work, because that is the cost of getting your money, and so recognized to that extent by the contract.

Q. I confess I could have a clearer impression than I have yet on that item, but I leave it for a moment, and maybe your subsequent explanation will tend to its clarification. Next is debt expense, $299,587; what is that? A. The debt expense differs from the debt discount in so much as it represents an expenditure in connection with the issuance of evidences of debt, such as bonds, and any other incident that may be issued in connection with the issue of bonds.

Q. Yes. Now, if you have any knowledge of the details that enters into that item account, specify in a general way what that item is composed of? A. It is the expense of registering the bonds, and printing bonds, paying the recording tax. I think those would be the principal items.

Chairman Thompson.— Lawyers for looking them over?

Mr. Gaynor.— I beg your pardon?

Chairman Thompson.— Lawyers for looking at them?

Mr. Gaynor.— No, sir.

Assemblyman Burr.— Special account for that.

Mr. Gaynor.— No legal account.

Mr. Quackenbush.— That comes under another class.

Chairman Thompson.— It is in, just the same.

Mr. Quackenbush.— There was never anything built in this world that did not have a lawyer's bill connected with it.

Q. I am warranted in saying this: Of these first two items, aggregating $1,100,000, not any part of that $1,100,000 has gone to the purchase of materials or payment of workmen or prosecution directly of the work of construction? A. You are, yes, sir.

Q. So those first two charges to construction account are, if correct, charges against construction theoretically rather than actually? A. Oh, no, they are absolutely charges against construction.

Q. From a bookkeeper's standpoint? A. From any standpoint.

Q. But when you have spent $1,100,000, you have not spent a dollar of it for building tunnels? A. But you could not spend a dollar for the digging of a tunnel if you did not undergo that expense to provide the money for the purpose.

Q. Now, the next is real estate, $355,000; what is that? A. That is very largely real estate that has been acquired by the city for the purposes of the dual subway, we having advanced the money to the city for the purpose.

Q. And does that come back to you? A. No, except as it comes back as part of the completed subway.

Q. You have, in other words, bought land for the city aggregating in value $355,000? A. To be exact, the city negotiates for the purchase of certain property necessary for the construction work, and calls upon the Interborough Company to provide the means to make the payment, which we do.

Q. I see. The next item is easements, $1,043,000. Have you acquired easements at that cost? A. How much is that?

Q. $1,043,000. Easements, $1,043,000.

Chairman Thompson.— That is real estate, rights and real estate?

Mr. Gaynor.— Let me refresh my recollection.

Mr. Colby.— Certainly.

(Witness refers to statement.)

Mr. Gaynor.— I will ask you to pass that for the present. I have not in mind the essential items of that.

Chairman Thompson.— Does that real estate you acquired — who takes title to that?

Mr. Gaynor.— The city.

Chairman Thompson.— Goes to the city?

Mr. Gaynor.— Yes, sir.

Senator Lawson.— But the Interborough pays for it?

Mr. Gaynor.— Yes, sir.

By Mr. Colby:

Q. The next is tunnels, $16,000,000; that is for the actual work of digging the tunnel, is it? A. Yes, sir.

Q. That includes labor, materials, engineering and superintendence? A. No, it is the actual labor and material entering into the performance of the work on the part of the various subcontractors engaged in digging and putting in the steel work.

Q. Is this a payment that you make to subcontractors, $16,000,000? A. Yes, sir.

Q. You, in other words, do not make any direct arrangements for the purchase of steel work or other materials, but this is the payment of a contract price to subcontractors; is that right? A. Yes, sir.

Q. Who in turn make those purchases? A. Yes, sir.

Q. The next item is elevated construction and foundation, $3,300,000? A. That follows the same description, the difference being that the item preceding it relates to tunnel work, while this is confined to elevated construction work.

Q. This is elevated construction in connection with the subway, and not in connection with the Manhattan Elevated? A. No relation to the elevated lines.

Q. Underground conduits, $257,000? A. Conduits in connection with the subway.

Q. Engineering and superintendence, $270,108? A. In connection with the subways. Expenditures for those purposes in connection with the subway.

Q. That is over a period of how long, up to December 31? A. From the beginning of the construction work.

Q. The next item I see is the law expenditures during construction, $106,701.40. A. Those are the legal expenditures which we have made in connection with the construction work.

Q. In other words, it is the aggregate of those evidences of payments made to outside lawyers? A. It is.

Q. Which have been charged to construction? A. Plus whatever may be included in representing our own law department's activities.

Q. Do you apportion the fixed expenses of your regular department to various accounts? A. The specific charges are carried there.

Q. The next item is interest during construction, $3,756,247; what is that interest on? A. That is interest upon the construction cost from the dates the company provided the money, to December 31.

Q. Well, let us see, now. The actual expenditures that are clear to me, are, we will say, real estate and casements, $1,400,000; tunnels and elevated structures, $19,600,000; then underground conduits, engineering and legal fees, about $650,000 more. That makes $21,650,000, in round numbers. And here is an interest charge of $3,756,000. How can such an interest charge

have mounted up in connection with expenditures relatively so
small? A. For the reason that interest chargeable to construction work is allied with the procuring of the funds necessary
for that work, rather than with the expenditures made after the
funds are obtained.

Q. In other words, you have charged this construction account
all the interest losses that you have sustained on your total bond
issue? A. No, sir.

Q. Well, the point is obvious that on actual expenditures for the
work of construction, including real estate, easements, tunnels,
elevated structure foundation, conduits, engineering and superintendence, and even excluding all expenses, all of which aggregate
only twenty-one millions and a half, you could hardly have incurred
an interest charge on such expenditures of $3,756,247? A. The
interest charge which you are looking at is the interest according
to the terms of the contract upon the moneys provided by the
Interborough Rapid Transit Company for the specific purpose
of building the subway.

Q. But I thought you said the debt discount of $809,861 repre-
sented an arbitrary 3 per cent. to cover cost of financing.

Chairman Thompson.— No. He said that represented 3 per
cent., that is all. He didn't say arbitrary or anything else, just
three per cent.

Mr. Colby.— I supplied the word "arbitrary," as it has not
any disclosed relation to anything else.

Chairman Thompson.— You don't pretend it has, do you?

Mr. Quackenbush.— It is all very simple. It is right here in
the contract.

Chairman Thompson.— Simple as can be. Three per cent.

Mr. Colby.— Three per cent. on what?

Chairman Thompson.— Whatever 3 per cent it takes to make
that money; whatever amount.

Mr. Quackenbush.— (Referring to pamphlet). Page 21, you
will find it, is the 3 per cent; and on page 23 is the interest charge.
All these items are in the contract.

Chairman Thompson.— I suspect they are all in the contract.

Mr. Quackenbush.—And our accounts are in accordance with the contract.

Chairman Thompson.— There are whole lot of things in that contract.

Mr. Quackenbush.— I am not endeavoring to get away from the contract.

By Mr. Colby:

Q. We have a total charge to construction here under the heading of " debt discount " and " debt expense " of $1,100,000, and a charge to construction for interest during construction of $3,756,000, making a total of $4,856,000, where the actual expenditure for construction seems to be about twenty-one million and a half. A. I would point out that you cannot satisfactorily analyze a construction interest account by dealing only with the moneys which you have spent. You must take into consideration the amount of money which you have raised for construction purposes, and which remains in a certain measure unprofitable until your construction work is finished.

Q. Well, how much money have you raised for this construction purpose which is costing you interest and which is to a certain extent unprofitable? A. You have a statement here which I prepared for you showing the exact balance in construction account December 31.

Chairman Thompson.— Yet Mr. Morgan charges you interest on $50,000,000 on deposit there for more than the amount you get back, or you charge that into construction, do you not?

Mr. Gaynor.— Not exactly that. When you raise money for construction purposes, it represents a loss from the time it is raised, diminished only by the amount of bank interest you earn until you apply the money.

Chairman Thompson.— That difference is charged to construction account?

Mr. Gaynor.— That's right.

Chairman Thompson.— So that my question you can answer
yes. When I asked if the money Morgan has got on deposit, when
he draws fifty million dollars of bonds, or has fifty million dollars on deposit, the difference between five and three-eighths per
cent which you are paying, and two and one-half per cent which
he gives you, you charge to construction account?

Mr. Gaynor.— No, sir.

Chairman Thompson.— What do you do? Or do you charge
the whole 5⅜ and credit the 2½ you receive? Is that the way
it is?

Mr. Gaynor.— The charge for interest —

Mr. Quackenbush.— Page 24.

Chairman Thompson.— I don't care if it is in the contract or
not. What do you actually do? I assume it is in the contract.

Mr. Gaynor.— Under the terms of the contract, from the time
money is provided, interest is charged at 6 per cent, and interest
credited at 2½ per cent. The difference between those two subdivisions accounts for the interest you are looking at.

Chairman Thompson.— So that comprehends what Mr. Morgan
gets on that $50,000,000 deposit?

Mr. Gaynor.— No, Mr. Morgan gets no — I am speaking now
— I cannot, say, of course, how much of the — how many of the
bonds Messrs. J. P. Morgan & Company may hold at any time.
The interest upon the bonds is paid to the bondholders, not to
J. P. Morgan & Company. Of course Morgan & Company allows
2½ per cent. on the balance in their hands.

Chairman Thompson.— That difference gets charged to construction?

Mr. Gaynor.— Yes; under the terms of the contract.

Mr. Colby.— Are you through, Senator?

Chairman Thompson.— Yes.

By Mr. Colby:

Q. Let me ask you this question, Mr. Gaynor, because the Chairman has indicated his desire to adjourn at 4:30, as I understand it. You and the city — you agreed in this contract to contribute $56,000,000 to construction? A. Fifty-eight million dollars.

Q. Fifty-eight million dollars. Now, did the city understand that by the time you had expended some twenty-six — some twenty-seven million dollars on account of construction — that there would be included in that expenditure $5,000,000 for debt discount, debt expense, lawyers' fees, and interest during construction? A. The city knew that those items would necessarily become a part of the construction cost of the subway.

Q. In other words, did the city when it agreed to make up any deficiency in construction work after the exhaustion of your agreed contribution, that they should figure as credits to you on contribution by the time you had advanced less than half of your agreed contribution, some $5,000,000 for these items that I have enumerated? A. Neither the city nor anyone representing the company, nor the bankers, could say at any time prior to the date of this contract what those amounts would be, but the principle was established and accepted by the city and the company.

Q. Now, the work of construction so far as the payments reflect the progress, is about half done? A. Approximately so.

Q. And if some $5,000,000 of the amount of your contribution to construction is at this point exhausted in interest charges, lawyers' fees, and these somewhat theoretical and technical items called debt discount and debt expense, do you mean to say that by the time 27,000,000 becomes 58,000,000, the total of those items will be $10,000,000? A. Collectively they might approach that.

Q. Might be $10,000,000? A. Possibly.

Q. And that is a fair guess as to the amount of the deficiency which the city will have to make up out of your contribution to construction account? A. Not necessarily so.

Q. Not necessarily, but you say it is a fair estimation, based upon your experience thus far? A. Well, the interest and discount might approach that sum. How much it will be depends entirely upon the dates when the various lines are open for operation?

Q. Yes.

Mr. Quackenbush.— And that is entirely beyond our control.

By Mr. Colby:

Q. Do you agree with the Comptroller that this contract from the city's standpoint is an admirable contract? A. It is.

Q. And your enthusiasm, looking at it from the city's standpoint, would not suffer any abatement because of this $10,000,000 deficit in the construction which the city would have to make up? A. Not one bit.

Mr. Colby.— Mr. Chairman, is it your pleasure to adjourn?

Chairman Thompson.— Yes. We reserve the right to disagree with you on this latter statement some time in the future, when we make up our mind.

Mr. Quackenbush,— Not when you have got all the facts.

Chairman Thompson.— I think we have got them now.

Mr. Quackenbush.— No, you haven't.

Chairman Thompson.— If I can find out anything the city got in this matter —

Mr. Quackenbush.— It got an increased assessment for the real estate in the outlying boroughs, more than this $10,000,000 ten times over.

Senator Lawson.— I would like to have you prove that.

Assemblyman Burr.— On the tax books, that's all.

Chairman Thompson.— The increases on assessments, on assessment rolls, is not a benefit to any institution, when you come with your corporation — you can bring your Interborough to Middleport, if you want to, and with your 3 per cent., we will spend that money in taking care of you and policing you and looking after you.

We will suspend now until to-morrow morning at 11 o'clock.

Whereupon, at 4:30 o'clock P. M.. an adjournment was taken to Tuesday, February 15, 1916, at 11 o'clock A. M.

FEBRUARY 15, 1916

NEW YORK COUNTY LAWYERS' ASSOCIATION BOARD ROOM,
165 Broadway, New York City.

The Committee was called to order, pursuant to adjournment, Senator Lawson, presiding.

Quorum present.

Senator Lawson.— The Committee will now come to order.

Mr. Colby.— I would like to have Mr. Fisher take the stand for just a moment or two, in order to introduce some material in evidence which we requested some days ago from Mr. Fisher, and which he has been working on in the meantime and some of which is completed.

FISHER, HORACE M., being recalled for further examination, testified as follows:

Examined by Mr. Colby:

Q. Mr. Fisher, you will recall in your examination when we were discussing the formation of the Interborough Consolidated Company and the reorganization affected through the organization of that company of the Interborough Metropolitan, you will also recall the testimony to the effect that the stated purpose of that reorganization was to escape from the burden of the losses and the depreciations of the securities owned by this holding company, the Interborough Metropolitan; that those losses chiefly arose through the acquisition of the stock of certain companies, such as the stocks of the Metropolitan Surface Railways, and stock of the Metropolitan Securities Company; I then asked you, in order to ascertain — how in order to gain some clew as to how this tremendous loss arose, and as one item therein to have prepared and delivered to the Committee a statement of all fees paid to counsel, and I ask you to go back to the beginning of the year 1906, as that was the year in which the so-called merger between the subway and the surface lines was brought about. So much for the purpose of recalling your mind to the point of my present question. You have supplied me with a statement of the payments made to out-

side counsel for services and disbursements by the Interborough
Rapid Transit Company and by it apportioned among the New
York Railways Company, the Interborough Consolidated Corporation, the Rapid Transit Subway Construction Company, the
New York and Queens County Railway Company, the Long
Island Electric Railway Company and the New York and Long
Island Traction Company; the total of such payments, as has
already been put in evidence, for the period from January 1,
1906, is $805,250.07; that has been testified to. Have you pre-
pared as supplemental to that statement and have you drawn
from the books of the Metropolitan Securities Company a statement of its payments to counsel during the same period? A. I
have had such a statement prepared by the secretary of the
company.

Q. Is this the statement? A. Yes, sir.

Q. Will you read it in full to the stenographer, as a part of the
record? A. Metropolitan Securities Company, payments made
to attorneys for services and disbursements from January 1, 1906,
to February 11, 1916. Taken for the year 1906: Guthrie, Cravath & Henderson, services and disbursements for the year 1906,
$81,051.31; Cravath, Henderson & de Gersdorff, disbursements,
$10,950.84; Henry D. Macdona, services and disbursements, $8,-
239.09; Lemuel E. Quigg, salary, $15,000; Quigg, Bostwick &
Coleman, disbursements, $1,309.85; James L. Quackenbush,
salary, $10,000; Elihu Root, retainer, $5,000; Henry D. Macdona, Sefton retainer, $500. Those are all the fees and expenses
for 1906.

1907: Guthrie, Cravath & Henderson, services, $42,500; Cra-
vath, Henderson & de Gersdorff, services and disbursements, $81,-
322.35; Henry D. Macdona, services and disbursements, $9,-
147.34; Lemuel E. Quigg, salary, $11,250; Quigg, Bostwick &
Coleman, disbursements, $409.91; Edwin Sefton, services, $2,500;
James L. Quackenbush, salary, $5,000; Franklin Bartlett, services,
$12,500; Nicoll, Anable & Lindsay, services and disbursements,
$4,228.50; William J. Wallace, retainer, $5,000.

For the year 1908: Cravath, Henderson & de Gersdorff, services
and disbursements, $41,234.69; Henry D. Macdona, services and
disbursements, $3,666; Lemuel E. Quigg, salary, $3,750; Charles
F. Kingsley, services, $1,600; Franklin Bartlett services, $6,100;

Nicoll, Anable, Lindsay & Fuller, services, $25,000; Paris S. Russell, taxable costs, $271.17; Guggenheimer, Untermeyer & Marshall, disbursements, $60.60.

For the year 1909: Cravath, Henderson & de Gersdorff, services and disbursements, $13,574.86; Nicoll, Anable, Lindsay & Fuller, services, $12,500; William J. Wallace, services and disbursements, $25,250. There was no expenses for 1910, and no expenses for 1911, and expenses for 1912, Cravath, Henderson & de Gersdorff, disbursements, $1,473.40. There have been no expenses for attorneys' fees or disbursements since that date.

Q. You are not an officer of this company, are you? A. No, sir.

Q. Have you any knowledge as to the services covered by these bills? A. No, sir, only in a very general way.

Q. The Metropolitan Securities Company is not an operating company? A. No, sir, a holding company.

Q. It merely owns the stocks and collects dividends of certain companies? A. It did own and control the stocks of the surface lines. To what extent, and what lines, I am unable to say.

Q. That was true in the year 1906, wasn't it? A. Yes, sir. that is the year I had reference to.

Q. In March, 1906, the Interborough Metropolitan Company acquired all the holdings of the Metropolitan Securities Company, didn't it? A. It acquired stock of the Metropolitan Securities Company.

Q. And notwithstanding that stock passed in 1906 to the Interborough Metropolitan, the Metropolitan Securities Company seems to have persisted in some form of activity? A. Yes, sir.

Q. What could it have been doing in 1907 to require, for instance, the payment to one firm of attorneys of $123,822? A. It negotiated certain loans and advanced the money to the surface lines for improvements and so forth.

Q. Were the services covered by these very substantial payments in 1906, for instance, the services in bringing the surface lines and the subway into this merger? A. I presume they were, yes, sir.

Q. The Interborough Rapid Transit Company never derived a dollar of gain or profit from that merger, did it? A. No, sir.

Q. And the losses to the Interborough Rapid Transit Company from that merger amount to approximately forty-five millions, do they not? A. That is more or less of a stock loss, or a security loss, a depreciation in the value of securities, and it does not represent a cash loss.

Q. That loss, and a considerable addition amounting, you have testified, amounting to approximately ninety millions, was the reason the Interborough Consolidation was formed? A. Yes, sir, it was to write off that depreciation in securities, and it does not represent a cash loss.

Q. A depreciation in securities, which have in turn, or which have been the basis of an issuance of your securities, has been a loss, although not a cash loss? A. Yes, sir, it is a loss on the books of the company.

Q. Your securities are still outstanding? A. All the securities of the Interborough Consolidated Corporation are still outstanding.

Q. And the thing they represent has shrunk in value? A. Its assets have depreciated, yes, sir.

Q. So that it would be very hard to make a substantial distinction between such depreciation and a loss; of course a man who has lost money has not necessarily dropped his wallet; there is such a thing as loss through depreciation of securities; it is no such loss, because the actual currency did not slip through his fingers? A. The answer is the Interborough Consolidated Corporation issued its securities for the securities of the underlying companies, and the securities were carried on the books of the company at that time at their full par value, and it was necessary to have the reorganization in order to wipe off of the books of the company the deficit or loss which occurred through the depreciation of those assets.

Mr. Colby.— I think, Mr. Chairman, the materiality of the information contained in this statement warrants me in putting it in evidence. I therefore offer it in evidence.

The same was received and marked exhibit 1, of this date.

(Exhibit I has been substantially copied into the record earlier during this morning's session through the answer by Mr. Fisher, the witness, to a question propounded him by Mr. Colby.)

Q. The stocks of these Metropolitan Companies were in the nature of a mill stone hung around the Interborough Rapid Transit Company's neck, weren't they ?   A. Not necessarily so, because the Interborough Rapid Transit Company did not assume any obligation of those stocks and to pay dividends on those stocks.

Q. It issued its securities, or turned over its securities which were valuable to the Interborough Metropolitan and allowed the Interborough Metropolitan to issue its stock protected by the junction between the valuable Interborough Rapid Transit Company's stock and the surface line stock which turned out to be worthless ?   A. That has nothing to do with the operation of the Interborough holding company?   The Interborough Metropolitan Company at that time issued its 4½ per cent. bonds for the stock of the Interborough Rapid Transit Company, plus $99 of common stock of the Interborough Metropolitan Company, and the Interborough Consolidated Company issued its preferred stock for the stock of the Metropolitan Street Railway Company and issued its common stock for the common stock of the Metropolitan Securities Company.   While the par value of these stocks amounted to $155,-000,000 authorized issue, the common stock never sold at par and the highest price was around fifty that it ever sold, and it is now selling around twenty.

Q. But the Interborough Metropolitan issued its preferred stock which has been taken over without diminution by the Interborough Consolidated Corporation?   A. Yes, sir, which is also a holding company.

Q. And the earnings of the Interborough Rapid Transit Company are relied upon by the Interborough Consolidated to make the payment of dividends on this Interborough Consolidated preferred stock, isn't it?   A. Nevertheless, the Interborough —

Q. That is true, isn't it?   A. Did use them for that purpose. I can't say it is relied upon.

Q. Possibly " use " is the better word?   A. Yes, sir.

Q. You could answer this question, which I wish to ask; what is the contract date for the completion of the East River Tunnel?   A. I could not answer that without looking it up.

GAYNOR, EDWARD F. J., being recalled for further examination, testified as follows:

By Mr. Colby:

Q. Mr. Gaynor, what is the East River tunnel, so called? A. Running from about Old Slip on this side to Clark street on the Brooklyn side of the East river.

Q. What is its relation to the combined dual system? A. It is the connecting link between the borough of Brooklyn and the borough of Manhattan in the subway line.

Q. Who is building that tunnel, which company? A. The Interborough Company.

Q. That is an Interborough tunnel? A. Yes, sir.

Q. Is it essential that that should be completed before the system can be put in operation as an entirety? A. Oh, yes, sir.

Q. What is the contract date for the completion of that tunnel? A. February 6, 1918.

Q. Has it been true of the past that these dates are reached by the contractors with completed work? A. As a rule, I think all work of that kind experience shows requires a little more time than the dates mentioned in the contract.

Q. What has been, in a general way, the average additional time required in the completion of contract work; has it been, in other words, one year or two years or three months, or six months? A. That is more of an engineering proposition than I would like to answer.

Q. As a general statement it is true, I understand, that the work is seldom completed at the time stated in the contract, and some considerable margin of time is necessary? A. That is true.

Q. I assume February 6, 1918, is the earliest date this work will be completed? A. I have heard it stated by the engineers of the Public Service Commission that so far as the work has progressed under that contract, the contractor is ahead of time.

Q. What do you understand by equipments as used in the contracts and as figuring the Interborough Rapid Transit Company's obligations? A. Equipment is the furnishing of the rolling stock, the power stations, substations, the third rail, the signalling and lighting apparatus necessary for the operation of the new subways.

Q. And your obligation is to supply how much money toward equipment of the new subways? A. $22,000,000.

Q. $22,000,000? A. Yes, sir.

Q. Which added to $58,000,000 makes a total contribution of how much? A. A total contribution of $80,000,000.

Q. And yet in the statements issued by Morgan & Company and the letters of Mr. Shonts he speaks of $77,000,000 as the total of your contribution? A. The $77,000,000 so mentioned was like a great many of the figures commented upon preliminary to the actualities. When the contract was finally made it was denominated $58,000,000 for construction and $22,000,000 for equipment.

Q. You have not entered upon the work of equipment to a very great extent as yet? A. Not nearly so active as the construction work of course.

Q. How much have you charged to cost of equipment under contract number 3? A. To December 31, 1915, $1,165,306.42.

Q. My attention is at once drawn to certain items of relative importance in this account which we discussed yesterday, such as debt discount, $34,959; debt expense, $55,718; miscellaneous equipment, $42,906; engineering and superintendence, $41,102; law expenditures, during construction, but charged to equipments, $40,830, interest during construction, $275,708; miscellaneous construction expenditures, $161,541; I see, however, that you have expended on tunnels, $59,266; on underground conduits, $4,703 — if I make an error, correct me — it is a little hard to carry the eye across these broad spaces — shops and car houses, $845; power plant electric equipment, $.20; furnaces, boilers and accessories, $1.79; miscellaneous power plant equipment, $354; other street railway land, $21,000 — what is that? A. That is the land purchased for the new substation.

Q. Interlocking and other signal apparatus, $59,266; are you putting your signals in the subway already? A. We are planning them, and so far as the Steinway tunnel line is concerned, which you will observe is much the greater portion of that charge, it is $51,613.96.

Q. Power plant buildings, $4,208; what does that mean? A. That is an expense in connection with either the sub-station building or the main power plant building, incidental to the development of our power plant to provide the necessary power to operate the new subways.

Q. What are revenue cars, $110,952? A. Of that amount, $107,071 refers to the cost of the cars now being operated in the Queens borough subway.

Q. Were those new cars or taken over? A. They were new cars.

Q. The old cars of the Steinway tube were taken over by the New York and Queens county? A. Yes, sir.

Q. And are now being operated there? A. I think they are.

Q. And are very heavy cars? A. Very much heavier than the ordinary surface car, ordinary.

(Chairman Thompson presiding.)

Chairman Thompson.— I want to inform counsel that Mr. MacInnis of the Comptroller's office was subpoenaed here for this morning at eleven o'clock, and he has not appeared. The deputy comptroller has rather attempted to impress me with the idea that Mr. MacInnis was excused, but I do not so understand it. He simply said Mr. MacInnis would come when we sent for him, we did send for him, and it developed since that that he had an ulcerated tooth, and he worked until one o'clock last night, and now he is gone to a funeral. I assume as soon as he recovers from all of these afflictions he will be here, because the Comptroller's office has been advised that the Committee, and the Chairman, and the counsel, and all the assistants, and all connected with the Committee, desire Mr. MacInnis' appearance before this Committee to-day, as soon as possible. I think that is understood up there now.

Mr. Colby.— Mr. MacInnis has a reputation of being a very capable and competent accountant and auditor, and his long identification with the department, antedating that of his chief officer, and his very close engagement in the work of subway building and particularly the accounting makes him an exceedingly desirable witness.

Chairman Thompson.— That is the reason why the Committee

disagree with the Comptroller in that we desire to hear Mr. Mac-Innis before we hear the Comptroller.

Assemblyman Burr.— I agree with the Chairman.

Chairman Thompson.— We are unanimous.

Q. In looking over cost of equipment, which up to December 31st, aggregates only $1,165,000, I am struck by the disparity between the items expended for actual work of equipments, actual in the sense of obviously proper charges against equipment, and the aggregate of the charges that are more or less technical and require explanation, such as debt discount, debt expense, interest during construction, and so forth; roughly figuring, a few of these so-called alien items, they aggregate out of the $1,100,-000 charge to equipment over $600,000; how do you account for the rapidity with which those items increased and the modesty of the amounts by contrast of the items that are obviously concerned with actual equipment? A. The sum that you mention as being the total of what is denominated as alien items rather surprised me. Under that caption, if I were to state any of those accounts, I would place debt discount and debt expense as alien items. They are alien only in the sense you have in mind, and they only amount to $80,000.

Q. How about interest during construction, $275,708? A. The interest during construction reflects nothing more and nothing less than the cost of the money which has been provided for equipment purposes to December 31st.

Q. But it does not represent interest on expenditures already made for purpose of equipment, does it? A. It does not.

Q. It represents the interest on some items that have not anything directly to do with equipment? A. It does not represent anything but items which have to do directly with equipment.

Q. On what principal sum is this interest charge of $275,708 calculated? A. If you will pass that I will give you that answer as soon as I can look it up. That reminds me, I would be very glad to add, if you are willing at this time, the information which I could not give you last evening with respect to charge for easements in the cost of construction.

Q. I will be glad to hear anything you have to say by way of elucidation of these charges. A. Under the cost of construction is the item Easements, $1,043,731.83. That represents the money which we have turned over to the comptroller of the city for the purpose of paying for easements acquired by the city in connection with the construction of the new subway lines.

Q. I understand, Mr. Gaynor, that your obligation on the score of equipment is limited to $22,000,000? A. Yes, sir.

Q. And if that does not suffice to equip the lines somebody is going to make up the deficiency; is that right; under the terms of the contract? A. Well, that thought has never occurred to me, for the reason that the $22,000,000 has been generally conceded to be ample to provide the equipment for initial operation.

Q. In other words, you do not apprehend a deficiency as you do on construction account? A. We do not.

Q. What is the amount that you believe will be employed or will be required for equipment for initial operations, as distinguished from these accompanying alien charges — I don't use that word " alien " for the purpose of characterizing, but merely for the purposes of distinction; that is to say, at the moment. A. Oh, I should say it was $21,000,000.

Q. That expended upon cars, sub-stations, conduits, signals, devices, in other words, $21,000,000 directly expended for concrete, tangible equipment would cover it? A. About that, yes, sir.

Q. How are you going to carry such charges as debt discounts, debt expense and interest during construction which with an expenditure here of $1,100,000 amounts to more than $600,000? A. We are now approaching the period when the payments for cars, motors and engines, power station equipment, sub-station buildings, tools and machinery, will be very much greater in proportion to the other sums than as exhibited during the period that you have before you.

Q. And yet you won't be ready for operation for two years at least? A. With respect to some of the lines.

Q. Do you expect to substantially operate the dual subway system within a shorter period than two years? A. I should say so.

Q. To what extent? A. Well, that —

Q. There has been some evidence given on that point, and I would like to have your impression on it. A. The general understanding is that it will be possible to open different sections of the line at various dates between now and June 30, 1918.

Q. Well, when is there to be a general inauguration of operation, according to your idea? A. I take it that that will depend upon the completion of the East River tunnel.

Q. You have testified that the earliest date at which the East River tunnel can be completed is the contract date February 6, 1918? A. Yes, sir.

Q. And your experience has been those contract dates are not closely kept? A. That is so.

Q. So, without attempting to suggest the form of your reply or to coerce your mind, may I not assume the subway will not be in substantial operation short of two years? A. It will not be wholly in operation.

Q. Substantially? A. There might be substantial sections, and probably will be very substantial sections of the subway opened before that date, but the line will not be wholly in operation until some time after February 6, 1918.

Q. And in the meantime the interest, for instance, upon the sums that are in excess of the actual money intended to be credited for equipment will continue to mount up? A. Yes, that is so. It is also true that so soon as you open any of the lines for operation the construction interest ceases.

Chairman Thompson.— Is that the reason they do not want to open the Lexington avenue line?

Mr. Gaynor.— It is not, so far as I know.

Q. Is it or is it not a fact the income to the Interborough Rapid Transit Company will be greater or less immediately after the inauguration of operation? A. The company would be very glad, so far as my judgment is concerned, to have the elevated lines —

Q. I ask you a simple question; I said is it or is it not a fact the income of the Interborough Rapid Transit Company will be less after the inauguration of operation than it is now during these preparatory years? A. No, sir; the income will be greater after the operation.

Q. The income that is apportionable and received by the Interborough Rapid Transit Company? A. It will be greater after the roads are fully in operation than it is now.

Q. You mean the aggregate, or the income derived by the Interborough Rapid Transit Company? A. The income to be derived by the Interborough Rapid Transit Company.

Q. Suppose the equipment account exceeds the $22,000,000, who will make that up? A. As I have testified, I have never heard anything that would indicate the $22,000,000 would not be sufficient to provide the initial equipment.

Q. What is the provision of the contract on that subject? A. We are to provide the equipment necessary for initial operation, while the equipment for extensions and additions, if provided by the company, will be allowed for in addition to the interest on the $22,000,000.

Q. If there is a deficiency on equipment account the city makes it up, that is the point, isn't it? A. No, sir, it does not, not as I understand it. The company's obligation is to furnish the equipment for initial operation.

Q. No matter what it costs? A. Not to exceed a cost of $22,000,000.

Q. Is there any provision with relation to equipment similar to the provision of the contract in relation to construction? A. There is one provision.

Q. And it is similar, isn't it? A. Not exactly, but there is a governing condition there which is that should the equipment cost us less than $22,000,000, whatever amount may be the difference, must be supplied by us towards the payment of the excess cost of construction.

Q. Is there any provision for an excess cost of equipment in the agreement? A. There is not.

Q. And if there should be your interpretation would be that that obligation rests upon the company? A. I could only tell you what I understand to be the situation. I have never heard anything that would lead me to believe other than that $22,000,000 will be sufficient.

Q. It is possible I should examine someone more familiar with that point. A. That is true.

By Chairman Thompson:

Q. With respect to your expenditures under this Contract No. 3, has your company installed the uniform system of accounts ordered by the Public Service Commission? A. We have.

Q. And you keep them according to that system of accounts? A. Yes, sir.

Q. Have any part of those accounts been passed upon or examined by the Public Service Commission? A. They have.

Q. The whole of them? A. The representatives of the Public Service Commission are in my office constantly.

Q. And up to what time have they been passed upon? A. We have filed with the Commission the details of our construction and equipment costs to December 31, 1915.

Q. Everything charged up to December 31, 1915, has been passed upon by the Public Service Commission? A. It has been reported by us to them, and we have filed the information with the Commission.

Q. They have not disapproved it? A. Not so far as we know.

Q. And as far as you assume it has been approved by the Commission? A. They have not raised any objection to it, apart from the objections raised at the time of the prior determination. They have not raised any objection to any of our items except in infinitesimal small amounts.

Q. As, for instance, this $125,000 item of Mr. Shonts, that has been passed upon by the Public Service Commission? A. That is part of the prior determination. It has not been passed upon as a specific item, but the Public Service Commission allowed in the prior determination, $327,041, of which this is a part.

Examination by Mr. Colby — resumed:

Q. You applied for the approval of a considerable aggregate of items under the prior determination, did you not? A. Yes, sir.

Q. What was the aggregate of the items that you applied for? A. Well, for subway construction and equipment and the elevated third-tracking, extension and improvement work, approximately $1,500,000.

Q. And of that amount all but $327,000 was disallowed; is that your understanding? A. No, sir. In addition to the $327,000 which was allowed in connection with the subway work, certain allowances were made in connection with the third-tracking and extension work, and the balance was disallowed.

Q. How much was allowed in connection with the third-tracking and the extension work? A. The total amount allowed was $589,286.02, of which $207,023.43 was in connection with the Manhattan third-tracking, $54,857.58 in connection with the elevated extension work and $327,405.01 in connection with the subway.

Q. Can you let me have the details of that transaction? A. Yes, sir.

Q. Let me see them.

(Witness hands sheet of paper, containing figures, to Mr. Colby.)

Q. Let me see the application that you made for the allowance of a million and a half. A. I do not happen to have that with me.

Q. Will you send for it right away? A. I am not sure it was in the form of an application.

Q. In what form else could it have been? A. I think it was in the form of an account submitted.

Q. With a request for approval? A. Yes, sir.

Q. Will you send for it at once, please? A. Yes, sir.

Q. Have you got the prior determination account there? A. I have not.

Q. I want that as quick as I can get it. A. The amounts entered in the prior determination are identical with those that you have in your hand.

Q. I would like to see the account, and I would like that right away, Mr. Gaynor. A. Very well. Will you excuse me while I get that?

Q. Yes, sir; I would like also the " other suspense " or any account that contains the book entries of the payments of $500,000, and I would like the original books; I would like to see them. A. Yes, sir.

Q. I would like your original books on that? A. I will go and get them.

Chairman Thompson.— We will take an elastic recess for about two minutes.

(Committee called to order at 1:15 P. M. by Chairman Thompson.)

Chairman Thompson.— I received the following letter, about an hour ago.

"J. P. MORGAN & CO.

"Wall street, corner Broad, New York

"NEW YORK, February 14, 1916.

"Hon. GEORGE F. THOMPSON, Chairman, The Joint Legislative Committee of the Senate and Assembly, care New York County Lawyers' Association, 165 Broadway, New York City:

"DEAR SIR.— You will recall that on February 3d we advised you by telephone that Mr. Morgan had gone to Europe on business, his trip having been planned many weeks ago — in fact last November — and that his date of return was necessarily uncertain. At that time we expressed to you our willingness to furnish you with any facts of which we may be possessed and in which the city is interested, relative to our relations with the Interborough Rapid Transit Company.

"This morning we are in receipt of a cable from Mr. Morgan in which he asks us to repeat our former message, as conditions have not changed and he has no more definite idea than he had on February 3d as to when he can return. We would say also that we believe ourselves possessed of all the information in connection with this business which Mr. Morgan possesses and concerning which he has not been examined already.

"Yours truly,

"J. P. MORGAN & CO."

Mr. Colby.— Mr. Quackenbush, I wonder if we could not have Mr. Gaynor with the books he has already, and possibly have somebody else do the searching?

(Mr. Quackenbush sends for Mr. Gaynor.)

(Committee in recess.)

(Committee called to order at 1:23 o'clock by Chairman Thompson.)

EDWARD F. J. GAYNOR, recalled.

By Mr. Colby:

Q. Mr. Gaynor, have you the items that you applied to the Public Service Commission to allow under the heading of special allowances for administration, engineering and legal expenses? A. I have in my hand a memorandum showing the subdivision of items, in the aggregate, $1,358,186.01, constituting the claim made by the company to the Public Service Commission for allowance in connection with new subways and elevated extensions.

(Witness hands memorandum to counsel.)

Q. I asked you for the original entries constituting this total. A. I have that; I have those.

Q. First, let me ask you from what is this memorandum compiled? A. This is compiled for the convenience of yourself, myself, and in answering the questions which I assume will be asked, and made from the original documents which I have here.

Q. Can you tell me —

Chairman Thompson.— May I see one of them? (Witness hands paper to Chairman.)

Q. Can you tell we when application was made to the Public Service Commission for approval of items aggregating $1,358,000 for these special expenses? A. In order that the record may be correct in this respect, I would like to say that I prepared statements for our general counsel, summarizing these disbursements, and the application that you speak of, I think, was an oral one made by him to the Public Service Commission.

Q. In a public statement made by the Comptroller, he says that you applied for an allowance of $1,532,000 and — A. I would like to say he is probably correct, but I am giving you these figures upon extremely short notice, and it is barely possible that

the difference between the Comptroller's statement and the figures
that you have before you can be accounted for during the day.

Q. Well now, what encouraged you to apply for these allowances? In other words, what took place leading you to make this
application? A. So far as my personal information in the premises is concerned, the belief was that the company had co-operated
with the city authorities in the plan for elaboration of the much
needed — the much-needed elaboration of rapid transit lines. And
we believed, and still believe, that the expenses which the company made in connection with that work should be recognized as
a part of the cost of the work.

Q. You were an applicant for franchises for the city, weren't
you? A. I think we were a little more than that.

Q. Well, that was — that is a very accurate statement; you
were seeking franchises, coupled with the city backing financially
for their operation, weren't you? A. We were, yes, sir.

Q. And was it your theory that the city should pay you for
your exertions in applying for public franchises? A. No; it was
not that. It was the theory that our best efforts being spent in the
work of developing a plan of subway and elevated development
that was expected to meet the city's needs for rapid transit lines,
the expenditures that we made in that connection would be considered as —

Q. In other words, you felt that you were putting the city
under an obligation by your efforts, by your persevering interest
in the application for new subway franchises? A. I would not
put it quite as strong as that.

Q. Put it as strong as that, up to $1,500,000, would you? A.
I would say that the very hearty co-operation of the company and
the city authorities in a plan which was of the tremendous scope
that this was, necessarily led us to believe, I for one, that our
expenses would be recognized as part of the cost.

Q. Well, isn't it a part of your duty, or that of the officers of
your company generally to co-operate very heartily with anybody
who will give you a guarantee of $14,568,000 per annum, with a
cumulative provision as to any deficits arising from subway earnings? A. That is a contract which has as many points of merit
for the city as it has for the company.

Q. Yes. But you feel that your efforts in arriving at an agreement with the city on those terms entitles your administrative officers and some of your lawyers to compensation directly from the city? A. I certainly do, and certainly did.

Chairman Thompson.— And you think the city ought to pay everything and the railroad company get all the benefit, because it is such a big undertaking; is that the way I understand it?

Mr. Gaynor.— No. And to be exact, there is no thought that the city was asked to pay any of these sums.

Chairman Thompson.— You didn't think about that, but it is the fact just the same. It turned out to be the fact, although you didn't think of it?

Mr. Gaynor.— If you will allow me, Mr. Chairman. As I view these expenditures, they represented skillful help in arriving at a plan for future subways and elevated extensions, and will undoubtedly, in my judgment, be reflected in the ultimate character of these enterprises, and a diminishment of what might otherwise be an excessive cost in certain directions.

By Mr. Colby:

Q. There was no way by which the city could reward its officials for co-operating with the Interborough in this great undertaking, was there? A. Not that I know of.

Q. Did it ever occur to your board of directors that if your co-operation was of so much value, that possibly the city officials should be rewarded for their co-operation? A. Well, now, that asks me to relate the mental operations of the board of directors; and of course, I cannot answer that question.

Q. Well, now, when did you, in fact, apply to the city for this $1,500,000, to recompense you for your ardent co-operation with the city in reaching this contract? A. Now, Mr. Colby, may I ask that that question be framed so that it will not appear that we were asking the city to pay this money? We were not asking the city to allow us this money. We were only asking the city to recognize this expenditure as part of the cost, which I think is a very different thing.

19

Chairman Thompson.— The Committee don't think so.   All
we are interested in, and we are not interested in any particular
eloquence in describing how this came about or in the use of
words; we are only interested that here is this expenditure, the
purpose for which it was made, and you have charged it to the
city. Now that is the important thing. You have charged it to
the city. The Committee don't care, I don't believe, about the
operation of the minds, that you have done it. We want to know
how it is done.

Mr. Colby.— The question was as to the date when the request
or application or suggestion — call it what you like —

Chairman Thompson.— We want that question answered. We
don't care about the details, about the operations of the men's
minds; or that it was a great undertaking. We know it is a
great undertaking. We also know the Interborough people had a
great jollification after it went through.

Mr. Quackenbush.— You are mistaken about that, Mr. Chairman. I wasn't there, and I think if they had one, I would have
been invited.

Chairman Thompson.— You didn't participate.

Mr. Gaynor.— Let me add this point —

Mr. Colby.— Just answer my point, please. When was this
application?

Mr. Quackenbush.— Well, let's be fair about this. I have not
interrupted very much —

Senator Lawson.— No, no, Mr. Quackenbush; our counsel has
asked a question.

Mr. Quackenbush.— With a lot of "ardent desire" on our
part —

Senator Lawson.— Just a moment. Mr. Quackenbush, will you
please?

Chairman Thompson.— Let him ask his question.

By Mr. Colby:

Q. When was the application, the invitation, the suggestion — call it what you like — made for the recognition, allowance, payment, call it what you like, of $1,500,000 for these —

Chairman Thompson.— Now, just a minute.

Q. — acts of co-operation, that you have described?

Chairman Thompson.— Now, Mr. Quackenbush, is there any objection to that?

Mr. Quackenbush.— No objection. My objection was with the "ardent" business. You didn't mean that?

Chairman Thompson.— Well, everything is all right now. A. Some time on or about, in or about June and July, 1913, to the best of my recollection.

By Mr. Colby:

Q. In what form was the application made? A. By our general counsel.

Q. Meaning? A. By our general counsel calling on, I think, the general counsel of the Public Service Commission.

Q. Do you mean Mr. Rogers? A. Yes, sir.

Q. Calling on whom? A. Mr. Coleman, the counsel for the Public Service Commission.

Q. What preliminary discussion had there been in the company concerning this application before Mr. Rogers called on Mr. Coleman? A. The only discussion that I know anything about was Mr. Rogers' request upon me to furnish the figures.

Q. And what did he say to you in explanation of the request? A. I don't recall exactly, except in a general way I was asked to advise him what our expenditures had been in connection with these elements of construction and equipment.

Q. What your past expenditures had been? A. Yes.

Q. Do you say "yes" with any hesitation? A. No, I am — you are using the word "past."

Q. I mean past in point of time as regards the time of that request from Mr. Rogers. A. Yes, sir.

Q. Had the — did he say that he had received some intimation or assurance from the Public Service Commission or the city that allowances would be considered on this score? A. He did not, so far as I can recollect. I think I would recollect that if he had said it.

Q. Did he say he wanted to get these items together and see if he could get them allowed? A. Generally, he must have stated that to me.

Q. You don't recall just what he stated? A. Specifically, no.

Q. What request did he make to you with regard to the compilation of these items? A. From time to time Mr. Rogers had often referred to the necessity of having these expenditures recognized as a part of the cost. And at the time that you speak of, he called upon me to produce the statement that would show what had been expended.

Q. Am I to understand you to say that all the payments included in this $1,500,000 had been actually expended by the company at the time Rogers made this request? A. They had not been.

Q. They had not been? A. No, sir.

Q. Where can I find out, without interrupting this examination, and without sacrificing time, just what items you assembled, just what had been actually expended, and just what had not been actually incurred? A. I can give you now the original record of the items which had been expended, and I can testify to the best of my knowledge what constituted the difference between these amounts which you will see, and the total of this memorandum that you have.

Q. I would like you to get those records at the moment. (Witness produces book.)

Mr. Colby.— I will ask you to yield place to Mr. MacInnes.

DUNCAN MACINNES, called as a witness, being first duly sworn, testified as follows:

By Mr. Colby:

Q. Mr. MacInnes, you are connected with the finance department of the city of New York? A. Yes, sir.

Q. How many years have you been connected with it? A. Since 1897.

Q. In what present capacity are you? A. Chief accountant in the Comptroller's office.

Q. Where do you reside, Mr. MacInnes? A. Brooklyn; No. 2 Glenada place.

Chairman Thompson.— Very well. On account of matters coming up, and we have got to suspend in a little while, our time will be taken until we suspend. You may be excused until 11 o'clock tomorrow morning.

EDWARD F. J. GAYNOR, recalled.

By Mr. Colby:

Q. Now, Mr. Gaynor, if you are ready: I think I will step around there, Mr. Gaynor, unless you could step around here, so that Mr. Dawson and I could run our eye in conjunction with that.

(Mr. Gaynor takes book and sits beside counsel.)

Q. Mr. Gaynor, have you preserved a copy of the statement that you compiled at the request of the company's counsel, of these items? A. Yes, sir; I think I have.

Q. Have you that statement with you? A. I have not. It is made from this original record you have before you.

Q. And consists of a selection of items appearing in this record? A. My recollection is it contains all of the items just as you see them here in this record.

Q. And running down to what point? A. Down to March 31, 1913.

Q. Now, do I understand you to say that the aggregate of all the items in this account entitled "Interborough Extensions from October 31, 1910, to March 31, 1913" were simply drawn off by you and rendered to Mr. Rogers as a statement in compliance with his request? A. Yes, sir.

Q. Is this a record of actual payments made at or about the time that they are charged? A. It is.

Q. What is the aggregate of the items appearing in this account, "Interborough extension up to March 31, 1913?" A. $26,718.19.

Q. Well, that is a good way from the $1,532,000, isn't it? A. Take the others up seriatim.

Q. Before I leave this account, tell me what it is; describe as "Interborough extensions"? A. This account refers to the disbursements made by the Interborough Company in connection with the proposed extension to the elevated lines.

Q. Let me just see them a moment here. This is the account, isn't it? A. Yes, sir.

Q. Let us see what this means.

Chairman Thompson.— Better have a copy of that made. (Referring to account in ledger.)

Q. Why are you buying soap cups and sheathes as far back as November 30, 1910, in connection with the application for these new franchises? A. Probably in the engineering work relating to the drawing of plans for the contemplated extensions.

Q. How do you happen to have a construction payroll account as far back as 1910 on this subject? A. The elevated extensions which are now in evidence, that is, the improvements as far as the third-tracking is concerned, were designed a great many years before the actual construction work was begun.

Q. I see items running through this period of years for rent and for service.

Chairman Thompson.— I think you better have a copy of that drawn up.

Mr. Colby.— Well, it will be quite an extensive thing, Senator, and most of the items are not long.

Chairman Thompson.— It could be run off this afternoon.

Mr. Colby.— That is only a small part of it, $26,718.19.

Chairman Thompson.— Well you have this drawn off in your office, Mr. Quackenbush?

Mr. Quackenbush.— Very glad to, if we have time. I doubt if there will be time —

Chairman Thompson.— Day after to-morrow.

Mr. Quackenbush.—As soon as we can get them, consistent with he other things.

By Mr. Colby:

Q. This account is entitled " Proposed subway routes "; did you begin to keep that account in 1909 ? A. We did.

Q. March 31 ? A. Yes, sir.

Chairman Thompson.— We will have to have it quiet here, gentlemen.

By Mr. Colby:

Q. I see some items here, labor performed during November, 1909, $1,681. Labor for what? Were you constructing new routes? A. The item you refer to refers to services of engineers engaged in the work of designing and studying proposed subway extensions.

Q. You had no thought at this time that you were ever going to enter into a dual contract such as the one entered into in 1913 with the city of New York? A. We did not.

Q. At this time the Interborough was considering the extension of its own subway route, wasn't it? A. Beginning in 1908, the Interborough began the study of necessary subway extensions and the dual plan is not the first, second, third or fourth proposition that was studied, but it was the ultimate one, of course.

Q. Now, wasn't the very first idea you had to extend your subway routes with your own resources, and to simply obtain the permission of the city to do that? A. I think the first thought was that the subway should be extended by the city on much the same lines as the original subways were designed.

Q. Do you mean to deny — I don't want to put the question that way — is it not a fact, Mr. Gaynor, that the first approaches to the city of New York, the first representations from your company, looked merely to permission on the part of the city to the expenditure of your own money in extending your own routes? A. I know such a proposal was made, though early in the study of the work.

Q. And a great deal of this expenditure which is carried in the earlier months and years under the head of " proposed subway routes " was in connection with the working out and the developing of that idea of your company? A. It is very difficult to segregate one subway plan from the whole plan which led up to the dual subway.

Q. But, my dear Mr. Gaynor, it would be easy to answer my question, and strike that out as evasive. A. I am answering it to the best of my ability.

Chairman Thompson.— Just read the question again.

(The question was read by the stenographer as follows: "And a great deal of this expenditure which is carried in the earlier months and years under the head of ' proposed subway routes ' was in connection with the working out and the developing of that idea of your company? ")

A. I think it had a relation to it.

Q. I see Mr. William Barclay Parsons received a quarterly payment of $6,250, on March 31, 1910; was he under regular salary to your company? A. He was.

Q. Beginning at that time? A. Prior to that time.

Chairman Thompson.— Civil engineer?

Mr. Gaynor.— Civil engineer.

Q. He had been on that salary for a number of years? A. I would have to refresh my recollection on that. He has been a consulting engineer for a great many years.

Q. Wasn't he in the employ of the Rapid Transit Subway Construction Company, and hasn't he been a consulting, if not a directing engineer, from the earliest days of the subway? A. He has been consulting engineer with the Interborough Rapid Transit Company since, I should say, about 1907.

Q. Well, didn't Mr. Parsons develop plans for the company's unaided extension of its routes? A. Undoubtedly co-operated in the study of that plan.

Q. And inasmuch as I have taken one of the earliest items in the account of " proposed subway routes," it is fair to say he was busy at that time on the earlier phases of the question? A. Yes, sir.

Q. His salary of $25,000 a year seems to be carried down through this account, uniformly appearing at each quarter. Here I see a number of newspapers and periodicals, in which advertising charges appear, also the Van Cleve Company, for ads. in the New York, Brooklyn and — New York and Brooklyn papers —

$27,939, June 10, 1911; and many other items, some very substantial, aggregating, maybe fifty or sixty thousand dollars, on this page alone.

Senator Lawson.— What was that for, Mr. Gaynor, the advertising?

Mr. Gaynor.— The company conducted at one time a publicity campaign to educate the people, so to speak, to the advantages of one plan of subway extension as compared with some other plan.

Chairman Thompson.— That was to educate them in favor of the dual subway contracts?

Mr. Gaynor.— No, I would not say that.

Mr. Quackenbush.— It was against the Brooklyn Rapid Transit system.

Mr. Gaynor.—And against the Tri-Borough.

Assemblyman Burr.— What was the Parsons plan; what was the subway plan of Mr. Parsons?

Mr. Gaynor.— I could not tell you.

Senator Lawson.— Mr. Gaynor, let me ask, who instructed you to make all these items?

Mr. Gaynor.— It fell within the scope of my official duties, without any specific instructions, and I received no specific instructions from anybody.

Senator Lawson.— The president or directors or anybody else?

Mr. Gaynor.— No, sir.

Senator Lawson.— You just carried along this suspense account?

Mr. Gaynor.— Done in the ordinary exercise of my official duties.

Senator Lawson.— I see. Just carried this suspense account along until it amounted close to a million and a half dollars?

Mr. Gaynor.— Well, it was carried in suspense account until the study of subways had reached the point where it was formulated into a contract when certain adjustments were made.

Senator Lawson.— Well, now, does your company now consider this a suspense account, or has it been transferred to some other account?

Mr. Gaynor.— In a large measure it has been transferred, and forms part of the many details that Mr. Colby was referring to in the statement I had before me this morning.

Chairman Thompson.— That is construction account.

By Mr. Colby:

Q. Now that Senator Lawson has asked this very pertinent question, I would like to bring out this fact, that of the total amount for which application was made for allowances, according to a memorandum handed to me this morning by Mr. Gaynor, $589,286.02 was allowed.

Chairman Thompson.— What were those two items?

Mr. Colby.—According to this memorandum. that. amount is separated into three items, three aggregates, rather: Manhattan third-tracking, $207,023.42; elevated extensions, $54,857.58; subway, $327,405.01.

Senator Lawson.— How does that compare —

Mr. Colby.— The total amounting to $589,286.

Senator Lawson.— How does that compare with the amount asked for?

Mr. Colby.—According to Comptroller Prendergast, the amount asked for was $1,532,000. That statement is not declared by Mr. Gaynor to be necessarily incorrect, but according to the information at Mr. Gaynor's disposal the total in his opinion is $1,358,186.

Chairman Thompson.— Let us see that $327,000 aggregated item. What is that? What is that made up of?

Mr. Colby.—According to this memorandum, that is made up of legal expenses and administration. $198,000.

Chairman Thompson.— Well, that is those lawyers that we have proved.

Mr. Colby.— Yes. Engineering and superintendence, $129,-
405.01; making a total of $327,405.01. The total for legal expenses and administration includes, according to this memorandum, $6,500 to Mr. Delancy Nicoll; $15,166.67 to Mr. Edward M.
Grout; $43,332.33 to Mr. Rogers; $125,000 to administration.

Chairman Thompson.— That is the Shonts bonus?

Mr. Colby.— I don't know.

Chairman Thompson (to Mr. Gaynor).— Is that what it is?

Mr. Gaynor.— It was allowed for administration expenses. Mr.
Shonts was paid that amount.

Chairman Thompson.— That is the Shonts $125,000 bonus,
voted to him?

Mr. Gaynor.— Whether allowed for administration expenses —
I cannot say that the Public Service Commission allowed it
specifically —

Chairman Thompson.— I know, but that is the $125,000 bonus
to Mr. Shonts; that is what it is.

Mr. Gaynor.— I cannot say that, because you have before you
a declaration of the Public Service Commission, not a declaration
on the part of any of our company officers.

Chairman Thompson.— Is there any other payment of $125,000
to Mr. Shonts?

Mr. Gaynor.— There is not.

Chairman Thompson.— Then that's right.

Mr. Colby.— Of course, Mr. Chairman. I have asked Mr.
Gaynor to hand me a copy of the memorandum handed to Mr.
Rogers, and which he says he can do. We can then see in what
form the request was made, and compare it with this memorandum,
which I assume from Mr. Gaynor's statement is the form in which
the allowances were stated by the Public Service Commission.

Chairman Thompson.— I would like to see the charge on the
book, of these figures, how they were charged on the book.

Mr. Gaynor.— You have it before you.

Mr. Colby.— I am coming to some items which will enlighten you.

Q. Here is an item of Edward M. Grout, special counsel, $10,000, July 7, 1911. That figured in the application for allowance? A. It did.

Q. I see here the payments to J. P. Morgan & Company, two payments, of $178,571.43 each; that figured in your application for allowance? A. It figured in my statement to Mr. Rogers, but he is the best witness to say how it was submitted to the Commission's counsel.

Q. Did it figure in this total which you asked to have allowed? A. It does.

Chairman Thompson.— Does it figure in the total that was allowed?

Mr. Gaynor.— No.

Senator Lawson.— This amount allowed by the Public Service Commission is now charged against the city, which the city will have to repay?

Mr. Gaynor.— It is a charge against the cost of the work.

Senator Lawson.— Yes; it is a charge that the city will have to repay.

Mr. Gaynor.— It is a charge against —

Chairman Thompson.— If it is more than fifty-eight millions — if it is enough more than fifty-eight millions to cover these, then the city pays it all.

Senator Lawson.— The city pays it all?

Chairman Thompson.— If it costs more than fifty-eight million.

Mr. Colby.— Most of our old friends, these familiar charges, Mr. Chairman, appear in this account. For instance, I see that bill of Hays, Hershfield & Wolf, including Guggenheimer, Untermyer & Marshall, $63,128.

Chairman Thompson.— Was that allowed?

Mr. Gaynor.— No.

Senator Lawson.— What authority did you have for entering up that million and some odd thousand dollars to Mr. Shonts, by whose authority did you enter that up to construction account, as administration?

Mr. Gaynor.— Upon the authority of the resolution passed by the board of directors.

Senator Lawson.— And do you recall the date of that resolution?

Chairman Thompson.— We have got that in evidence. But that resolution don't show anything about construction account.

Mr. Gaynor.— The resolution sets out why the amount was paid.

Senator Lawson.— Does it authorize you to charge that up to administration?

Mr. Gaynor.— In the exercise of my official duties, I must always charge a disbursement according to the facts related to that disbursement.

Chairman Thompson.— Senator Lawson wants to know who told you where to charge that.

Mr. Gaynor.— No one had any conference with me with respect to it.

Senator Lawson.— Did the resolution authorize you to charge it to administration?

Mr. Gaynor.— It does.

Chairman Thompson.— Well, he says so.

Mr. Gaynor.— For the reason that it sets out what the compensation was allowed for, and that was sufficient to justify me in placing it to the appropriate account, which was an expense in connection with proposed —

Chairman Thompson.— That don't bind the Committee. Let counsel proceed.

By Mr. Colby:

Q. And inasmuch as you are about to adjourn, I will ask a question on this point, without pursuing examination on those items. You say that some of the items, included in this total for which allowance was requested, had not been actually made, as expenditures were incurred, at the time this application was made? A. That is the best of my recollection.

Q. What are such items? A. The payment to Mr. Julian T. Davies, payment to Mr. Dillon, this payment to Mr. Nicoll, part of a payment to Mr. Grout was made prior to the date you are referring to, and part subsequent is my recollection. The payment to Mr. Rogers, the administration payment, and the payment to myself.

Q. Those had not been made? A. Those had not been made.

Q. At the time that this information was asked of you? A. That is the best of my recollection.

Q. It was felt, manifestly, that allowance could be obtained for a considerable total of payments; that must have been the occasion of this request of Mr. Rogers? A. Well, Mr. Rogers would be the best one to answer.

Q. Maybe he would, but I am asking you. A. I am giving you now my best recollection on those items. If you want it positively, I would be very glad to refresh my recollection.

Q. Give me your best recollection? It is a pretty good recollection. A. My recollection is those items I referred to were not paid as of March 31, 1913; paid subsequent to that time.

Q. And they were paid in order to be included in this allowance? A. No, sir.

Q. They were paid after the allowance was actually made? A. They were not paid to be included in the allowance.

Q. Well —

Chairman Thompson.— Just answer that question.

Mr. Gaynor.— What is the last question, please?

Chairman Thompson.— He wants to know if they were paid after this allowance was actually made?

Mr. Gaynor.— I think they were paid prior to the allowance.

By Mr. Colby:

Q. They were paid, however, after the application was made. A. I would like to refresh my recollection on that point.

Q. Are those matters of record? A. Oh, yes.

Q. Have you any correspondence with Mr. Rogers or in any other forms, memorandum on this subject? A. I have a copy of a statement which I made for him, and I have in mind that I compared the dates with the dates of payment of these vouchers, which I can do during recess, if you will allow me.

Q. I would like to get a copy of the memorandum which you supplied to Mr. Rogers.

Mr. Colby.— Mr. Quackenbush, I think it might not be well to encounter any — well, I understood you to say that Mr. Rogers was subpoenaed as a witness in an important case.

Mr. Quackenbush.— Mr. Rogers is subpoenaed as a witness in Minneapolis, I think, for next Monday, but he will be at the disposal of the Committee here to-morrow and the next day and the following day. He has to leave Friday night to be in court there on Monday. and he expects that that will take him a good part of the week.

Mr. Colby.— In view of the number of matters, crowding upon our attention, and the haste with which we are endeavoring to work, I think it would be recognized as fair that Mr. Rogers not go away without speaking to the Senator, and bringing the matter to mind.

Mr. Quackenbush.— I intended to bring it up now, because he spoke to me this morning.

Chairman Thompson.— Where does he go?

Mr. Quackenbush.— I think Minneapolis. It is some case that has been pending in which he is a witness, not a party, and he is under subpoena, he told me, and he said that if arrangements could be made so that he could be called here either Wednesday, Thursday or Friday, or go over that time —

Chairman Thompson.— Will you call that to the attention of the Chair to-morrow morning?

Mr. Quackenbush.— Yes, sir. Or, he would come down to-day.

Mr. Colby.— Mr. Chairman, I have a little feeling that you are under some pressure in point of time. I can continue as long as you permit me.

Chairman Thompson.— We want to suspend when you can.

Mr. Colby.— There is the point of these dates.

Chairman Thompson.— Can you leave that till to-morrow?

Mr. Colby.— Yes.

Chairman Thompson.— This approval by the Public Service Commission, have you got the copy of this?

Mr. Gaynor.— Here is a copy of what is called the " Priority Determinations," you asked me to produce this morning.

Chairman Thompson.— This is the action of the Public Service Commission as approving this five hundred odd thousand dollars?

Mr. Gaynor.— That is the finding of the chief engineer of the Commission, in which you will see that he enters these allowances as part of the cost of construction and equipment.

Chairman Thompson.— October 14, 1913. Will someone get from the — Mr. Shuster, will you get from the Public Service Commission two or three printed copies of this prior determination, October 14, 1913, in the matter of determination of chief engineer, under contract dated March 19, 1913, in relation to Interborough Rapid Transit Company of the cost of construction prior to March 19, 1913. Get a half dozen copies, and give this back to Mr. Gaynor.

Mr. Gaynor.— Before we adjourn, I have cleared up now all of the matters which I was asked for yesterday, and if you will kindly allow me to put this on the record, I think I will have cleared yesterday's transaction. in the interest account under the subdivision of construction, that Mr. Colby asked me about yesterday, amounting to upwards of three millions —

Mr. Colby.— Three million seven hundred and fifty-six thousand dollars.

Mr. Gaynor.— There is included a payment made by the company to the city of two hundred and two thousand odd dollars, which the city called upon us at one time to pay in the form of interest payable by the city. Otherwise, the account represents our own interest payments.

Chairman Thompson.— Well, we will suspend now until 11 o'clock to-morrow morning. Witnesses are required to attend at that time. Witnesses before the subcommittee will take the direction of the chairman of the subcommittee.

Whereupon, at 2:07 p. m., an adjournment was taken to Wednesday, February 16, 1916, at 11 o'clock a. m.

FEBRUARY 16, 1916

NEW YORK COUNTY LAWYERS' ASSOCIATION BOARD ROOM,
165 Broadway, New York City.

In the absence of Chairman Thompson, a recess was taken to 2:30 p. m.

AFTERNOON SESSION

The Committee was called to order, pursuant to recess, Chairman Thompson presiding.

Chairman Thompson.— The Committee will please come to order.

Mr. Colby.— I would like to ask Mr. MacInnes to resume the stand.

Chairman Thompson.— I apologize for being late to-day, but there was a Republican State Convention which had some very large and important questions to decide, and I could not get here before, which probably has inconvenienced this Committee some, but we will try to get along. We will expect you to furnish enough testimony this afternoon, Mr. MacInnes, to make up for the loss of the morning.

DUNCAN MACINNES, being recalled for further examination, testified as follows:

By Mr. Colby:

Q. Mr. MacInnes, I think you testified in the course of the few questions that we addressed to you yesterday that you had been connected with the Finance Department of the city of New York for a period of some thirteen years? A. Nineteen years.

Q. Your present position is Chief of the Accounting Department? A. Chief Accountant, Department of Finance.

Q. And all the work of keeping city accounts is under your direction and supervision? A. Well, to a great extent.

Q. Will you please state to me the various offices you have held under the city during your nineteen years of relations? A. I was appointed on the 5th of August, 1897, by the then Comptroller, Ashbel P. Fitch, as expert accountant to examine and clarify the situation over in Queens. I had the accounts of upwards of fifty of the municipalities, minor and large, in Queens to clear up for their consolidation, and when that was done the work of analyzing and reconstructing the accounts of the new city of New York to a great extent fell within my duties. The present Comptroller, Mr. Prendergast, appointed me auditor of receipts when he came into office in 1910, and later on as Chief Accountant of the Department of Finance. I think in the latter part of 1911 I was appointed by the present Comptroller, and have continued in that official position since.

Q. And during the period you have occupied the office of Chief Accountant the preliminaries as to the negotiations, the various tentative and finally the ultimate form of the contract relating to the new subways was considered by your department; is that not true? A. The ultimate form of the contracts, I can hardly say that. It was the prospective financial results of those contracts.

Q. Were estimated by you? A. Yes, sir, by me from time to time.

Q. From practically the beginning of the city's participation in the negotiations? A. From November, 1911, down to immediately preceding the authorization of the contracts, in March, 1913.

Q. You are familiar with the fact that one form of proposed agreement failed of approval in the Board of Estimate in July, 1911, are you? A. Yes, sir.

Q. You are also familiar with the fact doubtless, as has been testified here, that some months intervened before the negotiations were resumed? A. Yes, sir.

Q. When they were resumed it was upon a plan of participation by the city jointly with bankers and with the operating company in many respects revised, as compared with the plan that failed in July, 1911; is that true? A. I think there was very little difference between the plan as presented in July, 1911, and the plan that was ultimately adopted, excepting, as I recall it, in this important particular, the plan of 1911, contemplated a 9 per cent. return to the Interborough on all of its capital, new and old, and the new — the contract that was authorized on March 18, 1913, gave a preferential of $6,335,000 on the old capital estimated at $48,000,000, and 6 per cent. upon the new, which works out over the whole at 8.76 per cent., in other words a difference in favor of the new plan of about ¼ of 1 per cent. on the total capital to be invested by the Interborough. I might say further that into the new contract of March 18, 1913, there was placed this absolute condition which was not clear in the former one, that the Interborough Company as lessee of the present subways would continue to pay rental on the bonds for the present subways even after those bonds had been amortized or had matured.

Q. Was it contended by the Interborough that this rental should cease with the amortization of the bonds on the present subway? A. During the negotiations preceding 1911 the Interborough were contending that when the bonds on the present subways which had been issued by the city to build them were amortized that their rental on them would cease and that then they would go scot free until the end of the contracts.

Q. Notwithstanding the city had built the subway and owned it? A. Yes, sir. That phase of their contention was called attention to and the contract that was ultimately adopted placed a condition within it which while synchronizing the old contracts with the new contracts in point of duration, also requires the payment of the rental on these bonds no matter when they mature.

Q. Let me ask you this question, you say the revised plan contemplates a return of 6 per cent. to the company on the new capital? A. Yes, sir.

Q. What rate of return does the company receive under the plan finally adopted upon the capital invested in the present subways? A. It receives on its own statement of investments a little over forty-eight millions, it receives, or will receive, on the $6,335,000 of preferential, it will receive 13.18 per cent., or about, in round figures, 13 1/5 per cent.

Q. You say upon its own statement of its investment? A. Yes, sir.

Q. Do you mean to imply or do you regard that statement as in some particulars possibly an exaggerated statement of the actual investment of the Interborough Rapid Transit Company in the present subways? A. Well, I say — on its own statement of investment, I say, because I do not believe that ever a statement has been analyzed by the Public Service Commission with a view to determine what it really consists of.

Chairman Thompson.— You think the Public Service Commission never did it?

Mr. MacInnes.— I don't think they ever did.

Chairman Thompson.— What did they do?

Mr. MacInnes.— In saying —

Chairman Thompson.— Did you ever hear of anything they did do? You need not answer.

Q. The witness's smile is probably as expressive as an answer could be. A. The reason I say, "On their own statement," is this: As an accountant, I do not wish you to understand when I say their investments of forty-eight millions is an investment of which I know. I say on their own statement of forty-eight millions, a statement which I have no knowledge whatever has ever been analyzed with a view to be determined. I mean the Interborough statment.

Q. As an accountant you do not wish to assume any responsibility for their own statement? A. Just so.

Q. And you do not imply anything against them? A. No, sir.

Q. During the interval between the rejection of the first plan and the renewal of negotiations looking to a revised plan, did you carefully analyze the proposals of the Interborough Rapid Transit Company from the standpoint of the city? A. In compliance with the Comptroller's request or direction I made a careful estimate of what the probable financial results of the operation of the subways would be under the conditions outlined in the proposed contract and based upon passenger travel which year after year had been agreed to, the Public Service Commission engineers, the Interborough engineers, Mr. McAneny's own people who had made a study of transit conditions, and with these as a basis I proceeded to prepare estimates of what the financial results were likely to be to the city as a partner in the enterprise.

Q. That was a part of your duty as Chief Accountant of the city and a part of the specific assignments you had received from the Comptroller? A. Yes, sir.

Q. Did you preserve a copy of your calculations or of any report that you made? A. Yes, sir, I made quite a few.

Q. I mean at that time? A. Yes, sir, I have copies of the various statements I made.

Q. Are you in a position to produce the first discussion that you made of this question? A. As these reflect the labors of many a weary night and many a Sabbath afternoon —

Q. For which I assume no bonus was received by you? A. I was not on the pay roll.

Q. I might say, on this point, Mr. MacInnes, testimony has been placed upon this record that very large rewards were given and larger rewards even were sought for the pertinacity and the zeal with which the officers of the Interborough co-operated with the city in this matter; I suppose you pursued the matter with some degree of pertinacity and zeal? A. Well, I don't know whether I pursued it with much zeal, but I had to pursue it with a good deal of pertinacity. I find the first report I made was November 27, 1911, December 2, 1911, December 14, 1911, and December 21, and then I think it was along in 1912, April, the next one.

Q. May I see them all? A. Well, there is the first one. (Witness hands papers to Mr. Colby.)

Q. The reports with the annexed tables which you have handed me are too voluminous for me to examine them at this moment. I will, however, pass to what appears to be the latest in point of time, namely, a communication bearing date December 14, 1911, addressed to Mr. Prendergast, Comptroller, and I see from a hurried examination it is somewhat more general than the earlier reports, somewhat more in the nature of a summary of results and of views; that is true, is it not? A. Well, the summary is supported by tables that very clearly indicate the basis upon which these allegations were reached.

Mr. Colby.— There is a portion of this letter, Mr. Chairman, which I think I should read, and I believe the entire letter is of sufficient importance to warrant its being made a part of our record.

Chairman Thompson.— Very well.

Mr. Colby.— I offer in evidence this letter, from the Chief Accountant of the city, to the Comptroller, dated December 14, 1911.

(Same was received and marked Exhibit 1.)

Q. This was a report prepared by you at the request of the Comptroller? A. Yes, sir.

Q. And accompanied this elaborate table in which I notice there is an estimate of interest burden, deficits, returns, progress toward the wiping out of deficits, calculated from year to year and showing the true state of the operation at various times in its progress? A. Yes, sir.

Mr. Colby.— This discussion on operating and revenue seems interesting, and I will begin to read the letter at that point:

"All of the tables herewith submitted have been based upon the constant operating expense at 45 per cent of passenger revenue and taxes at 2 per cent, making an annual charge for such of 47 per cent of the passenger revenue. In the light of the practical experience in operating the present subway it would seem as if 45 per cent of passenger revenue was too large a ratio to be used as a constant factor upon which to estimate the operating expense. It would apparently follow that after the first four or five years' operation of the extended subway and the consequent largely increased per centum in its passenger revenue, which at the end of the first five years would be fully 40 per cent greater than during the first year, the operating expense would logically be expected to decrease in its relation to the greatly increased passenger revenue, and that therefore this constant factor of 45 per cent would in all likelihood prove to be far more than adequate after 1920 to meet and provide all operating expense, under an efficient business management. It was agreed, however, at the conferences which were held, that 45 per cent with an additional 2

per cent for taxes, should be used as a constant factor. A
reduction of the per centum of operating expenses to passenger
revenue, as compared with the ratio used in these tables,
would result in an increased amount of revenue available to
reduce the city's deficit and liquidate it much sooner than as
set forth on the tables herewith submitted.

"On the other hand, these tables do not make any provision
for obsolescence of equipment and machinery, or for depreciation of equipment, plants and machinery. I believe that it
could be safely assumed, however, that the 45 per cent charged
as operating expense would be sufficient not only to provide
all of the necessary operating expense under efficient and
careful management but would also yield sufficient revenue to
provide the necessary reserve funds for obsolescence and also
for such depreciation in rolling stock, other equipment and
machinery as could not be prevented by the best maintenance
and upkeep."

The report continues with an outline of an alternative method
for the financing of these subway extensions. This will appear
fully in the letter. The comment of the Chief Accountant on this
point is interesting and brief:

"These suggestions are respectfully submitted on the
ground that they will at least indicate a basis upon which
terms for the building and extension of subways and the
operation thereof could be entered upon by a lessee without
the city having to agree to any preferential application of
revenue, and which would not entail or bring into the proposition the vexing question of whether the actual expense of
operation was greater in amount or per centum than it should
be.

"The operating expense would be an all important factor
in determining to what extent the city would require to provide each year and for an extended period, either by bond
issue or from a tax burden or both, a deficit for interest and
sinking fund charges on its new investment in subways, and
it is quite possible that the adjustment of operating expense
within an amount such as would enable the city to liquidate

such deficit would be entirely beyond the control of the city
or its administrative officials.

" The general auditor of the Interborough at the conferences
held expressed himself as believing that the operating expense
and the taxes would amount, for a good many years at least,
to 50 per cent of the passenger revenue. If such should prove
to be the case it would mean that the city would require to
issue bonds for a much longer period of years than as indicated in the tables herewith submitted to provide the annual
interest and sinking funds on its new investment in subways.
This in turn would require a greater annual amount being
included in the tax budget and for a more extended period of
years, to provide the interest and carrying charges on such
bonds as would necessarily require to be issued to meet the
interest and sinking fund on the city's new investment.

"A table formulated on the basis of 50 per cent of revenue
for operating expense and tax indicates that the balance of
revenue available for the payment of interest and sinking fund
charges on the city's new investment, estimated at $57,000,000
would be so meagre as to require yearly issues of bonds for
such purpose ultimately aggregating over $40,000,000, the
principal of which could apparently never be redeemed from
the city's share of subway revenue.

" The conditions of the present operating lease required,
from the beginning, a payment by the lessee of all of the interest charges on the bonds issued by the city for the construction and 1 per cent for sinking fund to amortize said bonds.
It would seem that this is a provision that should enter into
any agreement for operating new subways, and that in addition thereto the city should receive a per centum of the gross
receipts, at any rate, from a period where it could approximately be assumed that there would be a resultant, reasonable
profit to the lessee, on this actual investment.

"Any agreement for the conjoint building of new subways
and their operation by a lessee, which would be predicated on
a return to the city from net revenue, viz., only after the
lessee had received his profits and carrying charges, would be
fraught with all the dangers of delay and the postponement
of result consequent upon a management and expense opera-

tion the cost of which would be entirely under the control and in the hands of the lessee, and which the city would apparently be powerless to influence."

Q. These views that you have so forcibly stated apparently were laid before the confreres on this important subject at a very early stage in the negotiations? A. Yes, sir, in December, 1911.

Q. Has the city any power of supervision or control under the new contracts on the subject of operating expense? A. The Public Service Commission are the only body that really have any control. The Public Service Commission are vested with whatever authority may be vested in those representing the city. The contract when operation begins gives to the Comptroller the right with the Public Service Commission to examine the account of the operating lessee with a view to determine their accuracy, but the Comptroller's office would have no control whatever over the operating expense. The Public Service Commission are vested with whatever authority may be vested in that direction.

Q. In other words, the city's participation in the revenue is confined entirely to net revenue? A. Net revenue.

Q. How long do you think it will be before the city participates in any of the earnings of the new subways? A. Well, I made a computation in January, 1913, prior to the adoption of the contracts, and these were based upon somewhat different conditions, under the same principle but different conditions —

Q. May I interrupt you there; different conditions, you mean conditions altered to the disadvantage of the city, as the result of delays? A. The conditions being the city were required to make a larger investment than was anticipated when these were prepared.

Q. In other words, to the disadvantage of the city, altered conditions? A. The lessee was required to also provide more money in construction under the new conditions, and upon which they would receive their interest and sinking fund charges.

Q. Now, if you will just allow me, a moment. Assuming a condition which closely approximated what ultimately the contract provided for, that does not include any interest on the deficits which the Interborough will likely have to carry for a few years and which will make a material difference in the outcome. This table trying to make a forecast of what was likely to be the result, shows that it would be 1933 if we began on the 1st of January, 1917, to operate, and that it would be 1933 before the city would have cleaned up its interest and sinking fund charges. That was based upon an investment by the city of sixty millions and by the Interborough Company of eighty millions. The increase of the investment by the city under the contract as it was finally adopted and the inclusion therein of interest on the company's deficit during the lean years of operation, and the fact that operation will not begin until very likely at least a year later than our estimates at that time, all indicate that instead of 1933 that that period will be put back for quite a few years. The condition of the contract also — one of the conditions of the contract also is that the city after having cleaned up its end and got its interest and sinking fund charges shall then begin to get an amount equal to 3.26 per cent. on its investment to bring it up even with the lessee, but it will be a long, long time before it overtakes that. This table indicated that in 1948 we would be $12,000,000 behind, and the prospects are a little better. With the increased amounts the city must put in the prospects are not improved.

Q. I want to develop that a little; on the assumption that operation would begin in 1917, and upon the assumption of the city's investment and the company's investment at the time that table was prepared, you say it would be at least 1933 before the city had caught up on the cumulative deficits of its own? A. Yes, sir.

Q. But the investment of larger sums by the company, the investment of larger sums by the city, the postponement in time of the beginning of operation, all operate to augment the amount of the company's preferential claim on earnings, also augment the city's deficit and also greatly prolong the period and postpone the day when the city will be in a position to participate at all in these net earnings; is that true? A. Well, I would like to put it more concisely.

Q. So would I, Mr. MacInnes. A. The factors that all tend to retard the period in which the city will come into its own, in which the city will get back its own, are one, the delay in operation; two, the interest charges on the Interborough's deficit, and three, the increased costs to the city for construction, because there will be no increased cost to the Interborough. So it is these three elements

that all, each and every one, has their influence, and the greatest
is the increased cost to the city.

Q. Is it possible that the entire period of these bonds may pass
without any participation by the city in subway earnings? A. No,
I think that the subway revenues will, if there is anything like
efficient management at all, if there is anything like a public supervision, the subway revenues, within the life of the contract, should
clean up the city's investment. How far it will go towards paying
to the city any of the 3.26 to put it on an even keel with the Interborough is problematical.

Chairman Thompson.— What do you mean by efficient public
supervision?

Mr. MacInnes.— I mean economical management is an absolute
essential, and as we have a right to expect some such thing as that,
and there will be no question in my mind of the passenger traffic,
and the only evasive and elusive quantity is the operating expenses.
There will be no question about the revenue. It will be coming in.

Chairman Thompson.— Are you able to state whether under the
present law, or the contracts made under the operation of the Rapid
Transit Act, whether they provide for such supervision as you have
in mind on the part of the city or the public?

Mr. MacInnes.— Well, I think, Mr. Chairman, that the law
gives the Public Service Commission the greatest latitude towards
making rules and regulations and enforcing them as it may consider essential to safeguard the city's interest.

Chairman Thompson.— You think that power has been modified
in any way by the subway contracts?

Mr. MacInnes.— No, sir.

Chairman Thompson.— If you have an efficient Public Service
Commission, they really would regulate this contract?

Mr. MacInnes.— Yes, sir.

Chairman Thompson.— From the city's standpoint?

Mr. MacInnes.— Yes, sir.

Mr. Colby, resuming:

Q. According to the table that assumed the beginning of operations in 1917, you calculated that you would clean up the city's deficit in 1933 and the city might then begin to participate in the earnings? A. Yes, sir.

Q. You have not stated how long a postponement of that desirable condition will result from these increased expenditures and from the increased delay; have you formed an impression in your mind? A. I have not had an opportunity after having read from the public press as to what the additional interest and debt expense charges are likely to be by the Interborough, and having some knowledge of what the additional real estate costs are likely to be I have not had an opportunity to make such a tabulation as I feel would justify me in giving expression to any opinion. I would like to have something that I can use to back up my conclusion with respect to a subject such as this.

Q. I understand you perfectly; in other words, there are indicated facts that would have a very direct bearing upon the calculations, and yet you have not any true measure of the extent or importance of those facts to proceed upon as yet? A. Well, I have not had an opportunity to give them the weight and consideration I should. Up to the present moment I have been trying to get my work in shape to come down here, and I worked until half past two this morning, and yesterday the same way.

Q. It has been testified, Mr. MacInnes, that the company's contribution to construction is not to exceed $58,000,000, and that any insufficiency of this sum to complete construction will have to be made by the city; that is true? A. That is true.

Q. If the city is called upon to make up some deficit on this account, will it have to issue new bonds, new corporate city stock, for that purpose? A. Yes, sir.

Q. That in turn, will add to its interest charges and increase its deficit? A. Yes, sir.

Q. And it follows logically that it will operate to postpone the date when the city begins to participate in revenue? A. Surely.

Q. Your calculation of 1933 and the beginning of operation in 1917 does not reckon upon any such insufficiency in construction contribution, does it? A. No, sir.

Q. It assumes the entire fifty-eight million will be contributed and spent upon proper items entering into construction account? A. Yes, sir, the only addition I have in here is two million instead of the fifty-eight, the city's sixty.

Q. What is the amount of bonds already issued by the city in connection with the Interborough contract No. 3; that is the contract for the extension of the subways. A. $40,000,000.

Q. What is the amount contracted to be issued? A. $65,625,000.

Q. What is the amount in excess of that figure which it is now indicated the city will have to contribute? A. Well, I think that it will probably be in the neighborhood of from $12,000,000 to $15,000,000 more.

Q. Twelve to fifteen million more? A. Yes, sir.

Q. What is the present amount of the debt margin, that is to say how much unappropriated borrowing power has the city at the moment? A. $22,000,000; $22,232,000.

Q. This additional issue of twelve million bonds is not deducted in arriving at that sum? A. No, sir.

Q. These additional bonds will come out of that sum? A. They will.

Q. The moment these additional bonds are issued there arises the concurrent necessity of issuing bonds to defray interest charges upon them; isn't that true? A. Yes, sir. Being issued for construction, the law authorizes the issue of other bonds to meet the interest upon them.

Q. And this estimate of yours that the city will have to issue ten or twelve millions more than they undertook to issue is not based upon any idea of the total of construction accounts except the idea you had when the contract was made; is that right? A. No, sir, that is based upon the additional extra costs that are looming up now, due to increased interest over and above the original estimates and to increased costs for real estate over and above the original estimates.

Q. Does it proceed upon any assumption that there may be a diminution of the Interborough's contribution on account of construction to the extent of ten or twelve millions for interest charges? A. No, sir, it does not include any more than a probable five millions for that.

Assemblyman Feinberg.— Do you refer to the cost of acquiring easements in the cost of real estate?

Mr. MacInnes.— Sometimes you have to acquire the property as well.

Assemblyman Feinberg.— Is that a large element in the cost?

Mr. MacInnes.— Yes, sir.

Chairman Thompson.— Have you anything to show how much interest has been incurred on account of the delay in operations?

Mr. MacInnes.— No, sir, I have not.

Chairman Thompson.— Can you give an estimate of that?

Mr. MacInnes.— Not at the moment. I have no knowledge at the present time of what the interest computations of the Interborough are.

Chairman Thompson.— You are the Chief Accountant in the Comptroller's office?

Mr. MacInnes.— Yes, sir.

Chairman Thompson.— If the Comptroller makes statements on this subject himself, he gets his information from you?

Mr. MacInnes.— Yes, sir.

Chairman Thompson.— And whenever the Comptroller makes a statement in relation to the finances, he gets his information from the department of which you are the head?

Mr. MacInnes.— Yes, sir.

Q. What price has the city realized upon the sale of bonds issued for subway purposes, at what rates of interest have the bonds been sold? A. 4, 4¼ and 4½ per cent. I would like to say, in further explanation, that preceding the sale of bonds by the city for Rapid Transit Construction and for any other public improvement the Comptroller sells corporate stock notes, and he is empowered to sell these notes for a short varying period and periods. The present Comptroller had the Legislature assist him by passing a law in 1911 which authorizes this, and the experience in 1915 of the city in financing subway construction prior to the issue of long term bonds is reflected in these rates of interest: In August, 3 per cent, 1915; September, 2⅜, 2¼, 2 3/16, 2½; October, 2 3/5, 2 7/16, 2½, 2 7/16; November, 2⅜; December, 2 1/5, 2¼; and now we have twenty-three millions of corporate stock notes for Rapid Transit purposes outstanding which will be taken up at the next bond sale, and the interest on these is from 2½ to 2 3/32 per cent; so you see that in the actual financing of the subways by this means we have borrowed just as we needed, carrying a very little on hand and getting lowest rates of interest. When these corporate stock notes finally crystallize into the long term bonds and are sold under sealed bids, the rate heretofore has not been under 4¼ and 4, 4¼ and 4½.

Q. You seem to have pursued a diametrically opposite policy in that respect to that pursued by the Interborough Rapid Transit Company; they have first issued their bonds carrying an interest charge of some 5⅜ per cent; they have first issued their bonds carrying an interest charge of some 5⅜ per cent aggregating recently over $50,000,000 cash on which they received 2½ per cent interest, and cleaning up the bank balance by subsequent expenditures for the work of construction, and I understand you have issued your notes for the purpose of raising money actually called for at the extraordinarily low rates of interest amounting to two and a small fraction per cent, and as the notes accumulated in amount you have cleaned up the notes by the issuance of city bonds at 4¼ and 4½ per cent? A. Yes, sir.

Q. Of course the method you have pursued is infinitely more saving and economical, is it not? A. No method could be more saving than the method pursued by the city in financing subway construction.

Q. The city has never, for instance, issued its bonds in a large amount and thereby built up a large cash balance on which it has drawn for its expenditures in construction work? A. Prior to 1911, the city found its money by two or three sales of long term bonds during the year, and that sometimes meant the carrying of quite large balances in bank, but in 1911, as I have already stated, the Legislature passed this corporate stock note act to enable the Comptroller to borrow from hand to mouth, and effected savings in interest costs, and it could not be possible the interest cost could be kept at any less, at a lower figure, than the city's interest costs are.

Chairman Thompson.— How do you save interest by borrowing money?

Mr. MacInnes.— In these cases I have cited, we borrowed it at 2⅜ and put in the bank, and as long as it lays there it gets 2 per cent, and costs ⅜ per cent.

Chairman Thompson.— If you have it in the bank, what would you want to borrow it for?

Mr. MacInnes.— We have to have it on tap, and could not possibly raise it any other way than by borrowing. The question of how long you should borrow it for is a mere matter of judgment, but it would be simply impossible to finance the construction of these Rapid Transit roads by the city without borrowing.

Chairman Thompson.— Why do you borrow it and put it in the banks and not use it?

Mr. MacInnes.— We don't put it there and not use it.

Mr. Colby.— One of the very important charges to construction account is for interest losses which result from the 5⅜ per cent paid by the Interborough, less the 2½ per cent received from Morgan & Company on the fifty million of cash balances, and the point of Mr. MacInnes' testimony is that the city by borrowing at 2½ or 2⅛ on notes the money it actually needs for expenditures for construction, is enabled when accumulated to a sufficient amount to clean up with bonds issued at 4 per cent, and there is not that loss on money in disuse.

Chairman Thompson.— You can borrow money on short term notes cheaper than on long term bonds?

Mr. MacInnes.— Yes, sir.

Chairman Thompson.— That is new to me.

Mr. MacInnes.— We do it.

Chairman Thompson.— What is the reason for that; is that because the notes are in smaller denominations?

Mr. MacInnes.— Yes, sir.

Chairman Thompson.— And more people willing to take them?

Mr. MacInnes.— Yes, sir.

Chairman Thompson.— If you issued your bonds in small denominations you would get them taken the same way?

Mr. MacInnes.— I don't know. In the past five years an observation of the money market has shown that bonds with a shorter term of years to run have sold better than they did twenty years ago. Twenty years ago it would seem long term bonds were more in preference. Now the short term notes we use, and we sell them when the market conditions are the very best. We keep a very close and careful attention to the progress of every subway contract, and as we have ten days in which to pay the vouchers, the contractors' vouchers, after they are in, and we try to pay them within that time, seven days, that gives us enough time to borrow. I have this statement of every contract we have, and a compilation of the vouchers tells us what we need to borrow for that particular month's outlay, and we borrow it to-day to pay your bills to-morrow, Senator. The interest costs are kept down to an irreducible minimum by the city in financing its subway construction.

Senator Lawson.— You mean that, Mr. MacInnes?

Mr. MacInnes.— Yes, sir; that is exactly what I mean.

Chairman Thompson.— It is entirely new to me, that a short term loan can be gotten at a less rate of interest than a long term. Up to this moment I supposed long-term loans bore the shortest interest, and of course, if you can do that, borrow money at two and seven-eighths on notes, it is easy to see how there is a saving there, and you issue your notes at $2\frac{1}{2}$ and your bonds at $4\frac{1}{2}$?

Mr. MacInnes.— Yes.

Chairman Thompson.— And sell them at par?

Mr. MacInnes.— Sell them at a premium.

Chairman Thompson.— At a premium.

20

By Mr. Colby:

Q. At what premium have these subway bonds been sold, speaking generally — I mean the city's bonds? A. The last sale brought a premium of somewhere about 1 — as to about 1.

Q. 101? A. Yes.

Q. Although they carried only 4½ per cent interest? A. Yes.

Q. These were sold to the public? A. Yes, sir, sold under sealed bid. The conditions are that they cannot be sold at less than par.

Q. Was any commission paid on their sales? A. None whatever.

Q. There was no necessity the city was under of carrying the proceeds of sale as a deposit balance with any bank or bankers? A. No. The method is that a bond sale by the city is used for the purpose of redeeming all of these short term notes that we have been borrowing money on, at the lowest possible rate of interest. We cannot borrow on those beyond one year. Now, we had to clean them up.

Q. And you have sought to restrict your borrowings on notes, even carrying so low a rate of interest as you have testified to, to your actual needs, as to expenditures? A. Yes, sir.

Q. Thus saving the city all avoidable interest charge? A. Yes, sir.

Mr. Colby.— I think that is very clear, Mr. Chairman.

Chairman Thompson.— Yes, it is. If it was not for the law that required you to issue those notes for one year only, it would be foolish to issue 4½ per cent bonds to take up 2⅞ per cent notes with.

Mr. MacInnes.— Well, you would require to have a law that would enable you to issue a longer term eventually, because we won't be in a position to redeem them — we could not redeem them in a short term of years. You must have a number of years in which to redeem them.

By Mr. Colby:

Q. Mr. MacInnes, I think the Committee would be interested in a statement of the interest cost to the city up to December 31. 1915. Could that be prepared in your office without too much exertion? A. Oh, that can be prepared very readily.

Q. Let me give you this little memorandum on that point, will you? (Counsel gives memorandum to witness.) Does the city aim to carry as moderate, not to say reduced, balances, as possible, of cash? A. They always do.

Q. You look upon a mounting cash balance as not necessarily an indication of careful financial management, do you? A. Not when we can raise it readily by an issue of notes. No need of incurring interest costs when the money itself is not actually necessary.

Q. The city has not any bank balance anywhere upon which — which is costing it 2⅞ or 3 per cent per annum interest, has it? A. Which is costing —

Q. Which is costing 2⅞ to 3 per cent in interest losses? A. No.

Q. Or which is costing it more than it receives in interest? A. Well, there may be — there may be two or three million dollars that may be costing us more. For instance, the proceeds of a bond sale that has not yet been used to liquidate the different bills and vouchers costing us 4½ per cent, and we are getting 2. Now, the proceeds of that bond sale would be very small, because the larger part of it is used to take up the notes. But there would be several millions, perhaps, in anticipation of obligations which we must meet, and which would be costing net 2½, until the money was all expended.

Q. How much of such money has the city on hand at the moment, applicable to these contracts? A. Not more than — I don't believe there is more than a couple of million dollars at the present time. It is a question if we have that.

Chairman Thompson.— You said some time ago, that in 1948, you would be $12,000,000 behind, according to some figures you have made. You got down to as far as 1948. When you were pressed for an idea as to how long it would be before the city would participate, you said there might be some obligations which you had not in mind. Assuming you had that $12,000,000 behind in 1948, figuring on that alone, how much further time would it take before the city participated, to catch up that twelve millions, according to your table?

Mr. MacInnes.— Well, it would probably take in the neighborhood of six years, at least.

Chairman Thompson.— Six years more. That would get you to '54· That is, if there is no waste and no foolishness charged to construction. Could these contracts have been made so that the city would have realized sooner on its investment?

Mr. MacInnes.— I beg your pardon?

Chairman Thompson.— Could these contracts have been made so that the city could have realized sooner on them?

Mr. MacInnes.— Well, when I made the report which — from which Mr. Colby has read certain extracts, I was very much of the opinion that the contract should not be predicated upon net revenue; that the contract should be predicated upon a recognition that the city as a partner, having little or no control over the operating expense, should at least have the interest on its bonds provided, and if in the lean years in the beginning, that it was necessary to divert the payment of its sinking funds. that could be done, because the debt could be amortized well within the period of the contract. It did not require the forty-nine years to amortize the debt, 1 per cent. My belief — my reason for suggesting this was because that would compel economical management. If, on the other hand, that the two partners. the one who had the control over all the revenue, was guaranteed his before the city. I felt that there would not be the same impelling force, the same impelling reason to economical management.

Chairman Thompson.— There is nothing — if you made it on net. there is nothing — there is no data on what they do — that is. there is nothing to impress upon the people operating the road anything beyond sufficient economy to get their own —

Mr. MacInnes.— Yes.

Chairman Thompson.— and not take care of the other.

By Mr. Colby:

Q. Now, Mr. MacInnes, is there any basis upon which operation was possible, on which those operating economies are enforced or necessary on the part of the operating company? A. Well, I have said already that the Public Service Commission is the only body vested with the authority to compel a proper recognition of efficient management and economical management in the roads — in the management of the roads.

Q. There are some important municipal operations of subways that are conducted on the basis of a division of gross, aren't there? In the city of Paris, for instance? A. Well, while this was under discussion I recall — while the contracts were under discussion, I recall that it was stated, and I believe it to be so, that the subways in Paris are operated under the very simple method of the city receiving 4, and the operator 6. It receives of every five cents at least — yes, of every five cents the city receives 2 and the operator 3 — 40 and 60 per cent; that is the division.

Q. And that automatically enjoins upon the operator economies and efficiencies of operation within that agreed division of gross receipts?

Chairman Thompson.— Well, you as a —

Mr. Colby.— Just a moment, Mr. Chairman. I would like to have that question answered, because it is a matter of significance to me in connection with some later questions. Will you read that question?

(The question was read by the stenographer.)

A. The operator has got to get all his carrying charges out of that, and consequently —

Q. That is his agreed share.

Mr. Colby.— Excuse me, Mr. Chairman.

Chairman Thompson.— All I wanted to observe was — it is rather out of my mind now — all I wanted — all I was suggesting, was observing — you were a resident of the city of New York in 1916, and suggested the city should get two cents out of every five cents?

Mr. MacInnes.— No.

Chairman Thompson.— You would not hope to have such ideas as that?

Mr. MacInnes.— I was merely stating a division. Oh, I don't expect to live to see that.

Chairman Thompson.— No. There is one more thing. Did you
ever make that suggestion in relation to this contract that you made
in answer to my question a few moments ago, in relation to the
city taking its share of the gross earnings? Did you make it to any
of the men interested in negotiating the contract at the time?

Mr. MacInnes.— You mean as to its being on the basis of gross
earnings?

Chairman Thompson.— Yes.

Mr. MacInnes.— Of course, it is in the report.

Chairman Thompson.— What is that?

Mr. MacInnes.— It is contained in the report that I made.

Chairman Thompson.— Report to whom?

Mr. Colby.— It is contained in the extracts I read on the record
to-day.

Chairman Thompson.— I just wanted to know. When was that
made?

Mr. MacInnes.— December, 1911.

Chairman Thompson.— Who was the report made to?

Mr. MacInnes.— It was a report made to the transit committee,
Comptroller and Mr. McAneny.

Chairman Thompson.— The Comptroller and the President of
the Board of Aldermen and the Mayor?

Mr. MacInnes.— Yes.

Chairman Thompson.— Is there any — did they ever take it up
further with you, or talk with you about it?

Mr. MacInnes.— We had quite some discussions about it, but
the kind of a contract that I was a believer in, was apparently a
contract which they could not get the lessees to agree to.

Chairman Thompson.— Do they agree now?

Mr. MacInnes.— I believe I may safely say that the views were
looked upon as being — as indicating the kind of a contract which

it would be a good thing if the city could have made, but the city could not make that contract, apparently.

Chairman Thompson.— Well, they didn't make it anyway.

Mr. MacInness.— No, they didn't.

By Mr. Colby:

Q. Mr. MacInnes, have the engineers of the Public Service Commission ever made an estimate of the increase on account of interest that would have to be taken care of by the city in connection with construction work? A. Yes, they have.

Q. Do you remember what they estimated that additional interest at? A. I think the additional interest was estimated at $7,500,000.

Q. Have you made any estimate as to operating deficit which will have to be carried or met by the issuance of new city bonds? A. Well, that is — I said that I had not had an opportunity of making any table yet based upon the probable additional cost to the city in construction.

Q. As I recall your testimony, it was fifteen millions? A. Yes.

Q. What is the amount of the item for Public Service engineering and superintendence that enters into the cost of the subway? A. About $15,000,000.

Q. In other words, the Public Service Commission has expended for engineering and superintendence — A. Not has, but will — has and will.

Q. Has partially and will ultimately expend $15,000,000? A. Yes, sir.

Q. What proportion of that is a burden upon the city, or is to be borne by the city? A. Oh, all of that will have to be borne by the city.

Senator Lawson.— Is that in addition to these amounts?

Mr. MacInnes.— Yes.

Senator Lawson.— In the subway — dual subway contract?

Mr. MacInnes.— Yes. They were not included in the original costs to be provided by the city.

By Mr. Colby:

Q. Is that also in addition to the charges for engineering and superintendence which the Interborough has paid? A. That is in addition.

Q. Now, it has appeared in the evidence already introduced that there are important items under construction account and under equipment account, representing payments by the engineers — by the Interborough to its engineers for engineering and superintendence; the city is a contributor to that payment as well, isn't it? A. The city is not a contributor to those payments.

Q. Would you not say so in the event that the city has a deficit under construction account to make up? A. The city is a contributor to all the additional costs of subway construction, whether these be due to increased costs for interest or increased cost for administration, or increased cost for acquiring real estate.

Q. Or increased cost for engineering and superintendence? A. Yes, sir. Whatever is recognized and included as part of the cost of construction, that carries the amount over and above the fifty-eight millions to be contributed by the Interborough, the city has to find.

Q. So that if engineering and superintendence amounting to large figures carry that increased cost beyond fifty-eight million, the city may be paying not only the fifteen millions for engineering and superintendence for the Public Service Commission, but the engineering and superintendence charges of the Interborough? A. Whatever is included in the cost of construction.

Mr. Colby.— I think that is clear. I believe that is also true.

Senator Lawson.— What does that $15,000,000 cover?

Mr. MacInnes.— It covers the cost of superintendence and engineering from the beginning of the construction of the Center street loop line.

Senator Lawson.— Covers special salaries to anybody?

Mr. MacInnes.— Well, I cannot tell.

Senator Lawson.— Any extraordinary salaries for services, extraordinary services?

Mr. MacInnes.— I believe that they have pro-rated the costs of the Commission during this time.

Senator Lawson.— Has the city made any compilation per month or per annum of this $15,000,000, since the inception of the idea of having these increased transit facilities?

Mr. MacInness.— Have they made —

Senator Lawson.— Has the Finance Department any detailed record of this $15,000.000 which has been expended?

Mr. MacInnes.— We have no detailed record. The Public Service Commission furnish us with the statements.

Senator Lawson.— You pay the money as they furnish the statements?

Mr. MacInnes.— A large part of the money has been paid.

Senator Lawson.— That is what I mean. And the Public Service Commission now has the figures on which you have paid out this money, a large part of fifteen millions?

Mr. MacInnes.— And the Public Service Commission are the commission vested with the authority to determine how much of their supervision and engineering shall be included as a part of the cost of construction; and that is their estimates that I am using.

By Mr. Colby:

Mr. MacInnes, did any such item as fifteen millions for superintendence and engineering enter into the discussion of the negotiations at the time these contracts were entered into? A. Yes, but it was clearly understood that they would be provided outside of the amount that was to be contributed by the city. At the time that these — that this contract was under discussion, the city had already over thirty-five millions — $35,400,000. in the construction of subways which came within, or which ultimately came within, the purview of this contract No. 3. And the city provided an additional $28,200,000 on the 18th of March, 1913, and that $28,200,000, or the $35,000,000 preceding it, did not contain any of the expenses for engineering and supervision. These had been paid by the city as each month went on going back, so far as the

Center street loop lines are concerned, to 1907. But the contract provided that while there was no debt incurred at that time, a good deal of money had been paid out — no debt incurred or money specifically set aside for the engineering and superintendence, yet it was to be capitalized by the city and made a part of the cost of construction, upon which it was to receive, when there was revenue enough, its interest and sinking fund. And the Public Service Commission will determine the amount for engineering and superintendence, which would be added to each one of these contracts.

Q. Let me ask you at that point: I understood you to say that the only reliance of the city for protection against these excessive costs is the Public Service Commission. Is there any way by which the city can protect itself from the Public Service Commission? In other words, is the Public Service Commission the absolute autocrat as to the amount of charges for engineering and superintendence that it shall roll over on the city in this matter? A. The lessee may take exception; if it does it within thirty days, the lessee may take exception to the Public Service Commission's statement of, or determination of, the amount for superintendence and engineering which the city is to charge.

Q. Yes.

Chairman Thompson.— Both of you are a little in error there. This is not fixed by the Public Service Commission. It is fixed by the chief engineer of the Public Service Commission, and the lessee or the Public Service Commission, either one, must appeal within thirty days from that determination; otherwise it becomes absolute under the Public Service Commissions Law. The engineer is the man that passes on all that, and if the Public Service Commission don't of its own initiative look at that and appeal in thirty days, they are stuck. That is correct, isn't it?

Mr. MacInnes.— Yes.

By Mr. Colby.

Q. When was the last determination by the Public Service Commission? A. With respect to the Interborough engineering and superintendence, there has been one and that was relating to the amounts prior to the 18th of March, 1913.

Chairman Thompson.— Has there ever been an appeal taken by the lessee or Public Service Commission or anybody else?

Mr. MacInnes.— Not to my knowledge.

Chairman Thompson.— Has anybody ever gone to look at the report of the engineer?

Mr. MacInnes.— I don't know.

Chairman Thompson.— Did you ever hear of anybody looking at the report of the engineer?

Mr. MacInnes.— No.

Chairman Thompson.— Or asking about it, or paying any attention to it?

Senator Lawson.— Did the city ever look at it or its financial officers?

Mr. MacInnes.— Well, now, that determination, I believe, was not published until after the time when any appeal could be taken from it. I believe that the Comptroller never saw or knew anything about the items entering into that determination until within a very short while ago.

Chairman Thompson.— As a matter of fact, the Public Service Commission's annual report is not published for a year and a half after the law requires it to be made and filed; that is correct, isn't it?

Senator Lawson.— Do you think, Mr. MacInnes, in view of what you have stated, that the law should be amended, that the Public Service Commission should submit to the city these financial matters that they pass upon before the time to appeal has expired — the time of the city to appeal?

Mr. MacInnes.— Well, I believe that no debt should be valid against the city of New York until the liability has been passed upon and accepted by the Board of Estimate.

Chairman Thompson.— Somebody representing the city ought to be permitted to help incur it?

Mr. MacInnes.— The Board of Estimate is composed of officials elected by the people. They should be the only board to determine.

Chairman Thompson.— They should have some responsibility in incurring it?

Mr. MacInnes.— Yes.

Senator Lawson.— I take it, Mr. MacInnes, from this statement, that the lessees of the operating companies might go to the Public Service Commission and present administration costs that might exceed $4,000,000 or $5,000,000, which would be a charge on the city, and at the present time the city would have no relative say as to whether that was proper or otherwise.

Mr. MacInnes.— Well, the engineers, with the determination, could be appealed from by the Commission.

Senator Lawson.— If the city knew of it. Where would the city come in on that? I am looking to the protection of the city of New York. Where does the city come in if the engineer passes an amount of $5,000,000 or more, which would become a charge on the city of New York?

Mr. Colby.— I have not been paying as much attention as I should to this. I heard just enough of Senator Lawson's question to be interested. I would like to hear that question.

(The question was read by the stenographer as follows: " Where does the city come in if the engineer passes an amount of $5,000,- 000 or more, which would become a charge on the city of New York? ")

Mr. MacInness.— Well, the Commission have the right, or the lessee has a right, to appeal from the engineer.

Senator Lawson.— What does the city gain? The lessee puts in the charge. The lessee goes to the Public Service Commission and says " Here is a schedule covering administration expenses, construction expenses, and so forth, that amounts to $5,000,000. The chief engineer passes that as correct. The report is not printed until the time for the appeal has elapsed. Where does the city come in to protect itself?

Mr. MacInnes.— Well, I have answered you, that the Commission have the right to appeal under the law.

By Mr. Colby:

Q. To appeal, Mr. McInnes, from the finding or determination of its own engineer? A. Yes.

Q. Isn't that a sort of perverted conception of relationship, that the Commission should be obliged to appeal from the determination or finding of its own employee, and if so, to whom do they appeal? A. The engineer.

Chairman Thompson.— The city themselves, through their own officers, have no right to appeal, except they can do it through the Public Service Commission? That is correct, isn't it? They appeal from the report of the engineer? And that is provided by the dual subway contract?

Mr. MacInnes.— Well, you gentlemen are lawyers, and I am merely a layman.

Senator Lawson.— You know something about these dual subway contracts. Now, do they permit things that are not contained in the Public Service Commissions Law?

Mr. MacInnes.— No, I don't think they do.

Senator Lawson.— Well, they do in this case, don't they?

Mr. MacInnes.— No, that is —

Senator Lawson.— I am asking you, Mr. MacInnes, if there is anything in the dual subway contracts that contravenes the Public Service Commission.

Mr. MacInnes.— I don't think so.

Mr. Colby.— Mr. MacInnes feels at the moment that he is not a lawyer.

Mr. MacInness.— I am not a lawyer. I don't know anything about that. That is simply between him (referring to Senator Lawson) and me.

By Mr. Colby:

Q. Isn't such a provision as this rotary system of appeals contained in the dual contracts also, and hasn't it received the approval of the Board of Estimate? A. Well, the contracts were authorized on the 18th of March, 1913, but I don't believe for a moment that the members of the Board of Estimate have realized that under this, that really one man —

Senator Lawson.— Would have all to say.

Mr. MacInnes.— Yes; and that the Commission, who have appointed it, is the only board representing the people that could take exception to his finding or his determination. I don't think they realize it. I think that this —the investigation of your Committee has brought this point out and made it very clear and forcible.

Chairman Thompson.— That was stated by Judge McCall way back last October.

Senator Lawson.— Mr. MacInnes, you don't have to be a lawyer to answer this question: Who is responsible for the delay in publishing these reports; that is, what part of the Public Service Commission is responsible for the publishing of these various reports. if you know?

Mr. MacInnes.— Oh. I don't know.

Senator Lawson.— Well, with the Commission itself or with the counsel, or with the secretary of the Commission? Did you ever confer with the Commission, or any part of it, to find what its functions are. or who is in charge of various departments?

Chairman Thompson.— Well, it is a — I think the requirement of the law is the secretary publishes these reports.

Senator Lawson.— I want to know if the secretary of the Public Service Commission is delinquent in his duty in not publishing these reports before the thirty days for appeal elapses.

Mr. MacInnes.— Isn't that determination signed by the engineer, Mr. Colby?

Mr. Colby.— This is signed — this is a determination of the chief engineer of the Public Service Commission.

Mr. MacInnes.— I think it comes from the chief engineer's office.

Mr. Colby.— And is signed by Alfred Craven, chief engineer of the Public Service Commission.

Chairman Thompson.— Is it endorsed by the secretary as an act of the Commission?

Mr. Colby.— It is a formal act of the engineer. It is entitled, " In the Matter of the determination of the Chief Engineer of the Public Service Commission for the First District, under the contract dated March 19, 1913."

Chairman Thompson.— The question Mr. Lawson wants to raise is whose duty it is, after the engineer makes a report, to print and publish it within thirty days.

Senator Lawson.— Do you know, Mr. MacInnes?

Mr. MacInnes.— I don't.

Chairman Thompson.— Perhaps you better get in touch with the Public Service Commission and ascertain that fact, whose duty it is to publish that.

Assemblyman Kincaid.— Has any complaint ever been made by any city official, as to the failure to print this report or determination within the time of appeal?

Mr. MacInnes.— I don't know.

Assemblyman Kincaid.— Have you ever been to the Public Service Commission with a complaint of that kind?

Mr. MacInness.— I never have.

Assemblyman Kincaid.— Have you ever suggested it to anyone?

Mr. MacInnes.— I never have.

Assemblyman Kincaid.— Has the Comptroller?

Mr. MacInnes.— I don't know whether he has.

Mr. Colby.— The contract between the city of New York and the Interborough Rapid Transit Company, described as contract

No. 3, provides for these determinations by the chief engineer, and in case either the lessee or the city is dissatisfied with his determination, there is a provision here for an appeal within thirty days, and in that event the chief engineer determines whether his prior determination was reasonable. Apparently the city and the lessee are left remediless and theoretically satisfied.

Mr. Quackenbush.— That is not correct. There is a provision for arbitration beyond that. That contract is understood by everybody. There is nothing ridiculous about it.

Chairman Thompson.— That was made by the city officials and the Interborough and the B. R. T., and the Public Service Commission, when they put this great public benefit over on the 19th of March, 1913.

Mr. Quackenbush.— There is no question about it, as far as Mr. Colby goes, and in that event there is a provision for arbitration.

Mr. Colby.— I have not come to that. Where is the arbitration provision?

Mr. Quackenbush.— There is no question about that, because we have been through it; under the present contract.

Mr. Colby.— It may be as diverting as the provision for the present determination. Let me see that determination.

Chairman Thompson.— Everybody will concede, inasmuch as this contract is signed by the city officials, and it needed their signature, they will be charged with knowledge of this condition. so that it should be their duty to have somebody get in touch with these decisions of the engineer some time within thirty days after they are made, regardless of any printed or published notice of it from the secretary. Isn't that true?

Mr. MacInnes.— I think it is true that the Public Service Commission have properly been looked upon as the body.

Chairman Thompson.— Shouldn't the city officials themselves — isn't it their duty? They signed the contract and made this condition possible. Wasn't it the duty of some city official to look into these determinations of the engineer. so that the city's rights would be protected, and an appeal could be had, whether it is printed or published or not? Don't you think so?

Mr. MacInnes.— Well, we didn't get that report from the Public Service Commission.

Chairman Thompson.— You never sent anybody to appear before the engineer when these things were done, did you? The city never did that?

Mr. MacInnes.— We didn't know that the engineer had them under consideration.

Mr. Quackenbush.— The contract provides that the engineer within six months from the beginning, must make this prior determination. That contract is executed by the Board of Estimate as well as by everybody else. It is in the contract.

Mr. Colby.— I will call the Committee's attention to this provision, which I am indebted to Mr. Quackenbush for referring to, with relation to the further procedure after an appeal from the chief engineer's determination. Under the caption " Final, if not objected to," I find this provision of the contract: " In such redetermination " — that is upon appeal to the chief engineer from the chief engineer — " any such redetermination shall be final and conclusive unless the Commission or the lessee shall within thirty days after its receipt of such redetermination, give written notice to the other that it requires the same to be submitted to arbitration of the court as hereinafter provided " — and I am perfectly willing to state what every lawyer would recognize as a principle of law, that the ground for successful appeal from a determination by the chief engineer which would be held to be probably a discretionary act, probably the exercise of a power confided in him by law, would be looked upon by the court as giving it very little scope, if any, for a third determination of a question of fact confined by law in the first instance to the designated public official. However, we cannot spend the afternoon arguing that fact. It may be stated.

Chairman Thompson.—No.

Mr. Colby.— I would like to call attention to this fact before we leave the question of determination: That the chief engineer's de-

termination on the subject of engineering and superintendence in
the so-called prior determination of October 14, 1913, is as follows: " The cost of lessee's expenses for superintendence, and so
forth, in and about construction for the specified lines of the railroad is as follows." After giving certain items, he says the total
cost for lessee's expenses for superintendence, and so forth, is
$271,965.01, and under the same determination he fixes the city's
expense for superintendence, and so forth, within the same period.
and over the same lines, as $1,261,353.07. Now, that determina-
tion is apparently made under this authority. The actual and
necessary net cost in money to the lessee for superintendence. insurance, damages, administration, engineering and legal expenses in
and about construction, including in respect of the cost of construction for initial operation the expense above referred to in this
paragraph actually and necessarily incurred or payable by the
lessee in and about construction prior to the date of this contract.
and in addition the actual and necessary expenses incurred or
payable by the lessee in printing, engraving, and so forth.

By Mr. Colby:

Q. Mr. MacInnes, do you happen to know, or are you able to
answer this question: Was the allowance of $589,000 on account
of administration and other expenses incurred by the Interborough
in connection with the subway — was that an allowance made by
the chief engineer of the Public Service Commission? A. I don't
know.

Q. Apparently under the authority in which he determines the
amount allowed for engineering and superintendence, there is a
power to determine the allowance for legal expense and administration expense. That is true, isn't it? A. That is what you have
read.

Q. That is a point on which we must examine someone more
cognizant with the facts. I would like to ask you this question.
Of course the city owns the present and the projected subways,
doesn't it? A. It owns the present subway and it should own the
projected one.

Q. I mean the projected subways will be operated by the Interborough as a lessee, and the city is the owner?

Chairman Thompson.—After eighty-five years.

A. Presumably.

Q. There is a provision for recapture after ten years or the expiration of the lease. The city is the owner of the fee.

Chairman Thompson.— Recapture don't mean anything, with the debt limit as close as it is now. Couldn't buy it.

Q. The question to which I am leading is this: The city is also really the guarantor of the income of the investors in the securities of this subway, in result and in final effect. It has submitted to the holders of the bonds issued by the bankers the preferential, giving them the right to participate prior to the city's participating to any extent? A. The contract gives the lessee —

Q. What justification can there be —

Chairman Thompson.— Let him answer.

A. — not only the right, but gives them an equivalent for their present profits of $6,335,000.

By Mr. Colby:

Q. Exactly. Now, what justification is there for the city allowing the Interborough Rapid Transit Company, those facts being true as stated, to issue its bonds at 93½, carrying five per cent interest, and a sinking fund payment, in addition, and when the city, which is the owner of this property or guarantor of this revenue, is able directly to finance itself and sell its bonds above par and at a rate of interest of 4½ per cent? A. The city, in the contract entered into between the Interborough and the city and also between the B. R. T. and the city, each one of these lessees were allowed to finance their obligations under the contract at a three per cent discount; that is all the discount that they will receive any credit for.

Chairman Thompson.— That is all they were supposed to, under the contract.

Mr. MacInnes.— No. They won't get any more. Three per cent discount on the bonds. Three per cent on 58 million, and on the 22 for equipment, or $2,400,000. in the case of the Interborough.

By Mr. Colby:

Q. The Public Service Commission, I believe, have got the power —

Assemblyman Burr.— You asked Mr. MacInnes a question. You asked what justification there was. Will he please answer?

Mr. MacInnes.— I answered the question by stating what the facts are.

Mr. Colby.— It is a pretty hard question.

Mr. MacInnes.— I should not be asked to indulge in my own conclusions.

Chairman Thompson.— We may ask you some time.

Senator Lawson.— I think the Committee is entitled to have your opinion on that.

Chairman Thompson.— How many years have you been in this position?

Mr. MacInnes.— Well, my opinion on that might be of very little interest to anybody.

Chairman Thompson.— We will give it credit for whatever it is worth, after we take it.

Mr. Colby.— I feel that Mr. MacInnes has been so studious and helpful to the Committee that it would possibly be —

Senator Lawson.— We appreciate that, Mr. Colby. That is the reason we want that opinion.

Assemblyman Burr.— I think he should answer that.

Mr. Colby.— Mr. MacInnes is the chief accountant, and possibly this carries him into controverted matters. Perhaps he is modest about giving his opinions.

Assemblyman Burr.— Well, if you don't want him to answer, I am satisfied.

Mr. Colby.— I would be interested in his opinion, but I feel a little disinclination to urge him to embark on that. Of course, the Committee has the right to direct its examination.

Assemblyman Burr.— Mr. MacInnes is a city official.

Mr. Colby.— Couldn't you give your —

Mr. MacInnes.— I am an employee.

By Mr. Colby:

Q. Couldn't you give us the benefit of your impression on that, Mr. MacInnes? A. Well, Mr. Colby, on the 18th of March, 1913, when the city had authorized this contract, and leading up to it, it was necessary to find, if the dual system was to be carried through, and if that was the only plan by which the city's congestion could be relieved, by which it could be made one great city in fact, by a system of transportation, it was absolutely necessary to find 160 millions for construction alone, and the city did not have any more — even after it received $69,943,000 bonds exempted, it could not find any more debt incurring power than 88 millions. It pledged $28,200,000 of that to the Interborough contract, and $60,000,000 to the B. R. T. contract. The $72,100 additional for construction was found or provided by the operators, by the two companies —

Mr. Quackenbush.— Millions, you mean.

Mr. MacInnes.— Millions, I should say. And the question of whether the city, the credit of which is as high as that of any municipality in the world, the question of whether it should justify discount at 97 per cent, can only be answered by considering the financial situation at the time, and the fact that the city could not go on of itself with these dual contracts. So, therefore, I confine my answer to the bare statement.

Senator Lawson.— That is all right; that is sufficient.

Mr. MacInnes.— I believe every member of the Board of Estimate at the time did the best they possibly could with respect to these contracts.

By Mr. Colby:

Q. Mr. MacInnes, I believe the Interstate Commerce Commission, as well as the Public Service Commission, promulgated a rule which both will observe, that debt discount or debt expense is not a proper charge to construction account; is that not true?

A. Yes, that is a part of their rule, part of their rules of the Public Service Commission with respect to public service corporations.

Q. Yes. A. With respect to electric and railway companies.

Q. Are the bonds of the Interborough Rapid Transit Company wholly or in part exempt of tax? A. Well, Counsellor, I cannot answer you that question. The subway itself is wholly exempt from any franchise tax. There was a mortgage tax. The company had to pay interest on some mortgage tax, or at least their recording some mortgage tax —

Chairman Thompson.— Recording tax, one per cent.

By Mr. Colby:

Q. The subway is entirely free of real estate tax? A. Yes, sir.

Q. And a special franchise is held to be real estate? A. Yes. All special franchises are held to be real estate, and are so taxed, but this franchise is not so taxed.

Q. You are not certain as to whether, for instance, the expenditures of this company for construction and equipment, the Interborough's 80 millions expended for construction and equipment would be taxable or exempt of tax? A. I don't know.

Mr. Colby.— Do you wish to suspend?

Chairman Thompson.— How much would that special franchise be worth?

Mr. MacInnes.— Well, before it is all completed, there will be an investment of approximately 200 millions, and you have a franchise of 49 years. The value of the franchise is X.

Chairman Thompson.— What do you mean by that?

Senator Lawson.— That is a lesson in algebra. That is what the Comptroller wants to teach us.

Mr. MacInnes.— It is a question for us to consider and discuss, as to what the value of that franchise would be. We would first begin to measure it according to the moneys there are in it.

Chairman Thompson.— Is there any complaint in your office — have you had complaint made as to these reports issued after the 30 days have expired, or the engineer — any complaints?

Mr. MacInnes.— I don't know of any.

Chairman Thompson.— If there is, will you look to-night and bring it in the morning?
We will suspend now unless there is something of account.

Mr. MacInnes.— Just a moment before you adjourn.

Chairman Thompson.— Yes.

Mr. MacInnes.— Now, you asked me about the probable results of this contract, this operating contract for the Interborough, and it does seem to me as if you ought to see the other side of the picture. There is another contract, and that is with the B. R. T., and a table prepared by me, prior to the adoption or authorization of the contracts was with a view to see how the city would likely come out financially, viewing these two contracts as one, so that you might see about the use of the profits to the city, the probable profits to the city, arising from the B. R. T. contract, to what extent the city could thereby avoid and obviate the necessity of raising moneys to meet the deficit on the Interborough.

Chairman Thompson.— We will take that up to-morrow morning.

Mr. MacInnes.—And that would give you a better general picture of what the financial outlook is likely to be —

Mr. Colby.— In other words —

Mr. MacInnes.— because the B. R. T. promises splendid returns after the —

Mr. Colby.— In other words —

Mr. MacInnes.— first few years to the city.

Chairman Thompson.— We will pursue that to-morrow. We cannot do everything in one day. I appreciate that I have not put in much time to-day.

Mr. MacInnes.— I would like to say this afternoon that I found that I had been evading you. But I haven't. The Comptroller was the man that found me. I didn't know you were looking for me. And I hope the newspaper men, at any rate, won't for a minute think that Comptroller Prendergast had anything to do with the fact that I was an elusive quantity yesterday.

Chairman Thompson.— The Committee now holds prematurely, possibly, that you are not an elusive quantity.

We will suspend now until to-morrow morning at 11 o'clock.

Whereupon, at 4:30 o'clock P. M., an adjournment was taken to Thursday, February 17. 1916, at 11 o'clock A. M.

FEBRUARY 17, 1916

NEW YORK COUNTY LAWYERS' ASSOCIATION BOARD ROOM,
165 Broadway, New York City

The Committee was called to order, pursuant to adjournment. Chairman Thompson presiding.

Quorum present.

Chairman Thompson.— I never have taken this into account at all with the Committee, this is a small room, and a lot of people get in here, and we are glad to have you come, and we have got to have you, if you want to come here, but you fill up the room with smoke and it is hard to get along. The pictures make a lot of smoke, too, and I suppose we have got to have them taken, and I wonder if we can make some suggestion that you take what pictures you want now and we will go on. I will request everybody to get in every kind of position you want and let them take the pictures.

THEODORE P. SHONTS, being first duly sworn, testified as follows:

By Mr. Colby:

Q. Mr. Shonts, you are the President of the Interborough Rapid Transit Company? A. I am.

Chairman Thompson.— Mr. Shonts, it has been the custom of this Committee with witnesses in transactions which in any way on the face of them look as though there might be something involving a conflict with the Penal Code, to ask those witnesses if they will sign a waiver of immunity, and while it is a rather disagreeable duty to perform, I think it is my duty to ask you at this time if you will sign such a waiver for the record.

Mr. Shonts.— I am advised by counsel that there is no statute which gives immunity to a witness appearing before a legislative committee, and therefore I am perfectly willing to sign, and for the additional reason I know of nothing for which I would ask immunity. So I would be very glad to sign such a waiver.

Chairman Thompson.— While we are waiting for that, I want to make a correction in the testimony. It seems the check to Elihu Root was made January 10, 1906, and I think our record made it appear the service was performed in 1906. The bill is for a retainer for six months ending August 1, 1905, so that that will show that his retainer was from February 1, 1905, to August 1, 1905, for which he was not paid until later.

(Waiver of immunity signed by Mr. Shonts and acknowledged.)

Mr. Colby.—As I recall the payment to Mr. Root, there was simply a statement made of payment to Mr. Root in 1906.

Chairman Thompson.— I think that is correct.

By Mr. Colby:

Q. You are the president of the Interborough Rapid Transit Company? A. Yes, sir.

Q. Are you president of other companies comprised in the transit system of New York? A. I am president of the Interborough Consolidated Corporation and of the New York Railways Company.

Q. Are you an officer of the Interborough — of the Rapid Transit Subway Construction Company? A. I am president of that also. I forgot that, excuse me. It may be I am of the Realty, but I am not sure; of the Subway Realty Company. I am.

Q. Do you draw any salaries other than that as president of the Interborough Rapid Transit Company? A. I draw from all of them, and division made by our staff, and the aggregate amount is one hundred thousand dollars.

Q. And apportioned among these companies? A. Apportioned among the various companies, and also, although I am not president of it, a small portion of that is from the New York & Queens County Railway Company.

Q. How long have you been president of the Interborough Rapid Transit Company? A. I came here as president of the old Interborough Metropolitan Company on April 1, 1907. I think about a year later I was made president of the Interborough Rapid Transit Company.

Q. The Interborough Metropolitan at that time being the holding company which owned the stocks of the Interborough Rapid Transit Company and of the New York Railways? A. At that time the Metropolitan Street Railway and affiliated companies. New York & Queens County, and Subway Construction, and Subway Realty, and so forth, and I think there has been no change in any excepting the old Metropolitan Street Railway Company.

Q. What position were you holding when you came to New York to accept these official positions? A. Chairman of the Isthmian Canal Commission.

Q. Had you had any prior experience in the conduct of railway operations? A. For many years had been a railroad builder and operator in the West.

Q. And had been officially connected with some of the railroads in the West? A. Yes, sir; I had been president and general manager, general superintendent, and I came up from the ranks.

Q. Had you been president of any railroads in the West? A. The Indiana, Illinois & Iowa, and Toledo, St. Louis & Western, and afterwards the Iowa Central, and the Minneapolis & St. Louis, the Chicago & Alton, and the Detroit & Toledo Shore Line, and I think some other roads.

Q. At the time you came here were you an officer of any of the western railroads? A. I was.

Q. What official positions did you hold with the western railroads? A. I was president of the Toledo, St. Louis & Western when I came here.

Q. And that is the only official position? A. That is my recollection.

Q. What salary did you receive upon coming to the Interborough road? A. At first $75,000 a year. I came here to take charge of the construction and operation of the properties. Those were the duties officially assigned to me.

Q. Did you continue to hold your official position in the railroads of which you were president in the West? A. For some years.

(Assemblyman Kincaid presiding.)

Q. For how long a period? A. I think until about two years ago.

Q. Two years ago? A. Yes, sir, about that time. That is my best guess now.

Q. And the discharge of your duties as such president occupied a portion of your time, as I understand? A. Yes, sir.

Q. And you made frequent visits to the West in connection with those duties? A. I made occasional trips to the West in connection with those duties.

Q. And I understand that you did not relinquish the western presidencies until about two years ago? A. That is my recollection.

Q. They were the Toledo, St. Louis & Western, and what other railroads? A. At that time, at the time I gave them up, I think was president of five railroads.

Q. The Toledo, St. Louis & Western, Chicago & Alton, Minneapolis & St. Louis Railroad, Iowa Central, and Detroit & Toledo Shore Line? A. Yes, sir; Minneapolis & St. Louis, and Detroit & Toledo Shore Line.

Q. Did you receive a salary from each of those railroads? A. I received a salary from the Clover Leaf, from the Alton, and the Minneapolis & St. Louis, and the Iowa Central, and from the Detroit & Toledo Shore Line.

Q. What salaries did you receive from the Toledo, St. Louis & Western Railroad? A. I would have to refresh my recollection on that. I don't remember what salaries, or how they were distributed.

Q. Can you tell me the aggregate of the four salaries? A. I think I received from the Detroit & Toledo, and the Alton combined, $25,000, and I think possibly $15,000 from the Iowa Central and the Minneapolis & St. Louis. That is my best guess.

Q. About $40,000? A. Yes, sir.

Q. And this continued until two years ago, until, say, January, 1914? A. That is — possibly Mr. Fisher can refresh my recollection on that.

Mr. Fisher.— That is approximately correct.

Q. How long did you receive a salary of $75,000 from the Interborough Rapid Transit Company and the other companies? A. I think until about the time I resigned those positions in the West.

Q. And then your salary was increased? A. To $100,000.

Q. Was it understood by the Interborough Rapid Transit Company that a portion of your time would be devoted to the discharge of those duties of those salaried positions in the West? A. Yes, sir, the same as understood with the United States government that I would continue as president of the Clover Leaf when I took the chairmanship of the Isthmian Canal Commission.

Q. Your salary from the Interborough has continued at $100,000 per annum? A. Since the date it was increased to $100,000 per annum.

Q. Do you recall that date? A. No, sir.

Q. I am perfectly willing Mr. Fisher should prompt you on these dates.

Mr. Fisher.— I should have to look them up.

A. Can I read this into the record a little later?

Q. Yes. A. I would say about two years ago.

Q. Have you received any emoluments from the Interborough Rapid Transit Company other than your salary? A. Yes, sir, I did.

Q. Have you received any additional pay or what I may describe as emoluments from any of the other transit companies? A. No, sir.

Q. What have you received by way of additional compensation? A. The directors of the Interborough Rapid Transit Company voted me as extra compensation for duties which they thought I did outside of the duties for which I was originally hired $125,000 at one time and $25,000 at another time, making $150,000 in all.

Q. Who suggested this extra award of $125,000? A. I don't know. It came to me as a surprise, and a very grateful surprise.

Q. I understand it was not upon any request or solicitation of yours? A. It was not.

Q. You say the directors took this action? A. Yes, sir, the directors took that action.

Mr. Colby.— Mr. Fisher, can you refer me to the minutes in which the payment of $125,000 was authorized by the board?

Mr. Fisher.— Yes, sir; June 5, 1913. I will confirm it.

Q. The secretary of the company prompts me as to the date on which this action of the board was taken and says it was June 5, 1913; that is the date as you remember it? A. It was about that time.

Q. How was the matter first broached to you, who acquainted you with the idea? A. I was invited to leave the room, the board room.

Q. By whom? A. By, I think, maybe the presiding officer, whoever it was. I don't remember who was presiding that day. He said there was a matter entirely personal coming up regarding myself, and asked me to leave the room, and I did, and in a few moments I was called back and was told a resolution had been passed voting me an appropriation for extra services of $125,000.

Q. That was not done at that meeting, was it; I mean to say the vote for this appropriation was not taken at that meeting, was it? A. At the meeting at which I was invited to leave the room, it was, as I understood it, and that is the reason they invited me to leave, so they could vote upon the subject.

Q. And your recollection is the directors without much delay came to an agreement and voted you this extra salary? A. That is my recollection.

Q. You do not recall a special committee was appointed on the matter, do you? A. No, sir. That may have been so, but I do not recall that.

Q. Nor do you recall that the minutes show the actual voting of this bonus — I don't know how you prefer me to describe it — was at a subsequent meeting? A. My recollection as to the exact date is not definite. I did understand, Mr. Counsel, that the matter was voted to me as extra compensation for work done.

(Chairman Thompson presiding.)

Q. Not in any sense as an honorarium? A. No, sir. As I

understood it, it was for work done outside of my usual line of duties.

Q. The secretary of the company hands me the minutes of the company, and I find on May 14, 1913, a resolution in which the matter is stated as follows: "In view of the extra and successful services rendered by the president in connection with the financial needs of the company and the negotiations recently concluded with the city for new subway and elevated extensions, extending over a period of about four years, it was, on motion duly seconded, resolved that a committee of three members of the board be, and they hereby are appointed," and so forth, to consider said extra service and report back to the board. Do you recall who were the members of that committee? A. No, sir, I don't. It was possible I was invited to leave the room when that committee was appointed. I only remember that I was invited to go out while they discussed something that pertained to me.

Chairman Thompson.— Was it a surprise to you they were going to take it up?

Mr. Shonts.— Yes, sir.

Q. You recall that you were present at the meeting prior to such action? A. I was present at one meeting, whether the smaller meeting or the full board meeting I do not remember. I remember the incident of my being asked to leave the room, and when I was recalled I was told that the purpose of it was to vote me for extra services this amount of money.

Q. You distinctly recall at one of the meetings at which action was taken you were present and were asked to leave the room? A. Yes, sir.

Q. I find that the special committee at a special meeting of the board held on June 4, 1913, submitted its report and made their recommendation? A. Was I noted as being present?

Q. You are not noted as being present at either meeting; may that be an inadvertent omission possibly? A. I do not know, I am sure. I cannot answer that. Mr. Fisher tells me that I was present at the meeting in which the salary was voted, and was requested to withdraw, but I was not present at either of the other meetings.

Q. Do you recall that the special committee made a report?
A. No, sir.

Q. Did you ever hear of them having made a report? A. Well, I heard afterward there was a committee, and it received consideration, and they made a report recommending this appropriation.

Q. Did you appear before the special committee in explanation of your services? A. No, sir.

Q. Nor did you participate in any discussion of their extent or value? A. No, sir.

Q. Did the committee, or any member of the committee, interrogate you on the question? A. No, sir. I think they were all pretty well acquainted with the extent of those negotiations that had been going on so long.

Q. Did the committee suggest to you what sum they had in mind? A. No, sir. I heard afterwards that among themselves they had thought of various sums of which they voted me the least.

Q. What were those various sums? A. I think it ranged from $125,000 to $250,000.

Q. Would you have been willing to accept $250,000? A. I would, and would have thought I earned it.

Q. Do you recall who the committee were that considered this question? A. No, sir, I don't.

Q. Do you recall Mr. Berwind was a member? A. No, sir, I do not recall who the committee was.

Chairman Thompson.— There is not any limit to the idea each of the officers of your company have as to the extent of their earning capacity, is there?

Mr. Shonts.— I read Mr. Hedley's testimony, and I will say seriously that I believe any officer that seriously realizes his responsibility in handling three to three and a half million people in this city a day under all the conditions that exist and does his full duty, I do not believe that officer can be overpaid.

Q. You mean to say the demands upon the chief executive of a company conducting such an operation are almost immeasurable? A. Yes, sir; you stated it better than I could.

Chairman Thompson.— Would you think that would justify an increase of fare up to ten cents, in order to increase their salary?

Mr. Shonts.— No, sir. You have touched upon a sociological question that I have very strong views on. I do not know that you want to hear them.

Chairman Thompson.— Not now.

Mr. Shonts.— What I mean, Mr. Chairman, there are two views. one of the zone fares used abroad and where the lower zone always results in the greatest density of population with the poorest health conditions, and the universal zone, as we have in this city, which means the broadest distribution for a nickel and the better health conditions in the outlying districts.

Q. In other words, reverting to my last question and your answer, you consider the demands of such a position are so great a tax upon the men as, in the way of mental and physical energy. that it would be hardly a possibility to err on the side of too liberal compensation, within reasonable bounds? A. Within reasonable bounds. Of course there is a sum beyond which you could not go.

Chairman Thompson.— I wanted to find out if there was a place where it would end?

Mr. Shonts.— Of course there is a limit.

Q. I judge at this time you were president of four railroads in the West? A. I think that was about the time I was resigning and getting out there.

Q. According to the testimony, it was about January 1, 1914, and yet here six months earlier you were in receipt of a bonus of $125,000 for services rendered some two or three years prior to 1913, so there is that basis at least for my question that although the demands and responsibilities of this position are as you have testified, you were president of the Toledo, St. Louis & Western, Chicago & Alton, the Iowa Central, and the Minneapolis & St. Louis, and also of a fifth road, but from only four of which you were drawing a salary of $40,000 per annum? A. As I recollect.

Q. And making numerous trips in connection with the earning of that salary? A. I would like to make the same answer, with your permission. that I made to the question when that question arose when I was with the Isthmian Canal Commission before a committee of Congress. I was still drawing a salary from the

Clover Leaf while drawing this salary from the government of the United States, and I was called before them and asked why I was permitted to do this, and I explained that it was a part of my contract with the President of the United States, because I had such large holdings of such a nature I could not dispose of readily without large personal sacrifice, and he said he did not think I should be required to make them, so I took a less salary and continued to draw a salary, and one of the members of the committee said to me, " Do you think you ought to draw a salary from both the government and the railroad ? " and I said, " Inasmuch as I am working eighteen hours a day for the government, it seems to me if anybody objects it should be the stockholders or the directors of the railroad," and I will say the same here, I was working probably eighteen hours a day on these measures here, and if there was anything I was not paying attention to it was the duties in the West, and that was the reason I resigned, because I felt I was not doing justice to those properties.

Q. And yet for the seven years after you came to New York to take the presidency of the subway you continued to fill the positions in the West ? A. I did.

Q. And you must within the six years that elapsed prior to the voting of this bonus have come to a very lively appreciation of the demands and burdens of your task here as chief executive ? A. Yes, sir, but God had given me a wonderful frame and constitution to back it up and a disposition to work like a horse, and I was working all the time, and trying to do my duty to all of them.

Chairman Thompson.— You think the stockholders ought to have something to say about it ?

Mr. Shonts.— Yes, sir, but I think if any one had objected it should have been the stockholders in the West. They did not object, but I objected to it myself, and I was trying to get out for maybe a year and a half before I finally was relieved.

Q. I understand that the relinquishment of those western positions with their salaries was entirely voluntary on your part ? A. Entirely voluntary on my part.

Q. It was not a question of failure of re-election ? A. No, sir.

21

Q. Did you file your resignation with those railroads as president? A. Yes, sir.

Q. With each of them? A. Yes, sir. I do not know that I filed them or whether at the annual meetings I said I would not stand for re-election. The records will show that my resignation was voluntary.

Q. And yet during the entire period when you had rendered these additional and highly valuable services to the Interborough which was the basis of this award of $125,000, you were occupying those western presidencies, and as far as your ability enabled you to were discharging the duties attached to those offices? A. I presume that is substantially correct.

Q. You have testified that an additional $25,000 was awarded beyond the $125,000 bonus? A. Yes, sir.

Q. Do you remember what period of time intervened? A. Some months. I do not know just how many. It was April the next year; April 22, 1914.

Q. Ordinarily, Mr. Shonts, when a special committee is appointed to consider a specific subject it is deemed at an end as a special committee when it disposes of that subject, is it not? A. Well —

Q. Let me make my question maybe a little clearer; if you appoint a special committee at a given session of your board to see whether a larger room with better ventilation can be obtained and instruct them to report, when that committee reports that no room can be obtained or that a room has been obtained you consider that that special committee has discharged its function, don't you? A. Ordinarily, yes, sir.

Q. That is a custom in all bodies, is it not, particularly when the report is made and adopted? A. I imagine so. I imagine that is the ordinary course.

Q. Well, I find that on April 22, 1914, more than ten months after the special committee on an extra award for you had made its report and that report had been adopted and acted upon with great promptness; I find that at a regular meeting of the board held on April 22, 1914, according to the minutes, the chairman brought up the subject of the report and the oral recommendation of the special committee that Mr. Theodore P. Shonts be allowed $150,000 for special services rendered in connection with the subway and elevated contract; are you aware that that special committee ever recommended the allowance of $150,000? A. Of course, I never attended a meeting of the special committee, and I do not know what transpired, and I do understand, as I told you a few minutes ago, there was a divergence of views as to what should be allowed me, from $125,000 up, and I do not know whether they felt that they had discharged their duty in the first instance or not. That is a matter that it seems to me you would have to get from the members of the committee, for, as I was never present at a meeting of them, I do not know.

Q. Yes, but a recipient of this substantial sum must have known with a fair degree of accuracy what this committee did in the first instance? A. I was told and have already testified —

Chairman Thompson.— The chairman of that committee at that time is beyond the reach of our subpoena.

Mr. Shonts.— Who is that?

Chairman Thompson.— Mr. Freedman.

Mr. Colby.— Mr. Berwind, I think.

Chairman Thompson.— Mr. Freedman reported on this second time.

Mr. Colby.— The testimony was Mr. Berwind acted, being the first name on the committee, and acted as chairman in the first instance. There is no mention of chairmen specially, however.

Mr. Shonts.— I would be very glad to answer, but never being present, I do not know what happened and I do not know whether they felt that they had only partially discharged their obligation when they made their first recommendation and held it open. In fact, that impression was left in my mind, if you want impressions. Impressions, I do not suppose, are testimony, however, but the matter was to have been followed up at a later time; but that would be, it seems to me, a matter for the committee to testify to.

Q. And yet on June 4, 1913, the minutes contain this entry: " The chairman submitted a report of the special committee appointed on May 14th," and then follows the resolution, as follows: " That in recognition of and in compensation for the extraordinary and efficient services rendered by Theodore P. Shonts, as aforesaid, he be paid the sum of $125,000 "; how do you explain the entry ten months later to the effect, and I am reading from the minute book, that the chairman brought up the subject of the report and oral recommendation of the special committee that Mr. Shonts be allowed $150,000? A. The only explanation I can make is as already indicated, not being present at any meeting of the committee, their first report was a partial report, and they finally decided to make that $150,000. I do not know how else to explain it.

Q. I see on April 22, 1914, that the resolution reads as follows: " Resolved, that Mr. Theodore P. Shonts be paid $25,000 additional in conformance with the oral recommendation of the special committee appointed by the board of directors on May 14, 1913." It would appear that that report made earlier, on June 4, 1913, was the special committee's report, wouldn't it? A. So far as it goes, yes.

Q. There is nothing indicated to your mind, is there, that that was a preliminary report? A. Not in that report. The impression I had was from outside of the record.

Q. Was your understanding at the time the $125,000 was paid you that it was a partial payment, that more was to follow? A. Yes, sir, I got that impression, that the most of the committee felt that the $125,000 was really not as much as they should have awarded me, that they hoped at some later date to make the compensation greater. I must have gotten that impression from some members of the committee.

Chairman Thompson.— In talking with them?

Mr. Shonts.— Yes, sir. After the action was taken.

Chairman Thompson.— But before the $25,000 was paid?

Mr. Shonts.— Yes, sir, before that was paid, and before the action was taken on it.

Q. And yet more than ten months elapsed before the committee carried out any reservation in its mind as to an additional award? A. Yes, sir.

Q. These two amounts were paid you in fact, were they not? They were.

Q. And in each instance rather promptly after the date of the meetings at which the resolutions were adopted? A. I don't remember about that. I suppose so, because we were always pretty strong in cash and aim to keep ourselves so. I have a check here. This is for the $125,000.

Q. Mr. Shonts hands me the check of $125,000; this is dated June 5, 1913, the day after authorizing this money and delivery to Mr. Shonts; you received this check? A. Yes, sir.

Q. What did you do with it? A. Endorsed it and gave it to my assistant to deposit it with Charles D. Barney & Company in partial payment of some securities I had bought there.

Q. Your assistant is whom? A. Mr. Pepperman, W. Leon Pepperman.

Q. You simply endorsed the check in blank? A. Yes, sir.

Q. And handed it to Mr. Pepperman with instructions to deliver it to Charles D. Barney & Company? A. Yes, sir, to deposit it with them in partial payment of those securities I had purchased.

Q. Had you a deposit or drawing account with C. D. Barney & Company? A. No, sir.

Q. What is the business of C. D. Barney & Company? A. Bankers and brokers.

Q. At what address? A. At that time it was 25 Broad street.

Q. Had you a running account there? A. No, sir.

Q. Of any kind? A. No, sir, not what you call a banking account. That is a note I got from a member of the firm which acknowledges receipt of the money.

Mr. Colby.— This letter is strictly pertinent to the inquiry at this point, and should be put in evidence, I think.

Mr. Shonts.— I wish to put in the dates of my resignation of the various roads. The Minneapolis & St. Louis Railroad and Iowa Central Railroad, October 15, 1911; Chicago & Alton, July 1, 1912; Toledo, St. Louis & Western Railroad, August 14, 1912, and the Detroit & Toledo Shore Line, October 7, 1912. That is longer ago than I thought it was.

Q. Were you indebted to Charles D. Barney & Company on June 5, 1913? A. Yes, sir.

Q. How did that indebtedness arise? A. By purchase of securities through them and which had not been fully paid for.

Q. You had an investment or speculative account with Charles D. Barney & Company? A. You call it what you please. I am not a speculator in the sense that I gamble in stocks, but I did buy more than I had money to pay for.

Q. Was Charles D. Barney & Company pressing you for payment or reduction of the debit balance at this time? A. Not that I recollect of.

Q. How much did you owe Charles D. Barney & Company at this time? A. I don't remember that. I would be very glad to get the information for you.

Q. You can produce the statement showing the amount of your debit balance — the amount of the debit charges against you? A. Yes, sir.

Q. And the receipt and credit to your account of this amount by Charles D. Barney & Company? A. Yes, sir, I would be very glad to.

Q. Were you indebted to any of your co-directors in the Interborough Rapid Transit Company at this time? A. No, sir.

Q. No member of the board of directors was interested in this account in any way with Charles D. Barney & Company? A. No, sir.

Q. Either as a guarantor of any deficiency or debit balance? A. No, sir.

Q. Or otherwise? A. In no way.

Chairman Thompson.— Were they bankers?

Mr. Shonts.— Yes, sir, they are one of the strong houses.

Mr. Colby.— I offer in evidence the letter produced by the witness written on the letterhead of Charles D. Barney & Company of 25 Broad street, apparently signed by Henry E. Butler, whose name appears on the letterhead as a member of the firm, as follows:

" New York, June 5, 1913. T. P. Shonts, Esq., 165 Broadway, New York city. My dear Mr. Shonts: In Mr. Harding's absence I have opened your missive to him, and beg to advise you that I take pleasure in acknowledging its contents and have credited the same, namely, $125,000, to your account."

Q. You received this letter, did you, from Mr. Butler, on or shortly subsequent to its date? A. Yes, sir.

Letter just read in evidence marked Exhibit 1 of this date, February 17, 1916.

Chairman Thompson.— Was that letter mailed to you or did it come back by Mr. Pepperman?

Mr. Shonts.— My mail is all opened when it reaches my desk, and I cannot tell you.

Chairman Thompson.— You say you gave a check to Pepperman?

Mr. Shonts.— Yes, sir.

Chairman Thompson.— Did Pepperman bring back the letter or the letter come by mail?

Mr. Shonts.— I tried to ascertain yesterday what the facts were, anticipating this inquiry. Mr. Pepperman's recollection is he took the original check to the Guaranty Trust Company and received for it a treasurer's check which he brought back to me and which I endorsed to Charles D. Barney & Company, and which I took down personally to them, and it has all passed from my mind except the letter, and this letter in my file would indicate that I put it in an envelope for Mr. Horace Harding, the active head of the firm, and left it evidently on his desk, and Mr. Butler comes in and opens it and finds it and acknowledges receipt of the check and credits my account, and the account shows it was credited by check on June 5th $125,000, and that completes the transaction so far as I know anything about it.

Q. There is one aspect of it that strikes my mind and which you could explain; there was great promptitude and dispatch in carrying out the transaction; the report of the special committee was made June 4, 1913, at a special meeting and the check was dated June 5, 1913, and it was apparently converted into a cashier's draft at the Guaranty Trust Company on the same date and delivered to Charles D. Barney & Company on the same date and the receipt of it acknowledged and advices to you that it had been credited to your account all on the same date. A. I hope that is true of all Interborough activities. We try to make it so.

Q. Had Charles D. Barney & Company called you for additional margin? A. No, sir.

Q. Had they been pressing you for the reduction of your account? A. No, sir.

Q. Can you tell me how much you were indebted to Charles D. Barney & Company at the time of this application? A. I told you I had forgotten, but I will be very glad to get that for you and furnish it to you.

Q. Could you give me an approximate idea? A. Half a million dollars.

Q. You have the statements of account rendered at this time, say on the 1st of June, 1915, from Charles D. Barney & Company? A. Yes, sir. Your accountant has seen it.

Mr. Colby.— I think for the complete discharge of the Committee's duty we should examine those and carry the witness over them.

Chairman Thompson.— Yes, sir; I think that is right.

Mr. Shonts.— There is one other feature occurs to me. Out of curiosity I inquired how much had been drawn out of that account since, and my office told me that $210 had been drawn out of it since, and that arose by reason of my buying three notes for one of my daughters bearing 7 per cent., and while paying for it with other money, when the interest came due $210 deposited erroneously in my account, and when my attention was drawn to it it was taken out and put in my daughter's box and that is the only money drawn out since that time.

Chairman Thompson.— I suppose you would like to know about that, and find out about the account as well as we would?

Mr. Shonts.— I see it every month.

Q. It was not a profitable series of stock transactions that you had with Charles D. Barney & Co.? A. It depends on what you call profitable.

Q. I should say if the debit balance was half a million dollars the use of the word unprofitable would not be an extravagant phrase? A. It is according to how much you paid for it. I had a good deal of margin against it, and I do not mean to convey the opinion I had a debit balance for half a million, but on the purchase price against which there was all of my collateral. The account was in good shape, and I do not want to be mislead about it. When you see the account you will see it is mostly Interborough Consolidated, in which I have great faith.

Q. I tremble to ask you if you were carrying any of the Interborough Metropolitan prior to the organization into the reorganization? A. I was.

Q. I understand in the course of that reorganization that the price of the Interborough Metropolitan stock was marked down as far as it could be under the law, in other words from par to $5 a share? A. I do not think that is a good way of stating it. I understand under the law that is the so-called Stetson law, I call it that because I heard of it first through Mr. Stetson, and it is that the par value should not be stated in the certificate, and that law provides that where there are two classes of stock, common and preferred, the preferred must be paid for at par and the common can be paid for in any multiple of five, commencing with five, and inasmuch as one of the objects of that reorganization was to take the ill repute out of the name of the Interborough Metropolitan, which the public seemed to have, that it was so saturated with water that it was not in good odor, our object was to make the capitalization as low as possible. The $5 did not affect in any way the intrinsic value of the securities. It had all the equities that it ever had after the preferred was taken care of.

Q. It never had very much, did it? A. I think it has yet.

Q. In other words, it was an effort on the part of the Interborough Metropolitan to hold its head above water? A. No, sir. It was an effort on the part of the management of the Interborough Metropolitan Company to get itself in a proper legal position so it could legally distribute the earnings coming to it from the various properties it had.

Q. In other words, so the amount of its liability on account of common stock did not stare it in the face in distributing the earnings? A. No, sir; there was an accumulative dividend on the preferred stock amounting to, as I recollect it, $42 a share, twenty odd million dollars. There is a statute on the books of this State which reads that if any director in conjunction with any other

·director or with any group of directors shall take any step toward
the declaration of a dividend, I do not know how you can get
language much broader, shall take any step toward the declaration
of a dividend except out of surplus profits, the same should be a
misdemeanor, etc., etc. The question is, what are surplus profits?
That question has never been settled in this conutry. In England
it has been held that a company has a right to carry on its balance
sheets securities at what it pays for them, in the absence of fraud,
but that has never been settled here.

Q. The Interborough Meropolitan adopted a very cautious
policy by suspending the payment of dividends about a year after
it was formed, didn't it? A. That was a matter that was forced
on it at that time. I am only trying to answer and I do not want
the record to show I sat here as president of this company. I do
not mean to discuss these things unless you want me to.

Q. We all know dividends can only be declared out of actual
profits? A. This was our means of settling this, without years
of litigation, and it was not that we did not believe that there was
substantial merit in the Interborough Metropolitan common stock.

Q. The only stock for which there was any prospect of dividends
was the Interborough Metropolitan preferred, wasn't it? A. Yes,
sir.

Q. Was there a pool in Interborough Metropolitan preferred
prior to the formation of the Interborough Consolidated? A. I
don't know. If there was I knew nothing about it.

Q. You were buying Interborough Metropolitan preferred? A.
I bought what I could and a little more than I could afford probably, but not in connection with any pool, and because I had faith
in it.

Q. Not to invite too rigid an interpretation of the word pool in
my questions that I have in mind to ask you, were several of the
directors of the Interborough Consolidated buying Interborough
Metropolitan preferred at the same time? A. I don't know.

Q. Do you know it not to be a fact? A. I don't know any thing
about it at all.

Q. The reorganization of the Interborough Metropolitan was
largely in the control of the men constituting your Board on the
Interborough Rapid Transit Company, wasn't it? A. They are
largely the same men.

Q. Mr. Berwind is a very large individual owner of the stocks of the Interborough Metropolitan and of the Interborough Rapid Transit Company, is he not? A. He was of the Interborough Metropolitan and now of the Interborough Consolidated.

Q. The Interborough Consolidated practically owns the stock of the Interborough Rapid Transit? A. Through that indirect means, if that is what you mean. The Interborough Rapid Transit is owned, about 97 per cent, by the Interborough Consolidated Corporation.

Q. When did you begin to buy substantial amounts of the Interborough Metropolitan preferred? A. I have had some since before I came here with the property, and never been out of them.

Q. Did you substantially increase your holdings recently in Interborough Metropolitan preferred? A. Within the last few months, yes.

Q. You knew that the reorganization into the Interborough Consolidated — A. This was after the reorganization.

Q. Did you substantially increase your holdings in the Interborough Metropolitan prior to the reorganization? A. No, sir.

Q. You did to some extent? A. I think not.

Q. The books of Barney & Company would show that? A. Yes, sir, but I don't think I did at all. I have taken on some since.

Chairman Thompson.— We will now suspend to this same place until 2:30 o'clock P. M.

Whereupon, at 1:10 P. M. a recess was taken to 2:30 o'clock P. M.

AFTERNOON SESSION

The Committee was called to order at 2:55 o'clock P. M., Chairman Thompson presiding.

Chairman Thompson.— We will have to dispense with smoking in here, I guess.

Mr. Colby.— Have you resumed, Mr. Chairman?

Chairman Thompson.— We are waiting to get chairs for the Committee, there don't seem to be any here. Will you ask Mr.

Bordwell to get some chairs of some kind here? The Committee will come to order. You may take this on the record. The question came up yesterday as to the fact which appeared to be under the law in the dual subway contracts, that matters, certain matters were required to be referred to the chief engineer of the Public Service Commission. His certificate then became final, unless appealed from in thirty days, and the question arose again that these decisions were made and no publication was given, and the further question arose as to whether or not the city did get notice of these determinations by the engineer at any time before the time to appeal had expired, even though the appeal was an appeal to the engineer himself. The point is a technical one, and we desire to have it cleared up, and we will refer this subject to the subcommittee now sitting, consisting of Assemblyman Feinberg, Senator Lawson and Assemblyman Burr.

I am also informed that the chief engineer, Mr. Craven, has left the city, and left the State. I will refer to this same subcommittee the duty of providing in some way for Mr. Craven's appearance in the city next week.

By Mr. Colby:

Q. Mr. Shonts, I think you testified that the check for $125,000 to your order was converted into a cashier's draft at the Guaranty Trust Company? A. That is what Mr. Pepperman told me.

Q. Do you know that as a fact? A. No.

Q. Why should that have been done? A. I don't know, I am sure; I didn't follow it further than to ask Mr. Pepperman to see that I received credit at C. D. Barney & Company.

Q. Wouldn't the check of the Interborough Rapid Transit Company have been acceptable to the C. D. Barney Company for immediate credit? A. I understand in checks of this size, private checks are not as acceptable as what they call treasurer's checks of these banks. If there is anything I know less about than any other, it is the details of banking forms.

Q. Well, why couldn't the check have been certified and delivered to Barney & Company?

Chairman Thompson.— We all don't know as much about that as we would like to.

A. I suppose it could have been certified and delivered. I am only telling you what I understand from Mr. Pepperman actually did happen.

Q. Was there any occasion for the immediate transmission of that check with the least possible delay to C. D. Barney & Company? A. Nothing except I didn't want to go around with a check for $125,000 in my pocket any longer than necessary, and I wanted to let the interest begin to operate as soon as possible.

Q. Why didn't you deposit it in your account in the ordinary manner? A. I didn't have any account in New York city at that time. I didn't have any account in New York city, because I hadn't had enough money here yet to open one. I did later on. I don't know that it is a crime to be poor. If it is, I am guilty of the crime.

Chairman Thompson.— I will have to go with you.

Mr. Shonts.— Well, I am glad to be in your company.

Q. But you had some occasion for a bank account, didn't you? A. Not in New York city. I maintained my old bank account in Chicago.

Q. Where? A. The Continental Trust & Savings, I think the present name. It was originally the American Trust & Savings Bank.

Q. Have you produced the statements of your account with Barney & Company? A. I have the amount in my pocket, yes, covering the one in — I find at the end of the month that it was $410,000 in place of 500, as stated. If you will turn over the page, you will get the recapitulation, Mr. Counsel. (Witness hands statement to counsel.) I sold out a lot of those things, among others that lovely 'Frisco proposition. (To the stenographer.) That is not testimony; that is just talk across the table.

Q. According to this statement which is dated June 30, 1913, on May 31, 1913, you owed C. D. Barney & Company $721,-435.10; that is correct, is it? A. If the statement shows it, yes.

Q. And during the month of June, 1913 — A. By sales and the deposit of that certificate, it was reduced to $410,000.

Q. You mean of that check? A. Check, yes.

Q. It was reduced, apparently, on the 30th of June to $410,-230.17? A. Not apparently, but actually, isn't it?

Q. Yes, but apparently is from the statement. Well, apparently on June 5, the day on which you deposited this check with — or rather, turned this check over to Barney & Company, they had sold a considerable amount of your securities — I should say, calculating roughly, about $285,000 worth of securities, in addition to the amount of the check? A. That was the date that I decided to clean up those items mentioned there.

Q. And there is a credit on your indebtedness as of June 5, 1913, of $308,702.59? A. Probably the result — the result of the sales plus the check.

Q. Yes. There are sales of some — what is that security (handing statement of witness)? A. Some steel 5s. Which do you mean?

Q. That is it; steel 5s. I could not read it. They apparently sold some sixty thousand dollars' worth of steel sinking fund 5s, some New York Railway Adjustment 5s, some shares of Reading, some sixty hundred shares of St. Louis & San Francisco. A. You will find more of that, I think.

Q. Sold on that day. That aggregates — the amount of sales on that day aggregated $283,702.59; that is correct, isn't it?

Mr. Dawson.— It is 183.

Q. It is $183,702.59? A. Whatever is there.

Q. Which, with the check of $125,000, reduced your indebtedness, $308,702? A. That is right.

Q. Well, now, I see that you were liquidating at a very rapid rate on that day. Do you wish to have us understand, Mr. Shonts, that your brokers were not anxious to reduce your debit? A. If they were, they didn't say anything to me about it. I didn't like the looks of the market. I thought things were going pretty fast. I decided to try to get out of debt.

Chairman Thompson.— What date is that, 1913?

Mr. Shonts.— Nineteen hundred and thirteen, yes.

By Mr. Colby:

Q. Had your brokers explained to you that it would be necessary to drastically liquidate your account unless it was re-enforced in some way? A. No.

Q. And your unfavorable situation at Barney & Company's had nothing to do with the granting of this bonus? A. I don't call that an unfavorable situation. If you will turn over the next sheet, you will find I had of my own securities a good deal more than the amount of the total indebtedness.

Q. Well, this sheet does not show exactly how you stood after that liquidation? A. Yes, it does show that. I beg your pardon.

Q. It doesn't show that. A. Yes, but I am putting down the market values of those things on the left there. It aggregates more than the total indebtedness of collateral loan, to say nothing of the things I had with them, not paid for.

Q. Well, I tell you, as I foot it up, roughly, the amounts that you have given me as footings, the values of the stocks amount to about $403,000, as against $410,000? A. Four hundred and thirteen, as I figured it up there. And in addition to all of the securities I had, not paid for.

Q. Four hundred and thirteen thousand as against an indebtedness of $410,000? A. That is right.

Q. So that with this check of $125,000, you brought yourself up even with Barney & Company's account against you? A. More than that. My own — what I owned with them was more than the total indebtedness they had against me.

Q. In other words — A. And in addition to which they had all of the securities they had on margin.

Q. Well, in other words, with the payment of $125,000, you practically brought your account to a balance with Barney & Company? A. No —

Q. That is to say, after the realizations in June, plus the $125,000? A. That had nothing to do with my balance. My balance was the value of what I owned, and —

Q. What you owned was worth $413,000, as against that $410,000? A. When I got through with the liquidation of the securities I sold, plus the $125,000.

Q. And without that $125,000, you could hardly have brought that account up? A. I would not have been on a parity, but would have had 60 or 70 per cent. margin. I think 10 per cent. is the usual rate.

Chairman Thompson.— Just let me understand that.

Q. On the contrary — I think I can explain that with a question, Mr. Chairman. On the contrary, if you had not paid in the $125,000 to Barney & Company, your indebtedness at the end of the month would have been $535,000? A. $535,000.

Q. And the total value of the securities not sold would have been $413,000? A. Of my own securities. No; that has nothing to do with all of the other securities which I have on the market value, as 4,500 shares of Inter-Met. preferred. I don't know what the value was that day. And the other things to be added to that. So you want to add to that $413,000, the market value of all those other items that are not marked T. P. S.

Q. I don't think the true aspect of this account can be reached without supplying — A. I have asked for those. I have asked my office to get those and send them down to me. As soon as I I get them, I will be glad to furnish them to you.

Q. You were carrying at that time 4,500 shares of the Interborough-Metropolitan preferred stock? A. Yes. At 60, that would be $270,000 more, in that one item alone.

Q. And another item of a thousand shares of Metropolitan? A. I don't know what that is. I have asked for those market values.

Chairman Thompson.— What is the Interborough Rapid Transit worth?

Mr. Shonts.— Now?

Chairman Thompson.— Then.

Mr. Shonts.— I don't know. That is what I have asked my office to get on that day.

Chairman Thompson.— What is it worth now?

Mr. Shonts.— About seventy-five.

Chairman Thompson.— The common stock?

Mr. Shonts.— No, the preferred.

Chairman Thompson.— What is the common stock?

Mr. Shonts.— About seventeen or eighteen, the common stock. I have not heard the last day or two, Mr. Chairman.

By Mr. Colby:

Q. Mr. Shonts, I don't want to make any suggestions that are not entirely in accord with the footings of the figures, and it is apparent what you say, that there are some stocks, the values of which are not stated, and that will affect — A. Well, I have asked for those, Mr. Counsel, and when they come down I will add them to these, and I hope to do so before the sitting is over. This is not in evidence. (Referring to statement.) I can send it up, and ask him to get the prices, market prices, as of that day.

Mr. Colby.— Mr. Fisher, did you bring back the vouchers?

Chairman Thompson.— Has this Interborough Rapid Transit ever declared a dividend?

Mr. Shonts.— Yes. It pays 20 per cent.

Chairman Thompson.— What is it that is worth 17?

Mr. Shonts.— The Interborough Consolidated Company is worth seventeen.

By Mr. Colby:

Q. To what fund or what account was this $125,000 charged? A. I have never followed that. The auditor — that is the auditor's duties, and I don't know, but I suppose that the voucher will show.

Q. Do you know whether it is charged to the company or to the city? A. Oh, I know that eventually — eventually we presented in connection with the Brooklyn Rapid Transit Company a statement of our preliminary expenses, antedating the contract between the city and the two companies. Our expenses amounted to something over a million and three hundred thousand dollars, as I recollect it. Out of that fund the city allowed us $327,000 as our share of preliminary expenses, and I am told that my $125,000 was part of that payment.

Q. What was the date of that application made to the city for the allowance of those preliminary expenses? A. That was handled by Mr. Rogers. I don't know the date. I suppose that was — certainly — (Mr. Quackenbush hands paper to witness.)

Mr. Quackenbush.— That is the date of the statement.

Mr. Shonts.— The date of the statement was rendered on July 25.

By Mr. Colby:

Q. What year? A. 1913. And this contains all of the items in making up, I imagine, the $327,000. Can I use this sheet of paper, Mr. Chairman?

Chairman Thompson.— Certainly.

Mr. Shonts.— Thank you. $129,659; $107,327; $105,957.

By Mr. Colby:

Q. We have those figures. A. You have those. Then this cuts no figure. (Witness hands statement to counsel.) That is right. Those aggregate $343,000. I understood that the allowance was $323,000.

Q. Who was this question of these allowances discussed with on behalf of the city? A. That was taken up by — that was entirely a legal question, and it was handled by Mr. Rogers, representing us.

Q. Mr. Gaynor has testified that some of the expenditures that were included in the total of $1,532,000 had been expended before their allowance, and some were expended only after the allowance? A. That is a million, five hundred thousand dollars?

Q. Yes. A. Yes, that is correct. My recollection is that the amount before we traded was a million three hundred thousand dollars.

Q. What do you mean by "traded?" A. Closed our contract as of March 19, 1913; so I imagine the discrepancies are those things that came in after that date.

Q. Did you give any instruction to have this $125,000 charged to construction account? A. No, I gave no instructions at all, because our general auditor followed the rulings of the Public Service Commission in the distribution of his accounts.

Q. Wasn't it known at the time this was considered by your Board, that this would come out of the city and not out of the company? A. I don't think the matter was thought of.

Q. Wasn't it stated as one reason for acquiescing in the vote?
A. I never heard —

Q. — that it would not come out of the company, but out of the city? A. I never heard it so stated. I don't believe it was so stated.

Q. When you accepted it, did you know that it would come out of the city? A. No.

Q. Did you suspect that it would? A. I did not think of it at all in that connection at that time. That was a matter that came up afterwards.

Q. Was this question of allowance of your so-called preliminary expenses under discussion at the time with the city? A. Oh, yes. The question of our preliminary expenses was discussed with the city before the date of our agreement with the city. It was discussed very frequently.

Q. And it was assumed at the time this bonus was awarded to you, that some allowance would be made on account of such preliminary or unclassified expenses? A. I cannot answer that question, because I don't know who you mean assumed it. I didn't assume it.

Q. Didn't you know it? A. No, I didn't think about it. It didn't occur to me.

Q. If the Committee examines Mr. Rogers on this point, I suppose that the Interborough Rapid Transit Company will release him from any question of privilege in testifying freely on this point? A. Oh, yes.

Q. Is he the man who knows all about it? A. I imagine he knows more about it than anyone else. We try to do team work in our organization. We have Mr. Gaynor, who handles and distributes all expenses according to the rules of the Public Service Commission, and in this matter and in all matters growing out of the original negotiations and up to the completion of the contract with the city, Mr. Rogers was the lawyer in charge; Mr. Quackenbush is our general attorney who has charge of all matters growing out of the operation. So we have a line of cleavage there. And that is the reason I say I suppose that Mr. Rodgers will — is most likely to be the man that can answer you fully about that.

Q. In other words, this allowance of some $589,000, because that is the amount which the evidence shows was the total allowance upon the $1,533,000 asked for, was made, you testify, on July 25, 1913? A. All I know is that memorandum that was handed me.

Q. That is what it says. A. I figured that it was 343.

Q. Well, the amount applied for was $1,532,000, and according to a memorandum supplied me by the auditor, the total amount allowed was $589,286. A. Well, I would say the auditor's figures would be the most reliable.

Q. Apportioned to the subway elevated extensions and Manhattan third tracking. I think what you are thinking of is the amount apportioned to the subway. A. To the subway, probably.

Q. That is, $327,405? A. I have got 323, in my head, I don't know where from, as the amount allowed for the elevated and subway.

Q. Now, what did you say Mr. Rogers' exact relation was to you and your company? A. The general attorney for our companies, our various companies, and in the distribution of duties, Mr. Rogers is our legal adviser in regard to general principles and general policies, and in this particular matter, in the negotiations with the city.

Q. Mr. Rogers has been associated with you for a long period? A. For many years.

Q. Before you came to the Interborough? A. Yes, before I came to the Interborough. I have known Mr. Rogers since he was a young man in college.

Q. Tell me just a little about him. Was he a practicing lawyer in New York before he went to Panama with you? A. Yes. He was in Cravath's — I have forgotten the exact name of the — Henderson & Cravath —

Mr. Stanchfield.— Cravath, Henderson & de Gersdorff.

Mr. Nicoll.— I think Guthrie left before —

Mr. Colby.— Guthrie, Cravath & Henderson.

Mr. Shonts.— Cravath is still there. And that it was that original firm, and he was connected with that office.

By Mr. Colby:

Q. And then you took him to Panama? A. I took him with me as our general counsel to Panama, and Mr. Taft, at that time secretary of war, did him the honor of asking me if I could not devise ways and means by which he could retain his services, after I came to New York, because he assumed I would want to bring him with me, in which assumption he was correct, and I remember him saying Mr. Rogers had done his work so well he did not think it was worth while to appoint a successor yet, and would like to be in a position to call upon him for advice and counsel when it was necessary, without coming to a private corporation —

Q. I am not disposed, Mr. Shonts, to disparage Mr. Rogers' ability in any way. Suppose we get along a little faster.

Chairman Thompson.— Why didn't Taft get his services after he became President, in the Attorney-General's office?

Mr. Shonts.— I suggested he make him general counsel for the Panama Railroad & Steamship Company, which he did, and which position he still retains.

Chairman Thompson.— Is that a government place?

Mr. Shonts.— Yes.

Chairman Thompson.— He still draws a salary from the government, besides working for you?

Mr. Shonts.— Yes.

Chairman Thompson.— He has got a fair earning capacity, too?

Mr. Shonts.— He has, and he deserves it.

Chairman Thompson.— I am going to make a rule of this Committee that every man who works for the Interborough Railroad Company thinks he deserves more salary than he gets, or allowance.

Mr. Shonts.— Do you find anybody objecting to that ruling?

By Mr. Colby:

Q. Now, before I pursue the matter of Mr. Rogers' relations to this matter, first I would like to ask a question or two with relation to this voucher just handed me, representing the second payment of $25,000 to you. A. Yes, sir.

Q. Which was authorized by the board on April 22, 1914. Have you the check which was given in payment of this amount? A. Yes. And I wish to say in this connection that it was upon receipt of this check that I was first placed in a position to open an account in the city of New York, and that I used that check for that purpose.

(Assemblyman Kincaid takes the Chair.)

Q. I have known accounts to be opened with a check of less magnitude. This you deposited in your first bank account in New York? A. Yes.

Q. Is that what you say? A. That is what I say.

Q. You deposited it to the Farmers' Loan & Trust Company? A. That is it.

Q. And endorsed it for deposit there. I understand, Mr. Shonts, that you have, at the request of the Committee, produced your personal bank books, showing this deposit and various checks subsequently deposited and checked out. A. I have.

Mr. Colby.— I will state, Mr. Chairman, that the Committee, through its counsel and actuary, Mr. Dawson, has examined those bank books and those checks, and Mr. Dawson has reported to me that there is no check drawn upon that account except for household expenses and personal expenditures, and other normal and moderate expenditures such as any man in receipt of Mr. Shonts' income, and living presumably upon his scale, would have drawn. Unless there is some desire on the part of the Committee that we should laboriously and toilsomely demonstrate that fact, which Mr. Dawson has reported, I think I will pass to other matters of Mr. Shonts' examination.

Acting Chairman Kincaid.— I am sure this report must be very gratifying to Mr. Shonts.

Mr. Shonts.— It is.

By Mr. Colby:

Q. Now, Mr. Shouts, you were instrumental in bringing about the award to Mr. Rogers of a large award, were you not? A. I recommended it.

Q. While there is some doubt in your mind as to who suggested your bonus, you are clear you suggested the bonus to Mr. Rogers? A. I am clear that I am one of them. There may have been others, probably were others. I think I was with him so closely and so long that I appreciated more the extent and value of his services than anyone else, and I was very glad to recommend that he be awarded with something for his extra services.

Mr. Colby.— Where is the Rogers voucher, Mr. Fisher; can you let me have it?

Mr. Quackenbush.— I think it is there.

Mr. Colby.— No, it doesn't seem to be there, Mr. Quackenbush.

Mr. Quackenbush.— My eyes deceive me, then. I saw it there this afternoon.

Mr. Colby.— It is not here, old man — here it is. Let me have the minute-book, please, Mr. Fisher, for September, 1913.

(Minute-book handed to counsel.)

By Mr. Colby:

Q. I turn to the minutes of the board of the Interborough Rapid Transit Company recording their proceedings on September 13, 1913. You are recorded as having stated as president that all legal matters in and about the contracts for the construction and equipment of the new subway and elevated lines of the city of New York, prior to March 19 — that is, March, 1913 — have been conducted by Mr. Richard Reid Rogers, counsel for the company, that the work was long continued and exacting, and had been performed in conjunction with his other duties in a highly satisfactory manner, and without the employment of associate counsel, thus resulting in a large saving to the company. He — the president — laid before the board the consideration of an amount to be allowed Mr. Rogers for his extra services in connection with such contracts, whereupon it was resolved that the

sum of $50,000 be paid Mr. Rogers for his services in connection with the contracts for the construction and equipment of the new subways and elevated lines, the sum to be charged· to the proper construction accounts.   That money was paid to Mr. Rogers?
A. Yes.

Q. Was it retained by Mr. Rogers? A. So far as I know, yes; but he can answer that question better than I can.

Q. Did you have any participation in that? A. I did not.

Q. There seems to be no doubt as to what account this amount should be charged to — construction account. A. I think that was a matter — if you will permit me to say, that the Public Service Commission and our representatives had agreed that a proper amount should be charged to legal expenses by both the B. R. T. and ourselves, before this matter came up.

Q. This amount, as well as the amount of your bonus was allowed to you by the city, was it not? A. It was finally made a part of the amount, $327,000, whatever this sum was they allowed as a portion of our million and a half — $1,300,000 — preliminary expenses.

Q. Well, apparently, Mr. Shonts, Mr. Gaynor is right when he says that some of these estimates that figure in the allowance had not been made by the company at the time they were allowed to the city. The date of this allowance — this payment to Mr. Rogers is some two months later than the date on which application was made for this allowance by the city? A. Well, that confirms what I meant a moment ago, by saying that I think in the meantime, that is between the time of mine for extra services in the matter, and the time Mr. Rogers' was considered, that the city had agreed with our people that a certain sum should be allowed for legal expenses.

Q. You applied not only for the allowance of what you had expended, but what you would like to expend? A. No, I think — of course, I was not present, but my understanding is that an arrangement was agreed upon that Mr. Rogers should receive a certain sum.

Q. Did you have any discussion with anyone representing the City as to the allowance of these expenditures totalling a million and a half? A. I had many discussions with them in principle —

I don't remember of having discussions in detail; I did as to principle, yes, many of them.

Q. And with whom did you have those discussions? A. The Public Service Commission.

Q. Mr. Craven? A. Oh, no.

Q. Not at all with Mr. Craven? A. Not that I remember of. Our chief conferences were with the members of the Public Service Commission and the committee of the Board of Estimate and Apportionment, which consisted of Mr. McAneny, Mr. — what is his name, from the Bronx — Miller; Mr.— what is his name from Staten Island — Cromwell.

Q. When was this matter conceded in principle, matter of allowance? A. I cannot carry those dates in my head.

Q. Relative to the presentation of the application to the city for the allowance? A. After the — I should say within a few months of the time the specific allowance was made. Very close to it; two or three months; three or four months; something of that kind. We were in almost constant session. That is the reason I cannot remember dates. Days and — particularly nights. I was going to say nights and days. But it was particularly nights, sometimes one, often one, sometimes two, occasionally to five in the morning.

Q. Well, what was the meaning of the statement that you made to the board that Mr. Rogers had obviated the necessity of employment of outside counsel in connection — A. In our negotiations.

Q. In the negotiations? A. Yes. As a rule in our negotiations, Mr. Rogers was the sole legal attendant.

Q. You don't mean to say outside counsel were not employed in the negotiations? A. No. We did have outside counsel in outside matters, but on the daily routine business —

Q. Only in the routine business? A. Routine negotiations such as I was following up myself every day.

Q. You are aware of the fact that substantial bills have been paid by the Interborough Rapid Transit Company to distinguished counsel for their services in negotiating the contract? A. I am aware that substantial sums have been disposed of for that matter.

Q. You are aware, for instance, that Mr. Stetson has rendered you a bill in which the first of two items is for his services to the Interborough Rapid Transit Company in — let me get it exactly — in connection with negotiations with Public Service Commisson and Board of Estimate Committee concerning new contracts for subway and extension of elevated railroads. I just want to ask you on that point, aren't those services in the bill covered by the Rogers' award? A. No; no.

Q. What does Mr. Rogers' service — A. I have never known a large loan negotiated with bankers, but what the bankers exacted a fee for their counsel, and this was no exception, and Mr. Stetson represented the bankers in all these negotiations, and he passed on the contract and everything of that kind.

Q. But Mr. Stetson has also charged for his services with the bankers in connection with the mortgage? A. Excuse me?

Q. Which services are rendered in the charge to you, pursuant to the contract with Morgan & Company, the amount of the charge having been approved by Mr. Morgan and yourself, but here is a specific charge of Mr. Stetson for services in connection with the negotiations with the Public Service Commission and the Board of Estimate. A. In conducting the negotiation of the magnitude this was, involving on our part one hundred and seventy millions and over one hundred millions for the city on our part, together with $171,000,000 for the city, but in which Morgan's were to furnish us — to buy $171,000,000 of bonds, as I recollect the figures — they insisted, and we were glad to have the services of Mr. Morgan and Mr. Davison and their counsel, in order — in these negotiations — in order to see that nothing should be written in any agreement, if we ever reached an agreement, that would make it unbankable. We could not see the usefulness of wasting all those weary months in the negotiations, to find at the last analysis that the city and ourselves had agreed, but that we could not sell any securities on that agreement, and therefore we had those gentlemen and their counsel, but in that matter Mr. Stetson represented only the bankers and not us.

Q. I see that in Mr.— in the bill rendered by Mr. Nicoll's firm, it is stated that one-half of the charge for services — it is stated in a memorandum attached to the voucher, that one-half of the charge for services represented — is represented by the numerous conferences with the president, members of the executive committee and other officers and directors, attending the conferences of the city authorities in matters of the new subway contracts and elevated certificates. A. Well, Mr. Nicoll was called in frequently, I cannot say on what subjects; on all important subjects in our firm.

Q. And the statement of Mr. Nicoll's firm on that point is as follows: "To professional services consisting of constant conferences and consultations with the president, members of the executive committee and other officers and directors, and advice and opinion on matters affecting the interests of the company, including the new subway contracts and Manhattan certificate, and the negotiations, controversies and litigations with respect to the same." That was another outside account, whom Mr. Rogers' services had not obviated the employment of? A. I think my first answer, Mr. Counsel, covers that. Mr. Rogers is the man who was in our daily — nightly sessions, the routine negotiations all the way through. Mr. Nicoll was not.

Q. You mean Mr. Rogers was the night shift? A. He had very few opportunities to wear a night shift, on account of the lateness of the hours to which these conferences lasted, but what I mean is that he was our regular salaried man, and we were in the saddle all the time, and we only called on —

Q. And as a salaried man, when he received $50,000 bonus — A. He was only compensated for that long-continued, enormous service you can expect of any salaried man.

Q. Now, the two bills I have mentioned that make specific mention in connection with these negotiations are not the only bills of outside counsel predicated upon services in that connection. A. I will be very glad to explain the rest to the best of my ability, if you will read them, call my attention to them.

Q. Mr. Davies. Further bills from Nicoll. A. Mr. Davies' bill was covered by a contract with the Manhattan road, which antedated my coming here.

Q. It has been testified here that a sum in excess of $183,000 was paid to outside counsel in connection with these negotiations. Did you know the amount was so large as that? A. I did not know the exact amount.   I am trying to explain each one as they come along.

Chairman Thompson.— Did you take the advice of all these lawyers, Mr. Shonts?

Mr. Shonts.— I listened to all their advice.

By Mr. Colby:

Q. Well, what did Mr. Mirabeau L. Towns do?   A. Mr. Mirabeau L. Towns?   Did he get some money?

Q. He got some too?   A. Much?   Not much.

Q. Do you remember he was employed in connection with the negotiations?   A. Not at this minute.   I will have to look that up.

Q. It was stated by one of the other officers of the company that you would know.   A. There are probably a lot of things I ought to know and do know, but which escape my mind for the moment.

Q. Do you know Mr. Mirabeau L. Towns?   A. Yes, I know Mr. Mirabeau L. Towns.

Q. When did you meet him last?   A. I have not seen him for several years.

Q. Did he ever have any connection — did he ever perform any work for the company except in connection with the subway contracts?   A. No.   If there is a voucher there for which he got money in connection with the subway, he must have done it. Just this minute I cannot tell you the nature of it.

Q. This is all the information afforded by the voucher: " In full for professional services rendered to date, $5,000."   A. Well, Fisher is no better off than I am.   We will have to look that up and tell you.

Chairman Thompson.— Haven't you any recollection at all that he was employed?

Mr. Shonts.— No.

Chairman Thompson.— Did you ever see him around at any of these negotiations, or anywhere?

Mr. Shonts.— I don't now think of any place I have met him

in connection with this thing. I will have to look it up. We have a record of it.

By Mr. Colby:

Q. How did you come to meet him? A. Oh, Lord, I don't remember, Mr. Counsel; I meet so many people that I would not — I would be afraid to guess, every day, and my memory for names and faces is bad, and I remember Mr. Town, know I met him, and if there is a voucher there that says he was employed —

Q. Towns, his name is, not Town. A. Towns; Mirabeau Towns. Well, no doubt he — I ought to remember, I admit, but I don't remember everything that ever happened.

Q. There was no attempt not to remember what he did when you paid him $5,000? A. There is never an attempt on my part not to remember anything connected with this company.

Q. There was apparently no request for specification of his services when that bill was paid. A. Well, all I can say is, you will have to let me look it up. I cannot tell you now a thing about it.

Chairman Thompson.—All these people you meet don't put in a bill for $5,000?

Mr. Shonts.— No.

Q. These other attorneys have made very careful specification of their services, apparently it being their practice, and apparently it was expected by your company. A. I don't know — I will have to look that up.

Q. Well, in the distribution to the proper account — A. Let me see it. That is my mark. I know my mark. *So it passed over my desk, and I will have to find out about it.*

Chairman Thompson.— That mark is " o. k."?

Mr. Shonts.— Yes, " o. k.", and that is my " o. k."

By Mr. Colby:

Q. Well, how did this come to be distributed among two accounts, " other suspense " and " proposed subway routes "? A. When it comes to distribution, that is for Mr. Gaynor. He is under the Public Service Law, and he follows it, and I never think of that.

Q. Did you know this is an amount that you asked the city to allow you? A. No, I don't. I don't know anything about it.

Chairman Thompson.— Just a minute. How could Mr. Gaynor split one item of $5,000 into two, without having somebody tell him? There is nothing on that bill to tell him.

Mr. Shonts.— I don't think he could. He is one of the men I will talk to. I will do my best to find out. I can find out, and I will tell you about it.

Chairman Thompson.— I know that is true. But, for instance, here he would not possibly have any authority to split one item into two, without somebody telling him.

Mr. Shonts.— Not unless he knew something of the service rendered.

Chairman Thompson.— How would he know?

Mr. Shonts.— Somebody has told him, possibly myself.

By Mr. Colby:

Q. Did you ever employ Edward M. Grout in connection with the subway negotiation? A. Yes, I did.

Q. You have got a little clearer impression about what he did? A. I know what he was hired for; He had been comptroller, and he knew the city's methods of doing business, and knew about their debt limit, and about the chances of their being able to carry out an obligation, and there were many things of that kind that now impress themselves on my mind, when I hear his name.

Q. In other words, you were anxious to get it through, and were willing to use any man who knew the ropes? A. Anxious to use anything I could get to put up in a good trading proposition against hard traders.

Q. You wanted inside information? A. I wanted actual information. I don't know whether you would call it inside or not.

Q. You wanted some man in touch with the atmosphere of the city offices? A. He had been comptroller, he ought to be able

,to give us a lot of definite information about conditions, about
,their methods, and matters of that kind.

Q. Whose methods? A. The city's methods.

Q. But the methods of the comptroller's office reflect, to some
,extent, the personality of the incumbent, do they not? A.
Possibly.

Q. In a negotiation with Mr. Prendergast, for instance, what
would be the benefit of having Mr. Grout's impressions as to his
administration? A. If a predecessor might — a recent predecessor might tell us a good deal about the city's finances, their
financial strength, their indebtedness, how it was carried, and a
lot of information that would be very useful.

Q. You have used the expression in a " trading proposition "?
A. Yes. We were negotiating with the city in a very large
transaction.

Q. In other words, an ex-comptroller might tell you what cards
,the city held? A. He might tell us about the condition of the
city, to carry out any contract they might enter into that might
be useful. It was a guess.

Q. Help you decide whether the city was bluffing or sincere?
A. I cannot remember all the facts that were in my mind.

Q. A whole lot of things like that? A. I wanted information
as to the situation.

Chairman Thompson.— Couldn't you get that from Mr.
MacInnes?

Mr. Shonts.— I didn't know him then.

Chairman Thompson.— Didn't you know there was a chief
accountant there who knew more of the details than any
comptroller?

Mr. Shonts.— If I had heard Mr. MacInnes' testimony of yesterday, and you had heard of how I disagreed with him, you
would not have thought I would have hired him.

, Chairman Thompson.— There are some things about this, Mr.
Shonts, that would be the real reason I would have in my mind
for your hiring him.

Mr. Shonts.— I didn't know Mr. MacInnes. I am giving you my impressions of what I sent for Mr. Grout for.

Chairman Thompson.— Detailed information you go to your auditor for. You have got somebody that knows about the inside in the Interborough more than you do, about details. That is true in the comptroller's office. The comptroller don't know details. He can't know them. He is only there for three or four years.

Mr. Shonts.— Well, if you had been there to advise me, may be I would have sent for Mr. MacInnes. I don't know whether it would have been proper for him to talk as freely as a man out of the city's service. There is a matter of ethics there.

By Mr. Colby:

Q. Did Mr. Grout deliver the goods? A. Mr. Grout told us in regard to his impressions of the city's condition, and so forth, yes.

Q. Did he ever render a bill stating what he did? A. I don't know about that. I know he rendered a bill, that we thought too big, and we pretty nearly had a lawsuit over it.

Q. Is your o. k. on that? A. Yes.

Q. What does that bill represent? A. Well, that was his retainer.

Q. It does not specify, however, what it was for? A. No; this was when he went to work.

Q. As soon as he went to work, you gave him ten thousand dollars? A. He demanded that as a retainer.

Q. He demanded that as a retainer? A. Yes, and as I say, he sent in a subsequent bill, which we almost had a lawsuit over.

Q. Well, what was the amount of his subsequent bill? A. I don't remember.

Q. Well, I guess — this is the voucher. You might refresh your mind there. (Hands voucher to witness.) A. Fifteen, and we compromised by splitting it in two.

Q. Still, there was no specification of what he had done? A. Well, I have not read it. (Reads voucher.) Well, what he did was along the lines I indicated, and you can appreciate we thought was not a very rich lead, and we tried to get rid of it, and that is the result.

Chairman Thompson.— Whom did he advise, come in contact with ?

Mr. Shonts.— He talked with me.

Chairman Thompson.— All the talks he had ?

Mr. Shonts.— So far as I remember, were with me.

Chairman Thompson.— He didn't advise any other officer ?

Mr. Shonts.— I don't remember referring him to other officers.

Chairman Thompson.— Ever sit in the meeting with city officials or Public Service Commission ?

Mr. Shonts.— All the talks were with me.

Chairman Thompson.— How many talks did you have with him ?

Mr. Shonts.— I don't know. Often.

Chairman Thompson.— How many; thirty-five or forty times ?

Mr. Shonts.— Oh, I could not say. Say twenty times. I am guessing. I don't remember.

Chairman Thompson.— He called at your office and talked with you ?

Mr. Shonts.— Frequently.

Chairman Thompson.— In the neighborhood of twenty times. That is the only service he performed ?

Mr. Shonts.— He looked up certain data for me.

By Mr. Colby:

Q. Did he ever appear openly as the counsel for the Interborough Rapid Transit Company ? A. I don't remember that he did.

Q. Did he ever take part in any negotiations with the Board of Estimate ? A. No.

Q. With the Public Service Commission ? A. No.

Q. Did he ever appear in court ? A. I don't remember that he ever appeared publicly.

22

Q. Your best recollection is that his services were advisory to you, along these personal and influential channels? A. Lines, yes.

Q. Did you ever take a trip with Mirabeau L. Towns? A. I think I did.

Q. Tell us where you went. A. I think that was the time I went to St. James.

Q. Did you go down there to enjoy the scenery? A. Well, you know what Joe Sherry said, when he was interrogated by the Interstate Commerce Commission as to why he shipped all his grain over the B. & O.— that it was on account of the scenery. No, I took a trip down to St. James, *hoping that I would catch the mayor of the city,* Mr. Gaynor, free and unencumbered, which I did. *I found him in his front yard, climbing over a fence toward a cattle yard.*

Q. Was he trying to get away when you saw him climbing over the fence? A. If he had recognized me, I might have had that conclusion, because he had not been saying very nice things about me. But I found him, I think it was in March. I know it was cold. *I know I was not invited* in the house. And I know we wore a path in the front yard, walking back and forth, for about three hours.

Q. But you paid $5,000, none the less, didn't you? A. Who? That is one of the things, probably. I had forgotten about that.

Chairman Thompson.— Now that your recollection has got refreshed by that, tell us what Towns did.

Mr. Shonts.— He did do this.

Chairman Thompson.— Oh, I know that. What else?

Mr. Shonts.— I don't remember now.

Chairman Thompson.— Did he do anything else?

Mr. Shonts.— Oh, yes. I will find out. I don't remember. I had forgotten that.

Chairman Thompson.— It is not a joking matter.

Mr. Shonts.— No. This was not a joking matter with me, either.

By Mr. Colby:

Q. Let me recall to you, Mr. Shonts, that it is a matter of common knowledge, that Mr. Grout was formerly the legal partner of the late Mayor Gaynor. Don't you know it to be a fact that Mr. Mirabeau L. Towns was an intimate personal friend of Mayor Gaynor? A. I had understood he had been, and that friendship had ceased.

Q. And is that the reason you took him down, to introduce you to the mayor? A. I didn't take him down to introduce me. I took him down — I thought that I could — if I would get an opportunity to say my speech to the mayor, that Mr. Towns or anybody else would not have any influence on the Mayor's mind, if he had an honest mind on the subject, which I think he had.

Q. Now, just allow me, there. In other words, you were seeking to change the mayor's attitude or ingratiate yourself with Mayor Gaynor, or obtain a more favorable attitude on his part toward your business? A. No. I wanted to tell Mayor Gaynor what I did tell him, that so far as the Interborough was concerned, that we were out of the situation, that we had no more propositions to make to the city, that we recognized he and other members of the board of estimate were elected on the platform which pledged themselves to city construction and city operation of subways, but that we were the largest taxpayer in this city, and that we had been in this business for a long time, and we thought we had more valuable information, and that we thought we could point out to him where for $70,000,000, he could build a better line, at least so far as distribution was concerned, than the line they were talking about building as the city line for $150,000,000.

Q. *Why did you take Towns down with you? A. I took Towns down to show me the way. I had never been to St. James. I am not sure whether it was Towns — before or after this, that Towns broke with the mayor — I am not sure.*

Q. Well, you could have gotten a village hack man for a dollar? A. I could have done this. The probability is this was before, but I have forgotten — but I know what I went there for, because I made a memorandum of it the next day I got back, when it was fresh in my mind, what I said to the mayor, and that was the gist, the object of my visit: there must be somebody in this city that

is honest and knows his business, and that you have got confidence
in. Now, if there is such a person, send him down to our office,
and we will open all our books to him. We have nothing to conceal from the city of New York. You have access to every record
we have, and I think we can show you —

Q. You have many to withhold but nothing to conceal? A.
Well, according to the way that you boys — and things have been
testified, we have not many to withhold. That is, we are not
withholding much. Well, what I was coming to was, there must
be some — there seemed to be such an antagonism on the part of
Mayor Gaynor toward our corporation, that I thought if there
was some person he had confidence in that would come down and
examine us and we would open all our books to him, everything
we had to him, he must be convinced. That is all I wanted.

Q. Sort of a quest for an honest man? A. A quest to have a
conversation which might result in something, and it did result
in his finally saying to me he would think it over, and if he
thought of anybody, he would send him down. And he did send
two men.

Q. Did it take him a long time to think of some men to send?
A. He did send two men.

Chairman Thompson.— What was the date of this meeting at
St. James?

Mr. Shonts.— My memorandum will show. I have it in my
office. I made this memorandum. It was on a Sunday, I know.

By Mr. Colby:

Q. Well, now, Mr. Shonts, when did you tell Mr. Towns you
wanted him to take you down to the mayor's house in St. James?
A. I don't remember. I suppose the day before I went.

Q. And was his trip as a companion *en courier,* as a part of his
professional services? A. I would not say it was not.

Q. It was included in his bill? A. I presume so.

Q. He was paid? A. He was paid, yes.

Q. Do you know of anything else he ever did? A. I don't
know. And I had forgotten that until you asked me about it. If
you have anything else you can ask me about, I will tell you as
frankly.

Q. How did you stop the Mayor from climbing over the fence when you and Towns got there? A. Well, I told him I wasn't as bad as I looked, that I didn't wear horns and didn't have any axes to grind, and we were on the level, and wanted to convince him so.

Q. And the Mayor came down off the fence a little slowly at that? A. He finally, if you want to use the figure of speech, he finally did come off. He sent an engineer by the name of and one by the name of Martin, and they spent months going through our records. I don't know the kind of report they made. I never saw it. But I know his attitude toward our company changed after they had spent months there, and after that we had a fair hearing, and that is all I wanted.

Q. What did Mr. Towns do on the occasion of that visit? A. I think Mr. Towns sat in the buggy while I walked the grass with the Mayor.

Q. The terms of his employment did not contemplate his getting out of the buggy? A. I don't remember what he did. I know I was on a serious matter, and I tried my best to dispose of it in a serious way.

Q. And you cannot recall anything else Mr. Mirabeau L. Towns did? A. I can't, as I say.

Chairman Thompson.— You interested me in one thing. You said your company was out of it, and you went to tell the Mayor you were.

Mr. Shonts.— Yes.

Chairman Thompson.— If you were, why tell the Mayor? What was your object?

Mr. Shonts.— We were out of it, because the Mayor was about to commit himself, as I understood, to what they call the Tri-Borough scheme, and the Tri-Borough scheme represented the building of a line down the East side and over into Brooklyn, at the expenditure running all the way from one hundred and thirty to one hundred and fifty millions of dollars. It gave no relief to the West side.

Chairman Thompson.— I know.

Mr. Shonts.— The point was that for seventy million dollars, I could point out to him, and we were willing to enter into that sort of a deal, if they would drop the question of public operation, and cooperate with us as the natural lessees of their present subways, I took the position just like a man, a tenant of a store. If I were a tenant in your store, and my business outgrew your facilities, and I want you to build an addition, I don't think it would be good business for you to start a rival store, and hurt me.

Chairman Thompson.— You don't want to be put out of it?

Mr. Shonts.— No. But the fact is that the City had elected the Mayor and these people on a platform pledged to municipal construction and operation, and I assumed we were out of it.

Mr. Colby.— Now, Mr. Shonts —

Chairman Thompson.— Just one more question, in reference to this matter. I think this matter is rather serious. First, you didn't remember Mr. Towns at all, as I understood you.

Mr. Shonts.— I remembered Mr. Towns, but I didn't remember the purpose for which he was employed.

Chairman Thompson.— You must have remembered him when the bill was first called to your attention. You must have remembered Towns was employed on a serious mission.

Mr. Shonts.— I did remember Towns, and that he was employed, but I didn't remember what the particular object I had in mind was when I employed him.

Chairman Thompson.— This conference that you had with the Mayor on this Sunday was one of the most important things you did, and one of the things you must have had in mind when you employed him, for extraordinary service, wasn't it?

Mr. Shonts.— I didn't have any particular thing in mind, but I do think that was a very important piece of work.

Chairman Thompson.— And if you performed extraordinary services for this company, for which you received a bonus, that was one of them?

Mr. Shonts.— I think it was.

Chairman Thompson.— Well, you didn't forget the name of Mr. Towns when counsel called his name to your attention?

Mr. Shonts.— I didn't say I forgot the name of Mr. Towns. I don't want to make that impression. I did remember the name of Towns; I did remember he was employed. I will let the reporter read my answer; but I didn't, and don't remember now, the particular purpose for which I employed him, and this incident is the first thing that refreshes my recollection.

Chairman Thompson.— These are important matters.

Mr. Shonts.— I have told you, that if you would let me, I would find out from the consultations with my men, all the details, and I will be very glad to find out.

By Mr. Colby:

Q. Mr. Shonts, did you preserve a memorandum — excuse me — I see your attention is taken up — A. Excuse me. I got those figures, that balance there, before the sale of $305,000, so you see there was not anything to disturb anybody. That is the point.

Mr. Colby.— I would like to state on the record that Mr. Shonts hands me a tabulation containing the worked out values of the stocks to his credit with Barney & Company on June 30, 1913.

Mr. Shonts.— June 30, or June 5?

Mr. Dawson.— June 30.

Mr. Colby.— Showing that the values, the aggregate values of the stocks in his account at that date was $715,550, against an indebtedness remaining after the liquidation of the month previous, which had reduced the debit to $410,230.

Mr. Shonts.— So there was almost —

Mr. Colby.— Leaving an excess of values in favor of Mr. Shonts in the account at that time of $305,320. We have not had an opportunity to verify, although we don't question —

Mr. Shonts.— These are brought down from the quotations they got upstairs. I suppose they are right.

Mr. Quackenbush.— Do you want to check it?

Mr. Colby.— Oh, no.   I assume they are right.

By Mr. Colby:

Q. Did you preserve the memorandum of your conversation with Mayor Gaynor on the occasion of that visit?   A. Yes, sir.

Q. It was quite a lengthy memorandum, was it?   A. Yes, it was.

Q. Is this it (showing paper to witness)?   A. (Witness takes memorandum.)   Memorandum of conversation with Mr. Gaynor, April 24, 1910; that is it, yes.

Chairman Thompson.— 1910?

Mr. Shonts.— Nineteen hundred and ten, yes.   He came into office, as I recollect it, on January 1, 1910.   The date of this memorandum is April 24, 1910.

By Mr. Colby:

Q. This memorandum is some ten typewritten pages?   A. I am —

Q. I think I don't want to spend time in any matter that is not strictly relevant, but I should like to read a few paragraphs from this memorandum.   It shows the attitude of mind of the Mayor of the city at that time, Mr. Shonts, who was the foremost spokesman and chief —   A. May I ask one question, Mr. Counsel?

Q. Yes.   A. This is a memorandum made by yourself, to refresh my recollection as to the substance of the conversation I had with the Mayor.   I never sent the Mayor a copy of it.   It was not in the shape of a letter which he could receive and answer, and I am just wondering out loud —

Q. The value of the memorandum, according to my opinion —
A. — if it is ethical for me to produce it.

Chairman Thompson.— Well, evidently you have.

Mr. Shonts.— But it was turned over to your boys, as I told them to turn over everything.   I am raising the question now, Mr. Chairman.

Chairman Thompson.— It was found from the files, the official files of the railroad company, wasn't it?

Mr. Shonts.— Personal files.

By Mr. Colby:

Q. I think you will be satisfied if I confine myself to reading nothing which the late Mayor might have wished to answer. A. I am making the point, because my boys turned everything over to you that I had there.

Chairman Thompson.— If it is a matter of the files of a railroad company, why, I think it is a public record.

Mr. Shonts.— A personal matter.

By Mr. Colby:

Q. This was a contemporaneous memorandum ? A. Within a day or two.

Q. Has all the presumptions of accuracy ?

Chairman Thompson.— I will leave it to the judgment of counsel, as to what he thinks about it.

Mr. Shonts.— If we can find out, Mr. Counsel, what day April 24th was on, we can know how many days after my visit, because it was on a Sunday I went down.

Mr. Colby.— Mr. Chairman, I don't want to seem insensible to any suggestion of impropriety, but I confess I don't —

Chairman Thompson.— The Committee will leave it to the judgment of counsel.

Mr. Colby.— See any impropriety of submitting this contemporaneous memorandum of what was probably the genesis of this whole negotiation.

Chairman Thompson.— The Committee leaves it to the judgment of counsel. You are familiar with the letter.

Mr. Colby.— The substance of Mr. Shonts' remarks is about as follows:

" He conveyed to the Mayor the fact that we had no proposition to make; that while we did make a proposition to Mr. Willcox on June 30, 1909, which proposition was emphatically declined, we realized then, as we do now, that the

carrying out of the proposition by the Interborough meant
a cut into its surplus immediately following the opening of
the new lines of about $3,000,000 per annum, nevertheless
at that time our people were not alarmed by the socialistic
trend of things; but that now they do have such fear, and
further, the fact that the City officials are committed, because
of the platform on which they were elected, to the building
of subways by the municipality.   Furthermore, the man
who would fall heir to the Mayor's chair if anything happened to him, has announced that the City will not even
give operating contracts to private corporations.

"The Public Service Commission has gone the full limit
in its idea of the creation of an independent subway system,
and, altogether, our people have become so alarmed that they
are afraid to make any venture whatever.   Therefore, all
that I am here to say is to tell you what I had in mind telling
you at our conference on last Monday, but because of the
presence of Chairman Willcox, and his request to me not to
tell you that we could not make a trade, I did not tell you
then.   I presume that Willcox's desire that I not make the
statement then was to hold back against the publication of
the first form of contracts and other data respecting the so-
called independent subway system, which has since appeared
in the public press.   Therefore, as the Mayor said in our
previous conversation, that it was very important for him
to know our position as soon as possible, and as I thought
he was entitled to know our position, I had come out to his
home to tell him.   Further, for the foregoing reasons, I had
nothing to say except the proffer of advice based on the
knowledge possessed by me of subway costs and earnings,
and I did not know that he wanted advice; but in the hope
and belief that he would not misunderstand the motive back
of giving such advice, I was willing to take the risk."

Then follows apparently some matters which the Mayor said
— the late Mayor said to the President, all very flattering, and
all of which I am certain the Mayor would — oh, no; this is
further what Mr Shonts said:

" It seems to me that you, as president of the corporation of the City of New York, with full responsibility on your shoulders of the chief executive, are confronted with a grave situation; and our people all admitting you to be a man of ability and courage and integrity, and desirous of undertaking great things, in which we would like to uphold your hands as far as we could, should know the facts as we view them. I think we all agree that a mistake would be made which would mean financial disaster and bring discredit on the administration, if it embarked on a system of subway building such as the Broadway-Lexington Avenue line contemplated, and others that would naturally follow suit, for when you commence this you will probably continue it — as against taking time to study for yourself and decide for yourself where you can spend the city's money to bring the greatest benefits to the citizens."

Apparently there was outlined here on a map the Broadway-Lexington route of the present subway line, which it was stated could be built for $71,000,000.

Mr. Shonts.— That was — if you will permit me, just a moment — that was the four lines down the West Side to Liberty, and two across Liberty and across the Manhattan bridge for a mile and a half, and two down to the Battery, and two up the Bronx, and two up Jerome avenue.

Mr. Colby.— Mr. Shonts apparently proposed to call the tunnel under the East river, the Gaynor tunnel. That was a little taffy, I suppose.

Chairman Thompson.— If there is anything here he don't read that you think ought to be read, why have him read it.

Mr. Colby.— The belief was expressed, after outlining —

" The situation may be summed up in that for $71,000,000 applied in the normal extensions above mentioned, a superior service will be furnished to the entire city than can be accomplished by the expenditure of 150 to 200 millions, in the creation of an independent system, which means to the citizen a ten cent fare as against a universal five cent fare.

" The belief was expressed that it would be a fatal mistake to permit such extravagant use of city money with such meagre results."

By Mr. Colby:

Q. Your company's attitude at this time was one that I may describe as solicitous about the waste of city moneys? A. It always has been. As a taxpayer, the largest taxpayer, it should be.

Q. Were you endeavoring to practice a form of urban economy when you applied to the city to allow you $1,532,000 for preliminary subway expenditures? A. I think it was perfectly proper. It must be taken care of some place.

Q. And your bonus and Mr. Rogers' bonus? A. I think whatever is the proper charge for the preliminary work of any construction enterprise, and I challenge anyone to controvert it, quoting any large work in the world, that does not contain in it the preliminary construction cost, the same as the subsequent construction cost.

Mr. Colby:

" The Mayor did not quite realize what was meant when he was told that we had no proposition to submit for he said it will be difficult to get the use of city money for our purposes. Whereupon I again said ' Please understand that we have no proposition at all; that the city having embarked in a policy of municipal construction, we felt bound to withdraw from the field, except that we stand ready, after the city has planned and built its subways, to operate them if the city so desires, and if a profit results, same to be divided, and if a loss, the city to stand same.' "

" It is true," continues he, " that this loss would not break the city of New York, as the city can afford to absorb a deficit of ten or twelve millions per annum, and not go into bankruptcy, but the Interborough would go broke the first year if it undertook to do so."

By Mr. Colby:

Q. In other words, you had, at that time, canvassed the city's capacities as an absorber of deficits? A. On the very plan which we were opposing. We always opposed the Tri-Borough plan; we always opposed the dual plan. And we spent large sums of money in the public press, by public advertisement, opposing it.

Chairman Thompson.— I cannot permit explanations of this letter. We must adjourn soon. If you want to put in the rest of the letter — or you can leave it where it is until tomorrow morning. Do you want to leave it where it is?

Mr. Colby.— I can conclude in about four or five minutes.

"I said to the Mayor that it looked to me, although I did not like to ascribe motives, that this independent subway idea was the product of an idea which developed in the minds of the Commission when it first came into existence, when it was popular to fight the Interborough, and when it might have been a popular thing to create an independent system, forgetting that the Interborough's subway is the city's own proposition, and anything that would help the same would help the city.

"The Mayor said to me that I might understand that if they commenced this system of city construction, they would have to continue it. I stated that I did understand that fully, and that we had nothing to say in regard to the wisdom of that policy; the city seemed to be embarked on it, and the public seemed to be educated up to the belief that this is the wise thing to do, and if we objected we would simply be misunderstood; and that inasmuch as they had decided on it, all we could do would be to gracefully withdrew. * * *

"I further said to the Mayor that there was a limit to the amount of transportation you can sell for five cents, and that that limit had been reached, and had a great deal to do with the bankruptcy of the surface lines; and that that limit could be reached and bankrupt other lines; and that it would be well to keep that thought in mind when planning the indiscriminate construction of subways."

Mr. Shonts.— I couldn't write a better letter today.

By Mr. Colby:

Q. What are people going to do when the limit of transportation is reached? A. I think it will be many years before the limit of transportation is reached, after all the new lines that are now under construction are finished and put in operation.

Chairman Thompson.— This ought to be a good place for jitney busses down here. What do you think?

Mr. Shonts.— They had them here years ago, and they took them off Broadway.

Chairman Thompson.— We will excuse the witnesses until to-morrow morning at 11 o'clock.

Mr. Quackenbush.— Just a minute. As I have said, the last two or three days, Mr. Rogers is under subpoena, and will be in Minneapolis for the next week, and while it probably will disarrange the order of things, he can be here tomorrow or the following Monday.

Mr. Colby.— Mr. Quackenbush, I have a great hesitation about asking any lawyer to take the stand, as he is under a great disability when it comes to testifying to things concerning his clients, or things he has done in his legal capacity. There has never been a moment when he would not have been welcome to the stand if he had asked to be heard, but there seems to be an expanding disposition to refer a great many important matters to Mr. Rogers for explanation. When you spoke to me a few days ago, I thought possibly we could elucidate these matters that are, maybe, only within Mr. Rogers' — in his recollection — through other witnesses. I don't know what the Chairman's idea is. We have had no opportunity to discuss the matter, I know the Committee wants to conclude its cursory survey of the Interborough conditions, and in view of the limit which it must observe, the limit already fixed to its existence, we must pass to other matters rather than to leave them entirely untouched.

Chairman Thompson.— When does he go, Monday?

Mr. Quackenbush.— He leaves tomorrow night.

Chairman Thompson.— Tomorrow night is Thursday night?

Mr. Shonts.— Friday night.

Chairman Thompson.— When will he be back?

Mr. Quackenbush.— He will be back a week from Monday. I brought it up because he will be available until Friday night.

Chairman Thompson.— Tomorrow isn't Friday.

Mr. Quackenbush.— I made a slip about that. I have seen what Mr. Colby has just said. I saw that Mr. Colby might have in mind just what he has expressed. I did not want a misunderstanding, because there has been no disposition on the part of Mr. Rogers to fail to be in attendance upon the Committee, but this matter is one that he is under subpoena in, and it is not anything of his own private nature at all, and he told me that it had been held because of his engagements in court here. He does not want to be in any equivocal position.

Chairman Thompson.— I think a subpoena better be issued. We will have to continue the examination of Mr. Shonts tomorrow, won't you? And I think you better issue a subpoena for Mr. Rogers, returnable a week from Monday.

Mr. Colby.— All right, Mr. Chairman. I should like to ask a question, one question, before we adjourn.

Chairman Thompson.— All right.

By Mr. Colby:

Q. Is it true that you sent a copy of the memorandum from which I have just read to Mr. J. P. Morgan, Jr., on the day after you had prepared the memorandum? A. I don't remember.

Q. Or on the day after you saw Mayor Gaynor? A. I don't remember.

Q. I find in your file a copy of a letter marked "personal," addressed to J. P. Morgan, Jr.

(Counsel hand letter to witness, which witness reads.)

A. No. Well, it may have been.   I don't know. I don't
remember just what is there.

Q. That letter does not completely refresh your recollection?
A. It doesn't show whether a resumé of what is here, or the whole
thing.

Q. But it was either a resumé on the whole thing? A. Yes.

Q. In other words, you reported upon your interview with
Mayor Gaynor to Mr. Morgan, Jr., practically immediately? A.
Yes; according to this letter, I told him of my talk with the mayor
— whether in extenso or in abbreviated form, I don't know.

Chairman Thompson.— When is that?

Mr. Colby.— 1910.

Chairman Thompson.— 1910. Did you have all these negotiations in reference to this matter with J. P. Morgan, Jr., when
J. P. Morgan, Sr., was alive?

Mr. Shonts.— Yes.

Chairman Thompson.— All with J. P. Morgan, Jr.?

Mr. Shonts.— All with J. P. Morgan, Jr., or in his absence
with Mr. Davison.

Chairman Thompson.— Back to 1907?

Mr. Shonts.— Always. I knew Mr. J. P. Morgan, Sr.; when I
began business, I began with J. P. Morgan, Jr., and never — and
when he was in the country I always dealt with him. When he
was abroad, then with Mr. Davison.

Chairman Thompson.— We will suspend now until to-morrow
morning at 11 o'clock, at this place.

Whereupon, at 4:30 o'clock P. M., an adjournment was taken, to
Friday, February 18, 1916, at 11 o'clock A. M.

FEBRUARY 18, 1916

NEW YORK COUNTY LAWYERS' ASSOCIATION BOARD ROOM,
165 Broadway, New York City

The Committee was called to order, pursuant to adjournment, Chairman Thompson presiding.

Quorum present.

Chairman Thompson.— The Committee will come to order.

SHONTS, THEODORE P., being recalled for further examination, testified as follows:

Examined by Mr. Colby:

Q. Mr. Shonts, you had other city employees or ex-city employees in your employment than Mr. Grout in connection with this subway negotiation, didn't you? A. I don't think now who you have in mind.

Q. What about the company's treasurer? A. Oh, Mr. Campbell, yes, he had been chamberlain for many, many, years.

Q. City chamberlain? A. City chamberlain, yes, sir.

Q. That is an office very closely allied to the finance department of the city, isn't it? A. Yes, sir; deputy chamberlain.

Q. Do you know in how many administrations Mr. Campbell, the treasurer of the company, held this office? A. I understood he was there for many years. I think, as I recollect it now, seventeen.

Q. Was he a friend of Dick Croker's? A. I don't know.

Q. How did he come to be employed by the Interborough Rapid Transit Company? A. We were looking for a treasurer, and he was recommended, and I have forgotten who by. He was employed, and that is all.

Q. Didn't he know as much about the inside of the finance department as Mr. Grout could possibly know? A. I had the benefit of all Mr. Campbell's knowledge. I know that.

Q. You have testified that you paid Mr. Campbell for some twenty or twenty-five conversations? A. Mr. Grout.

Q. I mean Mr. Grout. A. Yes, sir.

Q. And he rendered a bill for $25,000 ?   A. He received a
retainer for $10,000, as I recollect it, and then a subsequent bill
for $15,000, which we compromised.

Q. You mean you paid him $10,000 when you employed him ?
A. Yes, sir.

Q. And he rendered a bill subsequently for $15,000 ?   A. That
is my recollection, and we paid him $17,500.

Q. For a score or so of conversations ?   A. Yes, sir.

Chairman Thompson.— It might have been seventeen and a
half conversations he had.

Q. That is at the rate of about a thousand dollars a talk ?   A.
On that basis.   As a lightning calculator I would say you are a
glittering success.

Q. What else did he do besides having the conversations with
you ?   A. He did nothing I remember of except advise me in
regard to the situation.

Q. Don't you know the amount you paid Edward M. Grout
was allowed by the city as a part of the $589,000 that was allowed
on your application ?   A. Possibly I knew it at the time.   It was
a proper charge, as a preliminary cost of our work, and I have
no doubt was put in, and if allowed it must have been allowed on
the belief it was proper on the part of the city authorities.

Chairman Thompson.— Why was it proper ?

Mr. Shonts.— Because it was one of those items we expended
in the preliminary negotiations with the city.

Q. Who brought you on to New York ?   A. The first man that
spoke to me in regard to coming here was Mr. Paul Morton.

Q. He had just been brought on by Tom Ryan, hadn't he ?   A.
I think Mr. Ryan was very instrumental in bringing him here.

Q. And the thing you had to do was take charge of the Interborough Metropolitan, which was the name of the company under
which the surface lines were wished on to the subway; is that
right ?   A. It was the holding company and owned the Metropolitan and Interborough Rapid Transit and various other lines.

Q. Did Mr. Ryan ask you to come on and take the job ?   A. I
had a talk with him.

Q. Where ?   A. In New York city.

Q. What did he say? A. He pointed out the opportunities for great constructive work in this city, and thought that because of my large experience in constructive work that I might fit into the situation very nicely.

Q. Do you mean tunnel construction? A. No, sir; general construction.

Q. Mr. Ryan was opposed to the completion of the subways, was he not? A. At that time I was entirely unfamiliar with the history of the situation in New York city.

Q. At the moment, had he not? A. I understand he had proposed tunnel construction of his own.

Q. And had menaced the subway with a proposal to construct another line? A. No, sir; he told me he was very serious about it and believed in it.

Q. He had an opportunity to build a subway himself, had he not? A. I don't know how much of an opportunity.

Q. Don't you know at one time Mr. Ryan considered the proposal to construct a subway? A. That does not mean he had an opportunity. We might have an idea many times without an opportunity.

Q. Do you know that Mr. Ryan used his power and influence to harass Mr. Belmont in connection with the construction of the subway? A. I understood afterwards that there had been a good deal of contention between the two parties.

Q. Don't you know it had been testified to in court proceedings by Mr. Belmont that he went to see the late Mr. Whitney to see if this opposition could not be placated and ended? A. I have heard of it, but I did not read the testimony. I heard that in connection with the acquisition of the Pelham Bay Park Railroad.

Q. What is a slush fund? A. I have never had any connection with one.

Q. What is a slush fund? A. Never having had any connection with it, I don't know that I could define it.

Q. Did you ever hear of the term? A. Yes, sir.

Q. What idea was connoted in your mind? A. Connoted is good.

Q. I do not see why I should recede on a perfectly good word. A. Pardon me. I am trying to think of the derivation of it, to know what it means. I am trying to answer a question in which that is the verb, and I do not know what it means.

Q. What does it suggest to your mind? A. A fund that is used for improper purposes.

Q. What do you mean by improper purposes? A. I would say that if you were on the other side of a proposition from me and that I thought that you were vulnerable, which I do not think, and that I had a fund with which I thought I could change your mind and I would approach you and tell you that I had this fund and if you did so and so that you would be compensated, I would call that an improper use of a fund, and that is what I understand is meant by a slush fund. I may be mistaken.

Q. In the case of the utilization of such arguments to direct the judgment or course of a public official, it is tantamount to bribery, isn't it? A. If a man offers a public official a pecuniary reward for a change of his views I should think that it would be called bribery. I am not a lawyer. That is, I am not lawyer enough to hurt, so I am not an authority on the definition.

Q. What do you think about moneys expended for the use of irregular or secret influence? A. I do not think — I would not approve of money spent for irregular or secret influence.

Q. What was the real purpose of the payment of $1,500,000 for the Pelham Bay Park franchise? A. That was before my time, and I can only tell you what has been told me since.

Q. The amount paid for this franchise, however, is carried in the capital statement of the Interborough Rapid Transit Company, isn't it? A. Yes, sir. I say yes, this —

Q. That is so, is it not? A. I imagine it is so. I do not carry those balance sheets in my mind.

Q. Don't you know of an item such as $1,500,000 figuring in your capital statement? A. No, sir.

Q. Isn't it true, without any equivocation? A. I cannot tell you out of mind, because I do not carry balance sheets in mind. I am told it is true.

Q. That is a part of the estimate of the actual investment of the Interborough Rapid Transit Company in the present subways, or at least it is so regarded by you, is it? A. Yes, sir.

Q. That is drawing an income of 13 per cent. and a fraction

annually, is it not? A. If it is part of the Interborough Rapid
Transit capital, it is receiving more than that.

Q. It is a part of the principal sum on which the Interborough's
preferential of $6,335,000 is calculated, is it not? A. No, sir;
the Interborough — Yes, indirectly, indirectly, I imagine that
is true, because the —

Q. I ask you if it is true? A. Indirectly, I imagine that is
true.

Q. The preferential on the valuation placed upon the present
subway, according to the testimony of the chief accountant of the
city, is 13 and a fraction per cent.; is that right, under the new
subway contract? A. Say that once more.

Q. The preferential on the valuation placed upon the present
subway, according to the testimony of the chief accountant of the
city, is 13 and a fraction per cent.; is that right? A. Thirteen
and a fraction per cent. on what?

Q. On the valuation of forty-eight millions, according to the
testimony of Mr. MacInnes? A. I will tell you in a moment.

Q. You know the terms of the new dual contracts, do you not?
A. In a general way.

Q. Only in a general way? A. Well, as I know everything in
a general way.

Q. Don't you understand further, the first and most important
item, from the standpoint of the company, is the average of two
years' earnings, which is preferred to all other payments? A.
Yes, sir. The preferential payment was based on the average
earnings for the years 1910 and 1911, the surplus earnings for
those years, and they were averaged, and for 1910 were normal, and 1911 was not normal, and we always felt it was very
unfair, and the Public Service Commission forced us to rebuild
our equipments for a ten-car train, which cost a million and eight
hundred thousand dollars, and never in existence before, and a
million of that operating expense deducted from earnings, and
took the reduced earnings from one of the years, which we thought
was unfair.

Q. You took the years 1910 and 1911? A. Yes, sir.

Q. Yet the year 1910 was the year with lowest operating
cost in your history, was it not? A. I cannot tell you that out of

mind. Possibly that is so. I do not remember those things, out of my mind.

Q. I am not asking about figures, but about a fact, and of relation which I should think would be very strongly impressed upon your mind? A. If you ask me to tell you whether I absolutely know whether that was the lowest percentage of operation in the history, I say I don't remember.

Q. It was a very low year? A. Probably it was, but I don't remember it was the lowest year.

Q. This average of net earnings for two years — A. That is very close.

Q.— is designed to afford you or yield you what you claim to have been the actual net earnings upon the amount of investment represented by the present subways; is that true? A. The preferential payment was supposed to represent to us a fair average return on what we were earning under those years, and they selected the two years immediately preceding the agreement with the city.

Q. This is higher than the lowest and much lower than the highest? A. Our objection to 1911 was what I have stated.

Q. Mr. MacInnes has testified that that preferential amounts to 13 per cent. upon the valuation which was accepted as that of the present subways, and of course that is an accurate statement, isn't it? A. Mr. MacInnes is not working for us, and I do not know how he would arrive at his basis of valuation. I would have to look into that before I would approve his statement.

Q. You have had many discussions with the bankers as to the underlying basis of the new securities? A. Yes, sir.

Q. Don't you know what percentage of return the new contracts afford on the value of the present subways?

Chairman Thompson.— You can answer that yes or no.

Mr. Shonts.— It all depends upon the question of valuation, and that is in my mind.

Chairman Thompson.— I understand.

Mr. Shonts.— If I knew what that meant I could say yes or no, and inasmuch as I don't know what that means I couldn't say.

Q. Let me discuss the question of valuation; wasn't the question of the present value of the subways very earnestly debated between you and the city authorities before the contracts were made? A. It was.

Q. And wasn't there an agreement as to what should be taken as the valuation of the present subway? A. My recollection is that there was.

Q. And don't you recall what that valuation was? A. No, I don't.

Q. Don't you recall it was an amount much less than forty-eight million. A. No, sir, the forty-eight million, if you permit me to say, was the valuation agreed upon as to the value of the equipment in the present subway.

Q. Only the equipment; A. Yes, sir; only the equipment.

Q. Not the value of your leasehold? A. No, sir.

Q. And not the value of your right of operation during the former lease? A. I have not that figure in my mind, and I cannot answer that question.   Forty-eight millions is my recollection as to the value of the equipment.

Chairman Thompson.— I want to ask you a question. You said you didn't know about MacInnes; didn't you ever see the report MacInnes made in 1911?

Mr. Shonts.— No, sir.

Chairman Thompson.— It never came to your attention?

Mr. Shonts.— No, sir.

Chairman Thompson — Even though you had Mr. Grout and your treasurer and other people from the Comptroller's office?

Mr. Shonts.— I saw a report, Mr. Chairman — it was not a report, it was an estimate. I saw an estimate of the earnings of the B. R. T., and that is the only report I saw outside of our own estimates.

Q. Whatever the rate of return upon the value of the present subway, it is affected by such items as the $1,500,000 paid for the Pelham Bay Park franchise, isn't it? A. I have no doubt that is so.

Q. You know what the Pelham Bay Park franchise is? A.
Yes, sir; I was told, and I can tell it in a few words, all I know
about it. At the time Mr. Belmont was figuring for the bidding
on construction of the present subway there was not an operating
franchise in the city except the Pelham Bay and City Island
railroad, and there was a fight between the Whitney interests
and Mr. Belmont, and that he did not know whether he could get
a franchise from the Legislature to operate and that as a result
he bought the franchise of the Pelham Bay and City Island
railroads in order to have a franchise so he could operate the
subways.

Q. The battle ground of this fight was chiefly Albany, wasn't
it? A. That is as I understand it.

Q. And finding it impossible to secure certain amendments of
the law granting a franchise, it was proposed to buy this horse
car line up in the outskirts of the city? A. Not only was proposed, but Mr. Belmont did buy that, in order to get possession
of that franchise which gave him the right to operate the subway.

Q. It is also a fact, is it not, that shortly after that purchase
this titan struggle between these financiers was composed and
harmonized? A. Yes, sir; I understand so. That was before
my advent here.

Q. And that was before the Interborough Rapid Transit
Company acquired the franchise, wasn't it? A. How's that?

Q. It was before they acquired the Pelham Bay Park franchise? A. I was not in the city at all at that time. I was in
Panama, and I don't know except by hearsay about it, or about
any of those matters.

Q. The Interborough finally got its legislative relief in Albany,
did it not? A. Yes, sir.

Q. And thereafter acquired the Pelham Bay Park franchise?
A. I do not know which took precedence.

Q. Do you know whether testimony has been given in any legal
proceeding that the Pelham Bay Park franchise had no tangible
value? A. I know from a personal inspection of the property
it had no great intrinsic value.

Q. And have you ever appreciated the fact its charter or charter
privileges had any value? A. I imagine that its charter or

charter privileges had value at the time that Mr. Belmont purchased it, if that was the only franchise of the nature in the City of New York, and that would give it value.

Q. What did Mr. Ryan say to you when you were elected President of the Interborough Metropolitan as to what the scope of your duty should be? A. I was employed to take charge of the construction and operation of the properties of the Interborough Metropolitan which at that time composed the Interborough Rapid Transit, and the Interborough Rapid Transit covers the elevated and the subway, and the Metropolitan Street car lines, which covered all the street car lines except the B. R. T. system.

Q. When did Mr. Ryan first communicate with you? A. As I say, the first person that spoke to me was Mr. Morton.

Q. And did he say that Mr. Ryan asked him to speak to you? A. Mr. Morton asked me to come to New York, and I did, and he introduced me to Mr. Ryan.

Q. You came to New York to meet Mr. Ryan? A. I am not sure I knew when I came, but I did meet Mr. Ryan when I came to New York.

Q. When did you first meet Mr. J. P. Morgan, Jr.? A. Oh, that was some time afterwards. I don't remember when. I came to New York in April, 1907, and I don't think I met Mr. Morgan until late in 1908. I had known Mr. J. P. Morgan, Sr., before I came to New York.

Q. Did Mr. Morgan, Jr., suggest to you or did you suggest to him the building and equipment of the new subways as an interesting matter? A. I suggested it to Mr. Morgan.

Q. When? A. Very early in 1909, is my recollection.

Q. In what form did you make this suggestion? A. I went down to see Mr. Morgan.

Q. And what did you tell him? A. I was thinking of something, whether I ought to say it or not.

Chairman Thompson.— Say it; don't hold back anything.

A. I am not holding back anything, but I was taking an inventory with myself, and I was saying the results were not very flattering to myself, when I was thinking of what I had left and what I landed in here, with the surface lines immediately going

into the hands of the receiver and Mr. Ryan retiring from the
seat of activities, and not a strong financial party back of us, and
general ruin staring us in the face, and I said to myself, " You
are a fine bunch," and I said, "Where can I go?" I made up
my mind I would go to what I considered one of the strongest and
best houses in the city, and I said to myself, " I will go down to
see Mr. Morgan," and without any previous thought I put on my
hat and went there.

Q. You say general ruin was staring you in the face? A.
There was millions of dollars maturing, and I did not know
where we were going to get the money to meet the obligations,
and the surface lines already gone into bankruptcy.

Q. Was this general ruin you allude to a general result of the
disastrous Interborough Metropolitan merger? A. It was the
result of many things. The chief thing that was apparent to me
was the fact we were having, I think, ten or twenty millions dollars early maturing notes and I did not know where we were
going to get the money to pay it.

Q. You know that the losses of the Interborough Rapid Transit
Company under the Interborough Metropolitan merger were of
large amounts? A. Yes, sir.

Q. Have you the exact amount in mind, or approximately?
A. I think I can give you — as I recollect the figures, the Interborough Metropolitan paid something like forty-six million dollars for the acquisition of the Metropolitan Street Railways system, and I think what it has to show for it is fifteen million of
stock in the New York Railways.

Q. Was this done while you were President of the Interborough
Metropolitan? A. No, sir.

Q. That was done prior to your election? A. All done prior
to my advent, yes, sir.

Q. And if it had the millions that it paid for this street surface stock it possibly would not have found ruin staring it in the
face? A. I think the Interborough Rapid Transit Company in
and of itself would have been a very strong and successful
corporation.

Q. You might have been on a little more independent footing
in dealing with your bankers if you had not lost the millions that

you lost in this merger? A. If it had come, Mr. Counsel, to the question of raising $170,000,000, I think the market condition would have governed in any event. I think that our security at the time we made our large deal with the bankers was very good, and there had been some years elapsed, and we had rehabilitated ourselves and our Interborough was very strong, and it is very strong to-day.

Q. It has been testified here that the new bonds with the guarantee of the city and the preferentials that have been reserved in the contract to the company is as good as a security can imaginably be? A. I think that is true.

Q. When you went to see Mr. Morgan, that was with the idea of any such arrangement as was subsequently made with the city as to the use of its credit, was it? A. Yes, sir. I had visions, Mr. Counsel. Not only did I have the temporary interest of the companies in mind, but I had visions of the future, and I said very frankly to Mr. Morgan I wanted to talk to him in regard to the whole Rapid Transit problem of the city of New York.

Q. Had you talked with Mr. Ryan? A. No, sir.

Q. Did Mr. Ryan suggest that you see Mr. Morgan? A. He did not. Mr. Ryan has never, since my advent here, taken any interest in our affairs or given any advice, or insisted that any policy be pursued.

Chairman Thompson.— Is he a stockholder?

Mr. Shonts.— I don't think so. I don't know.

Q. He is the largest holder of underlying securities of the surface lines, is he not? A. I don't know. I think not. I have no way of knowing it.

Chairman Thompson.— You say Mr. Ryan is not a stockholder in the Interborough or Interborough Metropolitan or Consolidated?

Mr. Shonts.— Not to my knowledge.

Chairman Thompson.— Take a man interested in these matters, where the public knows he is interested in the concern, and still a small, comparatively small, holder of stock, how does that come about?

Mr. Shonts.— Mr. Chairman, that is one of the mysteries to me. I do not know. They continue to talk about Mr. Ryan and his dominance, and I never see him and he never talks to me.

Chairman Thompson.— Let us take Mr. Morgan; he don't own any stock either?

Mr. Shonts.— No, sir.

Chairman Thompson.— But he had an absolute power in respect to the management of your company's finances?

Mr. Shonts.— Only as a banker.

Chairman Thompson.— He had the power?

Mr. Shonts.— He had a right to say what he would sell his money for.

Chairman Thompson.— You must admit Mr. Morgan had the power?

Mr. Shonts.— Any banker has that power.

Chairman Thompson.— But Mr. Morgan had more power in relation to the financial management of the Interborough Company than you did, didn't he?

Mr. Shonts.— He had no power outside of the times we went and asked for money.

Chairman Thompson.— Those times he had more power than you did?

Mr. Shonts.— Yes, sir, he had the money to loan, and it was his job to say on what terms he would loan it.

Chairman Thompson.— Don't Mr. Ryan have a power somewhere?

Mr. Shonts.— Not with the Interborough.

Chairman Thompson.— Or any of your connecting lines?

Mr. Shonts.— Never since I have been here. That will be a great shock to a mass of people, but that is the truth. I cannot

understand how those ideas exist. Mr. Ryan has never said to
me once, " I wish you would do so and so," but Mr. Ryan has —
The Interborough Consolidated total indebtedness is two and a
half million dollars and of that amount I think Mr. Ryan owns a
million and a hundred and twenty thousand, and that is as far as
I know Mr. Ryan's total interest in any or all of our companies.

Mr. Colby resuming:

Q. Mr. Gary, of the Steel Trust, says he has never made any
suggestion to steel manufacturers as to prices; he only gives din-
ners ? A. Mr. Ryan gave a dinner last night and I did not go. I
was invited but I did not go, and I was sorry. If that is in line
with your remark, I missed a very good dinner no doubt.

Chairman Thompson.— If there wasn't any politics talked
there, we are not interested.

Mr. Shonts.— I should think you ought to.

Q. Did you speak to anybody else about financing the Interborough? A. No, sir, I did not, not until I had practically
reached an agreement with Mr. Belmont. Then I reported to the
Board.

Q. There was an agreement with Mr. Belmont? A. With Mr.
Morgan, and then I reported to the Board.

Chairman Thompson.— The Committee acknowledges with
pride and gratitude the presence of Senator Sanders, State
Senator.

Q. And from the time of your first approach to J. P. Morgan
& Company no one else occupied so close or so favored a relation
as to new financing as that firm? A. No, sir.

Q. Did you receive any proffers from other financial groups?
A. No, sir. I might say that one of the conditions that — Mr.
Morgan made two conditions when I said I wanted to talk with
him not only in regard to the present interests but also the whole
thing. He said he wanted to know if I had talked with anybody
else and I said I had not and I didn't suppose he wanted to take
up a matter that had been hocked about the streets, and he said
he wanted to know if I was authorized to talk, and I said that

nobody would know I was here unless we traded, and if we traded I would report to the Board, and if not, no harm was done.

Q. Did you write this letter to Mr. Freedman on September 13, 1910? A. Yes, sir, I did.

Q. Has that some relation to the subject we are discussing? A. It has. Mr. Belmont was not taken down there until — that is one of the things I did not want to bring out, and I say that we practically reached an agreement before I took Mr. Belmont down there.

Q. You mean with Morgan & Company? A. Yes, sir. You see that has no bearing and that is simply a courtesy. I say that to you, that has no bearing.

Mr. Colby.— I think this letter has a very definite bearing, and I think it is my duty to read it.

Mr. Shonts.— All right, read the letter, I don't care about the letter. It is the other features I am speaking about.

Q. I will explain to you, rather than to be under even your suspicion as to committing any matters to the record which are not in my opinion at least strictly pertinent, that the record discloses a rising note of domination in your financial negotiations on the part of Morgan & Company, and also a crescendo series of exactions and demands by Morgan & Company, and it does not disclose a single successful stand or murmer of dissent on the part of the company or any of its officers to the demands of Morgan & Company. The only justification I have heard uttered on the stand here is that the railroad was confronted by conditions which it could not cope with without the aid of Morgan & Company, and it was powerless to do anything except as they had aid upon such terms as were proper. This letter indicates to me that that was not necessarily the fact, and it is for that reason I read the letter. A. Can I say something in regard to that or not, at this moment?

Q. We would be very glad to hear what you have to say. A. If Morgan & Company ever had a desire to dominate our transactions it was never manifest to me and never made that impression on my mind. Our minds did meet on these problems, and there never was a time when I felt that they were undertaking to take any undue advantage of our necessities.

Q. I am sure that will be appreciated by Morgan & Company, that statement; however, it is somewhat at variance with the records and the inferences the records suggest. A. As to that I do not know.

Mr. Colby read the letter in evidence dated September 13, 1910, as follows:

"Dear Andy.—"

This is marked "Personal and Confidential," and continues:

"Mr. Belmont and I spent a couple of hours with the people on the corner yesterday. They announced that they, the National City and the First National Bank, were prepared to get under the Interborough securities, and put representatives of each institution on our board, and become publicly identified with the property. They are willing to now loan us the $30,000,000 required for financing the elevated improvements and extensions, and on May first next will loan us the $22,000,000 required to take up the maturing six per cent. notes now outstanding, and to sell $52,000,-000 five per cent. bonds at a price to be agreed upon for a fixed commission to themselves. While the terms proposed for the loan seem high, they claim the prices we will get for the bonds when sold because of their united backing and influence will probably be such as to more than compensate for the rates they are forced to charge us on notes at the present time, besides having the permanent advantage and protection of their association with us which will always help the property.

"Augy was rather of the opinion that we had better go on and trade with the Public Service Commission without making positive provisions for the money, thinking we might make a little better settlement with these gentlemen later on. I not only doubt the wisdom of our closing with the Public Service Commission until after we are fully financed, but also doubt our ability to make better terms than those proposed. For as you know, this combination not only makes the strongest financial group in this country, but probably in the world, and I think they fully realize their influence and power.

"I do not think it prudent to write more than is contained in this letter, and wish very much you could be with us, for I believe the situation is such as to require the earliest and most careful consideration.

"Very truly yours."

The letter is addressed to Mr. Andrew Freedman, Maplewood, New Hampshire.

Q. You sent that letter? A. Yes, sir.

Q. That is your letter to Mr. Freedman? A. Yes, sir; that is my letter to Mr. Freedman.

Q. Did he reply? A. If he did, it is there.

Q. There seems to be a telegram dated September 14 addressed to you by Mr. Freedman in which he says "Letter received. Arrangements very satisfactory. Will arrive home September 24th, trust in time to discuss matters. Will this date do? Write me arrangements. Regards." Mr. Shonts, is it your opinion that the strength of the bankers has been exerted wholly to the advantage of this company? A. I think that the strength of the bankers has been used wholly to the interest of this company, and I think they have exacted a fair compensation for their services.

Q. You admitted that the terms proposed for the loan seemed high to you, did you not? A. Yes, sir.

Q. And yet you stated that the bankers claimed the price that the company would realize for bonds would more than compensate? A. Yes, sir; more than compensate.

Q. You think 93½ is a good price for those bonds? A. That wasn't these bonds.

Q. Those were the old bonds? A. I imagine those were some of the fifty-five million issue which were refunded, and I don't remember what that price was.

Q. Do you remember what those bonds realized on refunding? A. On refunding I think we had the right to call them at 105. Those details I cannot keep, but I think we sold those bonds when we did sell them at a very satisfactory price. If I would guess,

I would guess 101 or 102, something like that. Mr. Fisher advises me that most of the notes were converted into the bonds direct.

Q. This letter was written subsequent to your interview with Mayor Gaynor? A. Yes, sir. What is the date of that letter?

Q. September, 1910. A. Yes, sir.

Q. And these financial transactions were for the purpose of raising money in connection with the contract you were supposed to make with the city? A. Partly, and partly to pay off our obligations, twenty-two millions, as I think it states are maturing obligations. I told you a few minutes ago ten or twenty millions. I have forgotten.

Q. You were of the opinion it was well to defer your financing until the negotiations were concluded with the Public Service Commission? A. No, sir; I would hate to finish my trade until I had to go out and get money.

Chairman Thompson.— You had to go to Mr. Morgan first, because you had to feel that you had some real financial backing before you went into the transaction?

Mr. Shonts.— Yes, sir.

Chairman Thompson.—And you tied up to somebody you could get the money from?

Mr. Shonts.— Yes, sir. If we traded with the city.

Chairman Thompson.— That is the reason you had to tie to Mr. Morgan?

Mr. Shonts.— We had to tie to somebody and selected him.

Chairman Thompson.— You tied in advance, so when you were in the negotiations you felt safe to go through?

Mr. Shonts.— Yes, sir; otherwise we might find ourselves with obligations and no ability to perform.

Chairman Thompson.— You didn't feel the Interborough was strong enough of its own financial resources?

Mr. Shonts.— No, sir, not at that time.

23

Chairman Thompson.— But you did feel that the realization of these contracts, as you said yesterday, would give you faith in this Interborough-Metropolitan stock so you could afford to buy it?

Mr. Shonts.— Yes, sir. I felt — here was a situation, we were the tenants of the city's only subway, and we were making good on all our obligations under our lease, and we felt that we normally ought to be allowed to make such extensions as the traffic requirements justified, and we were willing to do that with private capital, and we made three distinct offers to do it, and culminated in our offer of December 15, 1910, and it was finally rejected, and when these gentlemen were elected on the platform of city construction of city operations we felt everything we had might be ruined. They might build parallel lines and put in three cent fares, and it was very necessary for us, we felt, if possible, to make some fair trade with the city so as to protect the taxpayer on one side from what we thought was an extravagant use of money, and the citizens from paying two fares, and ourselves from being ruined by unjust and unfair competition.

Chairman Thompson.— The question is back to the idea — I don't yet understand, and I know what was in your mind, because I called it out before, and the question that I don't understand is why you had to tie yourselves up in that way; the city does not have to tie itself up in advance.

Mr. Shonts.— The city has power to levy taxes and can raise money, which the Interborough had not.

Chairman Thompson.— But the bonds of the city are protected entirely by the value of the security, aren't they?

Mr. Shonts.— That is real estate security.

Chairman Thompson.— Your securities were to be guaranteed practically by the same city?

Mr. Shonts.— We had no idea when we commenced these negotions with Morgan & Company, and it was long before the idea of a Tri-Borough system was born or the idea of the dual subway system was born, and we had not any idea of that kind. We were talking about raising money for private capital extensions of the subway system.

By Mr. Colby:

Q. How long did you proceed in this endeavor to extend the subways by private capital investment? A. I think our last offer was on December 5, 1910, which was our largest offer.

Q. December 5, 1910? A. That is my recollection.

Q. I find here a memorandum from Mr. D. L. Turner, engineer of subway construction, to the auditor of your company dated February 15, 1915, containing an estimate of prospective expenditures of the Interborough Company to cost of construction in the year 1915, and he sets forth various details, amounts disbursed, amounts of estimates, and so forth, and concludes with this interesting paragraph: "From the above tabulation it appears that there is sufficient cash now on hand to provide for all of the anticipated disbursements during this year and five million dollars to spare. It appears therefore that it will be unnecessary for the company to borrow any money during 1915, and that the further operation of the schedule can be deferred for twelve months. About January 1, 1916, a new estimate in the light of the facts then before us can be prepared"; was that memorandum ever submitted to you? A. No, sir. What is the date of it, please?

Q. The date of that memorandum is February 15, 1915, and it is stamped received by the auditor February 25, 1915, and I find a letter of the auditor, Mr. Gaynor, dated March 3, 1915, addressed to you as president, enclosing the memorandum. A. Probably reached Mr. Pepperman and was handled by him, my assistant.

Q. It was evidently considered a matter of importance, because I notice Mr. Gaynor says in his letter, "I am sending a copy of the memorandum to Mr. Hedley, Mr. Rogers and Mr. Quackenbush for their information," and he continues, "And with your approval will convey to Mr. Turner our understanding that the governing document on this point is the agreement with the bankers," and so forth. A. Those are the important words: "agreement with the bankers."

Q. Do you recall the receipt of this memorandum? A. No, sir; it probably was handled by Mr. Pepperman, because I understand it all thoroughly, and I can explain it all thoroughly.

Q. Let us first get the facts; I think may be you are entitled to such refreshing of your recollection as these documents will afford. A. Yes, sir.

Q. Is that a memorandum of yours to Mr. Quackenbush? A. No, sir. It is not signed, and my guess would be it was sent to Mr. Quackenbush by my assistant. I could say maybe, to save time, as a matter of fact, the whole thing did not amount to anything, because the bankers did not call for any more bonds until the last of the year, in December.

Q. The point I am getting at, did you go to the bankers and state the fact you had no further cash requirements for the year, and at the end of the year you would have the five million dollars? A. I have no remembrance of doing it.

Q. You felt that J. P. Morgan & Co. had a right to loan you money whether you needed it or not? A. We have a contract with them.

Q. But I am trying to arrive at your interpretation of its relative right and duty. A. I was trying to explain that when we entered into this contract with Morgan & Company it was all submitted to the Public Service Commission and their engineers and our engineers made a forecast as to the amounts required each year during the life of the contract.

Q. You mean Mr. Craven? A. It was done by Mr. Craven and his assistants; yes, sir.

Q. Mr. Craven is the man who makes the estimates of the expenditures? A. He is the chief engineer. I do not see Mr. Craven. I see the men of the Public Service Commission.

Q. You said the engineer. A. Because I told my engineers to do it, and I have no doubt they did do it. This matter was taken up at the time, and the Public Service Commission agreed first that this contract should be completed January 1, 1917, therefore, there was only the period left from April 19, 1913, to January 1, 1917, in which to carry out the contract, as decided by the Public Service Commission. Therefore, our time was limited with the bankers, and that was an operation of four years. It was a little less than four years, and we got together and our engineers and the engineers of the Public Service Commission, and made a forecast of the money required each year to make a memorandum to attach to the bankers' contract to show what they should be required to do each year, and under that contract they have a right to do —

Q. That has been fully explained, and in the record? A. Yes, sir.

Chairman Thompson.— Mr. Colby, in asking his questions, nor this Committee, do not stop at a contract as being conclusive. The fact that there was a contract does not make any difference. The fact that it is answered that there was a contract, that is no answer to the question at all.

Mr. Shonts.— Then what is the question?

Q. You could have saved a considerable amount of money for your company if you had been able to adjust your borrowings to your actual requirements, could you not? A. No, sir, because from the time this money was deposited it drew 6 per cent interest.

Q. You mean you paid 6 per cent? A. No, sir; 5⅜ per cent.

Q. You don't mean to say you received 6 per cent interest on it? A. Yes, sir; that was the basis of the allowance to both companies in the contract from the time the money was deposited.

Q. You don't mean to say you get 6 per cent from J. P. Morgan & Company? A. No, sir. The city gets 2½ per cent from J. P. Morgan.

Q. And you get 6? A. Yes, sir.

Q. And the city makes up the difference? A. It is — the amount that we are to contribute to the fund is credited to that amount.

Q. When you say that you would not have saved money had you been able to adjust your borrowing to your actual cash requirements, you refer merely to the fact that the losses on interest are to the city and does not fall upon your company? A. The 6 per cent we receive from the time money is deposited is credited to our contribution to the $58,000,000.

Q. In other words, your loss on interest is charged to construction? A. That is it.

Q. And constitutes a part of your contribution. A. Our interest.

Q. And in the event of any depletion of the fifty-eight million which you are under contract to contribute to construction, the city has to make it up? A. Yes, sir.

Q. So it does not make any difference to the Interborough Rapid Transit really what the loss on these large deposits with Morgan & Company is? A. Except as taxpayers, for any excess over the estimated amount, and we are the largest taxpayer in this city.

Chairman Thompson.— I do not think from the testimony up to date that you are entitled to claim much on the balance between you and the city on the tax proposition.

Mr. Shonts.— We are the largest taxpayer.

Q. In other words, your situation as a taxpayer does not entirely obscure from your mind the fact that you are also the operators of the Subway under very advantageous and long continuing guarantees from the City, does it? A. We have made it a rule, or I have made it a rule, to let each stump stand on its own bottom.

Q. In other words, you are not receiving a salary of a hundred thousand dollars a year as a president of a taxpayer? A. No, sir. I am receiving a salary of $100,000 to keep our taxes as low as consistent with the facts.

Chairman Thompson.—All there is about taxes, you ought to pay your share of what it costs, and it is not an asset to have a taxpayer to a locality. Every time a new taxpayer comes in it creates a new burden and your taxes meet your share.

Mr. Shonts.— Ordinarily, Mr. Chairman, that is true, but may I tell you something that I think is news to you, when I tell you the Manhattan Company pays in taxes more money per mile of road than the Pennsylvania system earns gross. That is rather a startling statement, isn't it?

Q. Is that one of the facts that entered into an award of a bonus to you, the extent of the taxes the Manhattan pays? A. All of my activities — the facts which entered into the award of the bonus were discussed by the Committee, and I was not present, as I told you yesterday, but all of my activities as an officer cover seeing that we do not pay more than our fair share of taxes.

Q. Did you go to J. P. Morgan & Company after the receipt of the Turner memorandum and state you would not need this money? A. As I say, I have no recollection of it.

Q. Didn't it occur to you to say it would be possibly acceptable to Morgan & Company and certainly advantageous to the company if they would suspend their rights of planting money on you and calling for bonds in accordance with the contracts? A. It may not seem possible, in view of some of my actions, but there are times when I have a little horse sense, and when there is no market for bonds and I know it is absolutely impossible for Morgan & Company to market a single bond, why disturb them?

Q. You mean that you had too much horse sense to suppose Morgan & Company would entertain such a suggestion? A. No, sir. There was no market for securities at that time and we were in the midst of the greatest panic, and that was in February, 1915.

Q. You had no occasion for the proceeds of securities in 1914, and there was no occasion to market? A. There wasn't, and we could not sell it. It is possible I told him if it reached me, and I don't remember a thing about it.

Q. Would you have asked Morgan & Company to suspend these loans upon you, if the interest charges had fallen upon the company and not upon the city? A. I think Morgan & Company —

Q. I mean the interest losses? A. I think Morgan & Company had a right under the contract, and I think it was their duty to take advantage during the time of the year when they thought was the best for marketing the bonds.

Q. Would you have done it if the interest loss owing to the fact you were paying 5⅜ per cent for money and you were only getting from Morgan & Company 2½ per cent, would you have done it if it affected the Interborough? A. I would not have done any different than I did do under any circumstances. I would not have asked them to modify a contract where I thought they were exercising their proper legitimate right under the contract.

Q. They had no hesitation in asking you to modify a contract with them? A. Wherein?

Q. Did they ever ask you to modify a contract? A. I don't remember it.

Q. Or relinquish any benefits under a contract? A. No, sir; I asked them to.

Q. Didn't you consent to the withdrawal from the syndicate of $40,000,000 of the bonds? A. Yes, sir; because I thought if they would place $40,000,000 where it would not come our during the life of the contract the remaining bonds would be much greater.

Q. The correspondence shows they asked you to do it? A. That may be, but I was glad to comply with it.

Q. Possibly they would have been glad to comply with a request from you to suspend the loans which you did not need? A. They did.

Q. When? A. Thirty-first of December, 1913. When they were obligated to take $78,000,000 on the 31st of December I went there and said, " I don't think we will need this ten million dollars, and I think we can get along without it, and I am going to ask you to waive your right to demand that ten million dollars of bonds."

Q. Of bonds you mean? A. Yes, sir, of bonds, and not of dollars, and after some talk they agreed and thereby waived.

Q. Why didn't you ask them to waive their right to call that thirty million bonds and put it on a 2½ per cent basis in 1913 when Turner said you would have five million dollars without borrowing a cent? A. Maybe I did. I don't remember about it. I remember of that other case.

Q. Is it a fact that you did? A. I don't know. I cannot tell you more than that.

Q. You testified yesterday that at the time you received the $125,000 bonus you owed none of your directors any money? A. That is right.

Q. Did you ever owe any of your directors any money? A. No, sir, not that I remember of now.

Q. Did you ever owe Andrew Freedman any money? A. No, sir. There was an occasion when I got some subscription for some bonds at his request and which were taken up and taken care of, in which he said he would care for a half interest, and that was the nearest to my ever owing him anything. To say I owed him money, no.

Chairman Thompson.— Do you remember yesterday you had some talk about Mr. Towns; did you find out anything else he did except what was testified to yesterday?

Mr. Shonts.— No, sir, except he went and studied our problem and qualified himself to talk.

Q. I show you a copy of a letter dated June 4, 1909; is that a letter of yours to Mr. Freedman? A. Yes, sir.

Q. Read it? A. "My dear Andy: I have yours of to-day enclosing checks for $12,500 and $15.62, respectively, in connection with the Armour bonds. Thank you very much for the same. It was very kind of you to take up and carry these bonds for me, and I appreciate it. Very truly yours." That is the matter I had in mind, and these bonds were being offered, and he did not think he would be awarded them and he thought I would, and he asked me to make the application which I did, and the bonds were awarded to me and he said "I am going to carry them right along," but I never got a cent out of it and it passed from his mind, and I never reminded him of it. I think that is the nearest I ever came to owing him.

Q. Mr. Freedman was the man who suggested the enlargement of the bonus from $125,000 to $150,000, wasn't he? A. I don't know.

Q. It has been so testified? A. I say I don't know.

Q. In the ten months that elapsed between the award of $125,000 to you and $25,000 did Mr. Freedman ever say to you the amount was insufficient? A. Yes, sir, often.

Q. Did he ever say, "I am going to try and get you some more"? A. Yes, sir, and since I have read what Mr. Schwab did to a couple of his men, I think we were all pikers. Mr. Freedman said he thought I ought to have had a quarter of a million, and he was one of the men said so, but I never got it.

Q. Then may be he would not have had to carry bonds for you? A. That had nothing to do with this, and I rather resent that, because it was a matter I have fully explained to you, and I think if you will read — I do not know what is in that file, but it was a suggestion to him that I make application for some of those bonds and I made it.

Q. Is that the only transaction ? A. That is the only one I have any recollection of.

Q. That you had with Mr. Freedman ? A. In which he even went that far. We had a sort of joint transaction in a couple of lots somewhere, which I put up, my share of the money. Three of us owned two lots somewhere in town, and I know the rent don't pay the interest charges, and we still have them.

Q. This was not the only occasion on which Mr. Freedman carried stock for you, was it ? A. That is the only one I remember of. There may be others, and if there are, you can remind me of them.

Q. Do you remember the Miami Copper transaction ? A. No, sir, I never had any Miami copper that I know of.

(Mr. Colby shows a letter to witness dated December 28, 1909.)

Mr. Shonts.— I do not remember a thing about this, but I will read it.

Q. Don't you recall the transaction now ? A. No, sir.

Q. It speaks of an allotment at your request ? A. Yes, sir, "At your request," but I don't remember a thing about it.

Q. Let me ask you this question: Have your directors ever participated, or any director ever participated by way of commission or rake off in the payment of any bills to your company in the supplies ? A. Not to my knowledge, ever.

Q. Have you ever had any information on that subject ? A. I have never heard of its being done.

Q. Would there be any record of deduction in the payment of your bills on that account ? A. What do you mean ?

Q. Would there be any record of diminution or reduction of bills on that account, commissions received or payments made ? A. I can only say this, that soon after I came here, Mr. Counsel, this was back in 1907 or 1908; it was within a year, I think, of my advent, I asked for a meeting of our full board, and we had it, and it had come to my attention that when we were in the market for certain large contracts, certain directors who had interests in some concerns who were going to bid on these contracts would send to my lieutenants and talk to them about it, and advocate the merits of their particular devices, and so forth, and I said, "I want to know," gentlemen, after we had finished the regular calendar, "whether I am a misfit here or not. I have never had but one rule of life, and I want it to apply here, and it is going to apply here if I remain, and for that reason I put that sign over the door," and they looked up over the door and there wasn't any sign there and some one said, "What does the sign say?" "Prices and quality must be equal before friendship commences," and I said, "That has always been my rule of life, and it is going to be my rule here, and it means exactly what it says, and more than that, all business has to be transacted over my table. If you gentlemen want to talk to any of my lieutenants, you can do it in my presence in my office, and I want to say that if you don't want that kind of a president you don't want me." I remember Mr. Freedman was the first man to laugh, and say "Well, I guess that maybe I have done as much of that sort of thing as anybody, because that has been the method, and I think our president is right." And I want to say here that from that day on I never heard of any director ever seeing one of our lieutenants or of ever mixing up in the purchase of any material for any contract we ever made except in open meeting or before my board, if that answers your question.

Q. When was that proclamation of emancipation made by you?
A. Early after I came here. I couldn't say whether in 1907 or 1908.

Chairman Thompson.— You did not have Mr. Hedley's patents in mind when you put up that notice, did you?

Mr. Shonts.— No, sir. We got all the benefits of all our men's devices without any expense to ourselves, and let them have the patents. There are different ways of looking at it, and that may be wrong.

Chairman Thompson.— We will suspend, if there is nothing more, until 2:30.

(Whereupon, at 1:05 o'clock P. M., a recess was taken to 2:30 o'clock P. M.)

AFTERNOON SESSION

The Committee was called to order at 2:55 o'clock P. M., Senator Towner presiding.

Chairman Towner.— The Committee will come to order. All right, Mr. Colby.

SHONTS, T. P., recalled.

By Mr. Colby:

Q. What had you in mind which you did not deem prudent to mention in your letter to Mr. Freedman that was read at the morning session? A. When you read that this morning I tried to think. I don't remember what I had in mind at that time, I am sure. Some of the details, I presume, of those negotiations, but what they are has escaped my memory.

Q. Something that you did not care to make a record of in writing? A. I presume so, from my language; but what it was I don't remember.

Q. Are there matters in connection with the affairs of the company which prudence requires should not be recorded? A. No, I imagine — I would have to guess. I have no recollection at all. I would have to guess there was something in regard to what led up to the taking of Mr. Belmont down to Mr. Morgan's, which I referred to this morning, which had no particular bearing —

Q. You mean referred to in your testimony this morning? A. In my testimony this morning, yes, which is more a matter of courtesy than anything else. That would be my best guess now. I have no recollection.

Q. Is there any imprudence in courtesy? A. Sometimes you do things, and you prefer, although no harm is occasioned to the other gentleman, you would prefer he would not know about it until after it was over.

Q. Did you consider it imprudent to be courteous to Mr. Belmont? A. No. It was not that.

Q. You would say, even if you were unable to recall what you had in mind when you used the expression in your letter, that it must have been of importance? A. If you want my best guess, and insist on it — for I say it was nothing of any importance at all. Mr. Belmont did not know that I was having these negotiations with Mr. Morgan until I took him down there. I didn't know whether anything would come out of it, and I think — I did know I thought it would be unwise.

Q. What was Mr. Belmont's position in the company at that time? A. Chairman of the board.

Q. And on a matter of such magnitude as this was it — A. If it developed into anything he should know, as it did develop, he would know, and he did know, and knew everything.

Q. Did you think it was correct to make overtures looking to the important arrangement that ensued with J. P. Morgan & Company without the knowledge of the chairman of your board of directors? A. I did so, and without the knowledge of any of the members of our board, because I did not know whether anything would come of it or not. If nothing came of it, it would not have been a matter of public gossip. If anything did, they would be advised.

Q. But Mr. Freedman knew about it? A. No. I am guessing that that was the matter I had in mind.

Q. Was it more prudent to confide these matters to Mr. Freedman than it was to Mr. Belmont? A. No. Mr. Freedman would not be as directly affected as Mr. Belmont.

Q. Did you assume that Freedman would know what you referred to as veiled imprudence? A. No. In fact, I don't remember what I had in mind when I wrote that phrase.

Q. You testified this morning, when I was questioning you on the memorandum of Engineer Turner, to the effect that the city did not need any money in 1915 for construction, that the company sustained no loss through this unnecessary borrowing, and through the adverse interest charge that was run up against the company, did you not? A. If there had been unnecessary borrowing, I testified to that —

Q. When I say "unnecessary borrowing," I am referring to the statement of Turner in his memorandum to you, that no borrowing was necessary. A. Well, no borrowing occurred as a matter of fact.

Q. But thirty millions of your bonds were issued to J. P. Morgan & Company? A. Not until December of that year.

Q. And the proceeds were placed on deposit with Morgan & Company to your credit? A. Yes.

Q. It has been testified to here that there is already charged to construction account, as of December 31st, interest losses, as I recall, the figure amounting to about $3,800,000. That is, out of an expenditure of only a little over twenty-six and a half million dollars on account of the fifty-eight contributions you were to make. It has been also testified that this arises through the fact that you were paying 5 per cent. on your bonds — in fact, 5⅜ on your bonds sold to Morgan & Company, and are receiving 2 and 2½ per cent. on your balances with Morgan & Company. That is the source of these interest charges. I understood you to testify this morning that it was not 2½ per cent. you received on the proceeds of your bonds, but 6 per cent.

(Chairman Thompson takes the Chair.)

A. You are right. The city receives the benefit of the 2½ per cent. we receive on balances with Morgan, and we receive 6 per cent as part of our contribution to the construction fund equipment from the date that we deposit the proceeds of the sale of bonds.

Q. In other words, when you mean that there is no loss on that, you mean the city pays you six per cent. on the amount of your contribution to construction? A. I mean that that is the amount that that fund receives as part of our contribution to the fifty-eight million.

Q. As a matter of fact, you pay for your money 5 3-8 per cent? A. Five and three-eighths per cent.

Q. So that every dollar that you don't need, and which is placed to your credit with Morgan & Company, and becomes the subject of interest, you are not only indemnified by the city for your losses in interest, but receive a profit by virtue of the city's six per cent? A. Five-eighths of one per cent from the date of the deposit of that money.

Q. Does that explain why you have on deposit with Morgan & Company on, I think, February 5, some fifty-four million dollars?

A. No. We have nothing to do with the term that Morgan & Company call the bonds, except as per the allotment agreed upon between the Public Service Commission and ourselves, when they limited the time to January 1, 1917. We agreed on an allotment, so much for the four years; the first year, seventy-eight million —

Chairman Thompson.— That is all in the evidence.

Q. So that you were not at all under the necessity of doing what the city is doing, that is to say, avoid the accumulation of large unused balances in connection with construction work? A. It was a matter that our construction — outside of the yearly allotments —

Q. You are at the mercy of the operation of your contract? A. Yes, if you wish to put it that way.

Mr. Colby.— I think the Chairman is not confining the Committee's inquiry to —

Chairman Thompson.— When you enter into a contract, that is an act of yours, you know.

Mr. Shonts.— And there can't be any blame, unless the contract is wrong.

Chairman Thompson.— Then you are entitled to credit. Take it either way you want. The Chair —

Mr. Shonts.— The Chair — the ruling is very fair.

By Mr. Colby:

Q. In other words, by virtue of the city's obligation to pay you this six per cent, the more money that you uselessly pile up at Morgan & Company, and the more interest, the more the differential of interest against the Interborough, the more profits you make? A. Out of that particular fund, that is true, sir.

Q. In the negotiation for these dual contracts, you were not averse to using any influential person, or availing yourself of any influential introduction that you could get, were you? A. We were not averse to using any legitimate means, whether person or by argument.

Q. And paying for that, if you felt it was valuable? A. We had to pay for the use of people.

Chairman Thompson.— Right there, I want to ask a question.

Mr. Shonts.— Yes, sir.

Chairman Thompson.— You took Towns down there to introduce you to Mayor Gaynor?

Mr. Shonts.— Yes, sir.

Chairman Thompson.— Now, would you think that if you had met a friend of yours up in the club that knew Mayor Gaynor just as well as Mr. Towns knew him, who wasn't a lawyer, would you think you would be justified in paying that man $5,000 to take you down and introduce you to the mayor?

Mr. Shonts.— I have refreshed my recollection since yesterday. Mr. Towns came and spent many days here studying our problem.

Chairman Thompson.— Well, would you think any other man, if he did —

Mr. Shonts.— Yes. That man should have been compensated the same as Mr. Towns was. We had occupied his time and energy.

Chairman Thompson.— Suppose there was somebody in the City Hall that knew him, the secretary?

Mr. Shonts.— I would not use an officer, I would not think —

Chairman Thompson.— You would think that would be wrong?

Mr. Shonts.— That would not be good ethics. If he had had a voice in it himself —

Chairman Thompson.— As I understood, Mr. Towns did not enter into the conversation at all.

Mr. Shonts.— Well, he had his talk before.

Chairman Thompson.— He had seen him before; fixed it up?

Mr. Shonts.— He had arranged the conference.

Chairman Thompson.— When you actually went down there, he simply went with you, and introduced you, and sat in a wagon?

Mr. Shonts.— I find it was not a wagon. I find it was an

automobile. And then I used the force of my arguments for
what they were worth.

Mr. Colby.— I will state, Mr. Chairman, that Mr. Dawson has
computed the interest paid by the city on the construction account
as revealed to us by the auditor, which shows only the expenditure
of some $26,000,000, that the city, in order to save the Inter-
borough from loss on that account, had already paid $2,500,000.
That is computed on the Morgan bank account alone.

Chairman Thompson.— Do you think his figures are correct
about that, Mr. Witness?

Mr. Shonts.— Why, I have not any way of guessing.

Mr. Colby.— Mr. Dawson also figures at the same time the city
is paying this $2,500,000 in order to make up this deficiency of
interest returns —

Mr. Shonts.— Is that after deducting the two and one-half per
cent, Mr. Dawson?

Mr. Dawson.— Yes.

Mr. Colby.— That the company derives from the city's payment a profit of $312,500 on the Morgan balance. I am not ask-
ing the witness questions on this point, because it has been fully
covered by the auditor, and by accounts described —

Chairman Thompson.—All the facts are already in the record.

Mr. Colby — Which are already exhibits.

Chairman Thompson.— It is simply computation. We will
take it for what it is worth. They say that figures don't lie, but —

Senator Towner.— They are sometimes misleading.

By Mr. Colby:
Q. What other influential persons besides Mr. Towns and Mr.
Grout did you have the aid of in connection with this negotiation?
A. I don't remember anyone else.
Q. You would say there were no others? A. Well, I don't
remember any one else.
Q. Could you refresh your memory? A. You don't mean

after our negotiations ended, and we thought we were out of it, when Mr. Ray came in, and Seth Low, and those men.

Q. I mean persons employed. A. Retained, no.

Q. I don't mean retained. That is an expression that is applied to lawyers, more particularly. I mean persons recompensed or compensated for their auxiliary aid to you by way of introduction or personal influence. A. I don't remember any one else.

Q. Do you remember any payments or gratuities given on this score? A. No.

Q. Or given on other reasons that were assigned, and in reality for this reason? A. No, sir.

Q. You said yesterday that Mr. Gaynor had been making some rather derogatory statements about the company, and about its officers prior to your visit to him. Do you recall making that statement? A. Yes.

Q. Do you recall what the mayor had been saying? A. That was in the fall preceding his campaign for mayor, and it was in certain magazines, the Outlook, and I remember of reading them in the magazine at the time. I did not remember the name of the magazine. Mr. Quackenbush tells me —

Q. Do you recall he said " The city is being over-reached by a few financiers of great ability?" A. Well, it was in — I don't remember his exact language, Mr. Counsel. I know it was very strongly condemnatory of ourselves, and in fact, so strongly condemnatory that some people said it was the platform upon which he was running for mayor.

Chairman Thompson.— He even called you rascals after you went and talked to him that time?

Mr. Thompson.— Well, I think that's true.

By Mr. Colby:

Q. Do you remember the late Mayor Gaynor saying, " I never expected to see the city officials give their aid to safely entrenching and perpetuating such baneful financing as this?" A. I don't remember that. Maybe that is the way he said it. I don't remember his exact language. I remember the fact that he did write articles, and it was in the public press and in the maga-

zines, strongly condemning us. And since the Chairman refreshes
my recollection, I think he called us rascals after I saw him.
I do remember that after my first — when I called to make what
you may call the courtesy call, that is to say, he was inaugurated
as mayor, and I as the chief executive of the most important
property the city owned, and as tenant of that property, I
thought it my duty to call upon him and pay my respects, and I
did so. I remember I went in with a feeling of fear and
trembling, as to the kind of reception I would have, and he
afterwards said he didn't see horns growing on me, or something
of that sort.

Chairman Thompson.— You are a pretty good-looking fellow,
I think, Mr. Shonts.

Mr. Shonts.— I thank you.

By Mr. Colby:

Q. Did you call Mr. Towns' attention to an expression used
by Mayor Gaynor, to the effect that he had too long written and
spoken against such damnable rescality to turn about now and
ally himself, as mayor, with these people? A. I don't remember
all the conversation with Mr. Towns, and more than that, I
wanted him to familiarize himself with the subway situation, as
we regarded it, so that he could discuss it fairly and impartially.
And we had no favors that were not based on a square statement
of facts, and that was the reason I told Mayor Gaynor in this
talk, that we opened our books to him, that we had nothing to
conceal. and if there was anybody he had confidence in that he
would send down there, we would be glad to show everything
we had.

Q. Did you open your books showing preliminary expenses
for proposed subways? A. We opened our books, and gave
instructions to show the engineers that came everything we had,
and I suppose they did.

Q. Well, did you tell him that bonuses to officers were to be
charged to construction? A. I think this antedated that by
some years.

Q. Did you tell him that the city would obtain no returns

from the subway operation until 1948, at the earliest? A. I did not tell him that, because I don't believe it.

Q. You know it is the testimony of the city's chief accountant? A. I read what Mr. MacInnes said the other day, but so far as the Interborough end is concerned, and that is the only end I am talking from, I very greatly differ from him.

Q. Did you intimate to him that the railroad having made an agreement to contribute $58,000,000 to construction, would possibly charge ten or twelve millions of unanticipated expenditures to that account, and the city would have to make it up? A. I could not very well have told him those things —

Q. Well, they are the truth, are they not? A. — because they did not develop until years after this conversation. I am not a prophet.

Q. But you were writing to Mr. J. P. Morgan, Jr., at that time, unfolding to him the fact that with the preferential which the city would guarantee on the present subway, the priority of the present subway, in receiving a six per cent. return on construction contribution, and other charges, that there would be built up a preferential of $14,568,000 ahead of the city's participation? A. I could not be writing that to J. P. Morgan at the time I was talking to Mayor Gaynor, because then Mayor Gaynor was dead.

Q. You did not intimate to the mayor any of these possibilities? A. No, sir, because they didn't exist at that time. We had not got that far along. We were talking on the broad principles of policy.

Q. You told him you were willing to contribute to the cost of construction? A. I told him — they had before them, as I think I testified this morning, all together three, I think, of our propositions, where we offered to build what we thought was a normal extension with — altogether with private capital.

Q. You did not tell him that your Vice-president and General Manager were drawing very substantial sums, running into thousands per annum, as revenue on inventions made in the company's shops and perfected there, did you? A. I didn't tell him that, because he had the general returns of what we were making before him. That included anything that he was at that time drawing. I don't know what the general manager was drawing at that time.

Q. Did you reveal to him in discussing the company's offer to expend a certain amount on construction, that you would include nearly $200,000 spent to counsel as part of your construction? A. How could I? The same answer applies.

Q. You discussed with the mayor? A. I discussed with the mayor the general principles involved, as to whether the city should enter upon an era of building municipally owned and operated railways, or whether they would allow us to build normal extensions with our own money, or whether they wanted us as a partner in the dual or triborough contracts with the city. I think the triborough, if I recollect that right, was altogether city's money. I think it was the dual contract where we first entered into the question of a combination of private capital and city's money. I think I can state, in a half dozen sentences, if it would clear the situation; we made three, as I recollect, three distinct offers, what we called normal extensions —

Q. What was the first offer? A. It was in 19 — early in 1909, and that was only a two-track down the West Side, two-track down the East Side, and that was promptly, and as, in the light of events, properly rejected.

Q. Were you going to build that with your own money? A. We were going to build that with our own money. Then we offered to build four tracks.

Q. When? A. Later in the year.

Q. What year? A. 1909, when financial conditions began to get a little better. At first we had no — we took a chance, we had no way of assuring ourselves of getting our money for the two-track, and that is the reason we limited ourselves to such a small outlet. When we got into the four-track, it was after I had seen the Morgans, and they had agreed to stand behind us with their associates. Then I offered to build a four-track up the West Side, and the East Side —

Q. Still with the company's money? A. Still with private money. That was rejected. Then, in the meantime, I offered — independent of the subway. I offered to third-track Second, Third and Ninth Avenue Elevated, to give some relief, an estimated cost, I think, of $30,000,000, and that we nearly closed on once, but finally it became merged in our third, and as I remember, our last offer with private capital, which was of December 5, 1910, and that was four tracks down the East Side and four tracks up the West Side, a line up White Plains road, one up to Jerome avenue, a new tunnel under the river, and a four-track extension of the present subway from its present terminus up to Nostrand avenue. I think that was our proposition of December 5, with private capital. That was the proposition, Mr. Counsel, that we supposed we had agreed upon with the Public Service Commission. Mr. Willcox told me they had decided to accept it, with slight modifications, and we sent it to the Public Service Commission.

Q. Now you have outlined your offers. A. Up to one more. They went over to the Board of Estimate and Apportionment, and that board appointed a committee with Mr. McAneny as chairman. That is how he came into the situation to discuss our proposition of December 5, 1910, with private capital. Finally that was refused, and I think — such conditions were made as we felt would bankrupt us, and I think it was on June 27, 1911, that I finally wrote the declination that put us out of it. Then the Triborough was working, and while this Triborough was working, I was trying to convince the city officials that it was wrong in principle, that it would cost the taxpayers an enormous amount of money, that it would not give as good distributing facilities as our last plan that I had suggested.

Q. You were afraid of municipal competition? A. Municipal ownership and operation, plus a two-cent fare for the people.

Q. That is what you feared? A. Of course. And municipal ownership and operation. Of course municipal ownership is all right, because the city owns our present subway, and it will own all these subways, and will get them for nothing. Then, only one more proposition. We finally were brought back into the situation when — after the city decided, as it had a perfect right to, although we fought it and we advertised it, and you will find we spent over a hundred thousand dollars there in public advertising, if you want to investigate, showing why in our judgment, the city was making a great mistake to agree upon a dual system, because

from our standpoint, it was uneconomic, it was financially uneconomic. We recognized the right of the city officials, however, to
be the judge of the city's policy. When they decided that, while
it might be, as it was —

Q. Just let me ask you. A. — uneconomic financially, they
took other elements into consideration, sociological elements, distribution of population and all that —

Q. Just a moment. I don't want you to talk all day. A. In two
minutes I can finish, and I am through.

Q. I want to ask you, at that point. A. I will stop right there.

Q. If you recognize the right of the city — A. To shape the
policy.

Q. — to pursue its own policy of operation, as well as ownership, why did you go to these great lengths to obtain friendly
access to the Mayor, why did you employ at such cost to the company, and eventually to the city, these men to assist you in your
effort to dissuade the city from pursuing its policy? A. You
injected one word I have not admitted. We have not admitted
their right to — outside of the Public Service Law — to operate.
The Public Service Law regulates them, as far as operation.

Q. Do you contend the city has no right to operate? A. Under
the Public Service Commission Law as expressed therein.

Q. You mean the city has no right to operate the subway which
it owns? A. Not when it leases it to a tenant, and requires the
tenant to live up to certain regulations, and the tenant complies
with all the conditions in that indenture. The city has a right, but
not in cases of terms set forth in its own indenture with a tenant,
but outside of that. We are living up to all the obligations that
the city sets forth in its lease to us. Outside of that, the Legislature of this State has passed what is called the Public Service
Commissions Law. and created the Public Service Commission
body, and that body has jurisdiction to almost the remotest detail
of our operation. They can schedule our trains, they can do
almost anything, and the owners of this company have no financial responsibility in it.

Q. But they don't? A. Yes, they do. I beg your pardon.

Q. Who? A. The Public Service Commission.

Q. Mr. Craven? A. No. He is the chief engineer.

Q. Did Mr. McCall harrass you with his regulations? A. Mr. McCall issued regulations that were — I would not say they were so drastic as to ruin us, but they were very drastic.

Q. Weren't you very much pleased with Mr. McCall's appointment as Public Service Commissioner? A. We were not unduly elated. We have not been unduly elated over any person there yet.

Q. What did you do to bring about Mr. McCall's appointment? A. Not a thing in the world, or any other man who had been appointed to that Public Service Commission. My policy has been we can get along with any set of men that are sent there, as long as we have got our constitutional rights, and that is the only protection that we finally have left, in the last analysis.

Q. Were you consulted about Mr. McCall's appointment? A. No, sir.

Q. Did you hear it discussed before its announcement? A. I suppose so. I suppose I hear everybody who is ever a candidate discussed. I don't remember of it now. I suppose I did.

Q. Were any of your attorneys active in connection with Mr. McCall's consideration? A. Not to my knowledge, and so far as that was concerned, there was an attorney that was active for the removal of a man, that I knew nothing about.

Q. I didn't ask about that. A. I know you didn't. I am volunteering it, because I might as well. I knew nothing about it until it was all over.

Q. Now, I call your attention to your letter to Mayor Gaynor of July 5, 1910, taken from your files. A. Yes.

Q. The question of gross operating revenue, the question of net profits, how calculated, how arrived at, you set forth very fully there? A. Yes. Isn't that the proposition where we offered to divide net profits — give the city the whole net profits for the first five years, and then divide it afterwards?

Q. That is right. But you didn't think there would be many profits the first five years, did you? A. I don't remember now what our estimates were on that.

Q. You are not going to get any profits the first five years on this present subway, are you? A. I think so.

Q. The first five years you didn't think the city would have a rofit on this, did you? A. Not on the first three years, perhaps.

We thought before the five years was out, they would. I will have to refresh my recollection on that.

Q. I notice you mention as elements of deduction in arriving at the net profits here, the actual annual charges of the company for carrying the cost of equipment, providing sinking fund, general and administration expenses, interest on bonds, to defray cost of construction, and so forth; if you didn't have in your mind the operation of those various items, you at least had those items in your mind when you talked to Mayor Gaynor? A. Oh, absolutely.

Q. And you didn't acquaint him with the possibility — or, let me put the question differently; did the possibility occur to you? A. What is the date of that letter?

Q. July 5, 1910. The possibility didn't occur to you that your offer of contribution on the subject of construction might turn out to be an obligation by the city of $12,000,000, did you? A. No. But I knew it would be a substantial sum. It always is, when you get into a large figure like that.

Q. On the present dual contracts, it is a fact that your contribution turns out to be a city contribution? A. No.

Q. To the extent of ten or twelve million? A. Whatever the interest is during the period of construction.

Q. And whatever the depletion of the actual funds devoted to construction may be, under fifty-eight million? A. Yes, whatever is allowed. The contract covers all those items, and I have not them all in my mind.

Q. In this letter of July 5, I see that you say, " Now that the city's debt limit has been enlarged, and self-supporting subway obligations are no longer included as a part of the city's debt limitation, the advantage to the city of construction with private capital is no longer apparent?" A. Yes.

Q. You believed that at the time? A. Yes, I was led to believe by our counsel, that until the new legislative act, that the city could not issue any securities, and if there was any extensions, it ought to be with private capital, and that is one reason we were trying so hard to do our duty in the situation by offering to build with private capital. After that law was passed, I understood the city was at a larger debt limit, and therefore not dependent on private capital.

(Senator Towner takes the chair.)

Q. In these items that are charged to construction, already there is a charge of some $63,000 paid to attorneys for the Admiral Realty Company. Do you know who those attorneys were? A. Yes. If you will let me answer it —

Q. No, I ask you, do you know who those attorneys were? A. Only in part. I don't remember it all, because Mr. Nicoll handled that, and he can tell you all about it. There were three suits, one by the B. R. T. and one by ourselves and one by Hearst. Those three suits were joined in one suit, in order that every angle might be presented to the court of last resort.

Q. You mean you brought one of these? A. And the constitutional question should be tested out, because it was clearly written in the proposition from the bankers that that had to be tested out by the court of last resort before they would furnish any money. We didn't want to issue bonds until we knew that they would be declared legal or not, and certainly the city didn't.

Q. You say one of these suits was brought by the Interborough? A. Instigated by ourselves.

Q. Which was? A. I think the Admiral Realty.

Q. They instigated the suit? A. That was done by Mr. Nicoll, and he can tell you all about it; I only have a general knowledge of it.

Q. Was it your suit from its inception? A. I don't know; I have only a general knowledge, not a very clear idea.

Mr. Delancey Nicoll.— The suit was brought in the interest of the company.

Mr. Colby.— In its inception?

Mr. Nicoll.— Yes.

Mr. Shonts.— He can tell you all about it. I trusted that to him. We wanted to test out that question.

Mr. Nicoll.— The first suit, Mr. Colby, was brought by Hays and Herschfield, with the Admiralty Realty Company as a taxpayer, and directed against the contract entered into between the city and the Brooklyn Rapid Transit, which was the first dual

contract made. That is the first participation contract. That suit
went through to the Appellate Division. You have probably read
the opinion. Now, when that suit was pending, at the time when
these negotiations were concluded, and Mr. Coleman represented
the Public Service Commission, Mr. Marshall and Mr. Hays
wanted to bring the new suit you are speaking about now for the
purpose of testing the questions required to be decided by the
Court of Appeals before there could be any bond issue.

Mr. Colby.— Let me ask you at that point. Is it at that point
that the attorneys for the Admiral Realty Company entered into
the employment of the Interborough Rapid Transit Company?

Mr. Nicoll.— Oh, no. They had already been acting at my
instance, for the purpose of testing these questions. They came
around to see me, Mr. Herschfield, I think, and Mr. Wolf, as his
partner, and told me Coleman proposed they should have this new
suit for the purpose of testing all these questions, and asked me
if I had any objection, and I told them to go ahead.

Acting Chairman Towner.— Would you like Mr. Shonts to
stand aside?

Mr. Colby.— No. I am willing to take Mr. Nicholl's statement
informally in this matter. There has been a considerable amount
of difficulty in getting at the facts in this matter, Mr. Nicoll.
Have you any objection to testifying on the subject?

Mr. Nicoll.— No, I have no objection to testifying at all on
the subject. I have this difficulty, Mr. Colby. I would have to
have a resolution by the Board of Directors before I could give
testimony here with regard to my conduct. A lawyer cannot
testify without the consent of his client.

Mr. Colby.— I appreciate that fact, and that is why I have
avoided seeking in the first instance testimony on any matters —

Mr. Shonts.— I think there would be no trouble about that.

Mr. Nicoll.— There would be no trouble about that, but I
would like — if you want to have me as a witness, I think I will
have a resolution passed first.

Mr. Colby.— Let me — there are some other matters I want to ask you in this connection, Mr. Shonts.

By Mr. Colby:

Q. You say that J. P. Morgan & Company stipulated that all questions affecting the validity of contracts or constitutionality, should be first tested in the courts? A. Yes, before our contract would be valid.

Q. And a final and authoritative decision on those questions?

Mr. Nicoll.— That is not only so — if you will excuse me for interrupting, to clear it up — there was an agreement between the president and the city from the very beginning that these whole matters should be tested.

Mr. Colby.— That is the point on which I wish to question Mr. Shonts.

Mr. Nicoll.— He already testified to that in the Continental Securities suit. All of this was brought out by Mr. Hodge.

Mr. Shonts.— It may be in the printed letter that was distributed. Maybe I could introduce it now. I don't know that you will want, it, Mr. Counsel, but I will show it to you, because it was meant to cover the very points you have in mind — I think you have in mind. (Witness takes paper from his pocket.) I see I have a lot of memoranda on the back, which you don't want.

Mr. Colby.— I won't look at the matter on it.

Mr. Shonts.—All right. You look at the letter, and I will send you a copy of it. I have been using it as a memorandum. (Witness hands paper to counsel.)

Mr. Colby.— You have no objection to my reading this?

Mr. Shonts.— Read it in the minutes.

Mr. Colby.— Mr. Chairman, the witness hands me a printed copy of a letter addressed by him as President to the Chairman of the Public Service Commission for the First District, Mr. William R. Willcox, dated February 27, 1912.

"INTERBOROUGH RAPID TRANSIT COMPANY

"165 Broadway, New York.

"THEODORE P. SHONTS, *President and Chairman of Executive Committee.*

"HON. WM. R. WILLCOX, *Chairman, Public Service Commission for First District,* 154 *Nassau street, New York city.*

"Dear Sir.— In connection with the proposal of this company regarding the subway and elevated lines and improvements described therein, I beg to state that the statement ment' marked "Schedule A," hereto attached, shows how the average annual income referred to in paragraph (b), section 12, of the proposal, under the heading "Pooling of Receipts and Payments Therefrom," is ascertained.

"Further, while it is not necessary to embody it in our proposal, I beg to advise you that we have informed our bankers that the city and the company reserve the right to submit, either severally or jointly, to the proper court the determination of any and all questions regarding the legal validity and sufficiency of the formal contract to be made. Therefore, the city and the company should within at least sixty days after due execution and delivery of the said formal contract, begin such proceedings as either or both may deem desirable or necessary for the foregoing purposes.

"Very respectfully,

"T. P. SHONTS, *President.*"

"INCL."

Mr. Shonts.— I have sent for a clean copy for you.

Mr. Colby.— Thank you.

y Mr. Colby:

Q. Do I understand you to say in this letter, or to mean, that he city concurred with you and agreed that this suit should be rought? A. Yes, sir.

Q. Who on behalf of the city made that agreement? A. The Chairman of the Public Service Commission.

Q. Anyone else? A. And, I understand, Mr. McAneny, Chairman of the Special Committee from the Board of Estimate and Apportionment.

Q. Are you certain as to the last? A. No, I am not certain. That is my impression. It was a matter of general conference.

Q. Anyone else? A. I think we all agreed, it was in our conferences.

Q. The reason I am questioning you somewhat earnestly at that point is because, if I understand correctly, Mr. Prendergast has denied that any consent to such litigation was ever given on behalf of the city? A. Well, there were many conferences at which Mr. Prendergast was not present. He may not have known.

Q. You say, "Therefore, the city after due execution and delivery of the formal contract." Did you mean to say that the execution and delivery of these contracts was all conditional upon arrival at a final decision in this action? A. Yes.

Q. An that although formally executed and although formally delivered, the agreement was tentative until that decision — A. Yes.

Q. — should have been delivered? A. If that decision had been hostile, the whole thing would have fallen down.

Q. If the decision was adverse to your contentions, the agreement would have fallen? A. Yes, sir.

Q. And there would have been no dual contract?

Mr. Nicoll.— It was very close. The court decided by four to three, and Judge Werner wrote the dissenting opinion.

Q. I would like also the statement marked " Schedule A." A. It is on the back of it.

(Schedule "A" is as follows) :

" Schedule A."

Showing average annual income of the Interborough Rapid Transit Company from operation of existing subway lines and equipment for the two years ending June 30, 1910 and 1911:

Year ending June 30, 1910 and 1911:

Gross operating revenue........	$13,932,505	$14,353,206
Operating expenses	4,756,449	5,929,653
Net operating revenue.....	$9,176,056	$8,423,553
Taxes......................	225,280	268,438
Income from operation.....	$8,950,776	$8,155,115
Interest and sinking fund on city bonds	2,181,204	2,254,692
Resulting net income.....	$6,769,572	$5,900,423

The average sum — as set forth in paragraph
(b) of section 12 of the company's proposal
of February, 1912, under the heading " Pooling of Receipts and Payments Therefrom "—
to be paid to the company during each of the
49 years of the proposed lease, is.......... $6,335,000

"Interborough Rapid Transit Company,
"By T. P. Shonts,
"President."

Mr. Shonts.— That is just those two years, 1910 and 1911,
the average.

By Mr. Colby:

Q. Will you give me a copy? A. I will give you a clean
copy, yes, Mr. Counsel.

Q. Were the attorneys of any of the three sets of plaintiffs in
the suit that we have been discussing paid by the Interborough,
except the attorneys for the Admiral Realty Company? A. No,
I don't think so.

Mr. Nicoll.— The other attorneys were Mr. Schoen, representing Mr. Hopper, and I have forgotten who represented Ryan
over there in Brooklyn.

Mr. Shonts.— We recalled among ourselves the B. R. T. suit.

By Mr. Colby:

Q. The Interborough Rapid Transit Company had nothing to do with the institution or prosecution or the course of the Hopper suit? A. No, or of the Ryan suit, until, as I understand it, they all merged.

Mr. Nicoll.— They were consolidated.

Q. You had nothing to do with the employment of the attorneys of either of the other two defendants or their compensation or in directing their course? A. No, sir.

Q. And your activity was entirely confined to the Admiral Realty Company?

Mr. Nicoll.— Right.

Q. And the only attorneys receiving recompense from the Interborough were the attorneys representing the Admiral Realty Company? A. That is right.

Q. Did you make an agreement to pay the attorneys of the Admiral Realty Company, or did Mr. Nicoll? A. Mr. Nicoll.

Q. Did he fix the amount of their compensation? A. He approved it.

Q. Well, I suppose they fixed it, but you left it to him for adjustment? A. We always do.

Q. And upon his approval you paid it? A. Yes.

Q. And charged it to construction account? A. I had nothing to do with that, but I don't know how it has been charged. The vouchers show.

(Chairman Thompson takes the chair.)

By Mr. Colby:

Q. Did the National City Bank have any representative on your Board in accordance with the suggestion of your letter to Mr. Freedman? A. That all fell through.

Q. Or the First National Bank? A. That all fell through. Neither Morgan, the National City or the First National, although it was agreed at one time, understood, that they were to.

Here is the clean sheet, Mr. Counsel. (Referring to printed letter of February 27, 1912.)

Q. Thank you. A. Some time, when it is convenient, I wish you would clean up that Miami matter.

Q. The participation offered to you in Mr. Freedman's letter in the stock of the Miami Copper Company, you didn't avail yourself of? A. I didn't.

Q. You have refreshed your recollection by examination of your file? A. That was shown a little later on, in that same memorandum.

Q. Did you know Mr. Gardiner M. Lane? A. Yes, sir.

Q. How long had you known him? A. Oh, I had known Mr. Lane, maybe, for twelve of fifteen years.

Q. How would you describe him, not in his personal appearance but in his standing and character? A. He was a member of the firm of Lee, Higginson & Company, who sold bonds. They had sold many of our bonds. He was a man of very excellent repute.

Q. The firm of Lee, Higginson & Company is one of the largest banking firms in the east? A. I think one of the largest in Boston, I don't know how that compares with the east.

Q. Is it not the correspondent of J. P. Morgan & Company in Boston? A. I think that the firms are very closely related.

Q. Did you ever meet Colonel Thomas Wentworth Higginson? A. Yes.

Q. Was he at any time a member of the firm of Lee, Higginson & Company? A. I suppose that is the one I know, Colonel Higginson, whom I have always regarded as really the head of Lee, Higginson & Company, the active head.

Q. He is a man who is universally respected, is he not? A. Yes, he is.

Q. Mr. Gardiner M. Lane had been for many years his partner? A. Yes, so I understand.

Q. Don't you know it to be a fact that he was a man, in his lifetime, of great business and social prominence in Boston? A. Mr. Lane?

Q. Yes. A. I knew nothing about his social position. I imagine he would be, because he was a cultured gentleman.

24

Q. A man of the very highest type, one might say? A. I would regard him so.

Q. Who suggested that he become a member of the Board of your company? A. He was a member of the Board when I came here, so I don't know.

Q. When did he resign as a member of the Board? A. Well, I have not the date in my mind. I think in 1914.

Mr. Colby.— Mr. Fisher, can you refresh the witness' mind as to the date of Mr. Lane's resignation?

Mr. Fisher.— Yes, sir.

(Mr. Fisher examines minute books.)

Mr. Shonts.— I think he died in 1914, and I think this was shortly before his death.

Mr. Fisher.— May 13, 1914.

Mr. Colby.— On May 13, 1914?

Mr. Fisher.— Yes.

Mr. Colby.— Do you know why he resigned as a director of your company?

Mr. Shonts.— He told me on account of ill-health.

Mr. Colby.— Were there other resignations at that time, or right about that time?

Mr. Shonts.— Mr. Read resigned not many months from then, but I don't remember the exact month.

Chairman Thompson.— Isn't it possible to tell the exact dates of these resignations? Can't somebody supply us? Don't spend time on it.

Mr. Shonts.— They got Mr. Lane's.

Chairman Thompson.— May 13, 1914. That is already in the record.

(Mr. Fisher examines minute books.)

Mr. Fisher.— Mr. Read's resignation was accepted December 31, 1913.

Mr. Colby.— When was it proffered?

Mr. Fisher.— It was dated December 29, 1913.

Chairman Thompson.— When did Mr. Young resign?

Mr. Colby.— He did not resign.

Mr. Fisher.— He was not re-elected at the annual meeting.

Chairman Thompson.— When did his time expire, December 31?

Mr. Fisher.— No, sir; his time expired at the annual meeting; I don't remember which year.

Chairman Thompson.— When does your fiscal year end? Can you tell that?

Mr. Fisher.— June 30, and the meeting is in September; so I presume he was not re-elected in September.

Chairman Thompson.— His term ran out in December, 1913?

Mr. Shonts.— Nineteen hundred and thirteen or 1914.

Mr. Fisher.— I don't know.

Mr. Shonts.— Nineteen hundred and fourteen, it must have been.

Chairman Thompson.— No, I think it was 1913.

Mr. Shonts.— Maybe; I am not sure.

Mr. Quackenbush.— He resigned before his term expired.

Chairman Thompson.— Who?

Mr. Quackenbush.— Mr. Read.

Chairman Thompson.— We are talking about Mr. Young. I say 1913, and the president says 1914. We will find out which one of us knows most about this business.

Mr. Shonts.— I would not want to go against anything you specialized in.

Mr. Fisher.— Must have been 1913, because I don't find him present at any meetings in 1914.

Mr. Colby.— When is the date of your fiscal meeting?

Mr. Fisher.— It is in September.

Mr. Shonts.— It is in September.

Mr. Colby.— When was Mr.— was Mr. Lane's resignation held without action for some time after it had been proffered?

Mr. Fisher.— He was present in 1913, so it was in the annual meeting of 1913 he went out.

Mr. Shonts.— Can you tell the date from there of Mr. Lane's resignation, how long we had it before it was acted upon?

Mr. Fisher.— Mr. Lane's resignation was dated May 11, 1914. It was accepted May 13, 1914.

By Mr. Colby:

Q. Was there any reason for Mr. Read's resignation, that he stated? A. I don't think he stated any. He simply resigned.

Q. Had there been any differences of opinion between you and Mr. Lane and Mr. Read prior to the resignations of these — prior to their resignations? A. There had been two matters that our minds had not met on. And two matters in which Mr. Read was interested — one which Mr. Lane was interested in. The two matters in which Mr. Read was interested was the Ward & Gow contract, and the suggestion I made, to making a deal with Mr. Stevens, to superintend our third-tracking and other work of the elevated nature. And with Mr. Lane, it was confined to the third-tracking and elevated improvements.

Q. The proposed agreement with Mr. Stevens? A. The proposed agreement with Mr. Stevens, yes.

Q. Who is Mr. Stevens? A. Mr. Stevens is an engineer who had 17 years' training under Mr. James J. Hill. He had built the Great Northern over the Rocky Mountains, and did other great engineering work.

Q. Had he been closely associated with you? A. I had taken him with me as chief engineer to Panama, where we had been closely associated for something over two years.

Q. Had you had any prior association with him? A. No.

Chairman Thompson.— Pull that window down.

(Window opened and then closed.) I must ask that we do not smoke any more. We will try to keep this fresh air.

By Mr. Colby:

Q. He had lived with you for two years in Panama? A. Yes.

Q. And since — did he come back with you? A. He came back soon after I did. He left the Great Northern, however, before he went with me, and went with the Rock Island.

Q. Immediately after? A. Left the Great Northern, went from the Great Northern to the Rock Island, went with me to Panama, came back shortly after I came from Panama, and became vice-president in charge of the operations of the New Haven, and then became consulting engineer.

Q. Did you have any business — A. Oh, no; he built some lines for Mr. Hill in the west after that, in the meantime.

Q. What business associations have you had with Mr. Stevens other than your association at Panama? A. No active business associations with him at all.

Q. You have had no — you have not undertaken any work together with Mr. Stevens? A. No.

Q. Is Mr. Stevens doing business individually or as a corporation? A. Well, he was doing business, both; he was doing business individually as a consulting engineer, and he had a construction company, and had a contract, I think the Harlem River contract of the present subway work.

Q. What was the name of that construction company? A. I don't know what it was. That is, I could not tell you accurately.

Q. Is it a good, solvent, going concern? A. No, it failed.

Q. When did it fail? A. It failed during the summer of 1913, when I was abroad.

Q. When you say " failed," did it go into bankruptcy? A. I understand it went into bankruptcy, through the death of its chief financial backer, Mr. Brady.

Q. Mr. Anthony Brady? A. Yes.

Chairman Thompson.— Did Stevens go along with it?

Q. No, he didn't. He is not in bankruptcy? A. No.

Q. When were these differences — when did these differences as to the Stevens agreement between you and Mr. Lane and Mr. Read first manifest themselves? A. They manifested themselves on June 24, I think it was, 1913.

Q. What occurred on that date? A. Can I tell you in a very brief way?

Q. Just answer my question. I want you to have every opportunity to answer, but I would like to direct the course of the examination. A. All right. I called the board together, because I had reserved passage for the Imperator the next day.

Q. This was on June 24th? A. Yes. I had asked the secretary to call the board together, if he could get a quorum, in view of a rumor I had heard that the Public Service Commission were about to act on a suggestion I had made to them, that I wanted to acquaint the board with what I had done, in case the Public Service Commission acted during my absence.

Q. What had you done?

Chairman Thompson.— Who did you get that rumor from?

Mr. Shonts.— I don't remember now. Just came down from some of my office force; they understood the Public Service Commission had before them the consideration of an application I had made to them. That is the first I had heard since I made it, and that was the first opportunity — first thing that caused me to take any action with regard to it.

Q. What had you done? A. I had suggested, and made an application really to the Public Service Commission that inasmuch as our contract No. 3, which is our present contract with the city — under that contract they had the right of supervision of any contracts for elevated extensions. We had the right for third-tracking. That if they would waive, inasmuch as — this, I think, I wrote in April. We had signed the agreement in March. I wanted to do something. I knew we could not do anything to promote the subway, because the initiative all rested there as to plans, specifications and awarding of contracts, in the hands of the Public Service Commission, but so far as third-tracking is concerned, the initiative rested with us, and I wanted to do something if I could to hurry matters, and get some relief in the city. I had suggested if they would waive that contracted right of theirs in regard to the supervision of the contracts so far as related to the elevated extensions, I would recommend to our board the making of a contract with Mr. Stevens, who had been associated with me at Panama, and who I knew to be an able and resourceful and experienced transportation man, upon some reasonable percentage basis, if we could agree on some, to take charge of that work.

Q. In other words, Mr. Shonts, you had asked the Public Service Commission to allow you, or the company, rather, to take the exclusive and unsupervised direction of the work of elevated extension? A. Yes.

Q. Although under the terms of the contract with the city there was a reservation in favor of the city of advisory rights, with reference to the rights? A. That is it, exactly. My object —

Q. Just a minute. With whom had you made that arrangement? A. What arrangement?

Q. That the right reserved to the city of supervising this work would be waived? A. That is part of our contract. I had not made any arrangement it should be waived.

Q. You say you had asked that it should be waived? A. I had written the Public Service Commission a letter, and said if they would waive it I would recommend to our board the making of this sort of an arrangement with Stevens.

Chairman Thompson.— Have you a copy of that letter?

Mr. Shonts.— Yes.

By Mr. Colby:

Q. Did they say they would waive it? A. They never acted on it.

Chairman Thompson.— I would like to see a copy.

By Mr. Colby:

Q. To whom did you address that letter? A. The Chairman, as I addressed all matters.

Q. Mr. McCall? A. Whoever was the Chairman at that time.

Q. Wasn't Mr. McCall the Chairman? A. I have forgotten, McCall or Mr.— I suppose he was, yes. When did he come in?

Q. Well, it was McCall, wasn't it? A. Wait. We signed — yes.

Chairman Thompson.— You must have pretty good recollection on that. You had to have Mr. McCall Public Service Commissioner in order to get the contracts signed? It was an important proposition, talked about a lot. I wasn't interested, but I can remember that.

Mr. Shonts.— Even in Niagara.

Chairman Thompson.— I was in the Senate, too.

Mr. Shonts.— I am trying to recall the dates. McCall came in just before the signing of the contracts with the city, which was in March, 1913. So it was Judge McCall.

By Mr. Colby:

Q. I find here a special meeting of the board was held on June 24, 1913, at 3:30 o'clock in the afternoon. A. That is a special meeting at which I —

Q. At which you were present and in the chair? A. Yes, sir.

Q. The only entry of any business is that the contract of the elevated railroad third-tracking extensions was discussed, but no action taken? A. Now, what actually happened, I submitted the proposed contract — I had instructed Mr. Quackenbush, who is our general counsel, to prepare a contract that would be satisfactory in form.

Q. When had he handed you that contract in form. A. Oh, some days prior to this; I don't remember.

Q. When did you show it to Mr. McCall? A. I don't remember that I ever showed it to Mr. McCall.

Q. Are you willing to say that you did not show it to Mr. McCall? A. I have no recollection of showing it to Mr. McCall. That would be a matter naturally between Mr. Quackenbush and Mr. Coleman, or Mr. Coleman's assistant.

Q. But you have said that you made this application to Mr. McCall. A. I wrote a letter, which I will produce.

Q. Did you see Mr. McCall on this subject? A. I think I did speak to him about it, and tell him what was in my mind, and he suggested that I write a letter.

Q. Did he also suggest what his attitude would be? A. No, he did not.

Q. Did you not state to the Board at this meeting that the contract had received Mr. McCall's approval? A. No.

Q. Was that a fact? A. No.

Q. You had the contract with you at this meeting of June 24? A. It was produced.

Q. Was the name of Mr. Stevens in the contract? A. I think so. Yes, it must have been.

Q. Was the percentage he was to receive — A. No.

Q. — on the work stated? A. No.

Q. Was it stated by you? A. It was never agreed to.

Q. I don't say "agreed." Was it stated by you? A. No, it was not stated by me.

Q. What percentage was discussed? A. Everything from five to twenty.

Q. Did you make a recommendation? A. I did not.

Chairman Thompson.— Didn't you state to the Board the percentage could not be less than 10 per cent?

Mr. Shonts.— No, I did not.

Chairman Thompson.— That is on the record here.

Mr. Shonts.— I can't help what is on the record.

Mr. Colby.— Well, why did the — as I understand you, you were going to Europe the following day? A. Yes.

Q. You had called this special meeting of the Board? A. Yes.

Q. And it was attended by Mr. Berwind, Mr. Fisher, Mr. Freedman, Mr. Lane, your assistant, Mr. Pepperman, Mr. Pierce, Mr. Read, Mr. Sullivan, Mr. Young; Mr. Hedley was also present as, not, apparently, as a director; Mr. Quackenbush was present? A. Yes; that is all true.

Q. It was discussed and no action taken? A. It was discussed and no action taken.

Q. Despite the urgent circumstances that had impelled you to summon a special meeting of all these gentlemen? A. The only urgent —

Q. Just answer the question; that is true, isn't it? A. No action was taken, yes.

Q. No action was taken. Now, I will give you the opportunity you want. Why was no action taken? A. Because no agreement was reached.

Q. No agreement with Stevens? A. No agreement was reached among the Board.

Q. There was discussion, though? A. Yes, a very free discussion.

Q. What was said? A. One of the first things said was an inquiry, as I recollect it, was an inquiry from Mr. Berwind. I had told Mr. Quackenbush to put everything in the contract that Mr. Stevens would suggest, but it would be very easy for the Board to delete anything they did not want him to do. The first question asked was by Mr. Berwind, and he asked me what particular assistance Mr. Stevens could be in the matter of equipment, which was in the contract. My answer was that I could not see that he would be of any particular assistance, as I thought the Interborough officials led the world in both the signalling and the rolling stock. And that was the end of the discussion of equipment, it being generally understood that the equipment would be removed. That matter was removed from the proposed contract. The next thing that I remember was a question as to who was to furnish the plant. I remember Mr. Freedman took the position that in his judgment no contractor ought to be allowed to take a contract without furnishing the plant. If the company furnished the plant, it would be at the mercy of the contractor, who would have no particular interest in using it carefully and prudently and economically, and in his judgment any contractor who ever took any sort of a contract should be required to own his own plant, and so far as my judgment went, which I said then, I not only agreed to that, but I agreed that every contractor should be required to pay his own administration expenses.

Q. You think that is proper in every contract? A. Yes, to furnish his plant and pay —

Q. Tools, and pay his own administration expenses? A. Pay his own administration expenses.

Q. You think no contract should be let except on that basis? A. That is my judgment, yes. Tools, you understand, is nearly always charged up to part of the cost, and as they are destroyed they are still continued as part of the cost. The plant is different from tools; that is the point.

Q. What I am trying to get also clear is that you — is that a proper construction contract presupposes the contractor should supply the plant and pay the administration expenses involved in the execution of the work? A. His own administration expenses.

Q. And that should be covered in the Commission? A. Yes.

Q. Go on. A. After the contract was read, Mr. Read — I think Mr. Lane's testimony in that regard is exactly like that — I think Mr. Read made a motion that the contract be not entered into in that form. And the meeting divided up into groups, each one began to discuss the various elements. I saw very plainly if I wanted to dispose of that before I went to Europe, I wasn't going to sail the next day.

Q. I don't gather exactly what the difference of opinion was. Mr. Freedman thought the contractor should pay for his plant, is that so? A. Yes.

Q. Did you mean to say that Mr. Lane and Mr. Read thought the company should pay for it? A. No, I don't. They didn't think they ought to pay for it. I will tell you very frankly the impression made on my mind by Mr. Lane's remarks was that he thought that because Mr. Stevens was a friend of mine there was some interest between Lane and myself.

Q. Who thought that? A. Between Stevens and myself. That was the impression that Mr. Lane's remarks made on my mind, and it was the first —

Q. Just a moment. What remarks did Mr. Lane make? A. Remarks in regard to my friendship with Stevens, my close intimacy with him.

Chairman Thompson.— State what he said?

Mr. Shonts.— I can't.

Chairman Thompson.— In substance.

Mr. Shonts.— As near as I can recollect, he said " You are very closely related, you are great friends, are you not ? " or words to that effect, and he says, " You are urging him in here." I said " I am urging him in here only for the reasons I have stated. This is a very difficult task. I don't believe you gentlemen realize how difficult it is, extending over this city as it does." It is not like an ordinary difficult task, like the Times Square subway is now diffi- cult and dangerous, but it is confined to one site.

Chairman Thompson.— Just state what occurred at that meeting.

Mr. Shonts.— I stated a good deal of this at the meeting.

Chairman Thompson.— This statement you are now making was made in the meeting ?

Mr. Shonts.— The substance of what I am saying. This was a difficult task —-

Chairman Thompson.— This is what you stated in the meeting ?

Mr. Shonts.— This is what I stated in the meeting, and that the only purpose I had in calling them together was to acquaint them with what I had done in case the matter came up while I was away, they would understand it, that no action could be taken by them, I didn't expect any action taken by them, unless the Board of Estimate, the Public Service Commission, took action on my application, but I wanted them to be advised of the situation in case it came up while I was gone.

By Mr. Colby:

Q. Well, Mr. Shonts — A. Yes.

Q. Do you mean to imply or to state that Mr. Lane suspected the relations between you and Mr. Stevens ? A. That was the impression left on my mind, and that was the reason I asked Mr. Lane to come with me into my next office, where I had a conversa- tion with him.

Q. But no percentage, I am told, was specified in the contract ? A. No percentage was specified in the contract.

Q. The only percentage specified was between five and twenty ? A. That is true.

Q. And you have testified the only discussion was apparently a concurrent expression of belief that the contractor should furnish the plant, administration expenses, and all the expenses of executing the work? A. Yes.

Q. On what did Mr. Lane's suspicions hinge? A. I don't know. That is what I asked him into the next room for. I asked him to come into my private office, and we went in there.

Q. Just a moment, before we get into the private office. A. Yes.

Q. Was there any dissent from Mr. Read's motion that the contract be not approved? A. It was not seconded, no action was taken.

Q. Why did Mr. Read make a motion that the contract be not approved before its terms were stated? A. I don't know, I am sure.

Q. Did the contract provide that rate of commission? A. It did not.

Q. What was it Mr. Read said should not be approved? A. He was against the contract as a whole, he said.

Q. But the contract was not a whole. It was incomplete. A. It was. I will say to you very frankly that Mr. Read's and Mr. Lane's attitude was a great surprise to me. I was trying to find out what was back of it.

Q. They both treated it with suspicion? A. Yes.

Q. They were both invited into your private office? A. I invited Lane.

Q. Why not Read? A. I had known Mr. Lane much longer, and I thought that he would be more likely to tell me the truth.

Q. Did you think Mr. Read might not tell you the truth? A. No; but Mr. Read is a very sarcastic man. I didn't know what his reply might be. I thought if I asked Mr. Lane what was back of it, he would tell me.

Chairman Thompson.— Mr. Lane was a very truthful man, was he, a man you had confidence in?

Mr. Shonts.— Yes; I had confidence in Mr. Lane.

Chairman Thompson.— And in his word?

Mr. Shonts.— Yes.

By Mr. Colby:

Q. Were you afraid of Read's sarcasm? A. Well, he was and he is a very sarcastic man.

Q. Did you feel there was anything in the discussion of the contract that had disposed you to his withering fire? A. No, I did not. It might have been an imprudent and unwise thing to have paid any attention to it. I did. You sometimes do those things on impulse. I, on impulse, said to Lane, " I would like to see you."

Q. Didn't you offer John F. Stevens 10 per cent commission on this contract? A. I did not.

Q. Hadn't you had talks with Mr. John F. Stevens? A. Many of them. I told him we were after his personal supervision. I asked if we could arrange for someone else to supervise. We wanted his personal work.

Q. What did you say to Lane in your private office? A. I said, " Mr. Lane, did you mean to intimate in there that you thought I had any interest in any suggestion that I would make to this company, any personal interest "— man-to-man fashion. He said " No, Mr. Shonts, I have always had and I still have the most absolute confidence in your personal integrity, but I cannot say as much about some of your associates."

Q. Did he mention their names? A. I said, " Whom do you mean," and he said he didn't think it was necessary to go into that. I said, " If it is going to influence your conduct, we should." After some hesitancy, he did mention one name. That name I don't think it is necessary for us to mention here. The man is dead.

Q. He was a member of your board? A. He was. And I said, " Mr. Lane, I heard loose talk about that gentleman when I first came here. I have been intimately associated with him ever since I have been here. I have formed a habit years ago to treat every man as I personally found him, and I want to say to you I have never known a man to have an eye more single to the interests of the company "— he was a director —" than that gentleman, and I think you have done him a great injustice." " Well," he says, " I am very glad to hear you say so." " Well," I said, " does that clear up the situation? Is that what was

behind your peculiar action in the other room?" He said "No."
"Well," I said, "what was it?" He said, "I don't like
Stevens." I said, "What is the matter with Stevens?" He said,
"I think Stone & Webster could do this work a great deal better."
I said, "I know you know Stone & Webster. You are a Boston
man and they are a Boston firm, and I know they are good men.
You have got just as much right to stand up for them as I have
to stand up for the man I know. I don't know them personally.
I do know this man personally. I have seen him work, I have
seen his resourcefulness; I have helped to divide with him many
millions of dollars of governmental money," and, I said, "Do
you think now that either Stone or Webster or anybody connected
with them approaches in skill, in experience and skill, the transportation judgment of Mr. Stevens?" "Well," he said, "I
think they are capable of doing this work as well as anybody.
That is what I think." And he says, "Besides that, who is back
of Stevens?" "Well," I says, "that is a matter for the board
to go into, to satisfy itself of his financial standing. That is a
proper question. The only one he has ever mentioned to me is
Mr. Mellen of Pittsburgh. He has told me Mr. Mellen was a
friend of his and would back him for almost anything." "Well,"
he said, "I don't like Stevens, and I don't like this arrangement,
and I am against it; and I don't know what associations he has
got here." I said, "I don't know what associations he has here.
I know he is not only an able and resourceful engineer, I know
he is not only a skilled and experienced transportation man, but
I know he is an honest and honorable gentleman, because I have
been side by side with him under very trying conditions, and I
know he would not make — enter into any obligations here or
elsewhere that were not honorable to himself and to the profession that he represents." And I says, "So far as myself, I have
never had but one rule of life, and that is that every obligation
I ever made, or every commitment I ever made, was on the basis
of quality and price being equal before our recognized friendship, and that is the basis on which this Stevens suggestion of
mine is made to this company." I said "Why should we quarrel
about that? You have just as good a right to stand up for your
people as I have for mine. I will give up my sailing to-morrow,

and we will adjourn over." I gave up my sailing; we held the regular meeting the next day. The matter came up. Somebody suggested a committee be appointed, and I appointed a committee of five, and put both Lane and Read on it. Now, what more could a person do, to be fair?

Q. Is that all you said to Mr. Lane? A. That is the substance of what I said to him, as I remember it. '

Q. The committee never reported? A. The committee never reported. We had many meetings — I won't say many — we had two or three meetings —

Q. You were not on the committee? A. No, but without me in it to give them data — I remember some of the data now. I remember I was advised that the Pennsylvania railroad, when it came into New York city, had a hundred million proposition, had retained Westinghouse, Church, Kerr & Company, and paid them 5 per cent commission to help them prepare plans and specifications for their work, and that later on had paid the same firm 7 per cent more to supervise thirty-one millions of that same hundred millions.

Mr. Colby.— Mr. Shonts, the Chairman calls my attention to the fact that he has exceeded the usual time, and I suppose he wants to adjourn.

Chairman Thompson.— Finish that.

Mr. Shonts.— I was going to say that I found the Long Island railroad paid 10 per cent for supervision, and that the per cents ranged in proportion to the work exacted all the way from 5 up to 20 per cent.

Chairman Thompson.— Our record shows that this is the only contract ever presented either Public Service Commission, up-State or down-State, where a percentage of profit was figured. That is what our record shows to date, either up-State or down-State.

Mr. Shonts.— Then, to supplement that, I will say that Stone & Webster, the firm that Mr. Lane recommended, and Westinghouse, Church, Kerr & Company, issued notices that they would take contracts on no basis except that. I have been in favor of percentage contracts ever since I was with the Panama canal, and if I had stayed there, I would have recommended the building of that on a percentage basis, and I think we would have saved hundreds of millions of dollars.

Chairman Thompson.— We will suspend now until to-morrow morning at 11 o'clock.

Whereupon, at 4:20 o'clock P. M., an adjournment was taken to Saturday, February 19, 1916, at 11 o'clock A. M.

FEBRUARY 19, 1916

NEW YORK COUNTY LAWYERS' ASSOCIATION BOARD ROOM,
165 Broadway, New York City

The Committee was called to order, pursuant to adjournment, Chairman Thompson presiding.

Quorum present.

Chairman Thompson.— I do not want anybody to think we have not done everything we can to get another room here. We have had a man at work for four days on it. The Committee will now come to order and we will dispense with smoking.

SHONTS, THEODORE P., being recalled for further examination testified as follows:

By Mr. Colby:

Q. Mr. Shonts, you have used the words " commitments " and " obligations " in your testimony; did you use those words in your talk with Mr. Gardner M. Lane, in your private talks after the break up of the special meeting? A. To the best of my recollection, one or both of them.

Q. When I asked you yesterday if what you narrated was all that you said to Mr. Lane you said that was substantially, but you did not say anything about commitments or obligations. A. I think I told him that all the commitments I had made were on the basis of quality and price being equal before I recognized a

friend. That is my recollection of what I said to him, and I think
I so testified yesterday.

Q. Your thought sometimes runs into phrases which are apt to
recur to you; in other words, phrases such as "Price and quality
must be equal before friendship begins." A. I have used that for
many years and it has become a common phrase.

Q. And when you are asked if you are a lawyer, you are apt to
say, "Not enough to hurt"? A. Yes, sir.

Q. Do you ever use phrases such as "Sharper than a serpent's
tooth," and "Honest hearts are more than coronets," and such as
that? A. My reading of poetry has not been quite as diversified
as counsel's and therefore I have not some of those literary
quotations at my tongue's end.

Q. Are "Commitments and obligations" two friends of yours?
A. No, sir, no more than any other language.

Q. What did you say to Mr. Lane about the obligations and
commitments you had incurred? A. I said the only obligations or
commitments, I don't remember which word or both, was to Mr.
Stevens. I had made them to him and I felt I should be backed
up in them, but we were not going to quarrel about them and if
he thought Stone & Webster were a better firm we would let the
matter rest over until the next day, and I would give up my
sailing, which I did.

Chairman Thompson.— You did tell Mr. Lane you had made
certain commitments and obligations to Mr. Stevens? A. Yes,
sir, and Mr. Stevens had gone on to say he was willing to turn
over his construction contract to other people and give us his
personal attention, and I was anxious for that.

Q. Why didn't you say that to the full Board? A. I don't
know but I did.

Q. Why did you ask Mr. Lane to come into your private office
to hear it? A. Because I wanted an explanation of what I
interpreted as an attitude toward me which I did not understand.

Q. Had you seen manifestations of this attitude of suspicion
before? A. No, sir, and it was a matter of great surprise to me.

Q. Wouldn't it have been of advantage to you to have made the
same explanation to the sarcastic Mr. Read? A. It might have

been. I think the scripture—I have read the scripture—speaks of two women grinding at the mill and one being taken and the other left. I do not know of any reason why one was taken and the other left, no more than I explained yesterday I thought Mr. Lane would be frank with me and tell me what was back of it.

Q. Did Mr. Lane and Mr. Read suggest to you two women grinding at the mill? A. I do not think we got into the petticoat discussion on that day.

Q. What did Mr. Lane say to you? A. Mr. Lane told me that he thought Stone and Webster could do this work better than Mr. Stevens.

Q. Did he say that in the Board meeting? A. I don't remember that he did. I know he said it to me. That was not the only discussion we had on that subject.

Q. Do you think it singular that Mr. Read and Mr. Lane should have promptly resigned after this incident? A. I do not think it was singular that Mr. Lane should have resigned, because he told me on account of his failing health he could not attend meetings. I had the curiosity to look up, and see how many meetings he did attend at which I was present after these meetings, and there were eight or nine, as I remember only.

Q. Why did you suspect there was anything back of the opposition of Lane and Read to the Stevens contract if this attitude which you noticed here had never previously been shown? A. From their remarks on that occasion.

Q. What did Mr. Read say on that occasion? A. I think I told yesterday that they made remarks in regard to my friendship for Mr. Stevens and my association with Mr. Stevens at Panama, and things of that kind, which I thought were unnecessary, if they wanted to treat the matter on its merits, as I was trying to treat it.

Q. How did you happen to say Mr. Freedman was not to have any share in this commission of two million dollars? A. I had not heard of any commission of two million dollars until I read it in the newspapers, and I do not see how there could be any commission named until a percentage was agreed upon.

Chairman Thompson.— Do you think Mr. Maltbie swore to a falsehood before this Committee?

Mr. Shonts.—I do not think he would swear to a falsehood. I did not read his testimony.

Q. Do you think, Mr. Harkness of the Public Service Commission, would write a memorandum on false information? A. I do not think Mr. Harkness is an untruthful man at all. On certain conditions I did stand ready, but the conditions were never complied with. On certain conditions I would have recommended a 10 per cent. allowance, and that was the elimination of the item of equipment and furnishing of plans and administration expenses of the contractor.

Chairman Thompson.— You are not familiar with our record, but there is no question from our record the Public Service Commission understood the percentage was to be not less than 10 per cent. under any circumstances and you were willing to recommend as high as 12½ per cent. on the Stevens contract as submitted to the Public Service Commission, and the same was blank and your instructions were the blank could be filled in with no less than ten and up as high as 12½.

Mr. Shonts.— We never had agreed, and it was not in Mr. Stevens' mind, and it was not in my mind.

Chairman Thompson.— Judge McCall swore before the Committee and made this statement, that you ought to be knocking at the door of this Committee to come here and explain this.

Mr. Shonts.— Possibly. I know you are quoting what is true, but I am trying to tell you the facts that Mr. Stevens and I never agreed on a per cent. I cannot do more than that.

Q. The most important feature of the contract was the percentage, wasn't it? A. You could not get at a percentage until you know what the contract was going to cover. Those percentages are all on sliding scales, and the less amount of money the contractor has to invest, the less his percentage.

Q. Who suggested twenty per cent? A. I don't remember.

Q. You say the discussion of percentages — A. I think Mr. Hedley quoted some twenty per cent. contract he was familiar with. I am not certain but that is my recollection.

Q. The contract in every feature except the percentage had been formulated by Mr. Quackenbush? A. It was formulated by Mr. Quackenbush under my instructions to put everything in Mr. Stevens asked for on the theory the board would decide, when it came before the board, if it ever came before the board, and it could not come before the board for action until after the Public Service Commission had acted, and they never acted, and therefore it could only come before the board for action after the Public Service Commission had acted. If it came there the board would decide what they thought Mr. Stevens could do advantageously.

Q. This was put up to the Public Service Commission, 'wasn't it, prior to the meeting on June 24th? A. Yes, sir, I think in April.

Q. And you called this special meeting on June 24th for the purpose of concluding this matter? A. No, sir, I had never mentioned it to the board, but I had to some individuals, but I had retained my passage for sailing the next day, the 25th, on the Imperator.

Q. And I think you testified you wanted to get the matter disposed of before you sailed? A. I heard the matter had come to life at the Public Service Commission, and if they acted while I was gone I wanted the board to understand what I had done, so they could act intelligently upon the subject in my absence.

Q. What had you done? A. What I had done was to have a contract prepared including everything Mr. Stevens asked for and I had made an application to the Public Service Commission to waive their contractural rights as to supervision of the elevated extension contracts.

Q. So Mr. Stevens could take upon himself the supervision and erection of the entire work of third-tracking and building the extensions if the board and Mr. Stevens agreed upon a per cent.— Mr. Stevens was not present at the meeting of the board? A. No, sir.

Q. You had had other contracts with Mr. Stevens? A. Yes, sir, and the only purpose was to acquaint the board with what I had done, if this matter came up while I was gone, so they would understand what I had done.

Q. What did you tell Mr. Stevens of the percentage? A. I said it would depend upon what they left in the contract.

Q. What percentage had he agreed to accept? A. Altogether depended upon what was left in the contract by the board.

Q. Did Mr. Read express himself as to the provisions of the contract or on the subject of percentages on June 24th? A. I suppose he did; that is my recollection about it.

Q. Your recollection is that he did? A. Yes, sir.

Q. What did he say? A. I don't remember. He was against the contract, and he said so. He said, " I am opposed to this whole contract."

Q. Did he move that the contract be not approved? A. I do not remember that distinctly, but Mr. Young so testified, and I have no doubt but what it happened. Of my own knowledge, I don't remember that.

Q. You had earnestly advocated the contract, had you not, in the board meeting? A. I had earnestly advocated the fact that in my judgment, Mr. Stevens was the best man available, and I had said, if I could go away, and I hadn't had a vacation for five years, if I could go away with Mr. Stevens in charge of construction, the same as Mr. Hedley was in operation, I would go away with a very free mind, but as to the percentage he should be allowed, that had not been arranged for, or any conclusion reached.

Q. Did you say anything to Mr. Lane, anything about commitments and obligations having to do with the dual contracts? A. No, sir.

Q. You absolutely deny that? A. I absolutely deny that.

Q. Did you endeavor to call a further informal meeting on the same day after the board had refused to take action at the special meeting? A. Yes, sir. While Mr. Lane and I were talking, the board up and left, and I was anxious to get away the next day, and some one suggested they thought if we had a meeting that night, it might be disposed of.

Q. Who suggested that? A. I don't remember.

Q. What steps did you take to bring about that meeting? A. I asked the secretary, as is my custom, to see if he could get hold of the members of the board, and he said he couldn't get hold of Mr. Lane, and I said I didn't want a meeting without his being present, and I had rather give up my sailing.

Chairman Thompson.— You say you would feel if you had Stevens in charge when you went away, you could go with a free mind. Did you expect to get Stevens tied up with a contract before you left?

Mr. Shonts.— I had been saying that for weeks. The only purpose of that afternoon was, as I have explained to you. To tell you the truth, I thought the matter died borning up at the Public Service Commission.

By Mr. Colby:

Q. Will you produce the letter you received from Mr. Morgan on this subject? A. I will if I have one from him on the subject. My secretary says it is in the file. I do not remember. That is the reason I said if there was one from Mr. Morgan, it is there. I do not remember any letter from Mr. Morgan on that subject.

Q. Do you deny you received a letter from Mr. Morgan on the subject? A. I have no recollection of receiving one, and I don't deny anything.

Chairman Thompson.— I do not want to be quarrelsome, but really this matter is a very important matter to you and the Committee.

Mr. Shonts.— If you want my best judgment, I did not receive such a letter.

Chairman Thompson.— It is awfully hard for me to understand, if you got a letter from Mr. Morgan, after Mr. Lane and Mr. Read called on him here, that you should not remember it.

Mr. Shonts.— My best recollection is I did not receive a letter from Mr. Morgan, and can I testify to more than that?

Chairman Thompson.— It seems to me under those circumstances, if you had one, you would remember it.

Mr. Shonts.— I probably would, but I don't remember it, and I don't think I ever got such a letter. I do not believe I got such a letter, and I have no recollection of such a letter from Mr.

Morgan. Mr. Morgan asked me to come down, and I went down
and we had a five minutes' conversation, and so far as I recollect,
that was the end of it.

By Mr. Colby:

Q. What did Mr. Morgan say? A. He said Mr. Lane, or Mr.
Lane and Mr. Read, had called on him in regard to an arrangement we had talked about making with Stevens, and he said,
"What is there to it?" And I said, "There is nothing to it,
outside of our usual arrangements you have heard me say so
often," and that it was — and I said, "I have made certain commitments to Mr. Stevens, and he has arranged, or is willing to
arrange, to turn over his contract he has here to other people and
give us his personal service, and I would like to have him give his
attention to this task."

Q. Do you mean obligations that you felt incumbent to redeem
or discharge, when you say "commitments"? A. May I say
again, "Other things being equal, I will stand by it."

Q. What did you tell him you would recommend? A. The
task of doing our work, if awarded to him.

Q. Was he willing to give up the contract without any understanding from you as to what he was to receive from you upon the
new work or substitute work? A. No, sir. He said he was
willing to turn the management over, if he agreed with us, to
others, and give his personal attention on this new work.

Q. Do you regard a promise to Mr. Stevens to do something
or other that was unparticularized, and without any definite meaning, as a commitment? A. I certainly do.

Q. How would you go ahead to discharge that commitment, if
you did not know what it was? A. If the board — if the Public
Service Commission first had complied with our request, and if the
board and Mr. Stevens in the second place had agreed upon what
he should do, and the percentage he should receive, I would have
felt I had complied with my commitment to Mr. Stevens.

Q. What did Mr. Morgan say was the reason why Mr. Lane
came to see him? A. That was all he said. I say I do not
think our conversation lasted over five minutes.

Q. I want to get what Mr. Morgan said Mr. Lane said to him.
A. He said either one or both of those gentlemen came down to

see him with regard to an arrangement we were about to make with Stevens, and they did not favor it, and if he would use his influence against it.

Q. Did Morgan express to you that Lane expressed suspicion in relation to your connection with Stevens? A. No, sir.

Q. Or that Mr. Read had? A. No, sir.

Q. Did he state to you they had expressed their opinion as opposed to the contract on its merits? A. No, sir, he said they did not like the contract.

Q. But the contract had not been completed in terms, according to your testimony? A. It had not been. They were opposed to that sort of arrangement being made with Stevens.

Q. What sort of an arrangement? A. That was being discussed by the board.

Q. Can you state what arrangement? A. Just what we have been discussing here, and I will repeat my testimony if you wish.

Q. Just answer the question. A. The character — the only character of contract that was up for discussion by Mr. Stevens and myself was that I would recommend to our board that things being equal, if we agreed on it, he should take charge of the construction of our third-tracking and our extensions, and possibly that was not fully settled, our power house improvements.

Q. In other words, do I understand you correctly, that Mr. Morgan objected to this work being undertaken by any contractor on a commission basis? A. Mr. Morgan did not object to anything in this conference with me. Mr. Morgan was telling me he had a call from either one or both of these gentlemen, and that they had objected to this arrangement.

Chairman Thompson.— Did he say he objected?

Mr. Shonts.— No, sir.

By Mr. Colby:

Q. You mean they had objected to giving this work to any contractor on a commission basis? A. Yes, sir.

Q. Because the amount of the Commission had not been inserted in the contract? A. No, sir.

Chairman Thompson.— Did Mr. Morgan tell you he thought this was an extravagant contract?

Mr. Shonts.— No, sir, nothing had gotten to a point where we could decide whether it was or not.

By Mr. Colby:

Q. Why did Mr. Morgan send for you? A. Because he was asked to, as I understand it.

Q. He was not a member of your board? A. No, sir.

Q. He was not an officer of any kind? A. No, sir.

Q. And he did not have any opinion, either favorable or adverse? A. Mr. Morgan was the head of the syndicate that was to sell our bonds, and I read somebody's testimony, I think it must have been, that Mr. Lane, as to why he went there, he said he would have more influence than any person else, and he was opposed to this contract, and asked him to send for me, and he did.

Q. The contract had already failed of approval at the meeting of June 24th; why should Mr. Lane go to Mr. Morgan for his puissant influence? A. You will have to ask Mr. Read, if he went with him, and I think that was testified to.

Q. At a meeting of the board held on June 25th, two days later, a committee had been appointed to consider the question, had they not? A. Yes, sir, I appointed that committee, and put both Mr. Lane and Mr. Read on that committee.

Q. Did the committee ever sit as such committee? A. Yes, sir.

Q. When? A. Either that day or the next.

Q. And what did they do? A. They asked for information, and I tried to give them what data I had at that time. As I started in to explain, as we adjourned yesterday, I told them I was advised that the Pennsylvania, the 100 million dollar proposition, their terminal plant, in New York City, that originally Westinghouse, Church, Kerr & Company had been paid 5 per cent for the preparation of those plans, and they had paid them an additional amount of 7 per cent on $31,000,000 of the work, that they supervised, and that I understood the Long Island Railroad paid 10 per cent to the same firm for supervising all of their electrical work, and that 10 per cent seemed to be the usual rate for that sort of work, as far as I had dug into it.

Q. You said that to the special committee? A. Yes, sir. I find —

Q. Was that a repetition of what you said at the special meeting of the board? A. Probably it was. I am not sure I had that information at the meeting of the board.

Q. But you are an engineer of long experience? A. It was not a question of being an engineer of long experience. It was getting information as to what other people were doing.

Q. You are the head of a corporation continuously dealing with contractors? A. Yes, sir.

Q. Continually giving out work? A. Yes, sir.

Q. You knew what contractors ordinarily exacted and companies ordinarily conceded? A. Yes, sir. I do not know of any successful contracting company in making up estimates ever putting in less than 15 per cent. as estimated price unless there is some special reason for it. We have occasionally put in 10 per cent in making up bids — I mean the construction company, which we own every share of, as, for instance, on the piece of work on Seventh avenue just south of 42d street, and we were anxious to get that work and get the Times Square job, and we put in an extra low bid on that account.

Q. That being so, and the only unspecified feature of the Stevens draft of contract being the commission for which a space was left blank, do you mean to say you did not say that to the board of directors June 24th? A. I say first that it was not the only unspecified thing in that. Everything was put in that contract that Mr. Stevens asked for, but there were things in the contract that I testified yesterday I never would have stood for. I never would have stood for the equipment, because I thought we knew more about it than Mr. Stevens did, and I thought that should be eliminated, and I think I said that if the equipment was eliminated and the contractor was required to furnish the plant and pay his own adminstrative expenses, I thought 10 per cent. was not an unfair allowance, and that was my judgment, and it is my judgment, and it is less than we finally paid.

Chairman Thompson.— You sent over to the Public Service Commission a contract which you now say you yourself would not have stood for?

Mr. Shonts.— We only sent it to them to get their O. K. as to form; but that don't mean anything in there. They had nothing to do with the items in there. They had nothing to do with equipments.

Chairman Thompson.— You sent it there, and it was not signed by Mr. Stevens?

Mr. Shonts.— No, sir.

Chairman Thompson.— And he did not know the terms of it in his mind?

Mr. Shonts.— His own mind had not met himself and everything in there. I told Mr. Quackenbush to put everything in there Mr. Stevens wanted.

Chairman Thompson.— There was a whole lot of things in it he did not know about?

Mr. Shonts.— I do not know about that.

Chairman Thompson.— He never spent a dollar looking over the work, and had not prospected the work in the slightest degree?

Mr. Shonts.— I do not know about that.

Chairman Thompson.— Your board of directors had not approved it?

Mr. Shonts.— That is true.

Chairman Thompson.— And you yourself say there are things in there you would not have stood for?

Mr. Shonts.— Yes, sir.

Chairman Thompson.— And still you sent it to the Public Service Commission for their approval?

Mr. Shonts.— As to form only.

Chairman Thompson.— If they had approved it as to form, that approval would have been all the approval they would have ever been asked to give, wouldn't it?

Mr. Shonts.— As to form.

Chairman Thompson.— As to anything else in it?

Mr. Shonts.— No, sir. We would be free to remove anything from that that we did not think was a wise thing to contract for.

Chairman Thompson.— If they had signed that order that you sent over there, you never would have had to go to the Public Service Commission again in reference to that particular contract, would you?

Mr. Shonts.— No, sir.

Chairman Thompson.— And you could have filled in those blanks any way you wanted to?

Mr. Shonts.— Yes, sir, and —

Chairman Thompson.— Do you think a Public Service Commission ought to perform any official act in just exactly that way, with that little information that they had?

Mr. Shonts.— It would depend altogether, Mr. Chairman, on the confidence they had in the integrity of the board of directors of the other company.

Chairman Thompson.— In other words, it would depend on the confidence they had in you as president of the Interborough?

Mr. Shonts.— No, sir; of the board of directors.

Chairman Thompson.— If the board of directors had passed this as you submitted it to them, it would have been up to you?

Mr. Shonts.— Yes, sir.

Chairman Thompson.— And if the Public Service Commission had approved it, it would have been signifying their confidence they had in you?

Mr. Shonts.— That would have been a case where both put their confidence in me to make the best trade I could.

Chairman Thompson.— Without any investigation on the part of either one?

Mr. Shonts.— Yes, sir.

By Mr. Colby:

Q. I have what has been stated to be a copy of your application to the Public Service Commission, for permission to enter into a contract for the construction and equipment of the third-tracking and the elevated extension, and I find a paragraph as follows: " The company therefore requests permission to enter into a contract with Mr. John F. Stevens for the construction and equipment of the railroad described in the second certificate referred to described in the first certificate for the actual costs and expense thereof, plus a reasonable percentage," and here is what I consider significant, " For the purpose of saving time, the Commission waive approval by it of such a contract in advance of its execution." You asked, in other words, the Public Service Commission to practically abdicate its function with regard to approving of a contract by issuing its approval in advance of the execution of the contract? A. I did.

Q. This was in May, 1913? A. Yes, sir.

Q. And towards the end of June, and in the early part of July, 1913, you still say that the terms of the contract had not been agreed to by the company or by the contractor? A. That is what I said.

Q. What did the Public Service Commission answer to this application? A. Never any answer.

Q. Did you get any informal assurances from the Public Service Commission? A. Not that I remember of.

Q. Did you make any statement at any of the meetings of the Board to consider this question as to what assurances or guarantees of approval, or what intimation you had from the Public Service Commission? A. I couldn't very well, if I don't remember that I had any.

Q. Will you deny that you did that? A. No, sir. I do not remember of having any assurances from the Public Service Commission, and I do not remember having said so to the Board.

Q. When did you call on Mr. Morgan? A. It was some time after our meeting. It was between June 25th and the date of my sailing, which I think was July 8th.

Q. Was it prior to the meeting of the special committee appointed to consider this contract? A. I could not tell you that.

Q. What was the attitude on this contract of Mr. Berwind? A. There was not any definite attitude taken by any member of our Board, outside the fact that if the Public Service Commission acted, and we got down to the things that we thought Mr. Stevens could safely and economically do, and we agreed on a percentage basis, he was a proper man. Mr. Berwind was perfectly willing to take my recommendation as to Mr. Stevens being a proper man.

Q. In other words, you considered Mr. Berwind to be an administration man? A. I think I can say that of all the directors, except Mr. Lane and Mr. Read.

Q. You could say that of Mr. T. DeC. Sullivan? A. I think of all of them.

Q. And you certainly could of Mr. Freedman? A. I think of all except those.

Q. They, with the exception of Mr. Read and Mr. Lane, constituted this special committee? A. Yes, sir, but that special committee had no authority except to report back to the Board.

Q. You would assume their recommendations to be persuasive to the Board, after giving them special instructions? A. I don't know.

Q. Why did you appoint Mr. Andrew Freedman on this committee, when you assured Mr. Lane Mr. Freedman had no interest? A. I regarded Mr. Freedman as one of the best posted transit men in New York city.

Q. Wasn't it a little singular that in appointing a committee which was to clear away confusion and reassure your doubting directors, and in a sense extract you from their suspicion, that you should appoint on that special committee a gentleman who was coupled with your name and Mr. Stevens, as an object of their suspicion? A. Mr. Lane assured me there never had been a time when I was an object of their suspicion, and he said I entirely misunderstood his attitude, and he was very glad to hear what I had to say in regard to Mr. Freedman, although I did not mention his name.

Mr. Colby.— The reason I mention Mr. Freedman's name, without any feeling that it involves any indelicacy, is that his name is already in this record.

Chairman Thompson.— We cannot help it.

By Mr. Colby:

Q. Mr. Lane made no concealment in his talk with you in the private office of the fact that he did entertain some suspicion of Mr. Freedman in this connection? A. Yes, sir; but after my explanation, that was the last time he ever referred to that.

Q. Had he, prior to that explanation? A. He said he had never had any question in his mind about my absolute integrity, but he could not say so much for some of my associates, and when I insisted who, he said he didn't think that was a matter we had to discuss, and I said, " If you are going to be guided by it, it seems to me, you ought to discuss it," and he finally mentioned the name that we have just referred to.

Q. Do you ascribe the fact Mr. Freedman was a member of this Committee as the reason that the Committee was unable to come to any agreement? A. I do not know that the Committee did not come to any agreement. They could not do anything until the Public Service Commission acted.

Q. The committee never made a report, you testified? A. I don't remember I have testified so, but I don't remember they did. I sailed on the 8th, and when I came back, things had happened, or one thing had happened, and one thing had not, and the thing that happened, Mr. Stevens, unfortunately, through the death of his chief backer, had failed with his construction contract, and was in difficulties of his own, and the thing that had not happened was that the Public Service Commission had never taken any action in regard to our application, and the thing died. I dropped it, so far as I was concerned.

Chairman Thompson.— Do you think the Public Service Commission ought to act on a contract in approving of it before the contract is made?

Mr. Shonts.— I do not see any harm in that instance.

By Mr. Colby:

Q. Had they ever done any such thing before? A. We had never had any such case before. We had never been confronted with a task that was so difficult and hazardous, and so far-reaching.

Chairman Thompson.— Understand, Mr. Shonts, that you must not be surprised if we ask you a great many questions about this, for this reason, we have had a great deal of testimony here, and Mr. Tench testified here that he said they took all the responsibility for this work, and the stoppage of trains and everything else, and had a profitable contract, and were proud of the fact that they had not delayed a single train since they had been there, and did all of that for less than five per cent.

Mr. Shonts.— But until I read their testimony in the public press, I had no idea of what each member of the firm — we treated them as a firm, and I have not yet an idea, except by hearsay, what each member of that firm contributed or how they divide their profits. That was not our province, as I understood it, and our province was to get by competition the most skilled men to do that work in the shortest time, and for the least money, and when you stop to think there was a possibility of work covering then practically this entire city, where we were operating over three thousand trains a day —

Chairman Thompson.— He testified to all of that.

Mr. Shonts.— It was a wonderful piece of work, but what they contributed and who financed it, and who put in the money, and what each one contributed, I did not go into that, and I do not think it was our province to go into it.

Chairman Thompson.— Mr. Tench testified further that you told him, I think he testified to it in that way, that you wanted that firm, Terry & Tench, to do the actual work.

Mr. Shonts.— That was no secret. I regarded — Stevens was an incident, and when I came back from Europe in September and got my desk cleaned up, I said, "We must do something and take up the third-tracking," and I said, "We won't get caught again with any criticism, and we will get competitive bids," and when you are going to get a man to take out an appendix, you have not so many surgeons to use as if you are going to lance a boil, and we could not get so many engineers who we felt were skillful to do the dangerous work, and we took up the question of a half dozen most available and skillful men, and we thought

25

Terry & Tench probably led the world in steel construction, and Snare & Triest were a good second, and Gillespie the greatest sub-surface expert living in the world.

By Mr. Colby:

Q. You do not use that word " sub-surface " rather figuratively, do you?   A. Both figuratively and literally.

Chairman Thompson.— There are some corporations both ways.

Mr. Shonts.— He was the greatest water-pipe man in the engineering world, and so regarded, and I remember back in the old Panama days when we were figuring doing the entire work on the percentage basis, he belonged to the only group that complied with all the requirements of the United States Government, and I know myself he is a great organizer, great driver, and very skillful in the part of the work we had to do with opening all the streets.

Chairman Thompson.— We do not want to lumber up the record with compliments.

Mr. Shonts.— I am telling you why we selected these men.

Chairman Thompson.— Mr. Gillespie did not do all the subsuface work, and some was done by people less skillful, I guess.

Mr. Shonts.— He promised as one of the conditions.

Chairman Thompson.— The facts are what we want, and I find it is not always the engineer or lawyer that has the great reputation that is always likely to win the law suit.

Mr. Shonts.— I am trying to tell you why we made the selection.

Q. Have you seen a copy of the memorandum which Mr. Gardiner M. Lane preserved of his talk with you?   A. I have never seen it.

Q. Have you been acquainted with its contents?   A. Never heard there was such a thing in existence until this investigation developed.

Chairman Thompson.— You had confidence in Mr. Lane right up to the time he died?

Mr. Shonts.— Yes, sir, I have so testified.

Chairman Thompson.— If he made a memorandum on this subject, I suppose you have not any objection to that, have you, and to our having it?

Mr. Shonts.— I have already written those people to that effect.

Chairman Thompson.— To whom?

Mr. Shonts.— The lawyer for the estate, I think it was. Somebody wrote me and I said we had offered to turn over everything we had to you.

Chairman Thompson.— You, on behalf of yourself or the Interborough Company, will not object to the production of the memoranda made by Mr. Lane?

Mr. Shonts.— If it has any bearing on our situation.

Chairman Thompson.— If it has any relation to the talk with you at the time of the directors' meeting?

Mr. Shonts.— I have already notified them.

Chairman Thompson.— Will you give us a letter to Mr. Cotting, the executor of the Lane estate, to that effect?

Mr. Shonts.— Well, I think that is going a little too far, but I will.

Q. You say you have written to the attorney for the executors about this matter? A. Yes, sir.

Q. Have you written more than once? A. No, sir.

Q. Have you preserved a copy of the letter? A. I suppose so.

Q. Would you have it exhibited to us? A. I would be very glad to.

Q. Mr. Shonts, did you have any conversation with any member of your Board after you had seen Mr. Morgan about the Stevens incident? A. Why, I probably did.

Q. Do you recall any conversation that you had with any member of the Board in which you endeavored to state what Mr.

Morgan had said or written? A. No, sir, I don't remember, but I probably did.

Q. Do you recall being angered at Mr. Morgan's position? A. I recall on the contrary I was not. There was nothing to be angered at.

Q. Do you recall expressing yourself with some freedom at Mr. Morgan's criticism of this transaction? A. I don't recall anything of the kind, and nothing of the kind happened.

Q. Do you recall expressing indignation that he should take it upon himself to criticise this transaction in view of all the facts and circumstances? A. To begin with, Mr. Morgan did not criticise the transaction. Mr. Morgan apologized to me for asking me to come down, and he said these gentlemen had called, one or both of them, and if I was going by he would like to have me run in, and he told me as I have already testified, and I do not think our conversation lasted over five minutes, and we were standing.

Q. Do these questions I have asked you tend to refresh your recollection as to any written communication being received by you from Mr. Morgan? A. I don't remember receiving any written communication from him on that subject.

Q. You are not positive of it, are you? A. I don't think I ever did.

Q. Will you glance at this letter which is in evidence? A. Yes, sir.

(Mr. Colby hands letter to witness.)

A. There is nothing in this that reminds me of any conversation I had with Mr. Morgan —

Q. Now, that you are familiar with its contents, I will ask you a question or two about it; it is apparent from this letter Mr. Lane had preserved a memorandum of his conversation with you? A. Yes, sir.

Q. And that he did so for his own protection? A. So he says.

Q. Does it seem an unnatural thing that Mr. Lane having recommended one contractor and you having recommended another should deem a difference of opinion on such a point of such moment to reduce to a contemporaneous memorandum everything that was said on the subject? A. I would not think so.

Q. Do you notice Mr. Lane's statement in his letter of October 1, 1913, that this is a very delicate matter? A. I notice that language.

Q. What could that mean? A. I don't know.

Q. Do you notice also that he says "While it seems to me wise that each of us who is conversant with the affair should preserve his own statement" (writing to Mr. Young, the co-director) "yet I think he should not have the responsibility of keeping the statement of others." What responsibility could there be in any such memoranda as to a choice of contractors for completing extensions of the elevated? A. I do not know, I am sure. That is all news to me, except that I have seen it in the print before.

Q. Mr. Lane was not a light or hysterical man, was he? A. During the last few months of his life, he was a very irritable man. I do not know what caused it.

Q. "Death, for example," says Mr. Lane, "might cause these statements to come into the possession of others than those to whom they were originally entrusted, and in that way they might even become public." Could there be any disaster or any reflection upon any man in his preference as to a choice of contractors becoming public? A. We are sitting here conjecturing. I do not know. There was nothing happened between Mr. Lane and myself to have been shrouded in such mystery. I did not remember, but I was reminded of it, one of my lieutenants, the same afternoon, says he remembers it exactly as I told it to him, and there was nothing either of us thought necessary to shroud in mystery or wrap up in papers and hide.

Q. Mr. Lane continues, "We who stood together know the understanding of one another"; that does not look as if Mr. Lane's understanding accorded with yours, does it? A. No, sir; it does not look so.

Q. That undoubtedly refers to the contractors who opposed the Stevens contract, doesn't it? A. It does.

Q. And Mr. Lane continues, "And if we each preserve for ourselves the notes made, we shall all be in a position to act together in case of need"; do you mean to say they would all need to act together in order to get Stone & Webster this contract? A. I don't know. In the light of what actually happened, that is a very remarkable document.

, Q. It is apparent from this letter that Mr. Lane enclosed a memorandum to the person to whom he addressed this letter; this was the memorandum which he thought it best not to have in his possession, and that memorandum is already in, and it is apparent from this letter Mr. Lane has preserved a memorandum. In this letter it is apparent Mr. Lane does not dispute the correctness of the memorandum made by Mr. Young and enclosed to him for his examination; he mentioned the fact it differs only in respect to one date from his own recollection; do you know the ground on which the executors of Mr. Lane have thus far resisted the production of his memoranda? A. I do not. `

Q. The memorandum made by Mr. Young and which he enclosed to Mr. Lane, and which Mr. Lane returned, have you read that? A. I read that in the public press, yes, sir.

Q. Is that in the main correct? A. How do you mean correct?

Q. Is it accurate? A. So far as reflecting Mr. Lane's and my talk?

. Q. In what respects is it inaccurate, if any? A. Mr. Lane and I did not have any talk in which the idea of my having made any commitments that in any way affected the dual subway contract was true.

Q. In that respect only? A. I am quoting now. That is the essential thing.

Q. The memorandum states this is a memorandum preserved by Mr. Young, who was at the time a director of the company and at this meeting; " Upon leaving the meeting of the Interborough Board to-day, Mr. Lane requested me to go around to his office with him. On reaching the office, we proceeded to Mr. Lane's private room, and Mr. Lane showed me a memorandum which he had drawn up stating what had taken place at the special meeting on Tuesday"; did you know at that time Mr. Lane had preserved the memorandum of what had taken place? A. No, sir.

Q. Did Mr. Lane ever tell you he had? A. No, sir. That is a remarkable thing. We sat in eight board meetings together, and he never mentioned anything of the kind to me again, and was in my office many times discussing the form of contract, and he never mentioned it.

Q. " This memorandum," says Mr. Young in his memorandum, which apparently has been found correct by Mr. Lane,
" in addition went on to state that following the special meeting
Mr. Shonts had taken him aside and stated that he wanted him,
Mr. Lane, to understand the reason for entering into such a
contract with Mr. Stevens; " that is correct? A. No, sir.

Q. You took him aside and asked him into your private office?
A. Yes, sir, and I asked him what was back of his attitude, and
I told him how I interpreted it.

Q. And the memorandum says: " Neither himself nor Mr.
Stevens nor Mr. Freedman was to receive any benefit from this
contract "; that is true, isn't it? A. That would be very remarkable, when you are talking about giving an excessive contract to
Mr. Stevens, he was not to get any benefit from it.

Q. I think you testified neither you nor Mr. Stevens nor Mr.
Freedman were to have any benefit? A. I said neither myself nor
Mr. Freedman, and the contract was to be with Mr. Stevens, and
he expected to receive benefit.

Q. As far as you and Mr. Freedman are concerned, the memorandum is correct? A. Yes, sir.

Q. " But that in connection with the securing of the contract
which had been closed between the city of Greater New York and
the Interborough, Mr. Shonts had found it necessary to make certain commitments and incur certain obligations "; you referred to
certain commitments and certain obligations in your talk to Mr.
Lane? A. To Mr. Stevens, yes, sir.

Q. But the point in divergence between the memorandum and
what you now testify is that those commitments and those obligations were with Mr. Stevens? A. Yes, sir, and had no relation
to the dual contract with the city of New York, which the records
show we fought and spent hundreds of thousands of dollars in
fighting.

Q. Mr. Lane further states that Mr. Lane, upon learning of
these facts, had gone to the office of J. P. Morgan & Company?
A. That is correct. Mr. Morgan told me he had been there.

Q. "And advised Mr. J. P. Morgan, Jr., of exactly what had
transpired at the meeting referred to in his memorandum, and
of the statement which had been made to him by Mr. Shonts ";
you see nothing to take exception to in those final statements?

A. I am taking exception to nothing. I testified to what Mr. Morgan said to me.

Q. So that in the portions of this memorandum which I have just read, there is no question but that you had this private talk with Mr. Lane, that you assured Mr. Lane that neither yourself nor Mr. Freedman were to receive any benefit from the contract? A. That is right.

Q. That you had found it necessary to make certain commitments and incur certain obligations to Mr. Stevens? A. I do not say it was necessary, but I said I had done it.

Q. And the only question as to which there is a difference between what you have testified and what this memorandum states is that these commitments and obligations which you had incurred were, as you say, to Mr. Stevens, your friend, and the prospective contractor, and not as this memorandum states, incurred in connection with the securing of the contract between the city of Greater New York and the Interborough? A. That is right.

Chairman Thompson.— You agree with the entire memorandum except with what detail he has stated?

Mr. Shonts.— I agree with what he has stated, as I have stated, I do not think I can say more after I have read it, than I have said. I did ask Mr. Lane to go into my private office, and asked him if he thought there was anything in this for me, and he assured me he did not, but he could not say so much of my associates. It developed Mr. Freedman's name was brought into it, and I told him, and I testified to what I said, that I had obligated myself to Mr. Stevens, other things being equal, to have him do the work, and I hoped that the board would back me up in it.

By Mr. Colby:

Q. Neither of these gentlemen who had opposed you on the Stevens contract negotiations continued to be a director for more than a very few months; in other words, Mr. Lane and Mr. Read resigned and at the next annual meeting of the company, Mr. Young, who makes this memorandum, was not re-elected? A. That is true.

Q. Who took their places on the board? A. I will have to refresh my recollection about that. We will tell you in a moment.

Q. One was Mr. W. Leon Pepperman, was he not? A. I don't think so. I think he had been on for a long time.

Q. While I am waiting for that information, there is produced and handed me a letter from Mr. Burton E. Eames, a member of the law firm of Tyler, Corneau & Eames of Boston, addressed to you. You received this letter dated October 15th? A. Yes, sir, and that is my answer attached.

Q. And annexed to it is your reply of October 18th? A. Yes.

Mr. Colby.— I will read this letter.

Mr. Colby reads the letter referred to which is as follows:

"Theodore P. Shonts, Esq., President, Interborough Consolidated Corporation, New York City.

"Dear Sir.—The enclosed copy of summons was served upon Mr. Cotting, executor of the will of Gardiner M. Lane, today. This follows a demand which was made upon us last week for the production of papers of Mr. Lane. As Mr. Cotting's counsel, I have advised him that he should not give up Mr. Lane's papers as a volunteer, but only under an order of a court having jurisdiction. I am writing you as a matter of courtesy, thinking that you may wish to make suggestions in the matter."

the summons enclosed was from the Commonwealth of Massachusetts to Charles E. Cotting, and called upon him, among other things, to produce at a time and place therein specified, all books, letters, copies of letters, written by or addressed to Gardiner M. Lane, and all papers of Gardiner M. Lane now in your possession or under your control, which in any manner relate to the affairs of the Interborough Rapid Transit Company, and particularly all books, letters, documents, memoranda, or other writings, relating in any manner to negotiations for the construction of third tracks on the Second, Third and Ninth avenue lines of the Manhattan Elevated Railroad Company of New York, and for the construction of additions and extensions to the said line. That was the committee proceeding in Boston, and the answer by Mr.

Shonts to this letter of Mr. Eames, which, however, is addressed to Mr. Charles Tyler, who, I take is, is the senior member of Tyler, Corneau & Eames, and the letter says:

"DEAR SIR.—I am in receipt of your letter of October 15, 1915, enclosing a copy of the summons served upon Mr. Cotting, executor of the will of Gardiner M. Lane, to produce Mr. Lane's papers before the Joint Committee of the New York Legislature sitting in Boston. I note that you have advised Mr. Cotting that he should not give up Mr. Lane's papers as a volunteer, but only under an order of a court having jurisdiction, and that you are writing as a matter of courtesy, thinking I may wish to make suggestions in the matter.

"I thank you for your courtesy, which is much appreciated. I am obliged to say, however, that I have no suggestions to make in view of the fact that our own attorney had assured the Chairman and counsel of this Committee that we would produce all papers upon request, without service of process.

"This was known to the Chairman of the Committee before he went to Boston, but he seemed to prefer a course which would attract newspaper attention.

"There is not the slightest objection on our part to the inspection by the Committee of any of Mr. Lane's letters to me, or to this company, relating to our affairs.

"Yours very truly."

By Mr. Colby:

Q. You signed that letter? A. I did.

Q. The permission that you expressed in the final paragraph is not broad enough to include the memorandum which Mr. Lane apparently had preserved of this transaction, is it? A. We did not mean to make any reservation. I do not think that was thought of then. I do not think we knew anything about it.

Q. The subpoena directly calls for documents, memoranda, or other items, and the permission is, I should say, quite definitely restricted to letters of Mr. Lane to you or to the company? A. I meant everything that was under investigation.

Q. You could have produced Mr. Lane's letters to you, and the company could have produced Mr. Lane's letters to it, and the Committee did, not have to go to Boston to get copies of those communications; that is true, isn't it? A. I did not keep those dates in my mind. I meant that to be a general release of any papers that had any bearing to your investigation. There are many matters, covering many years, having nothing to do with this investigation.

Q. Neither the executor, nor his counsel, Mr. Tyler, could infer from that that it was a general release? A. So you say, and I haven't heard from them since.

Q. All you said was, you had no objection to the Committee inspecting Mr. Lane's letters to you, or to the company; why should they go to Boston to get letters which were in your possession or in the possession of the Company? A. Is what I said this afternoon considered definite? If not, let us cure it now.

Q. You are willing to have the memorandum produced, are you? A. Yes, sir; I have so testified.

Q. Are you able to give us the names of the directors now who succeeded Mr. Read, Mr. Lane and Mr. Young? A. We have sent up for them.

Q. How long were you in Europe in 1913? A. About two months. I returned early in September.

Q. How soon after you returned did you take up the question of the third-tracking and the extension of the elevated? A. Two or three months; as soon as I got my work cleaned up and got around to it.

Q. What did you find was the attitude of your special committee on awarding the contract to Mr. Stevens? A. I did not call them together for the reason stated, the failure of his company had taken him out of consideration, and the Public Service Commission had taken no action, and I never took it up with them again.

Chairman Thompson.— I want to call attention to this letter of October 18th; was that dictated by you?

Mr. Shonts.— Yes, sir. As I recollect, it is. I usually dictate those letters and send them in to counsel to see if they are all right.

Chairman Thompson.— Did you know when you wrote this letter what this Committee was trying to get was some personal memorandum of Mr. Lane's?

Mr. Shonts.— No, sir.

Chairman Thompson.— Then you were misinformed as to what we were trying to get in Boston, weren't you?

Mr. Shonts.— If you were trying to get a personal memorandum, I knew nothing about it at that time.

Chairman Thompson.— Did you think this Committee went to Boston to get some copies of letters that were in your file?

Mr. Shonts.— I don't want to be disrespectful, but I have an awful lot of work to do, and I do not read everything that I really ought to read.

Chairman Thompson.— I wanted to see if you thought we would go to Boston and spend a lot of money hiring lawyers and going to court to get letters, copies of which were in your files?

Mr. Shonts.— If I was asked that question, I would say no.

Chairman Thompson.— Did you think that when you wrote this letter?

Mr. Shonts.— I don't know what I thought.

Chairman Thompson.— Your idea is, you rather wrote this letter without thinking?

Mr. Shonts.— Without either knowing or thinking of that feature of your work.

Chairman Thompson.— When you say that you had assured the Chairman that you would produce all papers upon request, you go on and say, " This was known to the Chairman of the Committee before he went to Boston, but he seemed to prefer a course which would attract newspaper attention "; did you think I had gone to Boston —

Mr. Shonts.— I didn't know you as well as I do now then.

Chairman Thompson.— Did you really think we were going to Boston to get something we could have produced from your files?

Mr. Shonts.— I do not remember that I knew about the special memorandum at that time.

Chairman Thompson.— You must have thought we were going there to get something you had on your files; is that true?

Mr. Shonts.— That must have been it.

Chairman Thompson.— Now that you know what we were in Boston for, do you think that letter was justified?

Mr. Shonts.— It may be justified by what was in my mind at that time, but not now.

Chairman Thompson.— That memorandum would be pretty important for this Committee to know, wouldn't it?

Mr. Shonts.— That is for you people to decide. I do not know what is in it.

Chairman Thompson.— I do not want a misunderstanding; newspaper attention is something we do not ask for except it helps in an investigation, and I want to say it is of great assistance in an investigation, and people ought to be under obligation for what the newspapers do.

Mr. Shonts.— I think you are seriously at work, Mr. Chairman.

Chairman Thompson.— We have had a great deal of help from the newspapers, without which we would not have succeeded as well as we have.

Mr. Colby.— I call the Chair's attention to the fact I have not as yet offered in evidence the memorandum handed me of the Stevens contract, as submitted to the Board of Directors of June 24th, but I would like to offer as a version of that contract this statement of the contract attached to the application to the Public Service Commission for its approval in advance of execution.

Chairman Thompson.— You have the contract, as it is.

Mr. Colby.— It seems to me this is the best evidence of what that contract was, although I have no reason to cast the least doubt upon the accuracy of the memorandum handed me. This is a statement, and before I leave that point, I would like to ask the witness this one question.

By Mr. Colby:

Q. Did you hear any expression in any manner, from the Public Service Commission, that your request for its approval of a contract in advance of execution was a preposterous request? A. I have no recollection of any member of the Commission going on record in regard to our request at all. Further than that, they would consider, and I think the Chairman said he would consider, "and you better write it out, and we will consider it."

Q. You asked them to do more than approve in advance of the execution of the contract, you asked them to waive approval? A. I asked them to waive their contractural rights which required us to submit to them any contracts for elevated extensions before they were awarded.

Q. In other words, a right that had been reserved by the Public Service Commission affecting public interests, you asked them to waive? A. I asked them to waive that specific reservation that we have referred to.

Q. Now, notwithstanding the failure of the Stevens contract and the collapse of his company, which took him out of the running, you made a very similar contract with T. A. Gillespie, didn't you? A. Not at all similar.

Q. With the T. A. Gillespie Company? A. Not at all similar with the Stevens proposed form of contract as drafted.

Q. In what respects was it dissimilar? A. Equipment was eliminated.

Q. What do you mean by that? A. I mean the signalling and rolling stock, which amounted to fully half of the contracts or approximately half, was eliminated. The contractor was required —

Q. What do you mean by eliminated? A. Taken out of the contract.

Q. Taken out of it? A. I am speaking of the difference. That was in as drafted.

Q. You mean the contractor had to supply it under the Stevens contract? A. No, sir; I mean under the Stevens contract Stevens would have had a right to supply the equipment consisting of signals and the other things, rolling stock, etc., and that was the question Mr. Berwind asked me when the matter first came up, what particular help I thought Mr. Stevens would give on that, and I told him I didn't think he would give us any, and I thought we were ahead of the world on signalling and rolling stock, and I did think so, and that was eliminated in —

Q. Mr. Stevens was to supply equipment, signalling and rolling stock? A. As the thing was drafted, everything he asked for was in there.

Q. But the contract with Mr. Gillespie eliminated signalling and equipment and rolling stock? A. Yes, sir.

Q. How was that to be supplied? We supplied that ourselves on competitive bidding.

Q. You, under the Gillsepie contract, were to supply — A. That has nothing to do with the Gillsepie contract. We buy that ourselves. That was entirely removed, and Gillespie had nothing to do with it at all.

Q. It had not ceased to be an essential feature of the work? A. No, sir, but our own organization is handling that itself.

Q. Under the proposed Stevens contract he was to supply signalling equipment and rolling stock, and under the Gillespie contract the Interborough supplied that? A. You are right in stating that under the proposed Stevens contract, as drafted, the equipment was included, but which was the first item eliminated when the matter came up in our Board, and from that time on it was out of the Stevens contract and it was never put back in any contract, and we handled that ourselves. .

Q. You are testifying as to the differences between the Stevens and the Gillespie contracts? A. Yes, sir, as framed up under the Gillespie contract the contractors have to furnish the plant.

Q. They have to furnish the plant? A. Yes, sir, and they pay their own administrative expenses. By administrative expenses I mean the members of the firm, just as in our office, those that administer the general affairs, and every man that is on the job and gives his whole time to the job, of course his salary is part of the cost in the Gillespie contract.

Q. And the administrative expenses means the salaries of the officers of the T. A. Gillespie Company? A. The principals themselves draw no salary, and if they do, we have nothing to do with it.

Q, What other differences were there? A. Those were the chief — we retained the same close personal supervision of the work; the Interborough retained the same close personal supervision of the work.

Q. Do you mean that the Interborough supplies engineering superintendence? A. Yes, sir, to supervise and see that the Gillespies carry out the terms of the contract, in accordance with the terms of the contract.

Q. And the Interborough does that at its own expense? A. Yes, sir; otherwise we would be turning over work to outsiders here.

Q. And what other differences were there between the two contracts? A. Those are the essential differences.

Q. Was this contract with the T. A. Gillespie Company entered into after discussion in your Board? A. Yes, sir.

Q. And under authority of resolutions adopted by the Board? A. Yes, sir. We received six bids, Mr. Counsel, with the right to reject any and all bids. None of the bids were satisfactory, and I so reported to the Board. You will find that in the various minutes.

Mr. Colby.— Is this the first mention of the Gillespie contract, Mr. Fisher?

Mr. Fisher.— I am not sure. I think it was a resolution before that, asking for bids.

By Mr. Colby:

Q. Mr. Fisher refers me to the minutes of the Executive Committee of the Board held on December 15, 1913; this is apparently a special meeting of the committee, and I understand, Mr. Secretary, that this is the first reference to contracts for the third-tracking and extension of the elevated lines in connection with T. A. Gillespie & Company in your minute book; is that correct?

Mr. Fisher.— Yes, sir.

By Mr. Colby:

Q. I read the following resolution: " Resolved that the proper officers of this company be, and they hereby are directed to prepare specifications and procure bids from the following firms for the construction of the third tracks and improvements on the Second, Third and Ninth Avenue Elevated Lines of the Manhattan Railway Company: Gillespie Brothers, Incorporated; the Pittsburg Contracting Company; Bradley Contracting Company; Snare & Triest Company; Kent Engineering Company; Terry & Tench Company "; how were those firms selected? A. Well, I started in to tell a while ago. We were trying to select the most skillful firms best qualified to do this particular class of work and all of our engineering force agreed, as I told you, that so far as the steel erection was concerned, they thought that Terry & Tench probably led the world, with Snare & Triest a close second. They all agreed that so far as organizing ability and driving force in sub-surface work, and I use their language, and they said they meant water pipe, and so forth, of which the streets are so full, and we had so many to remove, that there was no person in Mr. Gillespie's class. I think I said, " Isn't Bradley one of the biggest contractors, and hasn't he more contracts than anybody else for subway work in the city, and isn't he the fellow that had to go under us once or twice in Brooklyn and had relations with keeping up our structure under train movement?" and they said yes, and I said, "Why isn't he a good man?" and our chief engineer, Mr. Pegram, mentioned the Pittsburg Company, because he said " I think a man by the name of Swenson was chief engineer," and he has known him and he was a great iron and steel man in Pittsburg, and has done some wonderful work in the Catskills, and was a strong company, and good people, and that is how that name came in, and we, so far as Mr. Tench was concerned, someone suggested, one of our engineering staff — I don't mean Tench, but Kent had been a vice-president of the Westinghouse Church, Kerr Company, and had charge of all the Pennsylvania work here, and was wonderfully well qualified for this kind of work, and had started in for himself and could probably get a low bid from him. I know that suggestion was made, and his name was added, and so we made up the group, each of which we thought would be qualified to do this work, not that each would do the steel work as well as we hoped Terry & Tench and Snare & Triest would, and when the bids were finally all in, as is the custom with our company, to the chief engineer's office and opened it was reported to me by the chief engineer, or by Mr. Hedley, more likely, the vice-president to whom the chief engineer reports, that Mr. Gillespie was the lowest bidder, and I reported to the Board or the Executive Committee, I do not remember which, that I was not satisfied with any of the bids because we felt sure that Terry & Tench and Snare & Triest were the people we wanted to do that steel erection —

Q. I was questioning you on the point as to why you limited the bidding; why didn't you ask for bids generally? A. No one else was suggested that had particular skill.

Q. That was a stipulation against your interest, in restricting the bidding to six? A. That is always the case when you get very skillful men for any job, you don't find so many as in less important work.

Q. If you invited bids open and general — A. I would have resigned my job and split with the city on the question of that,— on that same question, and never made a contract with them before I would have taken on my conscience the crime of letting any incompetent men come in there to save a few dollars and undertake to do that work where we are handling over 3,400 trains a day.

Q. You could have passed also upon the competence of the bidders as well as the terms? A. We exercised our best judgment, and that was to get the most skilled men and limit the bidding to those we felt were competent, and that was our best judgment at the time, and it is my best judgment now. We are very proud of the way it has been accomplished, and we think it has been accomplished at a very reasonable sum.

Q. When was the invitation for bids issued? A. Soon following that. I do not follow those dates.

Q. The resolution was passed on December 15th and I am handed, Mr. Chairman, an invitation for bids dated December 16, 1913. When were the bids received? A. Doesn't that file of yours show? I haven't it in mind. I am told your file shows.

Chairman Thompson.— It was along about the 20th of December, 1914, I think it was.

Mr. Quackenbush.— December 23, 1913.

Mr. Colby.— Bids were opened on December 23, and the contract was let on what date?

Mr. Quackenbush.— February 13, 1914. The contract was executed on the 13th of February.

Q. Have you those dates clearly in mind? Do you know the number of days that elapsed between the invitation for bids and the dates that they were actually received? A. I think the bids were in eight days from the time, I think the specifications were submitted to them. We went into it very thoroughly. There is no doubt about that.

Q. Who is most likely to be able to give us that information? A. I think Mr. Fisher.

Q. Mr. Fisher, what is the date on which the contract was advertised? A. (By Mr. Fisher) January 20, 1914.

(Witness reading from book.)

Q. Let me have that book, will you please. I have the minutes of the meeting of the executive committee of January 20, 1914, Mr. Shonts. Was the president sitting formally and the subject submitted and bids requested for the construction of additional tracks on the Second, Third avenue and other lines which we have had under discussion? A. The form of the contract required that the obligation imposed upon the company was that the certificate should be under the provisions, or rather the specifications of the chief engineer of this company. The Interborough Rapid Transit Company to pay to the contractor the actual and necessary cost to be incurred by him,—

Chairman Thompson.— I don't think an explanation in detail of this is necessary, Mr. Shonts.

Q. There appears in this statement enumerations of the bids the William Bradley Company being for cost plus eighteen per cent., same amount for the Pittsburgh Constructing Company,—

Snare & Triest being cost plus fifteen and three-fourths per cent., and Terry & Tench cost plus fifteen and one-half per cent., and T. A. Gillespie Company, cost plus fifteen per cent., that being the lowest bid received.

Q. Was the contract made in pursuance of the terms of this resolution? A. I reported to the board that in my judgment none of these bids were satisfactory, because, as I have stated, we were most anxious to have Terry & Tench and Snare & Triest on the steel work. But I said to the board that if they would authorize me so to do, I would send to T. A. Gillespie Company and would ask them if they would have associated with them Terry & Tench and Snare & Triest and make a new bid under which the three applicants could join, that I would recommend the awarding of the contract to the combined firm and a resolution to that effect and a resolution giving me that authority was passed. I sent for Mr. Gillespie and stated the substance of what I have just testified to now. He agreed to undertake this proposition on the basis of fifteen per cent. and afterwards we received bids from them under that basis and the contract was awarded.

Q. Mr. Fisher, where is the contract under which the contract was authorized specifically? Where is the resolution specifically authorizing the contract? Is it this resolution. (Counsel indicating resolution to witness.)

Mr. Fisher.— I think it is that resolution of January 20th.

Q. Is there a later one? A. This is the resolution under which the contract was made. (Witness indicating resolution to counsel.)

Q. This is the resolution of January 20th, 1914, reading as follows: "That the president be and hereby is authorized to award contract third-tracking above described to the T. A. Gillespie Company upon the condition that they may associate with it Terry & Tench, Inc., and Snare & Triest on the basis of cost plus fifteen per cent., and that the bids be accepted as addressed." Was the form of the contract so approved at that time? A. Yes.

Q. Was it submitted to the board at that time? A. I imagine so.

Chairman Thompson.—Mr. Shonts, you say that you were

satisfied that Terry & Tench was the best firm and that Snare &
Triest was second? A. Yes.

By Chairman Thompson:

Q. Wasn't it a rather peculiar thing that this contract went to
the three people that you wanted? A. Well, it went to the three
that constituted the lowest bidder, because, Mr. Chairman —

Q. (Interrupting.) I don't think it is necessary for you to
make any long explanation about this thing, Mr. Shonts. The
question is do you think that kind of bidding, when you limit it
to these men, do you think you have a right to call that competitive bidding? A. Yes.

Q. Don't you think it is non-competitive? A. I do not.

Q. Pretty nearly everybody else does. A. Well, I am sorry.
But I think you have got to take into consideration the great
hazards connected with the work.

Q. I don't care about these explanations. It's perfectly easy
for six men to get together if they know who each other are before
they start. Isn't that so? A. Six men could get together,
certainly.

Q. They could all agree to whom the bid would go, too, couldn't
they? A. Why, I don't believe anyone was disregarded. I don't
believe they were. You have to select very efficient people for
this work, and I will tell you that in my judgment the hazard of
these enterprises exceeds the hazard of any structural undertaking
in this world.

Q. That is all right for you to sit here and talk and tell us
all about the hazards of this enterprise, but I want to say this to
you, that I am only a lawyer, and you give me the Stevens contract and I will take it for ten per cent. and do it satisfactorily
if you will associate me with a high-class engineer, and I don't
know a thing about engineering either. A. As an answer to this,
Mr. Chairman, I will tell you something. We have a contract
with the city of New York under which it is specifically stated
that we shall not make a profit. This is under contracts Nos. 1
and 2, and it is specifically provided that we shall not make a
profit. We have been running along under that contract for ten
years or more. We are required to do any work the city of New
York calls upon us to do. Now the city of New York authorized

us to charge as an overhead charge ten per cent. in addition to the cost of material, and fifteen per cent. in addition to the cost of labor, and since the last compensation law has been passed they allow us to charge ten per cent. more because of the cost of labor.

Q. Now, Mr. Shonts, I am not going to allow any long detailed statement to appear on the record about this thing. A. Well, Mr. Chairman, you are the arbiter. We can show you when there have been times that we lost money on that basis.

Q. Well now, that Stevens contract was presented to the board of directors by you, was it not? A. Not for any action in the form it was in. That was only a draft copy. Get that out of your mind clearly.

Q. You mean to say it was not for any action? A. No, not in the shape it was in.

Q. Was it not presented to the Public Service Commission for action? A. Only except as to form, which is entirely different.

Q. What do you mean by that? A. I mean as to the legal phraseology of it. We could take in or out anything we may please.

Q. You could take Stevens' name out and put in somebody else, could you not? A. Yes.

Q. You never in the world intended to do this work with Stevens, did you? A. I never had any other thought.

Q. Do you think, Mr. Shonts, that Stevens ever thought he was ever going to get the contract? A. If he didn't he was a damned fool, because he was making arrangements to turn over the construction contract to other people so that he could give the matter his personal attention.

Q. Isn't it a fact, Mr. Shonts, that that contract provided that Mr. Stevens or whoever the contractor might be would not pay a cent for the plant? A. I understand all that.

Q. That never was drawn for any other purpose except,—— A. (Interrupting) Mr. Chairman, I want to say ——

Q. (Interrupting) I want you to answer my question. That contract didn't provide that the contractor should provide one cent's worth of plant, did it? A. That isn't in the contract.

Q. Nor one cent for any office? A. It was never a contract.

Q. Nor a cent of insurance premium? A. I might say, Mr. Chairman, that I was advised by my lawyers——

Q. You cannot answer questions by explanations. I am not going to have that. A. I don't mean to be unfair, Mr. Chairman.

Q. Well, Mr. Shonts, I think we are entitled to have our questions answered. Now, Mr. Shonts, if that Stevens contract had been awarded Mr. Stevens would have been allowed 10 per cent. on the office rent, the stenographers, everything, but not only that, in the contract he got 10 per cent. of it as commission, is that not so? A. I suppose so.

Q. He even got a percentage on postage stamps. A. Well, that probably would have happened if he had signed the contract.

Q. That is what I wanted to get on the record, that you understood that. Now the members of the board of directors, they must have understood it in that way, didn't they? A. I don't see how they could have understood it in any other way. I told them very clearly and the very first question that was asked, as I have testified here, was the elimination of half of it right off by the taking out of the equipment. That was the very first question asked by Mr. Berwind, and I agreed with him. So I took out half of the whole contract at one scoop. I want to give the facts but I don't want to be placed in a position of testifying to something that is wrong, but I just want to make the observation that in this matter Mr. Lane, Mr. Berwind and Mr. Young all understood that the first thing that went out was the equipment. There wasn't one of them, in my judgment, but what understood that that was the case.

Q. You say you took out the equipment? A. Yes.

Q. You did leave in the third-tracking of the present line and extensions? A. Yes. And if they took that contract for that 10 per cent and furnished the plant and employees, etc., they would have lost money.

Q. Your contract didn't provide for furnishing the plant? A. We discussed it and it was agreed upon as far as we agreed to anything. The proof of it is that it went into the contract that was signed.

Q. It was not until after the Public Service Commission —— A. (Interruption by witness) Never had heard from the Public Service Commission from that day on. I never heard a word from them.

Q. Your third-tracking, your connection and your extensions outside of the equipment, would that amount to upwards of twenty million dollars? A. No. I think the entire proposition was estimated at twenty-two million dollars, and about ten million of it was for equipment and the total amount of the third-tracking, as we estimated it, and of the extensions, extensions two million, and as I recall the third-tracking cost would be about nine million aside from the percentage. I am speaking of the cost of labor and material.

Q. Well, Mr. Shonts, were the other directors in the same state of mind on this proposition as you were? A. The best thing I could suggest in that matter, Mr. Chairman, would be to get some of the other directors up here and put them on the stand.

Q. Well, we want to get your idea. A. That is what I want to tell you. That is my idea.

By Mr. Colby:

Q. Who were the directors who succeeded the three gentlemen who terminated their relations with the board March 15, 1914?

Mr. Fisher.— Charles B. Ludlow was elected a director to take the place of William A. Read. He is a member of the firm of August Belmont & Company. September 24, 1913, Mr. Edwin S. Morston was elected to take the place of Mr. Young, who would not be elected at that annual meeting. Mr. Morston is president of the Farmers' Loan & Trust Company. On January 18, 1916, Mr. G. E. Trippe was elected to take the place of Mr. Lane. Mr. G. E. Trippe is head of the Westinghouse concern.

Chairman Thompson.— Mr. Shonts has been kind enough to give us this letter, which I will read into the record:

The following letter was read into the record by Chairman Thompson:

"February 19, 1914.

"Dear Sir.— Under date of October 18, 1915, I wrote you advising you that there was not the slightest objection on our part to the inspection by the Legislative Committee of any of Mr. Lane's letters to me or to his company relating to our affairs. At that time I had not heard that there might be among Mr. Lane's affairs some personal memoranda bearing on this company's affairs, but it has recently been brought to my attention that such may be the case and I am writing you again to state that so far as I or this company are concerned we have no objection to the inspection by the Committee of any of Mr. Lane's letters or personal memoranda that have any bearing upon the affairs of this company, and I hereby, on my own behalf and of the Interborough Rapid Transit Company, request that you permit a copy thereof to be taken by Hon. George F. Thompson, Chairman of the Joint Committee, or his authorized representative.

" Very truly yours,

(sgd) " T. P. SHONTS,

" President."

" Mr. Chas. H. Tyler,
" Tyler, Corneau & Eames,
"Ames Building,
" Boston, Mass."

(In ink) " I make the same request of the executor.

" T. P. S."

Chairman Thompson.— This should be directed to the executors also.

Mr. Shonts.— I will be glad to add that.

At the bottom of the letter is the ink notation:

" I make the same request of the executors." (Signed) " T. P. Shonts."

Chairman Thompson.— We will adjourn now until Monday morning, February 21st, at 11 A. M., and all witnesses under subpoena are directed to be present at that time.

The Committee thereupon adjourned until Monday, February 21, 1916, at 11 A. M.

FEBRUARY 21, 1916

NEW YORK COUNTY LAWYERS' ASSOCIATION
165 Broadway, New York City

Assemblyman Burr acting as Chairman.

Chairman Burr.— The Committee will come to order. We
will take a recess for twenty minutes. All persons under subpoena will remain here, please.

———

The Committee reconvened after recess with Senator George
F. Thompson acting as Chairman.

Chairman Thompson.— The following letter was received by
the Chairman of the Committee:

FEBRUARY 19, 1916.

" Hon. George F. Thompson, Hotel Biltmore, New York
City.

My dear Senator Thompson.— I regret that I must ask
you to relieve me at once of my duties as counsel to the
Joint Committee of the Senate and Assembly, of which you
are Chairman, and to accept my resignation herewith.

" Yours very truly,

" Bainbridge Colby."

THEODORE P. SHONTS recalled.

Examination by Mr. Smith:

Q. Mr. Shonts, are you sure that after the visit of Mr. Lane,
the Director of the Interborough, to Mr. J. P. Morgan, in relation to the Stevens contract then pending, or presented to the
Interborough directorate, that you did not receive a letter from
Mr. Morgan in relation to that Stevens contract? A. I am very

positive of it, having searched carefully since I was asked the other day, and having no recollection of it.

Q. You have made an examination of your records for the purpose of discovering such a letter? A. Yes.

Q. And if you had received such a letter, you would consider it an Interborough matter, so it would appear in the Interborough files? A. Yes.

Q. Did you examine your personal files for it? A. Yes.

Q. And had the Interborough files examined? A. Yes. I am very sure there was no letter received on that subject from Mr. Morgan.

Q. You are just as certain about it as you were the other day, that you have not any recollection of it? A. Yes. Can I say one thing?

Chairman Thompson.— Yes.

Mr. Delancey Nicoll.— I received a letter from Mr. Grout, which I have given to Mr. Shonts to your attention.

Mr. Shonts.— Mr. Grout writes Mr. Lincoln a letter in which he shows at length various conferences that they had with public officials, and which is a matter of public record, and which I am very glad to submit as a part of my letter.

By Mr. Smith:

Q. Would it be possible that such a letter from Mr. Morgan as has been discussed here came within the range of your forgetfulness? A. I do not see how I could forget it.

By Chairman Thompson:

Q. Of course I have not any objection to you or Mr. Grout, or anybody, if it is a question of publicity, giving this letter to the press at all, but this is a matter that is very important, and I much rather Mr. Grout would be under oath.

Mr. Delancey Nicoll.— You take it under advisement. I give it to you to take it under advisement.

Chairman Thompson.— Having refused the other lawyers the privilege of making statements without being under oath, if you have no objection, we will give Mr. Grout an opportunity to come here and explain the letter, but cannot do it today.

Mr. Shonts.— All the point, I have, Mr. Chairman, is that I do not want to do any person any injustice.

Chairman Thompson.— And we do not.

Mr. Shonts.— And I know you do not, and I know I cannot remember everything, and this letter does refresh my recollection a little.

Chairman Thompson.— You may be excused until 2:30 P. M.

Now, I want to make this statement for the record. This morning Mr. George W. Young, who has been under subpoena before this Committee every day including today — I sent counsel to the place where he was found living at the time the subpoena was originally served upon him, to notify him to be here at twelve o'clock. Counsel reports that he went to the hotel, and that he went to the same quarters in the Hotel Netherland, where he was living at the time of the service of the original subpoena, and he was met by a man whom he did not know, not having seen him before, and was informed that Mr. Young was not in. He then desired to see Mr. Young's valet, or whoever he talked with when he was there before, and he was informed that he could not see him. He was then asked if he inquired at the desk before he came up to the room, and he said he had not; that he came right up the elevator and went directly to the room. He was then informed that it was the rule of the house that he must inquire at the desk before he came to the room and knocked at the door. He said he did not know anything about the rules of the house, and he was informed that he should know. I will say I did hear the instructions given to this same gentleman by Mr. Colby when he went to the hotel, and he was told by Mr. Colby specially not to inquire at the desk, but to go right up the elevator and inquire at the room. But it seems this morning, this man took great exception to his going to the room and not inquiring. He was told in ten minutes he could see the manager downstairs. He said he went downstairs and waited twenty-five minutes to see the manager and recognized him, and asked the manager where the other fellow was, and he says he was not down and would not come down. He was reminded that he said he would bring him down, and he said he would not do it, anyhow. Anyway, the manager of the hotel was served with a subpoena, under the name of John Doe, to be before this Committee forthwith. And the only reason why counsel believes he was the manager of the hotel, is that after he served this subpoena, he gave directions to some one in the hotel, if this representative of ours came in the hotel again to throw him out. So he don't know his name. I want to know if the man served with that subpoena is present. I also want to say I called up and attempted to get in communication with Mr. Colby, and I am informed at his office he is not there, and they do not know where he is, and they are unable to tell me where he is. I want a subpoena to issue at once for the manager of the hotel and the man in charge of Mr. Young's quarters, and Mr. Young, and Mr. Colby, and Mr. Dawson, all of them returnable forthwith before this Committee.

Whereupon, an adjournment was taken to 2:30 o'clock P. M., same day.

AFTERNOON SESSION

The Committee was called to order by Chairman Thompson at 3:15 P. M., a quorum being present.

Chairman Thompson.— We will take a recess now until 3:30 P. M.

The Committee thereupon took a recess until 3:30 P. M., at which time the meeting was called to order by Chairman Thompson, a quorum being present.

J. EDWARD SCHERWIN, being duly sworn, testified as follows:

Examination by Chairman Thompson:

Q. You are clerk in the office of Mr. Bainbridge Colby? A. I have charge of Mr. Colby's office.

Q. You know that this Committee has been inquiring for Mr. Colby since this morning? A. I do.

Q. Were you the gentleman to whom I telephoned about 11:30 A. M. ? A. No, that was at the office. I was at Mr. Colby's house this morning.

Q. Do you know where he is? A. I do not.

Q. Does anybody in his office know? A. Nobody. I left him at 1 o'clock this afternoon, and I think he was going to his garage to get his car. He said that he would be in the office later in the afternoon.

Q. Will you endeavor to get into communication with him and advise him that the Committee have a subpoena out for him and wish him to come here? A. I have been doing so, and will continue to do so.

Chairman Thompson.— We will take another recess for fifteen minutes.

(Recess for fifteen minutes.)

The meeting was called to order by Chairman Thompson at 3:50 P. M.

Chairman Thompson.— When we suspend it will be until Wednesday morning, and we will suspend to here, but in the meantime I hope to get a different, better and more healthy quarters to sit in, and we will adjourn to here and then meet at whatever quarters we arrange in the meantime.

THEODORE P. SHONTS, being recalled, testified as follows:

By Chairman Thompson:

Q. We don't want to hear anything more from you until day after tomorrow, and so that there will be no question about the legality, you are excused until Wednesday morning at 11 o'clock A. M. at this place. A. Thank you, Mr. Chairman.

MILES M. DAWSON, called as a witness, being first duly sworn, testified as follows:

By Chairman Thompson:

Q. You reside, Mr. Dawson, in the city of New York? A. I do.

Q. And you have been employed by this Commission up to Saturday? A. I was for about two weeks.

Q. You remember an occasion at Mr. Colby's house, when Mr. Colby and yourself and Mr. J. Frank Smith and myself were present one evening about a week ago? A. I remember being there when you and Mr. Colby were present, but I would not swear as to Mr. Smith.

Q. Do you remember a conversation in regard to a letter of great importance that passed between Mr. J. P. Morgan and Mr. Shonts. A. I don't recall that conversation.

Q. Do you remember at that time specifically talking of a letter that was written, from J. P. Morgan to Mr. Shonts, the date of the letter being some time after the death of Mr. Read and Mr. Lane as appearing in our former testimony? A. I do not recall such a letter.

Q. But do you recall the conversation about the letter? A. No, I do not.

Q. You don't remember any conversation at any time when I was present about such a letter? A. No, I do not.

Q. Don't you remember at that time of your saying that you had a very important letter and you had with you your brief bag, if that is what you call it, and pulled a paper out of your brief bag and showed it to me? A. I did not have copies of his letter, but I had access to what was represented to me to be the entire files of the Morgan and Shonts correspondence, and I had notes at that time concerning the correspondence, which notes I turned over to Mr. Colby for purposes of the examination, but I do not recall them specifically.

Q. Have these notes and papers been turned back to the Committee? A. All that were in my possession. They were either turned over to the Committee or were handed to Mr. Colby.

Q. Do you remember pulling a letter out of your brief bag? A. I didn't pull a letter out. I pulled my notes in reference to the correspondence.

Q. And showed them to me? A. No question about it.

Q. And put them back in the bag again? A. Yes.

Q. What became of those? A. Those notes were either given to Mr. Colby or are now in your possession. I handed all the remaining notes I had to Mr. Smith this afternoon.

Q. You don't know whether this letter was incorporated in

them or not? A. I do not. After Mr. Colby had completed the examination on the Morgan correspondence, which was some little time ago, as you remember, I am not sure what was done with the notes. They may have been possibly destroyed. That I could not say.

Mr. Moss.— Mr. Chairman, in order that the record may be complete, I suggest that you make a statement of just what occurred there, so that Mr. Dawson may know to what your question is addressed.

Chairman Thompson.— The statement I refer to is this; that there was a question came up in relation to certain matters of the Gillespie papers, and Mr. Dawson made the remark that he had a much more important letter than anything that had come out, and reference was made therein to the letter which passed between Mr. Morgan and Mr. Shonts. I think the reference was made by Mr. Colby to Mr. Dawson. Anyway, reference was made that he had a much more important paper than anything that had yet come out. He rather excitedly opened the bag and pulled up what, I say, was the paper. Mr. Colby then went on to talk about the letter between Mr. Morgan and Mr. Shonts and Mr. Dawson says the paper is there in that bag. I haven't seen it.

Mr. Dawson.— Mr. Colby had in his possession the entire correspondence between Mr. Morgan and Mr. Shonts and, I am sure, you will have a complete record of all the letters that I have found.

Chairman Thompson.— The letter I refer to, as you know perfectly well, is a letter passing between Mr. Shonts and Mr. Morgan in relation to the Stevens contract.

Mr. Dawson.— I have no recollection of a letter of that character.

By Mr. Moss:

Q. Was this stated to be the original letter or a copy?

Chairman Thompson.— A copy, as I understood.

A. If it was a copy, it would be one to Mr. Shonts. I don't recall that it had even the remotest reference to this Gillespie contract.

By Mr. Moss:

Q. Mr. Dawson, do you remember the incident that the Chairman speaks of? A. I remember being present at Mr. Colby's house when Senator Thompson was there; yes, sir.

Q. Do you remember any instance in which you took a paper out of your bag? A. I don't remember any particular instance, but it is certainly possible that I took the papers out of my bag.

Q. Didn't you say you had something important, more so than anything else? A. I don't recall.

Q. Well, will you say that you didn't? A. No.

Q. What was the paper that you did take out? A. That I couldn't answer.

Q. It was important? A. Yes.

Q. That's the reason you pulled it out? A. It was.

Q. You were then in the employ of the Committee? A. I was.

Q. Cannot you refresh your recollection and tell us something about it? A. I have no means to do it. If the file man of the Interborough Rapid Transit Company will bring all the files that were here on Saturday, and also the files of the Morgan papers, I shall be very glad to glance at them.

Q. Don't you know what the nature of the letter he has referred to is? A. No. That I could not say.

Q. Don't you remember any such letter? A. No, I have no recollection of any such correspondence between Mr. Shonts and Mr. Morgan about the Gillespie contract, or rather, the Stevens contract.

Q. I am not talking about the correspondence; I am talking about a specific letter that passed between Mr. Shonts and Mr. Morgan. A. I have not seen it as far as I know, and I am very sure that if I had seen it I would recall it.

Q. Has it occurred since you have been sitting here, what that important paper was? A. It has not, Mr. Moss, for the reason that a large proportion, a majority of the Morgan correspondence was important.

26

Q. Is that paper in the evidence in this hearing? A. I think it is.

Q. What is it, then? A. I think so because all the correspondence went into evidence.

Q. You were assistant counsel? A. I was, yes.

Q. Are you sure you were? A. I suppose I was, at least.

Q. As assistant counsel to this Committee I ask you what it was? A. I have answered you to the best of my ability.

Q. I say is it in evidence. A. To the best of my knowledge it is in evidence, because all of the correspondence between Mr. Morgan and Mr. Shonts that was in the file and that was turned over to me was put in by Mr. Colby when I was sitting at his right at this table.

Q. Did you have a talk with Mr. Colby about that particular paper? A. No.

Q. Not about the paper that you held up? A. Mr. Colby was there.

Q. Did you have a talk with him about it? A. Not at that time, as I remember it.

Q. Any other time? A. Not except in a general way.

Q. Did you ever talk to Mr. Colby about the letter which we are referring to? A. I must have done so.

Q. Have you any recollection? A. I have not.

Q. How is it that you have not? A. I don't know of such a letter.

Q. Is there anything more important in the testimony than the letter? A. I should say so.

Q. Have you had any talk with Mr. Colby about that particular letter? A. Not particularly.

Q. Have you made an effort to get such a letter? A. I have not seen it.

Q. Did you and Mr. Colby assume that there was such a letter? A. I have never, no, sir.

Q. Were you here last Saturday when Mr. Colby was interrogating Mr. Shonts about that letter? A. I was here when he asked where such a letter was.

Q. You say he didn't think there was such a letter? A. I didn't say so.

Q. Did you and he discuss the matter? A. No.

Q. Did you and he confer about it? A. No, we did not. If you will allow me to explain, I think it likely he asked that question. 'I think it likely he asked that question, because in the testimony of Mr. Young before I was brought here, before I was in the matter, I understand the statement had been made that the matter had been called to the attention of Mr. Morgan and that Mr. Morgan had called it to the attention of Mr. Shonts. I suppose that might have led Mr. Colby to believe that a letter might have been written to Mr. Shonts. I have no other reason, of course, to believe that the question should have been asked.

Q. You have been in conferences with the Chairman of the Committee? A. Yes.

Q. You know he believes there is such a letter? A. Yes, no doubt about it.

Q. You don't believe it was written? A. I don't think it was.

Q. Then there was a point of disagreement between you and the Chairman on that subject? A. As to whether it was written, I don't know.

Q. Don't you think it quite likely such a letter might be concealed? A. Yes.

Q. Don't you think such a letter was written and concealed? A. It is entirely possible. I think it much more probable, from the evidence that has been taken, that Mr. Morgan advised Mr. Shonts by telephone or in some other similar manner.

Q. Has the subject of this letter anything to do with your resignation? A. Nothing whatever.

Q. It was not a point over which you disagreed with the Chairman? A. I didn't know until I was called to the stand.

Chairman Thompson.— Now let's get down to this thing, Mr. Dawson. All I want to do is to get at these things. I don't like any personal controversy. Now, on this occasion things appeared to be rather acute because of a certain check of Gillespie's which had been published and you felt that way, didn't you, I mean this occasion when we were at the house?

Mr. Dawson.— I don't think so.

Chairman Thompson.— You had been talking about it, hadn't you? A. I think we may have talked about it.

Chairman Thompson.— Now, didn't you say when you pulled this out of your bag, didn't you say that here's a matter much more important and much more sensational, I think, is the word you used when you pulled that out of your bag?

Mr. Dawson.— I may have said it.

Chairman Thompson.— I would like to know what that was. There has been nothing in the testimony that was more sensational.

Mr. Dawson.— I think there was.

By Mr. Moss:

Q. Whom from? A. I shall be very glad to examine my notes and find out.

Q. Have you ever talked with Mr. Young? A. I met Mr. Young some years ago and I have seen him once since.

Q. Have you talked with Mr. Young about this case? A. I have not personally.

Q. Have you been present in which conversation was carried on between Mr. Young and somebody else? A. I have.

Q. Have you heard Mr. Young talk about the fact that a letter passed between Mr. Morgan and Mr. Shonts in reference to the Stevens contract? A. No; that subject did not come up.

Q. Not while you were present? A. No.

Chairman Thompson.— Well, now, I have held this matter until 4 o'clock, and it is our adjournment time, because I was in hopes I could meet Mr. Colby. I have tried since 11 o'clock this morning. We have waited until the last moment before swearing you, Mr. Dawson, and under the circumstances, the subpoena not having been served on Mr. Young, I will excuse you until Wednesday morning at 11 o'clock, and ask you to be here.

Mr. Dawson.— Do you really think I will have to be here, Mr. Chairman, because, you know, I have my own private business to take care of?

Chairman Thompson.— Well, Mr. Dawson, I will have to leave

it that you are excused until 11 o'clock Wednesday morning, and that you be where I can have you at any time. You are excused until Wednesday morning at 11 o'clock. I will ask that subpoenas issue for Mr. Young and Mr. Colby and the manager of the Hotel Netherlands, and Mr. Young's valet and his office boy, returnable at 11 o'clock Wednesday morning, February 23, 1916.

This Committee and that portion of the Committee examining the Gillespie books and other matters will adjourn until Wednesday morning at 11 o'clock at this place.

Mr. Colby's resignation is upon the record and is hereby accepted. The Chair announces the employment of Mr. Frank Moss as counsel to the Committee.

The Committee thereupon adjourned until Wednesday, February 23, 1916, at 11 A. M.

FEBRUARY 23, 1916

NEW YORK COUNTY LAWYERS' ASSOCIATION,
165 Broadway, New York City

Hon. George F. Thompson presiding.

Mr. Frank Moss, acting as Counsel to the Committee.

Mr. J. Frank Smith, Assistant Counsel, also present.

Chairman Thompson.— The Committee will come to order and I must ask of the spectators that we are glad to have you here of course, and we have got to because it is a public hearing, but we do not have to have the smoke, and you will all of you have time to go out and smoke if you want to. I might once in a while let a man who is tied in here take a whiff of a cigarette, but those who can go outside I am not going to let you smoke in here at all. We will see how that works.

BAINBRIDGE COLBY, presented as a witness.

Mr. Moss.— Mr. Chairman, we won't swear Mr. Colby.

Chairman Thompson.— I might say for the record Mr. Colby has not been subpoenaed. He came here because he was requested.

Examination by Mr. Moss.

Q. Mr. Colby, will you kindly tell us about where to find Mr. Young, where he is and where we might be able to see him? A. I learned yesterday that Mr. Young had left for Palm Beach on Monday. At the time he went there was no definite demand for his appearance, and the moment I learned in the newspapers that the Committee desired his presence, I sent him a wire on his train, with instructions to see it reached him at any point where he could be overtaken, calling his attention to the fact that the Committee wishes him and requesting his immediate return. I have received a reply telegram this morning, stating his entire willingness and readiness to return at any time the Committee wants him.

Q. Do you think we could get him here by Saturday? A. I haven't the least doubt of it.

Q. Will you telegraph the matter to him? A. I will, with pleasure. I might say, Mr. Moss, if you will allow me —

Q. Yes. A. That with the completest understanding with the Chairman of the Committee, Mr. Young has been held as what I might call a reserve witness. He has shown a very helpful disposition to tell the truth on all matters covered in his examination, and while we had not by any means exhausted Mr. Young's ability to aid the Committee, there was no definite idea as to just when he would be called. I learned from the doctor yesterday, whose office I went to, the fact that he had gone, and he said he was not in good shape; he had been suffering from a rasping and severe cough, which he had been unable to throw off, and the doctor recommended a few days under better climatic conditions.

Q. Of course, we would be glad to have any suggestion you will make to us concerning the further examination of Mr. Young? A. Certainly.

Chairman Thompson.— Is there any objection to showing that telegram, to putting it on the record?

Mr. Colby.— Not the least. He said in his telegram that he had wired to the Chairman of the Committee as well.

By Mr. Moss:

Q. The Chairman has not received any telegram, but he, no doubt thought you would show the Chairman. A. Shall I read it? This is sent from some point en route:

> " EAUGALLIE, FLA., *February* 23, 1916.

" Bainbridge Colby, 49 East 66th street:

> " Have telegraphed Thompson as follows: Stop en route Palm Beach; advice of physician, Dr. Campbell Douglas, West 58th street. No intention nor desire to avoid further examination. Expect to return before adjournment Committee; if you desire will return at once. Would appreciate few days here, if possible. Telegraph me care John N. Hanan stop. GEORGE W. YOUNG."

Chairman Thompson.— Does that mean we would have to telegraph him at that place it was sent from?

Mr. Colby.— No, I should telegraph him at Palm Beach or care of Mr. Hanan, who apparently is the man he wants you to telegraph in care of. He says John H. He means John W. Hanan.

Chairman Thompson.— Sent from Eaugallie.

By Mr. Moss:

Q. Now, Mr. Colby, you know the letter we are interested in? A. I am familiar, I think, with the entire discussion concerning that letter.

Q. What is your own opinion as to the existence of such a letter? A. I have been inclined to strongly suspect the existence of such a letter. I have questioned Mr. Young very carefully on that point. He, as the Senator knows, in discussing what contribution Mr. Young could make to our record here at an interview, Mr. Shonts, subsequent to the call of Mr. Lane on Mr. Morgan, and Mr. Young said that he has a rather clear impression that at the time of that call, some reference was made by Mr. Shonts to receiving such a letter. I never saw such a letter. It has never been — it has not been found in a very rigorous search that we made of the files of the correspondence furnished us by the president's office of the Interborough. Young never said he was positive that he saw such a letter, but he has stated to me that he was clearly of the impression that such a letter had been written and that Mr. Shonts in his interview with him on this occasion had referred to having heard from Mr. Morgan expressing disapproval or criticism of the Stevens contract. That was the occasion for the very persistent inquiry I made of Mr. Shonts on Friday or Saturday of the existence or receiving such a letter and you recall he testified he did not remember of receiving such a letter but later he declined to deny that such a letter had been received. That was where I left the point. This alleged or putative letter, because I have never seen it, has figured previously in the Committee. Mr. Morgan was asked if he had written such a letter and as I recollect the evidence he stated he did not recall it.

Q. He did not make a positive denial of it, did he? A. Not that I recall. It has been some weeks since I read the record on that point.

Q. Mr. Colby, you and I are old friends. I imagine there may be something you would like to say this morning. I have my confidence in your attitude and position and all that and you know it. I do not have to tell you that. I deem it an honor to have followed you and I shall want your help. A. You are sure to receive that in any manner in which I can render it to you, Mr. Moss. I would not have undertaken the quite arduous work of acting as counsel to this Committee had I not thoroughly believed that it was timely and that it had work of the highest importance to discharge and I want to say that at no time have I had the least suggestion of anything except the relentless determination of its Chairman and his colleagues to pursue this investigation wherever it might lead.

Q. Mr. Colby, I appreciate that statement and I am sure the Chairman does in view of some natural newspaper comments that have been made on the events of the last few days, and if I may, I will ask you to make that statement even more pointedly. You have referred to the purpose of this Committee. Have you ever questioned the honesty or sincerity of the efforts made by this Committee? A. Never for a moment.

Q. Your retirement is not for any reason that your hand was held back or anything of that sort? A. I certainly can assure you that no such reason entered into it. My reasons I thought were stated completely and were understood. I would like to state one further word about my colleague, Mr. Dawson.

Q. I would be glad to have you? A. I feel in his absence, and sustaining as I did the relation of chief counsel where he was merely an assistant, that I should say that it pains me very much to see any reflection made upon Mr. Dawson's zeal or his complete devotion to the purposes of this Committee. I know Mr. Dawson to be a man of the highest integrity and of a conscientious character. He won the regard and unlimited confidence of Justice Hughes during the Armstrong investigation. He was never absent from Judge Hughes' side, and he has served me and his Committee with the most indefatigable devotion, hardly ever leaving my house until past midnight. And I greatly regret to hear anything said whether it was authentic or even rantic that in any way reflects on him. I would like to say a word to the statement that I am counsel of Mr. George W. Young. I really do not sustain that relation in what that term suggests. I am not a keeper of his conscience or his volition. I do not think I am the attorney for Mr. Young. His attorney is the gentleman who appeared with him, Mr. Connell of Joline, Larkin & Rathbone. The only case I have had for Mr. Young that I can recall within a year was a matter which I argued for him at the request of Joline, Larkin & Rathbone in connection with the probate contest of his late wife's will in New Jersey. The New Jersey contestant made an application to enjoin the prosecution of the New Jersey case in the New York court and I suppose no one else being available I was asked to argue that motion. That is all I have ever done in that case.

Q. I know you are a public-spirited man and your relation to this inquiry was in the same public-spirit that has distinguished you for years, and I say to you, knowing your continued interest in the matter, that whenever you have any facts or any thoughts that would fit into the work of this inquiry I shall esteem it a favor if you will let me have it and I shall consult with you and get your advice whenever you will give it. A. Mr. Moss, I have already pledged you my most hearty co-operation and you may always depend upon it.

Q. Mr. Moss.— Is that all.

Chairman Thompson.— Except the chair in behalf of the Committee acknowledges its gratitude to Mr. Colby for his very satisfactory conduct in this matter even up to now and we agree with Mr. Colby in everything he said about himself and I could add a whole lot more very nice and complimentary and very decent things about Mr. Colby. There is only one thing, to get my idea clear, I do not want to be at all backward about expressing my idea about these things,— he said that Mr. Dawson was never absent from Mr. Hughes' side. I think that probably is the trouble. He never was here, and perhaps we won't have so much of that from now on. Mr. Dawson was requested to be here this morning at 11 o'clock. He may be excused. Mr. Smith will you frame a telegram for me to sign to Mr. George W. Young at Palm Beach, Florida in care of John W. Hannan. I want Mr. Shonts to come down here so that I can excuse him. I do not want any question about the validity of his appearance. After consultation with Mr. Morse we still think that there are more material witnesses in New York that the Committee want than are in Palm Beach, so we will continue our session in New York instead of adjourning down there, and with that in view, we will have Mr. Smith send a telegram to Mr. Young asking him to return in time so that he can be a witness here Saturday morning of this week.

At this point Mr. Shonts appeared before the Committee.

Chairman Thompson.— Mr. Shonts you may be excused until Saturday morning at eleven o'clock.

THOMAS H. GILLESPIE, on the stand.

Examination by Chairman Thompson:

Q. Mr. Gillespie there are certain documents we are advised are in your possession relating to matters under inquiry by our Sub-Committee that you have refused to deliver upon request this morning. My information is that your account shows that certain moneys are transmitted by you to your Pittsburgh office and that you received from the Pittsburgh office periodical reports in relation to that and that you refused to produce before the Sub-Committee those periodical reports from Pittsburgh? Is that correct? A. I have stated to the Committee and to Mr. Moss within the last few days, Senator, that we finance our Pittsburgh office — the New York office finances the Pittsburgh office. That there has been sums of money sent out there from time to time over the last two years to finance their work which amounted to somewhere about two millions and a half; that there has been a great deal of that money returned and that he can find and we will answer any questions pertaining to money which has been sent out and how it has been spent, but I have declined and do decline to produce any documents that he may roam through the same, as unfortunately we have had one experience.

Chairman Thompson.— Now I do not want to hear anything more about your unfortunate experience.

Mr. Gillespie.— Well, it has been unfortunate.

Chairman Thompson.— Yes. I assume that has been a great excuse for all you people in New York who do not want to show your books and transactions to the public, and that has been the excuse that you have used here for the last ten days and it is worn out.

Mr. Gillespie.—I beg your pardon, sir.

Chairman Thompson.— If you did not have documents there that made you feel bad to have the public see it would not bother you, those things.

Mr. Gillespie.— That may be —

Chairman Thompson.— If you did not make the payments of the kind mentioned in the so-called check of $2,500 to Mr. Quigg you would not have the embarrassment of having the public know about it and we will dismiss that proposition. That excuse don't go any further. The Chairman of this Committee is absolutely responsible for everything that occurs in respect to that check, and not Mr. Moss in the slightest degree, and I want that

thoroughly understood by you and such portion of the public that
proposed to hide behind this incident. Now we will go on. Now
these documents had been asked to be produced before this Committee and I want to know whether you are going to produce them
or not.

Mr. Gillespie.— As I have stated before I will answer any
questions in relation to them before the Sub-Committee but we will
not produce them because they do not pertain in any way or in any
manner whatever to this investigation.

Chairman Thompson.— That is for us to say, whether they
pertain or do not pertain. Is that correct Mr. Moss?

Mr. Moss.— Why, yes. If it was for a witness to say whether
a thing was pertinent or not, you would never get any evidence.
The Chairman has talked to you good and straight. My language
is in a different tone but means the same thing. You may trust
the Chairman and Counsel to look at this thing as fair and straight
men ought to look at it. If the matters that appear in those
documents are entirely private and they have no public relation,
they will be entirely forgotten and we will forget it. But Mr.
Chairman I notice in your record a great many of these passages
with witnesses and I want to tell you that I have the promise of
the district attorney of the county of New York to stand behind
this Committee for all legal purposes. That means to compel
witnesses to testify, to be here and to produce documents. I
suggest to you to give him *duces tecum,* and as the old gentleman
said to the board of aldermen at one time, let it take its course,—
nature take its course.

Chairman Thompson.— You said the account that was being examined, is the account of construction work for the Interborough.

Mr. Gillespie.— No, sir.

Chairman Thompson.— The account that is being examined is
account of construction work in the Interborough? A. Yes, sir.

Q. And in examining that account certain moneys appearing
in that account have been transmitted to your Pittsburgh office?
A. No, sir.

Q. Don't the books show that certain moneys — hasn't the books shown from the examination of this Interborough construction account? A. No, sir.

Q. How do they ascertain that certain moneys were sent to Pittsburgh? A. Because they have examined our fifty Church street account and the books were kept at the other office and the accounts were in the Park place office altogether. We have transferred money between those two offices.

Q. Then you transferred money from that office to your Pittsburgh account? A. No money pertaining to the Interborough account has been sent to Pittsburgh.

Q. They are moneys that have been sent from your uptown office to your 50 Church street office? A. Yes, there is one or two accounts.

Q. And there has been money sent from your 50 Church street office to Pittsburgh? A. Yes, sir.

Q. Now you have the record in your possession showing the expenditure of the moneys sent to Pittsburgh? A. Yes, and I offer to explain that.

Q. I don't want any explanation. I want to know have you those papers in your hands? A. We have reports in Pittsburgh showing how they made the disbursements.

Q. Those are in the State of New York? A. Yes, sir.

Q. And in your possession? A. Yes, sir.

Q. Now the Committee directs you to produce those papers; they are in your possession and in New York county, before this Committee, and so there will be no question about it, Counsel will prepare a subpoena *duces tecum* describing these papers and service forthwith.

Chairman Thompson.— For the record the following telegram to George W. Young, Palm Beach, Florida, care of John Hannan. "Accepting your assurance to Mr. Bainbridge Colby that you would return immediately upon request to give further testimony, the Joint Legislative Committee investigating Public Service, etc., requests that you present yourself at the place designated in the subpoena heretofore served on you on February 26th, 1916, at eleven o'clock A. M. for further examination. Signed George F. Thompson, Chairman."

Chairman Thompson.— I will state that Mr. Young has never been excused by the Chair, and I meant to have asked Mr. Colby whether he had ever excused him or not. There being certain subpoenaes that have been issued this morning and the witnesses who have not yet departed, returnable at 2.30, and so to properly welcome them we will suspend until half past two.

At this point the Committee took a recess until 2.30 P. M.

AFTER RECESS

Chairman Thompson.— The Committee will come to order. This telegram to Mr. Young, I suggest that it be sent to both places, and that the telegraph company be asked to report on the delivery.

LEROY T. HARKNESS, appearing as a witness, testified as follows:

Examination by Mr. Moss:

Q. And your position? A. Assistant counsel, Public Service Commission, First District.

Q. I want to call your attention, Mr. Harkness, to the case reported in 206 N. Y., at p. 110, the Admiralty Company against the City of New York — you remember that case, do you? A. Yes, sir.

Q. There seem to be three cases associated in this report. The case of which I have just given you the title, also the case of John R. Ryan against Willcox and others, Public Service Commissioners, and also the case of John J. Hopper against Willcox and others, Public Service Commissioners. I wish, Mr. Harkness, you would tell the Committee the history of those cases in a general way. A. The first case served was the Ryan case. I think that was the latter part of February, 1912, that the papers were served. Then came the Admiralty case, which was served a little later, and then finally, about the first of March, came the Hopper case. The cases came up on argument for injunction.

Q. Was the object in each case the same? A. Yes, sir.

Q. What was the object? A. To test the constitutionality of the proposed subway arrangement, perhaps dual subway plans.

Q. What law did it bring into question, if any? A. It brought in question the constitutionality, or those in the argument before Judge Blackmar — the statute also. And while the case was pending before Judge Blackmar, the so-called Wagner legislation in 1912 was obtained. Also the argument in the higher court was based on the constitutionality.

Q. Which was what? A. Which questioned the aid of the city in a private enterprise, and also the further constitutional question which was argued in the Court of Appeals, that the Rapid Transit Act was the private or local bill, and the further question was injected in the Hopper suit of the Rapid Transit Act requiring referendum, which was also passed on.

Q. The head-note of this report specifies Article VIII, section 10, of the State Constitution, and Article III, Section 18, of the State Constitution. A. The first is the faith and credit of the city, and the second the prohibition against a private or local bill giving the right to lay down railroad tax.

Q. The main question was whether the city or State had the right to enter into partnership with private individuals or corporations? A. More accurately, the faith of the city being given in aid of a private enterprise.

Q. Now, will you state the history of those cases in a general way? A. I gave about the dates I think they were started. They came on before Mr. Justice Blackmar, and on the argument demurrers were interposed to all three complaints, and the three cases heard together. Judge Blackmar handed down a decision sustaining the demurrer. The matter was then taken to the Appellate Division, Second Department, where it was argued, and the decision in the Appellate Division was an affirmance of Judge Blackmar's decision. Then the three cases were all taken to the Court of Appeals, heard together as in the lower courts, and the Court of Appeals sustained the Appellate Division and Special Term.

Q. And the opinion which I have just referred to is the opinion of the Court of Appeals in that case. The decision was rendered by a divided court, Judge Hiscock wrote the prevailing opinion,

Judge Cullen wrote the dissenting opinion, Judge Werner wrote a dissenting opinion, and Judges Haight, Vann and Collin concurred with Hiscock. Cullen and Werner dissented, and Gray took no part. Ryan was represented by counsel right through these litigations, wasn't he? A. Yes, sir.

Q. The brief on appeal appears to have been written by Willard M. Baylis? A. As I recall, a Mr. Baylis was both attorney and counsel throughout in that case.

Q. And the brief by Mr. Hopper was written by Clarence J. Shearn? A. I think Mr. Shearn was both attorney and counsel throughout in the Hopper case.

Q. So there were actual plaintiffs aside from the Hopper case and plaintiffs represented by counsel who remained in those cases from the beginning to the end, testing or trying to test the constitutionality of this question, and they were in from the beginning to the end of the litigation? A. Yes, sir. The counsel you mention argued those cases both before Judge Blackmar in the Appellate Division, as well as in the Court of Appeals.

Q. Was the Admiralty Company represented before Judge Blackmar? A. Yes, sir.

Q. The Admiralty Company appears in this report in the Court of Appeals to have been represented by Louis Marshall, Daniel Hays, Ralph Wolf, and Samuel Untermeyer. Were any of them in the case from the beginning? A. Mr. Marshall argued the case in the Court of Appeals. My recollection is Mr. Untermeyer argued it before Justice Blackmar and in the Appellate Division.

Q. The corporation counsel appeared by Louis H. Hohlo in the Court of Appeals. Was the corporation counsel represented throughout the litigation? A. Yes, sir.

Q. The Public Service Commission were represented by George S. Coleman, Oliver Semple, and Leroy T. Harkness. Was the Public Service Commission represented throughout these litigations? A. Yes, sir.

Q. The Interborough Rapid Transit was represented by Richard Reid Rogers and Alfred E. Mudge. Was it represented throughout? A. Yes, sir.

Q. The Brooklyn Rapid Transit was represented by its counsel, Charles A. Colin and George D. Youmans? A. Yes, sir.

Q. Was the road represented throughout the litigation? A. Yes, sir.

Q. At any time while these litigations were pending, do you know that counsel who appeared against the constitutionality of the act were in the pay of the Interborough Railroad Company? A. I did not know that, no, sir.

Q. Did you have any information of it until it was made to appear in the examination last week? A. Nothing more than a suspicion.

Q. When did you begin to have a suspicion? A. I suspected that when the suit came in.

Q. The original suit? A. Yes.

Q. Which suit, the Admiralty? A. The Admiralty suit is the one I am referring to now. There was a prior Admiralty suit in 1911, in which the same counsel and then the Admiralty counsel took part in at least one proceeding to modify the route and plan of Lexington avenue route. I am not sure whether they appeared in both proceedings or not, but from the past litigations I suspected that when the Admiralty suit of 1912 came in it was probably instigated by interests friendly to the Interborough Company.

Q. Did you have any facts upon which you could base your suspicion? A. No, sir.

Q. Did you confer with your associates, Mr. Coleman, Mr. Semple, or anyone connected as counsel with the Public Service Commission? A. I conferred with Mr. Coleman, I remember.

Q. Mr. Coleman was senior? A. Mr. Coleman is counsel to the Commission. The rest of us were assistants.

Q. Well, having that suspicion, did you, or did any of your associates, do anything to determine whether your suspicion was well founded? A. May I answer that somewhat at length?

Q. Yes, sir. Any way you like, Mr. Harkness. A. I took the matter up with Mr. Coleman and discussed it and the recollection is at that time I told Mr. Coleman of my suspicion, and he said, I remember his saying at that time if the question at issue were not properly raised in any of those suits, and all of them were not raised, that he would raise them himself or see that they were raised. I think I then discussed the matter somewhat with Commissioner Maltbie, and I remember afterward meeting Mr. Clarence J. Shearn at lunch. I used to meet him occasionally.

I don't know whether I told him of my suspicion or not. But I did talk with him over his bringing a suit, and I don't know to what extent the talk I had with him may have been instrumental in the bringing of the Hopper suit, which I believe did represent an interest really adverse to the subway contract.

Q. You had no such suspicion in the Hopper case as you had in the Admiralty case? A. No, sir.

Q. What about the Ryan case? A. I had no facts specially to base any conclusion on, but I had a suspicion they were probably instigated by interests friendly to the B. R. T.

Q. You thought that was helpful to the B. R. T. and the Admiralty case, helpful to the Interborough and not necessarily helpful. Inasmuch as they were probably instigated by those companies —

Q. Intended to be? A. I don't want to quibble about it.

Chairman Thompson.— They paid $62,000 for it. They do not hardly pay for them without they get help or assistance.

Mr. Harkness.— My understanding or suspicion was they were instigated by these companies in order to test the constitutionality of the act or arrangement.

By Mr. Moss:

Q. Did you or your associates make any inquiries to discover whether as a matter of fact any one representing the Admiralty Realty Company was receiving pay from the Interborough? A. No, sir.

Q. I asked the same question with reference to the Ryan suit? A. The same answer.

Q. Then, if I get the import of your testimony correctly, it is that possibly the Hopper case resulted from your discussion of the matter with Mr. Shearn and conveying your suspicions to him? A. I am not sure.

Q. I said possibly? A. Possibly, yes.

Q. Was it your intention to bring about some such result when you talked with Mr. Shearn? A. I was hopeful of such a result.

Chairman Thompson.— The Hopper suit was brought after those other two suits were commenced. A. Yes, sir.

Chairman Thompson.—And which was brought first?

Mr. Harkness.— The Ryan.

Chairman Thompson.—And then the Admiralty?

Mr. Harkness.— Yes.

Chairman Thompson.— You say you had these suspicions,— why,— what made them?

Mr. Harkness.— The prior litigation that had gone through with the Admiralty Company. I did not know of any reason why this Admiralty Realty Company were opposed, what real interest it had to enter into what must have been rather an expensive litigation years before, to hold up various projects of the Commission, and I suspected that the previous litigation had been instigated by interests friendly to the Interborough Company, or controlled by it.

Q. Do you remember whether or not, in the opinion of the court, one of the judges intimated that they were limited by the argument; that their discussion of the case was limited by the argument? A. No, sir; I don't remember that. Was that in the Court of Appeals?

Q. Yes. A. No, I don't remember.

Q. Do you believe that every question that could have been raised on the constitutional feature of the case was raised and argued? A. Yes, I do.

GEORGE S. COLEMAN, called as a witness, being first duly sworn, testified as follows:

Examination by Mr. Moss:

Q. You are senior counsel for the Public Service Commission, are you not? A. Yes.

Q. You heard the testimony of Mr. Harkness, did you? A. Yes, sir.

Q. He spoke of a conference with you — do you recall such a conference? A. I do not recall it, but I am willing to take Mr. Harkness' statement for it.

Q. That is, it does not come to your memory, but you believe he has told the facts? A. I believe he must have told the truth.

Q. Do you remember any question being raised or coming into your thought concerning this Admiralty case? A. I have no recollection of it whatever, because the same counsel and same attorneys had, I think, opposed the original route in the Appellate Division, and then they had afterwards opposed again some proceeding the Commission were interested in, and I then credited them as being hostile.

Q. Then did you believe the Admiralty company was hostile? A. I did.

Q. You did not share in the suspicion of Mr. Harkness? A. I cannot recollect having any suspicion until this matter came out in the newspapers. I was interested more in the Hopper case.

Q. The Hopper case was begun after the Admiralty case? A. It was begun after.

Q. Didn't you know that Mr. Harkness had spoken to Mr. Shearn? A. Yes, because we wanted to give Mr. Shearn all the ammunition we had on the law and the facts, knowing that he would oppose it on the merits fully, and that there was some things that had been omitted from the other complaint which should be before the court. Mr. Harkness has mentioned one, the question of referendum, which Mr. Shearn had raised, and the question about the private or local fact, and the question of law. The case was made up largely, one of facts, showing the length of time that would elapse before the city would get any profit. And Mr. Shearn was given the benefit of the latest estimate of our accounting department, and I think my recollection now is that matter was put in Mr. Shearn's complaint that was not contained in either of the others.

Q. Then Mr. Shearn's coming in enlarged the scope of the action, or enlarged the field, at any rate? A. I think it did.

Q. Didn't you know it had been suggested to Mr. Shearn that these two actions then pending, the Ryan and the Admiralty case, were in the interest of interested parties? A. No, I have not the slightest recollection of that. The only recollection I have is of having a suggestion made that the Ryan case was possibly brought at the instigation of the B. R. T.

Q. Who made that suggestion to you? A. I do not now recall it.

Q. Was it Mr. Harkness? A. I don't recall it.

Q. May it have been somebody else? A. Might have been.

Q. Was it common talk? A. I don't know about that. I don't suppose the matter was mentioned more than once or twice in a casual way. I am not sure but somebody made it in public, that the Ryan case was brought in the interest of the B. R. T.

Q. You say now that probably Mr. Harkness's statement of fact is correct, that is, that he told about his suspicions about the Admiralty case. Can't you recall it at all? A. I have not the slightest recollection of any such thing.

Q. How is that, Mr. Coleman? A. Because I was interested—

Q. Pardon me for putting it in this way,— Mr. Harkness seems to have a very distinct recollection, and it is of the more interest because I had not said a word to Mr. Harkness; there was no discussion between he and any member of the Committee. He was called here very suddenly, and really because looking through this list of attorneys, and desired to have all present,— I requested my associate here to include his name. Now that his testimony comes out without my expecting it really, because it appears clearly and comes out in your presence. You were sitting there while he testified as your subordinate. A. I do not question it.

Q. I want to account for his making what you believe to be a truthful statement, and you have no recollection of it? A. You will have to ask the Lord God Almighty.

Chairman Thompson.— Is that what runs your department?

Mr. Coleman.— We hope so, to some extent. What I was interested in was mainly the constitutional question, and I was also interested on the financial side so far as the complaint should be made full enough to show to the Court the worst possible feature of the financing of this large proposition. I wanted the worst possible that could be said against us to be in the complaint.

By Mr. Moss, resuming:

Q. But did you really desire to have the contract sustained? A. Well, I did not pass upon that.

Q. Well, you were on that side, weren't you? A. I was on that side. That was not my concern.

Q. But the Public Service Commission had approved it, hadn't they approved it? A. Yes.

Q. But had not formally, but had practically approved it,— they were not doing anything to stop it? A. Not that I know of. They wanted the rapid transit work to progress.

Q. They wanted that Gillespie contract to go through? A. I know nothing about it.

Q. But you were their counsel? A. That matter did not come to me.

Q. Didn't they talk to you about it? A. No.

Q. Didn't you understand they would be better satisfied if the contract was sustained than if it was defeated? A. Yes, if they could. If it could be sustained, they wanted rapid transit.

Q. Do you understand that the arrangement with Mr. Morgan for the floating of the bonds depended on the specific clause in the contract, upon the court establishing the validity of the contract,— do you know that? A. I do not remember as you put it. I have heard that Mr. Morgan, or whoever it was, whoever was going to put up the money, wanted to have some assurance from the court, if possible, that the bonds would be valid.

Q. Who told you that? A. I don't recall that.

Q. How did you learn? A. It probably was common talk.

Q. What did you care about it,— about that feature of it? A. All I cared about it was this. My business was the legal end of it, and if there was any question that touched the validity of the bonds or the validity of the statute, I wanted that question raised. I did not want to go out on a half-baked case. I didn't care how the question was raised if it was raised properly.

Q. Was it you that went to Mr. Shearn or Mr. Harkness? A. I had nothing to do with it.

Q. You had nothing to do with Mr. Shearn? A. I did not.

Q. Did Mr. Harkness go to Mr. Shearn on his own responsibility? A. Whatever Mr. Harkness says as a statement of fact, I should subscribe to.

Q. I want to know whether you directed him to go to Mr. Shearn, or whether he took it upon his own responsibility to go?

A. I have no recollection of telling him to go, and he stated here
he met Mr. Shearn occasionally at lunch and talked it over. Mr.
Shearn had always been a doughty fighter against the Commission.

Q. That was the reason I asked the question, because Mr. Harkness leaves it as though he was the moving cause for getting Mr.
Shearn into the case. A. If so, I would like to give him the
credit for it because it was a good move.

By Chairman Thompson:

Q. Will you give it to him? A. Yes, if he will take it, gladly.

Q. I will direct him to take it. Can you remember anything
that you personally did or any conference that you personally had
with any of the Commissioners relative to this suspicion that
either the Ryan or Berwind case or the Admiralty case was
brought in the interest of the contractors? A. Absolutely not.
No recollection of any such thing.

Q. Well when you heard a statement by somebody, public or
private, that the Ryan case might be in the interest of the B. R. T.,
what did you as senior counsel of the Public Service Commission
do to find out whether it was true? A. I don't know as I did
anything. I didn't care.

Q. Why didn't you? A. Because I knew there were other suits
pending that would raise every question we had.

Q. Didn't it occur to you that if it ever came to the attention
of the court that a suit if argued before it fair and square upon
its face was a collusive action that there might be of undoing the
decision and of upsetting the whole thing? A. No.

Q. Has it ever occurred to you that the Court of Appeals in
order to protect its own dignity, in order to protect the value of
its work might take some action itself to undo a decision which
was rendered in any way upon a collusive appearance of attorneys?
A. No, never occurred to me.

Q. Were you anxious to have a decision that would stand? A.
I wanted a final decision.

Q. Then I ask you again when you were informed, even though
it may have been publicly, of this suspicious condition of the
Ryan case, didn't you do anything to learn the truth? A. Never
did anything as I say. It was a suspicion. I don't know when
I heard it. I did not care what happened the Ryan case. I was

sure the points would all be raised in the case that did come up and went to the Court of Appeals. If there was one case out of the three that was genuine and raised all the points that was sufficient for my purpose. I wanted the court to pass on the law and that was the whole purpose of it.

Q. Have you in your mind any Public Service Commissioner to whom you communicated the suspicion that was in your mind? A. Not any. I haven't any recollection of any suspicion.

Q. You have, because you have told us voluntarily about the Ryan case? A. I have no recollection and would not know when that suspicion came. Probably long after the suit. I may but I do not remember speaking to any of the Commissioners about it.

Q. Did you have frequent conferences with Public Service Commissioners? A. Not on that particular case. They did not confer with me after a suit was brought. I do not confer with them after a suit is brought.

Q. Was it from any Public Service Commissioner that you learned of the arrangement for financing this great proposition depended upon the court sustaining its validity? A. No.

Q. Did you know that the financial arrangement was hanging upon the court decision? A. I can't recall. My present recollection. This case goes back over four years. My recollection is I had the information in some way. Whether it was from a newspaper or from counsel or associate counsel or counsel on the other side of the cases, that those who were going to lend the money wanted to be sure that the bonds were valid. That came to my mind and it was a thing that made me very anxious to have every question raised that could be raised.

By Chairman Thompson:

Q. Did you know Mr. Morgan wanted that done? A. I can't say that I did.

Q. Had you heard that he did? A. I say as I have already.

Q. Talked in the club or in the corridor of your office at any time? A. No.

Examination resumed by Mr. Moss:

Q. In the two route proceedings did the Admirality Realty Company appear? A. I don't remember whether they appeared twice.

Q. Mr. Harkness says they appeared before you know? A.
Yes. But there was one proceeding to base the approval of the
Appellate Division of the routes because they had not the proper
number of consents or property owners. I understand the
Admirality Realty Company was a realty company and they were
opposed for some reason to the route of Lexington avenue and
then there was some other provision or question came up where
they appeared later, and then after the route work they opposed
again and that was why I say my impression always was and my
present impression was before Mr. Harkness testified that the
Admiralty Company was always fighting us.

Q. Do you remember by whom the company was represented in
the first proceeding? A. No, I did not have anything to do with
it.

Q. Were you there in 1908? A. I went there the first of January, 1908. That is a matter that would have been handled by Mr.
Harkness or somebody in the Rapid Transit end of the office.

Q. Do you remember the applications to the Commission in
the First District for the three Commissioners? A. For the
routes?

Q. Yes. A. No. That was probably a form of proceeding with
a set of consents and necessity of it and probably my name was
attached to the papers but I do not remember.

Q. Do you remember the second proceeding in 1910 for a
modification of the Lexington avenue route? A. I have a recollection that there was such a proceeding and that is probably where
they opposed us the second time.

Q. Do you remember who appeared for them? A. No, but I
know I got a very strong impression that they were trying to block
all subway improvements.

Q. Do you remember in one of those proceedings the Commission questioned the bona fides of the people represented by Mr.
Wolf? A. I do not recollect.

Q. Did Mr. Wolf ever represent? A. I thought it was Hays,
Herschfield & Wolf.

Chairman Thompson.— You got a bill of costs out of this litigation?

Mr. Coleman.— I don't know. I don't remember that. I did

not get any of the cost. I don't know whether there were any in
the bill of cost or not.

Chairman Thompson.— You did not get any?

Mr. Coleman.— No, sir.

Examination resumed by Mr. Moss:

Q. Eighty-three dollars and fifty-eight cents, the item is so
small you perhaps would not remember? A. I cannot recall it.

Chairman Thompson.— The Interborough paid it and their
records show it was paid to you.

Mr. Coleman.— You will find in the records of the Commission
it was paid to the Commission and by the Commission to the city.

Q. Do you know any reason why the attorney should pay you a
bill of cost? A. They sent it to me and I sent it to the Commission.

Chairman Thompson.— For the successful litigants?

Mr. Coleman.— Who was the successful litigants? I thought
we were successful.

Chairman Thompson.— I said the Interborough Railroad Company have got in their records that they paid you a bill of cost —
do you remember.

Mr. Coleman.— I don't know where the cost came from.

Chairman Thompson.— It came from the Interborough Railroad Company.

Mr. Coleman.— I have no recollection.

Chairman Thompson.— Don't you remember anything about it?

Mr. Coleman.— Not at all.

Chairman Thompson.— They were the successful litigants?

Mr. Coleman.— I hope they regard it as successful.

Chairman Thompson.— How do you regard it?

Mr. Coleman.— I regard it as successful for the city.

Chairman Thompson.— How about the Interborough Railroad, do you think it was a success?

Mr. Coleman.— I don't know. The future will have to tell.

Chairman Thompson.— You are a lawyer and you are being paid $10,000 a year for being a good lawyer for the Public Service Commission. Now, I ask you if in this law suit the Interborough Railroad Company was not a successful litigant? Do you think you can answer that question?

Mr. Coleman.— I think you can draw your own inferences. What I might think about the success of the Interborough —

Chairman Thompson.— You knew the outcome of this lawsuit?

Mr. Coleman.— Yes.

Chairman Thompson.— And you knew the way the parties were before the court?

Mr. Coleman.— Yes.

Chairman Thompson.— You knew what the court decision was? Was the Interborough successful?

Mr. Coleman.— I don't know. I know we were successful in establishing our proposition of law.

Chairman Thompson.— The suit was decided in favor of the Interborough Company.

Mr. Coleman.— It was decided in favor of —

Chairman Thompson.— Was it decided in favor of the Interborough?

Mr. Coleman.— I presume they wanted it.

Chairman Thompson.— Is that as far as you will go.

Mr. Coleman.— They are not taking me into their confidence.

Chairman Thompson.— I am asking you what you thought.

Mr. Coleman.— I thought the city obtained a substantial victory.

Chairman Thompson.— I haven't asked you about the city. I am asking you about the Interborough Railroad Company.

Mr. Coleman.— I think it is the best —

Examination resumed by Mr. Moss:

Q. I want to ask you, during the pendency of this action, did you ever talk with Delancey Nicoll? A. No, not that I have the slightest recollection during the pendency of this action. But if Mr. Nicoll comes and says I did and gives you the date I will accept it, but I must confess I do not remember any little details that do not seem to be important. I remember ideas.

Q. Now you say that the city won a substantial victory? A. Well, I thought so.

Q. You thought it was a victory for the city of New York to establish this contract with the Interborough Railroad, did you? A. The constitutionality of the right to do it.

Q. But you were establishing a point of constitutionality? A. The contract had not been signed then.

Q. That was not merely sparring for points, you wanted the contract held in order that the city might be held? A. Not necessarily.

Q. Weren't you considering the end of the litigation, which was the contract? A. My private idea was to have that question of law determined. Suppose the Interborough had backed out. They backed out once.

Q. The real point of issue was the contract, wasn't it? A. No. The real point of issue was the constitutionality of the proposed contract. Afterwards we had as you know to get legislation to legalize as well. We had to apply to the Legislature.

Q. What bill was that? A. That was after the argument in the Court of Appeals. But we had one experience of working for two years to get something through and then having it all fall to pieces. It did not make any difference whether the Interborough or some other company. I believe at the time that there was other people from the outside might come in.

Q. That contract was the thing that was at stake. Did you ever read it? A. Yes, I read it. I have very often occasion to study it. It is an enormous document.

Q. It was a great victory for the city? A. I hope the time will show that it was, whether it is profitable or not we are going to get rapid transit. It will pay the city some time.

Q. You do not care anything about it in the meanwhile? A. I don't care anything about it. If they don't charge more than a nickel.

Q. Couldn't the legal questions in this case have been settled without the Admiral Realty suit, that is in the Hopper & Ryan proceedings? A. I suppose the Hopper suit could have settled it. I suppose so.

ALFRED E. MUDGE, being sworn as a witness, testified as follows:

Examination by Mr. Moss:

Q. You are one of the counsel for the Interborough? A. I am employed in the Law Department.

Q. Your superior is Mr. Richard Reid Rogers? A. Mr. Quackenbush.

Q. I beg your pardon. I saw your name associated with Mr. Rogers on the report. A. Mr. Quackenbush, and occasionally do work for Mr. Rogers.

Q. Then you as a part of Mr. Quackenbush's organization find yourself alongside of Mr. Rogers in the brief in the Court of Appeals? A. I did, yes, sir.

Q. Did you know of this suit by the Admiral Company? A. I knew of it, when it was brought, yes, sir. The first connection I had with it, I think, was when the complaint was turned over to me, and I drafted a demurrer, and after that I worked on the brief as the junior counsel in the preparation of the brief.

Q. Did you have a talk with Mr. Rogers about it? A. Many times.

Q. Did you know the suit was going to be brought? A. No. The only talk I had with Mr. Rogers was on the legal phases of the point.

Q. And was the first you knew of the Admiral case? A. Yes, sir.

Q. Are you quite sure you did not know that such a suit was in contemplation before it was brought? A. No, I did not.

Q. Did you know the attorneys for the Admiral Realty Company? A. I met them afterwards. I don't know that I met them before that, to my recollection.

Q. Did you see them at their office? A. No.

Q. Did you have any conference with them while the cases were pending? A. No, not that I recall, unless it was a matter over submission of briefs, or something of that kind.

Q. Do you know that the attorneys for the Admiral Realty Company were being paid by the Interborough Company? A. No, sir, I did not.

Q. Well, that knowledge would not necessarily come to you, would it? A. My only connection with the litigation was junior counsel, and working on the brief.

Q. Where is Mr. Rogers? A. I think he is out west.

JAMES L. QUACKENBUSH, sworn as a witness, testified as follows:

Examination by Mr. Moss:

Q. Were you attorney for the Interborough Company in these cases we have been discussing? A. No.

Q. Who was? A. Mr. Rogers.

Q. Was that handled entirely outside of your department? A. Yes, by Mr. Rogers with assistance from the law department whenever he required it.

Q. You simply loaned your assistance? A. Yes, that is, our organization.

Q. Did you have anything to do with these cases? A. Not personally.

Q. Did you have any knowledge of it? A. No, except to know there was such a litigation.

Q. Did you know that the Admiral Realty Company had intervened? A. I was in touch with the subway cases generally and knew that such a litigation was pending.

Q. Did you know that the Admiral Realty Company was going to bring a suit before it brought it? A. I did not.

Q. When the suit was brought, did you know it was in the interest of the Interborough Company? A. I did not.

Q. When did you first learn that fact, Mr. Quackenbush? A.

I think as a fact as you state it, probably only within the last week or so, when the matter became a subject of investigation.

Q. When did you have some knowledge or information on the subject? A. During the time the litigation was pending. I knew the case was in the court, and that the purpose of the action was to settle the questions that were involved.

Q. You knew that in the contract or arrangement with Mr. Morgan, there was a provision, did you not? A. I would not say so. I think, Mr. Moss, you will appreciate the transactions with regard to the subway matters were handled by Mr. Rogers and not by myself. Then you will understand.

Q. I think I understand that. I am simply reaching for what you may know about this matter. A. I do not want to seem to be in charge of a law department and not have knowledge of litigation. I knew that there was a litigation of the Admiral Realty Company. I knew it beginning back —

Q. Who first gave you to understand it was in the interest of the Interborough Company? A. I don't think anybody has given me to understand that yet.

Q. When did you get the idea, then? A. When that view of it began to be presented to this investigation.

Q. I thought you had some idea of it when the litigation was pending? A. I had an idea that such a litigation was pending; that is to say, I kept myself generally informed, and knew of the Hopper case that Mr. Shearn was conducting, and knew, although I could not recollect it by name, that the Ryan case was in the courts, and I knew also of the Admiral Realty case being in the court, because from time to time I took part in these transactions.

Q. Didn't you suspect that the Admiral Realty case was in the interest of the Interborough? A. No, and I do not now suspect it was in the interest of the Interborough. While I am on that subject,— do not misunderstand me about it,— during one phase of the subway negotiation with the Public Service Commission, when the Public Service Commission was carrying on negotiations, which looked as if they would make a contract with the Brooklyn Rapid Transit Company, to the exclusion of the Interborough, I personally had charge and to do with the presentation of the views of the Interborough in opposition to the validity of the proposed contract with the Brooklyn Rapid Transit. I made arguments and publicly — and debated the question with the President of the Brooklyn Rapid Transit, and argued the matter with the city officials. I contented myself that such a contract would be in violation of the constitution. Now, having made those contentions, I knew that the same contentions were being urged by the Admiral Realty case. I said that so it won't seem as if I was ignorant of what was involved in it, although personally I had nothing to do with the litigation.

Q. Did you ever hear Mr. Nicoll say who made arrangements? A. I heard him say it in the room the other day. I thought you meant some years ago. I have no recollection of ever discussing the question with Mr. Nicoll. It so happens Mr. Nicoll and Mr. Rogers were in charge of that phase of it.

Chairman Thompson.— Was it your opinion as a lawyer that contract with the Brooklyn Rapid Transit was unconstitutional? A. Yes.

By Chairman Thompson:

Q. Have you changed your opinion on it? A. No. I think the Court of Appeals was wrong. If I had been on the Court of Appeals, I would have voted against,— with the minority.

Q. Do you suppose if you had a good lawsuit up there with the Court of Appeals, with fellows hammering on both sides? A. Senator, I have not the slightest doubt that Clarence Shearn presented every possible question that was presented there. I haven't any notion at all that these facts that have been presented here would have swerved Louis Marshall from presenting every fact on that that could have been presented. I was not in the Court of Appeals when it was argued.

Examination resumed by Mr. Moss:

Q. How do you think Mr. Marshall was arguing? A. I know it was argued for the Admiral Realty side.

Q. He was not on your side? A. When you say my side,— my client's side. I made it perfectly plain here, or tried to, what my views were. I argued them at length. It was in the newspaper what my position was. In the Admiral Realty case, which was referred to as having been brought earlier, I knew it contained the same general fundamental proposition that I myself argued. I was in a position when they switched around and began talking about compromise, and to make a dual contract of it, and connected with a contract which I myself had assailed.

DELANCEY NICOLL, sworn as a witness, testified as follows:

Examination by Mr. Moss:

Q. Mr. Nicoll, you are counsel to the Interborough Company? A. Yes, I am one of the counsel.

Q. You have been connected with the company for a good many years? A. A great many years.

Q. We are talking about this Admiral Realty suit, and the various suits that were disposed of by the Court of Appeals in 206 New York. Did you make an arrangement with Mr. Hays to have the Admiral Realty Company bring suit there? A. Yes. That is, I made an arrangement with Mr. Hershfield, I think it was, to have a suit brought by a taxpayer, to test the validity of the Brooklyn contract. The contract made with the Brooklyn company. That was a contract very similar to the contracts which were finally made with the two companies, inasmuch as it contained the preferential feature. I doubted the constitutionality of any such contract, and sought to raise the question through the Admiral Realty Company suit. That was the first suit.

Q. Did you doubt the constitutionality? A. Yes, I think it was the gravest question in the world. You see in the court you have Judge Cullen and Judge Werner and some other very able judge, who dissented on that ground. In other words, I might say that Werner said if it was not a question of a municipality loaning its credit to the Interborough — I knew the Interborough was out after the Brooklyn company's contract was made, and no negotiations were taken up with the Brooklyn company or Interborough company until six months later, and then came the negotiations which resulted in the contracts which were afterwards examined by the Court of Appeals. The two contracts.

Q. You knew about the negotiations with Mr. Morgan? A. I had no particular interview.

Q. You knew about them? A. I consulted occasionally with them.

Q. Did you know about the clause in the letter of contract

27

which provided that there must be a determination by the court
as to the validity? A. I think Mr. Shonts advised in the Continental Securities Company litigation, that he had an understanding with the city that there would have to be a suit brought
on the validity of the contract.

Q. Your client really wanted to enter into the contract? A.
I think the contracts were forced upon my client.

Q. But they wanted to enter into them? A. They entered
into them when they could not make any better terms. You all
have a misunderstanding about that. The Interborough never
wanted to enter into —

Q. Why did they enter into it? A. They entered into it
because they were invited by the city and had a public duty to
perform as a public corporation.

Q. Do you mean to say they were doing the city— A. I
mean to say they were a quasi-public corporation; they were a
tenant of the city; they were invited to co-operate with the Brooklyn authorities to extend the facilities of the city.

Q. Had the city been standing out against the company? A.
It was all explained the other day to the Chairman. The attitude of the Interborough, as I recall it, was that as a tenant of
the city, it was their duty and it was their right to extend their
subway system throughout the city boroughs by the use of private
capital, and they made a number of offers from time to time, all
of which are in the record here. Those were all rejected.

Q. Do you mean to say that your company executed a contract
that it did not want to execute because of its public spirit or duty
to the city or people of the city? A. I mean to say they entered
into negotiations with the city authorities and finally made the
best contract they could.

Q. Exactly,— they wanted to make it. They wanted to complete their routes. A. I have answered it.

Q. They wanted to take the ground so somebody else would not
come in and take it? A. They wanted to do what their duty as
a public service corporation is, and at the same time to protect
the capital that was invested in it.

Chairman Thompson.— They spent quite a lot of money to help
to do that?

Mr. Nicoll.— They spent a great deal of money — hundreds of thousands.

By Mr. Moss:

Q. To get something better? A. They did not believe in a dual system.

Q. They wanted something better, and when they could not get anything better, they were glad to take this? A. I think that is so. They did the best they could.

Chairman Thompson.— Had an awful good time getting it through, and after it was done, giving a fellow $150,000?

Mr. Nicoll.— That was on account of the excessive time spent by the president on the operating.

Chairman Thompson.— I suppose that is the reason they charged the city ultimately, because the city got such a great benefit from the public spirit of the Interborough?

Mr. Nicoll.— I never heard of it.

By Mr. Moss:

Q. The point is, while your company wanted this contract to go through, you always had a grave doubt about the constitutionality of the scheme? A. Yes, sir.

Q. And you know in a general way the financing of this was depending entirely on Mr. Morgan? A. I knew you could not sell a bond.

Q. And then you made an arrangement with these legal gentlemen to bring a suit? A. No.

Q. Tell me when it was done and what was said.

Chairman Thompson.— You will have to answer the counsel's question.

The Witness.— I know how to conduct myself.

Chairman Thompson.— You will have to conduct yourself as the Committee —

Mr. Nicoll.— The Committee will put their questions, and I will decide whether they are pertinent and proper questions.

Chairman Thompson.— Mr. Moss will ask these questions, and he is authorized by the Committee to ask them, and after he has asked them, you either say you can answer them or say you cannot.

Mr. Nicoll.— Well, the next thing that I recollect about it was some time in the spring of 1913, after the contracts had been executed, when Mr. Hershfield and Mr. Wolf, I think, either one or the other of them, came in and told me that they had been talking with Mr. Coleman, and that Mr. Coleman wanted to utilize this Admiral Realty litigation.

Examination resumed by Mr. Moss:

Q. You mean George S. Coleman? A. Yes. That he wanted to utilize this Admiral Realty litigation, in conjunction with two other suits, one brought by a man named Hopper, and one brought by Ryan, for the purpose of raising all the questions concerning these contracts; whether or not there was any violation of the constitution; whether or not they were authorized by the act of the Legislature; whether or not there should be a referendum on the subject, and so on; wanted to know whether I had any objection to the Admiral Realty litigation being used for that purpose, and I said, "No, go ahead and raise all the questions possible; it has got to be done before the securities can be authorized."

Q. Then you did not originate the idea? A. No, I did not originate it.

Q. You simply gave your assent — the idea originated as you understood, in a conference between Mr. Hershfield and Mr. Coleman? A. Yes.

Q. You understood that from Mr. Hershfield? A. Or Mr. Wolf.

Q. Where was the conference held? A. At my office.

Q. Did they come to your office at your request? A. That I don't know. I don't think they did. I think they came in and told me; said that this matter —

Q. They wanted you to know about it? A. And see whether I approved of it. I thought it was an excellent opportunity and a necessary one to raise these questions, and I told them they could. That is all I had to do with it, except to afterwards certify to their bills and see they were properly paid for their services, which I did.

Q. What did you understand about the original purpose of the bringing of that Admiral Realty suit? A. The original purpose was for the purpose of testing the preferential payment of the Brooklyn contract on the very same grounds, namely, that this was a contract which the municipality was loaning its credit to a private corporation, in violation of the constitution. That question went to the Appellate Division, but the Appellate Division reserved their judgment on it.

Q. Well, that case did not directly touch the Interborough, but touched it indirectly? A. Yes.

Q. And the indirect touch was of sufficient importance to seize upon or to utilize it and to make the payments to the gentlemen who did the work on which it was made? A. Yes.

Q. Do you remember the Admiral Realty Company bringing an action against Mayor Gaynor in 1910? A. Yes.

Q. You knew about that? A. I did.

Q. Did you have anything to do with that? A. I did. I promoted that for the purpose of raising the question of the debt limit, as to whether the city had any money at all with which to go into the enterprise.

Q. How did you first learn of this suit? Did you suggest that it be brought? A. I think I suggested that it be brought. I think I was talking with Mr. Hershfield and told him there was a very grave question as to whether or not the debt limit had not been exceeded, and I told him I thought we ought to know that, and I wanted him to bring a suit by the Admiral Realty Company as plaintiff, for the purpose of testing that question.

Q. Was any compensation made to these gentlemen? A. Yes.

Q. In the same way? A. No. I paid him.

Q. How much? A. I don't know. Perhaps ten thousand dollars.

Q. Who did you pay it? A. I think I paid Mr. Hershfield. I am not sure, though.

Q. Of course, that came out of the Interborough? A. Yes, or one of the directors of the Interborough gave me that money. I think Mr. Freedman.

Q. Then it does not appear in the books? A. No.

Q. Mr. Freedman personally? A. Yes, sir. He was mostly interested.

Q. Was Mr. Freedman reimbursed by the company? A. I don't know.

Q. So far as you know the company took no action? A. Mr. Freedman was a large property owner in New York city himself, and he took a greater interest in the litigation than the company did, because he felt that the debt limit was being exceeded, and he wanted to test it out.

Q. Then Mr. Freedman wanted the action brought, and through you Mr. Hershfield or his firm were obtained, and then through you Mr. Freedman paid the fee? A. He gave me the fees, whatever they were. I forget what they were.

Q. And do you remember against whom that action was brought? A. No. It is all in the record.

Q. Wasn't it brought against the Interborough? A. I don't know.

Q. I will read you from the record of the Admiral Realty Company against William J. Gaynor, William A. Prendergast, John Purroy Mitchel, George McAneny, Alfred A. Steers, Tyrus C. Miller, Lawrence Greeser as members of and constituting the board of estimate and apportionment of the city of New York; William R. Willcox, William McCarroll, Milo R. Maltbie, John E. Eustis, J. Sargeant Cram as members of and constituting Public Service Commission for the First District, and the Bradley Contracting Company. The appearances were Hays, Hershfield & Wolf for the plaintiff, and they became the appellant afterwards; Archibald J. Watson, corporation counsel; George S. Coleman, attorney for the Public Service Commission; James R. Lindsay, attorney for the Bradley Contracting Company. Did you have any talk with Mr. Coleman about that matter? A. No But the Interborough was not a party to that suit.

Q. Were the Bradley Contracting Company taking any — A. They had a contract.

Q. For what? A. To build the Lexington avenue subway.

Q. They had a contract for building something for the Interborough? A. No. The Interborough had nothing to do with it.

Q. What was the result of that action? A. You will have to tell me. I have forgotten. But I think they held that the debt limit had not been exceeded.

Q. I guess that was so. A. I think that's so, but I have forgotten it now.

Q. 147 Appellate Division is the decision on appeal, page 719. Was not there a prior Admiral Realty suit brought affecting the Interborough? A. I do not recall any such one.

Examination by Chairman Thompson:

Q. This $10,000 that you paid to Hershfield, that was the retainer in the first place? A. I don't know. I don't know that it was $10,000. It may have been $15,000 or may have been $7,500 — whatever it was. It was not a retainer. It was after he had done a lot of work, perhaps all of it for all I know.

Q. In this case? A. No.

Q. In a prior case? A. Yes. If that is the date.

Q. That never was charged on the Interborough books? A. No.

Examination resumed by Mr. Moss:

Q. Now, Mr. Nicoll, you have said you have some knowledge about the provision that Mr. Morgan insisted upon, that there should be some test of the validity of the proceedings. Do you know how such a test could be made without some arrangement by which a suit should be brought? A. I think it is quite customary to decide these difficult constitutional questions by a taxpayer's suit. It has been done from time immemorial.

Q. That is by an inspired suit? A. Yes, it has been done constantly.

Q. Then the people who want the contract approved and want to borrow the money will give sort of an insurance policy to the man who has to loan the money by getting a friend to bring a suit and having it presented to the court and getting a decision which the money man can rely on as sort of a title policy? A. It was a very large transaction.

Q. That is about the way it goes? A. Yes, something like that.

Q. You say that is very common? A. Taxpayers —

Q. I did not say a taxpayer's suit but a proceeding of that suit for that purpose is very common? A. I think it is.

Q. In large financial operations? A. It often occurs or where

there is a grave constitutional question or legal question involved
which has to be settled before you can go ahead.

Examination by Chairman Thompson:

Q. You had a bill presented to the Interborough Railroad Company on June 1, 1915, in which one of the items for your services
appeared to be " an attack by a legislative committee appointed
to investigate Public Service Commission." A. Did I?

Q. Now what services did you render for the benefit of the
Interborough Railroad Company? A. Now, Mr. Chairman, that
in my judgment is not what I call a pertinent or proper question,
but I am going to assume it is for the purpose of answering your
question but without waiving any other objection I may make to
questions of that sort. The service I rendered to the Interborough
was to examine the resolution under which you were authorized to
make an investigation.

Q. It did refer then to this Committee? A. I think it did.
Must have been.

Q. I don't know of any other committee. A. I don't think
there was any other committee. I examined the resolution and
the scope of your authority and the extent of your authority and
then I made some examination concerning the personnel and the
character of the members of the Committee and reported highly
upon them.

Q. I think your bill was too small. What attack did this Committee make on the Interborough last winter? A. Well, in the
light of your findings on the personalty of the members of the
Committee I think your bill was very reasonable.

(At this point there was some explanation made by Mr.
Quackenbush to the Chairman of the Committee as to what constituted the bill.)

GEORGE D. YOUMANS, called as a witness, testified as
follows:

Direct examination by Mr. Moss:

Q. Mr. Youmans, you appeared in the report of the Admiral
Realty case as one of the counsel for the Brooklyn Rapid Transit
Company? A. Yes.

Q. Did you have full knowledge of the case?   A. Of the Admiral Realty case?

Q. Yes, this case in which you appeared.   A. I had appeared in the whole of that litigation.   I argued the case where the three joint cases were argued in the lower court, before Judge Blackmar.   Mr. Colin argued it in the lower court, and I argued it in the Appellate Division, and Mr. Colin argued it in the Court of Appeals, and I was present with him and we worked on the brief together.

Q. Did you know that the suit of John R. Ryan was brought in the interest of the Brooklyn Rapid Transit Company?   A. I did not.

Q. Did you ever hear of that?   A. Will you let me lead up just a little?

Q. Yes.   A. This original Admiral Realty case, that was brought, I think, some time in 1911, and my remembrance is that that was against the Public Service Commission and one of the construction companies.   I think it was the Bradley Construction Company.   We were not parties to that action, but there has been a great deal said about the constitutionality of our contract, and proposition, and I had in mind at that time, that that was an attempt to defeat our proposition.   The bringing of the Admiral Realty action was for the purpose of defeating the Brooklyn Rapid Transit Company proposition by a declaration that our proposition was unconstitutional.   I think both Mr. Colin and I asked Mr. Harkness and Mr. Coleman to argue the constitutionality of the questions that were raised.   They took the position, however, that the action was premature.   You know that action was brought, as I remember it, to enjoin the considering of the contract, the preparation of plans, and so forth, as being a waste, and I believe the entering into a contract.   Mr. Coleman and Mr. Harkness considered the action premature and they refused to argue the constitutional question.   Mr. Colin and I were in the court while the case was argued, without taking any part.   I do think that we talked over with Mr. Coleman and Mr. Harkness about the case.

Q. That is, about the Admiral Realty case?   A. That first case in 1911.   And then it went to the Appellate Division, and

I think that I expressed an opinion at that time to some of our people that it was unfortunate that that case was brought over in New York county, because as a lawyer I think that atmosphere has something to do with cases, and the whole atmosphere over here I think at that time was against the Brooklyn Rapid Transit Company, whereas over in our district the people of Brooklyn wanted the Brooklyn Rapid Transit Company to prevail. After that question was defeated, some time after that, I think that Mr. Baylis came into our office and asked for the Admiral Realty papers — some time after the Ryan case was brought.

Q. Mr. Baylis was counsel in the Ryan case? A. For the plaintiff Mr. Ryan. Then afterwards the Admiral Realty case was brought. I think almost immediately afterwards, including all of these parties, and soon afterwards this Hopper action.

Q. Do you know whether or not any of the moneys of the Brooklyn Rapid Transit, or any of the moneys of the New York Municipal Railways Corporation — do you know whether the moneys of either of those companies were ever paid to anybody in that Ryan case? A. I do not.

Q. It would not come within your knowledge? A. It would not.

Q. Who is Ryan? A. I don't know. I think Mr. Baylis at that time said when he came in there — I think he said he was a client of his who had considerable real estate.

Q. Well, you were desirous an action disposed of in Brooklyn for atmospheric reasons? A. I said at the time I thought it was unfortunate the action was over there.

Q. Didn't you have some friendly relations with the Ryan case, so you could move a Brooklyn forum? A. I did not.

Q. How does it happen that Mr. Baylis came in? A. I don't know how he came in there.

Q. Did you know that the Admiral Realty case was in the interest of the Interborough? A. I tell you I always felt the Admiral Realty case was brought for the purpose of defeating our proposition. I also knew from conversation or otherwise, whether about the time it was brought or whether it was not, that the counsel for the Interborough — I don't know that I knew what Mr. Quackenbush knew about it, but I know that Mr.

Rogers and also Mr. Nicoll thought that the Interborough proposition was probably constitutional and that ours was not, and that is the way the case was argued by the Interborough counsel all through the litigation — on the ground that their proposition was a constitutional proposition and that ours was not.

Q. The second Admiral Realty case was brought in the county of Kings? A. So the Hopper case — all of them. I felt in that case that we were the real defendants. I hadn't any doubt about any question being properly presented because Mr. Coleman had told me when the other Admiral Realty case was up, that he would see to it that in the litigation, if the cases went on, every possible question was raised and fought out.

Q. Do you know how it happened that the second Admiral Realty case was brought in Kings? A. I do not.

Q. Did you ever inquire? A. I never did.

Q. Had the B. R. T. and the Interborough come together? A. We had not. We were absolutely antagonistic.

Q. Did they ever get together? A. Never, except in one action. If you would like to know that.

Q. Go ahead. A. After the cases were brought out in the Court of Appeals and I think about the time that Mr. Wilcox's term was running out, the contracts I think were ready for execution and Mr. Shearn, again brought a new Hopper action, I think, to enjoin the Public Service Commission and the companies from executing those contracts. We were anxious to get the cases quickly heard. I think Mr. Quackenbush called me up,— I don't remember — at any rate we were both defendants in the action and I think he suggested that we go down and see Mr. Morgan J. O'Brien who had been acting for the Pennsylvania Railroad Company in these various — I did not that — but I think he told me that he had in these various conferences. We went down to see him and asked him if he would assist us in that litigation which was coming up in a day or two in the special terms. He said he would and did. He argued the case there. I think that the Judge refused to hear it and the next day it was argued before another Judge, and I think Mr. Shearn and everybody, Morgan J. O'Brien and everybody went up to see the Chief Justice and told him that this was a very important matter,— Mr. Shearn

agreeing to that, and asked him if he would not hear this litigation. I think he set the time about a week off. And the reason I
say we were joined was that as it appeared here the Interborough
Company finally paid Morgan J. O'Brien $2,500 for those serv-
ices and we paid $2,500 also. So far as I know the Interborough
and the Brooklyn Rapid Transit Companies were always antagonistic in this dual fight.

Examination by Chairman Thompson:

Q. What do you mean by atmosphere? A. I will tell you
exactly what I mean.

Examination resumed by Mr. Moss:

Q. You do not mean what the Chairman let out the window a
few minutes ago? A. No. I mean this. My meaning is perfectly legitimate so far as Judges and everybody is concerned.
Over here in New York, I think at that time there was a general
feeling — I don't know how general it was — at any rate there
was a general feeling in the Bronx and I think in other parts of
Manhattan that it was better for the Interborough to have this
subway business than for the B. R. T. to have it. As Mr.
Quackenbush has said —

Chairman Thompson.—Among whom was this feeling?

Mr. Youmans.— I think it was a feeling of the public. That
is what I mean. Whereas over in Brooklyn I do not think there
was any dissenting feeling over there that the Brooklyn Rapid
Transit Company if it operated a part of this system, especially
in Brooklyn, would be of an advantage to the Borough of Manhattan. I think there was a general feeling of that kind, which I
felt predominated.

Chairman Thompson.— You thought the B. R. T. had the
sentiment with it over in Brooklyn.

Mr. Youmans.— I knew the Interborough had been trying to
get the sentiment away from us. They had a variety of meetings
and advertised in the Brooklyn newspaper. They argued against
the possibility or probability of the B. R. T. doing this business.

They also argued against the advantages of having the B. R.
T. do it.

Chairman Thompson.— You say advertised in the newspapers.
You mean advertised for sentiment?

Mr. Youmans.— I think so.

Mr. Quackenbush.—All that advertising I was the author of it
and it was placarded all over Brooklyn and spoken of by everybody saying that they represented us and I endeavored with some
success to convince the people of Brooklyn that their interest lay
in having the Interborough people build these railroads.

Mr. Youmans.— I think my idea of the atmosphere was right.
I have never had any doubt about the constitutionality of our —

Examination resumed by Mr. Moss:

Q. Do you still doubt the constitutionality? A. How can I
when the Court of Appeals has decided it is. I accept my law
from the court. I thought it was a very grave difficult question
and very doubtful as it turned out to be. It was only by one
man's vote that these contracts were allowed.

Q. Didn't it ever occur to you that the question was so grave
that there was danger in submitting a collusive case to the court?
A. This case was not collusive at all.

Q. Well, an inspired case? A. It was not an inspired case. It
was a case agreed upon with two others for the purpose of raising
all the questions.

Q. Did you ever think what the Court of Appeals might have
thought about it if the facts were known? A. I haven't any
doubt about what any court would think about it being a perfectly
proper case.

Chairman Thompson.—You think the courts are in favor of
having one side pay both sides? A. It was not that and it was
not made out to be. I will undertake to defend it before the
courts.

(At this point Mr. Youmans who is on the stand continues his
answer.)

A. You see these were all argued together, and as I remember Mr. Coleman said in his opening brief he would take the complaint of the Hopper action as it included all the facts, etc. Now there isn't any doubt about the attitude of Mr. Shearn in this case. He argued from two to four hours before the Committee on the Wagner bill and frankly when the Admiralty Realty case was brought, first I thought I thought that the first Admiralty Realty case, I thought that Mr. Hays was behind it. You know at that time Mr. Shearn was the attorney for Mr. Hearst. But after I heard it argued over here I changed my opinion. That's all I know about it.

Chairman Thompson.— I just want to say that once I found that Mr. Quackenbush is correct. This bill of Mr. Nicoll, Anable & Fuller of June 1, 1915, says attacks of C. H. Venner and attacks by the New York American but it was American investigation of the Committee and all of the articles there. It did not say attacks on the Public Investigating Committee so I will say once you are right and once the Chair was wrong. What could you do to the New York American in reference to the benefit?

Mr. Nicoll.— I will answer no more questions on that. It is entirely my personal matter.

Chairman Thompson.— You think those were personal?

Mr. Nicoll.— Yes. I was willing to take that item up with you because you wanted me to.

Chairman Thompson.— If there is anybody connected with the New York American that wants this question asked, I will call you again and ask you.

Mr. Nicoll.— Well I won't answer it. You can call me all you want.

Mr. Coleman.— May I, while Mr. Nicoll is here, ask a question of counsel? Mr. Nicoll said in testifying that Mr. Hershfield and myself called at his office.

Mr. Nicoll.— No, sir, I never talked with you about it until this minute. I never have spoken to you on this subject.

Mr. Moss.— Mr. Nicoll said that Mr. Hershfield or whoever it was that called upon him said that he had talked with you.

Mr. Coleman.— I thought he said —

Mr. Moss.—He said that he had not talked with you.

Mr. Nicoll.— I am not sure whether it was Mr. Hays or Mr. Hershfield.

Mr. Moss.— That someone of the firm of Hays & Hershfield told Mr. Nicoll that he had been talking with you. Does that refresh your recollection.

Mr. Coleman.— No, sir.

Mr. Moss.— You have heard what Mr. Harkness said a little while ago and I am asking you if your memory is refreshed after your knowledge of the Admiral Realty Case.

Mr. Coleman.— No.

Mr. Moss.— You cannot say any more than when you testified a few minutes ago?

Mr. Coleman.— No.

(At this point Mr. Youmans resumes his testimony.)

A. I want to say that when the Hopper action was brought by the Interborough that it was not the result of my suggestion some months before.

Mr. Harkness.— I will say what Mr. Nicoll testified to does refresh my recollection in that I know Mr. Ralph Wolf did speak to me before the Admiral Realty case was tried.

DANIEL P. HAYS, sworn as a witness, testified as follows:

Examination by Mr. Moss:

Q. Mr. Hays, you are one of the gentlemen who appeared for the Admiral Realty Company in the litigation that I have mentioned in my question? A. Yes.

Q. Was the Admiral Realty Company a corporation with an office in Manhattan? A. I don't know that Mr. Moss.

Q. Do you know the Company? A. I knew there was such a Company, a client of my office, and Mr. Wolf, I think, can tell you more about that.

Q. How did your office come to bring the action, either one of the two actions? A. Shall I tell you what I know by hearsay?

Q. Yes. We are not bound by the rules of evidence, and what you want to say you can put in that way. A. When the first suit was brought by the Admiral Realty Company against the mayor and against the Bradley Construction Company, I was not here, I was in Europe, and I learned when I came back that that suit had been brought and had been argued before Justice Ford, by Mr. Louis Marshall, and he had held that the proposed agreement was constitutional, was not invalid, and that an appeal was being taken to the Appellate Division of the First Department.

Q. May I ask you where the Bradley Construction Company was working? A. I don't know. The Interborough were not interested in that at all. I understood afterwards that suit was brought at the suggestion of Mr. Nicoll, by our office, for the purpose of testing the validity of that proposed contract at that time. At that time, the Interborough was not a party to that suit, and it was the Brooklyn Rapid Transit Company's proposition which was being entertained by the city. I assisted in the preparation of the brief to the Appellate Division, but it was argued by Mr. Louis Marshall. In the Appellate Division, as you will see from the opinion, the court thought that the matter was premature. As has already been stated, Public Service counsel did not argue or state the constitutional question, and there was also a question raised on the brief that the Brooklyn Rapid Transit ought to be made a party to the suit, and that other parties ought to be brought in. I don't know the date of that, but thereafter.

Q. That finishes the first case, does it? A. That finishes the first case.

Q. Does Mr. Nicoll's statement of the paying of the fee coincide with your recollection? A. The payment of the fee, as I understand it, was paid in this, which included that suit and the Admiral Realty suit. The $35,000. I think Mr. Nicoll was mistaken. I think the voucher will show.

Q. You are speaking of the first case? A. I am speaking of the first Admiral Realty case. The matter you are now referring to. I do not think the Admiral Realty Company — I think it was the Fleischman Realty Company. I think it was some two years before that, and in which case the question was involved, what was to be included in a debt limit of the city of New York. I might say, so far as the finances of our office are concerned, I do not have anything to do with them.

Chairman Thompson.— Do you get any of it?

Mr. Hays.— Yes, sir, I always get my share of it.

Examination resumed by Mr. Moss:

Q. The first one you have already disposed of as premature? A. Now as I recollect it.

Q. That first one was brought over in this county? A. Yes, sir.

Q. And the second one was brought in Kings county? A. As I recollect it, about the time that the second suit was brought, there were propositions made through the Public Service Commission and Board of Estimate and Apportionment by both the Interborough and the Brooklyn Rapid Transit Company. So while the Interborough was not interested at all in the second suit, the propositions of both the Interborough and the Brooklyn Rapid Transit Company were then being made to the Public Service Commission and to the Board of Estimate and Apportionment. I know that Mr. Louis Marshall and Mr. Wolf of our office went to the office of the Public Service Commission and had several consultations with Mr. Coleman. He may not remember it now, but I am sure of that, with reference to the facts that should be alleged in our complaint, with reference to our making it so full that every question that could be involved in the legality or constitutionality of these contracts could be brought up, and I know it was also submitted to the corporation counsel.

Mr. Moss.— Is your recollection refreshed?

Mr. Coleman.— No.

Mr. Hays.— Well, I am so informed by Mr. Marshall. In fact, I have a letter in the office written to our firm by Mr. Marshall at that time, if you care to see it, in which he spoke of that fact that he had been in consultation with Mr. Coleman with reference to the allegations to be put in that complaint. I know that before the preparation of that complaint was completed, the Ryan suit was brought in Brooklyn. That is the reason why everything had been put in that complaint on consultation, so it would not only present every fact, but would present it so the city and Public Service Commission and everybody could demur to it, so as to raise the questions of law. Before that had been completed the Ryan suit was brought in Brooklyn, and that is why the Ryan suit was brought in Brooklyn.

Q. The forum had been established in Brooklyn? A. Yes. Now, if you want me to go on and tell —

Q. How did you come to bring this suit, Mr. Hays? A. Speaking of my own knowledge?

Q. Of your own knowledge, if you can state positively. A. I was informed by my partner that a serious question had been raised by the banking interests who were going to finance — who would be expected to finance the bonds which would be issued, and a test suit would be necessary to be brought in order to determine the validity of these proposed contracts. I was told also by them that I was to undertake the legal work in our office, and that I was to devote myself as far as I could to the preparation of that case, that I had both in the illegality of those contracts, and was to raise every possible question that I could which would in any way in my judgment affect the validity of those contracts, and which could be argued by me in good faith and a belief on my part that they were sound.

Q. Which one of your partners told you that? A. I think both Mr. Hershfield and Mr. Wolf. Now I did devote the greater part of my time while that suit was pending to the study of the questions involved. I was absolutely convinced that the contracts as proposed, both on the part of the Interborough and the Brooklyn Rapid Transit Company, were unconstitutional and illegal, and were not beneficial to the city of New York, and I in my whole professional career, never argued those questions which were raised by us in the Admiral Realty case with greater confidence and —ith greater vim, and with more earnestness than I did in that

Admiral Realty Company case. I argued the question first before Mr. Justice Blackmar. I opened the argument there for the Admiral Realty Company, and spoke for more than an hour or two hours. Mr. Samuel Untermyer, who was associated, closed the argument on our side, as to the validity of these contracts. In the Appellate Division I opened the argument, and Mr. Untermyer closed it. In the Court of Appeals, I opened the argument and argued for more than an hour, and Mr. Marshall made the closing argument on our side. There was no collusion in that suit, and if there had been any collusion, I would not have been in it.

Chairman Thompson.— What do you mean by collusion?

Mr. Hays.— Collusion, as I understand it, Mr. Chairman, is the submission to a court of some kind of a fake case, where it is nominally brought for the relief prayed for in the complaint, but actually brought to get a decision on the other side.

Chairman Thompson.— Your understanding of collusion don't mean for one side to pay all the lawyers?

Mr. Hays.— No, sir.

Chairman Thompson.— As long as you get your pay you don't care where you get it?

Mr. Hays.— Yes, I do. You have no right to make such a statement, I don't think I am here to be insulted.

Chairman Thompson.— You had $62,000.

Mr. Hays.— If I have done anything wrong or unethical, I am answerable to the Appellate Division of this district, and I am perfectly willing to answer every question you ask me. I was going to say to you and Mr. Moss, if you will examine the brief that was prepared by Mr. Marshall and myself, before Justice Blackmar, and before the Appellate Division of the Second Department, and before the Court of Appeals, you will see that the argument was made in absolute good faith.

Examination resumed by Mr. Moss:

Q. I have not the slightest doubt. A. I am glad to hear you say that, and that we argued it sincerely. By innuendoes you are criticizing me when you talk about collusive action.

Q. When I said collusive action, I am using the legal term, and I do not apologize for that. A. I do not agree with you that that was a collusive action.

Q. That is a question of terms. That you raised every question that an ingenious and well-trained mind could raise I haven't the slightest doubt, but the question that we are concerned about comes up in the investigation of the account for the Interborough company, when we find that the Interborough company was inspiring the action against its own contract, and paying for it. A. I would like to tell you what I think, and what I did think of it.

Q. Was the Admiral Realty Company in business? A. Yes, sir, so I understand.

Q. A building company? A. Real estate corporation.

Q. Owning real estate, and buying and selling real estate? A. Yes, sir, so I understand, but I have not any personal knowledge.

Q. Did they have a meeting of the board of directors and authorize this litigation? A. I couldn't tell you that. I know nothing about it.

Q. Who would know? A. Mr. Wolf.

Q. Do you know whether the Admiral Realty Company was consulted about the bringing of this action? A. I would only have to say that I don't know, but I presume that it was.

Q. Are the members of your firm stockholders in the Admiral Realty Company? A. I am not, and I don't know that any member of my firm is.

Chairman Thompson.— Who are the officers of the company?

Mr. Hays.— I don't know that.

Chairman Thompson.— Do you know any officer of the company?

Mr. Hays.— If I had the complaint here I could tell you who verified the complaint, but I will get you all the information you want on that subject. And Mr. Wolf, if Mr. Moss wants to examine him, can tell him all about it.

Examination resumed by Mr. Moss:

Q. Now, did you personally talk with any officer of the Interborough railroad concerning this suit? A. I never did, no, sir. I don't know any of them.

Q. Then, all of that conversation, if there was such, would come from Mr. Wolf and Mr. Hershfield? A. Well, I understand that Mr. Hershfield had a conversation with Mr. Nicoll, but I had no conversation with Mr. Nicoll about the suit.

Q. What I want to get at, Mr. Hays, is when you were doing this work, who were you looking to for pay? A. Well, I personally was not looking to anybody for it.

Q. You left that to the other members of the firm? A. I certainly did, but I understood when the check came that I was being paid by the Interborough. I knew I was going to be paid by some one else than the Admiral Realty Company, because I did not think the Admiral Realty Company would enter into such a litigation and go to the expense it did on its own initiative, as a taxpayer.

Q. Do you know that the Admiral Realty Company was informed that it would not be at any personal risk? A. I don't know; I presume it was, sir.

Chairman Thompson.— What is Mr. Wolf's name?

Mr. Hays.— Ralph.

By Chairman Thompson:

Q. In your firm? A. Yes.

Q. Who is Isaac Wolf? A. I think Isaac Wolf was his father. I think he is dead.

Q. Does it refresh your recollection any when I tell you that one of these complaints was verified by Isaac Wolf? A. It would not refresh my recollection, but I would say, hearing that, that Mr. Wolf, officer of the company, was father of Mr. Ralph Wolf.

Q. You do know Mr. Ralph Wolf's father was an officer of this company? A. I do. I know he was a real estate operator.

Q. You knew when you got the money it came from the Interborough? A. Yes, sir.

Q. How do you know that? A. I was told by my partner.

Q. Is that the only information you had on the subject? A. Well, I think that is the only information.

Q. Wasn't this money paid direct to you? A. I am informed now, sir, if you want my knowledge, that the check came directly to the firm; that the bill was rendered to the Interborough and the check came directly to the firm, and in that check was included the fee for Mr. Marshall of Guggenheimer, Untermyer & Marshall, and a letter was written by us on the date we received the check informing them—

Chairman Thompson.— Wasn't there a statement or letter or something attached to this bill you rendered to the Interborough saying to pay the money to you? A. I assume the check came with the bill.

Q. Wasn't there a letter or memorandum attached to the bill that was rendered to the Interborough Railroad Company requesting them to send the payment to you? A. I don't know. I know now the bill was sent by Mr. Hershfield.

Q. I don't know anything about how the bill was sent. I am asking whether the money was paid to you personally? A. No, sir, not to me personally.

Q. Do you know that there was a direction on the bill to pay it to you? A. To me personally?

Q. Yes. A. No, I never heard of that.

Q. You never heard of it? A. It was not paid to me personally.

Examination resumed by Mr. Moss:

Q. Do you know whether your office incorporated the Admiral Realty Company? A. I do not. I presume it did if it was Mr. Wolf's father.

Q. You don't know anything about the details of what stock or profit it had or anything? A. No, sir, I do not. I would like to say, Mr. Chairman, if Mr. Moss is through with me that I resent —

Chairman Thompson.— If you have got some fact you want to testify to?

Mr. Hays.— Yes, sir.

By Chairman Thompson:

Q. We have not got space to print presentments. A. I think when you put a lawyer on the stand who cares something for his reputation and you either by innuendo or otherwise —

Q. You will get a chance to make a statement. A. I know, but I think I ought to be entitled to make it here on the record.

Q. What is this in relation to? A. In relation to this being a collusive suit.

Q. You think that reflects on you personally? A. I think it reflects on me because I would not have been a party to a collusive suit. If I thought it was a collusive or unethical I would never have allowed my name to be used. I submit that both the Chairman and the learned counsel of the Committee are mistaken. Because the Interborough paid us for our services that it made it a collusive suit. I was informed it made no difference to the Interborough whether the contract was constitutional or unconstitutional. I was informed that it had made this proposition in the dual subway matter just about the time this suit was brought because they were practically forced into making it. They were satisfied with the situation as it was, having the subway here in New York city, and I did not know in my own mind whether they would be better satisfied to have it declared unconstitutional or not, but I knew that I was there for the purpose of attacking the contracts on any illegal grounds without regard to whether it hurt or helped the Interborough Railroad Company, and my whole efforts· and my whole purpose from the beginning to the end was directed to that result. And I convinced myself that the contract was illegal and unjust to the city, and I find that two of the judges were convinced by our arguments in the Court of Appeals that the contract was at least unconstitutional in that it created a partnership between, as we urged in our brief, between the city and the railway company, and it was virtually lending the credit of the city to a railroad corporation, to a citizen, to an individual, and I still believe, although I bow with deference to the Court of Appeals, I still believe that what we urged in our brief was right and just and fair.

Q. I have already expressed myself on the meaning as I meant it in that word collusive. It was an impersonal statement.

Chairman Thompson.— It is only the decision of the chair, but I think it is unethical and not proper legal ethics for a man to take a case and secretly get his pay from the other side.

A. There is nothing secret about it. If there was anything secret there would have been some subterfuge.

By Chairman Thompson:

Q. What do you say receiving a check of $10,000 from Mr. Freedman? A. I don't know anything about it. You will have to ask my partner.

Examination resumed by Mr. Moss:

Q. I just want to call your attention to the bill which is already in evidence. A. I did not prepare the bill.

Q. Here it is — Admiral Realty Company against Gaynor, revising complaint and affidavits on motion for temporary injunction; application to Judge Giegerich for temporary injunction to prevent and order to show cause; arguing motion and preparation of briefs at special terms, consultations with regard to appeal at Appellate Division; preparation of brief on such appeal and argument of appeal to the Appellate Division. A. I was away at the time that suit was brought.

Q. Second case — conferences with counsel for the Public Service Commission with regard to the preparation of complaint in a suit to test the constitutionality of the proposed contract between the city of New York and the Interborough Rapid Transit Company and the Brooklyn Rapid Transit Company for its construction of the new subways; revising the complaint, preparation of brief and argument of demurrer interposed by several defendants; arguments of issues of law at special terms held by Mr. Justice Blackmar; revision of brief for the Appellate Division of the Second Department and argument of the appeal in that court; preparation of the brief for Court of Appeals and argument of appeal in that court, $25,000. Then it includes the bill rendered by counsel Mr. Marshall, I presume, or his firm. Mr. Hays, your bill was $35,000. The bill of Guggenheimer, Untermyer & Marshall was $25,000, making outside of disbursements $60,000 and $3,228.72 for disbursements. Is there anything more about the bill? A. No, sir. I did not prepare the bill and I have only seen the bill since the matter came up before the Public Service Commission.

Mr. YOUMANS, recalled as a witness.

Examination by Mr. Moss:

Q. Calling your attention to your statement that the Brooklyn Rapid Transit was always at enmity with the Interborough Company except in one particular which you mentioned? A. That is my memory of it.

Q. Do you remember that the Brooklyn Rapid Transit Company had the whole field for twenty-one months? A. Well, I know that the Board of Estimate and Apportionment took up this question as to whether they would give to each one certain lines or give all the lines to one, and I think that seemed — I don't remember whether that was 1911 or 1912 — the Board of Estimate and Apportionment, the Interborough having refused to take any lines, granted all the lines.

Q. Granted all the lines to the Brooklyn Rapid Transit? A. Yes.

Q. And the Brooklyn Rapid Transit directors made and accepted it? A. I am not a director.

Q. Haven't you any information, they passed a resolution and accepted it? A. I think that is probably true, because I know Colonel Williams told me he apprised the city officials that we would take it all.

Q. Now, you remained in the possession of the confidence and apparent willingness of the Board of Estimate and Apportionment to take the whole field for twenty-one months? A. I don't know. This resolution was passed by the Board of Estimate and Apportionment. I know that then we at once proceeded, as I remember it, to get up a form of contract on the basis of the whole, and then from then on the city officials, as I understood, although I was not in the conference — the Board of Estimate and Apportionment, Mr. McAneny took up negotiations with the Interborough. I don't know how long that lasted. I don't think the Public Service Commission ever got out their form of contract until after that was settled, did they? I don't know how long it was.

Q. Some period of time? A. I was not in those negotiations.

Q. After you had the whole field, then they come along with this dual arrangement dividing it? A. Well, I think it was decided beforehand. At the time that the Board of Estimate and Apportionment took up the question of giving some of the lines to one company and some to the other, I think at that time they had it in mind.

Q. Having had the whole thing from the Board of Estimate, did your company make any objections to making negotiations and letting the other company in? A. You will have to ask Colonel Williams. I know nothing about those negotiations.

Q. Wasn't there a time when the Interborough and B. R. T. came together and virtually split the situation between them? A. I can't tell you that.

Q. I ask you that because you said they had been inimical except in one little matter. A. That is what I had in my mind from my personal contact with them.

Q. Isn't your information that the situation changed from the B. R. T. having it all to another situation where it had to divide it up, that the companies got together and became friendly? A. No. My information, whether it is good, bad or indifferent, that Colonel Williams was in negotiations all the time with the public officials and he has said, " While our company wanted all, they would take the part that they ultimately got or that was assigned to them." Now, whether he had any negotiations with the Interborough, I don't know. I don't believe I was ever in any conference with the Interborough.

Louis H. HAHLO, sworn as a witness, testified as follows:

Examination by Mr. Moss:

Q. You are an assistant corporation counsel? A. I am.

Q. Mr. Hahlo, you have been here this afternoon and heard the testimony of these various gentlemen? A. I have.

Q. When did you first learn that the suit brought by the Admiral Realty Company was brought in the interest of the Interborough Company? A. Of my own knowledge, only when I saw it published in the newspapers as to the matters that were brought out in this Committee.

Q. When did you first suspect that to be the case? A. I think when Mr. Harkness told me that he had asked Mr.— now Judge — Shearn to institute an action in the name of Mr. Hopper, or had suggested to do so.

Q. And that was while the action was pending? A. That was during the pendency of the suit.

Q. Did you confer with anybody connected with this office? A. I did not.

Q. Did you mention it to Mr. Watson? A. I don't think I did.

Q. Did you think it sufficiently important to discuss with him? A. I had nothing on which to predicate anything more than a suspicion.

Q. But suspicions are talked over among themselves? A. I did discuss that with Mr. Harkness.

Q. Well, had you entire charge of the case? A. I had.

Q. You did not have to confer with Mr. Watson? A. I had entire charge.

Q. Did you consider that an important case? A. I did.

Q. What did you do to verify your suspicion? A. I did not do anything, because I could not see anything to do.

Q. Well, why didn't you confer with your superiors, if you could not think of anything to do? A. I could not see that any good would be accomplished by doing it.

Q. Would you think it would have an important bearing on the case? A. If this action was brought by the Interborough?

Q. If the action of the plaintiff against sustaining the complaint was brought in the interest of the Interborough, which was a defendant? A. I did not think that the action had been brought in the interest of the Interborough. I had understood that the bankers who were to advance the money to enable the Interborough to enter this contract had announced publicly that they would not advance the money unless the question of the constitutionality of these contracts had been first judicially determined, and my suspicion was rather directed to the fact ——

Q. You thought that this was an action brought in the interest of the bankers? A. Yes, sir.

Q. Well, that was not what Mr. Harkness told you? A. No, sir. That was my dope, because I had heard that statement made publicly. I think it was even in the newspapers.

Q. Did you know, or did you have any information or any suspicion of a close relation between the bankers and the Interborough? A. I didn't know anything about it.

Q. Didn't you know who the bankers were? A. I did, sir.

Q. Did you know the attitude of the city officials towards that litigation? A. The city officials is a pretty broad term.

Q. Well, members of the Board of Estimate and Apportionment? A. I think they were divided on the subject. I know the present Mayor, that was President of the Board of Aldermen, was opposed to the contract. I knew Mr. Maltbie was opposed.

Q. I am asking about the Board of Estimate. A. I knew and I had reason to believe that Mayor Gaynor was favorable to it at that particular time.

Q. Did you have any conferences with any of those members of the Board of Estimate and Apportionment? A. I have no recollection of having conferred with any of the members of the Board of Estimate and Apportionment during the pendency of that action.

Q. Didn't you have instructions from anybody with regard to the attitude you should take and efforts you should make in that case? A. I had to examine the question of the constitutionality of these contracts before the action was brought, and when the action was brought, the action was assigned to me in the ordinary course of the business of the office.

Q. What were you driving at from your standpoint in that case? A. I was trying to defend the city officers who were attacked.

Q. Attacked for what? A. They were made defendants in this suit.

Q. What were you trying to establish in their defense? A. I was trying to establish the contract which they were contemplating making was constitutional and not violative of any law.

Q. Had you any direction from any members of the Board of

Estimate and Apportionment, or any of the members of the city government?   A. None whatever.

Q. Had you any instructions from the corporation counsel? A. None, except I spoke to him about the case when it first came into the office.

Q. It was just in your hands and you knew there was a contract there, and the constitutionality was discussed?   A. There was no contract then.

Q. Contract-to-be?   A. It was simply a draft contract.

Q. It was to be?   A. The Board of Estimate contemplated making, and its constitutionality had been assailed, and as the Board of Estimate contemplated making this contract, and as I was assistant to the counsel of the Board of Estimate, it was my duty to sustain its constitutionality.

Q. How did you work it out; it was your duty to stand by the contract which had not been executed?   A. Because I had learned that the Board of Estimate had in contemplation the entry into a contract of this kind.

Q. How did you learn that,— Who told you?   A. It is impossible for me now to tell you, Mr. Moss.   I don't know.   Possibly Mr. Watson told me, but no member of the Board of Estimate had discussed it with me.

Q. How did you know that your superiors, the Board of Estimate and Apportionment, the Mayor and the city officials desired to have that contract sustained, and it was not executed?   A. My superior was Mr. Watson.   I do not think the members of the Board of Estimate and Apportionment are my superiors.

Q. Well, did Mr. Watson tell you to fight for the contract? A. My impression is that he did.   He would not have said it in that many words, but he asked me to appear for the Board of Estimate and Apportionment.

Chairman Thompson.— You have the same idea, that the interests of the city could be well looked after by Clarence Shearn and the interests of the people looked after by the city on the other side?

A. I did not consider that.

Q. Was any of the officers attacked in his personal capacity? A. There was in the Shearn case an attack on the good faith of

the contract, but Mr. Shearn on the argument expressly said that
he did not attack these officers for the lack of good faith.

Q. Well, you did not take the position of saying to the court
substantially, " We are the wards of the court, and leave the court
to determine whether the contract is good or not," but you took
a positive position ? A. I argued to the best of my ability that
contracts of that kind would be constitutional if entered into.

Q. And when the question was raised that you spoke of by Mr.
Shearn, you argued that they were all right ? A. I did not have to.

Q. You argued the question of whether the contract in an impersonal way was in good faith or bad faith ? A. I cited the cases
that hold that unless a contract is wasteful, the court won't substitute its judgment for that of public officers charged with the
performance of a public duty.

Q. Did you argue that the contract was not wasteful ? A. I
don't know. It was not necessary.

Q. Did you say the contract was all right ? A. I argued in
favor of the contract.

Q. That it was all right ? A. I said it was not a waste, within
legal contemplation.

Q. Who told you to do that ? A. Nobody. Mr. Moss, we have
hundreds of cases in our office,— thousands of them, and when we
are given a case to defend, we defend it for all that is in us.

Q. I can understand that, Mr. Hahlo, if you were standing
for an executed contract, an act that the officers had really performed, that you might very well stand for them, and defend it
as right, but here you have merely a proposition that was held up
by an injunction. Why should you argue in favor of the proposition, unless you had received positive instructions to do it ? A.
Any instructions I did receive, I received from Mr. Watson.

Q. Well, did you receive them ? A. I can't say positively,
because I don't recollect.

Examination by Chairman Thompson:

Q. You say you suspected that the Admiral Realty people were
put up by the Interborough ? A. No, I did not. I said I thought
that possibly the Admiral Realty suit was instituted in behalf or
by the bankers who wanted that question settled before they
advanced the money.

Q. You never did think that Mr. Shearn was arguing for the bankers at all? A. I thought that Mr. Shearn who represented in effect, as I thought then, the New York Journal and Mr. Hearst, which was violently opposed to these contracts, was actually and in good faith, and without any question making a serious legal attack against us.

Q. Why do you use those words, " actually in good faith and without any question," with reference to Mr. Shearn? A. Because you gentlemen seem to have some question of the right of counsel in the Admiral Realty case.

Chairman Thompson.— Everybody else was either for the constitutionality of this contract.

Mr. Hahlo.— So far as the Ryan case was concerned, I had not any suspicion. The office was not in it.

Chairman Thompson.— But this Realty case, everybody was for the constitutionality of the contract, or else you had a suspicion?

Mr. Hahlo.— I want to say that Messrs. Untermyer, Marshall and Hays apparently did argue the case for all that was in it.

Chairman Thompson.— Apparently?

Mr. Hays.— You said " apparently." I said actually.

Mr. Hahlo.— I know all of these gentlemen, and I personally regard them as men of high reputation at the Bar.

Chairman Thompson.— Mr. Watson, when he came to the corporation counsel, did he come from the law firm of Nicoll, Anable & Fuller?

Mr. Hahlo.— I think Mr. Watson had offices with them, but what his connection was I don't know.

Chairman Thompson.— You don't know whether he was connected or not?

Mr. Hahlo.— I think he was connected, but what it was I don't know.

RALPH WOLF, being sworn as a witness, testified as follows:

Examination by Mr. Moss.

Q. Mr. Wolf, you are a partner of Mr. Hays? A. Yes, sir.

Q. Do you remember the bringing of the two suits by the Admiral Realty Company? A. Yes, sir.

Q. How did your firm come to bring those suits? A. I spoke to the president and secretary or treasurer of the company and asked them if they would mind bringing a suit to test the constitutionality of the contract or of the bonds to be issued under the contract, and they said they would.

Q. How did you come to do that? A. Because I suppose that Mr. Wolf, who is president of the company is my father, and Hocksteeter is secretary of the company.

Q. I don't mean that,— something caused you to undertake this? A. I was requested to do it.

Q. By whom? A. I don't know. Somebody in the office — Mr. Hershfield or Mr. Hays or some one.

Q. Do you think Mr. Hays told you? A. I don't think so.

Q. Do you think Mr. Hershfield? A. I think so.

Q. How did Mr. Hershfield come to request you to do that? A. I really don't know. I don't even know that he did.

Q. This was to be a large suit, of course? A. Yes.

Q. And it might involve the Admiral Realty Company in some expense unless it were protected in some way? A. Yes.

Q. Somebody requested you to do this, didn't they? A. Yes.

Q. Well, who was it? A. My impression is Mr. Hershfield, if I could talk to these gentlemen and obtain their consent on the understanding they would be held harmless from all expense.

Q. Who came to Mr. Hershfield? A. I don't know only from hearsay.

Q. What is your impression? A. Mr. Nicoll.

Chairman Thompson.— It is not any impression — you know it is Mr. Hershfield.

Mr. Wolf.— My impression is, it was.

Chairman Thompson.— Then it must be — then why put it on the record it is your impression?

Mr. Wolf.— Because it is my impression.

Chairman Thompson.— Isn't that your absolute recollection it was Mr. Hershfield?

Mr. Wolf.— No, sir, it is not.

Chairman Thompson.— There isn't anybody else in your office that could have asked you except him.

Mr. Wolf.— I don't believe anybody else did.

Examination resumed by Mr. Moss:

Q. Well, did you ever have any conversation with Mr. Nicoll? A. I think only on possibly one or two occasions I may have.

Q. Where was that? A. At his office.

Q. In connection with these matters? A. Yes.

Q. Do you mind telling us what the conversation was? A. Well, I really — I think the only thing that I can recall now is, was when I sent him a copy of the Court of Appeals' decision.

Q. That was when it was all over? A. Yes, I think so, and I think I saw him once prior to that time, but it was so unimportant, I haven't any recollection of what occurred, but I know I did see him.

Q. There was a good deal of work done and some liability incurred — who did you look to for recompense? A. I did not personally — did not look to anyone, because I personally did not make the arrangement.

Q. The Admiral Realty Company was your father's company? A. Yes. I was told by Mr. Hershfield, that Mr. Nicoll or his client would defray all the expenses of the suit.

Q. Did you know who was Mr. Nicoll's client? A. I understood so.

Q. Who was that? A. I understood the fees were to be paid by the Interborough Company.

Q. Supposing there had been a judgment of costs against the Admiral Realty Company, what was to be done by them? A. I understood the expenses of every kind were to be paid by the Interborough.

28

Q. Was there any meeting of the directors of the Admiral Realty Company? A. Not that I know of.

Q. You simply got instructions? A. I think the president and secretary. I think the same gentleman occupied both offices.

Q. And that was a company which was a client of the office? A. Yes, sir.

Q. Had some property in Manhattan? A. I don't know; it did at the time.

Q. It had two pieces of property in Manhattan at one time? A. I don't know.

Q. What is Mr. Hershfield's first name? A. A. Hershfield.

Chairman Thompson.— What does that stand for?

Mr. Wolf.— Abram.

Q. Didn't it hold two pieces of property in Manhattan which were transferred within a short time from the time it held them? A. I really don't know.

Q. You don't know anything about that? A. No. All I know is that it held some real estate. I really don't know just where. I undoubtedly knew at the time, but I do not remember any more.

Q. Now, did you have something to do with drawing the bill for services? A. No.

Q. Who did draw the bill? A. I really don't know.

Q. Who would draw it naturally — Mr. Hays says he had the legal end of the offices, and did not handle the finances. A. I suppose in the ordinary course of business, Mr. Hershfield would.

Q. Well, the bill was drawn directly to the Interborough Rapid Transit Company? A. Well, you say that. I have never seen it.

Q. I have a copy of it in the record here. Did you see that bill before it was sent out? A. No, I can't say that I did.

Q. Was the Interborough Company a defendant in the action? A. I believe it was, yes, sir.

Q. The Admiral Realty Company sued the Interborough Company as one of the defendants? A. As one of the defendants; they were a defendant.

Q. And the action in part was to defend the question of the validity of the contract which the Interborough Company had, wasn't it? A. Well, I don't believe there was any contract at the time.

Q. There was a form of contract, wasn't there? A. I am not sure there was even a form of contract.

Q. Wasn't there a form of contract? A. I don't believe so.

Q. What kind of an action did you bring, what for? A. Why, it was to test the constitutionality of the proposed arrangement.

Q. In what form — action for an injunction? A. Yes, it was an action for an injunction.

Q. To prevent the carrying out of a project? A. Of a program.

Q. And that program involved the making of a contract with the Interborough Company? A. A subway contract.

Q. I will read the second allegation of the complaint: "That the plaintiff is the owner of large tracts of land in the city of New York, aggregating in value thousands of dollars, and is the owner of which property is assessed for the amount of more than one thousand dollars, and is liable to pay taxes on said assessment to the city of New York, and within one year has paid the assessment exceeding said amount." That was drawn in your office? A. Yes, I haven't any doubt of it.

Q. Who did draw the complaint, do you know? A. I think the larger part of that complaint was prepared by Mr. Marshall.

Q. And who in your office passed upon it? A. I think probably Mr. Hays did. I am not sure. Either Mr. Hays did or I did. Probably I did.

Q. "Sixth. Upon information and belief, that the defendant Interborough Rapid Transit Company is a domestic railroad company, duly created and existing under and by virtue of the laws of the State of New York," and goes on to describe other defendants. The prayer is, "Wherefore the plaintiff demands judgment, and the defendant and each and all of them be restrained during the pendency of this action and permanently," and then comes on the provision regarding what they were going to do with the contract. That is what it was, an action for injunction, including the Interborough as defendant? A. Undoubtedly.

Q. Well, from the beginning, from the understanding you had, you were to make your bill and look for protection for the Realty

Company, from the Interborough Rapid Transit? A. That was the impression I had.

Chairman Thompson.— I would like to know who the stockholders are of this company.

Mr. Wolf.— I would be very glad to find out and let you know, except Mr. Wolf had one-third interest, and Mr. Hocksteeter had a third interest.

Chairman Thompson.— Who is he?

Mr. Wolf.— A friend of Mr. Wolf.

Chairman Thompson.— Who else?

Mr. Wolf.— I don't know who the other stockholders are.

Chairman Thompson.— Mr. Wolf is your father?

Mr. Wolf.— Yes.

Chairman Thompson.— Didn't he practically own the whole company?

Mr. Wolf.— He had a third interest in the company.

Chairman Thompson.— Didn't he control the rest of it?

Mr. Wolf.— No.

Chairman Thompson.— Are you sure of that?

Mr. Wolf.— No.

Chairman Thompson.— Where does he live?

Mr. Wolf.— He is dead now.

Chairman.— Who has got the stock now?

Mr. Wolf.— I think that the estate held it, but I think that it has been sold or liquidated.

Chairman Thompson.— Who was the executor?

Mr. Wolf.— My mother.

Chairman Thompson.— Are you attorney for the estate?

Mr. Wolf.— I don't think that they ever had an attorney.

Chairman Thompson.— You can get us the information tomorrow ?

Mr. Wolf.— I rather give it to you Monday morning.

Chairman Thompson.— I should like it tomorrow.

Mr. Wolf.— If I can get it, I will come in.

Chairman Thompson.— Has Mr. Coleman's recollection returned ?

Mr. Coleman.— I was thinking if the Interborough paid the expenses, that might account for the $83 coming through in the shape of costs.

Chairman Thompson.— We will suspend now until 11 A. M. tomorrow.

(At this point the Chairman handed the stenographer several papers as being offered in evidence, and asked that they be marked as exhibits. Whereupon the same were marked by the stenographer as of this date.)

The Committee then took an adjournment until February 24, 1916, at 11 A. M.

FEBRUARY 24, 1916

NEW YORK COUNTY LAWYERS' ASSOCIATION BOARD ROOM,
165 Broadway, New York City

Meeting called to order by Assemblyman Feinberg, acting Chairman, at 12:30 P. M.

Mr. Louis Marshall.— I came here for the purpose of making a statement with regard to the history of the Admiral Realty Company case, and I wish to state that I have not been subpoenaed. I have come here voluntarily. I was out of the city yesterday, and on my arrival I find that various gentlemen have been here and examined as witnesses, and I am very desirous of making a

full and complete statement of the history of that litigation, which
I do not think appears with sufficient accuracy upon the record, at
least from the newspaper accounts. I would like to explain the
history of that litigation, and I desire the opportunity to make a
complete statement giving a history of the case and of the various
phases of it.

Chairman Feinberg.— Mr. Marshall, I am glad to see you here.
I am always glad to see you here. I know that you are a very
respected member of the New York county bar, and any information that you might see fit to give to the Committee would be
highly appreciated by them. I wish to announce that Senator
Thompson has gone to Albany, and our chief counsel, Mr. Moss,
is not here, and I think it is only fair to you that you make your
statement and submit yourself to any questions that may be asked;
in other words, I think you should submit yourself to the
examination.

Mr. Marshall.— I hold myself subject to the orders of the Chairman or the Committee in that respect. Whatever they desire I am
willing to do.

Mr. Shuster.— Mr. Chairman, Mr. Wolf was instructed to
furnish this information this morning. He was a witness yesterday and was requested to bring a certain record which he has
here now. He has to be in Baltimore to-morrow and expects to
return some time Saturday, and I will suggest, Mr. Chairman, if
it is agreeable, that he be excused until Monday morning at 11
o'clock.

Mr. Wolf.— I came here voluntarily at the request of Mr.
Smith over the 'phone. I came here at once. I am glad to come
here any time the Committee wishes.

Chairman Feinberg.— You are excused until Monday morning
at 11 o'clock. The Committee will take a recess until to-morrow
morning, February 25th, at 11 o'clock. All witnesses are excused
except the Gillespie witnesses, who will continue in session, according to the stipulation already made.

The Committee thereupon adjourned until 11 A. M., February
, 1916.

FEBRUARY 25, 1916

NEW YORK COUNTY LAWYERS' ASSOCIATION BOARD ROOM,
165 Broadway, New York City

The Committee was called to order, pursuant to adjournment, Chairman Thompson presiding.

Quorum present.

Chairman Thompson.— The Committee will come to order.

Chairman Thompson.— I am in receipt of a letter from Roger Foster, who, according to the New York standard of value for lawyers' services spends $750 worth of time writing a letter explaining $750 he got, and he asks that it should go on the record, and it is right we should accommodate him, therefore we will put it on the record.

The letter referred to is as follows:

"Feb. 24th, 1916.

"Dear Sir.— To-day's newspapers reported that you have placed upon the record of your Committee a statement of counsel fee of seven hundred fifty ($750) dollars paid me by the Interborough Rapid Transit Company during the past nine years. This publication tends to give to the public the impression that I received this payment for services in connection with the contract under which the new subways are being constructed. That is not the fact. The payment was the balance of a bill due me for services upon an appeal to the Appellate Division for the First Department taken by the defendant in the case of the Mayor of the City of New York against the Manhattan Railway Company, reported in 119 App. Div. 240. The suit was brought to collect taxes or license fees, claimed from the Manhattan Railway Company because of the use of that part of the Ninth Avenue Elevated Railroad between Greenwich and Eighty-third streets. I assisted in the preparation of the brief, signed the brief and took part in the argument before the Appellate Division. My retainer was, I presume, because I have devoted considerable study to the law of taxation. I have done no other work for any elevated railway company for many years. I have never acted as general counsel for such a company. You will oblige me by placing this letter upon the records of your Committee.

" I remain,
" Very truly yours,
"(Signed)   Roger Foster.

" Hon. George Thompson, Chairman, Legislative Committee, 165 Broadway, New York."

Chairman Thompson.— I also have another letter, one from a gentleman by the name of Lemuel E. Quigg, written February 23, 1916, and received this morning. I think it is the same one which appeared in public this morning. That may also be incorporated in the minutes.

The letter above referred to is as follows:

" New York, Feb. 23, 1916.

" Mr. George F. Thompson, Chairman:

" Sir.— The Evening Post of to-night quotes you as saying, in respect of a certain check of $2,500 paid to me by T. A. Gillespie on January 13, 1915, you at the moment addressing his son, Mr. T. H. Gillespie, in respect of the books of T. A. Gillespie & Co., as follows:

" ' You wouldn't be so anxious to keep us from going through your books if you didn't have things you didn't want people to know. If you didn't make payments like that check of $2,500 to Mr. Quigg, you wouldn't be afraid to have your papers made public.'

" The Globe of to-night quotes you as saying, in the same relation:

" ' If there were not such things as the check for $2,500 to Lemuel E. Quigg, you would be willing enough to show your books.'

" The Evening Mail quotes you as saying:

" ' If there were not such things as the check for $2,500 to Lemuel E. Quigg in those books you would be willing enough to show them.'

" The Evening World quotes you as saying:

" 'And if you didn't have in your accounts that
$2,500 check to Mr. Quigg, you would not be so embar-
rassed.'

" The Evening Sun quotes you as saying:

" ' If you hadn't paid Mr. Quigg $2,500 things would
probably be different.'

" There has been no moment of time since your accountant
ran across Mr. Gillespie's check to me and his letters to his
brother in Pittsburgh when you might not have ascertained
precisely what the business was that this check related to by
even so slight an effort as calling me on the telephone at my
office. In causing Mr. Gillespie's letter to be printed on February 10, in causing that check to be photographed and exhibited in the newspapers on that date, and, two weeks later,
in making the remark you made to young Mr. Gillespie this
afternoon, without ever asking me about the check, your conduct is the conduct of a conscious blackguard.

"(Signed)   Lemuel E. Quigg."

Mr. Quackenbush.— I have not seen that letter, and I did not
know anything about it having been sent. I want to say I have
not any control over Mr. Quigg in his private business capacity
as representative of anybody excepting the Interborough, but he
is employed by the Interborough, and to that extent associated
with me, and I want to say that I deplore the language that he
used as I saw it in the newspapers, which I assume is in this
letter, in addressing the Chairman of this Committee, and I want
to add that I say by direction of Mr. Shonts that I voice his views
in that respect. Everybody connected with the Interborough
Rapid Transit Company has been treated with consideration by
you as Chairman of the Committee, and by everyone on the Committee, and by everyone connected with the Committee, and we
do not think under such circumstances that a lawyer who was
from time to time performing services for our Company should
of his own volition and without consultation with either the president or the general attorney of the company undertake to indulge
in vituperation. I do not do it, and the president has not done it.
I sincerely regret it.

Chairman Thompson.— I will say in answer to that, that from such perusal as I have gained from the morning papers the letter has been of great assistance to me. I really appreciate, not so much the spirit the writer has in writing it, but the result.

MARSHALL, LOUIS, being first duly sworn, testified as follows:

Examined by Mr. Moss:

Mr. Moss.— Mr. Chairman, Mr. Marshall communicated with me by telephone yesterday and suggested that he would like to make a statement, and would like to make it in his own way, and I think that is the proper thing to do. Mr. Marshall, you have the floor.

Mr. Marshall.— I will refresh my recollection with a memorandum which I have prepared. On July 28, 1911, while in the Adirondacks, I received a telegram from my partner, Mr. Alvin Untermyer, in which I was requested to come back to New York because some important new business had come into the office, and my attention was desired. I came to New York on the night train and arrived on the morning of July 29, 1911, and during the day Mr. Ralph Wolf, of Hays, Hershfield & Wolf, called upon me and informed me that he was about to bring a taxpayer's action against the Board of Estimate and Apportionment of the city of New York, the Public Service Commission of the First District and the Bradley Contracting Company for the purpose of restraining the execution of the contract with the Bradley Contracting Company on sections 6, 8, 10 and 11 of route 5 of the projected new subway, and restrain the Public Service Commission from preparing and executing any contract with the Brooklyn Rapid Transit Company for the construction, equipment and operation of the several lines of extension proposed for operation by it, the contention being that the proposed contracts with the Bradley Contracting Company were illegal and that the proposed contract of construction and operation between the city of New York and the Brooklyn Rapid Transit Company was in violation of the Constitution of the State, section 10, article 8, and also contrary to the provision of the Rapid Transit Act, and was therefore void.

I thereupon discussed with him the various questions involved, and concluded that it was a proper case to bring, since it would determine important and difficult questions of law of great interest to the entire public, and especially the constitutionality of the financing of the construction of the new subways as outlined in what is known as the McAneny reports. Mr. Wolf had a complaint practically completed in which all the necessary allegations were contained and references made to the various documents and resolutions which were involved in the consideration of the question. I made some suggestions as to the form of the papers, and then applied to Mr. Justice Giegerich for a restraining order and order to show cause. Judge Giegerich thought it was best just to grant an order to show cause, and he did so and made it returnable in Special Term, Part I, on August 3, 1911.

Q. You are speaking of the Admiralty case now entirely? A. Yes, sir. The plaintiff in that case was the Admiral Realty Company and the defendants in that case were the Board of Estimate and Apportionment and the Public Service Commission. It is known generally as the case of Admiral Realty Company against Gaynor.

Q. And you are now speaking of that one of the Admiral cases which Mr. Hays spoke of as prematurely brought, the first one? A. Not exactly. In one sense it might be so called. At any rate it is the case which was the first of the proceedings which involved the constitutionality of the new plan of financing the subway and operating the subway. The argument was postponed until the 9th of August, 1911, and came on for hearing before Mr. Justice Ford. The argument was a protracted one, voluminous briefs being filed by the counsel. I argued the case on behalf of the Admiral Realty Company, and Mr. Hollow on behalf of the Board of Estimate and Apportionment, and Mr. Harkness, one of the counsel of the Public Service Commission, argued the case on its behalf, and Mr. Lynch argued it on behalf of the Bradley Contracting Company. A decision was rendered by Judge Ford on September 6, 1911, and he denied our motion for an injunction, though he referred in the course of his opinion to the constitutional question and recognized it to be a very grave one, but relief was refused on the ground that the application for an injunction was premature, although he said: " In view of the magnitude of the public, quasi-public and private interests involved on this motion, it goes without saying that all parties concerned desire a speedy determination by the courts above of the questions raised by this motion."

An appeal was taken by the Admiral Realty Company to the Appellate Division of the First Department, where it was argued, I think, November, 1911. I appeared for the Admiral Realty Company, and Mr. Louis H. Hahlo for the Board of Estimate and Apportionment, Mr. George S. Coleman for the Public Service Commission, and ex-Lieutenant-Governor Thomas F. Conway for the Bradley Contracting Company.

On December 1, 1911, a decision was rendered affirming the order. The opinion is reported in 147 App. Div. Reports at page 719. As to the constitutional question involved Mr. Justice Scott said:

" The action proceeds upon the theory that the terms of the contract for operation have been finally determined upon, and that nothing remains but to prepare and execute a contract. It appears from the papers before us that early in the present year the general subject of a contract for a new rapid transit route or routes was taken up and considered by a joint committee consisting of the members of the Public Service Commission and certain members of the Board of Estimate and Apportionment. This joint committee invited and received informal proposals from two companies already operating lines in the city of New York, to wit, the Interborough Rapid Transit Company and the Brooklyn Rapid Transit Company. After consideration the joint committee made a report favoring the execution of an operating contract upon terms satisfactory to the Brooklyn Company, and which could apparently be carried out only by that company. It is a contract to be made as recommended by this joint committee that it is now sought to enjoin. The learned counsel for the plaintiff has argued before us with much force and earnestness that such a contract would be illegal (1) because it would violate Section 10 of Article VIII of the Constitution of this State, which forbids any county, city, town or village to give money or property, or loan its money or credit to or in aid of any individual, association or corporations, and (2) that it is ultra vires of the city of New York because no one could bid for the contract except the Brooklyn Rapid Transit Company, and hence that there can be no competition for the right to operate the railroad. The contract foreshadowed by the joint committee is in many respects an unusual and extraordinary one, doubtless because the problem to be solved was itself unusual and extraordinary, but we do not find it necessary at this time to consider or discuss the objections to it which are argued by the plaintiff, and expressly forbear to pass upon them, because their discussion and consideration at this time would be premature and academic. For this reason the learned counsel for the respondents has wisely and properly declined to undertake at the present time to enter upon a defense of either the legality or constitutionality of the proposed contract."

The court therefore affirmed, solely on the ground that the application for an injunction in the then state of affairs was premature, because it might have been upon advertising that contract the Board of Estimate and Apportionment and the Public Service Commission might have changed their minds and might have withdrawn their intended action.

The Bradley Contracting Company raised the objection that the city of New York was not a party to the action, and it was also urged that the Brooklyn Rapid Transit Company was a necessary party. It was argued also on behalf of the Public Service Commission that the Brooklyn Rapid Transit Company was a necessary party, and that their presence in the litigation was necessary. These questions were raised, but not decided.

The record and opinion show that, at this time, the only operating contract as to which action had been taken by the public authorities, was one by which it was contemplated that the Brooklyn Rapid Transit Company only was to be the operating corporation, that is, the Brooklyn Rapid Transit Company, or the Brooklyn Union Elevated Railroad Company, a majority of whose stock was held by the Brooklyn Rapid Transit Company. The

Interborough Rapid Transit Company was not brought in or involved in that situation, and the constitutionality of the plan which was involved was one which related to this proposed contract with the Brooklyn Rapid Transit Company.

After this decision had been rendered further proceedings were taken, which involved the operation under a dual system, it being proposed that parts of the subways were to be leased to the Brooklyn Union Elevated Railroad Company and part to the Interborough Rapid Transit Company.

Before anything was done with regard to that plan, the counsel for the Admiral Realty Company were considering an amendment to their complaint. The case was gotten on the calendar and had been noticed for trial, and it was felt that it would be desirable to amend the complaint so as to meet the various objections which had been made in the course of the litigation. On the argument before Judge Ford it was shown that the allegations in the complaint with regard to the nature of the contract proposed with the Brooklyn Rapid Transit Company were not entirely accurate in some of the allegations. Mr. Harkness on the argument of the motion produced the accurate documents from the records which we had not been able to procure, and we therefore decided that it would be necessary to amend our complaint so as to have in the complaint the precise document, the substance of which we had only pleaded in the original complaint.

At that juncture we thought it was necessary to confer with Mr. Coleman, the counsel for the Public Service Commission, in order that we might expedite the amendment of the complaint, and by stipulation bring in the parties that we thought would be essential, so that the case might be hurried along. It also appeared at that time that Mr. Coleman, representing the Public Service Commission, had made up his mind that it was desirable to get an expeditious hearing of the constitutional questions and an expeditious decision on the questions, because it became apparent that until there had been a determination by the Court of Appeals as to the validity of this plan of operation that it would be impossible for the city or for any corporation which might become the lessee, and might become the operating company, to finance the undertaking. So Mr. Wolf and I, and I think on one occasion

Mr. Hays, but I am sure Mr. Wolf and I, on a number of occasions had conferences with Mr. Coleman and with his associate, Mr. Harkness, with regard to the amendment of the complaint, and as I have said, they both indicated that the time had arrived when the Public Service Commission was desirous of obtaining a speedy adjudication as to the constitutionality and validity of the proposed operating contract. We then learned for the first time, while we were engaged in these conferences with Mr. Coleman and Mr. Harkness, representing the Public Service Commission, that an action similar to that of the Admiral Realty Company had been brought in Kings county by John R. Ryan, a taxpayer, against the Public Service Commission.

Mr. Moss.— Do you recall those conversations, Mr. Coleman?

Mr. Coleman.— I do not. I accept it, of course, as true.

Chairman Thompson.— Do you recall them, Mr. Marshall?

Mr. Marshall.— By personal recollection, yes, sir.

Chairman Thompson.— You recall meeting Mr. Coleman?

Mr. Marshall.— Yes, sir, Mr. Coleman, Mr. Harkness, and Mr. Harkness, I think, will be able to say he recollects these conversations.

Chairman Thompson.— You are a pretty busy man yourself?

Mr. Marshall.— Yes, sir.

Chairman Thompson.— Probably you are as busy as the chief counsel of the Public Service Commission?

Mr. Marshall.— I do not want to compare it; in this particular matter I had a memorandum.

Chairman Thompson.— Of course we know Mr. Marshall is a busy man.

Mr. Marshall.— Yes, sir. I remember the transaction, as I had occasion to communicate with my associate in this matter, and I had a memorandum on the proposition.

Mr. Marshall resuming.— Mr. Coleman and Mr. Harkness thought that perhaps the questions involved might be tried in that action. I expressed the opinion that the complaint in that action was in my judgment inadequate and that it lacked the necessary parties, and it was then thought advisable that the Admiral Realty Company should bring a new action in Kings county which could be disposed of with the Ryan case, there being a desire to have the whole subject determined at one time.

Q. On account of some other testimony that has come in the case, did it seem to you that the atmosphere of Brooklyn was as favorable to your proposition as the atmosphere of Manhattan? A. I did not see any difference. It seemed to me it would necessarily have to go to the Court of Appeals anyway, and in a constitutional case I always consider the Special Term and the Appellate Division as mere way stations, because the Court of Appeals will have to determine the constitutionality of the case, and it was therefore a question of expedition merely.

Q. The Court of Appeals might be affected by the form or terms of the decision rendered by the Appellate Division? A. I don't think that would make any difference in a constitutional question, where there is no inference to be drawn and where the entire question was a question as to the validity of a contract or of a statute, and the Court of Appeals would take up the questions de novo, and would have no greater light from the opinion of the lower court than the argument.

Q. Did it occur to you there might be some advantage in having the case proceed in Kings county, the Ryan case, and have your case proceed in New York county, the Admiral case, and reach the Court of Appeals with two Appellate Division decisions? A. It did not occur to me as of any moment at all, and the suggestion of bringing it in Kings county came from the Public Service Commission counsel, because they thought the whole thing could be decided at one and the same time. The general practice, of course, is that the court of first instance always holds a law constitutional, except in the most exceptional cases, and the tendency also of the Appellate Division is to hold the law constitutional unless it is very certain from the face of the law that it is unconstitutional, and generally the matter is left to the Court of Appeals to determine. Therefore, this fact might have been in our minds, but I cannot say it was at this moment; if the Appellate Division in the Second Department held the law was constitutional and the Appellate Division of the First Department also held it constitutional, we would have gone to the Court of Appeals with the adverse opinion of ten judges, and therefore would have had a struggle against that momentum which would have been larger than if only one court with five judges against us. Then we would not have been fighting against such odds.

Q. The Appellate Division in the Second Department wrote no opinion, did it? A. No, sir, they affirmed on the opinion of Judge Blackmar. We had already had a declaration by the Appellate Division of the First Department, in the Gaynor case, if you will recollect, that the constitutional questions were very grave and very important.

Q. If the Appellate Division of the First Department had said the constitutional questions were very grave, wasn't there possibly a chance of getting them to say they were grave in an opinion? A. They expressly refrained from indicating any view on the subject, as you will see, and my own personal view that it was, all things considered, much more desirable to have the case heard in the Second Department than in the First Department. That was merely a matter of feeling, however, and not a matter anybody could reason out.

Q. Did you ever have any question about the good faith of the Ryan suit? A. I had no ideas on the subject.

Q. Had you any information up to that time? A. No, sir, I had no information.

Q. Did you treat the Ryan suit as a suit brought in the interest of Ryan and not anybody else? A. I cannot say; at this time I can give you no light on that subject, but I will tell you what I did at that time have in mind.

Q. I asked that question because Mr. Coleman testified he expected the Ryan suit was not in the interest of the plaintiff, and I wondered if he expressed that to you? A. I cannot bring to my mind that point, but I made a memorandum of objection to the complaint in the Ryan case, why I thought it necessary to have a fuller complaint, to more fully state the constitutional questions involved. I made this objection, first, that the Board of Estimate and Apportionment in the city of New York should have been added as parties, and they were not parties to that case. It was only against the Public Service Commission. Next, the allegation as to the amount which was to be expended for subways by the city, namely, $150,000,000, by the Brooklyn Rapid Transit Company, $26,000,000 for extensions to its existing lines, and $24,-000,000 for equipment, the nature and character of the existing lines, the alleged net income derived therefrom, the fact that they were subject to mortgages for large amounts and that it was proposed to issue additional mortgages to cover the amount required to meet the cost of equipment and extension. None of those were contained in the complaint, and I thought it was necessary in the complaint, and to show that by a continuance of this plan the credits and money of the city were being used for the advantage of the Brooklyn Rapid Transit Company. I desired to make that as emphatic as possible, and therefore I did not feel that the Ryan case was in a situation for the argument of that question to the extent I thought it should be argued.

Then I thought there should be an allegation to the effect that the Public Service Commission and the Board of Estimate and Apportionment proposed to expend large sums of money for the preparation of plans and specifications and for advertising for bids in order to enable them to enter into a contract with the Brooklyn Rapid Transit Company on the lines proposed, which would involve an expenditure of a large sum of money; that, for the purpose of making and creating a case which in any event would enable the courts at that time to determine the constitutional questions, we have the question of prematureness raised which might have been because of the fact the contracts had not at that time been actually signed; also, that the Board of Estimate and Apportionment, the Public Service Commission and the city of New York have threatened and proposed to enter into a contract with the Brooklyn Rapid Transit Company in conformity with the terms of its proposal as modified by the subsequent resolution. Those were among the points which I pointed out as omitted from the complaint in the Ryan case, which I thought were absolutely essential.

Q. Serious omission. A. That therefore in the due course of
evolution allied to the proposition that the Admiral Realty Company should bring a new action in Kings county which could be
disposed of with the Ryan case, and that the complaint in the new
Admiral case should be very specific, very elaborate as to all the
facts, so that there should not be omitted a single fact, statement
or document which would have a bearing on the question of the
constitutionality of the contract and of its effect upon the taxpayers
of the city of New York. We then drafted a new complaint and
submitted that to Mr. Coleman, and to his associate, Mr. Harkness, and they produced various documents which we asked for
and which were deemed important to present every material fact
bearing on the constitutional question, and they were all put into
the complaint, so that there was not any question as to the fullness
of the statement, but the document itself was made a part of the
complaint, so that the complaint when completed covered nearly
three hundred and fifty printed pages.

It had the McAneny report in full, and all resolutions, all the
existing contracts with the different corporations also. I have here
before me the printed record of the case in the Court of Appeals,
which contains their complaint and the various appendices which
are part of it, all of which indicate the fullest and most complete
selection, so that I venture to say that the most careful investigation since that time would fail to disclose a single point, a single
document or a single fact which would have a bearing upon the
determination of the constitutional question. It was at first contemplated, as I have said, that the Brooklyn Rapid Transit Company and the Brooklyn Union Elevated Railroad Company only
were to be made co-defendants with the city of New York, the
Board of Estimate and Apportionment, and the Public Service
Commission in that second suit.

I have already indicated who the parties were in the Gaynor
case. Mr. Coleman and Mr. Harkness, however, called attention
to the fact that a proposal from the Interborough Rapid Transit
Company would be received within a few days which would probably be acceptable to the Public Service Commission, and that the
complaint might refer to that proposed contract as well as to the
Brooklyn Rapid Transit Company contract, in order that the

entire subject of the operation of the two subways might be before the court, and in view of the fact there were certain differences between the Interborough form of contract and the Brooklyn Rapid Transit Company's contract, if there was to be a distinction between the two they might be passed upon by the court. This was accordingly done, and my recollection is that a copy of that proposed contract with the Interborough Rapid Transit Company was furnished to me either by Mr. Harkness or Mr. Coleman, I rather think Mr. Harkness, because he had greater familiarity with the details of this matter, he having argued the case before Judge Ford, and having made affidavit at that time as to the general situation. So that we then, in compliance with that suggestion, brought in this proposed contract with the Interborough, the sole purpose of that action being to enable the court to render an authoritative decision which would determine once for all whether the operating plan was in violation of the constitution and statutes of the State or not. If unconstitutional, then it would become necessary for the public authorities to devise other methods for the operation of the new subways. If constitutional, then it would become possible to finance the new enterprise, since the cloud of unconstitutionality which overhung the financial phases of the project would be dissipated. It was at this time a third action was brought in Kings county for the purpose of determining the validity of this project, Mr. John J. Hopper being the plaintiff, and the Public Service Commission the defendant. Judge Shearn, a member of the bar, was the attorney for Mr. Hopper. He tried his action also in Kings county, the idea being that the three cases should be argued together so that they would have the fullest consideration. Judge Shearn obtained from my office a copy of the papers in the original action of the Admiral Realty Company against Gaynor and others, a copy of the brief which I used in the Appellate Division in that case, and it is my impression, although I am not positive, also a copy of our new complaint in the Kings county suit brought by the Admiral Company. At any rate, he had access to it, because he had all the acts in that complaint in his complaint.

As soon as that action was brought demurrers were interposed to the complaint in these several actions on behalf of the Public

Service Commission, the city of New York and the several railroad companies. These demurrers were argued together before Mr. Justice Blackmar in April, 1912. In an elaborate opinion judgment was rendered for the defendants. The decision is reported in 76 Misc. Reports at page 345. The parties then immediately took an appeal to the Appellate Division of the Second Department, where the judgment of the Special Term was affirmed on the opinion of Mr. Justice Blackmar, without any further memorandum.

Then the three cases were taken to the Court of Appeals, where they were elaborately argued on June 11, 1912. The court extended the time of counsel on account of the great public importance of the questions involved. My recollection is we took two full days and I think a part of a third day in the presentation of the case. I think we had about two and a half times the usual time allowed by the Court of Appeals for the discussion of such a case.

'On that occasion Mr. Hays argued for the appellant. Mr. Justice Shearn argued very elaborately on behalf of Hopper, and Mr. Baylis argued for Ryan, and Mr. Hahlo for the city of New York. Mr. Coleman argued for the Public Service Commission, and Mr. Collin for the Brooklyn Rapid Transit Company. Mr. Richard Reid Rogers argued for the Interborough Rapid Transit Company, and I closed the argument on behalf of the taxpayers. The Court of Appeals affirmed the judgment in all three cases by a bare majority, Judges Hiscock, Haight, Vann and Collin deciding in favor of the defendants, Chief Judge Cullen and Judge Werner delivering elaborate dissenting opinions, and Judge Gray taking no part in the decision. The case is reported in 206 N. Y. Reports at page 110. The opinions are of extraordinary length, covering some fifty-two pages. A reference to the brief of the Admiral Realty Company, to the record and to the opinions, will indicate that no case was ever fought with more earnestness and with deeper conviction as to the soundness of their position than was this case by the counsel for the Admiral Realty Company. I have here a copy of the brief which was submitted to the court, and I will produce and file with the Committee a copy of that brief which I would ask to have made a part of the record.

Mr. Moss.— That is all right.

Assemblyman Feinberg presiding.

Mr. Moss.— These briefs were handed me by Mr. Hays the other day, and perhaps we can mark those right in evidence.

Mr. Marshall.— I think he ought to have also the brief in the Appellate Division of the First Department in the first case.

Mr. Moss.— You may send that.

(The first three briefs received in evidence and marked Exhibits 1, 2 and 3 of this date, February 25, 1916.)

Mr. Marshall, resuming.— I spent a great many days in the preparation of the brief and in the investigation of the authorities. I do not think that there was a source to which I could have resorted for authorities which I did not exhaust, and I venture to say that nobody has to the present day discovered a single decision or a single authority which bears upon the questions involved which was not incorporated in the brief which I prepared and which was used before the court on the argument of this case. Nor was there any point of view bearing upon the question as to whether or not the property or credit of the city were being given or loaned for the benefit of the railroad companies which was not made use of and which was not elaborated. The brief which I filed was the longest of all briefs filed by all the numerous counsel in the case. That may not be to its credit, but it indicates the elaborateness with which the case was argued. I am sure it was read, because the Chief Judge, Judge Cullen and Judge Werner in their opinion gave us at least proof positive that our briefs were read, because they referred to the authorities and arguments presented in our briefs. I will also say I was never more serious, earnest or argued with more conviction as to the soundness of the propositions which I presented to the court than I was in that case, and I would personally rather have lost a large sum of money out of my own pocket rather than to be defeated in that case.

I have always taken a great interest in constitutional questions, and I took a great interest in this particular question, because I felt I was performing a public service in trying to protect the constitution of the State from invasion by means such as were employed in this case, and I desired to avoid the creation of a precedent which I feared might at some time mean a great injury to the municipalities of the State.

Q. Has not the argument of Judge Hiscock convinced you you were wrong? A. I have never been convinced I was wrong. I have said if it was the last thing I said on earth, I would think I was right in the argument of that case. I have the greatest respect for Judge Hiscock, with whom I practiced law while a resident of the city of Syracuse, and one of my warmest friends, but I feel that his decision was not as sound as the opinions that were rendered by the dissenting judges. But that is the case with any lawyer, he is frequently defeated in those cases in which he is the most confident he is right, and we are bound, after having done our duty, to acquiesce in the decision of the court, especially the highest court, and that is my attitude in respect to this case. I am sure if there was a higher court to go to, we would have attempted to determine whether or not our view was correct, or that of the Court of Appeals. The action was brought and prosecuted in the best of faith, with no other purpose than to enable the courts to pass upon purely legal questions, the speedy determination of which was of essential public importance. The presence of the railroad companies as defendants was, in my opinion, unnecessary. They were made parties solely because of the point that had been raised in the first case and in order that a prompt decision might not be delayed by the interposition of technical objections. The idea was the court itself might have said that these railroad companies were necessary parties, and therefore should be made parties and the case would not be decided until they were brought in, and therefore in order to bring about a more prompt decision, which was demanded by the public most vociferously at that time, the idea was that every party, every person, should be made a party who could from any point of view be regarded as necessary or proper in the determination of the questions involved. The important and the active defendants were the Public Service Commission and the city of New York. The case could have proceeded to judgment against them alone. The

actions were taxpayers' actions, and they were brought on the
theory that the Public Service Commission and the Board of
Estimate and apportionment were public agencies, were engaged
in acts which would, if carried out, operate as a waste of public
funds, and therefore the real litigation in the case was the litigation between the taxpayers and the public authorities whom I
have named. The burden of the defense was assumed by them,
by the Public Service Commission and the city of New York, and
they were consulted with respect to the framework of the complaint in order that the case could be presented fully and fairly.
In fact, Mr. Coleman manifested so much anxiety that every
possible question bearing on the constitutionality of the contracts
might be before the court, that he stated that if perchance the
plaintiffs overlooked any proposition which might strengthen the
argument as to the unconstitutionality of the plan, he would also
present that to the court, in order that an authoritative decision
of the merit might be obtained. He informed me a few days
ago that he had suggested certain facts to Mr. Shearn so that
they might be considered on the argument, as they were. I think
he was referring to the question of whether a referendum vote was
necessary. We did not raise that question, as I did not consider
it a sound proposition, and he presented it to Mr. Shearn, and
it was presented by him on the argument. Mr. Coleman informed
me he had suggested that point to Mr. Shearn, rather, and it was
argued, and the Court of Appeals did not consider the question
of any moment.

(Chairman Thompson presiding.)

Chairman Thompson.— Did you say Mr. Coleman informed
you of that?

Mr. Marshall.— He informed me recently he had suggested
that point to Mr. Shearn.

Mr. Marshall (resuming).— I have already shown that the
first action in no way referred to any contract with the Interborough Rapid Transit Company, the contract then contemplated
by the public authorities being solely with the Brooklyn Rapid
Transit Company, or the corporation the majority of whose stock

it held, the Brooklyn Union Elevated Railroad Company. The
second action was but the logical outcome of the first, since the
questions there presented were deemed by the court of such seri-
ousness as to make it inevitable that an adjudication by the Court
of Appeals with regard to such questions was essential to the
financing of the plan of operation which had been adopted by the
public authorities.

I think that states the history of both of those cases and indicates how the cases were presented and what the questions involved
were and how they were argued and how the case started as a test
against the contract with the Brooklyn Rapid Transit Company,
which, as the Appellate Division said, under the plan as adopted
was the only corporation which could have operated the subways
and which afterwards, when the new plan was adopted, was
changed, and it was at the suggestion of the counsel of the Public
Service Commission that we put into our complaint the Interborough Company as one of the defendants.

Mr. Moss.— Mr. Coleman, wouldn't you have some books which
would show the conversations and consultations?

Mr. Coleman.— I hardly think so.

Mr. Moss.— Don't you keep any desk book which would show
the consultations Mr. Marshall has testified about?

Mr. Coleman.— No, sir. The few times I have made memoranda they have been put in the files, and if important I would
dictate a memorandum and have it put in the files, but I find
nothing in these files, and I think Mr. Marshall will bear me
out, when he came to see me within the last two weeks, I said I
did not recall it, but when he said it I said it was what I should
have said if he stated it to me.

Chairman Thompson.— This is an important matter, the
matter of the Admiral lawsuit and the manner in which it was
conceived and presented to the courts, and the decisions upon it,
a pretty important proposition, wasn't it?

Mr. Coleman.— It had not impressed me so.

Chairman Thompson.— It had not?

Mr. Coleman.— No, sir.

Chairman Thompson.— Isn't the question of the dual subway contracts and their constitutionality about as important a matter as has been before the Public Service Commission since you have been its attorney?

Mr. Coleman.— I wouldn't say that, not the way it went through. Possibly financially it was the most important.

Chairman Thompson.— I wish you would go to the Chairman of the Public Service Commission today and state to him that in this matter concerning this litigation that you have no recollection on subjects that have been brought before this Committee and concerning which other witnesses do have a recollection, and that you have no recollection of conversations which other witnesses state under oath they had with you, and also that you have no memorandum in your office on this subject. I wish you would state that to the Chairman today.

Mr. Coleman.— I will do so.

Chairman Thompson.— I will state to counsel, Mr. Smith, that I wish you would have the stenographer make a transcript of the testimony here in reference to this matter and see that the Chairman of the Public Service Commission gets it as soon as possible.

Mr. Smith.— Very well.

Examination by Mr. Moss resumed:

Q. Mr. Marshall, the Interborough Rapid Transit Company was not a party to the first action that was brought? A. It was not.

Q. Do you know who retained your firm to bring that first action? A. All that I know I have told, namely, that I came down from the Adirondacks, and on the morning of my arrival Mr. Wolf, of Hays, Hershfield & Wolf, saw me with regard to this case and told me that he was the attorney for the Admiral Realty Company, and presented the complaint which he had prepared and asked me to pass upon it and to cooperate with him in the action.

Q. Did you know or did you learn of the retainers, who retained and what the retainer was? A. I did not.

Q. Did you know anything about the fact of the retainers for the second action? A. There was no special transaction there. As I have shown you, that was a mere matter of natural evolution from the first. There was no discussion of the subject in any way. We have gone on with the case to a point, and when we found it necessary to amend and bring in new parties, and when the suggestion was made we would have to make quite a number of changes in the complaint and the action should be brought in Kings county, we then naturally started over again by bringing the second suit in Kings county.

Q. Do I understand you correctly in saying that you came into this case because of the request of members of the firm of Hays, Hershfield and Wolf, and did not concern yourself with the persons that had retained them? A. I did not make inquiry or have any interest in that subject.

Q. Did you render your bill to them? A. I did, that is, I rendered a bill to the Admiral Realty Company and sent it to them. That is my recollection. I mean the office. I do not recollect that I personally rendered any bill at all.

Q. Did your office receive the check of Hays, Hershfield and Wolf? A. Yes, sir, it was the check of Hays, Hershfield and Wolf that paid us.

Q. Did you ever talk with Mr. Nicoll about this case, or any matter involved in it? A. Not while the suit was pending, and never had a moment's conversation with him or anybody connected with the Interborough Company with regard to this litigation. The only persons with whom I ever conferred with regard to the case were my associates in the case and the counsel for the Public Service Commission, and I think Mr. Hahlo.

Q. Did you ever talk with anyone connected with the Admiral Realty Company? A. I did not.

Q. Had you any information at the time that you argued the case in the Court of Appeals that the retaining client was the Interborough Railroad Company? A. I hadn't any such information.

Q. Did you know that Hayes, Hershfield & Wolf had rendered a bill to the Interborough Company for their services and your services? A. I did not, no.

Q. When you received their check did you know that fact?
A. I did not receive the check personally.

Q. When your office received it? A. I did not know the details of it. I knew we got our pay through them, and I had nothing —

Q. Through them, you mean the lawyers, your associates? A. Yes, sir, through the lawyers. The check came from them, and that is all I know about it. It came to the office and I learned that it was the check of Hays, Hershfield & Wolf.

Q. Who asked you to come down from the Adirondacks? A. It was a telegram came from my partner, Mr. Alvin Untermyer.

Q. Did you have any conference with Mr. Wolf after your arrival from the Adirondacks? A. Certainly.

Q. Was Alvin Untermyer present at any of those conferences? A. He was not.

Q. Are you clear in your recollection that no member of the firm of Hays, Hershfield & Wolf told you who their real client was? A. I am very sure that they did not. I am sure the question was not discussed. That is my very strong recollection.

Q. You believed you were representing nobody but the Admiral Realty Company? A. I had no knowledge of anybody but the Admiral Realty Company. Whether there was anybody who asked them to bring the action or not, I did not know and I did not investigate.

Q. Of course you look upon a man who pays the fee as the client, don't you? A. Yes, that is, I regarded the Admiral Realty Company as the person with whom I was doing business, through Mr. Wolf, who represented them.

Q. You thought they were paying the fee? A. I did not think very much, I did not give very much thought to the fee at that time. The thing that interested me was the legal question.

Q. You did not think of anyone other than the Admiral Realty Company as the party or person paying the fee? A. I had no one suggested in my mind, as I did not give that subject any serious consideration, as is very apt to be the case in my experience when an interesting question of law, or constitutional question is presented to me.

Chairman Thompson.— There must be somebody in your firm gives the question of how much you are going to get, serious consideration?

Mr. Marshall.— Eventually we get paid for most of the things, but I have performed some of the most important services without compensation or thought of compensation. I might say there was so important a case as the constitutionality of the private banking law, I argued the case without reward, and without hope of reward, and took the case to the Supreme Court of the United States; and recently in the case of Leo Frank I argued that case without expecting or receiving a dollar.

Chairman Thompson.— That does not answer my question; the point was there must be somebody in your firm looks out for the fact the Admiral Realty Company were to pay, wasn't there?

Mr. Marshall.— Doubtless.

Chairman Thompson.— Who was that?

Mr. Marshall.— It all depended upon various — what the matter —

Chairman Thompson.— Who in your firm would see that the Admiral Realty Company paid for the services; who do you suppose that talk was with?

Mr. Marshall.— I don't know.

Chairman Thompson.— Isn't there some one in your firm looks after that?

Mr. Marshall.— Various persons in the firm with regard to various matters. There is no rule about the thing. Sometimes the bookkeeper asks the question as to what the charge should be in certain litigation, and he makes an entry.

Chairman Thompson.— Wasn't there any talk with Hays, Hershfield & Wolf or the Admiral Realty Company as to how much you were to get or where your pay was to come from, when you entered the case?

Mr. Marshall.— No, sir. I did not discuss it at all.

Chairman Thompson.— Did any other member of your firm?

Mr. Marshall.— I don't know.

By Mr. Moss (resuming):

Q. You did not think that you were going to do this work as a labor of love? A. No, sir, I expected to be paid.

Q. And weren't you told you would be paid? A. The matter was not mentioned. I took it for granted.

Q. If it was expected of you that you were to take a case like this for nothing, you would have been told? A. Yes, sir.

Q. And as you were not told it was a labor of love you expected to be paid? A. I assumed somebody would pay us.

Chairman Thompson.— What did Mr. Alvin Untermeyer say when you arrived from the woods?

Mr. Marshall.— In substance, the case was about to be brought and I was expected to take part in the argument.

Chairman Thompson.— Did he say anything to you about Wolf, or Hershfield & Wolf?

Mr. Marshall.— I think he told me counsel would see me, the attorneys in the case.

Chairman Thompson.— Had you ever had any other retainers from Hays, Hershfield & Wolf?

Mr. Marshall.— Not that I recollect at present.

Q. It seemed important when you were brought by a telegram from your rest? A. Undoubtedly it was important. I could see the importance of it as soon as I heard what the question was. I could see it involved a very important public question and a very large amount of money, so far as the city of New York was concerned.

Q. Who first suggested the bringing of the Hopper case, as far as you know? A. I have no idea. Some time or other in the course of these discussions we had prior to the argument of the case in Kings county I learned that Mr. Shearn was about to bring such a case, and we furnished such papers as we were called upon to supply and I am quite sure our brief, and I think our complaint.

Q. Did you find difficulty in getting documents from the Public Service Commission at the time of the Bradley Contracting action? A. Well, at that time I think Mr. Wolf had certain documents, or certain papers or statements which related to the subject matter of that action. I do not know that we had any — personally I made no application to the Public Service Commission for documents. I took it for granted that we had the exact documents, and I knew we had the McAneny report, because that was a printed document which had been generally circulated throughout the city; at least the newspapers had it, and I have no recollection as to making any application to the Public Service Commission for any documents.

Q. You do not know of any difficulty of that kind? A. No, sir. I assumed Mr. Wolf had made those investigations before I came, because such facts as we had and data which were inserted in the complaint were data which he had collected, and with the collection of which I had nothing to do.

Q. In arguing against the constitutionality of the law and in trying to show in that argument the practical partnership which was proposed between the city of New York and the railroad company, what point in the proposed contract did you particularly rely upon as an illustration of your claim? A. I can only refer to my brief.

Q. Wasn't it the preferential payment? A. That was one of the important features of it, but it was the fact of there being a common adventure, a common undertaking which I claimed made of the case one of partnership, and because of the fact it was a partnership I argued that there was necessarily a giving of property and credit of the city, so that the usual consequences of a partnership would result.

Q. Did you in your brief — A. If you will wait one moment.

Q. Yes. A. I call attention to these facts. The Brooklyn Company in its offer said, " In making this concession, therefore, and inviting the city into partnership with us not as compensation for new privileges which we sought, but with the idea of creating thereby new and greatly improved facilities for public travel, we merely asked that when this partnership went into effect we should be allowed to retain the net earnings we would be then making — and that all increase and all gain from saving and operating cost by reason of better facilities and terminals should be shared with the partners." Again: "Hereafter, if contract is made with the city, there will be other calls upon the surplus revenue, as set forth in Appendix A, and it is essential that we should continue to get substantially the full measure of the net earnings which we are now enjoying and shall be enjoying when we begin partnership with the city. There would not seem to be equity in asking the Brooklyn Company to be content with a reservation of net earnings less than it will be earning when the pooling begins."

There was, right on the record, so far as the Brooklyn Rapid Transit Company was concerned, an interpretation of the transaction as being a partnership.

Q. I want to call your attention to one feature specifically which the proposed contract provided, that the operating expenses should be deducted before net profits might be arrived at, provided that the operating expenses should be taken to include damages for accidents. What did you understand to be the meaning of damages for accidents in that connection? A. As I now recollect it, if any accident occurred in the course of construction —

Q. These are operating expenses? A. I cannot at this moment bring to mind.

Q. Doesn't that mean that after the contract is completed that if a man is run over, and if there is a collision and anybody hurt, the damages have to be paid by the Interborough Company, that those damages paid by the Interborough Company shall be taken out of the income of the railroad before there are any net profits to be divided by the city? A. I am unable to express an opinion on it now.

Q. I am asking your opinion; you have been over it? A. In analyzing the Interborough subject, the brief says: "It is then provided that when the new subway lines shall have been equipped and put in operation the gross receipts from the operation of the existing subway line and equipment and from the proposed new subway line and equipment will be pooled for and during the full term of forty-nine years, and that from the total of such gross receipts deductions shall be made as follows:

"(1) Operating Expenses, including damages for accidents.

(2) Provisions for deterioration, renewals and obsolescences."

Q. Did you discuss that phrase, "Damages for accidents," in any other way than by just referring to it as you have read it there? A. I discussed the proposition as to what the charges were against the results of the operation of the company.

Q. Was it brought out in your brief, and brought out in your argument before the Court of Appeals that the city would practically have to pay the damages for people hurt by the Interborough Railroad Company on running its trains? A. I do not recollect that specific case. That was negligible in importance compared with the tremendous amounts of money involved.

Q. It might be negligible in volume, but wasn't it very emphatic as an illustration? A. That was all argued.

Q. Where is there anything on that? A. I think on the oral argument I referred to that.

Q. Having in mind such an accident as occurred some time ago, when a pick being driven through a wall struck a rail charged with electricity, and a lot of people hurt, and damage resulted, and damages paid which were charged up against the city, don't you think that an illustration of that sort might have been very effective in your brief and in your argument in your effort to drive home to the conscience and intelligence of the court that this was a partnership arrangement in which most of the gainful sides were upon the railroad and the most of the losing sides upon the city? A. I made an expression in the argument, "Heads I win, and tails you lose," and I illustrated it by various matters, and I do not think it could be more strongly illustrated than by going through the existing contracts and comparing the merits of brokerage charges, etc.

Q. They all follow. I notice in the reading of the summary of the contract that the very first matter, the very first item to be deducted from income, was operating expenses, page 16 of the brief, including damages for accidents? A. That is the first thing I mentioned.

Q. But I am asking whether that matter was illustrated and discussed, and brought out and illustrated? A. I am very sure it was discussed, but as I say, compared with the millions upon millions of dollars involved in the idea of the city investing an unlimited amount, subject to all of these preferential charges, that that dwindles into insignificance compared with the great big questions.

Q. It may dwindle into insignificance as far as the volume of money is concerned, but don't you think it is a large item? A. I don't think so.

Q. How can you tell what accidents will happen, or how much money will be involved in them? A. Let me call our attention to what I consider to be the important thing. "This investment of the Interborough Company is not to be less than and is not to exceed $77,000,000, or $56,000,000 for new construction and $21,000,000 for equipment, so that with the Interborough Company's capital investment in the present subway, which on June 30, 1911, aggregated approximately $48,000,000, it would make its total investment amount to $125,000,000. It is contemplated that the city shall expend for these new subway lines $56,000,000, and if additional capital is required for their construction, the city is to furnish the excess," and this I emphasized:

"If any deficiency shall arise in any year in meeting the aforesaid payments to the company, such deficiency shall be cumulative and shall be paid off and discharged annually out of the said subway earnings before the payments herein defined shall be made to the city.

Thus far, these provisions all contemplate that out of the pooled earnings of the old and new subway, constructed partly with funds supplied by the city and upon its credit and partly by moneys provided or to be provided by the Interborough Company, and upon its credit, the latter is to receive a preferential payment not only of the foregoing items of operating expenses, but also a sum equal to the average annual income from the operation of the existing subway line, amounting to $6,335,000, and a sum equal to 6% upon the $77,000,000 which are to be invested by the Interborough Company for construction and equipment of the new subway, the latter two items amounting to 8.76% per annum on a total investment of $125,000,000, all of these payments being cumulative.

It is only after all of these cumulative payments have been made that the city is to receive any return on its investment of upwards of $56,000,000, the provision of the proposed contract being:

"After the payment of the foregoing obligations to the company, there shall be deducted out of the profits, interest and sinking fund upon the capital provided by the city for the construction of the new line and such further sum as will bring the payment to be made to the city during the entire period of the forty-nine year lease up to an amount equal to 8.76 per centum per annum upon its capital investment in the original construction of the new subways. Upon its capital investment in the betterments or improvements of the old or new subways chargeable to capital account, it shall then receive the same rate of compensation as is provided for in Section 12 hereof, with respect to investment by the company in betterments or improvements upon new equipment.

"This payment to the city is also made cumulative, subject, however, to the preferential payments to the Interborough Company, and is to be discharged annually out of the said subway earnings before the equal division of profits provided for in the following paragraph becomes effective."

That is an analysis.

Q. But where is there anything in that brief which draws it to the conscience and the intelligence of the court that when the Interborough Railroad by its own negligence kills a man, the city of New York must pay the damages that that man sustains or pay the amount for which his estate is given a judgment? A. That was presented and discussed.

Q. Where was it presented and discussed? A. I have read to you where it was stated, but I cannot ——

Q. I mean to get it sharply; where is there any direct reference to such a situation as that which it seems to me would powerfully affect the mind and conscience of the court? A. I cannot give so much importance to that element as you do.

Q. Don't you think the majority of the court was obtuse? A. I don't think so.

Q. Doesn't it seem so, on Mr. Hiscock's opinion? A. I don't think so.

Q. When you compare Mr. Hiscock's opinion with the opinion of Cullen and Werner, doesn't it seem to you, even in the phraseology of the language of the opinion, that Mr. Hiscock at least missed a point of the case? A. I wouldn't say that. I am sure he did not miss the point. He interpreted the contracts and the results of them differently from the way they were interpreted by the other judges, and from the way I interpreted them.

Q. When he dwells on preferential payments to the city, isn't he a little off? A. It is not an accurate statement. The city comes last.

Q. Judge Hiscock puts that down as a part of the contract, the preferential payment to the city, and he is incorrect, isn't he? A. I have not the opinion before me, and I would not venture to make any special criticism of any phrase of the opinion. I will say I was strongly convinced our position was right, and fortified in that conclusion by the other opinions written by Chief Judge Cullen, one of the very ablest judges ever had in the Court of Appeals, and also Judge Werner, a very brave judge. I must say, however, when such men as Judge Hiscock, for whose legal ability and conscientiousness I have the highest regard, and men as good as Judge Vann, and so experienced a judge as Judge Haight and Collin voted the other way, and when a case had been argued so fully, and necessarily the subject of so much discussion in the consultation room as is evidenced by the fact there was a difference of opinion among the judgments, it would be unseemly for me to make a comment upon the majority opinion of the court.

Q. I do not mean it in that way, but we are dealing with something that comes before us and it occurred to me in the reading of Judge Hiscock's opinion that the court was obtuse to some of the salient points of the case, and it appeared where Judge Hiscock refers so strongly to the preferential payments to the city, and I was wondering whether there was not one judge

of those four who might have been shocked into more activity of
expression and thought if forced upon his attention by your
eloquence that the city of New York has to pay for the negligence
of the Interborough Railroad Company when it kills a man.
You told me last night — I do not think I do any harm in quoting
you — you would have rather lost $100,000 than to have lost
that case? A. I will say it again, as a witness.

Q. That shows your intense earnestness and ardor in that case,
and I was wondering how it is in that splendid brief that the very
first point, the very first element of deductions in favor of the
railroad company contains that, including "damages for accidents," is a phrase challenging attention, and I was wondering
if you could not show me somewhere in the brief where you
deevloped that thing sharply? A. I do not know that I elaborated
that particular phrase because it seemed to me when it got to the
question of dollars and cents that amounted to what we might
call the "chicken feed" of the proposition.

Q. On the other side it would be the human life, and that
cannot be measured in dollars and cents, even by the verdicts of
juries obtained by good lawyers and never is properly measured.
A. Let me say:

"It would be none but a deceptive answer to say that the public
will, as a result, have the benefit of better transportation facilities
and will enjoy the advantages of rapid transit. So would the
public receive like advantages were the city of New York to
subsidize the two corporations by paying into their treasuries the
millions of dollars required to enable them to extend their lines,
or if the city were to loan them, with or without interest, for a
term of years, such sum of money, or if it were to guarantee bonds
of the two corporations for such an amount, as the recipients of
its bounty would have to employ, in order to afford to the public
better transportation facilities than it now possesses. Nor is it
an answer to this proposition, that it is quite possible that the
pooled lines may eventually be operated so profitably, that the
city of New York will be reimbursed for the interest which it is
required to pay on the bonds issued by it, in payment for the
construction of its new subways. It is certainly equally, if not
more probable, that they may not.

" It cannot be said with any degree of certainty, that any profit will ever result from the operation of the pooled lines. The existing lines may be a drawback on each of the undertakings. The lean kine of the Brooklyn Company may devour the fat kine of the subway lines. The old may swallow the new. The deficiency in its preferential payments which the Interborough Company contemplates by making them cumulative, may render the city's investment a vanishing quantity. It is quite possible that the result of the operation of these lines may prove disastrous to the city of New York. These beneficiaries of the city's money and credit, far from being willing to guarantee the payment to the city of any return on its investment, recognize the potentiality of failure, and seek to protect themselves against that contemplated contingency, by insisting on the preferential payment of their operating expenses, of their fixed charges, plus a profit of $3,500,000 in the one case, and $6,335,000 in the other, and a return on their new investments for construction, additions and equipment.

" In spite of the enormous population of the city of New York, there have been disastrous failures among the public service corporations, which have operated railroads within the present boundaries of the city. All of the elevated railroads have passed through the ordeal of foreclosure and reorganization, including those now operated by the Brooklyn company. The Metropolitan Street Railway Company and the Third Avenue Railroad Company, with most of their allied lines, have just passed out of the hands of receivers. Some or all of the surface lines now owned or controlled by the Brooklyn company have suffered financial vicissitudes. The Interborough Railroad Company was well-nigh wrecked by its alliance with the Metropolitan Street Railway Company. What has occurred in the past may happen again. The same mismanagement, or misfortune, if that term be preferred, which necessitated railroad reorganizations heretofore may not spare these operating companies in the future. It is not impossible that they may become involved in financial complications, which may lead to the foreclosure of the mortgages resting on the lines which they are now operating, and which are to be pooled with the subways to be constructed by the city. They may be subjected to severe losses

on account of strikes, the destruction or disintegration of their
property, new methods of transportation, or in consequence of
some or all of the other causes which have already been considered.

" This case cannot, therefore, be considered on the assumption
that there will inevitably result from the operation of the con-
joined properties, income sufficient to make to the two corporations
the preferential payments for which they have shrewdly stipulated,
and to the city of New York, the deferred payments which are
vouchsafed to it, after the two corporations have received the
colossal sums which are guaranteed to them respectively, out of
the joint enterprise."

Q. I am glad you have read that, and I still fail to find what
I am driving at; you had only to push one of those four judges
over; you knew it was a close question, of course, and I told you
the picture I had when I saw that sentence there, and realized
that this is the contract we are-working under; here are your tubes
full of trains this morning, and we had an illustration when we
could not use the tube this morning, because stopped by the water;
supposing through the negligence of some workman in some power
station or at some point, I don't know where he works, but if the
river should suddenly fill those tubes when full of trains, and you
are talking about finances; suppose the water of the river should
be let in through some action and fill the tubes and drown hundreds and thousands of people, and there would be a case for re-
covery of damages against the Interborough Railroad Company,
and the damages would be charged against the city of New York,
and the city of New York would have to pay for it no matter what
negligence caused it. A. Your suggestion is, if you argued that
case you might have been stronger on the question of damages?

Q. No, sir. I am asking whether it did not occur to you as a
man of experience, and desiring to the extent of a hundred thousand dollars to win this case, that in the first provision for assisting of this other partner of the enterprise, that sharp situation
was presented which might have pushed a judge over? A. Don't
you see the real point in the case was the constitutional question
whether or not the credit and the property of the city was being
given or loaned to a private enterprise?

Q. And the four judges said it was not? A. Yes, sir.

Chairman Thompson.— Was this point that Mr. Moss now brings to your attention, was that brought to the attention of the court?

Mr. Marshall.— I referred to it on the brief, as I have already shown.

Chairman Thompson.— If it was not contained in what you have read in the record, it was not presented; that is correct, is it?

Mr. Marshall.— I have read into the record ——

Chairman Thompson.— Won't you answer my question? If it was not presented to the court in the language you have read in our record, then it was not covered; is that correct?

Mr. Marshall.— I won't say that, because I cannot say now that I orally dwelt on that particular question, because I cannot conceive it is half as strong a point as the point I did dwell on. It is there, however.

Chairman Thompson.— Mr. Baylis is excused until three o'clock P. M. Mr. Ryan is also excused until that time.

So that you may have time to take up your errand with the Chairman, Mr. Straus, we will excuse you, Mr. Coleman.

Mr. Coleman.— There was one small matter of the last hearing I could explain now, that question of $83 and some cents I am supposed to have received from the Interborough. I could do it in three minutes.

Chairman Thompson.— We will give you four minutes.

Mr. Coleman.— On January 22, 1912, I received a letter from the Corporation Counsel's office stating that the costs and disbursements had been taxed in the Admiral Realty Company's case against Gaynor and others, and apparently there had been ten dollars costs plus disbursements, and the Corporation Counsel said $3.33 of the ten dollars should go to Mr. Willcox and others of the Commission, and our disbursements, $80.25, making $83.58, and I acknowledged that letter on the same day. I received it on the 23rd, and the next day, on the 24th, I have a letter from Mr.

Hershfield; Hays, Hershfield & Wolf, received January 25th, in the same case, stating, " Enclosed please find check, $83.58, costs and disbursements awarded Appellate Division," etc., " Please acknowledge receipt and oblige." On the same day, the 25th, I received the letter, I acknowledged the receipt.

Chairman Thompson.— Who awarded against ?

Mr. Coleman.— The Admiral Realty Company. That was the Admiral Realty Company against Gaynor. That was in the first case, against Gaynor and others. Mr. Conway represented Bradley and I represented the Commission, and that was the reason the ten dollars was divided into three parts, and the city took the odd cent.

Chairman Thompson.— That is the first odd cent we have found the city received.

Mr. Coleman.— In the final letter, dated January 25th, I transmitted the check to the Public Service Commission in the usual course. It was made to my order as attorney for William Willcox and others, and I endorsed it and sent it to the Commission, and the only dollar I have ever received that did not go to the Commission was a one dollar bill Mr. Whitridge sent to satisfy a judgment of one dollar, and I put that in a frame and it hangs in my office, and I took a dollar out of my pocket and sent it up to the Commission.

Chairman Thompson.— That is the only judgment the Public Service Commission ever recovered ?

Mr. Coleman.— Yes, sir, that is the only one.

Chairman Thompson.— And the city did not share in that?

Mr. Coleman.— No, sir, it did not,

Chairman Thompson.— We will suspend now until 2 :30 o'clock P. M.

Whereupon at 1 :30 o'clock P. M. a recess was taken to 2 :30 o'clock P. M.

AFTERNOON SESSION

The Committee was called to order at 2:50 o'clock P. M., Chairman Thompson presiding.

ABRAHAM HERSHFIELD, being called as a witness, was first duly sworn, testified as follows:

By Mr. Moss:

Q. Mr. Hershfield, you were one of the attorneys in the Admiral Realty suit? A. Yes, sir.

Q. One of the counsel? A. Yes, sir.

Q. While Mr. Nicoll was on the stand, he spoke about a case of Fleischman, which he said he had obtained in your office. Do you remember the case? A. It was a small case.

Q. Will you tell us what you remember about it, what it was and what it was for? A. Debt limit proposition, so far as I recall.

Q. Was it a taxpayer's action? A. It was a taxpayer's action.

Q. How far did it go in the courts? A. I don't recall that.

Q. Do you remember what year it was? A. Seven or eight years ago, I understand; six or seven years ago.

Q. Is it in the reports? A. Not that I know of.

Q. Then it didn't get beyond special term? A. I should imagine not.

Chairman Thompson.— Do you keep an office docket?

Mr. Hershfield.— We do.

Chairman Thompson.— Would this case appear?

Mr. Hershfield.— It would if there was litigation, yes.

By Mr. Moss:

Q. Can you hear, Miss Stenographer? A. I will speak louder. I did not know you gentlemen (referring to newspaper men) were interested.

Mr. Moss.— They seem to be.

Chairman Thompson.— I think the witness concedes now the fact.

By Mr. Moss:

Q. Do you remember who employed you? A. Mr. Nicoll.

Q. For whom? A. I don't recall that.

Q. Who was the plaintiff, Fleischman; was it a man or a woman? A. The Fleischman Realty Company.

Q. Were they clients? A. Real estate corporation, and clients of ours.

Q. Yes. Did you know that the suit was brought in the interest of the Interborough Railroad Company? A. I did not.

Q. In whose interest did you suppose it was brought? A. I have no recollection.

Q. Who would have some recollection? A. I don't think anybody would any more than I have.

Chairman Thompson.—I don't hear you very well myself.

Mr. Hershfield.— I don't think anyone would of our firm, other than myself.

By Mr. Moss:

Q. Is it not recorded in the books of your office in some way? A. It must be if it was a litigation, if it went as far as litigation.

Q. Well, will it say who was the party in whose interest this suit was brought? A. It certainly would not.

By Chairman Thompson:

Q. What do you mean by its being a litigation? A. If the suit was brought.

Q. We assume there was one brought? A. I assume you know it was.

Q. If we did not know it was, we knew you would tell us. A. If I recollect it, yes. But I am telling you everything I know, and I am going to answer every question frankly and without evasion.

By Mr. Moss:

Q. Mr. Hershfield, you don't know? A. I really don't know.

Q. My first intimation of this Fleischman case came from Mr.

Nicoll, who at first thought it was an Admiral Realty case, and someone else touched up his recollection, and finally he agreed it was the Fleischman case. Haven't you any recollection? A. If you had not mentioned Fleischman, I would not have even recalled that as much as I did.

Q. Do you remember whose check it was you received? A. I don't know that.

Q. Would you be kind enough to look up your papers and records, so that it may be inquired into fully at a later time? A. I will.

Q. Do you know whether it was Andrew Freedman's check? A. I don't think it was. I have no recollection at all about it.

(Assemblyman Burr takes the Chair.)

By Mr. Moss:

Q. Well, now, I want to ask you about the Admiral Realty. suit. Who first spoke to you about the bringing of that suit? A. Mr. Nicoll.

Q. What did he say? A. He wanted to know whether I was not willing to bring a taxpayer's action.

Q. For whom? A. To test the validity of the proposed contract to the Brooklyn Rapid Transit. I went into the details with him, and saw that the interest of the Interborough that he represented was coincident with that of any taxpayer, and I consented to bring the action.

Q. Well, who was your client? A. The Admiral Realty Company.

Q. Did the Admiral Realty Company pay you? A. No, sir. It was agreed between me and Mr. Nicoll that he would see the Interborough paid us for our services.

Q. Who was your client? A. The Admiralty Realty Company.

Q. Did Mr. Nicoll's check go to the Admiral Realty Company? A. It did not. We were paid by the Interborough directly. We brought an action for one party, the expense of which action was borne by another.

Q. Did you discuss that with the directors of the Admiral Realty Company? A. I did not.

Q. Was there any discussion whatever with the — A. There was not.

Q. — officers of the Admiral Realty Company? A. There was not.

Q. Was there any resolution put on the books of the Admiral Realty Company? A. I am not in their secrets. The complaint was verified by an officer, I take it. The only one I knew of that bunch was Mr. Wolf.

Q. In bringing a suit in their name, you knew that legally you were committing them to certain costs and obligations? A. Possibly.

Q. What did you do to see that those costs and obligations did not fall upon the Admiral Realty Company? A. Did nothing.

Q. Did you tell the officers of the Admiral Realty Company that they would be protected against costs and liabilities? A. I never had any conversation with them personally.

Q. The fees outside of disbursements, paid to your firm and to Mr. Marshall's firm was $60,000. Why, the capital stock of the Admiral Realty Company is $50,000? A. I have not the faintest idea what the capital stock of the Admiral Realty Company was. Might have been $500.

Q. Well, it wasn't. They were a client of your office, weren't they? A. Yes, sir.

Q. Didn't you know whether they had stocks sufficient to meet any obligation? A. I did not. We have forty such little realty companies.

Q. Was this a little realty company? A. I imagine so.

Q. It was a big action? A. Little in a sense. Under the statute, any taxpayer of a thousand dollars can bring an action.

Q. But he assumes the responsibility of any other party, doesn't he? A. I presume that is a matter between him and his counsel.

Q. Doesn't he assume more responsibility than the ordinary — A. Not that I know of.

Q. Aren't there certain circumstances in which the defeated taxpayer may have more to pay than the ordinary litigant? A. I don't see how.

Q. Aren't there provisions to that effect? A. Provisions of law?

Q. Yes. A. Not that I know of.

Mr. Moss.— I offer in evidence Certificate of Incorporation of the Admiral Realty Company, filed and recorded June 5, 1906, which shows a capital stock of $50,000. The names of the first directors — directors for the first year, are Jonas B. Weil, 68 William street; Isaac Wolf, 19 Liberty street; Morris F. Hochstadter, 19 Liberty street; Isador H. Kramer, 68 William street; Jacob Wolf, 68 William street. Then comes the ninth provision: "The names and post-office addresses of the subscribers of the certificate and a statement of the number of shares of stock which each agrees to take in the corporation, are as follows: Jonas B. Weil, five shares; Isaac Wolf, five shares; Morris F. Hochstadter, five shares." The shares are $100 each.

By Mr. Moss:

Q. But did you know from the beginning, Mr. Hershfield, that the responsibilities of the action, so far as they might relate to a defeated party, and the responsibilities of the action so far as they related to the compensation of the attorneys, would be borne by the Interborough? A. I did.

(Certificate of Incorporation of the Admiral Realty Company was received in evidence and marked Exhibit No. 4, February 25, 1916.)

Q. Did you have anything for that in writing? A. Absolutely nothing.

Q. Did you have any letter upon that subject from anybody? A. Nothing at all.

Q. Did you know whether that matter was discussed with the officers of the Interborough, president or any other officers? A. Not at all.

Q. You made no inquiry on that subject? A. None whatever.

Q. You relied upon Mr. Nicoll? A. Entirely upon Mr. Nicoll's word, and that was not binding in law, as he was simply verbally being answerable for the debt of another. I was willing to take my chances.

Q. You knew he was counsel for that company, and had been for many years? A. I did know that — and I didn't know how long he would live.

Q. You knew you had handled the Fleischman case and that it had been paid for? A. Yes, sir.

Q. Did you talk with Mr. Coleman? A. Never.

Q. Did you talk with any of the counsel in the other cases? A. Never had any active participation in the management of the litigation at all.

Q. I think it appears from the testimony of Mr. Hays that he handled that, with some assistance from Mr. Wolf? A. Yes, sir.

Q. Where did you have that conversation with Mr. Nicoll? A. In Mr. Nicoll's office.

Q. Did he send for you? A. He telephoned, yes.

Q. And at the conversation that you had with him, was any officer of the company present? A. No one whatever.

Q. Have you had any other suit than this Fleischman suit or the two Admiral suits for the Interborough, or brought to you in the same way as those were, substantially? A. None that I recall.

Mr. Moss.— I think that is all I want to ask Mr. Hershfield.

Mr. Hershfield.— I would like to add —

Mr. Moss.— Put in any statement you want to make.

Mr. Hershfield.—— that in the suit number one, the Interborough was not a party at all, not a defendant. The only defendants in that suit were the Board of Estimate and Apportionment, the Bradley Construction Company and the Public Service Commission, and the Interborough were not a party to that suit whatever. The suit number 2 — the way this suit naturally evoluted into suit number 2, has been fully explained by Mr. Marshall.

By Mr. Moss:

Q. In this conversation with Mr. Nicoll, was anything said as to the reason why the Interborough wanted this action brought? A. Not that I recall.

Q. Was there anything said about the purposes of the action, so for as the Interborough was concerned? A. Oh, I understood the purposes of the action.

Q. So far as they affected the Interborough? A. No, that was not stated at all. It was apparent enough.

Q. Well, what did you understand? A. I understood that the awarding of this proposed contract to the Brooklyn Rapid Transit was unjust and illegal, invalid, according to Mr. Nicoll's opinion. Of course, that was — naturally it was to the interest of the Interborough that contract should be set aside, and when I went to him in the second action, after I was drawn into that, and I asked him again whether the Interborough was interested in sustaining the dual subway, he said, no, that we establish the unconstitutionality of the dual subway contract — it was to the interest of the Interborough to have it established, because they would be left in sole possession of the subway field, so that it was coincident with the interest of the taxpayer that the unconstitutionality of the dual subway should be established — just as much to the interest of the Interborough as to the interest of the taxpayer.

Q. Did you notice that the attorneys and counsel for the Interborough in the arguments in the courts stood for the contract? A. I don't know. They were only nominally defendants, anyway. It was really a fight between the city and the Public Service Commission. I don't think they counted for any more than appendages.

Q. Didn't they argue and submit their briefs? A. I suppose so.

Q. Didn't they take pains in the argument to the court, and didn't the counsel for the Interborough and Brooklyn Rapid Transit Companies stand for the contract and for the power of the authorities to make that contract? A. I don't know that.

Q. The record shows they did? A. Then it is so.

Q. You have read the report in 210 N. Y., haven't you? A. I have not.

Q. Let us look at it. A. I read the opinions when they came out.

Q. Let us look at it. A. I don't dispute you. What I am trying to establish is that they were nothing but figureheads, that the real contention was between the taxpayer and the Public Service Commission and the city.

Q. How many figureheads were there in this case? A. They were nominal defendants. You get my meaning as a lawyer, what I mean by that; not substantially defendants.

Q. You have said in a case that seriously went up to the Court of Appeals, and in which counsel stood up and seriously argued to the court, and got a decision, by one, that the parties were figureheads; who were the figureheads, please name them? A. You misunderstand by meaning. I mean to say they were figureheads in this sense. They each had an interest, and that therefore the court, having before it the Public Service Commission and the city arguing to the constitutionality of the bill, that they didn't count — that it what I mean.

Q. Well, now, you told me a minute ago that Mr. Nicoll told you the interest of the Interborough Company was to defeat this contract? A. They didn't care, they were indifferent.

Q. Their interest was to defeat it, and they were employing you to defeat it, but their own counsel, representing them directly, stood up in court and fought for the contract? A. I can't help that.

Q. How do you explain it? A. The fact remains, just the same, the Interborough would have been better off if the contract had been defeated.

Q. Why did these counsel — A. I am not in their secrets; I can't tell you what they did. I don't even know what they did. But I take your word for it.

Q. Now, just a minute; hold on. Well, now, I read from 206 N. Y., at page 122, in the statement of a summary of the brief of each party:

"Richard Reid Rogers and Alfred E. Mudge for the Interborough Rapid Transit Company, respondent.

"The proposed agreement with the Interborough Rapid Transit Company does not violate Article VIII of section 10 of the Constitution."

Then follow a number of authorities.

"The Rapid Transit Act does not violate Article III, section 18 of the Constitution."

Then follow a number of authorities. Then comes:

"Charles A. Collin and George D. Yeomans for Brooklyn Rapid Transit Company at al." It goes on with his brief — with their brief. quoting "Neither the purpose nor the effect of the ' preferential payments ' from the ' pooled earnings,' or of the division of profits after deduction of all ' preferential payments ' from the 'pooled earnings,' as provided in the contemplated lease to the Brooklyn Company, can possibly be a gift of money or property or a loan of money or credit of the city to the Brooklyn Company." Citing the Sun case. Next, "The proposed lease to the Brooklyn Company does not effect such a quasi partnership, or joint enterprise between the city and the Brooklyn Company as can possibly work out the result of a gift or loan of property, money or credit of the city to the company in violation of Article VIII, section 10 of our State Constitution," citing authorities.

Next, "The limitation of the Rapid Transit Act to Cities having over one million inhabitants does not make that act special or local within the meaning of the Constitutional prohibition of special or local legislation."

Authorities cited.

Now, was the Brooklyn Rapid Transit Company a nominal or figurehead party in your judgment? A. I don't know that; I certainly think so.

Q. Your testimony, if I understand the record right, is that Mr. Nicoll told you that the interest of the Interborough was to defeat the contract? A. I don't think I put that quite as strongly — that it was utterly indifferent as to the result but in his opinion the Interborough was better off if these contracts were defeated, because they would then be left in sole possession of the subway field.

Q. And he was willing to back that up by the employment of you for over $60,000 for the Interborough Company? A. That was not discussed.

Q. But it was coming from the Interborough Company? A. Right.

Q. Now, that being the purpose of the leading counsel of the Interborough Railroad Company, in employing you to bring a taxpayer's action, I find in reading the official report, that their counsel stood up in court and argued for the contract? A. Well, I am not party to that.

Q. Well, didn't you ask Mr.— your firm was? A. Not a party to these people standing up in court, no.

Q. Why, yes. Here is Louis Marshall, Daniel P. Hays, Ralph Wolf and Samuel Untermeyer, for the Admiral Realty Company. Two of those gentlemen were your partners and the other two men

are men you employed as special counsel? A. We didn't employ
them.

Q. Your firm did? A. No, sir.

Q. Who employed Mr. Marshall? A. We did not.

Q. He says you did? A. I can't help that, sir; we did not.

Q. Let me remind you that Mr. Marshall said this morning that
he never met Mr. Nicoll, met anyone, or had communication with
anyone connected with the railroad company. That he was employed solely by your firm, and knew no one else in the transaction,
— and I think he said by you. A. No, he said by Mr. Wolf. I
don't know who employed him. I don't think my firm employed
him. Mr. Nicoll told me in that conversation, when I told him it
was midsummer — and I generally go away in August — that my
partner, Mr. Hays, in whose province this would naturally fall,
was absent in Europe, and he said he would see Mr. Marshall would
be associated with us.

Q. Now you knew Mr. Marshall was sent for; you knew Mr.
Wolf telephoned for him, or had telegraphed? A. I have heard so
since. I suppose hearsay —

Q. At least, whatever may be your personal knowledge, so far
as I can understand you, you were not in court; these are two
members of your firm who were present in the Court of Appeals
and whose names are signed to the brief, and who stood alongside
of the counsel for the B. R. T. and the I. R. T. when these arguments were made. Now, in view of the fact it appears upon your
testimony, and upon the other testimony that is given, that on the
one side were the regular attorneys for the companies fighting for
the constitutionality of the law, and on the other side was your
firm. nominally appearing for a taxpayer, fighting for the unconstitutionality of the law, I ask you if you can give any explanation
of that inconsistent situation? A. I cannot characterize the action
of those gentlemen or their sincerity. I can characterize our own,
and that is from start to finish, with whatever talent we possessed,
or Mr. Marshall possessed, we fought this conscientiously on the
ground of unconstitutionality and illegality of that contract. I
took care of my end of it. I know nothing about that other and if
anybody can read that letter and listen to Mr. Marshall to-day, and
have that idea, and we spent a hundred per cent. of all the energy,
labor and talent within us, to have that agreement declared uncon-

stitutional, I have nothing more to add, and I don't think you have,
too.

Q. Not at all. I am willing to put myself on record that your
briefs were extraordinary briefs. A. I thank you for that and I
will never forget it.

Q. That the two judges that dissented at all, built up their
opinion upon those two briefs though I did argue with Mr. Marshall this morning that he might have made his brief more pic-
turesque and put more atmosphere in it. A. You certainly did
pick out a very graphic illustrative point, that certainly would have
created an atmosphere to a court, but Mr. Marshall, from the top
of his head to the bottom of his feet is all technical law, and that
was not a question that had a bearing on the unconstitutionality
that he was arguing.

Q. He showed up graphically the partnership? A. The assumption of liability for accident would not establish partnership.

Q. If there was partnership, then the contract was unconstitutional and the court was on the edge of declaring it to be unconstitutional, and it only needed a little psychology to put it over.
Psychology is an important element, as Mr. Quigg will tell you,
in drawing a contract. A. But the assumption of a specific liability would not have any bearing on the question either upon
partnership or unconstitutionality.

Q. But it might affect a judge in his disposition to bust up an
arrangement that appeared to be unjust? A. I think it would
have been wise to have added it, but there are lawyers that stick to
the record, and there are others who adorn and decorate their
cases, and know how to appeal to a court, and you have done it
very nicely.

Q. I ought to have been employed? A. You certainly should.
I am mighty sorry you were not. I would have been questioning
you.

Mr. Moss.— " Full many a gem was born," etc.

Mr. Hershfield.— Don't take that down.

Mr. Moss.— " Full many a flower " — I didn't know I got so
high.

By Mr. Moss:

Q. Now, then, I want, Mr. Hershfield, that you see this situation as I am seeing it. I am very interested in getting out the facts. A. I appreciate your fairness.

Q. And my friendship to you and your partners, and Mr. Marshall, and all of them, is a matter I could not get away from if I wanted to. We all know it. But here is a situation upon which we want the facts, however they may lie, and whatever they may lead to, and I thoroughly agree with you in your statement that you are not to blame for whatever the counsel to this railroad company did. But we have this situation, at least: That the senior counsel to the railroad company employed you to bring a taxpayer's action to attack the contracts, while the other counsel for the railroad company, who presumably were under his direction, or subject to his advice, at any rate, were standing for the contracts, and both sides, with the same money — same kind of money — in their pockets, stood before the Court of Appeals and argued both sides. A. I think your point is well taken. Haul them over the coals, and not me. I attended to my end of it.

Q. But your testimony is valuable to us, I don't care who it hits? A. Thank you.

Q. Very valuable? A. Thank you, sir.

Mr. Quackenbush.— May I suggest, as Mr. Rogers is not here?

Mr. Moss.— Yes, Mr. Quackenbush.

Mr. Quackenbush.— I apparently did not make plain when I was explaining this situation yesterday, that our contention all the time was that the proposed contract for the Brooklyn Rapid Transit Company was in violation of the Constitution. I myself argued that up and down this State, and with all the public officials, before these suits were brought, and probably while they were pending. In the same breath I contended with equal sincerity, and with all the force that I possessed, and I contend at this moment, that it was competent for the city of New York to make a contract with the Interborough Rapid Transit Company, and that that would not be a partnership in violation of the Constitution, and you will find in the brief to which you referred, no argument inconsistent with what I now state, an argument all the time that the city could make

a contract with the Interborough, that it could not make one with
the Brooklyn Company, and nowhere there will you find a single
word, I believe that, that the contract with the Brooklyn Company was a valid contract. Now, the situation
was this: That the taxpayer was attacking them both.
If the taxpayer succeeded, the Brooklyn Company was
eliminated from the field. The Interborough was interested in having the Brooklyn Company eliminated from the
field, and at the same time sustaining the competency of the city
to make a contract with us. I then believed that was the law, and
I still believe it was the law, and I believe it was the economics of
the situation. Just a word, and I am done. The city, for reasons
of its own, acting through the committee of the Public Service
Commission and the Board of Estimate undertook to lay out this
so-called dual system. I argued then, and I believe now, that they
laid out more railroads than the public needed, an economic waste,
at the interest of the Brooklyn Rapid Transit Company which they
brought into the situation against us. Our position in the courts
was then, and is to-day, the city had a right to make a contract with
us, it could not make it with the Brooklyn Company. And that is
what I meant yesterday when I said I was still of the same opinion.
But, of course, the law of the case has been fixed, and it is a rule
of property, and our securities have been issued on the strength of
the decision of the Court of Appeals, and it is beyond the court to
change. That is an explanation which has not occurred to Mr.
Hershfield, which I am sure Mr. Rogers would make if he were
here, that all the time that Mr. Nicoll — I only know by hearsay —
was urging the taxpayer's suit to get the Brooklyn Company out
of it, the counsel of the Interborough were asserting the right of
the city to make a contract with the Interborough.

Mr. Moss.— Well, Mr. Quackenbush —

Mr. Quackenbush.— And the interest of the Interborough and
of the taxpayer were not adverse interests and therefore the same
counsel — the same counsel, Mr. Nicoll or anybody associated with
him, could represent those two interests; and that in my judgment,
and I say this now, because my colleague is absent, and there has
been so much said about it that in my judgment, what I now tell

you, will be the ultimate decision of any tribunal to which this mess ever goes.

Mr. Moss.— That is a prognostication —

Mr. Quackenbush.— I make it with all —

Mr. Moss.— You will strike out the word "mess." No, let it stand.

Mr. Quackenbush.— I am willing.

Mr. Hershfield.— I consent that it be stricken out.

Mr. Moss.— I withdraw that motion. That is a designation by one of the witnesses which should stay. Mr. Quackenbush, did you know that the Admiral Realty Company was a dummy plaintiff?

Mr. Quackenbush.— I don't think it was. I don't know anything of the kind. I said yesterday that while I did not have that intimate connection with the situation that my colleague, Mr. Rogers had, I was the head of the law department and I knew that the suit was pending, and the issues it involved, and I have tried to say to you in the last few minutes it was not a dummy, that it was a taxpayer, that it had a right to bring the action, that the Interborough had a right to press its position, to sustain its act, to make a contract with the city, and if the taxpayer got rid of the Brooklyn Rapid Transit Company, they were then free to make a successful contract with us.

Mr. Moss.— Mr. Hershfield says he resents my suggestion it was a dummy. Why wasn't it?

Mr. Hershfield.— Because it is an actual plaintiff.

By Mr. Moss:

Q. So is the man who signed a deed? A. He is an actual statutorily created plaintiff.

Q. Did he pay a dollar? A. He complied with the statute. He answers the requirement of the statute. He gave a bond, as the statute requires.

Q. How much? A. A thousand dollars.

Q. Who paid the premium? A. I don't know.

Q. You better find that out. Did the Admiral Realty Company pay one dollar of premium or anything else? A. The court don't call that a dummy plaintiff.

Q. That hasn't been known before? A. They say it is against sound policy that any taxpayer's suit should be criticised for motive. I have looked up the authorities. You probably have not.

Q. It is not a question of motive. A. It must not be inquired into. It should be encouraged, say the authorities, so long as the purpose is to restrain public officials from wasting the funds of the city. Those are the authorities.

Q. Where one party is ringing the bell both ways? A. I never heard the bell ringer on the other side. I can't help his ringing the bell.

Q. He rang your bell? A. Ringing his own bell.

Q. And paid you $60,000 for the privilege? A. Mr. Quackenbush explained it.

Mr. Feinberg.— Try to get the witness to answer questions.

Mr. Hershfield.— There is none.

Acting Chairman Burr.— He asked if the Admiral Realty Company paid anything?   .

Mr. Hershfield.— I said I did not know.

By Mr. Moss:

Q. Do you know of a single dollar that the Admiral Company paid for the bonds or for lawyers or for anything? A. I don't think they did. It never was the intention. ·

Q. Exactly. A. And yet they were not dummy plaintiffs in this statutory —

Mr. Feinberg.— I would not go any further than the answer, Mr. Hershfield.

Mr. Moss.— Will you, Mr. Quackenbush, answer a question?

Mr. Shuster.— Are we to understand from what you have said in regard to this litigation, that the court could have found the B. R. T. contract violative of the Constitution, while at the same time holding the Interborough contract not violative of the Constitution?

Mr. Quackenbush.— No. If they had decided that the B. R. T.'s position was different from the Interborough, the whole thing would have fallen, and we would have had to reopen the negotiations as of the date anterior to the time when the so-called dual subway plan was agreed upon.

(Chairman Thompson resumes the Chair.)

Mr. Shuster.— Then I don't quite understand the force of your explanation of why your counsel should have been contending for the contract, which it appears here they wished destroyed.

Mr. Quackenbush.— For this reason. That we had argued everywhere that they could not make a contract with the Brooklyn Rapid Transit Company. We had also argued that they could make a contract with the Interborough Company. Therefore, to be consistent,— and of course we were sincere about the position — our counsel must argue in the Court of Appeals that it was competent for the city to make a contract with the Interborough. While not arguing against the Brooklyn Company in the case you now refer to, our record for arguing against it is so clear —

Mr. Shuster.— That was before the court of public opinion, but not before the Court of Appeals.

Mr. Quackenbush.— No, but I say — I have been trying to answer your question, Mr. Shuster — that if the Court of Appeals sustained the attitude of the plaintiff as against the Brooklyn Rapid Transit Company, we did not want the Court of Appeals at the same time committed to any proposition that would prevent the making of a contract with the Interborough Company, and therefore, we argued naturally in our own interest, to say nothing about our belief in the law, that the Interborough's right to make this contract was unquestioned. That is my answer to your question, and I will be very glad to expatiate.

Mr. Shuster.— The Interborough Company did not want the Court of Appeals to decide the city did not have a right to make a contract with the Interborough Company?

Mr. Quackenbush.— It did not.

Mr. Shuster.— But that it didn't have the right under the Constitution to make a similar contract with the B. R. T.

Mr. Quackenbush.— This is the position of the Interborough. in respect to that — one of absolute good faith with the city. We had had our day with the city in which we had argued against the intrusion, if I may so use the phrase of the Brooklyn Rapid Transit Company. The Public Service Commission and the Board of Estimate — they disagreed with us and said in effect, we believe the Brooklyn Rapid Transit Company should go up Broadway. We said, "All right. We don't retract a word of what we have said about the illegality of your performance. but if that can be done. we will travel along with you," all the time — and I am speaking now about my own views of the thing,— believing and hoping the Court of Appeals would not sustain the attitude of the city in proposing to build more railroads here than they would need, and that they would say in their opinion that the contract did create a partnership with them. Now, we undertook in all the courts to sustain our right to make a contract of the same general sort with the city. We did not, having acquiesced in the plan, undertake to go up there and defeat the city's plan as to the Brooklyn Rapid Transit Company. We left the Brooklyn Rapid Transit Company to assert its own position and maintain it — if we could. Do I answer your question?

Mr. Shuster.— Well, the same facts with regard to preferential payments, with regard to partnership relations was involved in the contract proposed with the Interborough as with the B. R. T.

Mr. Quackenbush.— No. That is where we differ. That is what the Brooklyn Rapid Transit Company contended and they succeeded in the Court of Appeals.

Mr. Shuster.— I cannot construe your contracts differently.

Mr. Quackenbush.— This would require an argument of it. The Interborough Rapid Transit Company at the time we sued was in possession of the city's subway. This subway we are operating to-day belongs to the city of New York. We proposed that our money and the city's money be used for the extension of that city owned subway and we proposed to put our money into that property. which became the city's. The Brooklyn Rapid Transit Company proposed that the city put a great many million dollars into the improvement of its elevated railroad lines, which it owned. And there is a pretty big difference, Mr. Shuster, and that was lending the aid and credit of the city of New York for the rehabilitation of the Brooklyn Elevated lines, which is being done from day to day since. We did not ask them to put anything into our elevated lines. We asked them to put the city money in the city's own lines.

Chairman Thompson.— They have to put in everything you don't spend over the $58,000,000.

Mr. Quackenbush.— Not our elevated lines. There is all the difference in the world between the Brooklyn system and ours. Theirs is a system of elevated lines, going down to the river, crossing the bridges, and getting into the city subway. The subway owned by the city of New York is tied up by an elevated railroad in Brooklyn, owned by the Brooklyn Rapid Transit Company or its subsidiaries. No such situation exists or can exist between the city and the Interborough. Everything we operate, into which a part of the city moneys goes, is the property of the city of New York. If we are successful operators, we will earn enough to amortize the cost and turn it over to the city, free and clear. That is what the service is that we perform for the city of New York. The Brooklyn Rapid Transit Company, in its partnership relation with the city, is benefiting the city, but also the Brooklyn Elevated lines. That point is what I have had in mind all these years. Mr. Burr heard me argue it in public in Brooklyn. I still believe it, and if the Court of Appeals had been convinced, as I hope you will be, they would have decided the city could not make that arrangement for the benefit of the Brooklyn Rapid Transit Company, but they could make an arrangement of the kind we proposed with the Interborough, the result of which would have been that the negotiations of the city, upon the decision of the Court of Appeals as I have indicated it might have been, would have been reopened. The city's money, instead of being for the benefit of the Brooklyn system, would have been all available for the greater extension of our own system, for the immediate relief of the people, and the city would not have had more railroads in the next few years — more railroads to pile up, but would be in a condition to earn something for the sinking funds and the bonds.

Mr. Shuster.— It is expected that the returns to the city from the Brooklyn Rapid Transit Company will be earlier than that from the Interborough.

Mr. Quackenbush.— That is another story. The city has loaned its aid, its money, its credit, has got behind the rehabilitation of the Brooklyn Elevated Railroads. It has not done that for our lines.

Mr. Shuster.— The city has not aided with its credit or money the Interborough?

Mr. Quackenbush.— No, sir; it has built its own railroad. We own it as a tenant.

Mr. Shuster.— Hasn't it loaned its credit and its assistance to the enterprise?

Mr. Quackenbush.— The enterprise of constructing the subway which it owns.

Mr. Shuster.— Operating rapid transit facilities in the city of New York?

Mr. Quackenbush.— That was settled in the Sun case, under which we are operating the present subway. That point is beyond discussion. You are quite right there. But the Court of Appeals in that case said they could do it, and in the case that now is before you, the Interborough contract carried with it the B. R. T. contract and the necessities of the public here, probably —

Mr. Moss.— We will go into that again, Mr. Quackenbush. It opens a field that we will take up. Mr. Quigg, will you take the stand?

Mr. Quackenbush.— I just wanted to make clear —

Mr. Moss.— Did you make that point in the Court of Appeals, that your contract would be constitutional, and the Brooklyn contract would be unconstitutional?

Mr. Quackenbush.— No, I think not. I am speaking from memory, because I think I explained that.

Mr. Moss.— I have got that. We will take that up again.

Mr. Quackenbush.— It will take only a moment. I appeal — as the question was asked — only a minute.

Mr. Moss.— You will have a chance.

Mr. Feinberg.— I think full opportunity should be given, but Mr. Quackenbush fails to see that now is not the time.

Mr. Quackenbush.— The time to give it is when you are taking things. That is only fair.

Chairman Thompson.— The question — it is a perfectly clear one — was whether this question was in the Court of Appeals or not.

Mr. Quackenbush.— It will only take a moment. Good faith on our part with the city of New York required that we should acquiesce in their proposed plan with the Brooklyn Company, if the Court of Appeals would sustain it. If they did not sustain it, then they were free to deal with us again.

Mr. Moss.— That answers that question; and it will all be opened up to you at any time.

Chairman Thompson.— This Committee is — we will listen to an appeal from that decision of the Court of Appeals; you can have all these same lawyers.

Mr. Quackenbush.— While I don't agree that they decided it right, their decision has become a rule of property now, and our bonds have been issued on it. The Supreme Court of the United States can't change it now.

LEMUEL ELY QUIGG, called as a witness, being first duly sworn, testified as follows:

By Mr. Moss:

Mr. Moss.— I invited Mr. Quigg to attend, Mr. Chairman, because of a letter which I read in the newspapers.

Chairman Thompson.— I received the letter this morning, I think it was, after the papers printed it.

Mr. Moss.— It appeared he wanted to make some statement concerning the check of $2,500, and I presume Mr. Quigg will tell us —

Mr. Quigg.— It did not so appear, Mr. Moss. I said in my letter there was no time when Mr. Thompson could not have ascertained what that check was for simply by asking me. Now, I will tell what it is.

Mr. Moss.— You tell what it is, and we will have that on the record.

Mr. Quigg.— Yes, sir.

Chairman Thompson.— Better put the check in evidence, and have that done with.

(Check No. 529, signed T. A. Gillespie, dated New York, January 13, 1915, drawn on the Liberty National Bank, to the order of Lemuel E. Quigg, for $2,500, was received in evidence, and marked Exhibit No. 5 of February 25, 1916, V. E. Valva.)

Mr. Quigg.— A day or two before Mr. Gillespie sent this check to me, he asked me to take luncheon with him at the Lawyers' Club, and he talked with me about two matters: His contract with the city for the disposition of garbage, and a sanitation system of sewage disposal that he had, known as the Reinsch-Wurl Screen. There was no definite employment at the time, but he discussed those two matters with me. A day or two later he sent me this check. In the garbage —

By Mr. Moss:

Q. What is the date of that check, Mr. Quigg? A. January 13, it seems to be.

Q. January 13, 1915? A. Yes, sir. He sent to me his contract with the city in the garbage matter, and many papers, and I went over all of the matter as closely as I could and talked with Mr. Cravath about it, advising Mr. Cravath that an action lay against the city. It was not brought, and that was the end of that matter. In the sanitation disposal matter, the sewage matter, I did a great deal of work. I had his engineers with me; talked over the matter with them and —

(Photograph taken.)

Chairman Thompson.— You are now famous.

Mr. Quigg.— Sir?

Chairman Thompson.— I say you are now famous.

Mr. Quigg.— I did not need that, Mr. —

Chairman Thompson.— I didn't know that.

Mr. Moss.— Well answered.

Mr. Quigg.— Went out to Ann Arbor, and Grand Rapids for him, and have it now in hand. And that is the whole of it, sir.

By Mr. Moss:

Q. That check is divided, as I am informed by voucher, divided on the books, one-third to pipe lines, one-third to garbage, one-third to general expenses. When you — have you covered pipe lines in your testimony? A. I don't keep his books.

Q. No, but can you appreciate the meaning of that expression? A. Yes, sir, it has relation to the sanitation disposal company.

Q. Yes. Well, was there a bill pending in the Legislature relating to the subject of garbage, which would have affected the garbage business of Gillespie? A. Of my own knowledge, I don't know. I have seen in the newspapers something about it. But I had nothing to do with the bill in any way whatever, if there was such.

Q. But if I follow it right, there was a garbage bill which was introduced and passed in both Houses, and vetoed by the Governor? A. Yes, sir.

Q. Did you have anything to do with the garbage bill? A. Nothing whatever.

Q. Did you see anyone in Albany with reference to that bill? A. Nothing whatever — no, no one.

Q. You say it was simply with reference to the bringing of a suit that you were — A. Yes. I never knew just what that bill was. If I caught the sense of it from the newspapers — from their statement of it, it would be much in Gillespie's interest, in my opinion, but I never spoke of it — nobody spoke to me about it. Gillespie didn't, and I never spoke to anybody else about it.

Q. Well, if that bill passed, wouldn't Gillespie have lost the garbage contract? A. I don't know.

Q. If that bill had been passed and acted upon, if the garbage plant had been built and if certain people had used the garbage plant, instead of giving the contract to Gillespie, it would have been against him — A. I understand you. I don't know; because I don't know the terms of the bill, but assuming that the bill meant what the newspapers said it meant, he might have lost the contract, and I wish he would have lost it. It would have been very much in his interest to have lost it, as the city construed the contract.

Q. Did he tell you so? A. I told him so.

Q. He didn't know it until you told him? A. I don't know that. I suspect he suspected it.

(Photographs taken.)

Chairman Thompson.— We will suspend now, and if Mr. Quigg will consent, we will have pictures taken.

Mr. Quigg.— I wish you would finish that, Mr. Chairman, if it has got to be done.

Mr. Moss.— Mr. Chairman, unless you have some —

Chairman Thompson.— It makes a lot of smoke in here and I would like to have it done with.

Mr. Moss.— Mr. Chairman, any question?

Chairman Thompson.— One more photograph, I am told, and then we will get this smoke out of here.

(Recess while windows are opened.)

By Mr. Moss:

Q. What is the meaning of this general expense, do you know that? A. I don't, sir.

Q. East Jersey Pipe Line, New York Disposal Company, general expense; three items. What does general expense cover? A. I don't know anything about it.

Q. Did you render any bill for this? A. No.

Q. You gave no voucher at all? A. I acknowledged receipt of it.

Q. Yes. But nothing specifying your services? A. No.

Q. There is nothing in writing to show what your services are for? A. Oh, yes.

Q. What? A. There is a great deal of correspondence between Mr. Gillespie and I on the — between me and Mr. Gillespie's companies on the subject of my services, on the work I did, reports to him about what I had done in the matter.

By Chairman Thompson:

Q. Over what period of time? A. Sir?

Q. Over what period of time? A. Why, from then until now.

Q. When was your last correspondence? A. I don't remember. You can see it, if you want to.

Q. Haven't you got the slightest idea when your last correspondence was about it? A. No, I have no very definite idea.

Q. I see. Is this the only money you received? A. No.

Q. You had more money afterwards? A. Yes.

Q. Can you tell us how much and when? A. I have had, I think, $2,500 since then.

Q. Do you know when you got it? A. I got a thousand dollars before I went to Grand Rapids and $1,500 afterwards.

Q. What date was that? A. I don't know.

Q. Can you find out? A. Oh certainly, I can find out, but it is none of your business, of course.

Q. I understand. I got a letter from you in which you promised to come and explain this matter. I think you should have brought the information with you when you came? A. I am doing it now.

Q. You should go and get informed on the subject yourself. A. I got it before I went to Grand Rapids, a thousand dollars, and I got $1,500 afterwards.

By Mr. Moss:

Q. Does that cover any different services than those? A. No, sir.

Q. Relating to this same matter? A. Relating to this one matter, which, except for the examination of the law in connection with the garbage contract, and my conferences with Mr. Cravath on that subject, are the only services of any kind I have rendered to Mr. Gillespie.

Mr. Moss.— Well, suppose we withdraw Mr. Quigg now. I want to ask Mr. Gillespie a question.

30

Chairman Thompson.— I think perhaps we had better excuse Mr. Quigg long enough for him to get informed on the details, and come again. When can you come?

Mr. Quigg.— Mr. Thompson, I wish you would finish with me. Mr. Gillespie — what do you want more?

Chairman Thompson.— I would like the dates when you received these payments and the date of your service and the period over which it extended.

Mr. Quigg.— Well, I can give you that now. It extends to now.

Chairman Thompson.— Yes; I asked you when you had the last — you said the service consisted of certain correspondence. I asked you the date of the last correspondence. I would like to know the dates. I would like to know the dates of the receipt of these payments.

Mr. Quigg.— I went West for Mr. Gillespie last summer,— in the fall, after the adjournment of the Constitutional Convention. I was there about a week, I think. And I suspect that is the last time that I made any report in writing. I am quite sure it is.

By Chairman Thompson:

Q. What are the dates of the checks you received? A. I don't know the dates of the checks, but one was before I went, the thousand dollars was before I went, and the $1,500 was, I should say, about three or four months ago.

Q. Were the checks drawn by the Gillespie Company, the same as that check now in evidence? A. I can't say whether they were drawn by the Pipe Line Company or the Disposal Company, I cannot say — or by Gillespie himself — I cannot say.

Q. You don't know what bank they were drawn on? A. They are drawn either by Gillespie or by his Pipe Line Company, or by his disposal company.

Q. One or the other? A. One or the other.

Q. What has pipe line got to do with sanitation? A. A great deal to do with it.

Q. I mean sanitation of the city of New York? A. I don't mean anything about the city of New York.

Q. The garbage matter did have something to do with the garbage matter in the city of New York? A. Yes.

Q. And that garbage situation was affected by this legislation that Mr. Moss talked about? A. I don't know whether it was or not. The legislation failed. I advised Mr. Gillespie that if it had succeeded, it would have been very much in his interest.

By Mr. Moss:

Q. Failed by veto? A. Failed by veto.

Mr. Moss.— I want to ask Mr. Gillespie a question. He has been sworn, hasn't he?

Chairman Thompson.— You may be excused, Mr. Quigg.

T. H. GILLESPIE, recalled.

By Mr. Moss:

Mr. Gillespie, I want to ask you what this portion of this check of $2,500 that was charged to general expense, one-third to general expenses, what that represented? A. That was the portion that I thought belonged to T. A. Gillespie Company.

Q. Did you tell Mr. Perley Morse what that was for? A. I don't recollect that I did. I had some talk with Mr. Morse, as I remember. What I told him was that I saw Mr. Quigg several times with relation to the Pipe Company business, meaning the Sanitation Company. The Sanitation Company is financed by the Pipe Company. It is merely a small business, and is only starting. That is the reason why it has no account of its own.

Q. I am speaking now particularly of general expense. Do you remember what you told Mr. Morse about that? A. No; I think the general expense — the reason we charged it to general expense was because —

Chairman Thompson.— He didn't ask that. He asked you what you told Mr. Morse about that.

Mr. Gillespie.— I don't recollect.

By Mr. Moss:

Q. Let me refresh you recollection. Is Mr. Morse a sworn witness?

Chairman Thompson.— He has been.

Mr. Moss.— Mr. Morse, will you tell me, so as to refresh the recollection of the witness, what he said to you concerning this "general expense?"

Mr. Morse.— Mr. Gillespie said that about this time the Thompson Committee was to be appointed and Mr. Quigg was more or less familiar with different members of the Legislature, and he advised his father at that time about this Committee.

Mr. Moss.— That is. Mr. Quigg advised his father about this Committee?

Mr. Morse.— Yes, sir.

Mr. Moss.— So that a portion of this voucher of $2.500 on that statement related to the work of this Committee?

Mr. Morse.— According to what Mr. Gillespie told me.

Mr. Gillespie.— That refreshes my memory.

Examination of Mr. Gillespie resumed by Mr. Moss:

Q. State what it was? A. Mr. Morse asked me if my father had talked to Mr. Quigg.

Mr. Quigg.— I am a little bit deaf.

Chairman Thompson.— Get up here, and we will all have our memories refreshed.

Mr. Moss.— We will soon find out what the facts are.

Mr. Quigg.— Yes, we shall.

Mr. Gillespie.— I remember now very well what the conversation was. Mr. Morse asked me if the general expense charge had anything to do with the investigation of the Thompson Committee. I told him that my father had had the talks with Mr. Morse (witness apparently means Mr. Quigg), and I was not familiar with what he had said, that it may have had connection with the Thompson Committee but I didn't know anything about it.

Mr. Moss.— Well, now, Mr. Morse, you have heard the statement of Mr. Gillespie. Have you any amendment to make to the testimony you gave?

Mr. Morse.—No, sir.

Chairman Thompson.— Who suggested — in the conversation who suggested first the fact that this had to do with the Committee investigating the Public Service Commissions?

Mr. Morse.— Mr. Gillespie, because I was very much surprised that he said that to me. I didn't think that it could have anything to do with the Thompson Committee because my understanding was the Thompson Committee was appointed after the date of this check. I was surprised to hear him say that.

Mr. Gillespie.— Mr. Morse asked me the question, saying, as I remember now, this was about the time of the Thompson Investigating Committee starting, and my answer was my father had done the talking. I think Mr. Morse will remember my saying that my father had talked to him, but I did not know what he had said.

Chairman Thompson.— Where is your father?

Mr. Gillespie.— In Florida.

Chairman Thompson.— Have you had any talks about your father returning to New York?

Mr. Gillespie.— No, sir.

Chairman Thompson.— With anybody?

Mr. Gillespie.— Yes, I have talked to Mr. Cravath about it.

Chairman Thompson.— Anybody else?

Mr. Gillespie.— May have talked to several people about it.

Chairman Thompson.— Talked with Mr. Morse about it?

Mr. Gillespie.— Possibly.

Chairman Thompson.— Talked to Mr. — anyone connected with this Committee about it, anybody else?

Mr. Gillespie.— Not that I know of; no, sir; I may have.

Chairman Thompson.— Didn't you make a promise that your father would return from Florida if this Committee wanted him?

Mr. Gillespie.— If he was needed, yes, sir.

Chairman Thompson.— If he was needed.

Mr. Gillespie.— I made the statement also that he had been thrown out of an automobile last fall and that he was — went down there for his health — he was a sick man.

Chairman Thompson.— When did he go?

Mr. Gillespie.— He went three weeks ago last Saturday, I think it was.

Chairman Thompson.— When was it he was thrown out of the automobile?

Mr. Gillespie.— Last fall.

Chairman Thompson.— What time, November, October or December?

Mr. Gillespie.— I think it was September.

Chairman Thompson.— September?

Mr. Gillespie.— I think so.

Chairman Thompson.— He fell out of an automobile in September and three weeks ago went to Florida on account of it?

Mr. Gillespie.— No, sir, not on account of it. Been trying to get away for a good while. He has been here. We have had a great deal of work to do.

Chairman Thompson.— Has he made any arrangements to come back while this Committee is sitting?

Mr. Gillespie.— No, sir.

Chairman Thompson.— When can he come back?

Mr. Gillespie.— I don't know.

Chairman Thompson.— Will you find out?

Mr. Gillespie.— I will ask him, yes, sir.

Chairman Thompson.— Will you wire him to-day?

Mr. Gillespie.— I will find out, yes, sir.

Chairman Thompson.— And let me know to-morrow, or as soon as you hear from the wire?

Mr. Moss.— Mr. Quigg, you have no recollection of Mr. Gillespie, Senior, speaking to you about this at all?

Mr. Quigg.— Mr. Gillespie never spoke to me about this Legislature or this Committee. Nobody ever has spoken to me about this Committee except the wayfarer on the highway.

Mr. Moss.— Well, have the wayfayers spoken to you about the Committee?

Mr. Quigg.— Yes.

Mr. Moss.— There is a passage in the Scripture that says, " The wayfaring man, though a fool, need not err therein."

Mr. Quigg.— May I go away now?

Mr. Moss.— Mr. Gillespie, while you are on the stand —

Chairman Thompson (to Mr. Quigg).— If we need you later, we can find you in your office?

Mr. Quigg.— At any time later.

Chairman Thompson.— You will be just as willing to appear?

Mr. Quigg.— On the subject of Gillespie, yes.

Chairman Thompson.— Or any other subject that might be within the scope of our investigation?

Mr. Quigg.— If my clients wish me to testify, I am very glad to be of any service to you that I can.

Chairman Thompson.— All I care for is the date of those other two checks.

Mr. Quigg.— Would you like me to get them for you and send them to you?

Chairman Thompson.— Yes.

Mr. Quigg.— I will do so.

Examination of Mr. Gillespie resumed by Mr. Moss:

Q. Mr. Gillespie, I understood from Mr. Cravath yesterday that the reports from the Pittsburgh Company would be produced; are you ready to produce them? A. I understood that there was to be a subpoena issued for those, Mr. Moss. We have not yet received any subpoena.

Q. That is, you did not know you were to produce them until you got a subpoena?

Chairman Thompson.— Better issue subpoena at once.

Mr. Moss.— Yes.

In that view, we will excuse you for the present, and the subpoena will issue. Mr. Ryan.

Examination of Mr. Gillespie resumed by Mr. Moss:

Q. What about those two other checks given to Mr. Quigg, what were they for? A. Sanitation Company business, in connection with this same contract.

Chairman Thompson.— Were they drawn the same as this check?

Mr. Gillespie.— I think by the pipe company probably, because the pipe company was financing the sanitation.

Chairman Thompson.— Will you look it up this afternoon and let us know?

Mr. Moss.— We would like to have what you have on that point.

Mr. Gillespie.— In relation to the disposal company, may I say a word?

Mr. Moss.— Yes, sir.

Mr. Gillespie.— We are in the New York Disposal Company which has the garbage contract, or the contract with the city for the disposal of garbage. We have a suit or are about to start proceedings against the city in connection with that contract.

By Mr. Moss:

Q. What is the nature of that suit, what is it for?

Chairman Thompson.— Has not started yet, he says.

Mr. Moss.— In contemplation? A. I believe the city has not fulfilled its present contract with us, Mr. Moss, in that it is not delivering us all the garbage which it stipulated to do in the contract. It was on the question of the law in relation to that matter that Mr. Quigg talked to my father.

Q. If that bill had passed in Albany, you would have been out with the city? A. Our contract would have run.

Q. You would not fight for it? A. Wouldn't bother about it at all.

Chairman Thompson.— You don't like it because they don't give you enough garbage to remove?

Mr. Gillespie.— The garbage — we have to have so much garbage to — the only way we get our pay out of that is by the grease that comes out of it. If we don't get what they stipulated —

Chairman Thompson.— The Committee is in favor of your having all of it.

Mr. Moss.— Now, Mr. Ryan.

JOHN R. RYAN, called as a witness, being first duly sworn, testified as follows:

By Mr. Moss:

Q. Now, Mr. Ryan, you were the plaintiff in an action against the city of New York some time ago that went to the Court of Appeals, if you remember? A. Yes, sir.

Q. And I suppose you signed the complaint and verified it? A. I did.

Q. Who asked you to do it? A. Why, the action was brought through Mr. Willard N. Baylis.

Q. Who asked you to do it, is my question. Who asked you to sign the complaint? A. Why, it was submitted to me by Mr. Willard N. Baylis, my attorney.

Q. Did you tell him to start the suit first? A. Surely.

Q. Who asked you to do it? A. I don't know that I can answer that question. The suit was brought after a conference between Mr. Baylis, as my attorney, and myself. Mr. Baylis has been my attorney for twenty years, and the proposition came —

Chairman Thompson.— Will you please answer Mr. Moss's question?

Mr. Ryan.— I have tried to.

Chairman Thompson.— Just read it to him.

By Mr. Moss:

Q. Who asked you to do it? A. Why, I presume Mr. Baylis.

Q. I didn't ask you to presume anything. Who asked you to do
it? A. I will answer definitely, Mr. Willard N. Baylis, my
attorney.

Q. Anyone else? A. No, no one whatever.

Q. Mr. Baylis asked you to do it? A. I don't see how I can
answer the question any other way than yes but,—

Chairman Thompson.— That answers it.

Q. Had you begun any such action as this at any other time
before that? A. No.

Q. Did you meet anyone connected with the Brooklyn Rapid
Transit Company? A. I did not.

Q. Did Mr. Baylis? A. I don't know.

Q. Did he tell you whether he had or not? A. He did not.

Q. Do you know whether or not the Brooklyn Rapid Transit
Company wanted this action started? A. I did not know.

Q. What did you think about it? A. I had no knowledge in the
matter at all.

Q. No. But what did you think about it, I asked. A. I assumed that one of the large railroad interests were directly interested in the proposition.

Q. And wanted the suit brought? A. I presume that they
wanted the matter tried out in some form.

Q. They wanted to try it out, and your action would try it?
Which of the great interests wanted it done? A. I don't know.

Q. You assumed which? A. I did not assume.

Q. You said you assumed one of the big interests wanted it
brought out and tried. Which interest did you assume? A. I did
not know.

Q. What did you think? A. I had no positive information on
the matter.

Q. What did you think, I asked? A. I don't know that I can
answer.

Q. Did you have any thought about it at all? A. Yes, I presume I did.

Q. Did you worry about this case any ? A. Not at all.

Q. Not at all about the possible expense of it ? A. No, sir.

Q. Did you pay for printing the briefs ? A. I did not.

Q. Who did ? A. I don't know.

Q. Did you pay any bill of costs ? A. I did not.

Q. Who did ? A. I don't know. No bill has ever been rendered to me in this matter.

Q. Did anybody ever ask you for any money ? A. No.

Q. For counsel fee ? A. None.

Q. None ? A. None whatever.

Q. For a bond ? A. No, I never paid anything at all in the way of a charge.

Q. Did you sign a bond ? A. I did.

Q. How much ? A. My impression is about a thousand dollars.

Q. How much was the premium ? A. I don't know.

Q. Did you pay it ? A. I did not.

Q. Who did ? A. I don't know.

Q. Did you ask ? A. No.

Q. Why ? A. I wasn't interested. The matter was left entirely to my attorney.

Q. When you started this action did you own any real estate ? A. A great deal.

Q. In Brooklyn ? A. A great deal, and I still do.

Q. How many times did you see Mr. Baylis in his office about this case ? A. Why, I have kept no record of it. Several times, whenever he wished to consult with me.

Q. What did he confer with you about ? A. We had several conferences ; one before the case was started, and some conferences in connection with the case, and I called to sign the complaint, and I think on two or three other occasions.

Q. Tell me anything he did say to you about it ? A. Why, the chief conversation we had was when the proposition was first started ; that is one.

Q. Yes. A. Mr. Baylis —

Q. Speak a little louder. A. Mr. Baylis and myself met in my club over in Brooklyn, and we discussed this general subway proposition.

Q. Mr. Baylis cannot hear you. A. I have a little huskiness in my voice.

Q. Do the best you can. Speak out. A. We — are you ready?

Q. Fire away. A. We talked over the proposition of the subway situation, which at that time was in a somewhat muddled condition. Mr. Baylis knew that I owned a great deal of property down in South Brooklyn, particularly along the route of the Fourth Avenue Subway and the Sea Beach Road, which was the only subway at that time which made very much progress.

Mr. Baylis.— Might Mr. Ryan state the assessed value of the property he owned?

Chairman Thompson.— The questions will be asked by Mr. Moss.

Mr. Ryan.— And we discussed, as I recollect it, in effect that the delay in providing the means of completing and operating the subway, the depression it had on real estate along that particular line, and he told me that the question of the legal right of a city to enter into the contracts with the transportation companies was somewhat doubtful and that it would probably be necessary to test out that right by a taxpayer's action, and in view of the fact we were very intimate friends and we had business relations for twenty odd years, he asked me if I would be willing to join in this action, or to start this action, and I agreed to do so.

By Mr. Moss:

Q. Did he ever tell you who was paying the bills? A. He did not.

Q. Did you ever ask him? A. I did not.

Q. Did you ever do anything more in the action than to sign the complaint? A. Why, practically nothing, as I recollect.

Q. Are you a stockholder in the B. R. T.? A. I am not.

Q. Or on any railroad? A. Not in any Brooklyn railroad.

Q. In any New York or Brooklyn railroad? A. No; I own some stock in the Lehigh Valley Railroad and some bonds in some of the western railroads. I have no securities of any transportation company in New York city.

Mr. Moss.— Any question, Mr. Chairman?

Chairman Thompson.— You may be excused, Mr. Ryan.

Mr. Baylis.— Might Mr. Ryan be asked the value of his property along the Fourth Avenue Subway in Brooklyn?

Mr. Ryan.—At the time this action was started?

Mr. Baylis.— Yes.

Mr. Ryan.—At that time I owned, I should say, between fifty and sixty lots, with an assessed valuation of probably $70,000. The bulk of the lots were free and clear. Some of this property I still own.

Mr. Baylis.— You owned other properties in Brooklyn at the time, free and clear?

Mr. Ryan.—And fully as much in value in other sections of the city.

Chairman Thompson.— Did they give you any guarantee at that time against loss in the case?

Mr. Ryan.— I asked for none. I relied on my friend and attorney, Mr. Baylis, to take care of the matter for my protection. Is that all?

Chairman Thompson.— That is all.

WILLARD N. BAYLIS, called as a witness, being first duly sworn, testified as follows:

By Mr. Moss:

Q. Mr. Baylis, I want to ask you about the beginning of that suit? A. Yes, sir.

Q. That your client has just talked about. A. Might I ask, Mr. Ryan, you are an officer of the Chauncey Company in Brooklyn, are you, at present?

Mr. Ryan.— Chauncey Real Estate Company.

Mr. Baylis.— Officer of that corporation, and doing business in Brooklyn.

By Mr. Moss:

Q. Now Mr. Baylis, who asked you to start this action? A. Mr. Ryan authorized it.

Q. Who asked you to start it? A. Nobody.

Q. Who paid your bill? A. Nobody paid the bill for this action, unfortunately.

Q. Did you render a bill to any one? A. No, sir.

Q. Have you received any moneys from the B. R. T. or any one connected with it? A. That is a very broad question, Mr. Moss.

Q. I know it is, but your answer forces me to ask it. A. I think I have sued the B. R. T. and received moneys in settlement of suits, possibly, in years gone by. I have had business dealings with various of the directors and officers of the B. R. T. during my life, in which we have had money transactions, but not in connection with this suit. Your question was very broad.

Q. Yes. Did you have any conversation with any one connected with the Interborough before you brought this action? A. No, not that I know of.

Q. Did you have any conversation with any one representing the B. R. T. before you brought this action? A. Yes.

Q. Who? A. Col. Timothy S. Williams.

Q. And what was that conversation? A. Col. Williams has been my client in personal matters more or less for a number of years. He was in my office one day in New York, and in substance said to me — I forget the instance which brought him there — said to me in substance that in the subway agitation then prevailing he did not think it was possible to proceed until the constitutionality of these proposed contracts was tested, and the validity of the bonds determined. And he said that would make a very interesting lawsuit. That is all he said on the subject.

Q. How long have you known Col. Williams, did you say? A. Every since he lived at Huntington. I have been his attorney in various matters and was attorney in some land matters, including Mr. Williams and others, the Center Syndicate, and searched about forty or fifty titles, and had to do with their money transactions, but all matters not connected with railroad matters. I secured a grant from the State for lands under water adjacent to his home, and have had various personal dealings with him.

Q. Have you done anything for his corporation? A. Never. One minute — never directly.

Q. How indirectly? A. I — after the determination of this suit in the Court of Appeals. I was consulted about the contract, which I think was finally executed.

Chairman Thompson.— The Chair wishes to announce the presence of Senator Emerson from Warren county.

By Mr. Moss:

Q. Well — A. Where did I leave off, Mr. Moss?

Q. You were saying that you did do something afterwards for the company? A. Yes, I did — no, I beg your pardon; I said I did not do it for the company.

Q. Whom did you do it for? A. I did it in consultation with Professor Collin of Collin, Wells & Hughes.

Q. Professor Collin. Is he a relative of Judge Collin of the Court of Appeals? A. I think he is related to Judge Collin, but he appeared in the Court of Appeals in this matter for the B. R. T. or some of the defendants, in which Ryan was plaintiff.

Q. Was Judge Collin sitting in that case? A. I think he was. He was.

Q. Yes, yes, he was. A. I know he was. I argued it in the Court of Appeals.

Q. You were present. Was he on the bench? A. Yes, I know him.

Q. Judge Collin concurs with Judge Hiscock. You say it was his brother that was arguing? A. I don't know the relation. I think they are related. I am not certain whether it is his brother or not.

Q. Let us see which side Mr. Collin argued on? A. For the constitutionality of the B. R. T. and the Brooklyn Union Elevated.

Q. Represented the Brooklyn Rapid Transit Company and argued for the constitutionality of the law? A. I don't know how he represented them, but —

Q. He and Youmans? A. Yes, sir. I think he argued for the constitutionality.

Q. You prepared a brief? A. Oh, yes.

Q. Cost you something? A. Yes.

Q. Who paid for it? A. No one.

Q. Who paid it, yourself? A. Yes.

Q. Just because of the conversation you had with Col. Williams? A. Because I believed my association with this suit would yield results in other ways; and it did.

Q. Then — yes, you were called into consultation promptly afterwards? A. I knew the situation. I had briefed it just as well as I knew how. I wish to file a copy of my brief and see if I have not done it with all the energy possible, in claiming that the proposed contract was unconstitutional.

Q. Unquestionably your entrance in the case was due to the remark made by Mr. Williams? A. Correct.

Q. And you discovered it would be agreeable to Mr. Williams for you to bring such an action as this? A. He did not say that.

Q. You discovered that. You would not have brought it if you had not believed that? A. If I had thought Mr. — Col. Williams would have been offended by an action, I would not have brought it. I am friendly with him.

Q. You have said you were willing to bring an action because you thought it would produce more business, and it did? A. I didn't say that.

Q. In substance. Wait a minute.

Chairman Thompson.— You will have plenty of time. I am going to stay until 6 o'clock, if necessary.

Mr. Baylis.— Well, I must be correctly quoted.

Chairman Thompson.— Let him ask the question first, and then you can interrupt him after he is all through.

Mr. Baylis.— That would not be an interruption; that would be a correction.

Chairman Thompson.— That is the only kind of an interruption I will allow.

Mr. Baylis.— That is a left-handed one.

Mr. Moss.— We are dealing with a left-handed subject.

By Mr. Moss:

Q. The business you got afterwards was Williams' business? A. I don't think so.

Q. B. R. T. interests? A. I think the B. R. T. was interested, but I did not —

Q. You know it was? A. — deal with the B. R. T.

Q. Oh. pshaw. I think I am willing to leave that record just where Mr. Baylis has left it.

Mr. Baylis.— I am glad to answer any question, or to be excused at this moment.

By Mr. Moss:

Q. You did this work because you knew it would be acceptable to the B. R. T.? A. No, I had no interest in the B. R. T., and never had.

Q. You knew it would be acceptable to Mr. Williams? A. I was on friendly relations with Mr. Williams.

Q. You did it because you thought it would be acceptable to Mr. Williams? A. No, I did not, entirely.

Q. Well, what did you do it for? A. I did it because I thought it was an interesting question, and that it had to be tried out before the subway conditions in New York or Brooklyn would be improved, and that I believed no bonds could be issued until that was settled, and I believed that, after talking to Mr. Ryan. it was the desirable thing to do, and I believed it would do me no harm in a business way ultimately.

Q. And you remarked that it did not? A. No.

Q. And what was the circumstance you had in your mind when you said it did not do you any harm? What was that? A. Had to do with the details of the final contract, which was signed between the city and the B. R. T.

Q. Mr. Collin was counsel for the B. R. T.? A. I understand so.

Q. This circle is complete. You don't claim as a lawyer to be an eleemosynary institution? A. Not entirely; although I do many things —

Q. You didn't start out to settle the subway question for New York? A. That was an element —

Q. Yes, you are glad to do a good thing on the way, as you go along.

Mr. Moss.— I think we have got all we want, Mr. Chairman.

By Chairman Thompson:

Q. How much did you get finally? A. Well, for my services in this — which I rendered in conjunction with Collin, having to do with this contract, I received approximately $3,000. The exact amount I don't remember.

Q. Ever get back your money you paid for the bonds and briefs?
A. It was never mentioned.

Q. Did you pay for it? A. Most of them. ·

Q. How much money did you pay out in all, disbursements, in this Ryan case? A. The printing of the briefs?

Q. All the disbursements you paid out in the Ryan case, from beginning to end? A. I would estimate it at $150 to $200. That is my best estimate.

By Mr. Moss:

Q. Mr. Baylis, do you mean to say — now listen to me, please — do you mean to say that you, a lawyer, because of something Mr. Williams said to you, called upon a man, or called a man to you. and asked him to bring a lawsuit out of which you might get some advantage incidentally, and that you paid the disbursements and carried the thing along at your own expense? You induced the man to be the plaintiff, and you financed and carried the action, do you say that? A. I did not say anything like that.

Q. I am asking you if you do? A. I don't say yes to what you say.

Q. Didn't you do that? A. No.

Q. In what way does my statement fail to indicate the facts? A. Many ways.

Q. Please state them? A. Among others —

Q. I want to be sure you know what you are saying. A. Among others — among the various criticisms of your suggestion are the following —

Q. The criticisms are in your testimony. I am calling your attention to it. A. I didn't say it the way you do.

Q. Go ahead.

Chairman Thompson.— Do what Mr. Moss says. Let the stenographer read the question.

(The question was read by the stenographer as follows):

" Q. Mr. Baylis, do you mean to say — now listen to me, please — do you mean to say that you, a lawyer, because of something Mr. Williams said to you, called upon a man, or called a man to you. and asked him to bring a lawsuit out of which you might get some advantage incidentally, and that you paid the disbursements and carried the thing along at your own expense? You induced the man to be the plaintiff, and you financed and carried the action; do you say that?"

A. I didn't say I induced him to be a plaintiff. I said after talking with him he authorized me to bring the action. Now, there are various other things that I —

Q. You heard his testimony. A. One moment. I also did not bring it entirely because Col. Williams had made the suggestion that such a suit would be a desirable one, or words to that purport. I did presume that out of my work in connection with the suit, and my familiarity with the situation, I would be able to do work which would be remunerative, which conclusion the result justified.

Q. I guess that is all, Mr. Baylis? A. Thank you.

Chairman Thompson.— Have you any further explanation?

Mr. Baylis.— Oh, no. I would be very glad to leave this brief here.

Mr. Moss.— Yes. Let us mark it right in evidence.

(The brief referred to is received in evidence and marked Exhibit 6 of February 25, 1916, V. E. Valva.)

Mr. Baylis.— I endeavored to win. I want to say in the Court of Appeals I expected to win. I felt confident we would win, and the differences in those two contracts are brought out in my brief, namely, that as to the B. R. T., that was taking a subway built with city money and entering into a partnership with property privately owned by the B. R. T.; whereas to a large extent the Interborough was hitching up with a new subway, a city owned subway, already constructed; and the B. R. T. didn't get any charity in my brief or in my argument. I did the best I could to win and believed it was unconstitutional.

By Chairman Thompson:

Q. Weren't you afraid you would hurt the feelings of Mr. Williams? A. I didn't care. If I go into a lawsuit I go in to win.

Q. If you had won the lawsuit, do you think you would have got this subsequent recognition? A. I did not know nor care. I was not dependent upon one lawsuit.

Q. Did you get excited in the lawsuit, or anything? A. I am energetic in anything I do, Mr. Thompson.

By Mr. Moss:

Q. Mr. Baylis, I would like to ask your opinion. Almost all the lawyers have given their opinions about this case. But take this accident that occurred up here on Seventh avenue, which resulted in some damage? A. Yes.

Q. Now, that was not a case where there was damage in the operation of a railroad, but damage in the construction of the railroad. Is there any view of that case — that situation where damages have been paid and will be paid, and which throw any burden upon the city of New York, regarding the damages? A. And my answer to that would be if the city itself owned the subway, it would have to pay those damages. But be that as it may, it did not enter into the constitutionality of this proposed contract. It had to do with whether or not the city, through its subway commission, had made a good bargain. But it has no bearing whatever upon the constitutionality —

Q. I didn't ask you that.

A. — of the contract in question.

Mr. Moss.— I think that is all, Mr. Baylis.

Chairman Thompson.— You don't get any pay for this advice, either.

Mr. Baylis.— I am used to that misfortune. But I have done very well at it.

Mr. Moss.— The expense of $150 to $200 then produced a good retainer. I want to ask another question of Mr. Morse. Mr. Morse, referring to these transactions in the Gillespie Company's accounts, you have been examining them, haven't you?

Mr. Morse.— Yes, sir.

Mr. Moss.—And have you found any items in their accounts which go back of January 1, 1914, that were made the subject of our inquiry? If so, point them out.

Mr. Morse.— Up to now we have not been allowed to examine ? accounts before January 1, 1914. We found, however, vouchers and correspondence to do with the third-tracking contract in December, 1913, as early as December 23.

Mr. Moss.— Now, will you specify those, and point out anything which relates to the question which I have given you.

(Mr. Moss hands papers to Mr. Morse.)

I am assisting, Mr. Chairman, to lay a foundation which may be useful in the future, at this time. While Mr. Morse is looking through those vouchers, I want to call your attention. Mr. Chairman, to the fact that that check of $2,500, identified by Mr. Quigg, now on the testimony, is a part of this investigation and is germane to this investigation. I don't know whether that attracted your attention, but that is part of this inquiry now, on the testimony that has been given.

Chairman Thompson.— That is true. That was the information of the Chair all the time.

Mr. Moss.— Yes.

Chairman Thompson.— I have not seen fit to retract anything I have said about the $2,500 check yet.

Mr. Moss.— Go ahead, Mr. Morse.

Mr. Morse.— I have in my hand a voucher of Griggs, Baldwin & Baldwin, attorneys, dated March 31, 1914. From that I read: "Consultations and advice relative to meaning and interpretation of construction contracts of Interborough Rapid Transit Company with Terry & Tench, Snare & Triest, or T. A. Gillespie Company, or letters relating to the same, to wit, T. A. Gillespie Company, to Interborough Rapid Transit Company, December 23, 1913; T. A. Gillespie, President, to Theodore P. Shonts, President, December 31, 1913; " which shows that these contracts were being considered in December, 1913.

Chairman Thompson.— There isn't any question. Our record shows these contracts were considered, and Mr. Gillespie was in touch with the Interborough Railroad with reference to them as far back as, at least, November, and I think October, 1913; our record already shows that.

Mr. Moss.— Yes, and I think, Mr. Chairman, the general scope of the investigation shows that we have more — no question about it — legal right to inquire — as far as we care to go.

Chairman Thompson.— No question about that, because the bidding is not competitive bidding; it was non-competitive bidding. The record shows that up to date.

Mr. Moss.—Now, I will ask you further to state the conversation you had with Mr. Gillespie.

Mr. Morse.— Mr. Gillespie, Jr., stated to me this morning that his father was probably in conference with Mr. Shonts regarding this contract six or seven days before December 23, 1913, and that most of the details leading up to this contract were discussed between them in different conversations that they had, and it was not put down in writing.

Mr. Moss.— Now, was that subpoena served upon Mr. Gillespie? Did you receive it?

Mr. Gillespie.— Yes.

Mr. Moss.— Now, I understand, Mr. Gillespie, from my conversation with Mr. Cravath, that you are going to bring those reports, bring them here to the Committee to-morrow.

Mr. Gillespie. — Eleven o'clock. Called for 11 o'clock to-morrow morning.

Chairman Thompson.— We won't be up much before that.

Mr. Moss.— I don't think there is any other witness I have forgotten.

Chairman Thompson.— We will suspend now until 11 o'clock to-morrow morning.

Whereupon, at 4:40 P. M., the Committee adjourned to meet to-morrow morning, Saturday, February 26, 1916, at 11 o'clock A. M.

FEBRUARY 26, 1916

NEW YORK COUNTY LAWYERS' ASSOCIATION BOARD ROOM,
165 Broadway, New York City

The Committee was called to order at 11:37 o'clock A. M., Chairman Thompson presiding.

Mr. Moss.— Mr. Chairman, can we make some announcement concerning Mr. Shonts, so as to relieve Mr. Stanchfield?

Mr. Stanchfield.— Mr. Shonts is upstairs, if the Chairman please, and I am informed by Mr. Moss, the counsel for the Committee, that he does not desire to examine Mr. Shonts until the return of Mr. Young, and his examination is finished, and I would like to ask if it be satisfactory if I agree that Mr. Shonts — in my capacity as counsel —

Chairman Thompson.— You are simply here in his place, and you will agree Mr. Shonts will abide by the direction of the Committee?

Mr. Stanchfield.—Absolutely.

Chairman Thompson.— Well, we will direct that he appear Wednesday morning at 11 o'clock. Will that be agreeable?

Mr. Stanchfield.— Certainly.

Chairman Thompson.— Very well.

Mr. Moss.— Will you swear Mr. Towns?

Chairman Thompson.— I had a letter here from Mr. Quigg, somewhere, that I wanted to find. I can't find it.

Letter subsequently handed to stenographer is as follows:

" Mutual Life Building, 32 Liberty Street,
   " New York, February 25, 1916.
" Hon. George F. Thompson, Chairman.
   " Sir: Referring to your request that I advise your committee of the dates of checks paid to me by Mr. Gillespie or his companies subsequently to the check sent to me January 13,

1915, I beg to inform you that a check for $1,000 was paid to me on April 30, 1915, and another check on October 22, 1915, in payment of a bill that I rendered to him on October 19, 1915. This check was for $1,500.

" These checks have to do only with the business of Mr. Gillespie's Sanitation Company.

" Faithfully yours,

"(Signed) LEMUEL E. QUIGG."

MIRABEAU L. TOWNS, called as a witness, being first duly sworn, testified as follows:

By Mr. Moss:

Q. Mr. Towns, you have been practicing at the bar a great many years, haven't you? A. I have been practicing, yes, since 1876.

Q. Yes. Do you know Mr. Shonts, the president of the Interborough Railroad? A. Yes, I have met him.

Q. How long have you known him? A. Well, I think I have known him since December, 1909.

(Assemblyman Burr takes the chair.)

By Mr. Moss:

Q. Do you remember the first occasion on which you met him? A. Yes, I think so.

Q. What was it about? A. Well, I have no objection to telling, but I wish to keep within section 835 of the Code.

Q. Surely. A. If Mr. Shonts has any representative here who will relieve me from the obligation of that, why I have no objection.

Q. Mr. Stanchfield has just stepped out, and I suppose he represents him. Is Mr. Quackenbush here?

Mr. Quackenbush.— Is it a question as to Mr. Shonts as an individual, or —

Mr. Moss.— I don't know.

Mr. Towns.— I never had any individual business with Mr. Shonts.

Mr. Quackenbush.— So far as the Interborough Rapid Transit Company is concerned, it consents to the testimony, without any question of privilege.

Mr. Towns.— Yes; now, what is the question?

By Mr. Moss:

Q. The question is, what was the occasion of your meeting him in 1909, when you first met him? A. To discuss the plans of the Interborough — the construction of the new subway.

Q. Yes. And did you meet him frequently after that? A. Yes. I wish to say — I think it is appropriate to say here that I had been first spoken to by a representative of the Interborough as far back as 1909, before the election, and from that time on I had conversations with representatives of the Interborough, concerning — first, concerning a campaign in the interest of the subways as against the tri-borough proposition.

Q. Yes. A. And then afterwards all of my conversations related to that, and what could be done in order to favor the accomplishment of the — not having the city enter into competition with the railroad that was already in existence, the present subway. I never demanded or received any retainer. These first conversations were informal. Afterwards they became formal and I was requested to do certain things and which I tried my best to accomplish. That is all.

Q. Did you introduce Mr. Shonts to Mr. Towns — to Mayor Gaynor? A. Well, I was present on the occasion when he met Mayor Gaynor.

Q. Did you introduce him? A. Well, I don't think I did. Mr. Shonts got out of the automobile, and I think they recognized each other. I did not get out and make any formal introduction of them.

Q. Did you go with him for the purpose of meeting the Mayor? A. I had arranged that the Mayor should meet — Mr. Shonts should meet the Mayor —

Q. Then the Mayor was expecting — pardon me. A. — on a former occasion, but appointments prevented their meeting, and afterwards the day was set that he should meet him at St. James.

Q. You fixed the time and place for the meeting of Mr. Shonts and Mr. Gaynor? A. I think the time was fixed by the parties themselves. I simply communicated one to the other that it would be agreeable to meet.

Q. And so far as you know, was that the first meeting between

Mr. Shonts and Mr. Gaynor? A. So far as my personal knowledge goes, that was the first meeting.

Q. Were you requested by Mr. Shonts to arrange for the meeting? A. I think so. I cannot tell now whether it was at the suggestion of the Mayor or whether it was Mr. Shonts. Both at that time were anxious to meet each other in order to clear up the conditions that existed.

Q. They were both anxious to meet each other? A. I think so.

Q. And the Mayor knew he was coming, did he? A. Of course he knew.

Q. So far as you can judge? A. Well, I have positive knowledge that he knew, if a statement means anything — that is, a message means anything.

(Chairman Thompson resumes the chair.)

Q. Well, Mr. Shonts, in his examination the other day, gave the impression that he did not know you very well. A. Well, I am not socially familiar with Mr. Shonts. I only know him in this transaction. I have met him once or twice since then, just to say good-day, informally.

Q. He seems to have forgotten all about you; didn't know your name, even? A. Yes, I regretted that when I saw it, that I was forgotten, but I imagine he was a man of great affairs.

Q. And he just took it in his head to go down and see the Mayor, as it were, to take the bull by the horns; but you say it had all been arranged, and each was desirous of meeting the other? A. That is my recollection of it. Yes. Well, each was willing to meet the other. I don't wish to be too strong about it.

Q. Well, the Mayor told you to have Mr. Shonts come down, didn't he? A. Yes.

Q. Mr. Shonts said he wanted to go down, didn't he? A. Yes.

Q. And this really brought two great men together? A. Well, I won't pass on their greatness.

Q. Now, this inquiry which was made by Mr. — A. I wish to say — which I consider in justification of myself, in reading the testimony of Mr. Shonts, it seemed as if an impression generally went out that I received $5,000 for the privilege of taking him down there. I had worked diligently and faithfully in the interest of my client, the Interborough, from October until about the 1st of May, 1909.

Q. What did that work consist of, as this is an inquiry into the affairs of the Interborough, which is represented by its counsel, and counsel says they are perfectly willing to have you testify why it is germane to the inquiry, and there is nobody making an objection — so go right into it. A. It consisted of submitting plans, of conveying to Mayor Gaynor the desires of the Interborough. Mayor Gaynor had written an article in I think it was Pearson's Magazine, in which he denounced this scheme of the effort of the railroads to get charge and monopolize the rapid transit system of the city, in which he had criticised the result of the present management of the Interborough, and the giving of the tunnel under the East River, and I had had something to do with that with the Mayor, Van Wyck, on the last day, it was said he was going to veto the resolution, and Mr. Baldwin, who represented the Long Island Railroad, asked me to go up and see the Mayor, at that time Mr. Van Wyck, and ask him if he would not approve of the aldermanic resolution, or at least let it pass without signing it. I did. I went to the Democratic Club on Fifth avenue and laid the facts before him, and he did not approve of it, but he did not veto it. And that went through, so that I had some knowledge of that, and my endeavor was to try and convince Mayor Gaynor that he was wrong in his premise, and necessarily must be wrong in his conclusions, with regard to the over-reaching of the railroad company, over-reaching of the city or railroad company, and I worked on that before the election, and spoke to him frequently, thought it was inadvisable to commit himself too strongly to that proposition. Then I continued afterwards to try and convince him that it would be for the best interests of the city to have — not to enter into competition with the existing road, and then when he came to a question of routes — this all goes to your question as to what I did.

Q. Yes, certainly. A. Came to a question of routes, there were many suggestions, and as they would come up we would go over the matter. Then I would report to the Interborough.

Q. Whom did you report to, what persons? A. Well, at first I reported to Mr. Campbell.

Q. That was the treasurer? A. He was my friend, and I had known him for a long time, and he had got me interested in this question. I was very much anxious to —

Q. Who else? A. I don't know what attracted him to me, but I had charge of the case of Duffy against Bingham, and brought

that about, and the result of it was to make the Mayor a very
prominent candidate for the Mayoralty, and I got up a petition
which nominated him independently and filed it, and in that way
I was connected with Mayor Gaynor, I suppose.

Q. Who else did you report to in the Interborough, besides Mr.
Campbell? A. Mostly to Mr. Campbell.

Q. Who else? A. Except I never had but about three — I
think it was three meetings with Mr. Shonts, in which he laid out
the different routes, see? And finally came to a conclusion. He is
quite right about his statement that it was the intention of naming
the tunnel the Gaynor tunnel. I remember that distinctly as being
one of the — one of the arguments used why the Seventh avenue
route should be adopted, and the tunnel should go under — I think
it was Beekman street.

Q. That is that the — A. It has passed out of my mind. I
don't know now whether it was to go under the river at the foot of
Beekman street, or some other street, but at any rate, it was to be
named the Gaynor tunnel.

Q. That was one of the arguments, you say, that was used? A.
What?

Q. You say that was one of the arguments that was used? A.
Of course that was one of the arguments. I tried to show Mayor
Gaynor that it would be better to confer a great benefit upon pos-
terity than to nurse an unreasonable grouch.

Q. And you thought naming the tunnel after him would help
him to get over that grouch? A. I don't know anything about it.
I conveyed the intelligence.

Q. You evidently have an atmospheric judgment? A. I am
only dealing with facts; I am not giving an opinion.

Q. You dealt with men, and you overcame Mayor Gaynor's
opposition? A. I don't know whether I overcame it or not.

Q. Aren't you the one who did it? A. It would perhaps be
rather presumptuous on my part to say I overcame his opposition.
I did all I could. and the results speak for themselves.

Q. And you only received $5,000? A. That is all. I never —
when I had gotten through — let me see the date. Is that the
voucher?

Q. That is the voucher (hands voucher to witness). At least —
', Yes, I received that about — well, about two years after my

services had been rendered. That date refreshes my recollection.

Q. Did you receive this money two years after — A. I never did any work for the Interborough, or had any consultations with them, after, I think, about May, 1910.

Q. How long was it after you had seen the Mayor with Mr. Shonts that this bill was paid? A. It was paid — when is the receipt signed? Paid on that day.

Q. Signed on March 25, 1912. A. Well, it was paid on that day.

Q. I know, but how long was that after you saw the Mayor with Mr. Shonts? A. Well, I saw the Mayor — now, I can fix the date exactly; if I had known I was going to be called.

Q. Yes. A. I know there was snow on the ground. Now, these matters, when I had finished, it was not a matter that, like a case in court, in which I kept a diary and entered each particular item upon my book, of my activities; and so the date I can't recall, but I see in Mr. Shonts's testimony, that he fixes it — fixed it in April. I always thought — I know there was snow on the ground, and it was quite cold; quite cold. It was freezing.

Q. Well, then, it would be some time prior to that? A. Why, it was in 1910.

Q. Yes; I am trying — A. It was in 1910; that is my —

Q. That would be about two years? A. As I say, if I had known I was going to be called — Mr. Thompson rang me up about twenty minutes ago — I could have fixed the date exactly, but I should think it could be fixed by the railroad company.

Q. Yes. Is that the only money you received from the Interborough Company? A. That is every cent, covering disbursements and everything else. I must have had about $160 disbursements, and the way it happened was this: After the thing was finished I said — they said, " Well, what are you going to charge? " I said, " Well, you send me a check for whatever you think my services are worth." He said, " No, we prefer that you should make a bill." I made a bill for $10,000; I received $5,000, and I signed a receipt.

Q. You received no money from any other person connected with the company? A. Not a cent; not a cent; nor any other consideration.

Q. Did you ever take part in any negotiations with any members of the Board of Estimate regarding these matters? A. No. My activities were confined entirely to taking reports to the Mayor, going over them, showing him the proposed routes, and arguing with him as to the relative advantage of having the subway controlled by the people who understood it and who had managed it effectively, and who, as I argued, were efficient, and who could represent the city better than any municipal staff that the city might necessarily entrust the business of the management of a big enterprise like that to.

Q. Well, your work was altogether in dealing with the Mayor, was it? A. In dealing with the Mayor and Mr. Shonts, or the railroad.

Q. You stood between the railroad and the Mayor? A. Had to take their views and —

Q Yes, I understand. That is all I want. A. I did that until one day when I was informed that my services were no longer needed. I had finished then. I want it distinctly — I hope — I felt humiliated when I — the atmosphere that was put upon this, or the aspect that I had received $5,000 to introduce two people. I felt aggrieved at that, and I want to state most emphatically here that I received no such sum for such a purpose. It was only in the course of my employment that I made this appointment and it was part of the fee that I had received for what I considered diligent and effective work. I really believe that my representations — this is my personal belief — resulted in the acceptance of the proposition of the railroad.

By Chairman Thompson:

Q. Mr. Towns, how often did you see the Mayor? A. Oh, I saw him every night, three or four times a week, whenever he was not otherwise engaged. We lived near each other.

Q. From October to around May? A. Yes, but I didn't necessarily see him about this all the time. We talked. I would mention — I think I would be within the mark if I said forty or fifty times.

Q. You say that extended in relation to this matter until — I understood you to say from October around to May? A. Well, October to May. The Mayor became a candidate in October for election.

Q. October, 1911? A. Naturally I went — he called me up, I would go down to St. James and see him.

Q. What year did the Mayor run? A. Ran in 1909.

Q. Yes. Well, you mean that — when you said you had taken this up with the Mayor from October around until May, did you mean from 1909 to May, 1910? A. I didn't say that. I said I was first spoken to by a representative of the Interborough in October, 1909. If you want to know what that was about, I am willing to tell you what that was about. This is what I said. I didn't say I saw the Mayor then, but I talked with him, but about an entirely different thing — that he spoke to me —

Q. I was going to ask if that talk in October, 1909, had anything to do with what you received that $5,000 for? A. Yes.

Q. Well, then, what? A. I considered so. It was first — you see there was the campaign instituted. There were two interests, the tri-borough route in which the — naturally the wish or desire on the part of the railroad company to maintain what they had, and I was consulted with regard to suggestions of what could be done in order to educate the public up to the idea that the Interborough — their interests would be conserved by the Interborough remaining in control.

Q. Well, what did that have to do with the Mayor? A. Had nothing to do with the Mayor —

Q. Did they want to know — A. — I said that distinctly.

Q. Have this conference in reference to seeing whether the Interborough would support Mayor Gaynor's candidacy? A. No; I understand the Interborough supported both candidates.

Q. You said you had a great activity in relation to the service you performed for $5,000, and as I understood you to say, it commenced in October, and continued until the following May? A. Quite correct.

Q. Now, what year? A. I thought I had told you, in 1909.

Q. And your service was all performed, for which you received this $5.000 — your service was all performed between October, 1909, and May, 1910? A. Yes, sir.

Q. And did you think that you had accomplished the result that you state, by bringing the Mayor friendly to signing these dual subway contracts? A. That was an incident of my employment. That was not — it was an incident. That was one of the things that I sought to do.

Q. And you say you accomplished it in that time? A. Well, no. You have misunderstood me. I never said I accomplished it, Mr. Moss, if I remember the question asked me, and I said that modesty forbade me to say —

Q. Well, I am a stranger here, you see. That is why I ask these questions. A. We would recognize that.

Q. We will get back, now.

Mr. Moss.— He has too blunt a way about him, hasn't he?

By Chairman Thompson:

Q. Then we will take out the word " accomplished "; but I understand that you felt that within the limits of modesty that any New York lawyer can have, you want to have us understand that these talks and activities that you had between 1909, October, and 1910, May, had considerable to do with making the Mayor friendly to the signing of the dual subway contract? Now, am I getting that down fair? A. Rather confused, Mr. Chairman.

Q. Just put it your way. A. I said I did certain things; the results speak for themselves. Now, it may be attributed to anybody. Far be it from me to attribute it to myself, except in my closet.

Q. What you did was between those dates? A. Done between those dates.

Q. Begun in October, 1909, and your activity ceased in May, 1910? A. All, at least — twenty-five or — between twenty-five and fifty conferences.

Q. Now, do you know, Mr. Towns, that in 1911. July, this matter came up for a vote in the Board of Estimate, and at that time Mayor Gaynor refused to vote for it, and wrote a letter where he used the word " rascality " in relation to it? A. I don't know that. I have heard it.

Q. Now, if that was so, and that occurred in July, 1911, then your accomplishment did not amount to much. did it, up to that time? A. It would seem so.

Q. You never saw him again afterwards? A. I never had any conferences with him in relation to this subway matter.

Q. And your bill was paid on March 26. 1912? A. I was told my services —

Q. Your bill was not paid until March 26, 1912, was it? A. That is the date of it. It was paid on the day I signed the receipt.

Q. Pretty near two years after you rendered the last service? A. I am painfully aware of that, yes.

Q. And that was a little bit before the Mayor did finally sign the contracts? A. I don't know.

Q. Signed in May, 1912; that is, he voted for it in 1912? A. It had nothing to do with that.

Q. You don't know about that? A. I had no contingent fee.

Q. Can you give us any facts or circumstances that might enlighten us as to why the Mayor felt so badly about these contracts, in July, 1911, and then wrote a letter, using the word "rascality," and refusing to vote for them, and later, in May, 1912, did vote for them? A. Except to say that men and women are emotional; may cry to-day and laugh to-morrow, I cannot account — I was not in the Mayor's advice or confidence.

Q. Pretty intimate with him? A. I was not intimate with him upon that subject afterwards.

Q. After you performed this service, you never talked to him about it, or anybody? Didn't know anything about it? A. Well, I never spoke to him about the subway.

Q. Well, now, we will get back. You were pretty well interested in his being elected as Mayor? A. Very well interested.

Q. You were the gentleman who had charge of the Duffy case, and that made a — there was considerable publicity attached to that, and that brought him into favor with the people? A. Yes.

Q. Made considerable strength to his campaign? A. I am not volunteering any opinion about that. The result speaks for itself.

Q. You were very active, and wanted to see him elected Mayor? A. I was. I wanted him to be elected Mayor.

Q. Did you have any activity with relation to his campaign other than the Duffy case? A. Yes.

Q. Did everything you could to help see him elected? A. Did everything I could to help see him elected.

Q. You advised with him about his campaign? A. Yes.

Q. And as to the manner in which it should be conducted? A. Yes.

Q. And as to the public questions that he would take a side on, in relation to the campaign? A. I don't quite understand that.

31

Q. Well, certain questions always come up in a campaign, where a candidate has to take a stand before the people, and make certain promises as to how he is going to conduct himself if he gets elected. That is the ordinary case down here, isn't it? A. Well, Mayor Gaynor was not a man that took advice. You might operate on him by suggestions, but not advice.

Q. You were advising with him during that campaign? A. What?

Q. You were advising him during that campaign? A. Influencing —

Mr. Moss.— Suggesting.

By Chairman Thompson:

Q. Making suggestions? A. No doubt I made many suggestions.

Q. You say in October you had a talk with Mr. Shonts in relation to these dual contracts; did you get convinced — A. I did not say that. I said the first time I saw Mr. Shonts, I think, was the latter part of December, after Christmas.

Q. After election? A. Yes.

Q. Were you convinced these dual contracts were good things, during the campaign of 1909? A. I was always convinced, provided a proper contract could be made to serve the interests of the city, that it was better to have the arrangement that was sought to be put through. Whether that was the final arrangement or not I don't know. But my impression is that after the first arrangement was made, the Brooklyn Rapid Transit came upon the field very suddenly and upset everything.

Q. That doesn't quite answer my question. A. What was your question?

Q. As to whether in the fall of 1909, during that campaign, you were convinced these dual subway contracts were a good thing? A. I thought so. That is, there was not any dual subway contracts at that time.

Q. They were talked about? A. There was not a dual subway contract at that time. It was all upon the knees of the gods. Nobody had any very direct idea. There was one fundamental idea, if I understood it, and that was that the management of the subway, what we call the Interborough — that is what it is called —

Q. Yes. A. Did not wish the property which they had then destroyed by public competition, and I thought it was in morals and in business —

Q. The question was as to whether or not the city should enter into partnership with the railroads, or build their own subway. That was about the situation then? A. Yes.

Q. And you were convinced the proper thing to do was for the city to enter into contracts with the railroads? A. I was convinced public ownership would not be to the advantage of the city.

Q. You wanted the city to enter into contracts with the railroads. Did you disagree — A. Don't say that, Mr. Chairman. I didn't use the word "contracts." I didn't have anything to do about that. I was convinced it would be better for the city to come to some arrangement with the present management than to enter into competition with them. Whether it was to be done by contract or by some other method, legislative enactment, or what not, that was —

Q. Let's see, now. Take another phase of it. Did you think Mayor Gaynor made a successful campaign when he ran for Mayor? A. Huh! He was elected.

Q. You were with him in this campaign? A. We only measure everything by success.

Q. You were with him in this campaign? A. Well, I wasn't a part of his overcoat or his undershirt, but I saw him every now and then.

Q. And you think that the course of conduct that he had during that campaign was a proper course to insure his election? A. Well, *Vox Populi, Vox Dei.* He was elected.

Q. You thought he didn't make any mistake. You thought that was a proper way, the subjects he stood for in that campaign? A. I thought he didn't make any disastrous mistakes.

Q. Now, I am told — I may be wrong entirely about this, because I was not here — I am told pretty near every time he appeared in public in that campaign he brought up the question of this extension of subways, and declared against the plan of the city entering in with the railroad. A. Yes, and every time I saw him, I told him I thought he made a mistake.

Q. You thought that was a mistake? A. Yes.

Q. Do you think he would have been elected if he had not done that? A. I don't know. I don't measure convictions by success. If a man has a conviction of what is moral and right, it does not make any difference.

Q. Was he convinced he was right in the campaign? A. I don't know.

Q. What do you think? A. I would not deal with his numerous thoughts.

Q. Did you advise him to be any other way in the campaign? A. I told him I thought his attitude was not a proper one to take.

Q. Did you think he was honest in his advocacy of the plan he made in that campaign? A. If I must express an opinion —

Q. Now, you were friendly to the Mayor. A. Wait a minute. One question at a time.

Q. You are right about that. A. I think he was honest. I think he was honest, in his opinion.

Q. And you were interested in him? A. What is that?

Q. You were interested in him? A. Only as a friend.

Q. You wanted him to succeed, didn't you? A. I had no other interest —

Q. I mean that. I mean that. I am not — A. — or for appointment to any office.

Q. After he got elected you were interested to see him succeed? A. What?

Q. You were interested to see him succeed, interested in him? A. I, to some extent, started the fire. I was successful in the Duffy case, and naturally, whenever I could, I put more fagots on it.

Q. After he was elected, you wanted him to succeed as a Mayor? A. Most assuredly I wanted him to succeed.

Q. Well, how in the world could you possibly advise him to vote for these contracts, after the campaign he made against it? A. These contracts, as they at present exist, were not the contracts under consideration at that time. The Brooklyn Rapid Transit had never been heard of. They thought they would confine themselves to their own system. Nobody had ever thought of them, given them a thought. When they came in, it entirely changed the aspect of affairs. If you ask me about whether I approved of the

signing of these contracts, I had nothing to do with it. I was never
consulted about it, and I am not called upon to express an opinion.

Q. They were not approved until after your work was finished?
A. Long after my work was finished. I had nothing to do with it.

Q. I wanted to see what you thought about this. I felt interested in it. A. I wish to say that as far as my relations with the
company were concerned, there was never a suggestion of anything
ulterior or sinister or immoral in the whole business. I have told
you what I did, except that they should try and get something, and
whether they got it or not is for you to determine.

Chairman Thompson.— I have no more questions.

Mr. Moss.— That is all.

(Senator Towner takes the Chair.)

J. ASPINWALL HODGE, called as witness, being first duly
sworn, testified as follows:

By Mr. Moss:

Q. You have been a lawyer a good many years, Mr. Hodge?
A. Since the eighties, some time.

Q. Have you any knowledge or information, Mr. Hodge, as to
how this Admiral suit was begun? A. My positive information
is that derived from Mr. Shonts, the president of the Interborough.

Q. Yes. Was there some circumstance that occurred in your
office? A. There was.

Q. Now, I ask you, in your own way, to state your knowledge,
and what occurred in your office? A. I have always supposed
until the last few days that everybody in New York who knew
anything about the Interborough, knew that the Admiral suit was
begun at the instigation of the Interborough, so much so, that in
July, 1912, I drew a complaint, a supplementary bill, a complaint
in the Federal Court, in which that fact was alleged, and on the
12th of July, I think it was — it was certainly in the first two
weeks of March — not July — Mr. Shonts in my office testified,
stating that as early as July, I think he said July, 1911, there was
an agreement between the city and the Interborough that the question of the legality of the contracts that might be entered into, and

were then in contemplation, owing to an offer of the Interborough, would be tested by a case submitted by agreement.

Q. That is in a familiar form where the law provides for a submission of a controversy? A. It is in the Appellate Division.

Q. Yes. A. And that subsequently to that — that was never accomplished — Mr. Nicoll suggested to Mr. Shonts that a taxpayers' action might be brought, and that that would accomplish the same result, or words to that effect. Mr. Shonts then stated that that received his approval, and as he expressed it, he instructed Mr. Nicoll to take such steps that were taken in that regard. Of course that testimony by Mr. Shonts is, of course, all of record. I have not got the minutes except as they were afterwards printed. I have not the stenographer's minutes; but in my office at the time that that was taken, this was three months before the argument of the Admiral Realty case in the Court of Appeals, there were present the representatives of such firms as Winthrop & Stimson, Mr. Cravath's firm — I have forgotten the whole name of it — Mr. Nicoll's firm — Mr. Nicoll himself was there, Mr. Rogers of the Interborough, Rollins & Rollins, representing the Windsor Trust Company; and therefore I always took it for granted that everybody, of the Bar, at any rate, knew that that was the fact. It appears now that some of the counsel for the plaintiff did not know it, and the court did not know it. But my impression was, and I am testifying now very suddenly, because I have not looked up my records — my impression was that until recently, that the court was informed of the facts, as they were known by the counsel in the office, and certainly by the lawyers that were in my office when that testimony was given, that the Interborough instigated the suit with the consent and approval, as I understood it, of the city.

Q. Of the city itself? A. I only know what Mr. Shonts testified, and I know he testified that the city has agreed to submit it to the Appellate Division, and that this was — this other arrangement was afterwards adopted at Mr. Nicoll's suggestion and with Mr. Shonts' approval.

Q. At this event in your office, was there any representative of the city present? A. There was not. That is, unless somebody was there that I didn't know.

Q. If an agreed case had been made and submitted to the Appellate Division, the court would have been informed by the very form of the papers that it was a submission by arrangement? A. Certainly.

Q. But if the case was presented to the Court of Appeals in the way that the reported volume shows, with counsel apparently appearing for litigants taking opposite positions and appearing to represent real parties and not dummy parties, that presents a very different situation from what would be presented to the courts by an agreed case? A. Unless the court was informed by counsel or on the briefs as to who the real parties were, and I always supposed until recently that that had been done.

Q. There was no information on the briefs — no information whatever in the case to be found — not a thing. A. I had a conversation with Mr. Shearn at that time, who I understand was an intervenor in the case. I don't know even whether he argued the case. And that conversation I don't care to repeat, without looking up my notes, and see if I have any notes about it, so that my memory of four years ago can be somewhat refreshed. Mr. Shonts' testimony made a very great impression upon me, because it was so absolutely free and frank, I did not have to cross-examine him. He stated the whole case as if there was nothing to conceal and I never supposed there was anything to conceal.

Q. What hearing was that you were holding? A. It was a hearing in the case of the Continental Securities Company against the Interborough and the Inter-Met, and the New York Railways and Guaranty Trust Company and others, in an endeavor, in which we were at first successful, to convince the court that a combination of the subways, of all transit facilities of New York, underground and on the surface, and above the surface, was a monopoly in restraint of trade, against the statutes of this State, which statutes are almost identical with the Sherman Act.

Q. And what was the title of the case? A. I have given it.

Q. The Continental Securities Company against the — A. I think the first name among the defendants was the Interborough. It also included the Inter-Met and the Guaranty Trust Company, the Windsor Trust Company, and I think that was all. Oh, there may have been individual defendants, but if there were individual defendants, they were all directors of one of the two companies.

Q. When you spoke of the testimony of attorneys for the plaintiff, or counsel for the plaintiffs, I suppose you referred to the

testimony of Mr. Marshall yesterday, who said substantially that
he supposed he was representing the Admiral Company in a litigation actually brought by them for their own purposes, substantially that? A. I merely noticed that Mr. Marshall stated that he
did not know that he had been retained by the Interborough, in
the sense of having the Interborough back of the Admiral Company.

Q. Yes. A. And that was, I think, the first intimation — I
have not read the papers — the first intimation I had that any
lawyer in New York City did not know what was made known in
a public hearing, as I say, as early as three or four months before
that argument.

Q. When you speak of a public hearing, of course it was in a
legal sense public, but it was restricted to the persons in your office?
A. That is true.

Q. Your private office? A. Sometimes there were reporters
there, and for the most part there were not. I don't know just how
far there was a publication of the facts that were brought out at
that particular hearing. I know that my action did not receive
any support from the Public Service Commission or from the city
or from the press of New York. And I attribute the final decision
in the action largely to that, because upon the original complaint
the court held that the facts alleged in that complaint constituted
a right to the plaintiff to dissolve that merger. And all the facts
in the complaint we believed were entirely and utterly proved by
the testimony of the witnesses for the defendants, and no fact in
the complaint was left unproved.

Q. Was one of the issues, or one of the subjects touched upon
in that case, the issuing of 15,000 shares of stock to August Belmont and some of his associates for the City Island Railroad up
there? A. No, sir.

Q. That was not in that case? A. Not in that case.

Q. I think that is all, Mr. Hodge.

Mr. Quackenbush.— In view of a statement I made before you
were counsel, would you mind asking Mr. Hodge if in any other
litigation in which he was attorney that was the subject?

By Mr. Moss:

Q. Yes. Was that involved in some other litigation? A. It
as.

Q. What was that litigation? A. That was a suit to endeavor to procure the return to the treasury of the Interborough, of $1,500,000, and all the accruing benefits that Mr. Belmont had derived from the ownership of that stock, to the treasury of the company. That suit is still pending, I believe, in the Court of Appeals. I am not attorney in either of those cases, nor counsel at the present time, and have nothing whatever to do with that litigation now.

Q. Is that the litigation in which Mr. Venner was interested? A. Mr. Venner was the president of the Continental Securities Company. He was the plaintiff in both actions.

Q. Yes, and in this other action, to which Mr. Quackenbush has called attention, I think the point of it was that a railroad worth not more than $350,000, had been taken in at a million and a half, and that the stock of that railroad had been issued to Mr. Belmont and his associates, who held the stock for themselves. A. I would not state it in that way.

Q. How would you state it? A. In the first place, I think the railroads were worth a little less than nothing, as has been subsequently proved, by sales on the auction block.

Q. That is what Mr. Shonts called the "mule" railroad? A. Yes. The facts proved in that action were that Mr. Belmont of the Interborough had bought that railroad for $1,500,000 of stock, from Mr. Belmont, who was the president of the Interborough, who had been acting as its agent, and who had secured, as he said, the purchase of the road, for between three and four hundred thousand dollars. It had been carried upon the books — and that transaction was carried upon the books of the Interborough as the purchase of that railroad for that price — $1,500,000. And, as I have said, the determination of that case is — that case is still pending in the Court of Appeals, but I retired from that case, and all other cases of the Continental Securities Company last September.

Mr. Moss.— I think that is all.

Mr. Quackenbush.— Would you mind asking Mr. Hodge to state what the judgment of the court below was on the question involved?

Mr. Moss.— We might as well have that on the record.

Mr. Hodge (to Mr. Quackenbush).— Can you give me the volume of that case — 167 Appellate Division?

Mr. Quackenbush.— I can't from memory.

Mr. Hodge.— I think that was reported in 167, and I have never understood the opinion rendered by the Appellate Division, notwithstanding that they considered the case for fourteen months, and decided 1,000 cases that were argued after that case, before they reached a determination, and then gave a short *per curiam* opinion. I have never been able to understand it — and which will give you an intimation of how the case was decided.

Mr. Moss.— It is up to the Court of Appeals to try to understand it.

Mr. Hodge.— I hope it will be. It is true that in that case it has already been to the Court of Appeals on a demurrer to the complaint, and every issue of law was determined in favor of the plaintiff there, and I cannot see any possibility of the court reversing itself, although they may reverse the Second Department, as they sometimes do.

T. H. GILLESPIE, recalled as a witness, having previously been duly sworn, testified as follows:

By Mr. Moss:

Q. Mr. Gillespie, in obedience to the subpoena of the Committee, have you produced some reports? A. I have the reports, yes, sir.

Q. Let me have them? A. Just the same as I had ten days ago before the sub-committee.

Q. How far back do they go? A. Just as called for in the subpoena, to February 13, 1914.

Q. Is that what the subpoena called for? A. Yes.

Mr. Shuster.— That is the date of the contract, whatever that is.

Mr. Gillespie.— The date of the contract.

By Mr. Moss:

Q. Well, we will take those, and I will change this subpoena.

Mr. Moss.— Please mark those in evidence, Miss Stenographer.

Mr. Gillespie.— I understand I am to keep them in my pos-

Mr. Moss.— They are subpoenaed now, and they are going to be turned over to the sub-committee.

Chairman Thompson.— You can't keep them.

Mr. Gillespie.— I don't understand so, sir. I am advised that I am not compelled to submit these papers; I am only doing so in line with our general stand; that we do not wish to interfere with this Committee, with the — with what they are trying to get at. I am perfectly willing to answer any questions, which is the same stand we have taken for the last two or three weeks; I am perfectly willing to answer questions with relation to the disposal of moneys we sent to Pittsburgh, but I cannot submit all the records for Mr. Moss or anybody else to go through.

Chairman Thompson.— You are not advised that by any member of the Committee.

Mr. Gillespie.— By my own counsel.

Chairman Thompson.— You just offer those papers in evidence.

Mr. Moss.— Mr. Gillespie, do those reports which you hold in your hand show transactions between your firm and your Pittsburgh office, being the transfer of money from New York to Pittsburgh, or the transfer of money back from Pittsburgh to New York, since the execution of the contract?

Mr. Gillespie.— Yes, sir, and shows what the Pittsburgh office did with this money. For instance, if you will allow me, we —

Chairman Thompson.— No, we won't allow you to state what you did.

Mr. Gillespie.— Just the same things as I offered to state before the sub-committee ten days ago.

Mr. Moss.— We are not asking for any favors now. Let me have those reports.

Mr. Gillespie.— I cannot do so.

Chairman Thompson.— I direct you to deliver those reports to the Committee.

Mr. Gillespie.— I am advised by counsel, on the ground that they have nothing in them whatever pertaining to this contract —

Mr. Moss.— How do we know that? The Committee is to pass on that. I may say to you — I want you to understand, Mr. Gillespie, that the Committee and the counsel know what is right about these matters, and we are going to treat these things right. There is no disposition on the part of the Committee and counsel to take your private affairs, and separate them from the matters that are germane to this inquiry, and give them to the press, or anything of that sort. There are in those papers matters germane to this inquiry. There may be other matters too — I don't know. But certainly, if those relate to the passage of funds between your two offices since this contract was made, in view of the testimony given in this inquiry, they are germane. I give you the assurance — the Chairman is here — all concerned are at this table — that these reports will not be used to harass you or to annoy you, or to publish the affairs of your concern to the community, or anything of that sort. But those things that, on examination of them, appear to be germane to this inquiry, will be brought out and treated properly, as an investigation of this kind is intended to do. We don't want you to have any misunderstanding about it.

Chairman Thompson.— Now, you are directed by the Chair, and by the Committee, to produce those papers which you have.

Mr. Gillespie.— For the reason stated, I decline to produce them.

Chairman Thompson.— So you decline to produce them.

Mr. De Gersdorff.— May I be allowed to take a —

Chairman Thompson.— No, you need not take any statement. (To the stenographer.)

Mr. Moss.— May I suggest, Mr. Chairman, that you —

Chairman Thompson.— I want a certified copy of the record.

Mr. Moss.— give one more direction, and that is that he hand to you the papers in his hands that he has produced under this subpoena.

Chairman Thompson.— I direct you to hand them — the Committee authorizes me to direct you to hand those papers to the Chairman of this Committee.

Mr. Gillespie.— On the advice of counsel, and for the reasons stated, that they have nothing in them whatever which pertains to this contract, I must decline to do so.

Chairman Thompson.— That is all.

Mr. Moss.— The witness makes himself the judge of the contents of the papers.

Chairman Thompson.— Oh, yes. We will have to find that out. That is all.

(To the stenographer). You may certify a transcript of this record of Mr. Gillespie's testimony. I think he has already testified there were items here of money from this contract that had gone to Pittsburgh — he has already testified to that, hasn't he?

Mr. Gillespie.— Yes, sir — no, not from this contract, no; no, sir.

Mr. Moss.— How is he to be allowed to say, by an operation of his own mind, whether it is connected with this contract? They are moneys that have gone from his office in New York to his office in Pittsburgh during the time this contract was running, and while receiving money on this contract.

Mr. Gillespie.— That is true.

Mr. Moss.— And it is for the Committee to decide.

Mr. Gillespie.— As a matter of fact, Mr. Moss, we actually sent $514,000 during the two years, and received back from there $335,000 —

Mr. Moss.— You are making a statement upon the record in your own way, without submitting your vouchers and reports. You are making yourself the judge of what those reports cover. The Committee, as it is investigating, has a right to follow those reports.

Chairman Thompson.— You may stand aside, but remain in attendance before the Committee.

Chairman Thompson.— Now, yesterday afternoon I appeared before the sub-committee, and asked them to submit a report this morning in reference to the testimony taken regarding the making of a prior determination by the Engineering Department of the Public Service Commission, and various claims of the Interborough Railroad submitted to them, and I am informed this morning by the Chairman of the sub-committee that they are still taking evidence on that, and he thinks perhaps a report now — it would perhaps be wise to permit him to take the rest of the day. So, under the circumstances, we will permit them to take evidence in the sub-committee. I will state that there is no — the sub-committee is not sitting in executive session because there is any reason why the public should not know what is going on in the sub-committee. If there is anything you want to know, you have our consent to talk with the Chairman of the sub-committee, or see the evidence. We are not holding it there for that purpose, but because they can go on without us and get the work along. So if that is agreeable, Mr. Moss, I shall not ask the sub-committee to report until they get ready later in the day.

Mr. Moss.— All right.

Chairman Thompson.— Or Monday.

CHANDLER WITHINGTON, called as a witness, being first duly sworn, testified as follows:

By Mr. Moss:

Q. You have some official position? A. Chief Engineer, Department of Finance.

Q. Has the city at some recent time condemned property at the foot of Rector street for use by the Lehigh Valley Railroad as a pier? A. I cannot answer that directly.

Q. What is your information about it? A. They are, or have — I don't know.

Q. Well, if you have information that is sufficient for our purpose — this is a committee of investigation. A. Yes.

Q. And is the railroad company to advance the funds for the purchase of the property and for the construction of the pier? A. Yes, sir.

(Senator Towner in the Chair.)

Q. Does the city agree to allow the Lehigh Valley 5 per cent annually on the moneys it invests in the pier? A. No; I don't know; no.

Q. What income — what interest does it allow? A. Term of lease.

Q. How much lease? A. Thirty-seven years, if I remember rightly.

Q. Well, what does the company get for the money which it invests? A. A lease of thirty-seven years.

Q. What becomes of the property at the end of the lease? A. The city's — the city's property as soon as the title vests — it vests in the city, the title does.

Q. Yes. A. But the railroad company pays the money.

Q. How much rental does it pay on the lease? A. I think the city did own some property there other than private property.

Q. Is there a contract in existence for the construction of a pier? A. I will have to answer that — I see the pier is going up, so I presume there is a contract, but it is a contract by the Lehigh Valley Railroad. The city don't make the contract; the company makes the contract, and the work is done under the supervision of the Chief Engineer.

Q. Haven't you a copy of the contract in those books? A. No, sir, I only have the resolution of the Commissioner of the Sinking Fund which authorizes the lease.

Q. Let me see that, please.

(Book, being proceedings of the Commissioner of the Sinking Fund of the city of New York, is handed to counsel by the witness.)

Q. You have no copy of the agreement in your office? A. No, sir.

Q. Other than this which you have produced in the resolutions? A. No, sir.

Q. I suppose a copy of that contract is with the Lehigh Valley Company? A. Presumably. I presume so, yes, sir.

Q. Does that other book which you have contain anything relating to this? A. That is a resolution in 1914 which moved the location of the piers; that is all.

Q. That is all? A. It don't change the lease.

Mr. Moss.— Just let us mark this in evidence, and you may leave this, and we will study it over.

(Page 1392 of the proceedings of the Commissioner of the Sinking Fund of the City of New York is marked in evidence as Exhibit No. 1 of February 26, 1916, V. E. Valva.)

Mr. Moss.— Now we will have Mr. Ross.

DAVID W. Ross, called as a witness, being first duly sworn, testified as follows:

By Mr. Moss:

Q. Mr. Ross, what is your business and your position? A. I am vice-president of the Interborough Rapid Transit Company and the New York Railways Company, in charge of the purchasing of materials and real estate, insurance.

Q. Do you have to do with the purchase of coal? A. Yes, sir.

Q. Who does the buying of coal? A. I do.

Q. Who authorizes or approves of the purchase? A. Well, the president, of course, approves my acts.

Q. Anybody else? A. The board, the board of directors approve all contracts.

Q. Yes. Well, when you make your arrangements to purchase coal, you report to somebody. Whom do you report to? A. To the president.

Q. And does the president submit these reports to the board of directors? A. As a rule, yes, sir.

Q. Is there any committee of the board that you have to deal with? A. No, sir.

Q. Your dealings are directly, then, with Mr. Shonts? A. Yes, sir.

Q. Do you ever come in contact with Mr. Berwind in these matters? A. Yes, sir, I have.

Q. How so? A. We have had a contract with Mr. Berwind's company, Berwind-White Coal Company.

Q. You have a contract for the purchase of coal from Mr. Berwind's company, and this is the same Mr. Berwind who is one of the directors of the company? A. Yes, sir.

Q. Who tests and passes on the coal? A. Our superintendent of motive power.

Q. Who is that? A. Mr. H. G. Scott.

Q. Is that test final which he makes? A. Yes, sir.

Q. Does he certify the test to you? A. Yes, sir.

Q. Do you go behind his report at all? A. No, sir.

Q. Do you — A. He has chemists.

Q. You consider him an expert and accept his report? A. Yes, sir.

Q. What quantity of coal does the company use annually? A. About 475,000 tons approximately.

Q. That is distributed among how many stations? A. Two power houses, one at Fifty-ninth street and North River, and one at Seventy-fourth street and East River.

Q. What is the proportion between those two power houses? A. Almost — it is about equally divided.

Q. Is the coal which you supply to these power houses bituminous or anthracite? A. Bituminous.

Q. No anthracite at all? A. No, sir.

Q. How do you receive your coal, by rail or by water? A. It comes in by rail, then is delivered to our power houses by lighters.

Q. These lighters take it from the docks and carry the cars around? A. No, delivered in lighters carrying from 700 to 1,200 tons.

Q. They don't take the cars? A. No.

Q. The coal is shifted? A. Dumped into the lighters and then taken to our power houses.

Q. Is your coal that is received that way — do you have any by water at all? A. No, sir. It all comes by rail to New York.

Q. Well, do you pay for the coal as delivered on the cars, or as delivered at the power houses? A. As delivered at the power houses. Our own weights.

Q. The same coal would be — that you buy, would be satisfactory to each power house plant, I suppose? A. Yes.

Q. Do you weigh the coal as it is taken out of the lighter, or when it is put into the lighter? A. As it is taken out of the lighter.

Q. Does the company require a special quality of coal, or can they use ordinary grades? A. No, we require a coal that makes very little smoke, low in bond, and we want also a coal that has large heat units, with as large number of heat units as possible. We buy our coal on a B. R. U., which is British Thermo Unit basis, and as it is analyzed, we either pay so much above the base price, or if it is lower in heat units than the contract calls for, why we make a deduction, if it runs under the standard number of heat units, which my recollection is 14,250 British Thermal Units.

Q. Do you use the underfeed or the overfeed stoker system? A. Underfeed.

Q. What is the chemical requirement for your coal further than you have stated? A. My recollection is that 20 per cent of volatile matter, the standard is. Coal must be of good steam, caking, run of mine, bituminous coal, free from all dirt and excessive dust, a dry sample of which will approximate the company's standard in heat value and analysis, as follows: Carbon, 71 per cent; volatile matter, 20 per cent; ash, 9; British Thermal Units, 14,100; sulphur, 1½ per cent. (Witness refers to specifications.) This is evidently an old specification.

Q. Will you send us a specification such as is used now? A. The last one, yes, sir. The British Thermal Unit has been changed.

Q. Is the price at which you purchase, a flat figure, or do you pay premiums, and exact penalties? A. It is a base price, based on our specifications, and we pay a premium when the coal runs higher in B. T. U. than the standard, or make a deduction if it runs under the standard.

Q. Yes. And that appears — all this appears on the regular specification, of which you are going to send me a copy? A. Yes, sir.

Q. When in the market for coal, is it your custom to advertise for prices, or do you send tenders asking for bids? A. We send out inquiries. We don't advertise.

Q. We will ask you to send us a copy of those last ones you have used. You will do that, will you? A. Yes, sir.

Q. Will you state the names of the concerns to whom you send invitations? A. We have only been sending them to two companies, the only companies we would feel safe in placing our contracts with. You see, we have but very little storage capacity, probably about enough for probably ten days, and we have to be sure of having a supply of coal at all times, of course, so they are practically the only two companies we would feel safe in placing coal contracts with.

Q. What are their names? A. One is the Consolidation Coal Company and the other is the Berwind-White Company.

Q. Are there any persons connected with the Interborough Railroad interested in the Consolidation Company? A. No, sir, not that I know of.

Q. Are there any persons in the Interborough Company interested in the Berwind Company besides Mr. Berwind? A. No, sir.

Q. Are you under any contracts now for the supplying of coal? A. Yes, sir.

Q. What contracts? A. We have a contract with those two companies.

Q. Will you state the quantities of the coal that you are under contract for? A. My recollection is that our contract with the Consolidation is for 200,000 tons a year, 10 per cent more or less, and with the Berwind-White I think 200,000 or 250,000 tons a year, 10 per cent more or less.

(Assemblyman Kincaid takes the Chair.)

Q. When do those contracts expire? A. Two years from next July, first of July.

Q. Those two contracts cover all the coal you are buying? A. All the coal we are using in the power houses. We use some blacksmith coal and some anthracite coal for heating purposes, but —

Q. How much would that amount to? A. That probably would amount to about 30,000 tons a year.

Q. Where do you get that from? A. Various people. We get bids from nearly everybody that handles it, and give it to the low bidder. I think right now we have got contracts with — our with order was placed with Parrish, Phillips & Company.

Q. How many years have you been buying from these concerns, the Consolidation Company and the Berwind Company? A. Well, I have been buying from them ever since I have been with the company, and I think they did for a number of years before that — I presume ten years or more.

Q. Those two companies for ten years or more have supplied this large quantity of bituminous coal? A. Practically all the coal.

Q. What prices are you paying each concern? A. Just the same price, $3.23 a ton is my recollection. We pay them both the same.

Q. What would that be at the mines, f. o. b.? A. I don't know exactly that.

Q. What is your best judgment? A. I imagine somewhere around $1.25 a ton at the mine.

Q. And are those prices, $3.23, which you have mentioned, in any important way varied by the premiums or penalties in practice? Have those prices been appreciably varied by penalties and premiums? A. Not very much. Sometimes there is an increase in the price. Sometimes there is a decrease. But it does not vary very much.

Q. A negligible amount? A. It doesn't vary very much from the standard price, because they select the coal. They try to get coal that comes up to the specifications. In some cases the Berwind-White coal runs a good deal higher in heat units than some we get from the Consolidation and lower in volatile. We have to have coal that makes little smoke.

Q. Which makes more? A. Berwind makes more.

Q. And produces more heat? A. And produces more heat.

Q. Then the Berwind coal is much better than the Consolidation? A. Very considerably better for our purpose.

Q. Why don't you try to get it all from the Berwind Company? A. We feel safer in having contracts with two companies. Right now —

Q. Who tells you that? A. Well, I don't know that anybody tells me.

Q. Have you talked that over with Mr. Shonts? A. I have talked with Mr. Shonts every year.

Q. What did he ever say to you about it being safer by having two companies? A. I don't know that he ever told me.

Q. You never mentioned that to him. He is interested in practically every detail in this matter? A. Yes, sir.

Q. How is it you haven't talked with him upon that subject? A. I have talked with him about the coal contracts.

Q. Did you ever tell Mr. Shonts that the Berwind coal was a great deal better than the Consolidation? A. Yes.

Q. At the same price? A. Yes, sir.

Q. Did he ever tell you not to buy it all from the Berwind Company? A. Well, I don't know, we never discussed it.

Q. Did he — never discussed it? Why didn't you? A. Well, I discussed coal contracts with him a good many times.

Q. This particular matter? A. I never discussed the matter —

Q. Why didn't you? A. — of placing it all with the Berwind Company.

Q. Well, why didn't you? A. It didn't enter my head.

Q. Why didn't you? You say the coal is much better, makes less smoke, produces more heat, and you think it is better to have — safer to have your contract with two companies. Well, now, when you have a question in your mind as between a much better coal on the one side, and possibly on the other side the safety of having two contracts, why did you take the responsibility, when you can share it with Mr. Shonts? A. You see, we pay for it —

Q. You pay the same price? A. — the same in each case.

Q. But one coal is much better than the other, you say? A. We pay for it when it is better.

Q. What? A. We pay for so many B. T. U.'s, you know, so we get the same thing from each company.

Q. Well, you mean so far as the going out of the money is concerned, but isn't it much better so far as space and practical operations are concerned to have the best coal? A. There is not enough difference to amount to anything. They are close to the same.

Q. You told me there was considerable difference? A. There is a difference.

Q. A noticeable difference. One produces less smoke. A. Higher in heat units, and some lower in smoke.

Q. Better coal; burns itself out and does not throw out its substance in smoke upon the atmosphere? A. The other is good coal, too.

Q. The other is good coal too, or you wouldn't buy it. Well, I guess we have all there is on that subject. Now, then — do you pay premiums, or make deductions mostly on this coal? A. Well,—

Q. Do you pay premiums mostly, or make deductions? A. We do both.

Q. Which is — exceeds — if you figure it up, is it greater on the premium or — A. On the average we pay a premium on the Berwind-White Company, because their coal runs higher than our standard requirements. And on the average we make a deduction from the other company.

Q. Then most of the deduction is done on the Consolidation, most of the premium is on the Berwind coal. How much does the premium amount to in a year? A. Oh, very little, a few cents a ton, I should say.

Q. How much in the course of a year on all these tons; how much does it amount to? A. Probably around $25,000, maybe, in a year.

Q. Yes, and how is that — A. The deduction on the other company would be pretty near the same.

Q. Then there is a premium given to the Berwind-White of $25,000, and a deduction against the Consolidation of about $25,000 a year. How are those premiums and deductions determined? A. By the analysis of the coal.

Q. By your chemists? A. You will find in the specifications they say how they are made.

Q. You might read it in the record (referring to the specifications). A. This is not the latest copy.

Q. How far back is that? A. I see it is preliminary specifications, 1906 and 1907, gotten out then. It has been changed some since then.

Q. Perhaps you had better give me the later one and not put that on the record. Now, you have a record showing how these different coals have been running chemically, haven't you? A. Yes, sir.

Q. Will you produce that record? A. Copies of our — I don't have it in my office, but I can get it from the Superintendent of Motive Power.

Q. Will you send that to me? A. Yes, sir. You just want an average statement, I suppose? You don't want a record.

Q. I would like to have a record. A. They analyze several samples from each lighter, you know. It would be very voluminous. If you wanted them all, of course — over what period?

Q. I will take an average, and see how it works out. A. Per month?

Q. Per month. A. Per month.

Q. And see how it works out. A. You see —

Q. Have you conferred with any other dealers in coal with the object of getting a better price? A. No, I have only talked with these two companies.

Q. Why haven't you conferred with other dealers, to get a better price? A. Well, because — I would not feel safe in doing business —

Q. Well, why? A. There are other companies that I might feel safe with, but they don't handle the right kind of coal; but these are the only two companies that handle the kind of coal we want, that we feel safe in doing business with. The Berwind-White has its own coal equipment, owns its own coal cars, its own lighters, they use their coal cars and their lighters practically as a storage place for coal for us.

Q. Well, they could afford to do it. They have had a monopoly for ten years. A. Not a monopoly. The Consolidation Coal Company —

Q. Well, a monopoly between the two of them. The Consolidation has some coal cars, too? A. They don't own their own cars.

Q. They are fit to furnish that goods at the same price and they don't own their own cars? A. That is a very strong substantial concern.

Q. Are there no others? A. Not that I know; not as strong as those two.

Q. Are you going to swear there are none? A. I said I don't know of any as strong as those two.

Q. You are an expert and have been on this job for a good many years. I ask you, are there no other strong coal companies that could supply coal to your company? A. I don't know of any, with the kind of coal we want.

Q. Have you tried to find out? A. Yes, sir.

Q. How? A. I don't know of any.

Q. How have you tried to find out? A. Well, I have the subject in mind all the time.

Q. How have you tried to find out? Having the subject in mind don't help us very much to know what you have been doing. A. Well, I don't know how I could explain what I mean.

Q. Well, try and explain what you mean. What have you done to try to find out whether you cannot get a better price for your coal? A. Well, there would not be any use in getting a price from a company you would not do business with.

Q. Why wouldn't you do business with it? A. I don't know of any other company who could furnish us the amount of coal we want.

Acting Chairman Kincaid.— Answer the question. Have you tried to find out whether any other company could do that or not?

By Mr. Moss:

Q. What have you done? A. I have made inquiries.

Q. Have you asked for bids from other companies? A. No, sir.

Q. Why haven't you? A. Because I don't know of any other companies we would want to do business with.

Q. Wouldn't you find out by asking for bids? A. No,

Q. Supposing you were to submit offers to all of the coal companies to supply this great amount of coal that you use, then they would furnish you with their bids, and you could determine whether there is a likelihood of their supplying the coal. Maybe they would even give you bonds. Maybe they would like to have a look-in? A. Bonds wouldn't do us any good if we did not get the coal.

Q. It would be some assurance from the people that gave the bonds that the people behind them would give the coal? A. It would help.

Q. You have not made an effort? A. I have.

Q. Well, what effort have you made? A. It does not require effort.

Q. But you say you have made an effort. What was the effort you made? A. I am on the lookout all the time.

Q. What does that mean? A. If I learn of some companies, some other company that furnishes as good coal as they do, and is as strong as they are —

Q. How do you find that out? Now, you say you are on the lookout,— looking up or looking down? A. Straight ahead.

Q. Is that the way to get coal, by looking straight ahead? A. If there is anybody in the coal business that wants to do business, they come around and see me.

Q. Aren't there other companies who are anxious to do business? A. I don't know of any other.

Q. Don't you know any at all, any other? A. Other companies are anxious to do business, but I don't know of any company that can furnish us what we want.

Q. Have you tried to find out? Isn't this coal question a burning question to the coal trade? A. Yes.

Q. You say it is. What have you tried to do to find out whether or not these gentlemen in the burning industry could furnish you some coal at a cheaper price? A. Well, I have asked companies for prices —

Q. Do you know that this question — A. — that I would feel safe in doing business with.

Q. Do you know that this question of the price of coal affects the city of New York, and the people, and the treasury of the city of New York, as well as it does the treasury of the Interborough? A. It does not yet, but it will.

Q. Doesn't it? A. It will when the new contract becomes effective.

Q. Doesn't the operating expense interest the city of New York? A. Not at present.

Mr. Quackenbush.— Not in the slightest.

Q. Well, this contract runs on for two years, doesn't it? A. Yes, sir.

Acting Chairman Kincaid.— The witness testified he made inquiries, and he has not testified of whom nor where.

By Mr. Moss:

Q. Whom did you make those inquiries of? A. Just those two companies, the Consolidation and the Berwind-White.

Q. Did you make inquries of any other companies? A. No, I didn't ask any other company.

Q. Why? A. Because I didn't know of any other company.

Q. Whom did you make inquiries of? A. Just those companies.

Q. And they told you their competitors couldn't do any better? A. No. They didn't tell me that.

Q. What did they tell you? A. They gave me their prices.

Acting Chairman Kincaid.— It comes to the fact they didn't make any inquiries.

Mr. Moss.— It looks that way.

Mr. Ross.— Not from any other than those two companies.

By Mr. Moss:

Q. Is August Belmont interested in the Consolidation Company?
A. No.

Q. Are you sure he isn't? A. Quite sure he isn't.

Q. Hasn't he some of the bonds of that company? A. I don't
know. I never heard of his having. He may have. If he has I
never heard about it.

Q. Your inquiries did not go as far as that? A. No.

Q. Have you tested any coal and found it unsatisfactory coal,
offered by other companies? A. I don't know as to that.

Q. You haven't, have you? A. I don't know as to that.

Q. You have no knowledge or information on that subject? Do
you honestly believe that the concerns you are taking coal from are
the only coal producing companies that could take proper care of
you, both as to quality and service? A. Yes, sir.

Acting Chairman Kincaid.— That belief does not seem to be
founded on anything.

Q. Now I am going to ask you what foundation you put under
that belief? A. They are the only companies that I know of, doing
business in this territory, that we would feel safe in doing business
with. If I learn or can find any others, I can send them inquiries
or try to do business with them. I don't know of any others at
present.

Q. Don't you think, Mr. Ross, that if you should get some other
company to take the place of the Berwind Company, that if you,
using your discretion, should find some other company that could
supply or would supply this coal, that your job might be in danger?
A. No, I don't think it would.

Q. Don't you think it is advantageous to you personally, having
some power of discretion, to prefer the company in which Mr. Berwind is interested? A. Well, I never made any change in that
respect. They were buying coal from those two companies.

Q. You found it, and you have continued it, thought it was a
wise thing to do? A. I never thought about it in that light at all.

Q. You never thought of changing? A. I didn't think of it in
that light.

Q. Really, the matter of changing has never come to you seriously, has it? A. I wouldn't know who to change to.

Q. It has never come to you seriously? You have no serious interest in trying to change, have you? A. Not as long as we are taken care of as well as we have been.

Q. If you get coal for fifty cents a ton less, it would not interest you? A. I don't think there is a chance.

Q. If you could get coal for fifty cents a ton less, it would not interest you? A. It would interest me very much if we got it five cents a ton less.

Q. Do you think it might lose you your job? A. I am quite sure it would not, if I could get it for a lower price.

Q. Well, if you had competitors trying to come in, they would have to pass the chemical test which is under you, wouldn't they? A. Yes, sir.

Q. And the finding of that chemist is a matter you would not interfere with at all? A. The chemist does not report to me. He reports to the Superintendent of Motive Power.

Q. You would not interfere with it? A. I could not interfere with it. I don't have anything to do with it.

Q. Have you ever been requested by any one for the company to continue with your present suppliers of coal? A. No, sir.

Q. In what respect do you require a better coal than the New York Edison requires? A. I don't know that it would require any better coal than they do, as far as that is concerned.

Q. Do you require as good a coal as they require? A. Yes, sir. We want the best coal we can get.

Q. But no better than they require? A. We want the best we can get.

Q. But their demands are just as great as yours, aren't they, as to quality? A. Approximately.

Q. Yes. Did you ever buy any coal from the Fairmount or Somerset Companies? A. The Somerset is part of the Consolidation Coal Company. Formerly known as the Somerset. Our contract used to be with the Somerset Coal Company.

Q. Then the Fairmount and the Somerset are combined with the — A. Part of the Consolidation.

Q. How many big operatives offered you coal last year? A. I don't recall.

Q. Did any? A. No.

Q. Are you sure no other companies offered you coal, or no other operatives offered you coal last year? A. No, I think — probably during the past year, probably have been several.

Q. Who would? A. I don't recall the names of them.

Q. Who were they? A. I can find out, but I don't recall.

Q. I know.

Assemblyman Burr.— Don't you know the names of the different operators?

Mr. Ross.— Davis Coal & Coke Company.

By Mr. Moss:

Q. Have they quoted you any price? A. Some time ago they did.

Q. How long ago? A. About — oh, I guess about a year and a half ago.

Q. Who else? A. I don't recall the names of any others.

Q. Did the Evansburg Coal Company ever offer you any prices? A. I don't remember they ever did.

Q. Do you know the company? A. What is the name of it?

Q. The Evansburg? A. No, sir.

Q. Have you told all you can in answer to Senator Burr's question? A. Yes, sir.

Chairman Thompson.— He is going to be Senator some day.

Mr. Moss.— I am only taking time by the forelock.

Assemblyman Burr.— That is the only big operator you know? Aren't there other big operators in New York?

Mr. Ross.— There are other big operators, but not suitable for our firm.

Mr. Moss.— Perhaps there are some members of the Committee would like to ask some questions.

Assemblyman Burr.— I wanted to find out if he knew any of the coal operators, that was all.

Mr. Moss.— I am going to continue, Senator Burr.

By Mr. Moss:

Q. Can you answer that? A. I know of the representatives of the Davis Coal & Coke Company; I have talked with them at times; and I think at one time, a long time ago, we did try some of their coal, but —

Q. The question is not now with whom you have tried to deal, but do you know the names of any of the operators? A. Yes; I have given you the names.

Q. Any others? A. Yes, I know the names of others.

Q. Name them, please? A. But —

Q. Prominent operators? A. I don't know any other prominent ones.

Q. In this whole territory? A. Not handling the kind of coal we use.

Q. I didn't ask you that. I asked you if you knew the names of prominent operators? A. Well, there is the Berwind-White, the Consolidation and Pittsburgh Coal Company, and Davis Coal & Coke Company. I don't know any others.

Q. What is the Pittsburgh Company? A. They handle a lower grade of coal than we use. It makes more smoke than the coal we use. We could not use their coal.

Q. Will you send me also a copy of your contract? A. Yes, sir.

Q. Is there any unusual clause in your contract? A. Well, there is no — in our contract, no strike clause, as there usually is in coal contracts, because we have to have coal, and these two contractors we get our coal from are bound to give it to us, whether there are strikes or not. If they have trouble, they are bound to give us coal. Right now, on account of the roads, and congestions on the railroads, the Consolidation Coal Company has been getting very little coal in, and had to go out and buy coal to furnish us, and paid as high as $1.25 a ton more than we are paying them. The price of coal now in this market is about $1.25 a ton higher than our contract price. They went out and bought several thousand tons to protect us.

Q. Who owns the Consolidation Coal Company, do you know? A. I don't know who the principal owner is. I think Senator Watson is president, I believe, and chairman of the board. I imagine he is one of the largest stockholders.

Q. Who else do you know in that company? Who else have you heard of in that company? A. As stockholders, I don't know.

Q. Or as persons interested in it? A. There is Mr. Landstreet, who is vice-president. Mr. F. S. Landstreet.

Chairman Thompson.— Who is Senator Watson? Where from?

Mr. Ross.— I think from West Virginia.

By Mr. Moss:

(Mr. Moss writes something on a piece of paper and hands it to witness.)

. A. Yes, sir.

Q. Put the institution underneath that? A. (Witness writes on the paper and hands paper to counsel.)

Q. Do you know what mines this coal comes from the Berwind Company? A. Mines in Pennsylvania.

Q. Whereabouts? A. I don't know exactly the localities.

Q. What county is it in? A. I don't know.

Mr. Shuster.— Probably Clearfield, Indiana.

By Mr. Moss:

Q. Indiana? A. I don't know what county the mines are in. I can find out.

(Counsel writes on paper and hands it to Chairman Thompson, and then hands it to the witness.)

Q. There is a little direction. A. All right.

Chairman Thompson.— Can you file that?

Mr. Ross.— Yes, sir.

Mr. Moss.— I think that will do.

By Senator Thompson:

Q. How much of a salary do you get? A. $18,000 a year.

Q. Do you get a commission on purchases? A. No, sir.

Q. Who are the men in your office — what is your title? A. Vice-president in charge of real estate, purchase, and the store-house —

Q. Who is your principal assistant? A. Mr. Fuhrer.

Q. Have you more than one? A. Mr. Fuhrer is my assistant so far as purchasing is concerned, and I have another man in charge who is my assistant so far as real estate is concerned, Mr. Warner.

Q. Those are your two principal assistants? A. Yes.

Senator Thompson.— That is all.

OSCAR W. PALMENBERG, called as a witness, being first duly sworn, testified as follows:

By Mr. Moss:

Q. What is your business, Mr. Palmenberg? A. I am an analytical chemist and fuel engineering expert.

Q. How long have you followed that occupation? A. My work has been affiliated with coal and its investigation for sixteen years.

Q. And you have followed it practically, have you? A. I made a study of coal in its application to power, and the arts.

Q. Yes, and you have a knowledge of the practical uses of coal, have you? A. Yes, I have the knowledge of the practical use of coal.

Q. You analyze mostly? A. I analyze very extensively.

Q. And have you ever been employed by the Interborough? A. I have.

Q. How long were you with them? A. Why, in the year 19 — in the spring of 1902 I became employed, and stayed in there, with them, until 1910.

Q. In this same line, or what did you do? A. I was called at the time of the starting of the Seventy-fourth street power station to investigate their fuel conditions, to obviate the production of smoke. And I instituted the chemical laboratory and carried on the fuel investigation and chemical work which came up in connection with the power plants.

Q. During this period? A. During this period, to 1910. Since then I have had my own establishment.

Q. Where is your office? A. My office and laboratory is in the Chemist Building, 50 East Forty-first street.

Q. Are you familiar with the requirements of the coal that is needed by the Interborough Company, particularly the power houses? A. I am, up to the time I left their services.

Q. Are you aware of any change in their requirements? A. I don't believe they have made any great changes.

Q. Are you familiar with the coal ordinarily supplied by the Berwind Company? A. Yes, I am familiar with that.

Q. And the Consolidation Company? A. Yes.

Q. And other companies? A. Other companies.

Q. You know the supply that comes into New York pretty well, don't you, practically? A. Yes, sir.

Q. Are there any other companies that supply a coal equal for the purposes of the Interborough Railroad — equal to that of the Berwind-White or Consolidation companies? A. There are other coals equal in quality and action.

Q. Name some of them? A. But as to quantity, I could not state.

Q. Yes; because your specialty is in the coal itself? The examination of the coal? A. The examination of problems; but as to quantity.

Q. Leave that out; name some of the companies that supply coal that will meet the requirements, so far as the constituent elements in the coal are concerned? A. Well, I cannot name the companies in particular. They may have a supply of typical types — typical coals which classify as these which are used by the Interborough, and which should act very much the same when used with the same installation.

Q. Can you name such companies, for furnishing or supplying coal? A. Well, broadly, many of the coals coming from the same districts where these coals are mined, should certainly meet with the same value.

Q. Are there other companies, broadly, that sell coal from those districts? A. There are companies that sell coal from those districts.

Q. Well, name some of them? A. Well, I cannot name all the companies.

Q. I only asked you to name some of them. A. Some of them. Well, the United Coal Company has a coal similar to that of the Consolidation. The Pennsylvania Coal & Coke Corporation, they handle coals which are adjoining to the Berwind operations. And there is the Loyal Hanna Coal & Coke Company; the Pocahontas Fuel Company, probably they would have difficulty in making rail shipments; the J. H. Weaver Company —

Q. Can they make water shipments, that company? A. Oh, the best coals available are nearest the port of Norfolk.

Q. Norfolk? A. All the New River and Pocahontas type coals are nearest that port. It is nearest to ship there, or Philadelphia, and therefore the direct route is to Norfolk.

Q. What was that last company you mentioned? I did not get the name? A. Well, the Chesapeake & Ohio Coal & Coke Corporation, and then there is the Pocahontas Company.

Q. Did you speak of J. H. Weaver? A. J. H. Weaver. Weaver ships to this port. His mines are located — that is, they have a direct rail connection.

Q. Do you know the tonnage of Weaver's? A. Why, yes, I have that.

Q. Approximately, of course? A. I think upwards of a thousand tons a day, if not two thousand tons now; they have extended their operation.

Q. What is the quality of that coal? A. Very high class coal.

Q. Does it come into the port of New York now? A. Yes. It is higher in volatile than the other two; and perhaps might not be as well adaptable for the purpose.

Q. You say perhaps. Can you make that a little clearer? A. Well, with the present installation of furnaces, the higher volatile might cause more smoke to emit from the stack. Otherwise, the coal would probably be almost equal to the other two.

Q. Is the Weaver output almost, about 4,000 tons a day? A. I am not informed on that. I cannot say. It may be.

Mr. Moss.— I think that is all.

By Senator Thompson:

Q. Who furnishes the coal to the New York Edison Company? A. The New York Edison Company?

Q. Yes? A. I cannot answer that.

Q. They have the same style furnaces, don't they? They make their power the same way the Interborough make it? A. I think

32

— I think they are supplied by a number of companies. I don't know exactly how many, though.

Q. I say they make the power the same way the Interborough make it, by turbine steam engines? A. The power is generated — that is, the water is evaporated in about the same class boiler; have the underfeed Taylor stoker; same installation.

Q. They make the power by the steam turbine system? A. That has nothing to do with the coal.

. Q. They have the same kind of a power generating station? A. Yes; the boiler equipment is very much the same.

Q. Yes. Do you know how much coal the New York Edison Company use in a year? A. I suppose close on to half a million tons. The most important proposition with regard to coal is to have a coal which will be of uniform grade. In taking coals from various coal companies, unless the coal can be held to a uniform grade, and of the same character, it will give difficulty, with a large unit, as the modern power station; there are so many boilers to operate frequently, and that is the main feature in obtaining a coal which will be of uniform grade.

By Mr. Moss:

Q. Did you say that several companies were supplying the Edison? A. I think so. If several companies can supply the same grade of coal, then there would be no trouble, but the moment you have a mixture of coals, coming into a power station, you are going to have variable conditions to meet.

Q. Do you know the names of some of the companies that supply the Edison? A. No, I don't.

Q. Not one of them? A. Not positively.

Q. What is your information on that subject? A. What?

Q. What is your information on that subject, as to the names of those companies? You say not positively, but you have some information? A. I have never inquired into who furnished the coal to the Edison Company.

Q. All right.

By Senator Thompson:

Q. You say you quit the Interborough in 1910? A. 1910 I left them.

Q. Why? A. I established myself.

Q. Have you ever been called in by Mr. Ross since, and talked over coal with him? A. Never.

Q. And you never — they never desired your service since that time? A. I have never had any contact with Mr. Ross except perhaps —

Mr. Quackenbush.— I think, Senator, the witness was probably associated with Mr. Stott. Am I right?

Mr. Palmenberg.— Mr. Stott was my superior.

Mr. Quackenbush.— That is the Superintendent of Motive Power.

Senator Thompson.— When did you go to work for the Interborough?

Mr. Ross.— 1908.

Mr. Moss.— That is all.

    CLARENCE C. HARRIS, being called as a witness, first duly sworn, testified as follows:

By Mr. Moss:

Q. Mr. Harris, what do you know about coal? That is a big question. A. That is a big question.

Q. Tell us. A. Well, I know that there are several million tons of coal mined yearly, of excellent quality, that are shipped into this market at fair and reasonable market prices. I am acquainted with the quality of a great deal of this coal, and I know who ships some of it.

Q. What is your business? A. I am in the coal business.

Q. Will you speak just a little louder? A. Yes, sir. I am in the coal business.

Q. In what line, and how? Just describe your business? A. I am an officer of a company.

Q. What is the name of it? A. George D. Harris & Company, dealing in coal.

Q. Yes. Are you a wholesaler? A. At wholesale, yes, sir.

Q. How much coal do you handle? A. Well, I would not want

to say that without reference to the records. In our business that is something that varies greatly with the supply and demand.

Q. But you are familiar with the coal in large quantities? A. Yes, sir.

Q. Do you know anything about the coal used by the Edison Company? A. Yes, I know what some of the coals that they use are.

Q. Do you know the names of any of the companies that supply coal that goes to the Edison Company? A. Yes, sir.

Q. State them. A. Quemahoning Coal Company; Blaine Mining Company; Davis Coal & Coke Company. I think, Mr. Moss, I may be mistaken about some of these. Piedmont & Georges Creek Coal Company. I believe the Knickerbocker Coal Company. I am not sure about that.

Assistant to Mr. Moss.— Fuel, isn't it?

Mr. Harris.— Knickerbocker Fuel Company.

By Mr. Moss:

Q. Do you believe that the Berwind Company or the Consolidation Company supply any coal to the Edison Company? A. I don't think they do.

Q. Do you know where most of this Edison coal comes from, what district? A. Well, these companies I have enumerated ship from different districts. I know substantially where the coal of these different companies I have mentioned comes from.

Q. Where? A. Come from the Somerset district of Pennsylvania, Cambria county. I believe some comes from West Virginia, and also some from what is called the Georges Creek district.

Q. Yes. Is there any considerable amount of coal coming into New York by water? A. Yes.

Q. What companies handle that mostly? A. Well, there are probably seventy-five or a hundred companies ship coal into New York by water.

Q. And is coal brought in from certain districts by water at such prices as can compete with coal that is brought by rail, such coal as the Consolidation and the Berwind people bring in? A. Well, I would like to correct the last answer. I guess I did not understand you. There are not many companies that bring coal into New York by water, that is from outside.

Q. That is — A. What I meant was, companies bring coal into New York city by water, but it is brought from railroad connections across the river, the Jersey terminals.

Q. Oh, yes. Well, are there companies shipping direct to New York from the coal fields? A. You mean by water?

Q. Yes. A. From outside?

Q. Yes. A. Well, that is not done to any great extent. I believe that one company does a little of that, but on account of the long distance that the coal would have to come by boat, and the conditions in freight rates, it is not considered practicable to —

Q. That is what I have been inquiring about. A. Yes, it is not practicable.

Q. So that the market here, so far as price is concerned, is mostly to the companies that send in by rail, is that so? A. Yes, sir, that is right.

Q. And those that you say deliver by water, to what point do they come, how near the city? A. Well, that is, Norfolk, and, that is, Hampton Roads — those piers there that load coal. I have known of coal to be shipped to New York from those piers, but of course that is a long trip by boat.

Q. Yes. Now, what can you say about the prices of coal, and, of course, I am speaking now of bituminous coal such as used by the Edison Company and the Interborough Company for five years back? A. Well, you want a general average price covering five years?

Q. No, make it for each year, if you can? A. Well, I think the same price would answer your question. There has been —

Q. No change of any consequence? A. Not a great deal of variation.

Q. All right. A. I should say a price ranging from $1.20 to $1.35 at the mines would be a fair average for such coal as you refer to, covering a period of five years.

Q. Now, what would be the freight rate during that period? A. The freight rate to New York tidewater is $1.55 a ton, and it costs about twenty cents a ton to boat it.

Q. That is what is called alongside? A. That puts it alongside.

Q. That would be $1.75? A. Yes.

Q. That would deliver it in at $3.00 — at $1.25 at the mines? A. Yes.

Assemblyman Burr.— Did you say $1.25 or $1.35? You said
$1.35 to $1.50.

Mr. Harris.— I said $1.20 to $1.35.

By Mr. Moss:

Q. And I am taking $1.25 as an average. A. That would
deliver it at $3.00.

Q. Now, will you name some of the companies that, in your
opinion, would furnish coal to meet the requirements of the Edison
Company or of the Interborough Company? A. J. H. Weaver &
Company; Pennsylvania Coal & Coke Company; Sterling Coal
Company; Stineman Coal Company; Quemahoning Coal Com-
pany; the United Coal Company; Knickerbocker Fuel Company;
Davis Coal & Coke Company. Any more, Mr. Moss?

Q. Well, all that you have. I would like to get advantage of all
your knowledge while you are here. A. (referring to memorandum book) Loyal Hanna Coal & Coke Company; Baker-Whitely
Coal Company; Commercial Coal Mining Company; Vinton Col-
liery Company; Miller Coal Company; Lincoln Coal Company;
Rock Hill Coal & Iron Company.

Q. Now, Mr. Harris, is there any feeling in the coal trade that
there is a discrimination against the trade generally in the contracts of the Interborough Railroad; is there? A. Why, yes. I
should say there was.

Q. What is that feeling? Let us have it. A. It is a difficult
thing to put into words.

Q. Put it as well as you can. I don't want to frame the words
for you, Mr. Harris. What is the feeling of the trade? That is
what we want to get at.

(Chairman Thompson resumes the chair.)

Mr. Moss.— I may say, Senator, it is because of complaints
made to us by people in the trade that this inquiry has been had.
We are only interested in knowing what the facts are.

Mr. Harris.— The people in the trade think that it is unfair for
a public service corporation to award their contracts for coal without any competition and that without even inviting other people
to bid, and to confine their purchases of this large quantity of coal,

which, if it were distributed around, would be of great benefit to
the trade, to two or three people. There always has been that feeling amongst the trade, and it is nothing the trade felt they could
overcome. We are not invited to bid, and the company does not
know what other people would be willing to take the contract for.

Q. Now, Mr. Ross has intimated that he has been looking out —
looking out for others that might make better terms with the company. As an interested coal man, have you been aware of the fact
that Mr. Ross has been looking out for other bidders? A. I never
heard of him looking out for other bidders, no.

Chairman Thompson.— He might have been looking out for fear
other bidders would come.

Mr. Harris.— Possibly.

Q. Has there been a feeling that the door was shut to the trade?
A. Yes, that is a good way to express it.

Mr. Moss.— Well, I think that is all I want to ask.

By Chairman Thompson:

Q. What I am interested in more than anything is, could these
people buy coal cheaper than they pay Berwind for it? A. Yes,
certainly.

Q. How much cheaper a ton? A. Well, according to the scale
of prices I gave Mr. Moss, it would be at least twenty-three cents
a ton.

Q. Just as good coal? A. Yes.

Q. Adaptable for their purposes? A. Certainly.

Mr. Moss.— That is all.

Mr. Quackenbush.— I don't suppose you expect to allow cross-
examination?

Chairman Thompson.— Do you want to ask questions? I am
going to let you, if you want to. This won't create any precedent,
Mr. Quackenbush.

Mr. Quackenbush.— I assume not.

Mr. Moss.— Of course, Mr. Quackenbush is interested. Go
ahead.

Mr. Quackenbush.— It occurred to me that one thing to ask would be whether these companies that the witness has named are all as able to furnish such quantity of coal as the Interborough needs, as Berwind-White or the Consolidation Company.

Chairman Thompson.— What do you say to that?

Mr. Moss.—Answer that.

Mr. Harris.— I am not acquainted with the capabilities of these people. That is their own private business as far as I am concerned. But I do know that practically all the concerns I mentioned have very large outputs and presumably have enough output to take care of a contract of that size.

By Mr. Quackenbush:

Q. Do you know whether or not they would be prepared to make a contract which did not contain any strike clause, which requires them absolutely and at all events to deliver the coal? A. That is a question that there would be some consideration given to, before any one would sign such a contract as that.

Q. That would affect the price, would it not? A. Well, if a contract is made with a strike clause eliminated, the maker of the contract expects to get something for it.

Q. And could you state whether or not these concerns that you have mentioned have the same facilities as to the ownership of their own cars and means of transportation, so that they would be able to make good their deliveries against strike troubles on the railroads or steamship lines, to the extent that these other two companies do? A. These other two companies — the Consolidation Coal Company, as I understand it, does not own any cars or boats.

Q. How about the Berwind-White? A. The Berwind-White own both boats and cars.

Mr. Moss.— The Consolidation, by the way, has half — supplies half the coal.

Q. Exactly. Take the companies that you have mentioned. I would like to know whether you know whether they are equipped in that way, so that the public, who are interested in this question, won't be inconvenienced by any breakdown in the transportation system? A. I believe many of those companies could take care of half of that contract, the way you have it awarded, as well as the Consolidation, and possibly the Berwind. I don't know about that.

Mr. Quackenbush.— Well, those occurred to me, Mr. Chairman.

Mr. Moss.— I am glad you asked that.

Mr. Quackenbush.— My understanding is indicated by the questions.

By Mr. Moss:

Q. Mr. Harris, J. H. Weaver represents the Evansburg Coal Company, doesn't he? A. Yes, sir.

Q. What is their output a year, about? A. The Evansburg Coal Company's output, I believe, is about 4,000 tons a day.

Q. About a million tons a year? A. At least that.

Q. Probably more? A. Probably more, yes.

Q. Have they any railroad facilities? A. Yes, they have.

Q. What are they? A. They are located on a railroad which I understand they control.

Q. Yes.

Mr. Moss.— Now, may I ask Mr. Ross right here, do you know all the companies that this witness has enumerated?

Mr. Ross.— No, sir. I have heard of them. I know of some of them.

Mr. Moss.— How many of those — about half of what Mr. Ross enumerated — Mr. Harris enumerated? Do you know half of them?

Mr. Ross.— Possibly that, I think.

Chairman Thompson.— I think it is fair to say Mr. Ross has not given this feature any attention at all. You have not tried to find another contract. You have assumed to go on with the conditions there. Mr. Berwind is a director, and you go on with him and the Consolidation. Haven't tried, have you?

Mr. Ross.— Yes, sir, I have tried.

Chairman Thompson.— You have tried? When?

Mr. Ross.— When we make our coal contract.

Mr. Moss.—Ask him what he has done to find out whether Mr. Weaver, of the Evansburg Company, could do this work?

Chairman Thompson.— I just asked that question to show him the Committee's idea is, from your testimony, that you have not tried at all. I wondered if that was not the truth.

Mr. Moss.— You mean to give him a chance to show, not by grilling him with questions — to show definitely. He has heard the testimony. What have you done? That is the point of it.

Mr. Ross.— I don't know that I could add anything to what I said before.

Mr. Moss.— Let us take the Evansburg Company. There is a tremendous company, with railroad facilities, owning a railroad, and supplying more than a half million tons to this port a year. Have you looked into their system, into their coal?

Mr. Ross.— No, sir.

Mr. Moss.— Haven't thought about it, have you?

Mr. Ross.— No, sir.

Mr. Moss.— Nobody asked you to. Now, the Quemahoning Company has about the same, hasn't it, about the same output?

Mr. Harris.— Yes, I believe it has.

Mr. Moss.— Have you ever looked into that, Mr. Ross?

Mr. Ross.— No, sir.

Mr. Moss.— Did you know of the great output of those two concerns before you were told this morning?

Mr. Ross.— I did not know it was as large.

Mr. Moss.— Did you know it was half as large as Mr. Harris has testified?

Mr. Ross.— No, sir, I did not know what their output was.

Mr. Moss.— This is news to you this morning, a liberal education in coal. Now, I have another witness, and I am going to ask him just a general question in the same line as Mr. Harris. He is here. Mr. Chairman, I presume you want to adjourn about 2 o'clock.

Chairman Thompson.— Do you think this difference in this strike clause contract would consume the difference of twenty-three cents you suggest? Would that — would that make up that difference of twenty-three cents a ton? You say the coal can be furnished for twenty-three cents a ton less than they are buying it for. Now, do you think the elimination of a strike clause would account for that twenty-three cents?

Mr. Harris.— Well, I don't know, Mr. Chairman, about that. I do know they don't get twenty-three cents for eliminating their strike clause.

Chairman Thompson.— Don't get that.

Mr. Moss.— Don't get it. But your point, as I understand, is they have had no chance to figure on those bids.

Mr. Harris.— No, they have not; not the trade in general.

Mr. Moss.— If the trade in general had a look-in on this Interborough business, they might be willing to take some chances, just as much as these fellows, for keeping what they have?

Mr. Harris.— They would be.

Mr. Moss.— If they had a chance at these large contracts, they might take some risks, too. Mr. Lesher.

G. F. LESHER, called as a witness, testified as follows:

By Mr. Moss:

Q. Mr. Lesher, you are in the coal business too? A. Yes.

Q. And you know this coal subject as it has been discussed here? A. Yes, sir.

Q. Practically? A. Yes, sir.

Q. I am going to ask you a general question.

Chairman Thompson.— The witness has not been sworn.

(Witness sworn.)

Chairman Thompson.—All you have said in evidence is included?

Mr. Lesher.—All included.

By Mr. Moss:

Q. Now, you have listened to the testimony of these witnesses that we have examined on this coal subject, have you? A. Yes, sir.

Q. You heard the testimony of Mr. Harris? A. Yes, sir.

Q. Do you agree with the testimony of Mr. Harris? A. Yes, in a general way I do.

Q. If there is any point of difference, either in matters of fact or matters of opinion, I wish you would state it, as between you and Mr. Harris? A. No, there is not.

Q. What do you say about price, price at the mines and hauling charges, and that — A. I consider an average price for coal of that description, during the past five years, would run — that is, on contracts of —

Q. Large contracts? A. Large contracts, would run from $1.20 to $1.30 at the mines.

Q. At the mines? A. At the mines.

Q. That is about the same figure? A. The rate of the freight from tidewater to the piers is $1.55, and the boating charge from eighteen to twenty cents a ton.

Q. So that on the figures, you agree with Mr. Harris? A. Yes, sir.

Q. And do you believe there are large concerns in New York that would furnish all of this coal, or a portion of the coal, a large portion of the coal at a lower price — A. I believe there are.

Q. — than is now being paid? A. I believe there are, that would be glad to have an opportunity.

Q. And do you believe the feeling of the trade on the subject of the closed door to be as Mr. Harris expressed it? A. Has always been so understood by the trade, that it was not open to competition.

Q. And if other concerns had a chance to bid, to get in on this important business, do you believe they would take chances on strike clauses, and chances on prices, just as well as the companies that have? A. At a little advance in price I believe they would, a number of them.

Q. Yes. At any rate, they have not been given a chance to figure and try to compete, have they? A. No.

Mr. Moss.—All right.

Chairman Thompson.— I am in receipt of a letter which I will read in the record.

"28 Nassau Street, New York,

"February 26, 1916.

"Dear sir:— I hand you herewith a copy of a letter I am to-day sending to the New York Tribune. In view of what is contained in it, I should be much obliged if you would furnish me with an official copy of the record of my examination before your Committee, in order that I may understand exactly how I am reported as having testified.

"Yours very truly,

"Encl.   "(Signed)   WM. A. READ."

"Hon. Geo. F. Thompson, Chairman.

Joint Legislative Committee to Investigate Public Service Commissions, 165 Broadway, City."

The letter enclosed is — this is a copy of the letter, evidently, that he has written to the Tribune:

"Feb. 26th, 1916.

"Dear Sir:— My attention has been called to a letter signed by Mr. Shonts, dated February 21, 1916, which was published in your edition to-day.

"While regretting the necessity of noticing it, I feel forced to say that I thought the questions quoted by Mr. Shonts were confined to the operation of my mind at the time the Stevens contract was first brought up before the Executive Committee of the Interborough Rapid Transit Company.

"One of the questions, at least, as it is quoted, seems to have called for my thought at the date of my examination. If this is not a stenographer's error, then I certainly misunderstood the time to which the question referred.

"Yours very truly,

"WM. A. READ."

"Editor, New York Tribune,
"154 Nassau Street,
"New York City."

Mr. Moss.— It would be well to state your purpose.

Chairman Thompson.— My purpose — I will read into the record the letter in the New York Tribune. This is the letter referred to, and appeared in the Tribune to-day:

"MR. READ TESTIFIED.

" To the Editor of The Tribune:

" Sir:— In an editorial appearing in this morning's paper you state:

" ' Mr. Read, fortunately, is alive, and from the description Mr. Shonts has given of him should provide entertaining testimony.'

" The above creates an impression that Mr. Read has not testified, and I ask permission to call your attention to the fact that he testified before the Thompson legislative committee on September 29, 1915. I quote the following from his testimony:

" ' Q. Did you know, Mr. Read, of any statement being made by any one in the board of directors that a fund had been raised by voluntary contributions for the purpose of promoting the execution of the dual contracts, so called? A. No, sir.

" ' Q. Ever hear that subject discussed? A. No, sir.

" ' Q. Either in or out of the board? A. No, sir.

" ' Q. Had you any reasons to suppose at the time the proposition was presented for the approval of the executive committee that any such fund had been created and expended? A. No, sir.

" ' Q. Don't you think Mr. Shonts had some other object? A. No.

" ' Q. Didn't the suspicion occur to you that there might be something behind a thing like this? A. I don't like to have suspicions.

" T. P. SHONTS, President."

" New York, Feb. 21, 1916."

I put this in the record because Mr. Read is an important witness in this Committee and he evidently disagrees with Mr. Shonts in some way we don't know about, and we shall want to hear from

Mr. Read further about this matter. And the stenographer can furnish me with a copy of the record of his examination, and we will take it up later, as to forwarding it to Mr. Read, after consultation with counsel.

Mr. Quackenbush.— Senator, may I suggest, in case you conclude, after consultation with counsel, that you will send a copy of the minutes to Mr. Read, that a copy also be sent to Mr. Shonts?

Chairman Thompson.— Yes, but I think we will conclude after consultation with counsel not to send a copy of it at all, because we would rather have the recollections without being reinforced.

Mr. Quackenbush.—As to that, I have no request.

Mr. Moss.— Mr. Quackenbush means, if it goes one way, it should go another.

Chairman Thompson.— It shows that Mr. Shonts is very technically familiar with the testimony that appears here.

Mr. Quackenbush.— Mr. Chairman, that was before you made the rule. At that time we had our stenographer here.

Chairman Thompson.— Mr. Alvin Untermyer has been reported to me by the Sergeant at Arms to be in California.

Mr. Moss.— Did the Sergeant at Arms report when he left?

Chairman Thompson.— I didn't ask that. I am getting so used to that, I didn't ask that detail. Any other witness?

Mr. Moss.— That is all. I don't think that I have overlooked anybody that is anxious to sit in the chair.

Chairman Thompson.— Mr. Gillespie, I asked you yesterday when your father would be likely to return.

Mr. Gillespie.— I sent him a telegram. I have not heard.

Chairman Thompson.— When you have received a reply, will you communicate to Mr. Moss or myself?

Mr. Shuster, I think there ought to be a copy of our record, so far as it relates to this Admiral Realty Company case, made and turned over to the Bar Association.

Mr. Shuster.—And the District Attorney?

Chairman Thompson.— Well, he gets a copy of the minutes, anyway. Will you, Mr. Shuster, take care of that and see that is made in shape?

I want a certified copy of the record — I want it made and certified by the stenographer, relative to Mr. Gillespie's testimony this morning. I would like that out to-night. And there is one other thing. A copy of the testimony relative to Mr. Coleman, that investigation in search for his memory. Will you see that is made out, too, if you please, and forward that to the Public Service Commission?

Is there anything more? Then we will suspend. Now the matters Monday — Tuesday — we are going to suspend the Committee, because Mr. Moss may find he desires to have us in session — there probably will not be and cannot be — we have got to be in Albany, most of us, and for that reason the sessions won't be very full in evidence on Monday and Tuesday.

Mr. Moss.— Make it to Tuesday and Wednesday; put both dates in.

Chairman Thompson.— We will adjourn in that way, to Tuesday morning at 11 o'clock, and to Wednesday morning at 11 o'clock, same place.

They have also refused to produce, or haven't produced the books that the accountant has been working on, and not only stopped with the record they have here, but stopped with all other records (referring to Mr. Gillespie), and I don't make these things for any particular purpose, except to say that the Committee gets the impression that this is all for the purpose of gaining time on the part of Mr. Gillespie. Then we will take a recess for fifteen minutes, to allow a conference of counsel.

(A recess from 2:05 o'clock P. M. to 2:45 o'clock P. M.)

———

Committee called to order at 2:45 P. M.

Chairman.— The Committee will come to order. In the speculating over adjournment to Wednesday, I overlooked the sub-committee is in session and they will — we will adjourn, and this

Committee will adjourn, but the sub-committee will be in session Monday, and probably Tuesday, and it is up to them. So that they will be running along. The sub-committee — the matters before the sub-committee — they are not executive or private, and any matters there, if anybody desires, he can ascertain, if he desires by requesting of Senator Lawson, who is acting as Chairman of the sub-committee.

We will suspend, then, until Wednesday morning, at 11 o'clock, at this place.

Whereupon, at 2:46 P. M., the Committee adjourned to meet on Wednesday, March 1, 1916, at 11 o'clock A. M.

Lightning Source UK Ltd.
Milton Keynes UK
UKHW020332071218
333420UK00007B/185/P